The Econometrics of Financial Markets

The Econometrics of Financial Markets

John Y. Campbell
Andrew W. Lo
A. Craig MacKinlay

Princeton University Press
Princeton, New Jersey

Library of Congress Cataloging-in-Publication Data

Campbell, John Y.
      The econometrics of financial markets / John Y. Campbell, Andrew
W. Lo, A. Craig MacKinlay.
            p.   cm.
      Includes bibliographical references and index.
      ISBN 0-691-04301-9 (cloth : alk. paper)
      1. Capital market—Econometric models. I. Lo, Andrew W. (Andrew
Wen-Chuan). II. MacKinlay, Archie Craig, 1955– . III. Title.
HG4523.C27 1997
332′.09414—dc20   96–27868

This book was composed in ITC New Baskerville with LaTeX by Archetype Publishing Inc.,
15 Turtle Pointe Road, Monticello, IL 61856.

Second printing, with corrections, 1997

http://pup.princeton.edu

Printed in the United States of America

10 9 8 7 6 5

To Susanna, Nancy, and Tina

Contents

List of Figures

List of Tables

xv

Preface

The seeds of this book were planted over fifteen years ago, at the very start of our professional careers. While studying financial economics, and as we began to teach it, we discovered several excellent textbooks for financial theory—Duffie (1992), Huang and Litzenberger (1988), and Ingersoll (1987), for example—but no equivalent textbook for empirical methods.

During the same period, we participated in research conferences on Financial Markets and Monetary Economics, held under the auspices of the National Bureau of Economic Research in Cambridge, Massachusetts. Many of the papers that captured our attention at these meetings involved new econometric methods or new empirical findings in financial economics. We felt that this was some of the most exciting research being done in finance, and that students should be exposed to this material at an early stage.

In 1989 we began to discuss the idea of writing a book that would cover econometric methods as applied to finance, along with some of the more prominent empirical results in this area. We began writing in earnest in 1991, completing this arduous project five years and almost six hundred pages later. This book is considerably longer than we had originally planned, but we have finally overcome the temptation to include just one more new topic, and have put our pens to rest. Of course, the academic literature has evolved rapidly while we have been writing, and it continues to do so even as this book goes to press. We have attempted to provide broad coverage, but even so, there are many subjects that we do not touch upon, and many others that we can only mention in passing.

We owe many more debts—personal and intellectual—than we can possibly acknowledge. Throughout our professional careers our colleagues and mentors have offered us advice, debate, inspiration, and friendship; we wish to thank in particular Andy Abel, Ben Bernanke, Steve Cecchetti, John Cox, Angus Deaton, Gene Fama, Bruce Grundy, Jerry Hausman, Chi-fu Huang, Mervyn King, Nobu Kiyotaki, Pete Kyle, Greg Mankiw, Bob Merton, Whitney Newey, Bob Shiller, Jim Tobin, and Arnold Zellner.

Many individuals have also provided us with invaluable comments and discussions regarding the contents and exposition of this book. We thank David Backus, Nick Barberis, David Barr, David Bates, Ken Bechmann, Dimitris Bertsimas, Tim Bollerslev, Peter Christoffersen, Susan Kerr Christoffersen, George Constantinides, John Cox, Xavier Gabaix, Lorenzo Giorgianni, Jeremy Gold, Lars Hansen, Campbell Harvey, John Heaton, Ludger Hentschel, Roger Huang, Ravi Jagannathan, Shmuel Kandel, Gautam Kaul, Jung-Wook Kim, Todd Mitton, Dan Nelson, Amlan Roy, Bob Shiller, Marc Shivers, Robert Stambaugh, Tom Stoker, Jean-Luc Vila, Jiang Wang, and the Ph.D. students at Harvard, MIT, Princeton, and Wharton on whom this material was "test-marketed" and refined.

We have relied heavily on the able research assistance of Petr Adamek, Sangjoon Kim, Martin Lettau, Terence Lim, Constantin Petrov, Chunsheng Zhou, and particularly Matt Van Vlack and Luis Viceira, who undertook the difficult tasks of proofreading the manuscript and preparing the index.

We are grateful to Stephanie Hogue for her great skill and care in preparing the electronic version of this manuscript, and the typesetters at Archetype for producing the final version of the book.

We thank Peter Dougherty, our editor at Princeton University Press, for his patience, encouragement, and support throughout this project.

Several organizations provided us with generous support during various stages of this book's gestation; in particular, we thank Batterymarch Financial Management, the National Bureau of Economic Research, the National Science Foundation, the John M. Olin Foundation, the Alfred P. Sloan Foundation, and research centers at Harvard, MIT, Princeton, and Wharton.

And finally, we owe more than we can say to the support and love of our families.

JYC
AWL
ACM

The Econometrics of Financial Markets

1
Introduction

FINANCIAL ECONOMICS is a highly empirical discipline, perhaps the most empirical among the branches of economics and even among the social sciences in general. This should come as no surprise, for financial markets are not mere figments of theoretical abstraction; they thrive in practice and play a crucial role in the stability and growth of the global economy. Therefore, although some aspects of the academic finance literature may seem abstract at first, there is a practical relevance demanded of financial models that is often waived for the models of other comparable disciplines.[1]

Despite the empirical nature of financial economics, like the other social sciences it is almost entirely nonexperimental. Therefore, the primary method of inference for the financial economist is model-based statistical inference—financial econometrics. While econometrics is also essential in other branches of economics, what distinguishes financial economics is the central role that uncertainty plays in both financial theory and its empirical implementation. The starting point for every financial model is the uncertainty facing investors, and the substance of every financial model involves the impact of uncertainty on the behavior of investors and, ultimately, on market prices. Indeed, in the absence of uncertainty, the problems of financial economics reduce to exercises in basic microeconomics. The very existence of financial economics as a discipline is predicated on uncertainty.

This has important consequences for financial econometrics. The random fluctuations that require the use of statistical theory to estimate and test financial models are intimately related to the uncertainty on which those models are based. For example, the martingale model for asset prices has very specific implications for the behavior of test statistics such as the autocorrelation coefficient of price increments (see Chapter 2). This close connection between theory and empirical analysis is unparalleled in the

---

[1]Bernstein (1992) provides a highly readable account of the interplay between theory and practice in the development of modern financial economics.

3

social sciences, although it has been the hallmark of the natural sciences for quite some time. It is one of the most rewarding aspects of financial econometrics, so much so that we felt impelled to write this graduate-level textbook as a means of introducing others to this exciting field.

Section 1.1 explains which topics we cover in this book, and how we have organized the material. We also suggest some ways in which the book might be used in a one-semester course on financial econometrics or empirical finance.

In Section 1.2, we describe the kinds of background material that are most useful for financial econometrics and suggest references for those readers who wish to review or learn such material along the way. In our experience, students are often more highly motivated to pick up the necessary background *after* they see how it is to be applied, so we encourage readers with a serious interest in financial econometrics but with somewhat less preparation to take a crack at this material anyway.

In a book of this magnitude, notation becomes a nontrivial challenge of coordination; hence Section 1.3 describes what method there is in our notational madness. We urge readers to review this carefully to minimize the confusion that can arise when $\hat{\beta}$ is mistaken for β and X is incorrectly assumed to be the same as $\mathbf{X}$.

Section 1.4 extends our discussion of notation by presenting notational conventions for and definitions of some of the fundamental objects of our study: prices, returns, methods of compounding, and probability distributions. Although much of this material is well-known to finance students and investment professionals, we think a brief review will help many readers.

In Section 1.5, we turn our attention to quite a different subject: the Efficient Markets Hypothesis. Because so much attention has been lavished on this hypothesis, often at the expense of other more substantive issues, we wish to dispense with this issue first. Much of the debate involves theological tenets that are empirically undecidable and, therefore, beyond the purview of this text. But for completeness—no self-respecting finance text could omit market efficiency altogether—Section 1.5 briefly discusses the topic.

1.1 Organization of the Book

In organizing this book, we have followed two general principles. First, the early chapters concentrate exclusively on stock markets. Although many of the methods discussed can be applied equally well to other asset markets, the empirical literature on stock markets is particularly large and by focusing on these markets we are able to keep the discussion concrete. In later chapters, we cover derivative securities (Chapters 9 and 12) and fixed-income securities (Chapters 10 and 11). The last chapter of the book presents nonlinear methods, with applications to both stocks and derivatives.

Second, we start by presenting statistical models of asset returns, and then discuss more highly structured economic models. In Chapter 2, for example, we discuss methods for predicting stock returns from their own past history, without much attention to institutional detail; in Chapter 3 we show how the microstructure of stock markets affects the short-run behavior of returns. Similarly, in Chapter 4 we discuss simple statistical models of the cross-section of individual stock returns, and the application of these models to event studies; in Chapters 5 and 6 we show how the Capital Asset Pricing Model and multifactor models such as the Arbitrage Pricing Theory restrict the parameters of the statistical models. In Chapter 7 we discuss longer-run evidence on the predictability of stock returns from variables other than past stock returns; in Chapter 8 we explore dynamic equilibrium models which can generate persistent time-variation in expected returns. We use the same principle to divide a basic treatment of fixed-income securities in Chapter 10 from a discussion of equilibrium term-structure models in Chapter 11.

We have tried to make each chapter as self-contained as possible. While some chapters naturally go together (e.g., Chapters 5 and 6, and Chapters 10 and 11), there is certainly no need to read this book straight through from beginning to end. For classroom use, most teachers will find that there is too much material here to be covered in one semester. There are several ways to use the book in a one-semester course. For example one teacher might start by discussing short-run time-series behavior of stock prices using Chapters 2 and 3, then cover cross-sectional models in Chapters 4, 5, and 6, then discuss intertemporal equilibrium models using Chapter 8, and finally cover derivative securities and nonlinear methods as advanced topics using Chapters 9 and 12. Another teacher might first present the evidence on short- and long-run predictability of stock returns using Chapters 2 and 7, then discuss static and intertemporal equilibrium theory using Chapters 5, 6, and 8, and finally cover fixed-income securities using Chapters 10 and 11.

There are some important topics that we have not been able to include in this text. Most obviously, our focus is almost exclusively on US domestic asset markets. We say very little about asset markets in other countries, and we do not try to cover international topics such as exchange-rate behavior or the home-bias puzzle (the tendency for each country's investors to hold a disproportionate share of their own country's assets in their portfolios). We also omit such important econometric subjects as Bayesian analysis and frequency-domain methods of time-series analysis. In many cases our choice of topics has been influenced by the dual objectives of the book: to explain the methods of financial econometrics, and to review the empirical literature in finance. We have tended to concentrate on topics that involve econometric issues, sometimes at the expense of other equally interesting material—including much recent work in behavioral finance—that is econometrically more straightforward.

1.2 Useful Background

The many rewards of financial econometrics come at a price. A solid background in mathematics, probability and statistics, and finance theory is necessary for the practicing financial econometrician, for precisely the reasons that make financial econometrics such an engaging endeavor. To assist readers in obtaining this background (since only the most focused and directed of students will have it already), we outline in this section the topics in mathematics, probability, statistics, and finance theory that have become indispensable to financial econometrics. We hope that this outline can serve as a self-study guide for the more enterprising readers and that it will be a partial substitute for including background material in this book.

1.2.1 Mathematics Background

The mathematics background most useful for financial econometrics is not unlike the background necessary for econometrics in general: multivariate calculus, linear algebra, and matrix analysis. References for each of these topics are Lang (1973), Strang (1976), and Magnus and Neudecker (1988), respectively. Key concepts include

- multiple integration
- multivariate constrained optimization
- matrix algebra
- basic rules of matrix differentiation.

In addition, option- and other derivative-pricing models, and continuous-time asset pricing models, require some passing familiarity with the *Itô* or *stochastic calculus*. A lucid and thorough treatment is provided by Merton (1990), who pioneered the application of stochastic calculus to financial economics. More mathematically inclined readers may also wish to consult Chung and Williams (1990).

1.2.2 Probability and Statistics Background

Basic probability theory is a prerequisite for any discipline in which uncertainty is involved. Although probability theory has varying degrees of mathematical sophistication, from coin-flipping calculations to measure-theoretic foundations, perhaps the most useful approach is one that emphasizes the intuition and subtleties of elementary probabilistic reasoning. An amazingly durable classic that takes just this approach is Feller (1968). Brieman (1992) provides similar intuition but at a measure-theoretic level. Key concepts include

- definition of a random variable
- independence
- distribution and density functions
- conditional probability
- modes of convergence
- laws of large numbers
- central limit theorems.

Statistics is, of course, the primary engine which drives the inferences that financial econometricians draw from the data. As with probability theory, statistics can be taught at various levels of mathematical sophistication. Moreover, unlike the narrower (and some would say "purer") focus of probability theory, statistics has increased its breadth as it has matured, giving birth to many well-defined subdisciplines such as multivariate analysis, nonparametrics, time-series analysis, order statistics, analysis of variance, decision theory, Bayesian statistics, etc. Each of these subdisciplines has been drawn upon by financial econometricians at one time or another, making it rather difficult to provide a single reference for all of these topics. Amazingly, such a reference does exist: Stuart and Ord's (1987) three-volume *tour de force*. A more compact reference that contains most of the relevant material for our purposes is the elegant monograph by Silvey (1975). For topics in time-series analysis, Hamilton (1994) is an excellent comprehensive text. Key concepts include

- Neyman-Pearson hypothesis testing
- linear regression
- maximum likelihood
- basic time-series analysis (stationarity, autoregressive and ARMA processes, vector autoregressions, unit roots, etc.)
- elementary Bayesian inference.

For continuous-time financial models, an additional dose of stochastic processes is a must, at least at the level of Cox and Miller (1965) and Hoel, Port, and Stone (1972).

1.2.3 Finance Theory Background

Since the *raison d'être* of financial econometrics is the empirical implementation and evaluation of financial models, a solid background in finance theory is the most important of all. Several texts provide excellent coverage of this material: Duffie (1992), Huang and Litzenberger (1988), Ingersoll (1987), and Merton (1990). Key concepts include

- risk aversion and expected-utility theory
- static mean-variance portfolio theory
- the Capital Asset Pricing Model (CAPM) and the Arbitrage Pricing Theory (APT)
- dynamic asset pricing models
- option pricing theory.

1.3 Notation

We have found that it is far from simple to devise a consistent notational scheme for a book of this scope. The difficulty comes from the fact that financial econometrics spans several very different strands of the finance literature, each replete with its own firmly established set of notational conventions. But the conventions in one literature often conflict with the conventions in another. Unavoidably, then, we must sacrifice either internal notational consistency across different chapters of this text or external consistency with the notation used in the professional literature. We have chosen the former as the lesser evil, but we do maintain the following conventions throughout the book:

- We use boldface for vectors and matrices, and regular face for scalars. Where possible, we use bold uppercase for matrices and bold lowercase for vectors. Thus $\mathbf{x}$ is a vector while $\mathbf{X}$ is a matrix.
- Where possible, we use uppercase letters for the levels of variables and lowercase letters for the natural logarithms (logs) of the same variables. Thus if P is an asset price, p is the log asset price.
- Our standard notation for an innovation is the Greek letter ϵ. Where we need to define several different innovations, we use the alternative Greek letters η, ξ, and ζ.
- Where possible, we use Greek letters to denote parameters or parameter vectors.
- We use the Greek letter ι to denote a vector of ones.
- We use hats to denote sample estimates, so if β is a parameter, $\hat{\beta}$ is an estimate of β.
- When we use subscripts, we always use uppercase letters for the upper limits of the subscripts. Where possible, we use the same letters for upper limits as for the subscripts themselves. Thus subscript t runs from 1 to T, subscript k runs from 1 to K, and so on. An exception is that we will let subscript i (usually denoting an asset) run from 1 to N because this notation is so common. We use t and τ for time subscripts;

i for asset subscripts; k, m, and n for lead and lag subscripts; and j as a generic subscript.

- We use the timing convention that a variable is dated t if it is known by the end of period t. Thus R_t denotes a return on an asset held from the end of period $t-1$ to the end of period t.
- In writing variance-covariance matrices, we use Ω for the variance-covariance matrix of asset returns, Σ for the variance-covariance matrix of residuals from a time-series or cross-sectional model, and $\mathbf{V}$ for the variance-covariance matrix of parameter estimators.
- We use script letters sparingly. $\mathcal{N}$ denotes the normal distribution, and $\mathcal{L}$ denotes a log likelihood function.
- We use $\Pr(\cdot)$ to denote the probability of an event.

The professional literature uses many specialized terms. Inevitably we also use these frequently, and we italicize them when they first appear in the book.

1.4 Prices, Returns, and Compounding

Virtually every aspect of financial economics involves *returns*, and there are at least two reasons for focusing our attention on returns rather than on prices. First, for the average investor, financial markets may be considered close to perfectly competitive, so that the size of the investment does not affect price changes. Therefore, since the investment "technology" is constant-returns-to-scale, the return is a complete and scale-free summary of the investment opportunity.

Second, for theoretical and empirical reasons that will become apparent below, returns have more attractive statistical properties than prices, such as stationarity and ergodicity. In particular, dynamic general-equilibrium models often yield nonstationary prices, but stationary returns (see, for example, Chapter 8 and Lucas [1978]).

1.4.1 Definitions and Conventions

Denote by P_t the price of an asset at date t and assume for now that this asset pays no dividends. The *simple net return*, R_t, on the asset between dates $t-1$ and t is defined as

$$R_t = \frac{P_t}{P_{t-1}} - 1. \tag{1.4.1}$$

The *simple gross return* on the asset is just one plus the net return, $1 + R_t$.

From this definition it is apparent that the asset's gross return over the most recent k periods from date $t-k$ to date t, written $1 + R_t(k)$, is simply equal to the product of the k single-period returns from $t - k + 1$ to t, i.e.,

$$
\begin{aligned}
1 + R_t(k) &\equiv (1 + R_t) \cdot (1 + R_{t-1}) \cdots (1 + R_{t-k+1}) \\
&= \frac{P_t}{P_{t-1}} \cdot \frac{P_{t-1}}{P_{t-2}} \cdot \frac{P_{t-2}}{P_{t-3}} \cdots \frac{P_{t-k+1}}{P_{t-k}} = \frac{P_t}{P_{t-k}},
\end{aligned} \qquad (1.4.2)
$$

and its net return over the most recent k periods, written $R_t(k)$, is simply equal to its k-period gross return minus one. These multiperiod returns are called *compound* returns.

Although returns are scale-free, it should be emphasized that they are *not* unitless, but are always defined with respect to some time interval, e.g., one "period." In fact, R_t is more properly called a *rate* of return, which is more cumbersome terminology but more accurate in referring to R_t as a rate or, in economic jargon, a *flow* variable. Therefore, a return of 20% is not a complete description of the investment opportunity without specification of the return horizon. In the academic literature, the return horizon is generally given explicitly, often as part of the data description, e.g., "The CRSP *monthly* returns file was used."

However, among practitioners and in the financial press, a return-horizon of one year is usually assumed implicitly; hence, unless stated otherwise, a return of 20% is generally taken to mean an *annual* return of 20%. Moreover, multiyear returns are often *annualized* to make investments with different horizons comparable, thus:

$$
\text{Annualized}[R_t(k)] = \left[\prod_{j=0}^{k-1} (1 + R_{t-j}) \right]^{1/k} - 1. \qquad (1.4.3)
$$

Since single-period returns are generally small in magnitude, the following approximation based on a first-order Taylor expansion is often used to annualize multiyear returns:

$$
\text{Annualized}[R_t(k)] \approx \frac{1}{k} \sum_{j=0}^{k-1} R_{t-j}. \qquad (1.4.4)
$$

Whether such an approximation is adequate depends on the particular application at hand; it may suffice for a quick and coarse comparison of investment performance across many assets, but for finer calculations in which the volatility of returns plays an important role, i.e., when the higher-order terms in the Taylor expansion are not negligible, the approximation (1.4.4) may break down. The only advantage of such an approximation is convenience—it is easier to calculate an arithmetic rather than a geometric average—however, this advantage has diminished considerably with the advent of cheap and convenient computing power.

Continuous Compounding

The difficulty of manipulating geometric averages such as (1.4.3) motivates another approach to compound returns, one which is not approximate and also has important implications for modeling asset returns; this is the notion of continuous compounding. The *continuously compounded return* or *log return* r_t of an asset is defined to be the natural logarithm of its gross return $(1+R_t)$:

$$r_t \equiv \log(1 + R_t) = \log \frac{P_t}{P_{t-1}} = p_t - p_{t-1}, \qquad (1.4.5)$$

where $p_t \equiv \log P_t$. When we wish to emphasize the distinction between R_t and r_t, we shall refer to R_t as a *simple* return. Our notation here deviates slightly from our convention that lowercase letters denote the logs of uppercase letters, since here we have $r_t = \log(1 + R_t)$ rather than $\log(R_t)$; we do this to maintain consistency with standard conventions.

The advantages of continuously compounded returns become clear when we consider multiperiod returns, since

$$
\begin{aligned}
r_t(k) &= \log(1 + R_t(k)) = \log((1 + R_t) \cdot (1 + R_{t-1}) \cdots (1 + R_{t-k+1})) \\
&= \log(1 + R_t) + \log(1 + R_{t-1}) + \cdots + \log(1 + R_{t-k+1}) \\
&= r_t + r_{t-1} + \cdots + r_{t-k+1}, \qquad (1.4.6)
\end{aligned}
$$

and hence the continuously compounded multiperiod return is simply the sum of continuously compounded single-period returns. Compounding, a multiplicative operation, is converted to an additive operation by taking logarithms. However, the simplification is not merely in reducing multiplication to addition (since we argued above that with modern calculators and computers, this is trivial), but more in the modeling of the statistical behavior of asset returns over time—it is far easier to derive the time-series properties of additive processes than of multiplicative processes, as we shall see in Chapter 2.

Continuously compounded returns do have one disadvantage. The simple return on a portfolio of assets is a weighted average of the simple returns on the assets themselves, where the weight on each asset is the share of the portfolio's value invested in that asset. If portfolio p places weight w_{ip} in asset i, then the return on the portfolio at time t, R_{pt}, is related to the returns on individual assets, R_{it}, $i = 1 \ldots N$, by $R_{pt} = \sum_{i=1}^{N} w_{ip} R_{it}$. Unfortunately continuously compounded returns do not share this convenient property. Since the log of a sum is not the same as the sum of logs, r_{pt} does not equal $\sum_{i=1}^{N} w_{ip} r_{it}$.

In empirical applications this problem is usually minor. When returns are measured over short intervals of time, and are therefore close to zero, the continuously compounded return on a portfolio is close to the weighted

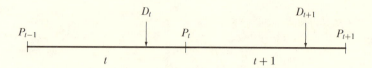

Figure 1.1. *Dividend Payment Timing Convention*

average of the continuously compounded returns on the individual assets: $r_{pt} \approx \sum_{i=1}^{N} w_{ip}r_{it}$.[2] We use this approximation in Chapter 3. Nonetheless it is common to use simple returns when a cross-section of assets is being studied, as in Chapters 4–6, and continuously compounded returns when the temporal behavior of returns is the focus of interest, as in Chapters 2 and 7.

Dividend Payments

For assets which make periodic dividend payments, we must modify our definitions of returns and compounding. Denote by D_t the asset's dividend payment at date t and assume, purely as a matter of convention, that this dividend is paid just before the date-t price P_t is recorded; hence P_t is taken to be the *ex-dividend* price at date t. Alternatively, one might describe P_t as an end-of-period asset price, as shown in Figure 1.1. Then the net simple return at date t may be defined as

$$R_t = \frac{P_t + D_t}{P_{t-1}} - 1. \tag{1.4.7}$$

Multiperiod and continuously compounded returns may be obtained in the same way as in the no-dividends case. Note that the continuously compounded return on a dividend-paying asset, $r_t = \log(P_t + D_t) - \log(P_{t-1})$, is a nonlinear function of log prices and log dividends. When the ratio of prices to dividends is not too variable, however, this function can be approximated by a linear function of log prices and dividends, as discussed in detail in Chapter 7.

Excess Returns

It is often convenient to work with an asset's excess return, defined as the difference between the asset's return and the return on some reference asset. The reference asset is often assumed to be riskless and in practice is usually a short-term Treasury bill return. Working with simple returns, the

---

[2]In the limit where time is continuous, Ito's Lemma, discussed in Section 9.1.2 of Chapter 9, can be used to relate simple and continuously compounded returns.

simple excess return on asset i is

$$Z_{it} = R_{it} - R_{0t}, \qquad (1.4.8)$$

where R_{0t} is the reference return. Alternatively one can define a log excess return as

$$z_{it} = r_{it} - r_{0t}. \qquad (1.4.9)$$

The excess return can also be thought of as the payoff on an *arbitrage portfolio* that goes long in asset i and short in the reference asset, with no net investment at the initial date. Since the initial net investment is zero, the return on the arbitrage portfolio is undefined but its dollar payoff is proportional to the excess return as defined above.

1.4.2 The Marginal, Conditional, and Joint Distribution of Returns

Having defined asset returns carefully, we can now begin to study their behavior across assets and over time. Perhaps the most important characteristic of asset returns is their randomness. The return of IBM stock over the next month is unknown today, and it is largely the explicit modeling of the sources and nature of this uncertainty that distinguishes financial economics from other social sciences. Although other branches of economics and sociology do have models of stochastic phenomena, in none of them does uncertainty play so central a role as in the pricing of financial assets—without uncertainty, much of the financial economics literature, both theoretical and empirical, would be superfluous. Therefore, we must articulate at the very start the types of uncertainty that asset returns might exhibit.

The Joint Distribution
Consider a collection of N assets at date t, each with return R_{it} at date t, where $t = 1, \ldots, T$. Perhaps the most general model of the collection of returns $\{R_{it}\}$ is its joint distribution function:

$$G(R_{11}, \ldots, R_{N1}; R_{12}, \ldots, R_{N2}; \ldots; R_{1T}, \ldots, R_{NT}; \mathbf{x} \mid \boldsymbol{\theta}), \qquad (1.4.10)$$

where $\mathbf{x}$ is a vector of *state variables*, variables that summarize the economic environment in which asset returns are determined, and $\boldsymbol{\theta}$ is a vector of fixed parameters that uniquely determines G. For notational convenience, we shall suppress the dependence of G on the parameters $\boldsymbol{\theta}$ unless it is needed.

The probability law G governs the stochastic behavior of asset returns and $\mathbf{x}$, and represents the sum total of all knowable information about them. We may then view financial econometrics as the statistical inference of $\boldsymbol{\theta}$, given G and realizations of $\{R_{it}\}$. Of course, (1.4.10) is far too general to be of any use for statistical inference, and we shall have to place further restrictions on G in the coming sections and chapters. However, (1.4.10) does serve as a convenient way to organize the many models of asset returns to be developed here and in later chapters. For example, Chapters 2 through 6 deal exclusively with the joint distribution of $\{R_{it}\}$, leaving additional state variables **x** to be considered in Chapters 7 and 8. We write this joint distribution as G_R.

Many asset pricing models, such as the Capital Asset Pricing Model (CAPM) of Sharpe (1964), Lintner (1965a, b), and Mossin (1966) considered in Chapter 5, describe the joint distribution of the cross section of returns $\{R_{1t}, \ldots, R_{Nt}\}$ at a single date t. To reduce (1.4.10) to this essentially static structure, we shall have to assert that returns are statistically independent through time and that the joint distribution of the cross-section of returns is identical across time. Although such assumptions seem extreme, they yield a rich set of implications for pricing financial assets. The CAPM, for example, delivers an explicit formula for the trade-off between risk and expected return, the celebrated security market line.

The Conditional Distribution

In Chapter 2, we place another set of restrictions on G_R which will allow us to focus on the *dynamics* of individual asset returns while abstracting from cross-sectional relations between the assets. In particular, consider the joint distribution F of $\{R_{i1}, \ldots, R_{iT}\}$ for a given asset i, and observe that we may always rewrite F as the following product:

$$F(R_{i1}, \ldots, R_{iT}) \;=\; F_{i1}(R_{i1}) \cdot F_{i2}(R_{i2} \mid R_{i1}) \cdot F_{i3}(R_{i3} \mid R_{i2}, R_{i1})$$

$$\cdots F_{iT}(R_{iT} \mid R_{iT-1}, \ldots, R_{i1}). \tag{1.4.11}$$

From (1.4.11), the temporal dependencies implicit in $\{R_{it}\}$ are apparent. Issues of predictability in asset returns involve aspects of their *conditional* distributions and, in particular, how the conditional distributions evolve through time.

By placing further restrictions on the conditional distributions $F_{it}(\cdot)$, we shall be able to estimate the parameters θ implicit in (1.4.11) and examine the predictability of asset returns explicitly. For example, one version of the random-walk hypothesis is obtained by the restriction that the conditional distribution of return R_{it} is equal to its marginal distribution, i.e., $F_{it}(R_{it} \mid \cdot) = F_{it}(R_{it})$. If this is the case, then returns are temporally independent and therefore unpredictable using past returns. Weaker versions of the random walk are obtained by imposing weaker restrictions on $F_{it}(R_{it} \mid \cdot)$.

The Unconditional Distribution

In cases where an asset return's conditional distribution differs from its marginal or unconditional distribution, it is clearly the conditional distribution that is relevant for issues involving predictability. However, the properties of the unconditional distribution of returns may still be of some interest, especially in cases where we expect predictability to be minimal.

One of the most common models for asset returns is the temporally independently and identically distributed (IID) normal model, in which returns are assumed to be independent over time (although perhaps cross-sectionally correlated), identically distributed over time, and normally distributed. The original formulation of the CAPM employed this assumption of normality, although returns were only implicitly assumed to be temporally IID (since it was a static "two-period" model). More recently, models of asymmetric information such as Grossman (1989) and Grossman and Stiglitz (1980) also use normality.

While the temporally IID normal model may be tractable, it suffers from at least two important drawbacks. First, most financial assets exhibit limited liability, so that the largest loss an investor can realize is his total investment and no more. This implies that the smallest net return achievable is -1 or -100%. But since the normal distribution's support is the entire real line, this lower bound of -1 is clearly violated by normality. Of course, it may be argued that by choosing the mean and variance appropriately, the probability of realizations below -1 can be made arbitrarily small; however it will never be zero, as limited liability requires.

Second, if single-period returns are assumed to be normal, then multi-period returns cannot also be normal since they are the *products* of the single-period returns. Now the *sums* of normal single-period returns are indeed normal, but the sum of single-period simple returns does not have any economically meaningful interpretation. However, as we saw in Section 1.4.1, the sum of single-period continuously compounded returns does have a meaningful interpretation as a multiperiod continuously compounded return.

The Lognormal Distribution

A sensible alternative is to assume that continuously compounded single-period returns r_{it} are IID normal, which implies that single-period gross simple returns are distributed as IID *lognormal* variates, since $r_{it} \equiv \log(1 + R_{it})$. We may express the lognormal model then as

$$r_{it} \sim \mathcal{N}(\mu_i, \sigma_i^2). \tag{1.4.12}$$

Under the lognormal model, if the mean and variance of r_{it} are μ_i and σ_i^2, respectively, then the mean and variance of simple returns are given by

$$\mathrm{E}[R_{it}] = e^{\mu_i + \frac{\sigma_i^2}{2}} - 1 \tag{1.4.13}$$

$$\mathrm{Var}[R_{it}] = e^{2\mu_i + \sigma_i^2}[e^{\sigma_i^2} - 1]. \tag{1.4.14}$$

Alternatively, if we assume that the mean and variance of simple returns R_{it} are m_i and s_i^2, respectively, then under the lognormal model the mean and variance of r_{it} are given by

$$E[r_{it}] \;=\; \log \frac{m_i + 1}{\sqrt{1 + \left(\frac{s_i}{m_i+1}\right)^2}} \qquad (1.4.15)$$

$$\text{Var}[r_{it}] \;=\; \log\left[1 + \left(\frac{s_i}{m_i + 1}\right)^2\right]. \qquad (1.4.16)$$

The lognormal model has the added advantage of not violating limited liability, since limited liability yields a lower bound of zero on $(1 + R_{it})$, which is satisfied by $(1 + R_{it}) = e^{r_{it}}$ when r_{it} is assumed to be normal.

The lognormal model has a long and illustrious history, beginning with the dissertation of the French mathematician Louis Bachelier (1900), which contained the mathematics of Brownian motion and heat conduction, five years prior to Einstein's (1905) famous paper. For other reasons that will become apparent in later chapters (see, especially, Chapter 9), the lognormal model has become the workhorse of the financial asset pricing literature.

But as attractive as the lognormal model is, it is not consistent with all the properties of historical stock returns. At short horizons, historical returns show weak evidence of skewness and strong evidence of excess kurtosis. The *skewness*, or normalized third moment, of a random variable ϵ with mean μ and variance σ^2 is defined by

$$S[\epsilon] \;\equiv\; E\left[\frac{(\epsilon - \mu)^3}{\sigma^3}\right]. \qquad (1.4.17)$$

The *kurtosis*, or normalized fourth moment, of ϵ is defined by

$$K[\epsilon] \;\equiv\; E\left[\frac{(\epsilon - \mu)^4}{\sigma^4}\right]. \qquad (1.4.18)$$

The normal distribution has skewness equal to zero, as do all other symmetric distributions. The normal distribution has kurtosis equal to 3, but *fat-tailed* distributions with extra probability mass in the tail areas have higher or even infinite kurtosis.

Skewness and kurtosis can be estimated in a sample of data by constructing the obvious sample averages: the sample mean

$$\hat{\mu} \;\equiv\; \frac{1}{T} \sum_{t=1}^{T} \epsilon_t, \qquad (1.4.19)$$

the sample variance

$$\hat{\sigma}^2 \equiv \frac{1}{T} \sum_{t=1}^{T} (\epsilon_t - \hat{\mu})^2, \tag{1.4.20}$$

the sample skewness

$$\hat{S} \equiv \frac{1}{T\hat{\sigma}^3} \sum_{t=1}^{T} (\epsilon_t - \hat{\mu})^3, \tag{1.4.21}$$

and the sample kurtosis

$$\hat{K} \equiv \frac{1}{T\hat{\sigma}^4} \sum_{t=1}^{T} (\epsilon_t - \hat{\mu})^4. \tag{1.4.22}$$

In large samples of normally distributed data, the estimators $\hat{S}$ and $\hat{K}$ are normally distributed with means 0 and 3 and variances $6/T$ and $24/T$, respectively (see Stuart and Ord [1987, Vol. 1]). Since 3 is the kurtosis of the normal distribution, sample *excess kurtosis* is defined to be sample kurtosis less 3. Sample estimates of skewness for daily US stock returns tend to be negative for stock indexes but close to zero or positive for individual stocks. Sample estimates of excess kurtosis for daily US stock returns are large and positive for both indexes and individual stocks, indicating that returns have more mass in the tail areas than would be predicted by a normal distribution.

Stable Distributions
Early studies of stock market returns attempted to capture this excess kurtosis by modeling the distribution of continuously compounded returns as a member of the *stable* class (also called the *stable Pareto-Lévy* or *stable Paretian*), of which the normal is a special case.[3] The stable distributions are a natural generalization of the normal in that, as their name suggests, they are stable under addition, i.e., a sum of stable random variables is also a stable random variable. However, nonnormal stable distributions have more probability mass in the tail areas than the normal. In fact, the nonnormal stable distributions are so fat-tailed that their variance and all higher moments are infinite. Sample estimates of variance or kurtosis for random variables with

---

[3]The French probabilist Paul Lévy (1924) was perhaps the first to initiate a general investigation of stable distributions and provided a complete characterization of them through their log-characteristic functions (see below). Lévy (1925) also showed that the tail probabilities of stable distributions approximate those of the Pareto distribution, hence the term "stable Pareto-Lévy" or "stable Paretian" distribution. For applications to financial asset returns, see Blattberg and Gonedes (1974); Fama (1965); Fama and Roll (1971); Fielitz (1976); Fielitz and Rozell (1983); Granger and Morgenstern (1970); Hagerman (1978); Hsu, Miller, and Wichern (1974); Mandelbrot (1963); Mandelbrot and Taylor (1967); Officer (1972); Samuelson (1967, 1976); Simkowitz and Beedles (1980); and Tucker (1992).

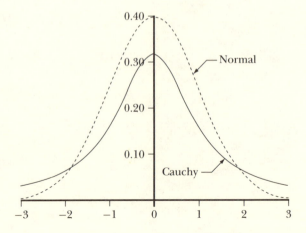

Figure 1.2. *Comparison of Stable and Normal Density Functions*

these distributions will not converge as the sample size increases, but will tend to increase indefinitely.

Closed-form expressions for the density functions of stable random variables are available for only three special cases: the normal, the Cauchy, and the Bernoulli cases.[4] Figure 1.2 illustrates the Cauchy distribution, with density function

$$f(x) = \frac{1}{\pi} \frac{\gamma}{\gamma^2 + (x - \delta)^2}. \qquad (1.4.23)$$

In Figure 1.2, (1.4.23) is graphed with parameters $\delta = 0$ and $\gamma = 1$, and it is apparent from the comparison with the normal density function (dashed lines) that the Cauchy has fatter tails than the normal.

Although stable distributions were popular in the 1960's and early 1970's, they are less commonly used today. They have fallen out of favor partly because they make theoretical modelling so difficult; standard finance theory

---

[4]However, Lévy (1925) derived the following explicit expression for the logarithm of the characteristic function $\varphi(t)$ of any stable random variable X: $\log \varphi(t) \equiv \log E[e^{itX}] = i\delta t - \gamma|t|^\alpha [1 - i\beta \operatorname{sgn}(t) \tan(\alpha\pi/2)]$, where $(\alpha, \beta, \delta, \gamma)$ are the four parameters that characterize each stable distribution. $\delta \in (-\infty, \infty)$ is said to be the *location* parameter, $\beta \in (-\infty, \infty)$ is the *skewness index*, $\gamma \in (0, \infty)$ is the *scale* parameter, and $\alpha \in (0, 2]$ is the *exponent*. When $\alpha = 2$, the stable distribution reduces to a normal. As α decreases from 2 to 0, the tail areas of the stable distribution become increasingly "fatter" than the normal. When $\alpha \in (1, 2)$, the stable distribution has a finite mean given by δ, but when $\alpha \in (0, 1]$, even the mean is infinite. The parameter β measures the symmetry of the stable distribution; when $\beta = 0$ the distribution is symmetric, and when $\beta > 0$ (or $\beta < 0$) the distribution is skewed to the right (or left). When $\beta = 0$ and $\alpha = 1$ we have the Cauchy distribution, and when $\alpha = 1/2$, $\beta = 1$, $\delta = 0$, and $\gamma = 1$ we have the Bernoulli distribution.

almost always requires finite second moments of returns, and often finite higher moments as well. Stable distributions also have some counterfactual implications. First, they imply that sample estimates of the variance and higher moments of returns will tend to increase as the sample size increases, whereas in practice these estimates seem to converge. Second, they imply that long-horizon returns will be just as non-normal as short-horizon returns (since long-horizon returns are sums of short-horizon returns, and these distributions are stable under addition). In practice the evidence for non-normality is much weaker for long-horizon returns than for short-horizon returns.

Recent research tends instead to model returns as drawn from a fat-tailed distribution with finite higher moments, such as the t distribution, or as drawn from a mixture of distributions. For example the return might be conditionally normal, conditional on a variance parameter which is itself random; then the unconditional distribution of returns is a mixture of normal distributions, some with small conditional variances that concentrate mass around the mean and others with large conditional variances that put mass in the tails of the distribution. The result is a fat-tailed unconditional distribution with a finite variance and finite higher moments. Since all moments are finite, the Central Limit Theorem applies and long-horizon returns will tend to be closer to the normal distribution than short-horizon returns. It is natural to model the conditional variance as a time-series process, and we discuss this in detail in Chapter 12.

An Empirical Illustration

Table 1.1 contains some sample statistics for individual and aggregate stock returns from the Center for Research in Securities Prices (CRSP) for 1962 to 1994 which illustrate some of the issues discussed in the previous sections. Sample moments, calculated in the straightforward way described in (1.4.19)–(1.4.22), are reported for value- and equal-weighted indexes of stocks listed on the New York Stock Exchange (NYSE) and American Stock Exchange (AMEX), and for ten individual stocks. The individual stocks were selected from market-capitalization deciles using 1979 end-of-year market capitalizations for all stocks in the CRSP NYSE/AMEX universe, where International Business Machines is the largest decile's representative and Continental Materials Corp. is the smallest decile's representative.

Panel A reports statistics for daily returns. The daily index returns have extremely high sample excess kurtosis, 34.9 and 26.0 respectively, a clear sign of fat tails. Although the excess kurtosis estimates for daily individual stock returns are generally less than those for the indexes, they are still large, ranging from 3.35 to 59.4. Since there are 8179 observations, the standard error for the kurtosis estimate under the null hypothesis of normality is $\sqrt{24/8179} = 0.054$, so these estimates of excess kurtosis are overwhelmingly statistically significant. The skewness estimates are negative for the daily index returns, -1.33 and -0.93 respectively, but generally positive for the individual stock returns, ranging from -0.18 to 2.25. Many of the skewness estimates are also statistically significant as the standard error under the null hypothesis of normality is $\sqrt{6/8179} = 0.027$.

Panel B reports sample statistics for monthly returns. These are considerably less leptokurtic than daily returns—the value- and equal-weighted CRSP monthly index returns have excess kurtosis of only 2.42 and 4.14, respectively, an order of magnitude smaller than the excess kurtosis of daily returns. As there are only 390 observations the standard error for the kurtosis estimate is also much larger, 0.248. This is one piece of evidence that has led researchers to use fat-tailed distributions with finite higher moments, for which the Central Limit Theorem applies and drives longer-horizon returns towards normality.

1.5 Market Efficiency

The origins of the Efficient Markets Hypothesis (EMH) can be traced back at least as far as the pioneering theoretical contribution of Bachelier (1900) and the empirical research of Cowles (1933). The modern literature in economics begins with Samuelson (1965), whose contribution is neatly summarized by the title of his article: "Proof that Properly Anticipated Prices Fluctuate Randomly".[5] In an informationally efficient market—not to be confused with an allocationally or Pareto-efficient market—price changes must be unforecastable if they are properly anticipated, i.e., if they fully incorporate the expectations and information of all market participants.

Fama (1970) summarizes this idea in his classic survey by writing: "A market in which prices always 'fully reflect' available information is called 'efficient'." Fama's use of quotation marks around the words "fully reflect" indicates that these words are a form of shorthand and need to be explained more fully. More recently, Malkiel (1992) has offered the following more explicit definition:

> A capital market is said to be efficient if it fully and correctly reflects all relevant information in determining security prices. Formally, the market is said to be efficient with respect to some information set ... if security prices would be unaffected by revealing that information to all participants. Moreover, efficiency with respect to an information set

---

[5]Bernstein (1992) discusses the contributions of Bachelier, Cowles, Samuelson, and many other early authors. The articles reprinted in Lo (1996) include some of the most important papers in this literature.

Table 1.1. *Stock market returns, 1962 to 1994.*

Security	Mean	Standard Deviation	Skewness	Excess Kurtosis	Minimum	Maximum
		Panel A: Daily Returns				
Value-Weighted Index	0.044	0.82	−1.33	34.92	−18.10	8.87
Equal-Weighted Index	0.073	0.76	−0.93	26.03	−14.19	9.83
International Business Machines	0.039	1.42	−0.18	12.48	−22.96	11.72
General Signal Corp.	0.054	1.66	0.01	3.35	−13.46	9.43
Wrigley Co.	0.072	1.45	−0.00	11.03	−18.67	11.89
Interlake Corp.	0.043	2.16	0.72	12.35	−17.24	23.08
Raytech Corp.	0.050	3.39	2.25	59.40	−57.90	75.00
Ampco-Pittsburgh Corp.	0.053	2.41	0.66	5.02	−19.05	19.18
Energen Corp.	0.054	1.41	0.27	5.91	−12.82	11.11
General Host Corp.	0.070	2.79	0.74	6.18	−23.53	22.92
Garan Inc.	0.079	2.35	0.72	7.13	−16.67	19.07
Continental Materials Corp.	0.143	5.24	0.93	6.49	−26.92	50.00
		Panel B: Monthly Returns				
Value-Weighted Index	0.96	4.33	−0.29	2.42	−21.81	16.51
Equal-Weighted Index	1.25	5.77	0.07	4.14	−26.80	33.17
International Business Machines	0.81	6.18	−0.14	0.83	−26.19	18.95
General Signal Corp.	1.17	8.19	−0.02	1.87	−36.77	29.73
Wrigley Co.	1.51	6.68	0.30	1.31	−20.26	29.72
Interlake Corp.	0.86	9.38	0.67	4.09	−30.28	54.84
Raytech Corp.	0.83	14.88	2.73	22.70	−45.65	142.11
Ampco-Pittsburgh Corp.	1.06	10.64	0.77	2.04	−36.08	46.94
Energen Corp.	1.10	5.75	1.47	12.47	−24.61	48.36
General Host Corp.	1.33	11.67	0.35	1.11	−38.05	42.86
Garan Inc.	1.64	11.30	0.76	2.30	−35.48	51.60
Continental Materials Corp.	1.64	17.76	1.13	3.33	−58.09	84.78

Summary statistics for daily and monthly returns (in percent) of CRSP equal- and value-weighted stock indexes and ten individual securities continuously listed over the entire sample period from July 3, 1962 to December 30, 1994. Individual securities are selected to represent stocks in each size decile. Statistics are defined in (1.4.19)–(1.4.22).

... implies that it is impossible to make economic profits by trading on the basis of [that information set].

Malkiel's first sentence repeats Fama's definition. His second and third sentences expand the definition in two alternative ways. The second sentence suggests that market efficiency can be tested by revealing information to market participants and measuring the reaction of security prices. If prices do not move when information is revealed, then the market is efficient with respect to that information. Although this is clear conceptually, it is hard to carry out such a test in practice (except perhaps in a laboratory).

Malkiel's third sentence suggests an alternative way to judge the efficiency of a market, by measuring the profits that can be made by trading on information. This idea is the foundation of almost all the empirical work on market efficiency. It has been used in two main ways. First, many researchers have tried to measure the profits earned by market professionals such as mutual fund managers. If these managers achieve superior returns (after adjustment for risk) then the market is not efficient with respect to the information possessed by the managers. This approach has the advantage that it concentrates on real trading by real market participants, but it has the disadvantage that one cannot directly observe the information used by the managers in their trading strategies (see Fama [1970, 1991] for a thorough review of this literature).

As an alternative, one can ask whether hypothetical trading based on an explicitly specified information set would earn superior returns. To implement this approach, one must first choose an information set. The classic taxonomy of information sets, due to Roberts (1967), distinguishes among

Weak-form Efficiency: The information set includes only the history of prices or returns themselves.
Semistrong-Form Efficiency: The information set includes all information known to all market participants (*publicly available* information).
Strong-Form Efficiency: The information set includes all information known to any market participant (*private* information).

The next step is to specify a model of "normal" returns. Here the classic assumption is that the normal returns on a security are constant over time, but in recent years there has been increased interest in equilibrium models with time-varying normal security returns.

Finally, abnormal security returns are computed as the difference between the return on a security and its normal return, and forecasts of the abnormal returns are constructed using the chosen information set. If the abnormal security return is unforecastable, and in this sense "random," then the hypothesis of market efficiency is not rejected.

1.5.1 Efficient Markets and the Law of Iterated Expectations

The idea that efficient security returns should be random has often caused confusion. Many people seem to think that an efficient security price should be smooth rather than random. Black (1971) has attacked this idea rather effectively:

> A perfect market for a stock is one in which there are no profits to be made by people who have no special information about the company, and in which it is difficult even for people who do have special information to make profits, because the price adjusts so rapidly as the information becomes available.... Thus we would like to see *randomness* in the prices of successive transactions, rather than great continuity.... Randomness means that a series of small upward movements (or small downward movements) is very unlikely. If the price is going to move up, it should move up all at once, rather than in a series of small steps.... Large price movements are desirable, so long as they are not consistently followed by price movements in the opposite direction.

Underlying this confusion may be a belief that returns cannot be random if security prices are determined by discounting future cash flows. Smith (1968), for example, writes: "I suspect that even if the random walkers announced a perfect mathematic proof of randomness, I would go on believing that in the long run future earnings influence present value."

In fact, the discounted present-value model of a security price is entirely consistent with randomness in security returns. The key to understanding this is the so-called *Law of Iterated Expectations*. To state this result we define information sets I_t and J_t, where $I_t \subset J_t$ so all the information in I_t is also in J_t but J_t is superior because it contains some extra information. We consider expectations of a random variable X conditional on these information sets, written $E[X \mid I_t]$ or $E[X \mid J_t]$. The Law of Iterated Expectations says that $E[X \mid I_t] = E[E[X \mid J_t] \mid I_t]$. In words, if one has limited information I_t, the best forecast one can make of a random variable X is the forecast of the forecast one would make of X if one had superior information J_t. This can be rewritten as $E[X - E[X \mid J_t] \mid I_t] = 0$, which has an intuitive interpretation: One cannot use limited information I_t to predict the forecast error one would make if one had superior information J_t.

Samuelson (1965) was the first to show the relevance of the Law of Iterated Expectations for security market analysis; LeRoy (1989) gives a lucid review of the argument. We discuss the point in detail in Chapter 7, but a brief summary may be helpful here. Suppose that a security price at time t, P_t, can be written as the rational expectation of some "fundamental value" V^*, conditional on information I_t available at time t. Then we have

$$P_t = E[V^* \mid I_t] = E_t V^*. \tag{1.5.1}$$

The same equation holds one period ahead, so

$$P_{t+1} = E[V^* \mid I_{t+1}] = E_{t+1} V^*. \tag{1.5.2}$$

But then the expectation of the change in the price over the next period is

$$\mathrm{E}_t[P_{t+1} - P_t] \;=\; \mathrm{E}_t[\mathrm{E}_{t+1}[V^*] - \mathrm{E}_t[V^*]] \;=\; 0, \qquad (1.5.3)$$

because $I_t \subset I_{t+1}$, so $\mathrm{E}_t[\mathrm{E}_{t+1}[V^*]] = \mathrm{E}_t[V^*]$ by the Law of Iterated Expectations. Thus realized changes in prices are unforecastable given information in the set I_t.

1.5.2 Is Market Efficiency Testable?

Although the empirical methodology summarized here is well-established, there are some serious difficulties in interpreting its results. First, any test of efficiency must assume an equilibrium model that defines normal security returns. If efficiency is rejected, this could be because the market is truly inefficient or because an incorrect equilibrium model has been assumed. This *joint hypothesis* problem means that market efficiency as such can never be rejected.

Second, perfect efficiency is an unrealistic benchmark that is unlikely to hold in practice. Even in theory, as Grossman and Stiglitz (1980) have shown, abnormal returns will exist if there are costs of gathering and processing information. These returns are necessary to compensate investors for their information-gathering and information-processing expenses, and are no longer abnormal when these expenses are properly accounted for. In a large and liquid market, information costs are likely to justify only small abnormal returns, but it is difficult to say how small, even if such costs could be measured precisely.

The notion of *relative* efficiency—the efficiency of one market measured against another, e.g., the New York Stock Exchange vs. the Paris Bourse, futures markets vs. spot markets, or auction vs. dealer markets—may be a more useful concept than the all-or-nothing view taken by much of the traditional market-efficiency literature. The advantages of relative efficiency over absolute efficiency are easy to see by way of an analogy. Physical systems are often given an efficiency rating based on the relative proportion of energy or fuel converted to useful work. Therefore, a piston engine may be rated at 60% efficiency, meaning that on average 60% of the energy contained in the engine's fuel is used to turn the crankshaft, with the remaining 40% lost to other forms of work such as heat, light, or noise.

Few engineers would ever consider performing a statistical test to determine whether or not a given engine is perfectly efficient—such an engine exists only in the idealized frictionless world of the imagination. But measuring relative efficiency—relative to the frictionless ideal—is commonplace. Indeed, we have come to expect such measurements for many household products: air conditioners, hot water heaters, refrigerators, etc. Similarly, market efficiency is an idealization that is economically unrealizable, but that serves as a useful benchmark for measuring relative efficiency.

For these reasons, in this book we do not take a stand on market efficiency itself, but focus instead on the statistical methods that can be used to test the joint hypothesis of market efficiency and market equilibrium. Although many of the techniques covered in these pages are central to the market-efficiency debate—tests of variance bounds, Euler equations, the CAPM and the APT—we feel that they can be more profitably applied to measuring efficiency rather than to testing it. And if some markets turn out to be particularly inefficient, the diligent reader of this text will be well-prepared to take advantage of the opportunity.

2

The Predictability of Asset Returns

ONE OF THE EARLIEST and most enduring questions of financial econometrics is whether financial asset prices are forecastable. Perhaps because of
the obvious analogy between financial investments and games of chance,
mathematical models of asset prices have an unusually rich history that pre-
dates virtually every other aspect of economic analysis. The fact that many
prominent mathematicians and scientists have applied their considerable
skills to forecasting financial securities prices is a testament to the fascination
and the challenges of this problem. Indeed, modern financial economics is
firmly rooted in early attempts to "beat the market," an endeavor that is still
of current interest, discussed and debated in journal articles, conferences,
and at cocktail parties!

In this chapter, we consider the problem of forecasting future price
changes, using only past price changes to construct our forecasts. Although
restricting our forecasts to be functions of past price changes may seem too
restrictive to be of any interest—after all, investors are constantly bombarded
with vast quantities of diverse information—nevertheless, even as simple a
problem as this can yield surprisingly rich insights into the behavior of asset
prices. We shall see that the martingale and the random walk, two of the most
important ideas in probability theory and financial economics, grew out of
this relatively elementary exercise. Moreover, despite the fact that we shall
present more sophisticated models of asset prices in Chapters 4–9, where
additional economic variables are used to construct forecasts, whether future price changes can be predicted by past price changes alone is still a
subject of controversy and empirical investigation.

In Section 2.1 we review the various versions of the random walk hypothesis and develop tests for each of these versions in Sections 2.2–2.4.
Long-horizon returns play a special role in detecting certain violations of
the random walk and we explore some of their advantages and disadvantages in Section 2.5. Focusing on long-horizon returns leads naturally to

the notion of long-range dependence, and a test for this phenomenon is presented in Section 2.6. For completeness, we provide a brief discussion of tests for unit roots, which are sometimes confused with tests of the random walk. In Section 2.8 we present several empirical illustrations that document important departures from the random walk hypothesis for recent US stock market data.

2.1 The Random Walk Hypotheses

A useful way to organize the various versions of the random walk and martingale models that we shall present below is to consider the various kinds of dependence that can exist between an asset's returns r_t and r_{t+k} at two dates t and $t + k$. To do this, define the random variables $f(r_t)$ and $g(r_{t+k})$ where $f(\cdot)$ and $g(\cdot)$ are two arbitrary functions, and consider the situations in which

$$\text{Cov}[f(r_t), g(r_{t+k})] = 0 \qquad (2.1.1)$$

for all t and for $k \neq 0$. For appropriately chosen $f(\cdot)$ and $g(\cdot)$, virtually all versions of the random walk and martingale hypotheses are captured by (2.1.1), which may be interpreted as an *orthogonality* condition.

For example, if $f(\cdot)$ and $g(\cdot)$ are restricted to be arbitrary *linear* functions, then (2.1.1) implies that returns are serially uncorrelated, corresponding to the *Random Walk 3* model described in Section 2.1.3 below. Alternatively, if $f(\cdot)$ is unrestricted but $g(\cdot)$ is restricted to be linear, then (2.1.1) is equivalent to the martingale hypothesis described in Section 2.1. Finally, if (2.1.1) holds for all functions $f(\cdot)$ and $g(\cdot)$, this implies that returns are mutually independent, corresponding to the *Random Walk 1* and *Random Walk 2* models discussed in Sections 2.1.1 and 2.1.2, respectively. This classification is summarized in Table 2.1.

Although there are several other ways to characterize the various random walk and martingale models, condition (2.1.1) and Table 2.1 are particularly relevant for economic hypotheses since almost all equilibrium asset-pricing models can be reduced to a set of orthogonality conditions. This interpretation is explored extensively in Chapters 8 and 12.

The Martingale Model

Perhaps the earliest model of financial asset prices was the *martingale* model, whose origin lies in the history of games of chance and the birth of probability theory. The prominent Italian mathematician Girolamo Cardano proposed an elementary theory of gambling in his 1565 manuscript *Liber de*

Table 2.1. *Classification of random walk and martingale hypotheses.*

$\mathrm{Cov}[f(r_t), g(r_{t+k})] = 0$	$g(r_{t+k})$, $\forall g(\cdot)$ Linear	$g(r_{t+k})$, $\forall g(\cdot)$
$f(r_t)$, $\forall f(\cdot)$ Linear	Uncorrelated Increments, Random Walk 3: $\mathrm{Proj}[r_{t+k}\vert r_t] = \mu$	—
$f(r_t)$, $\forall f(\cdot)$	Martingale/Fair Game: $\mathrm{E}[r_{t+k}\vert r_t] = \mu$	Independent Increments, Random Walks 1 and 2: $\mathrm{pdf}(r_{t+k}\vert r_t) = \mathrm{pdf}(r_{t+k})$

"Proj[y | x]" denotes the linear projection of y onto x, and "pdf(·)" denotes the probability density function of its argument.

Ludo Aleae (*The Book of Games of Chance*), in which he wrote:[1]

> The most fundamental principle of all in gambling is simply equal con-
> ditions, e.g., of opponents, of bystanders, of money, of situation, of the
> dice box, and of the die itself. To the extent to which you depart from
> that equality, if it is in your opponent's favour, you are a fool, and if in
> your own, you are unjust.

This passage clearly contains the notion of a *fair game*, a game which is neither
in your favor nor your opponent's, and this is the essence of a *martingale*, a
stochastic process $\{P_t\}$ which satisfies the following condition:

$$E[P_{t+1} \mid P_t, P_{t-1}, \ldots] = P_t, \tag{2.1.2}$$

or, equivalently,

$$E[P_{t+1} - P_t \mid P_t, P_{t-1}, \ldots] = 0. \tag{2.1.3}$$

If P_t represents one's cumulative winnings or wealth at date t from playing
some game of chance each period, then a fair game is one for which the
expected wealth next period is simply equal to this period's wealth (see
(2.1.2)), conditioned on the history of the game. Alternatively, a game is fair
if the expected incremental winnings at any stage is zero when conditioned
on the history of the game (see (2.1.3)).

  If P_t is taken to be an asset's price at date t, then the martingale hypothesis states that tomorrow's price is expected to be equal to today's price,
given the asset's entire price history. Alternatively, the asset's expected price
change is zero when conditioned on the asset's price history; hence its price
is just as likely to rise as it is to fall. From a forecasting perspective, the
martingale hypothesis implies that the "best" forecast of tomorrow's price is
simply today's price, where "best" means minimal mean-squared error (see
Chapter 7).

  Another aspect of the martingale hypothesis is that nonoverlapping
price changes are uncorrelated at all leads and lags, which implies the in-
effectiveness of all *linear* forecasting rules for future price changes based
on historical prices alone. The fact that so sweeping an implication could
come from as simple a model as (2.1.2) foreshadows the important role that
the martingale hypothesis will play in the modeling of asset price dynamics
(see the discussion below and Chapter 7).

  In fact, the martingale was long considered to be a necessary condition
for an *efficient* asset market, one in which the information contained in past
prices is instantly, fully, and perpetually reflected in the asset's current price.[2]
If the market is efficient, then it should not be possible to profit by trading on

---

[1] See Hald (1990, Chapter 4) for further details.
[2] See Samuelson (1965, 1972, 1973). Roberts (1967) calls the martingale hypothesis *weak-
form* market efficiency. He also defines an asset market to be *semistrong-form* and *strong-form*

the information contained in the asset's price history; hence the conditional expectation of future price changes, conditional on the price history, cannot be either positive or negative (if shortsales are feasible) and therefore must be zero. This notion of efficiency has a wonderfully counterintuitive and seemingly contradictory flavor to it: The more efficient the market, the more random is the sequence of price changes generated by the market, and the most efficient market of all is one in which price changes are completely random and unpredictable.

However, one of the central tenets of modern financial economics is the necessity of some trade-off between risk and expected return, and although the martingale hypothesis places a restriction on expected returns, it does not account for risk in any way. In particular, if an asset's expected price change is positive, it may be the reward necessary to attract investors to hold the asset and bear its associated risks. Therefore, despite the intuitive appeal that the fair-game interpretation might have, it has been shown that the martingale property is neither a necessary nor a sufficient condition for rationally determined asset prices (see, for example, Leroy [1973], Lucas [1978], and Chapter 8).

Nevertheless, the martingale has become a powerful tool in probability and statistics and also has important applications in modern theories of asset prices. For example, once asset returns are properly adjusted for risk, the martingale property does hold (see Lucas [1978], Cox and Ross [1976], Harrison and Kreps [1979]). In particular, we shall see in Chapter 8 that marginal-utility-weighted prices do follow martingales under quite general conditions. This risk-adjusted martingale property has led to a veritable revolution in the pricing of complex financial instruments such as options, swaps, and other derivative securities (see Chapters 9, 12, and Merton [1990], for example). Moreover, the martingale led to the development of a closely related model that has now become an integral part of virtually every scientific discipline concerned with dynamics: the random walk hypothesis.

2.1.1 The Random Walk 1: IID Increments

Perhaps the simplest version of the random walk hypothesis is the independently and identically distributed (IID) increments case in which the dynamics of $\{P_t\}$ are given by the following equation:

$$P_t = \mu + P_{t-1} + \epsilon_t, \qquad \epsilon_t \sim \text{IID}(0, \sigma^2) \qquad (2.1.4)$$

where μ is the expected price change or *drift*, and $\text{IID}(0, \sigma^2)$ denotes that ϵ_t is independently and identically distributed with mean 0 and variance σ^2. The

efficient if the conditional expectation of future price changes is zero, conditioned on all available public information, and all available public and private information, respectively. See Chapter 1 for further discussion of these concepts.

independence of the increments $\{\epsilon_t\}$ implies that the random walk is also a fair game, but in a much stronger sense than the martingale: Independence implies not only that increments are uncorrelated, but that any nonlinear functions of the increments are also uncorrelated. We shall call this the *Random Walk 1* model or RW1.

To develop some intuition for RW1, consider its conditional mean and variance at date t, conditional on some initial value P_0 at date 0:

$$\mathrm{E}[P_t \mid P_0] \;=\; P_0 + \mu t \qquad\qquad (2.1.5)$$

$$\mathrm{Var}[P_t \mid P_0] \;=\; \sigma^2 t, \qquad\qquad (2.1.6)$$

which follows from recursive substitution of lagged P_t in (2.1.4) and the IID increments assumption. From (2.1.5) and (2.1.6) it is apparent that the random walk is nonstationary and that its conditional mean and variance are both linear in time. These implications also hold for the two other forms of the random walk hypothesis (RW2 and RW3) described below.

Perhaps the most common distributional assumption for the innovations or increments ϵ_t is normality. If the ϵ_t's are IID $\mathcal{N}(0, \sigma^2)$, then (2.1.4) is equivalent to an *arithmetic Brownian motion*, sampled at regularly spaced unit intervals (see Section 9.1 in Chapter 9). This distributional assumption simplifies many of the calculations surrounding the random walk, but suffers from the same problem that afflicts normally distributed returns: violation of limited liability. If the conditional distribution of P_t is normal, then there will always be a positive probability that $P_t < 0$.

To avoid violating limited liability, we may use the same device as in Section 1.4.2, namely, to assert that the natural logarithm of prices $p_t \equiv \log P_t$ follows a random walk with normally distributed increments; hence

$$p_t \;=\; \mu + p_{t-1} + \epsilon_t, \qquad \epsilon_t \; \text{IID} \; \mathcal{N}(0, \sigma^2). \qquad\qquad (2.1.7)$$

This implies that continuously compounded returns are IID normal variates with mean μ and variance σ^2, which yields the lognormal model of Bachelier (1900) and Einstein (1905). We shall return to this in Section 9.1 of Chapter 9.

2.1.2 The Random Walk 2: Independent Increments

Despite the elegance and simplicity of RW1, the assumption of identically distributed increments is not plausible for financial asset prices over long time spans. For example, over the two-hundred-year history of the New York Stock Exchange, there have been countless changes in the economic, social, technological, institutional, and regulatory environment in which stock prices are determined. The assertion that the probability law of daily stock returns has remained the same over this two-hundred-year period is simply implausible. Therefore, we relax the assumptions of RW1 to include processes with independent but not identically distributed (INID) increments, and we shall call this the *Random Walk 2* model or RW2. RW2 clearly contains RW1 as a special case, but also contains considerably more general price processes. For example, RW2 allows for unconditional heteroskedasticity in the ϵ_t's, a particularly useful feature given the time-variation in volatility of many financial asset return series (see Section 12.2 in Chapter 12).

Although RW2 is weaker than RW1 (see Table 2.1), it still retains the most interesting economic property of the IID random walk: Any arbitrary transformation of future price increments is unforecastable using any arbitrary transformation of past price increments.

2.1.3 The Random Walk 3: Uncorrelated Increments

An even more general version of the random walk hypothesis—the one most often tested in the recent empirical literature—may be obtained by relaxing the independence assumption of RW2 to include processes with dependent but uncorrelated increments. This is the weakest form of the random walk hypothesis, which we shall refer to as the *Random Walk 3* model or RW3, and contains RW1 and RW2 as special cases. A simple example of a process that satisfies the assumptions of RW3 but not of RW1 or RW2 is any process for which $\text{Cov}[\epsilon_t, \epsilon_{t-k}] = 0$ for all $k \neq 0$, but where $\text{Cov}[\epsilon_t^2, \epsilon_{t-k}^2] \neq 0$ for some $k \neq 0$. Such a process has uncorrelated increments, but is clearly not independent since its squared increments are correlated (see Section 12.2 in Chapter 12 for specific examples).

2.2 Tests of Random Walk 1: IID Increments

Despite the fact that RW1 is implausible from *a priori* theoretical considerations, nevertheless tests of RW1 provide a great deal of intuition about the behavior of the random walk. For example, we shall see in Section 2.2.2 that the drift of a random walk can sometimes be misinterpreted as predictability if not properly accounted for. Before turning to those issues, we begin with a brief review of traditional statistical tests for the IID assumptions in Section 2.2.1.

2.2.1 Traditional Statistical Tests

Since the assumptions of IID are so central to classical statistical inference, it should come as no surprise that tests for these two assumptions have a long and illustrious history in statistics, with considerably broader applications than to the random walk. Because of their breadth and ubiquity, it is virtually impossible to catalog all tests of IID in any systematic fashion, and we shall mention only a few of the most well-known tests.

Since IID are properties of random variables that are not specific to a particular parametric family of distributions, many of these tests fall under the rubric of *nonparametric* tests. Some examples are the Spearman rank correlation test, Spearman's footrule test, the Kendall τ correlation test, and other tests based on linear combinations of ranks or R-statistics (see Randles and Wolfe [1979] and Serfling [1980]). By using information contained solely in the ranks of the observations, it is possible to develop tests of IID that are robust across parametric families and invariant to changes in units of measurement. Exact sampling theories for such statistics are generally available but cumbersome, involving transformations of the (discrete) uniform distribution over the set of permutations of the ranks. However, for most of these statistics, normal asymptotic approximations to the sampling distributions have been developed (see Serfling [1980]).

More recent techniques based on the empirical distribution function of the data have also been used to construct tests of IID. These tests often require slightly stronger assumptions on the joint and marginal distribution functions of the data-generating process; hence they fall into the class of *semiparametric* tests. Typically, such tests form a direct comparison between the joint and marginal empirical distribution functions or an indirect comparison using the quantiles of the two. For these test statistics, exact sampling theories are generally unavailable, and we must rely on asymptotic approximations to perform the tests (see Shorack and Wellner [1986]).

Under parametric assumptions, tests of IID are generally easier to construct. For example, to test for independence among k vectors which are jointly normally distributed, several statistics may be used: the likelihood ratio statistic, the canonical correlation, eigenvalues of the covariance matrices, etc. (see Muirhead [1983]). Of course, the tractability of such tests must be traded off against their dependence on specific parametric assumptions. Although these tests are often more powerful than their nonparametric counterparts, even small departures from the hypothesized parametric family can lead to large differences between the actual and nominal sizes of the tests in finite samples.

2.2.2 Sequences and Reversals, and Runs

The early tests of the random walk hypothesis were largely tests of RW1 and RW2. Although they are now primarily of historical interest, nevertheless we can learn a great deal about the properties of the random walk from such tests. Moreover, several recently developed econometric tools rely heavily on RW1 (see, for example, Sections 2.5 and 2.6), hence a discussion of these tests also provides us with an opportunity to develop some machinery that we shall require later.

Sequences and Reversals

We begin with the logarithmic version of RW1 or geometric Brownian motion in which the log price process p_t is assumed to follow an IID random walk *without* drift:

$$p_t = p_{t-1} + \epsilon_t, \qquad \epsilon_t \sim \text{IID}(0, \sigma^2) \qquad (2.2.1)$$

and denote by I_t the following random variable:

$$I_t = \begin{cases} 1 & \text{if} \quad r_t \equiv p_t - p_{t-1} > 0 \\ 0 & \text{if} \quad r_t \equiv p_t - p_{t-1} \leq 0. \end{cases} \qquad (2.2.2)$$

Much like the classical Bernoulli coin-toss, I_t indicates whether the date-t continuously compounded return r_t is positive or negative. In fact, the coin-tossing analogy is quite appropriate as many of the original tests of RW1 were based on simple coin-tossing probabilities.

One of the first tests of RW1 was proposed by Cowles and Jones (1937) and consists of a comparison of the frequency of *sequences* and *reversals* in historical stock returns, where the former are pairs of consecutive returns with the same sign, and the latter are pairs of consecutive returns with opposite signs. Specifically, given a sample of $n+1$ returns $r_1, \ldots, r_{n+1}$, the number of sequences N_s and reversals N_r may be expressed as simple functions of the I_t's:

$$N_s \equiv \sum_{t=1}^{n} Y_t, \qquad Y_t \equiv I_t I_{t+1} + (1 - I_t)(1 - I_{t+1}) \qquad (2.2.3)$$

$$N_r \equiv n - N_s. \qquad (2.2.4)$$

If log prices follow a driftless IID random walk (2.2.1), and if we add the further restriction that the distribution of the increments ϵ_t is symmetric, then whether r_t is positive or negative should be equally likely, a fair coin-toss with probability one-half of either outcome. This implies that for any pair of consecutive returns, a sequence and a reversal are equally probable; hence the Cowles-Jones ratio $\widehat{CJ} \equiv N_s/N_r$ should be approximately equal to one. More formally, this ratio may be interpreted as a consistent estimator of the ratio CJ of the probability π_s of a sequence to the probability of a reversal $1 - \pi_s$ since:

$$\widehat{CJ} \equiv \frac{N_s}{N_r} = \frac{N_s/n}{N_r/n} = \frac{\hat{\pi}_s}{1 - \hat{\pi}_s} \xrightarrow{pr} \frac{\pi_s}{1 - \pi_s} = CJ = \frac{\frac{1}{2}}{\frac{1}{2}} = 1,$$

where "$\overset{pr}{\rightarrow}$" denotes convergence in probability. The fact that this ratio exceeded one for many historical stock returns series led Cowles and Jones (1937) to conclude that this "represents conclusive evidence of structure in stock prices."[3]

However, the assumption of a zero drift is critical in determining the value of CJ. In particular, CJ will exceed one for an IID random walk with drift, since a drift—either positive or negative—clearly makes sequences more likely than reversals. To see this, suppose that log prices follow a normal random walk with drift:

$$p_t = \mu + p_{t-1} + \epsilon_t, \qquad \epsilon_t \sim \mathcal{N}(0, \sigma^2).$$

Then the indicator variable I_t is no longer a fair coin-toss but is biased in the direction of the drift, i.e.,

$$I_t = \begin{cases} 1 & \text{with probability } \pi \\ 0 & \text{with probability } 1 - \pi, \end{cases} \qquad (2.2.5)$$

where

$$\pi \equiv \Pr(r_t > 0) = \Phi\left(\frac{\mu}{\sigma}\right). \qquad (2.2.6)$$

If the drift μ is positive then $\pi > \frac{1}{2}$, and if it is negative then $\pi < \frac{1}{2}$. Under this more general specification, the ratio of π_s to $1 - \pi_s$ is given by

$$CJ = \frac{\pi^2 + (1 - \pi)^2}{2\pi(1 - \pi)} \geq 1.$$

As long as the drift is nonzero, it will *always* be the case that sequences are more likely than reversals, simply because a nonzero drift induces a trend in the process. It is only for the "fair-game" case of $\pi = \frac{1}{2}$ that CJ achieves its lower bound of one.

To see how large an effect a nonzero drift might have on CJ, suppose that $\mu = 0.08$ and $\sigma = 0.21$, values which correspond roughly to annual US stock returns indexes over the last half-century. This yields the following estimate of π:

$$\hat{\pi} = \Phi\left(\frac{0.08}{0.21}\right) = 0.6484$$

$$\hat{\pi}_s = \hat{\pi}^2 + (1 - \hat{\pi})^2 = 0.5440$$

$$\widehat{CJ} = 1.19,$$

---

[3]In a later study, Cowles (1960) corrects for biases in time-averaged price data and still finds CJ ratios in excess of one. However, his conclusion is somewhat more guarded: "...while our various analyses have disclosed a tendency towards persistence in stock price movements, in no case is this sufficient to provide more than negligible profits after payment of brokerage costs."

which is close to the value of 1.17 that Cowles and Jones (1937, Table 1) report for the annual returns of an index of railroad stock prices from 1835 to 1935. Is the difference statistically significant?

To perform a formal comparison of the two values 1.19 and 1.17, we require a sampling theory for the estimator $\widehat{CJ}$. Such a theory may be obtained by noting from (2.2.3) that the estimator N_s is a binomial random variable, i.e., the sum of n Bernoulli random variables Y_t where

$$
Y_t = \begin{cases} 1 & \text{with probability } \pi_s = \pi^2 + (1-\pi)^2; \\ 0 & \text{with probability } 1 - \pi_s \end{cases}
$$

hence we may approximate the distribution of N_s for large n by a normal distribution with mean $E[N_s] = n\pi_s$ and variance $Var[N_s]$. Because each pair of adjacent Y_t's will be dependent,[4] the variance of N_s is not $n\pi_s(1-\pi_s)$—the usual expression for the variance of a binomial random variable—but is instead

$$
\begin{aligned}
Var[N_s] &= n\pi_s(1 - \pi_s) + 2n\,Cov[Y_t, Y_{t+1}] \\
&= n\pi_s(1 - \pi_s) + 2\left(\pi^3 + (1-\pi)^3 - \pi_s^2\right). \quad (2.2.7)
\end{aligned}
$$

Applying a first-order Taylor approximation or the *delta method* (see Section A.4 of the Appendix) to $\widehat{CJ} = N_s/(n - N_s)$ using the normal asymptotic approximation for the distribution of N_s then yields

$$
\widehat{CJ} \stackrel{a}{\sim} \mathcal{N}\left(\frac{\pi_s}{1 - \pi_s} , \; \frac{\pi_s(1 - \pi_s) + 2\left(\pi^3 + (1-\pi)^3 - \pi_s^2\right)}{n(1 - \pi_s)^4} \right). \quad (2.2.8)
$$

where "$\stackrel{a}{\sim}$" indicates that the distributional relation is asymptotic. Since the Cowles and Jones (1937) estimate of 1.17 yields $\hat{\pi}_s = 0.5392$ and $\hat{\pi} = 0.6399$, with a sample size n of 99 returns, (2.2.8) implies that the approximate standard error of the 1.17 estimate is 0.2537. Therefore, the estimate 1.17 is not statistically significantly different from 1.19. Moreover, under the null hypothesis $\pi = \frac{1}{2}$, $\widehat{CJ}$ has a mean of one and a standard deviation of 0.2010; hence neither 1.17 or 1.19 is statistically distinguishable from one. This provides little evidence against the random walk hypothesis.

On the other hand, suppose the random walk hypothesis were false— would this be detectable by the CJ statistic? To see how departures from the random walk might affect the ratio CJ, let the indicator I_t be the following

---

[4]In fact, Y_t is a two-state Markov chain with probabilities $Pr(Y_t = 1 \mid Y_{t-1} = 1) = (p^3 + (1 - p)^3)/p_s$ and $Pr(Y_t = 0 \mid Y_{t-1} = 0) = 1/2$.

two-state Markov chain:

$$I_{t+1}$$

$$\begin{array}{cc} & \begin{array}{cc} 1 & \quad\ \ 0 \end{array} \\ I_t \ \begin{array}{c} 1 \\ 0 \end{array} & \begin{pmatrix} 1-\alpha & \alpha \\ \beta & 1-\beta \end{pmatrix} \end{array} \qquad (2.2.9)$$

where α denotes the *conditional* probability that r_{t+1} is negative, conditional on a positive r_t, and β denotes the *conditional* probability that r_{t+1} is positive, conditional on a negative r_t. If $\alpha = 1 - \beta$, this reduces to the case examined above (set $\pi = 1 - \alpha$): the IID random walk with drift. As long as $\alpha \neq 1 - \beta$, I_t (hence r_t) will be serially correlated, violating RW1. In this case, the theoretical value of the ratio CJ is given by

$$CJ = \frac{(1-\alpha)\beta + (1-\beta)\alpha}{2\alpha\beta}, \qquad (2.2.10)$$

which can take on any nonnegative real value, as illustrated by the following table.

		0.10	0.20	0.30	0.40	0.50	0.60	0.70	0.80	0.90	1.00
	0.10	9.00	6.50	5.67	5.25	5.00	4.83	4.71	4.63	4.56	4.50
	0.20	6.50	4.00	3.17	2.75	2.50	2.33	2.21	2.13	2.06	2.00
	0.30	5.67	3.17	2.33	1.92	1.67	1.50	1.38	1.29	1.22	1.17
	0.40	5.25	2.75	1.92	1.50	1.25	1.08	0.96	0.87	0.81	0.75
α	0.50	5.00	2.50	1.67	1.25	1.00	0.83	0.71	0.63	0.56	0.50
	0.60	4.83	2.33	1.50	1.08	0.83	0.67	0.55	0.46	0.39	0.33
	0.70	4.71	2.21	1.38	0.96	0.71	0.55	0.43	0.34	0.27	0.21
	0.80	4.63	2.13	1.29	0.87	0.63	0.46	0.34	0.25	0.18	0.12
	0.90	4.56	2.06	1.22	0.81	0.56	0.39	0.27	0.18	0.11	0.06
	1.00	4.50	2.00	1.17	0.75	0.50	0.33	0.21	0.12	0.06	0.00

(column header group: β)

As α and β both approach one, the likelihood of reversals increases and hence CJ approaches 0. As either α or β approaches zero, the likelihood of sequences increases and CJ increases without bound. In such cases, CJ is clearly a reasonable indicator of departures from RW1. However, note that there exist combinations of (α, β) for which $\alpha \neq 1 - \beta$ and CJ=1, e.g., $(\alpha, \beta) = (\frac{3}{4}, \frac{3}{8})$; hence the CJ statistic cannot distinguish these cases from RW1 (see Problem 2.3 for further discussion).

Runs
Another common test for RW1 is the *runs test*, in which the number of sequences of consecutive positive and negative returns, or runs, is tabulated and compared against its sampling distribution under the random walk hypothesis. For example, using the indicator variable I_t defined in (2.2.2), a particular sequence of 10 returns may be represented by 1001110100, containing three runs of 1s (of length 1, 3, and 1, respectively) and three runs

of 0s (of length 2, 1, and 2, respectively), thus six runs in total. In contrast, the sequence 0000011111 contains the same number of 0s and 1s, but only 2 runs. By comparing the number of runs in the data with the expected number of runs under RW1, a test of the IID random walk hypothesis may be constructed. To perform the test, we require the sampling distribution of the total number of runs N_{runs} in a sample of n. Mood (1940) was the first to provide a comprehensive analysis of runs, and we shall provide a brief summary of his most general results here.

Suppose that each of n IID observations takes on one of q possible values with probability π_i, $i = 1, \ldots, q$ (hence $\sum_i \pi_i = 1$). In the case of the indicator variable I_t defined in (2.2.2), q is equal to 2; we shall return to this special case below. Denote by $N_{\text{runs}}(i)$ the total number of runs of type i (of any length), $i = 1, \ldots, q$; hence the total number of runs $N_{\text{runs}} = \sum_i N_{\text{runs}}(i)$. Using combinatorial arguments and the properties of the multinomial distribution, Mood (1940) derives the discrete distribution of $N_{\text{runs}}(i)$ from which he calculates the following moments:

$$\mathrm{E}[N_{\text{runs}}(i)] = n\pi_i(1 - \pi_i) + \pi_i^2 \qquad (2.2.11)$$

$$\mathrm{Var}[N_{\text{runs}}(i)] = n\pi_i(1 - 4\pi_i + 6\pi_i^2 - 3\pi_i^3)$$
$$+ \pi_i^2(3 - 8\pi_i + 5\pi_i^2) \qquad (2.2.12)$$

$$\mathrm{Cov}[N_{\text{runs}}(i), N_{\text{runs}}(j)] = -n\pi_i\pi_j(1 - 2\pi_i - 2\pi_j + 3\pi_i\pi_j)$$
$$- \pi_i\pi_j(2\pi_i + 2\pi_j - 5\pi_i\pi_j). \qquad (2.2.13)$$

Moreover, Mood (1940) shows that the distribution of the number of runs converges to a normal distribution asymptotically when properly normalized. In particular, we have

$$x_i \equiv \frac{N_{\text{runs}}(i) - n\pi_i(1 - \pi_i) - \pi_i^2}{\sqrt{n}}$$

$$\overset{a}{\sim} \mathcal{N}\left(0, \pi_i(1 - \pi_i) - 3\pi_i^2(1 - \pi_i)^2\right) \qquad (2.2.14)$$

$$\mathrm{Cov}[x_i, x_j] \overset{a}{=} -\pi_i\pi_j(1 - 2\pi_i - 2\pi_j + 3\pi_i\pi_j) \qquad (2.2.15)$$

$$x \equiv \frac{N_{\text{runs}} - n(1 - \sum_i \pi_i^2)}{\sqrt{n}}$$

$$\overset{a}{\sim} \mathcal{N}\left(0, \sum_{i=1}^{k} \pi_i^2(1 + 2\pi_i) - 3\left(\sum_{i=1}^{k} \pi_i^2\right)^2\right). \qquad (2.2.16)$$

where "$\overset{a}{=}$" indicates that the equality holds asymptotically. Tests of RW1 may then be performed using the asymptotic approximations (2.2.14) or

Table 2.2.   *Expected runs for a random walk with drift μ.*

n	μ	π	$E[N_{\text{runs}}]$
1,000	0	0.500	500.5
1,000	2	0.538	497.6
1,000	4	0.576	489.1
1,000	6	0.612	475.2
1,000	8	0.648	456.5
1,000	10	0.683	433.6
1,000	12	0.716	407.2
1,000	14	0.748	378.1
1,000	16	0.777	347.3
1,000	18	0.804	315.5
1,000	20	0.830	283.5

Expected total number of runs in a sample of n independent Bernoulli trials representing positive/negative continuously compounded returns for a Gaussian geometric Brownian motion with drift $\mu = 0\%, \ldots, 20\%$ and standard deviation $\sigma = 21\%$.

(2.2.16), and the probabilities π_i may be estimated directly from the data as the ratios $\hat{\pi}_i \equiv n_i/n$, where n_i is of the number of runs in the sample of n that are the ith type; thus $n = \sum_i n_i$.

To develop some sense of the behavior of the total number of runs, consider the Bernoulli case $k = 2$ corresponding to the indicator variable I_t defined in (2.2.2) of Section 2.2.2 where π denotes the probability that $I_t = 1$. In this case, the expected total number of runs is

$$E[N_{\text{runs}}] = 2n\pi(1-\pi) + \pi^2 + (1-\pi)^2. \qquad (2.2.17)$$

Observe that for any $n \geq 1$, (2.2.17) is a globally concave quadratic function in π on $[0, 1]$ which attains a maximum value of $(n+1)/2$ at $\pi = \frac{1}{2}$. Therefore, a driftless random walk maximizes the expected total number of runs for any fixed sample size n or, alternatively, the presence of a drift of either sign will decrease the expected total number of runs.

To see the sensitivity of $E[N_{\text{runs}}]$ with respect to the drift, in Table 2.2 we report the expected total number of runs for a sample of $n = 1,000$ observations for a geometric random walk with normally distributed increments, drift $\mu = 0\%, \ldots, 20\%$, and standard deviation $\sigma = 21\%$ (which is calibrated to match annual US stock index returns); hence $\pi = \Phi(\mu/\sigma)$. From Table 2.2 we see that as the drift increases, the expected total number of runs declines considerably, from 500.5 for zero-drift to 283.5 for a 20% drift. However, all of these values are still consistent with the random walk hypothesis.

To perform a test for the random walk in the Bernoulli case, we may calculate the following statistic:

$$z = \frac{N_{\text{runs}} - 2n\pi(1-\pi)}{2\sqrt{n\pi(1-\pi)[1-3\pi(1-\pi)]}} \overset{a}{\sim} \mathcal{N}(0,1)$$

and perform the usual test of significance. A slight adjustment to this statistic is often made to account for the fact that while the normal approximation yields different probabilities for realizations in the interval $[N_{\text{runs}}, N_{\text{runs}}+1)$, the exact probabilities are constant over this interval since N_{runs} is integer-valued. Therefore, a *continuity correction* is made in which the z-statistic is evaluated at the midpoint of the interval (see Wallis and Roberts [1956]); thus

$$z = \frac{N_{\text{runs}} + \frac{1}{2} - 2n\pi(1-\pi)}{2\sqrt{n\pi(1-\pi)[1-3\pi(1-\pi)]}} \overset{a}{\sim} \mathcal{N}(0,1).$$

Other aspects of runs have also been used to test the IID random walk, such as the distribution of runs by length and by sign. Indeed, Mood's (1940) seminal paper provides an exhaustive catalog of the properties of runs, including exact marginal and joint distributions, factorial moments, centered moments, and asymptotic approximations. An excellent summary of these results, along with a collection of related combinatorial problems in probability and statistics is contained in David and Barton (1962). Fama (1965) presents an extensive empirical analysis of runs for US daily, four-day, nine-day, and sixteen-day stock returns from 1956 to 1962, and concludes that, "...there is no evidence of important dependence from either an investment or a statistical point of view."

More recent advances in the analysis of Markov chains have generalized the theory of runs to non-IID sequences, and by recasting patterns such as a run as elements of a permutation group, probabilities of very complex patterns may now be evaluated explicitly using the *first-passage* or *hitting* time of a random process defined on the permutation group. For these more recent results, see Aldous (1989), Aldous and Diaconis (1986), and Diaconis (1988).

2.3 Tests of Random Walk 2: Independent Increments

The restriction of identical distributions is clearly implausible, especially when applied to financial data that span several decades. However, testing for independence without assuming identical distributions is quite difficult, particularly for time series data. If we place no restrictions on how the marginal distributions of the data can vary through time, it becomes virtually impossible to conduct statistical inference since the sampling distributions of even the most elementary statistics cannot be derived.

Some of the nonparametric methods mentioned in Section 2.2.1 such as rank correlations do test for independence without also requiring identical distributions, but the number of distinct marginal distributions is typically a finite and small number. For example, a test of independence between IQ scores and academic performance involves two distinct marginal distributions: one for IQ scores and the other for academic performance. Multiple observations are drawn from each marginal distribution and various nonparametric tests can be designed to check whether the product of the marginal distributions equals the joint distribution of the paired observations. Such an approach obviously cannot succeed if we hypothesize a unique marginal distribution for each observation of IQ and academic performance.

Nevertheless, there are two lines of empirical research that can be viewed as a kind of "economic" test of RW2: *filter rules*, and *technical analysis*. Although neither of these approaches makes much use of formal statistical inference, both have captured the interest of the financial community for practical reasons. This is not to say that statistical inference *cannot* be applied to these modes of analysis, but rather that the standards of evidence in this literature have evolved along very different paths. Therefore, we shall present only a cursory review of these techniques.

2.3.1 Filter Rules

To test RW2, Alexander (1961, 1964) applied a *filter rule* in which an asset is purchased when its price increases by $x\%$, and (short)sold when its price drops by $x\%$. Such a rule is said to be an $x\%$ *filter*, and was proposed by Alexander (1961) for the following reasons:

> Suppose we tentatively assume the existence of trends in stock market prices but believe them to be masked by the jiggling of the market. We might filter out all movements smaller than a specified size and examine the remaining movements.

The total return of this dynamic portfolio strategy is then taken to be a measure of the predictability in asset returns. A comparison of the total return to the return from a buy-and-hold strategy for the Dow Jones and Standard and Poor's industrial averages led Alexander to conclude that "... there *are* trends in stock market prices. . . ."

Fama (1965) and Fama and Blume (1966) present a more detailed empirical analysis of filter rules, correcting for dividends and trading costs, and conclude that such rules do not perform as well as the buy-and-hold strategy. In the absence of transactions costs, very small filters (1% in Alexander [1964] and between 0.5% and 1.5% in Fama and Blume [1966]) do yield superior returns, but because small filters generate considerably more frequent trading, Fama and Blume (1966) show that even a 0.1% roundtrip transaction cost is enough to eliminate the profits from such filter rules.

2.3.2 Technical Analysis

As a measure of predictability, the filter rule has the advantage of practical relevance—it is a specific and readily implementable trading strategy, and the metric of its success is total return. The filter rule is just one example of a much larger class of trading rules arising from *technical analysis* or *charting*. Technical analysis is an approach to investment management based on the belief that historical price series, trading volume, and other market statistics exhibit regularities—often (but not always) in the form of geometric patterns such as *double bottoms, head-and-shoulders*, and *support* and *resistance* levels—that can be profitably exploited to extrapolate future price movements (see, for example, Edwards and Magee [1966] and Murphy [1986]). In the words of Edwards and Magee (1966):

> Technical analysis is the science of recording, usually in graphic form, the actual history of trading (price changes, volume of transactions, etc.) in a certain stock or in "the averages" and then deducing from that pictured history the probable future trend.

Historically, technical analysis has been the "black sheep" of the academic finance community. Regarded by many academics as a pursuit that lies somewhere between astrology and voodoo, technical analysis has never enjoyed the same degree of acceptance that, for example, fundamental analysis has received. This state of affairs persists today, even though the distinction between technical and fundamental analysis is becoming progressively fuzzier.[5]

Perhaps some of the prejudice against technical analysis can be attributed to semantics. Because fundamental analysis is based on quantities familiar to most financial economists—for example, earnings, dividends, and other balance-sheet and income-statement items—it possesses a natural bridge to the academic literature. In contrast, the vocabulary of the technical analyst is completely foreign to the academic and often mystifying to the general public. Consider, for example, the following, which might be found in any recent academic finance journal:

> The magnitudes and decay pattern of the first twelve autocorrelations and the statistical significance of the Box-Pierce Q-statistic suggest the presence of a high-frequency predictable component in stock returns.

---

[5]For example, many technical analysts no longer base their forecasts solely on past prices and volume but also use earnings and dividend information and other "fundamental" data, and as many fundamental analysts now look at past price and volume patterns in addition to more traditional variables.

Contrast this with the statement:

> The presence of clearly identified support and resistance levels, coupled with a one-third retracement parameter when prices lie between them, suggests the presence of strong buying and selling opportunities in the near-term.

Both statements have the same meaning: Using historical prices, one can predict future prices to some extent in the short run. But because the two statements are so laden with jargon, the type of response they elicit depends very much on the individual reading them.

Despite the differences in jargon, recent empirical evidence suggests that technical analysis and more traditional financial analysis may have much in common (see, in particular, Section 2.8). Recent studies by Blume, Easley, and O'Hara (1994), Brock, Lakonishok, and LeBaron (1992), Brown and Jennings (1989), LeBaron (1996), Neftci (1991), Pau (1991), Taylor and Allen (1992), and Treynor and Ferguson (1985) signal a growing interest in technical analysis among financial academics, and so it may become a more active research area in the near future.

2.4 Tests of Random Walk 3: Uncorrelated Increments

One of the most direct and intuitive tests of the random walk and martingale hypotheses for an individual time series is to check for *serial correlation*, correlation between two observations of the same series at different dates. Under the weakest version of the random walk, RW3, the increments or first-differences of the level of the random walk are uncorrelated at all leads and lags. Therefore, we may test RW3 by testing the null hypothesis that the autocorrelation coefficients of the first-differences at various lags are all zero.

This seemingly simple approach is the basis for a surprisingly large variety of tests of the random walk, and we shall develop these tests in this chapter. For example, tests of the random walk may be based on the autocorrelation coefficients themselves (Section 2.4.1). More powerful tests may be constructed from the sum of squared autocorrelations (Section 2.4.2). Linear combinations of the autocorrelations may also have certain advantages in detecting particular departures from the random walk (Sections 2.4.3 and 2.5). Therefore, we shall devote considerable attention to the properties of autocorrelation coefficients in the coming sections.

2.4.1 Autocorrelation Coefficients

The autocorrelation coefficient is a natural time-series extension of the well-known correlation coefficient between two random variables x and y:

$$\text{Corr}[x, y] \equiv \frac{\text{Cov}[x, y]}{\sqrt{\text{Var}[x]} \sqrt{\text{Var}[y]}}. \tag{2.4.1}$$

Given a covariance-stationary time series $\{r_t\}$, the kth order autocovariance and autocorrelation coefficients, $\gamma(k)$ and $\rho(k)$, respectively, are defined as[6]

$$\gamma(k) \equiv \text{Cov}[r_t, r_{t+k}] \tag{2.4.2}$$

$$\rho(k) \equiv \frac{\text{Cov}[r_t, r_{t+k}]}{\sqrt{\text{Var}[r_t]}\sqrt{\text{Var}[r_{t+k}]}} = \frac{\text{Cov}[r_t, r_{t+k}]}{\text{Var}[r_t]} = \frac{\gamma(k)}{\gamma(0)}, \tag{2.4.3}$$

where the second equality in (2.4.3) follows from the covariance-stationarity of $\{r_t\}$. For a given sample $\{r_t\}_{t=1}^{T}$, autocovariance and autocorrelation coefficients may be estimated in the natural way by replacing population moments with sample counterparts:

$$\hat{\gamma}(k) = \frac{1}{T}\sum_{t=1}^{T-k}(r_t - \bar{r}_T)(r_{t+k} - \bar{r}_T), \qquad 0 \le k < T \tag{2.4.4}$$

$$\hat{\rho}(k) = \frac{\hat{\gamma}(k)}{\hat{\gamma}(0)} \tag{2.4.5}$$

$$\bar{r}_T \equiv \frac{1}{T}\sum_{t=1}^{T}r_t. \tag{2.4.6}$$

The sampling theory for $\hat{\gamma}(k)$ and $\hat{\rho}(k)$ depends, of course, on the data-generating process for $\{r_t\}$. For example, if r_t is a finite-order moving average,

$$r_t = \sum_{k=0}^{M}\alpha_k \epsilon_{t-k},$$

where $\{\epsilon_t\}$ is an independent sequence with mean 0, variance σ^2, fourth moment $\eta\sigma^4$, and finite sixth moment, then Fuller (1976, Theorem 6.3.5) shows that the vector of autocovariance coefficient estimators is asymptotically multivariate normal:

$$\sqrt{T}\left[\,\hat{\gamma}(0)-\gamma(0)\ \ \hat{\gamma}(1)-\gamma(1)\ \cdots\ \hat{\gamma}(m)-\gamma(m)\,\right]' \overset{a}{\sim} \mathcal{N}(0, \mathbf{V}), \tag{2.4.7}$$

where

$$\mathbf{V} = [\,v_{ij}\,]$$

$$v_{ij} \equiv (\eta - 3)\gamma(i)\,\gamma(j) + \sum_{\ell=-\infty}^{\infty}\left[\,\gamma(\ell)\,\gamma(\ell-i+j)\right.$$

$$\left. + \gamma(\ell+j)\,\gamma(\ell-i)\,\right]. \tag{2.4.8}$$

[6]The requirement of covariance-stationarity is primarily for notational convenience—otherwise $\gamma(k)$ and $\rho(k)$ may be functions of t as well as k, and may not even be well-defined if second moments are not finite.

Under the same assumptions, Fuller (1976, Corollary 6.3.5.1) shows that the asymptotic distribution of the vector of autocorrelation coefficient estimators is also multivariate normal:

$$\sqrt{T}\left[\ \hat{\rho}(0)-\rho(0)\ \ \hat{\rho}(1)-\rho(1)\ \ \cdots\ \ \hat{\rho}(m)-\rho(m)\ \right]'\ \overset{a}{\sim}\ \mathcal{N}(0,\mathbf{G}), \qquad (2.4.9)$$

where

$$\mathbf{G}\ =\ [\ g_{ij}\ ]$$

$$g_{ij}\ \equiv\ \sum_{\ell=-\infty}^{\infty}\left[\ \rho(\ell)\,\rho(\ell-i+j)+\rho(\ell+j)\,\rho(\ell-i)-2\rho(j)\,\rho(\ell)\,\rho(\ell-i)\right.$$

$$\left.-\ 2\rho(i)\,\rho(\ell)\,\rho(\ell-j)+2\rho(i)\,\rho(j)\,\rho^2(\ell)\ \right]. \qquad (2.4.10)$$

For purposes of testing the random walk hypotheses in which all the population autocovariances are zero, these asymptotic approximations reduce to simpler forms and more can be said of their finite-sample means and variances. In particular, if $\{r_t\}$ satisfies RW1 and has variance σ^2 and sixth moment proportional to σ^6, then

$$\mathrm{E}[\hat{\rho}(k)]\ =\ -\frac{T-k}{T(T-1)}+O(T^{-2}) \qquad (2.4.11)$$

$$\mathrm{Cov}[\hat{\rho}(k),\hat{\rho}(\ell)]\ =\ \begin{cases}\frac{T-k}{T^2}+O(T^{-2}) & \text{if}\ \ k=\ell\neq 0 \\[2mm] O(T^{-2}) & \text{otherwise.}\end{cases} \qquad (2.4.12)$$

From (2.4.11) we see that under RW1, where $\rho(k)=0$ for all $k>0$, the sample autocorrelation coefficients $\hat{\rho}(k)$ are negatively biased. This negative bias comes from the fact that the autocorrelation coefficient is a scaled sum of cross-products of deviations of r_t from its mean, and if the mean is unknown it must be estimated, most commonly by the sample mean (2.4.6). But deviations from the sample mean sum to zero by construction; therefore positive deviations must eventually be followed by negative deviations on average and vice versa, and hence the expected value of cross-products of deviations is negative.

For smaller samples this effect can be significant: The expected value of $\hat{\rho}(1)$ for a sample size of 10 observations is -10%. Under RW1, Fuller (1976) proposes the following bias-corrected estimator $\tilde{\rho}(k)$:[7]

$$\tilde{\rho}(k)\ =\ \hat{\rho}(k)+\frac{T-k}{(T-1)^2}\left(1-\hat{\rho}^2(k)\right). \qquad (2.4.13)$$

---

[7]Not that $\tilde{\rho}(k)$ is not unbiased; the term "bias-corrected" refers to the fact that $\mathrm{E}[\tilde{\rho}(k)]=O(T^{-2})$.

With uniformly bounded sixth moments, he shows that the sample auto-correlation coefficients are asymptotically independent and normally distributed with distribution:

$$\sqrt{T}\hat{\rho}(k) \overset{a}{\sim} \mathcal{N}(0,1) \tag{2.4.14}$$

$$\frac{T}{\sqrt{T-k}}\tilde{\rho}(k) \overset{a}{\sim} \mathcal{N}(0,1). \tag{2.4.15}$$

These results yield a variety of autocorrelation-based tests of the random walk hypothesis RW1.

Lo and MacKinlay (1988), Richardson and Smith (1994), and Romano and Thombs (1996) derive asymptotic approximations for sample autocorrelation coefficients under even weaker conditions—uncorrelated weakly dependent observations—and these results may be used to construct tests of RW2 and RW3 (see Section 2.4.3 below).

2.4.2 Portmanteau Statistics

Since RW1 implies that *all* autocorrelations are zero, a simple test statistic of RW1 that has power against many alternative hypotheses is the Q-statistic due to Box and Pierce (1970):

$$Q_m \equiv T\sum_{k=1}^{m} \rho^2(k). \tag{2.4.16}$$

Under the RW1 null hypothesis, and using (2.4.14), it is easy to see that $\hat{Q}_m = T\sum_{k=1}^{m} \hat{\rho}^2(k)$ is asymptotically distributed as χ_m^2. Ljung and Box (1978) provide the following finite-sample correction which yields a better fit to the χ_m^2 for small sample sizes:

$$Q'_m \equiv T(T+2)\sum_{k=1}^{m} \frac{\rho^2(k)}{T-k}. \tag{2.4.17}$$

By summing the squared autocorrelations, the Box-Pierce Q-statistic is designed to detect departures from zero autocorrelations in either direction and at all lags. Therefore, it has power against a broad range of alternative hypotheses to the random walk. However, selecting the number of auto-correlations m requires some care—if too few are used, the presence of higher-order autocorrelation may be missed; if too many are used, the test may not have much power due to insignificant higher-order autocorrelations. Therefore, while such a portmanteau statistic does have some appeal, better tests of the random walk hypotheses may be available when specific alternative hypotheses can be identified. We shall turn to such examples in the next sections.

2.4.3 Variance Ratios

An important property of all three random walk hypotheses is that the variance of random walk increments must be a linear function of the time interval.[8] For example, under RW1 for log prices where continuously compounded returns $r_t \equiv \log P_t - \log P_{t-1}$ are IID, the variance of $r_t + r_{t-1}$ must be twice the variance of r_t. Therefore, the plausibility of the random walk model may be checked by comparing the variance of $r_t + r_{t-1}$ to twice the variance of r_t.[9] Of course, in practice these will not be numerically identical even if RW1 were true, but their ratio should be statistically indistinguishable from one. Therefore, to construct a statistical test of the random walk hypothesis using variance ratios, we require their sampling distribution under the random walk null hypothesis.

Population Properties of Variance Ratios
Before deriving such sampling distributions, we develop some intuition for the population values of the variance ratio statistic under various scenarios. Consider again the ratio of the variance of a two-period continuously compounded return $r_t(2) \equiv r_t + r_{t-1}$ to twice the variance of a one-period return r_t, and for the moment let us assume nothing about the time series of returns other than stationarity. Then this variance ratio, which we write as VR(2), reduces to:

$$
\begin{aligned}
\text{VR}(2) \quad &= \quad \frac{\text{Var}[r_t(2)]}{2\,\text{Var}[r_t]} \quad = \quad \frac{\text{Var}[r_t + r_{t-1}]}{2\,\text{Var}[r_t]} \\[2mm]
&= \quad \frac{2\,\text{Var}[r_t] + 2\,\text{Cov}[r_t, r_{t-1}]}{2\,\text{Var}[r_t]} \\[2mm]
\text{VR}(2) \quad &= \quad 1 + \rho(1), \qquad\qquad\qquad\qquad\quad (2.4.18)
\end{aligned}
$$

where $\rho(1)$ is the first-order autocorrelation coefficient of returns $\{r_t\}$. For any stationary time series, the population value of the variance ratio statistic VR(2) is simply one plus the first-order autocorrelation coefficient. In particular, under RW1 all the autocorrelations are zero, hence VR(2)=1 in this case, as expected.

In the presence of positive first-order autocorrelation, VR(2) will exceed one. If returns are positively autocorrelated, the variance of the sum of two

---

[8]This linearity property is more difficult to state in the case of RW2 and RW3 because the variances of increments may vary through time. However, even in these cases the variance of the sum must equal the sum of the variances, and this is the linearity property which the variance ratio test exploits. We shall construct tests of all three hypotheses below.

[9]Many studies have exploited this property of the random walk hypothesis in devising empirical tests of predictability; recent examples include Campbell and Mankiw (1987), Cochrane (1988), Faust (1992), Lo and MacKinlay (1988), Poterba and Summers (1988), Richardson (1993), and Richardson and Stock (1989).

one-period returns will be larger than the sum of the one-period return's variances; hence variances will grow faster than linearly. Alternatively, in the presence of negative first-order autocorrelation, the variance of the sum of two one-period returns will be smaller than the sum of the one-period return's variances; hence variances will grow slower than linearly.

For comparisons beyond one- and two-period returns, higher-order autocorrelations come into play. In particular, a similar calculation shows that the general q-period variance ratio statistic VR(q) satisfies the relation:

$$\text{VR}(q) \equiv \frac{\text{Var}[r_t(q)]}{q \cdot \text{Var}[r_t]} = 1 + 2 \sum_{k=1}^{q-1} \left(1 - \frac{k}{q} \right) \rho(k), \qquad (2.4.19)$$

where $r_t(k) \equiv r_t + r_{t-1} + \cdots + r_{t-k+1}$ and $\rho(k)$ is the kth order autocorrelation coefficient of $\{r_t\}$. This shows that VR(q) is a particular *linear* combination of the first $k-1$ autocorrelation coefficients of $\{r_t\}$, with linearly declining weights.

Under RW1, (2.4.19) shows that for all q, VR(q)=1 since in this case $\rho(k)=0$ for all $k \geq 1$. Moreover, even under RW2 and RW3, VR(q) must still equal one as long as the variances of r_t are finite and the "average variance" $\sum_{t=1}^{T} \text{Var}[r_t]/T$ converges to a finite positive number. But (2.4.19) is even more informative for alternatives to the random walk because it relates the behavior of VR(q) to the autocorrelation coefficients of $\{r_t\}$ under such alternatives. For example, under an AR(1) alternative, $r_t = \phi r_{t-1} + \epsilon_t$, (2.4.19) implies that

$$\begin{aligned}
\text{VR}(q) &= 1 + 2 \sum_{k=1}^{q-1} \left(1 - \frac{k}{q} \right) \phi^k \\
&= 1 + \frac{2}{1-\phi} \left[\phi - \frac{\phi^q}{q} - \frac{\phi - \phi^q}{q(1-\phi)} \right].
\end{aligned}$$

Relations such as this are critical for constructing alternative hypotheses for which the variance ratio test has high and low power, and we shall return to this issue below.

Sampling Distribution of $\widehat{\text{VD}}(q)$ and $\widehat{\text{VR}}(q)$ under RW1

To construct a statistical test for RW1 we follow the exposition of Lo and MacKinlay (1988) and begin by stating the null hypothesis H_0 under which the sampling distribution of the test statistics will be derived.[10] Let p_t denote the log price process and $r_t \equiv p_t - p_{t-1}$ continuously compounded returns.

---

[10]For alternative expositions see Campbell and Mankiw (1987), Cochrane (1988), Faust (1992), Poterba and Summers (1988), Richardson (1993), and Richardson and Stock (1989).

Then the null hypothesis we consider in this section is[11]

$$H_0 : \qquad r_t = \mu + \epsilon_t, \qquad \epsilon_t \text{ IID } \mathcal{N}(0, \sigma^2).$$

Let our data consist of $2n+1$ observations of log prices $\{p_0, p_1, \ldots, p_{2n}\}$, and consider the following estimators for μ and σ^2:

$$\hat{\mu} \equiv \frac{1}{2n} \sum_{k=1}^{2n} (p_k - p_{k-1}) = \frac{1}{2n} (p_{2n} - p_0) \qquad (2.4.20)$$

$$\hat{\sigma}_a^2 \equiv \frac{1}{2n} \sum_{k=1}^{2n} (p_k - p_{k-1} - \hat{\mu})^2 \qquad (2.4.21)$$

$$\hat{\sigma}_b^2 \equiv \frac{1}{2n} \sum_{k=1}^{n} (p_{2k} - p_{2k-2} - 2\hat{\mu})^2. \qquad (2.4.22)$$

Equations (2.4.20) and (2.4.21) are the usual sample mean and variance estimators. They are also the *maximum-likelihood* estimators of μ and σ^2 (see Section 9.3.2 in Chapter 9). The second estimator $\hat{\sigma}_b^2$ of σ^2 makes use of the random walk nature of p_t: Under RW1 the mean and variance of increments are linear in the increment interval, hence the σ^2 can be estimated by one-half the sample variance of the increments of even-numbered observations $\{p_0, p_2, p_4, \ldots, p_{2n}\}$.

Under standard asymptotic theory, all three estimators are strongly consistent: Holding all other parameters constant, as the total number of observations $2n$ increases without bound the estimators converge almost surely to their population values. In addition, it is well known that $\hat{\sigma}_a^2$ and $\hat{\sigma}_b^2$ possess the following normal limiting distributions (see, for example, Stuart and Ord [1987]):

$$\sqrt{2n}\,(\hat{\sigma}_a^2 - \sigma^2) \overset{a}{\sim} \mathcal{N}(0, 2\sigma^4) \qquad (2.4.23)$$

$$\sqrt{2n}\,(\hat{\sigma}_b^2 - \sigma^2) \overset{a}{\sim} \mathcal{N}(0, 4\sigma^4). \qquad (2.4.24)$$

However, we seek the limiting distribution of the *ratio* of the variances. Although it may readily be shown that the ratio is also asymptotically normal with unit mean under RW1, the variance of the limiting distribution is not apparent since the two variance estimators are clearly *not* asymptotically uncorrelated.

But since the estimator $\hat{\sigma}_a^2$ is asymptotically efficient under the null hypothesis RW1, we may use Hausman's (1978) insight that the asymptotic

---

[11]We assume normality only for expositional convenience—the results in this section apply much more generally to log price processes with IID increments that possess finite fourth moments.

variance of the difference of a consistent estimator and an asymptotically efficient estimator is simply the difference of the asymptotic variances.[12] If we define the variance difference estimator as $\widehat{\text{VD}}(2) \equiv \hat{\sigma}_b^2 - \hat{\sigma}_a^2$, then (2.4.23), (2.4.24), and Hausman's result implies:

$$\sqrt{2n}\,\widehat{\text{VD}}(2) \overset{a}{\sim} \mathcal{N}(0, 2\sigma^4). \tag{2.4.25}$$

The null hypothesis H can then be tested using (2.4.25) and any consistent estimator $2\hat{\sigma}^4$ of $2\sigma^4$ (for example, $2(\hat{\sigma}_a^2)^2$): Construct the standardized statistic $\widehat{\text{VD}}(2)/\sqrt{2\hat{\sigma}^4}$ which has a limiting standard normal distribution under RW1, and reject the null hypothesis at the 5% level if it lies outside the interval $[-1.96, 1.96]$.

The asymptotic distribution of the two-period variance ratio statistic $\widehat{\text{VR}}(2) = \hat{\sigma}_b^2/\hat{\sigma}_a^2$ now follows directly from (2.4.25) using a first-order Taylor approximation or the delta method (see Section A.4 of the Appendix):[13]

$$\widehat{\text{VR}}(2) \equiv \frac{\hat{\sigma}_b^2}{\hat{\sigma}_a^2}, \qquad \sqrt{2n}\,(\widehat{\text{VR}}(2) - 1) \overset{a}{\sim} \mathcal{N}(0, 2). \tag{2.4.26}$$

The null hypothesis H_0 can be tested by computing the standardized statistic $\sqrt{2n}(\widehat{\text{VR}}(2)-1)/\sqrt{2}$ which is asymptotically standard normal—if it lies outside the interval $[-1.96, 1.96]$, RW1 may be rejected at the 5% level of significance.

Although the variance ratio is often preferred to the variance difference because the ratio is scale-free, observe that if $2(\hat{\sigma}_a^2)^2$ is used to estimate $2\sigma^4$, then the standard significance test of VD=0 for the difference will yield the same inferences as the corresponding test of VR-1=0 for the ratio since:

$$\frac{\sqrt{2n}\widehat{\text{VD}}(2)}{\sqrt{2\hat{\sigma}_a^4}} = \frac{\sqrt{2n}(\hat{\sigma}_b^2 - \hat{\sigma}_a^2)}{\sqrt{2}\,\hat{\sigma}_a^2} = \frac{\sqrt{2n}(\widehat{\text{VR}}(2) - 1)}{\sqrt{2}} \sim \mathcal{N}(0, 1). \tag{2.4.27}$$

Therefore, in this simple context the two test statistics are equivalent. However, there are other reasons that make the variance ratio more appealing

---

[12]Briefly, Hausman (1978) exploits the fact that any asymptotically efficient estimator of a parameter θ, say $\hat{\theta}_e$, must possess the property that it is asymptotically uncorrelated with the difference $\hat{\theta}_a - \hat{\theta}_e$, where $\hat{\theta}_a$ is any other estimator of θ. If not, then there exists a linear combination of $\hat{\theta}_e$ and $\hat{\theta}_a - \hat{\theta}_e$ that is more efficient than $\hat{\theta}_e$, contradicting the assumed efficiency of $\hat{\theta}_e$. The result follows directly, then, since:

$$\text{aVar}[\hat{\theta}_a] = \text{aVar}[\hat{\theta}_e + \hat{\theta}_a - \hat{\theta}_e] = \text{aVar}[\hat{\theta}_e] + \text{aVar}[\hat{\theta}_a - \hat{\theta}_e]$$

$$\Rightarrow \quad \text{aVar}[\hat{\theta}_a - \hat{\theta}_e] = \text{aVar}[\hat{\theta}_a] - \text{aVar}[\hat{\theta}_e],$$

where aVar[·] denotes the asymptotic variance operator.

[13]In particular, apply the delta method to $f(\hat{\theta}_1, \hat{\theta}_2) \equiv \hat{\theta}_1/\hat{\theta}_2$ where $\hat{\theta}_1 \equiv \hat{\sigma}_b^2 - \hat{\sigma}_a^2$, $\hat{\theta}_2 \equiv \hat{\sigma}_a^2$, and observe that $\hat{\sigma}_b^2 - \hat{\sigma}_a^2$ and $\hat{\sigma}_a^2$ are asymptotically uncorrelated because $\hat{\sigma}_a^2$ is an efficient estimator.

and these are discussed in Cochrane (1988), Faust (1992), and Lo and MacKinlay (1988, 1989).

The variance difference and ratio statistics can be easily generalized to multiperiod returns. Let our sample consist of $nq+1$ observations $\{p_0, p_1, \ldots, p_{nq}\}$, where q is any integer greater than one and define the estimators:

$$\hat{\mu} \equiv \frac{1}{nq} \sum_{k=1}^{nq} (p_k - p_{k-1}) = \frac{1}{nq} (p_{nq} - p_0) \qquad (2.4.28)$$

$$\hat{\sigma}_a^2 \equiv \frac{1}{nq} \sum_{k=1}^{nq} (p_k - p_{k-1} - \hat{\mu})^2 \qquad (2.4.29)$$

$$\hat{\sigma}_b^2(q) \equiv \frac{1}{nq} \sum_{k=1}^{n} (p_{qk} - p_{qk-q} - q\hat{\mu})^2 \qquad (2.4.30)$$

$$\widehat{\text{VD}}(q) \equiv \hat{\sigma}_b^2(q) - \hat{\sigma}_a^2, \qquad \widehat{\text{VR}}(q) \equiv \frac{\hat{\sigma}_b^2(q)}{\hat{\sigma}_a^2}. \qquad (2.4.31)$$

Using similar arguments, the asymptotic distributions of $\widehat{\text{VD}}(q)$ and $\widehat{\text{VR}}(q)$ under the RW1 null hypothesis are

$$\sqrt{nq}\,\widehat{\text{VD}}(q) \overset{a}{\sim} \mathcal{N}\big(0, 2(q-1)\sigma^4\big) \qquad (2.4.32)$$

$$\sqrt{nq}\,\big(\widehat{\text{VR}}(q) - 1\big) \overset{a}{\sim} \mathcal{N}\big(0, 2(q-1)\big). \qquad (2.4.33)$$

Two important refinements of these statistics can improve their finite-sample properties substantially. The first is to use *overlapping* q-period returns in estimating the variances by defining the following alternative estimator for σ^2:

$$\hat{\sigma}_c^2(q) = \frac{1}{nq^2} \sum_{k=q}^{nq} (p_k - p_{k-q} - q\hat{\mu})^2. \qquad (2.4.34)$$

This estimator contains $nq-q+1$ terms, whereas the estimator $\hat{\sigma}_b^2(q)$ contains only n terms. Using overlapping q-period returns yields a more efficient estimator and hence a more powerful test.

The second refinement involves correcting the bias in the variance estimators $\hat{\sigma}_a^2$ and $\hat{\sigma}_c^2$ before dividing one by the other. Denote the unbiased estimators as $\overline{\sigma}_a^2$ and $\overline{\sigma}_c^2(q)$, where

$$\overline{\sigma}_a^2 = \frac{1}{nq-1} \sum_{k=1}^{nq} (p_k - p_{k-1} - \hat{\mu})^2 \qquad (2.4.35)$$

$$\overline{\sigma}_c^2 = \frac{1}{m} \sum_{k=q}^{nq} (p_k - p_{k-q} - q\hat{\mu})^2$$

$$m \equiv q(nq - q + 1)\left(1 - \frac{q}{nq}\right), \qquad (2.4.36)$$

and define the statistics:

$$\overline{\text{VD}}(q) \equiv \overline{\sigma}_c^2(q) - \overline{\sigma}_a^2, \qquad \overline{\text{VR}}(q) \equiv \frac{\overline{\sigma}_c^2(q)}{\overline{\sigma}_a^2}. \qquad (2.4.37)$$

This yields an unbiased variance difference estimator, however, the variance ratio estimator is still biased (due to Jensen's Inequality). Nevertheless, simulation experiments reported in Lo and MacKinlay (1989) show that the finite-sample properties of $\overline{\text{VR}}(q)$ are closer to their asymptotic limits than $\widehat{\text{VR}}(q)$.

Under the null hypothesis H, the asymptotic distributions of the variance difference and variance ratio are given by

$$\overline{\text{VD}}(q) \overset{a}{\sim} N\left(0, \frac{2(2q-1)(q-1)}{3q}\sigma^4\right) \qquad (2.4.38)$$

$$\sqrt{nq}\,(\overline{\text{VR}}(q) - 1) \overset{a}{\sim} N\left(0, \frac{2(2q-1)(q-1)}{3q}\right). \qquad (2.4.39)$$

These statistics can then be standardized in the usual way to yield asymptotically standard normal test statistics. As before, if σ^4 is estimated by $\overline{\sigma}_a^4$ in standardizing the variance difference statistic, the result is the same as the standardized variance ratio statistic:

$$\begin{aligned}\psi(q) &\equiv \sqrt{nq}\,(\overline{\text{VR}}(q) - 1)\left(\frac{2(2q-1)(q-1)}{3q}\right)^{-1/2} \qquad (2.4.40)\\[2mm] &= \frac{\sqrt{nq}\overline{\text{VD}}(q)}{\sqrt{\overline{\sigma}_a^4}}\left(\frac{2(2q-1)(q-1)}{3q}\right)^{-1/2} \overset{a}{\sim} \mathcal{N}(0,1).\end{aligned}$$

Sampling Distribution of $\overline{\text{VR}}(q)$ under RW3
Since there is a growing consensus among financial economists that volatilities change over time (see Section 12.2 in Chapter 12), a rejection of the random walk hypothesis because of heteroskedasticity would not be of much interest. Therefore, we seek a test for RW3. As long as returns are uncorrelated, even in the presence of heteroskedasticity the variance ratio must still approach unity as the number of observations increases without bound, for the variance of the sum of uncorrelated increments must still equal the sum of the variances. However, the asymptotic variance of the variance ratios will clearly depend on the type and degree of heteroskedasticity present.

One approach is to model the heteroskedasticity explicitly as in Section 12.2 of Chapter 12, and then calculate the asymptotic variance of $\overline{\text{VR}}(q)$ under this specific null hypothesis. However, to allow for more general forms of heteroskedasticity, we follow the approach taken by Lo and MacKinlay (1988) which relies on the heteroskedasticity-consistent methods of White (1980) and White and Domowitz (1984). This approach applies to a much broader class of log price processes $\{p_t\}$ than the IID normal increments process of the previous section, a particularly relevant concern for US stock returns as Table 1.1 illustrates.[14] Specifically, let $r_t = \mu + \epsilon_t$, and define the following compound null hypothesis H_0^*:

(H1) For all t, $E[\epsilon_t] = 0$, *and* $E[\epsilon_t \epsilon_{t-\tau}] = 0$ *for any* $\tau \neq 0$.

(H2) $\{\epsilon_t\}$ *is* ϕ-*mixing with coefficients* $\phi(m)$ *of size* $r/(2r-1)$ *or is* α-*mixing with coefficients* $\alpha(m)$ *of size* $r/(r-1)$, *where* $r > 1$, *such that for all t and for any* $\tau \geq 0$, *there exists some* $\delta > 0$ *for which* $E[|\epsilon_t \epsilon_{t-\tau}|^{2(r+\delta)}] < \Delta < \infty$.

(H3) $\displaystyle\lim_{nq \to \infty} \frac{1}{nq} \sum_{t=1}^{nq} E[\epsilon_t^2] = \sigma^2 < \infty$.

(H4) For all t, $E[\epsilon_t \epsilon_{t-j} \epsilon_t \epsilon_{t-k}] = 0$ *for any nonzero j and k where* $j \neq k$.

Condition (H1) is the uncorrelated increments property of the random walk that we wish to test. Conditions (H2) and (H3) are restrictions on the maximum degree of dependence and heterogeneity allowable while still permitting some form of the Law of Large Numbers and the Central Limit Theorem to obtain (see White [1984] for the definitions of ϕ- and α-mixing random sequences). Condition (H4) implies that the sample autocorrelations of ϵ_t are asymptotically uncorrelated; this condition may be weakened considerably at the expense of computational simplicity (see note 15).

This compound null hypothesis assumes that p_t possesses uncorrelated increments but allows for quite general forms of heteroskedasticity, including deterministic changes in the variance (due, for example, to seasonal factors) and Engle's (1982) ARCH processes (in which the conditional variance depends on past information).

Since $\overline{VR}(q)$ still approaches one under H_0^*, we need only compute its asymptotic variance [call it $\theta(q)$] to perform the standard inferences. Lo and MacKinlay (1988) do this in two steps. First, recall that the following equality holds asymptotically under quite general conditions:

$$\overline{VR}(q) \overset{a}{=} 1 + 2 \sum_{k=1}^{q-1} \left(1 - \frac{k}{q}\right) \hat{\rho}(k). \qquad (2.4.41)$$

[14]Of course, second moments are still assumed to be finite; otherwise, the variance ratio is no longer well defined. This rules out distributions with infinite variance, such as those in the stable Pareto-Levy family (with characteristic exponents that are less than 2) proposed by Mandelbrot (1963) and Fama (1965). However, many other forms of leptokurtosis are allowed, such as that generated by Engle's (1982) autoregressive conditionally heteroskedastic (ARCH) process (see Section 12.2 in Chapter 12).

Second, note that under H_0^* (condition (H4)) the autocorrelation coefficient estimators $\hat{\rho}(k)$ are asymptotically uncorrelated.[15] If the asymptotic variance δ_k of each of the $\hat{\rho}(k)$'s can be obtained under H_0^*, the asymptotic variance $\theta(q)$ of $\overline{VR}(q)$ may be calculated as the weighted sum of the δ_k's, where the weights are simply the weights in relation (2.4.41) squared. Denote by δ_k and $\theta(q)$ the asymptotic variances of $\hat{\rho}(k)$ and $\overline{VR}(q)$, respectively. Then under the null hypothesis H_0^* Lo and MacKinlay (1988) show that

1. The statistics $\overline{VD}(q)$, and $\overline{VR}(q)-1$ converge almost surely to zero for all q as n increases without bound.

2. The following is a heteroskedasticity-consistent estimator of δ_k:

$$\hat{\delta}_k = \frac{nq \sum_{j=k+1}^{nq} (p_j - p_{j-1} - \hat{\mu})^2 (p_{j-k} - p_{j-k-1} - \hat{\mu})^2}{\left[\sum_{j=1}^{nq} (p_j - p_{j-1} - \hat{\mu})^2\right]^2}. \tag{2.4.42}$$

3. The following is a heteroskedasticity-consistent estimator of $\theta(q)$:

$$\hat{\theta}(q) \equiv 4 \sum_{k=1}^{q-1} \left(1 - \frac{k}{q}\right)^2 \hat{\delta}_k. \tag{2.4.43}$$

Despite the presence of general heteroskedasticity, the standardized test statistic $\psi^*(q)$

$$\psi^*(q) = \frac{\sqrt{nq}(\overline{VR}(q) - 1)}{\sqrt{\hat{\theta}}} \overset{a}{\sim} \mathcal{N}(0, 1) \tag{2.4.44}$$

can be used to test H_0^* in the usual way.

2.5 Long-Horizon Returns

Several recent studies have focused on the properties of long-horizon returns to test the random walk hypotheses, in some cases using 5- to 10-year returns over a 65-year sample. There are fewer nonoverlapping long-horizon returns for a given time span, so sampling errors are generally

[15] Although this restriction on the fourth cross-moments of ϵ_t may seem somewhat unintuitive, it is satisfied for any process with independent increments (regardless of heterogeneity) and also for linear Gaussian ARCH processes. This assumption may be relaxed entirely, requiring the estimation of the asymptotic covariances of the autocorrelation estimators in order to estimate the limiting variance θ of $\overline{VR}(q)$ via (2.4.41). Although the resulting estimator of θ would be more complicated than equation (2.4.43), it is conceptually straightforward and may readily be formed along the lines of Newey and West (1987). An even more general (and possibly more exact) sampling theory for the variance ratios may be obtained using the results of Dufour (1981) and Dufour and Roy (1985). Again, this would sacrifice much of the simplicity of our asymptotic results.

larger for statistics based on long-horizon returns. But for some alternatives to the random walk, long-horizon returns can be more informative than their shorter-horizon counterparts (see Section 7.2.1 in Chapter 7 and Lo and MacKinlay [1989]).

One motivation for using long-horizon returns is the permanent/transitory components alternative hypothesis, first proposed by Muth (1960) in a macroeconomic context. In this model, log prices are composed of two components: a random walk and a stationary process,

$$p_t = w_t + y_t \tag{2.5.1}$$

$$w_t = \mu + w_{t-1} + \epsilon_t, \qquad \epsilon_t \sim \text{IID}(0, \sigma^2)$$

$$y_t = \text{any zero-mean stationary process,}$$

and $\{w_t\}$ and $\{y_t\}$ are mutually independent. The common interpretation for (2.5.1) as a model of stock prices is that w_t is the "fundamental" component that reflects the efficient markets price, and y_t is a zero-mean stationary component that reflects a short-term or transitory deviation from the efficient-markets price w_t, implying the presence of "fads" or other market inefficiencies. Since y_t is stationary, it is mean-reverting by definition and reverts to its mean of zero in the long run. Although there are several difficulties with such an interpretation of (2.5.1)—not the least of which is the fact that market efficiency is tautological without additional *economic* structure—nevertheless, such an alternative provides a good laboratory for studying the variance ratio's performance.

While VR(q) can behave in many ways under (2.5.1) for small q (depending on the correlation structure of y_t), as q gets larger the behavior of VR(q) becomes less arbitrary. In particular, observe that

$$r_t \equiv p_t - p_{t-1} = \mu + \epsilon_t + y_t - y_{t-1} \tag{2.5.2}$$

$$r_t(q) \equiv \sum_{j=0}^{q-1} r_{t-j} = q\mu + \sum_{k=0}^{q-1} \epsilon_{t-k} + y_t - y_{t-q} \tag{2.5.3}$$

$$\text{Var}[r_t(q)] = q\sigma^2 + 2\gamma_y(0) - 2\gamma_y(q). \tag{2.5.4}$$

where $\gamma_y(q) \equiv \text{Cov}[y_t, y_{t+q}]$ is the autocovariance function of y_t. Therefore, in this case the population value of the variance ratio becomes

$$\text{VR}(q) = \frac{\text{Var}[r_t(q)]}{q\,\text{Var}[r_t]} = \frac{q\sigma^2 + 2\gamma_y(0) - 2\gamma_y(q)}{q\left(\sigma^2 + 2\gamma_y(0) - 2\gamma_y(1)\right)} \tag{2.5.5}$$

$$\rightarrow \quad \frac{\sigma^2}{\sigma^2 + 2\gamma_y(0) - 2\gamma_y(1)} \quad \text{as} \quad q \rightarrow \infty \qquad (2.5.6)$$

$$= \quad 1 - \frac{2\gamma_y(0) - 2\gamma_y(1)}{\sigma^2 + 2\gamma_y(0) - 2\gamma_y(1)}$$

$$= \quad 1 - \frac{\text{Var}[\Delta y]}{\text{Var}[\Delta y] + \text{Var}[\Delta w]}$$

$$\text{VR}(q) \quad \rightarrow \quad 1 - \frac{\text{Var}[\Delta y]}{\text{Var}[\Delta p]}, \qquad (2.5.7)$$

where (2.5.6) requires the additional assumption that $\gamma_y(q) \rightarrow 0$ as $q \rightarrow \infty$, an asymptotic independence condition that is a plausible assumption for most economic time series.[16] This shows that for a sufficiently long horizon q, the permanent/transitory components model must yield a variance ratio less than one. Moreover, the magnitude of the difference between the long-horizon variance ratio and one is the ratio of the variance of Δy_t to the variance of Δp_t, a kind of "signal/(signal+noise)" ratio, where the "signal" is the transitory component and the "noise" is the permanent markets component. In fact, one might consider extracting the "signal/noise" ratio from $\text{VR}(q)$ in the obvious way:

$$\frac{1}{\text{VR}(q)} - 1 \quad \rightarrow \quad \frac{\text{Var}[\Delta y]}{\text{Var}[\Delta w]} \ .$$

2.5.1 Problems with Long-Horizon Inferences

There are, however, several difficulties with long-horizon returns that stem from the fact that when the horizon q is large relative to the total time span $T = nq$, the asymptotic approximations that are typically used to perform inferences break down.

For example, consider the test statistic $\overline{\text{VR}}(q) - 1$ which is asymptotically normal with mean 0 and variance:

$$V = \frac{2(2q-1)(q-1)}{3nq^2} = \frac{4}{3n}\left[\frac{q^2 - \frac{3}{2}q + \frac{1}{2}}{q^2}\right] \qquad (2.5.8)$$

under the RW1 null hypothesis. Observe that for all $q > 2$, the bracketed term in (2.5.8) is bounded between $\frac{3}{8}$ and 1 and is monotonically increasing in q. Therefore, for fixed n, this implies upper and lower bounds for V are $\frac{4}{3n}$ and $\frac{1}{2n}$, respectively. Now since variances cannot be negative, the lower

---

[16]This is implied by ergodicity, and even the long-range-dependent time series discussed in Section 2.6 satisfy this condition.

bound for $\overline{\mathrm{VR}}(q)-1$ is -1. But then the smallest algebraic value that the test statistic $(\overline{\mathrm{VR}}(q)-1)/\sqrt{V}$ can take on is:

$$\mathrm{Min}\,\frac{\overline{\mathrm{VR}}(q)-1}{\sqrt{V}} \;=\; \frac{-1}{\mathrm{Min}\,\sqrt{V}} \;=\; -\sqrt{2n} \;=\; -\sqrt{2T/q}. \tag{2.5.9}$$

Suppose that q is set at two-thirds of the sample size T so that $T/q=\frac{3}{2}$. This implies that the normalized test statistic $\overline{\mathrm{VR}}(q)/\sqrt{V}$ can never be less than -1.73; hence the test will *never* reject the null hypothesis at the 95% level of significance, regardless of the data! Of course, the test statistic can still reject the null hypothesis by drawing from the right tail, but against alternative hypotheses that imply variance ratios less than one for large q—such as the permanent/transitory components model (2.5.1)—the variance ratio test will have very little power when q/T is not close to zero.

A more explicit illustration of the problems that arise when q/T is large may be obtained by performing an alternate asymptotic analysis, one in which q grows with T so that $q(T)/T$ approaches some limit δ strictly between zero and one. In this case, under RW1 Richardson and Stock (1989) show that the unnormalized variance ratio $\widehat{\mathrm{VR}}(q)$ converges in *distribution* to the following:

$$\widehat{\mathrm{VR}}(q) \quad \overset{d}{\to} \quad \frac{1}{\delta}\int_{\delta}^{1} X_{\delta}^{2}(\tau)\,d\tau \tag{2.5.10}$$

$$X_{\delta}(\tau) \quad \equiv \quad B(\tau) - B(\tau-\delta) - \delta B(1), \tag{2.5.11}$$

where $B(\cdot)$ is standard Brownian motion defined on the unit interval (see Section 9.1 in Chapter 9). Unlike the standard "fixed-q" asymptotics, in this case $\widehat{\mathrm{VR}}(q)$ does not converge in probability to one. Instead, it converges in distribution to a random variable that is a functional of Brownian motion. The expected value of this limiting distribution in (2.5.10) is

$$\mathrm{E}\!\left[\frac{1}{\delta}\int_{\delta}^{1} X_{\delta}^{2}(\tau)\,d\tau\right] \;=\; \frac{1}{\delta}\int_{\delta}^{1} \mathrm{E}[X_{\delta}^{2}(\tau)]\,d\tau \;=\; (1-\delta)^{2}. \tag{2.5.12}$$

In our earlier example where $q/T = \frac{2}{3}$, the alternative asymptotic approximation (2.5.10) implies that $\mathrm{E}[\widehat{\mathrm{VR}}(q)]$ converges to $\frac{1}{9}$, considerably less than one despite the fact that RW1 holds.

These biases are not unexpected in light of the daunting demands we are placing on long-horizon returns—without more specific economic structure, it is extremely difficult to infer much about phenomena that spans a significant portion of the entire dataset. This problem is closely related to one in spectral analysis: estimating the spectral density function near frequency zero. Frequencies near zero correspond to extremely long periods, and it is notoriously difficult to draw inferences about periodicities that exceed the span of the data.[17] We shall see explicit evidence of such difficulties in the empirical results of Section 2.8. However, in some cases long-horizon returns can yield important insights, especially when other economic variables such as the dividend-price ratio come into play—see Section 7.2.1 in Chapter 7 for further discussion.

2.6 Tests For Long-Range Dependence

There is one departure from the random walk hypothesis that is outside the statistical framework we have developed so far, and that is the phenomenon of *long-range dependence*. Long-range-dependent time series exhibit an unusually high degree of persistence—in a sense to be made precise below—so that observations in the remote past are nontrivially correlated with observations in the distant future, even as the time span between the two observations increases. Nature's predilection towards long-range dependence has been well-documented in the natural sciences such as hydrology, meteorology, and geophysics, and some have argued that economic time series are also long-range dependent. In the frequency domain, such time series exhibit power at the lowest frequencies, and this was thought to be so commonplace a phenomenon that Granger (1966) dubbed it the "typical spectral shape of an economic variable." Mandelbrot and Wallis (1968) used the more colorful term "Joseph Effect," a reference to the passage in the Book of Genesis (Chapter 41) in which Joseph foretold the seven years of plenty followed by the seven years of famine that Egypt was to experience.[18]

2.6.1 Examples of Long-Range Dependence

A typical example of long-range dependence is given by the fractionally differenced time series models of Granger (1980), Granger and Joyeux (1980), and Hosking (1981), in which p_t satisfies the following difference equation:

$$(1 - L)^d p_t = \epsilon_t, \qquad \epsilon_t \sim \mathrm{IID}(0, \sigma_\epsilon^2), \qquad (2.6.1)$$

where L is the lag operator, i.e., $Lp_t = p_{t-1}$. Granger and Joyeux (1980) and Hosking (1981) show that when the quantity $(1-L)^d$ is extended to noninteger powers of d in the mathematically natural way, the result is a

---

[17] See the discussion and analysis in Section 2.6 for further details.

[18] This biblical analogy is not completely frivolous, since long-range dependence has been documented in various hydrological studies, not the least of which was Hurst's (1951) seminal study on measuring the long-term storage capacity of reservoirs. Indeed, much of Hurst's research was motivated by his empirical observations of the Nile, the very same river that played so prominent a role in Joseph's prophecies.

well-defined time series that is said to be *fractionally differenced* of order d (or, equivalently, *fractionally integrated* of order $-d$). Briefly, this involves expanding the expression $(1-L)^d$ via the binomial theorem for noninteger powers:

$$(1-L)^d = \sum_{k=0}^{\infty} (-1)^k \binom{d}{k} L^k,$$

$$\binom{d}{k} \equiv \frac{d(d-1)(d-2)\cdots(d-k+1)}{k!} \qquad (2.6.2)$$

and then applying the expansion to p_t:

$$(1-L)^d p_t = \sum_{k=0}^{\infty} (-1)^k \binom{d}{k} L^k p_t = \sum_{k=0}^{\infty} A_k\, p_{t-k} = \epsilon_t, \qquad (2.6.3)$$

where the autoregressive coefficients A_k are often re-expressed in terms of the gamma function:

$$A_k = (-1)^k \binom{d}{k} = \frac{\Gamma(k-d)}{\Gamma(-d)\,\Gamma(k+1)}. \qquad (2.6.4)$$

p_t may also be viewed as an infinite-order MA process since

$$p_t = (1-L)^{-d} \epsilon_t = B(L)\,\epsilon_t, \qquad B_k = \frac{\Gamma(k+d)}{\Gamma(d)\,\Gamma(k+1)}. \qquad (2.6.5)$$

It is not obvious that such a definition of fractional differencing might yield a useful stochastic process, but Granger (1980), Granger and Joyeux (1980), and Hosking (1981) show that the characteristics of fractionally differenced time series are interesting indeed. For example, they show that p_t is stationary and invertible for $d \in (-\frac{1}{2}, \frac{1}{2})$ (see Hosking [1981]) and exhibits a unique kind of dependence that is positive or negative depending on whether d is positive or negative, i.e., the autocorrelation coefficients of p_t are of the same sign as d. So slowly do the autocorrelations decay that when d is positive their sum diverges to infinity, and collapses to zero when d is negative.[19]

To develop a sense for long-range dependence, compare the autocorrelations of a fractionally differenced p_t with those of a stationary AR(1) in Table 2.3. Although both the AR(1) and the fractionally differenced ($d=\frac{1}{3}$)

---

[19]Mandelbrot and others have called the $d<0$ case *antipersistence*, reserving the term *long-range dependence* for the $d>0$ case. However, since both cases involve autocorrelations that decay much more slowly than those of more conventional time series, we call both long-range dependent.

Table 2.3. *Autocorrelation function for fractionally differenced process.*

Lag k	$\rho_p(k)$ $[d=\frac{1}{3}]$	$\rho_p(k)$ $[d=-\frac{1}{3}]$	$\rho_p(k)$ $[AR(1), \phi = .5]$
1	0.500	−0.250	0.500
2	0.400	−0.071	0.250
3	0.350	−0.036	0.125
4	0.318	−0.022	0.063
5	0.295	−0.015	0.031
10	0.235	−0.005	0.001
25	0.173	−0.001	2.98×10^{-8}
50	0.137	-3.24×10^{-4}	8.88×10^{-16}
100	0.109	-1.02×10^{-4}	7.89×10^{-31}

Comparison of autocorrelation functions of fractionally differenced time series $(1-L)^d p_t = \epsilon_t$ for $d = \frac{1}{3}, -\frac{1}{3}$, with that of an $AR(1)$ $p_t = \phi p_{t-1} + \epsilon_t, \phi = .5$. The variance of ϵ_t was chosen to yield a unit variance for p_t in all three cases.

series have first-order autocorrelations of 0.500, at lag 25 the AR(1) correlation is 0.000 whereas the fractionally differenced series has correlation 0.173, declining only to 0.109 at lag 100. In fact, the defining characteristic of long-range dependent processes has been taken by many to be this slow decay of the autocovariance function.

More generally, long-range dependent processes $\{p_t\}$ may be defined to be those processes with autocovariance functions $\gamma_p(k)$ such that

$$\gamma_p(k) \sim \begin{cases} k^\nu f_1(k) & \text{for} \quad \nu \in (-1,0) \quad \text{or,} \\ -k^\nu f_1(k) & \text{for} \quad \nu \in (-2,-1) \end{cases} \quad \text{as} \quad k \to \infty, \quad (2.6.6)$$

where $f_1(k)$ is any slowly varying function at infinity.[20] Alternatively, long-range dependence has also been defined as processes with spectral density functions $s(\lambda)$ such that

$$s(\lambda) \sim \lambda^{-\alpha} f_2(k) \quad \text{as} \quad \lambda \to 0, \quad \alpha \in (-1,1), \quad (2.6.7)$$

where $f_2(k)$ is a slowly varying function. For example, the autocovariance

---

[20]A function $f(x)$ is said to be slowly varying at ∞ if $\lim_{x\to\infty} f(tx)/f(x) = 1$ for all $t \in [a, \infty)$. The function $\log x$ is an example of a slowly varying function at infinity.

function and spectral density near frequency zero of the fractionally differenced process (2.6.1) is

$$\gamma_p(k) = \frac{\sigma_\epsilon^2\, \Gamma(1-2d)\, \Gamma(k+d)}{\Gamma(d)\, \Gamma(1-d)\, \Gamma(k+1-d)}$$

$$\sim\ c_o\, k^{2d-1}\quad \text{as}\quad k \to \infty \tag{2.6.8}$$

$$s(\lambda)\ \cong\ (1 - e^{-i\lambda})^{-d}(1 - e^{i\lambda})^{-d}\, \sigma_\epsilon^2$$

$$\sim\ \sigma_\epsilon^2\, k^{-2d}\quad \text{as}\quad \lambda \to 0, \tag{2.6.9}$$

where $d \in \left(-\frac{1}{2}, \frac{1}{2}\right)$. Depending on whether d is negative or positive, the spectral density of (2.6.1) at frequency zero will either be zero or infinite.

2.6.2 The Hurst-Mandelbrot Rescaled Range Statistic

The importance of long-range dependence in asset markets was first studied by Mandelbrot (1971), who proposed using the range over standard deviation, or R/S, statistic, also called the *rescaled range*, to detect long-range dependence in economic time series. The R/S statistic was originally developed by the English hydrologist Harold Edwin Hurst (1951) in his studies of river discharges. The R/S statistic is the range of partial sums of deviations of a time series from its mean, rescaled by its standard deviation. Specifically, consider a sample of continuously compounded asset returns $\{r_1, r_2, \ldots, r_n\}$ and let $\bar{r}_n$ denote the sample mean $\frac{1}{n}\sum_j r_j$. Then the classical rescaled-range statistic, which we shall call $\tilde{Q}_n$, is given by

$$\tilde{Q}_n \equiv \frac{1}{s_n}\left[\underset{1 \le k \le n}{\mathrm{Max}} \sum_{j=1}^{k} (r_j - \bar{r}_n) - \underset{1 \le k \le n}{\mathrm{Min}} \sum_{j=1}^{k} (r_j - \bar{r}_n) \right] \tag{2.6.10}$$

where s_n is the usual (maximum likelihood) standard deviation estimator,

$$s_n \equiv \left[\frac{1}{n}\sum_j (r_j - \bar{r}_n)^2 \right]^{1/2}. \tag{2.6.11}$$

The first term in brackets in (2.6.10) is the maximum (over k) of the partial sums of the first k deviations of r_j from the sample mean. Since the sum of all n deviations of r_j's from their mean is zero, this maximum is always nonnegative. The second term in (2.6.10) is the minimum (over k) of this same sequence of partial sums, and hence it is always nonpositive. The difference of the two quantities, called the *range* for obvious reasons, is always nonnegative and hence $\tilde{Q}_n \ge 0$.[21]

---

[21] The behavior of $\tilde{Q}_n$ may be better understood by considering its origins in hydrological studies of reservoir design. To accommodate seasonalities in riverflow, a reservoir's capacity

In several seminal papers Mandelbrot, Taqqu, and Wallis demonstrate the superiority of R/S analysis to more conventional methods of determining long-range dependence, such as analyzing autocorrelations, variance ratios, and spectral decompositions. For example, Mandelbrot and Wallis (1969b) show by Monte Carlo simulation that the R/S statistic can detect long-range dependence in highly non-Gaussian time series with large skewness and/or kurtosis. In fact, Mandelbrot (1972, 1975) reports the almost-sure convergence of the R/S statistic for stochastic processes with infinite variances, a distinct advantage over autocorrelations and variance ratios which need not be well-defined for infinite variance processes. Further aspects of the R/S statistic's robustness are developed in Mandelbrot and Taqqu (1979). Mandelbrot (1972) also argues that, unlike spectral analysis which detects periodic cycles, R/S analysis can detect *nonperiodic* cycles, cycles with periods equal to or greater than the sample period.

Although these claims may all be contested to some degree, it is a well-established fact that long-range dependence can indeed be detected by the "classical" R/S statistic. However, perhaps the most important shortcoming of the rescaled range is its sensitivity to short-range dependence, implying that any incompatibility between the data and the predicted behavior of the R/S statistic under the null hypothesis need not come from long-range dependence, but may merely be a symptom of short-term memory.

In particular Lo (1991) shows that under RW1 the asymptotic distribution of $(1/\sqrt{n})\, \tilde{Q}_n$ is given by the random variable $\mathcal{V}$, the range of a Brownian bridge, but under a stationary AR(1) specification with autoregressive coefficient ϕ the normalized R/S statistic converges to $\xi \mathcal{V}$ where $\xi \equiv \sqrt{(1+\phi)/(1-\phi)}$. For weekly returns of some portfolios of common stock, $\hat{\phi}$ is as large as 50%, implying that the mean of $\tilde{Q}_n/\sqrt{n}$ may be biased up-

---

must be chosen to allow for fluctuations in the supply of water above the dam while still maintaining a relatively constant flow of water below the dam. Since dam construction costs are immense, the importance of estimating the reservoir capacity necessary to meet long-term storage needs is apparent. The range is an estimate of this quantity. If X_j is the riverflow (per unit time) above the dam and $\overline{X}_n$ is the desired riverflow below the dam, the bracketed quantity in (2.6.10) is the capacity of the reservoir needed to ensure this smooth flow given the pattern of flows in periods 1 through n. For example, suppose annual riverflows are assumed to be 100, 50, 100, and 50 in years 1 through 4. If a constant annual flow of 75 below the dam is desired each year, a reservoir must have a minimum total capacity of 25 since it must store 25 units in years 1 and 3 to provide for the relatively dry years 2 and 4. Now suppose instead that the natural pattern of riverflow is 100, 100, 50, 50 in years 1 through 4. To ensure a flow of 75 below the dam in this case, the minimum capacity must increase to 50 so as to accommodate the excess storage needed in years 1 and 2 to supply water during the "dry spell" in years 3 and 4. Seen in this context, it is clear that an increase in persistence will increase the required storage capacity as measured by the range. Indeed, it was the apparent persistence of "dry spells" in Egypt that sparked Hurst's lifelong fascination with the Nile, leading eventually to his interest in the rescaled range.

ward by 73%! Since the mean of $\mathcal{V}$ is $\sqrt{\pi/2}\approx1.25$, the mean of the classical rescaled range would be 2.16 for such an AR(1) process.

Lo (1991) develops a modification of the R/S statistic to account for the effects of short-range dependence, derives an asymptotic sampling theory under several null and alternative hypotheses, and demonstrates via Monte Carlo simulations and empirical examples drawn from recent historical stock market data that the modified R/S statistic is considerably more accurate, often yielding inferences that contradict those of its classical counterpart. In particular, what the earlier literature had assumed was evidence of long-range dependence in US stock returns may well be the result of quickly decaying short-range dependence instead.

2.7 Unit Root Tests

A more recent and more specialized class of tests that are often confused with tests of the random walk hypotheses is the collection of *unit root* tests in which the null hypothesis is

$$X_t = \mu + X_{t-1} + \epsilon_t, \tag{2.7.1}$$

often with the following alternative hypothesis:

$$X_t - \mu t = \phi\big(X_{t-1} - \mu(t-1)\big) + \epsilon_t, \qquad \phi \in (-1,1), \tag{2.7.2}$$

where ϵ_t is any zero-mean stationary process, such that

$$0 < \sigma_o^2 = \lim_{T\to\infty} \mathrm{E}\left[\frac{1}{T}\left(\sum_{t=1}^{T}\epsilon_t\right)^2\right] < \infty. \tag{2.7.3}$$

Heuristically, condition (2.7.3) requires that variance of the partial sum $\sum_{t=1}^{T}\epsilon_t$ increase at approximately the same rate as T, so that each new ϵ_t added to the partial sum has a nontrivial contribution to the partial sum's variance.[22] This condition ensures that the usual limit theorems are applicable to the ϵ_t's, and it is satisfied by virtually all of the stationary processes that we shall have occasion to study (except for those in Section 2.6).

---

[22] If the partial sum's variance were to grow slower than T, so that the limit in (2.7.3) were 0, the uncertainty in the sequence of ϵ_t's would be "cancelling out" over time and would not be a very useful model of random price dynamics. An example of such a process is an MA(1) with a unit root, i.e., $\epsilon_t = \eta_t - \eta_{t-1}$, where η_t is white noise.

If the partial sum's variance were to grow faster than T, so that the limit in (2.7.3) were ∞, this would be an example of *long-range dependence*, in which the autocorrelation function of the ϵ_t's decays very slowly. An example of such a process is a fractionally differenced process $(1-L)^d\epsilon_t = \eta_t$, where η_t is white noise. See Section 2.6 and Lo (1991) for further discussion.

The unit root test is designed to reveal whether X_t is *difference-stationary* (the null hypothesis) or *trend-stationary* (the alternative hypothesis); this distinction rests on whether ϕ is unity, hence the term *unit root hypothesis*. The test itself is formed by comparing the ordinary least squares estimator $\hat{\phi}$ to unity via its (nonstandard) sampling distribution under the null hypothesis (2.7.1), which was first derived by Dickey and Fuller (1979).[23] Under the null hypothesis, any shock to X_t is said to be *permanent* since $E[X_{t+k} \mid X_t] = \mu k + X_t$ for all $k>0$, and a shock to X_t will appear in the conditional expectation of all future X_{t+k}. In this case X_t is often called a *stochastic trend* since its conditional expectation depends explicitly on the stochastic variable X_t. In contrast, under the alternative (2.7.2), a shock to X_t is said to be *temporary*, since $E[X_{t+k} \mid X_t] = \mu(t+k) + \phi^k(X_t - \mu t)$, and the influence of X_t on the conditional expectation of future X_{t+k} diminishes as k increases.

Because the ϵ_t's are allowed to be an arbitrary zero-mean stationary process under both the unit root null (2.7.1) and alternative hypothesis (2.7.2), the focus of the unit root test is not on the predictability of X_t, as it is under the random walk hypotheses. Even under the null hypothesis (2.7.1), the increments of X_t may be predictable. Despite the fact that the random walk hypotheses are contained in the unit root null hypothesis, it is the permanent/temporary nature of shocks to X_t that concerns such tests. Indeed, since there are also nonrandom walk alternatives in the unit root null hypothesis, tests of unit roots are clearly not designed to detect predictability, but are in fact insensitive to it by construction.

2.8 Recent Empirical Evidence

Predictability in asset returns is a very broad and active research topic, and it is impossible to provide a complete survey of this vast literature in just a few pages. Therefore, in this section we focus exclusively on the recent empirical literature.[24] We hope to give readers a sense for the empirical relevance of predictability in recent equity markets by applying the tests developed in the earlier sections to stock indexes and individual stock returns using daily and weekly data from 1962 to 1994 and monthly data from 1926 to 1994. Despite

---

[23] Since then, advances in econometric methods have yielded many extensions and generalizations to this simple framework: tests for multiple unit roots in multivariate ARIMA systems, tests for cointegration, consistent estimation of models with unit roots cointegration, etc. (see Campbell and Perron [1991] for a thorough survey of this literature).

[24] However, we would be remiss if we did not cite the rich empirical tradition on which the recent literature is built, which includes: Alexander (1961, 1964), Cootner (1964), Cowles (1960), Cowles and Jones (1937), Fama (1965), Fama and Blume (1966) Kendall (1953), Granger and Morgenstern (1963), Mandelbrot (1963), Osborne (1959, 1962), Roberts (1959), and Working (1960).

the specificity of these examples, the empirical results illustrate many of the issues that have arisen in the broader search for predictability among asset returns.

2.8.1 Autocorrelations

Table 2.4 reports the means, standard deviations, autocorrelations, and Box-Pierce Q-statistics for daily, weekly, and monthly CRSP stock returns indexes from July 3, 1962 to December 31, 1994.[25] During this period, panel A of Table 2.4 reports that the daily equal-weighted CRSP index has a first-order autocorrelation $\hat{\rho}(1)$ of 35.0%. Recall from Section 2.4.1 that under the IID random walk null hypothesis RW1, the asymptotic sampling distribution of $\hat{\rho}(1)$ is normal with mean 0 and standard deviation $1/\sqrt{T}$ (see (2.4.14)). This implies that a sample size of 8,179 observations yields a standard error of 1.11% for $\hat{\rho}(1)$; hence an autocorrelation of 35.0% is clearly statistically significant at all conventional levels of significance. Moreover, the Box-Pierce Q-statistic with five autocorrelations has a value of 263.3 which is significant at all the conventional significance levels (recall that this statistic is distributed asymptotically as a χ_5^2 variate for which the 99.5-percentile is 16.7).

Similar calculations for the value-weighted indexes in panel A show that both CRSP daily indexes exhibit statistically significant positive serial correlation at the first lag, although the equal-weighted index has higher autocorrelation which decays more slowly than the value-weighted index. The subsample autocorrelations demonstrate that the significance of the autocorrelations is not an artifact of any particularly influential subset of the data; both indexes are strongly positively autocorrelated in each subsample.

To develop a sense of the *economic* significance of the autocorrelations in Table 2.4, observe that the R^2 of a regression of returns on a constant and its first lag is the square of the slope coefficient, which is simply the first-order autocorrelation. Therefore, an autocorrelation of 35.0% implies that 12.3% of the variation in the daily CRSP equal-weighted index return is predictable using the preceding day's index return.

---

[25]Unless stated otherwise, we take returns to be continuously compounded. Portfolio returns are calculated first from simple returns and then are converted to a continuously compounded return. The weekly return of each security is computed as the return from Tuesday's closing price to the following Tuesday's closing price. If the following Tuesday's price is missing, then Wednesday's price (or Monday's if Wednesday's is also missing) is used. If both Monday's and Wednesday's prices are missing, the return for that week is reported as missing; this occurs only rarely. To compute weekly returns on size-sorted portfolios, for each week all stocks with nonmissing returns that week are assigned to portfolios based on the beginning of year market value. If the beginning of year market value is missing, then the end of year value is used. If both market values are missing the stock is not assigned to a portfolio.

Table 2.4. *Autocorrelation in daily, weekly, and monthly stock index returns.*

Sample Period	Sample Size	Mean	SD	$\hat{\rho}_1$	$\hat{\rho}_2$	$\hat{\rho}_3$	$\hat{\rho}_4$	$\hat{Q}_5$	$\hat{Q}_{10}$
A. Daily Returns									
		CRSP Value-Weighted Index							
62:07:03–94:12:30	8,179	0.041	0.824	17.6	−0.7	0.1	−0.8	263.3	269.5
62:07:03–78:10:27	4,090	0.028	0.738	27.8	1.2	4.6	3.3	329.4	343.5
78:10:30–94:12:30	4,089	0.054	0.901	10.8	−2.2	−2.9	−3.5	69.5	72.1
		CRSP Equal-Weighted Index							
62:07:03–94:12:30	8,179	0.070	0.764	35.0	9.3	8.5	9.9	1,301.9	1,369.5
62:07:03–78:10:27	4,090	0.063	0.771	43.1	13.0	15.3	15.2	1,062.2	1,110.2
78:10:30–94:12:30	4,089	0.078	0.756	26.2	4.9	2.0	4.9	348.9	379.5
B. Weekly Returns									
		CRSP Value-Weighted Index							
62:07:10–94:12:27	1,695	0.196	2.093	1.5	−2.5	3.5	−0.7	8.8	36.7
62:07:10–78:10:03	848	0.144	1.994	5.6	−3.7	5.8	1.6	9.0	21.5
78:10:10–94:12:27	847	0.248	2.188	−2.0	−1.5	1.6	−3.3	5.3	25.2
		CRSP Equal-Weighted Index							
62:07:10–94:12:27	1,695	0.339	2.321	20.3	6.1	9.1	4.8	94.3	109.3
62:07:10–78:10:03	848	0.324	2.460	21.8	7.5	11.9	6.1	60.4	68.5
78:10:10–94:12:27	847	0.354	2.174	18.4	4.3	5.5	2.2	33.7	51.3
C. Monthly Returns									
		CRSP Value-Weighted Index							
62:07:31–94:12:30	390	0.861	4.336	4.3	−5.3	−1.3	−0.4	6.8	12.5
62:07:31–78:09:29	195	0.646	4.219	6.4	−3.8	7.3	6.2	3.9	9.7
78:10:31–94:12:30	195	1.076	4.450	1.3	−6.3	−8.3	−7.7	7.5	14.0
		CRSP Equal-Weighted Index							
62:07:31–94:12:30	390	1.077	5.749	17.1	−3.4	−3.3	−1.6	12.8	21.3
62:07:31–78:09:29	195	1.049	6.148	18.4	−2.5	4.4	2.4	7.5	12.6
78:10:31–94:12:30	195	1.105	5.336	15.0	−1.6	−12.4	−7.4	8.9	14.2

Autocorrelation coefficients (in percent) and Box-Pierce Q-statistics for CRSP daily, weekly, and monthly value- and equal-weighted return indexes for the sample period from July 3, 1962 to December 30, 1994 and subperiods.

The weekly and monthly return autocorrelations reported in panels B and C of Table 2.4, respectively, exhibit patterns similar to those of the daily autocorrelations: positive and statistically significant at the first lag over the entire sample and for all subsamples, with smaller and sometimes negative higher-order autocorrelations.

2.8.2 Variance Ratios

The fact that the autocorrelations of daily, weekly, and monthly index returns in Table 2.4 are positive and often significantly different from zero has implications for the behavior of the variance ratios of Section 2.4 and we explore these implications in this section for the returns of indexes, portfolios, and individual securities.

CRSP Indexes

The autocorrelations in Table 2.4 suggest variance ratios greater than one, and this is confirmed in Table 2.5 which reports variance ratios $\overline{\text{VR}}$ defined in (2.4.37) and, in parentheses, heteroskedasticity-consistent asymptotically standard normal test statistics $\psi^*(q)$ defined in (2.4.44), for weekly CRSP equal- and value-weighted market return indexes.[26] Panel A contains results for the equal-weighted index and panel B contains results for the value-weighted index. Within each panel, the first row presents the variance ratios and test statistics for the entire 1,695-week sample and the next two rows present similar results for the two subsamples of 848 and 847 weeks.

Panel A shows that the random walk null hypothesis RW3 is rejected at all the usual significance levels for the entire time period and all subperiods for the equal-weighted index. Moreover, the rejections are not due to changing variances since the $\psi^*(q)$'s are heteroskedasticity-consistent. The estimates of the variance ratio are *larger* than one for all cases. For example, the entries in the first column of panel A correspond to variance ratios with an aggregation value q of 2. In view of (2.4.18), ratios with $q=2$ are approximately equal to 1 plus the first-order autocorrelation coefficient estimator of weekly returns; hence, the entry in the first row, 1.20, implies that the first-order autocorrelation for weekly returns is approximately 20%, which is consistent with the value reported in Table 2.4. With a corresponding $\psi^*(q)$ statistic of 4.53, the random walk hypothesis is resoundingly rejected.

The subsample results show that although RW3 is easily rejected over both halves of the sample period, the variance ratios are slightly larger and the rejections slightly stronger over the first half. This pattern is repeated in Table 2.6 and in other empirical studies of predictability in US stock

---

[26]Since in our sample the values of $\psi^*(q)$—computed under the null hypothesis RW3—are always statistically less significant than the values of $\psi(q)$ calculated under RW1, to conserve space we report only the more conservative statistics.

Table 2.5. *Variance ratios for weekly stock index returns.*

Sample period	Number nq of base observations	Number q of base observations aggregated to form variance ratio			
		2	4	8	16
A. CRSP Equal-Weighted Index					
62:07:10–94:12:27	1,695	1.20	1.42	1.65	1.74
		(4.53)*	(5.30)*	(5.84)*	(4.85)*
62:07:10–78:10:03	848	1.22	1.47	1.74	1.90
		(3.47)*	(4.44)*	(4.87)*	(4.24)*
78:10:10–94:12:27	847	1.19	1.35	1.48	1.54
		(2.96)*	(2.96)*	(3.00)*	(2.55)*
B. CRSP Value-Weighted Index					
62:07:10–94:12:27	1,695	1.02	1.02	1.04	1.02
		(0.51)	(0.30)	(0.41)	(0.14)
62:07:10–78:10:03	848	1.06	1.08	1.14	1.19
		(1.11)	(0.89)	(1.05)	(0.95)
78:10:10–94:12:27	847	0.98	0.97	0.93	0.88
		(-0.45)	(-0.40)	(-0.50)	(−0.64)

Variance-ratio test of the random walk hypothesis for CRSP equal- and value-weighted indexes, for the sample period from July 10, 1962 to December 27, 1994 and subperiods. The variance ratios $\overline{VR}(q)$ are reported in the main rows, with heteroskedasticity-consistent test statistics $\psi^*(q)$ given in parentheses immediately below each main row. Under the random walk null hypothesis, the value of the variance ratio is one and the test statistics have a standard normal distribution asymptotically. Test statistics marked with asterisks indicate that the corresponding variance ratios are statistically different from one at the 5% level of significance.

returns: the degree of predictability seems to be declining through time. To the extent that such predictability has been a source of "excess" profits, its decline is consistent with the fact that financial markets have become increasingly competitive over the sample period.

The variance ratios for the equal-weighted index generally increase with q: the variance ratio climbs from 1.20 (for $q=2$) to 1.74 (for $q = 16$), and the subsample results show a similar pattern. To interpret this pattern, observe that an analog of (2.4.18) can be derived for ratios of variance ratios:

$$\frac{VR(2q)}{VR(q)} = 1 + \rho_q(1) \tag{2.8.1}$$

where $\rho_q(1)$ is the first-order autocorrelation coefficient for q-period returns $r_t + r_{t-1} + \cdots + r_{t-q+1}$. Therefore, the fact that the variance ratios in panel A of Table 2.5 are increasing implies positive serial correlation in multiperiod returns. For example, $\overline{VR}(4)/\overline{VR}(2)=1.42/1.20=1.18$, which implies that 2-week returns have a first-order autocorrelation coefficient of approximately 18%.

Panel B of Table 2.5 shows that the value-weighted index behaves quite differently. Over the entire sample period, the variance ratios are all greater than one, but not by much, ranging from 1.02 for $q=2$ to 1.04 for $q=8$. Moreover, the test statistics $\psi^*(q)$ are all statistically insignificant, hence RW3 cannot be rejected for any q. The subsample results show that during the first half of the sample period, the variance ratios for the value-weighted index do increase with q (implying positive serial correlation for multiperiod returns), but during the second half of the sample, the variance ratios decline with q (implying negative serial correlation for multiperiod returns). These two opposing patterns are responsible for the relatively stable behavior of the variance ratios over the entire sample period.

Although the test statistics in Table 2.5 are based on nominal stock returns, it is apparent that virtually the same results would obtain with real or excess returns. Since the volatility of weekly nominal returns is so much larger than that of the inflation and Treasury-bill rates, the use of nominal, real, or excess returns in volatility-based tests will yield practically identical inferences.

Size-Sorted Portfolios

The fact that RW3 is rejected by the equal-weighted index but not by the value-weighted index suggests that market capitalization or size may play a role in the behavior of the variance ratios. To obtain a better sense of this intuition, Table 2.6 presents variance ratios for the returns of size-sorted portfolios. We compute weekly returns for five size-sorted portfolios from the CRSP NYSE-AMEX daily returns file. Stocks with returns for any given week are assigned to portfolios based on which quintile their beginning-of-year market capitalization belongs to. The portfolios are equal-weighted and have a changing composition.[27] Panel A of Table 2.6 reports the results for the portfolio of small firms (first quintile), panel B reports the results for the portfolio of medium-size firms (third quintile), and panel C reports the results for the portfolio of large firms (fifth quintile).

Evidence against the random walk hypothesis for the portfolio of companies in the smallest quintile is strong for the entire sample and for both subsamples: in panel A all the $\psi^*(q)$ statistics are well above the 5% critical value of 1.96, ranging from 4.67 to 10.74. The variance ratios are all greater

---

[27]We also performed our tests using value-weighted portfolios and obtained essentially the same results. The only difference appears in the largest quintile of the value-weighted portfolio, for which the random walk hypothesis was generally not rejected. This, of course, is not surprising, given that the largest value-weighted quintile is quite similar to the value-weighted market index.

Table 2.6. *Variance ratios for weekly size-sorted portfolio returns.*

Time period	Number nq of base observations	Number q of base observations aggregated to form variance ratio			
		2	4	8	16

A. Portfolio of firms with market values in smallest CRSP quintile

62:07:10–94:12:27	1,695	1.35	1.77	2.24	2.46
		(7.15)*	(9.42)*	(10.74)*	(9.33)*
62:07:10–78:10:03	848	1.34	1.76	2.22	2.46
		(5.47)*	(7.33)*	(8.03)*	(6.97)*
78:10:10–94:12:27	847	1.37	1.79	2.22	2.49
		(4.67)*	(5.91)*	(6.89)*	(6.60)*

B. Portfolio of firms with market values in central CRSP quintile

62:07:10–94:12:27	1,695	1.20	1.39	1.59	1.65
		(4.25)*	(4.85)*	(5.16)*	(4.17)*
62:07:10–78:10:03	848	1.21	1.43	1.66	1.79
		(3.25)*	(4.03)*	(4.27)*	(3.67)*
78:10:10–94:12:27	847	1.19	1.33	1.44	1.47
		(2.79)*	(2.74)*	(2.63)*	(2.14)*

C. Portfolio of firms with market values in largest CRSP quintile

62:07:10–94:12:27	1,695	1.06	1.10	1.14	1.11
		(1.71)	(1.46)	(1.38)	(0.76)
62:07:10–78:10:03	848	1.11	1.21	1.30	1.32
		(2.05)*	(2.15)*	(2.12)*	(1.59)
78:10:10–94:12:27	847	1.01	1.00	0.98	0.92
		(0.29)*	(0.05)	(-0.13)	(-0.41)

Variance-ratio test of the random walk hypothesis for size-sorted portfolios, for the sample period from July 10, 1962 to December 27, 1994, and subperiods. The variance ratios $\overline{VR}(q)$ are reported in the main rows, with heteroskedasticity-consistent test statistics $\psi^*(q)$ given in parentheses immediately below each main row. Under the random walk null hypothesis, the value of the variance ratio is one and the test statistics have a standard normal distribution asymptotically. Test statistics marked with asterisks indicate that the corresponding variance ratios are statistically different from one at the 5% level of significance.

than one, implying a first-order autocorrelation of 35% for weekly returns over the entire sample period.

For the portfolios of medium-size companies, the $\psi^*(q)$ statistics in panel B shows that there is also strong evidence against RW3, although the variance ratios are smaller now, implying lower serial correlation. For the portfolio of the largest firms, panel C shows that evidence against RW3 is sparse, limited only to the first half of the sample period.

The results for size-based portfolios are generally consistent with those for the market indexes: variance ratios are generally greater than one and increasing in q, implying positive serial correlation in multiperiod returns, statistically significant for portfolios of all but the largest companies, and more significant during the first half of the sample period than the second half.

Individual Securities

Having shown that the random walk hypothesis is inconsistent with the behavior of the equal-weighted index and portfolios of small- and medium-size companies, we now turn to the case of individual security returns. Table 2.7 reports the cross-sectional average of the variance ratios of individual stocks that have complete return histories in the CRSP database for our entire 1,695-week sample period, a sample of 411 companies. Panel A contains the cross-sectional average of the variance ratios of the 411 stocks, as well as of the 100 smallest, 100 intermediate, and 100 largest stocks.[28] Cross-sectional standard deviations are given in parentheses below the main rows. Since the variance ratios are clearly not cross-sectionally independent, these standard deviations cannot be used to form the usual tests of significance—they are reported only to provide some indication of the cross-sectional dispersion of the variance ratios.

The average variance ratio with $q=2$ is 0.96 for the 411 individual securities, implying that there is negative serial correlation on average. For all stocks, the average serial correlation is -4%, and -5% for the smallest 100 stocks. However, the serial correlation is both statistically and economically insignificant and provides little evidence against the random walk hypothesis. For example, the largest average $\psi^*(q)$ statistic over all stocks occurs for $q=4$ and is -0.90 (with a cross-sectional standard deviation of 1.19); the largest average $\psi^*(q)$ for the 100 smallest stocks is -1.67 (for $q=2$, with a cross-sectional standard deviation of 1.75). These results are consistent with French and Roll's (1986) finding that daily returns of individual securities are slightly negatively autocorrelated.

For comparison, panel B reports the variance ratio of equal- and value-weighted portfolios of the 411 securities. The results are consistent with those in Tables 2.5 and 2.6: significant positive autocorrelation for the equal-weighted portfolio, and autocorrelation close to zero for the value-weighted portfolio.

That the returns of individual securities have statistically insignificant autocorrelation is not surprising. Individual returns contain much company-specific or *idiosyncratic* noise that makes it difficult to detect the presence of predictable components. Since the idiosyncratic noise is largely attenuated

---

[28]Mid-sample market values are used as the size measure.

Table 2.7. *Variance ratios for weekly individual security returns.*

Sample	Number nq of base observations	Number q of base observations aggregated to form variance ratio			
		2	4	8	16
A. Averages of variance ratios over individual securities					
All stocks (411 stocks)	1,695	0.96 (0.04)	0.92 (0.07)	0.89 (0.11)	0.85 (0.14)
Small stocks (100 stocks)	1,695	0.95 (0.06)	0.90 (0.09)	0.88 (0.12)	0.85 (0.15)
Medium stocks (100 stocks)	1,695	0.96 (0.04)	0.93 (0.07)	0.90 (0.09)	0.85 (0.13)
Large stocks (100 stocks)	1,695	0.95 (0.03)	0.91 (0.06)	0.89 (0.11)	0.86 (0.15)
B. Variance ratios of equal- and value-weighted portfolios of all stocks					
Equal-weighted portfolio (411 stocks)	1,695	1.11 (2.75)*	1.20 (2.83)*	1.30 (2.88)*	1.29 (1.99)*
Value-weighted portfolio (411 stocks)	1,695	0.99 (-0.26)	0.97 (-0.43)	0.96 (-0.42)	0.93 (-0.53)

Means of variance ratios over all individual securities with complete return histories during the sample period from July 10, 1962 to December 27, 1994 (411 stocks). Means of variance ratios for the smallest 100 stocks, the intermediate 100 stocks, and the largest 100 stocks are also reported. For purposes of comparison, panel B reports the variance ratios for equal- and value-weighted portfolios, respectively, of the 411 stocks. Parenthetical entries for averages of individual securities (panel A) are standard deviations of the cross section of variance ratios. Because the variance ratios are not cross-sectionally independent, the standard deviation cannot be used to perform the usual significance tests; they are reported only to provide an indication of the variance ratios' cross-sectional dispersion. Parenthetical entries for portfolio variance ratios (panel B) are the heteroskedasticity-consistent $\psi^*(q)$ statistics. Asterisks indicate variance ratios that are statistically different from 1 at the 5% level of significance.

by forming portfolios, we would expect to uncover the predictable *systematic* component more readily when securities are combined. Nevertheless, the weak negative autocorrelations of the individual securities are an interesting contrast to the stronger positive autocorrelation of the portfolio returns.

2.8.3 Cross-Autocorrelations and Lead-Lag Relations

Despite the fact that individual security returns are weakly negatively autocorrelated, portfolio returns—which are essentially averages of individual security returns—are strongly positively autocorrelated. This somewhat paradoxical result can mean only one thing: large positive cross-autocorrelations across individual securities across time.

To see this, consider a collection of N securities and denote by $\mathbf{R}_t$ the $(N \times 1)$ vector of their period-t simple returns $[\, R_{1t} \;\cdots\; R_{Nt} \,]'$. We switch to simple returns here because the focus of our analysis is on the interaction of returns within portfolios, and continuously compounded returns do not aggregate across securities (see Section 1.4.1 in Chapter 1 for further discussion). For convenience, we maintain the following assumption throughout this section:[29]

(A1) $\mathbf{R}_t$ *is a jointly covariance-stationary stochastic process with expectation* $\mathrm{E}[\mathbf{R}_t]$ $= \boldsymbol{\mu} \equiv [\, \mu_1 \; \mu_2 \;\cdots\; \mu_N \,]'$ *and autocovariance matrices* $\mathrm{E}[(\mathbf{R}_{t-k} - \boldsymbol{\mu})(\mathbf{R}_t - \boldsymbol{\mu})'] = \boldsymbol{\Gamma}(k)$ *where, with no loss of generality, we take* $k \geq 0$ *since* $\boldsymbol{\Gamma}(k) = \boldsymbol{\Gamma}'(-k)$.

If ι is defined to be a vector of ones $[\, 1 \;\cdots\; 1 \,]'$, we can express the equal-weighted market index as $R_{mt} \equiv \iota'\mathbf{R}_t / N$. The first-order autocovariance of R_{mt} may then be decomposed into the sum of the first-order own-autocovariances and cross-autocovariances of the component securities:

$$\mathrm{Cov}[R_{mt-1}, R_{mt}] = \mathrm{Cov}\left[\frac{\iota'\mathbf{R}_{t-1}}{N}, \frac{\iota'\mathbf{R}_t}{N}\right] = \frac{\iota'\boldsymbol{\Gamma}(1)\iota}{N^2}, \qquad (2.8.2)$$

and therefore the first-order autocorrelation of R_{mt} can be expressed as

$$\frac{\mathrm{Cov}[R_{mt-1}, R_{mt}]}{\mathrm{Var}[R_{mt}]} = \frac{\iota'\boldsymbol{\Gamma}(1)\iota}{\iota'\boldsymbol{\Gamma}(0)\iota} = \frac{\iota'\boldsymbol{\Gamma}(1)\iota - \mathrm{tr}(\boldsymbol{\Gamma}(1))}{\iota'\boldsymbol{\Gamma}(0)\iota} + \frac{\mathrm{tr}(\boldsymbol{\Gamma}(1))}{\iota'\boldsymbol{\Gamma}(0)\iota}. \quad (2.8.3)$$

where $\mathrm{tr}(\cdot)$ is the *trace* operator which sums the diagonal entries of its square-matrix argument. The first term of the right side of (2.8.3) contains only

---

[29]Assumption (A1) is made for notational simplicity, since joint covariance-stationarity allows us to eliminate time-indexes from population moments such as μ and $\Gamma(k)$; the qualitative features of our results will not change under the weaker assumptions of weakly dependent heterogeneously distributed vectors R_t. This would merely require replacing expectations with corresponding probability limits of suitably defined time-averages. See Lo and MacKinlay (1990c) for further details.

Table 2.8. *Cross-autocorrelation matrices for size-sorted portfolio returns.*

$$\widehat{\Upsilon}_0 = \begin{array}{c} R_{1t} \\ R_{2t} \\ R_{3t} \\ R_{4t} \\ R_{5t} \end{array} \begin{array}{ccccc} R_{1t} & R_{2t} & R_{3t} & R_{4t} & R_{5t} \\ \left(1.000 \right. & 0.938 & 0.892 & 0.839 & 0.728 \\ 0.938 & 1.000 & 0.976 & 0.944 & 0.856 \\ 0.892 & 0.976 & 1.000 & 0.979 & 0.914 \\ 0.839 & 0.944 & 0.979 & 1.000 & 0.961 \\ \left. 0.728 \right. & 0.856 & 0.914 & 0.961 & 1.000 \end{array}$$

$$\widehat{\Upsilon}_1 = \begin{array}{c} R_{1t-1} \\ R_{2t-1} \\ R_{3t-1} \\ R_{4t-1} \\ R_{5t-1} \end{array} \begin{array}{ccccc} R_{1t} & R_{2t} & R_{3t} & R_{4t} & R_{5t} \\ 0.352 & 0.226 & 0.171 & 0.115 & 0.024 \\ 0.330 & 0.232 & 0.182 & 0.129 & 0.037 \\ 0.324 & 0.244 & 0.197 & 0.147 & 0.053 \\ 0.310 & 0.242 & 0.201 & 0.153 & 0.059 \\ 0.265 & 0.223 & 0.187 & 0.147 & 0.057 \end{array}$$

$$\widehat{\Upsilon}_2 = \begin{array}{c} R_{1t-2} \\ R_{2t-2} \\ R_{3t-2} \\ R_{4t-2} \\ R_{5t-2} \end{array} \begin{array}{ccccc} R_{1t} & R_{2t} & R_{3t} & R_{4t} & R_{5t} \\ 0.163 & 0.089 & 0.057 & 0.032 & -0.010 \\ 0.141 & 0.078 & 0.051 & 0.029 & -0.010 \\ 0.135 & 0.079 & 0.051 & 0.032 & -0.005 \\ 0.121 & 0.071 & 0.046 & 0.028 & -0.006 \\ 0.084 & 0.045 & 0.025 & 0.012 & -0.016 \end{array}$$

$$\widehat{\Upsilon}_3 = \begin{array}{c} R_{1t-3} \\ R_{2t-3} \\ R_{3t-3} \\ R_{4t-3} \\ R_{5t-3} \end{array} \begin{array}{ccccc} R_{1t} & R_{2t} & R_{3t} & R_{4t} & R_{5t} \\ 0.155 & 0.106 & 0.074 & 0.050 & 0.027 \\ 0.141 & 0.100 & 0.071 & 0.050 & 0.031 \\ 0.143 & 0.105 & 0.077 & 0.058 & 0.039 \\ 0.137 & 0.104 & 0.079 & 0.061 & 0.044 \\ 0.120 & 0.093 & 0.074 & 0.061 & 0.047 \end{array}$$

$$\widehat{\Upsilon}_4 = \begin{array}{c} R_{1t-4} \\ R_{2t-4} \\ R_{3t-4} \\ R_{4t-4} \\ R_{5t-4} \end{array} \begin{array}{ccccc} R_{1t} & R_{2t} & R_{3t} & R_{4t} & R_{5t} \\ 0.104 & 0.063 & 0.036 & 0.016 & -0.007 \\ 0.097 & 0.062 & 0.036 & 0.017 & -0.006 \\ 0.095 & 0.060 & 0.033 & 0.015 & -0.011 \\ 0.100 & 0.067 & 0.039 & 0.023 & -0.004 \\ 0.094 & 0.064 & 0.038 & 0.025 & -0.001 \end{array}$$

Autocorrelation matrices of the vector $\mathbf{X}_t \equiv [\ R_{1t}\ \ R_{2t}\ \ R_{3t}\ \ R_{4t}\ \ R_{5t}\ ]'$ where R_{it} is the week-t return on the equal-weighted portfolio of stocks in the ith quintile, $i = 1, \ldots, 5$ (quintile 1 contains the smallest stocks), for the sample of NYSE-AMEX stocks from July 10, 1962 to December 27, 1994 (1,695 observations). Note that $\Upsilon(k) \equiv \mathbf{D}^{-1/2} \mathrm{E}[(\mathbf{X}_{t-k}-\mu)(\mathbf{X}_t-\mu)']\mathbf{D}^{-1/2}$ where $\mathbf{D} \equiv \mathrm{diag}(\sigma_1^2, \ldots, \sigma_5^2)$; thus the (i, j)th element is the correlation between R_{it-k} and R_{jt}. Asymptotic standard errors for the autocorrelations under an IID null hypothesis are given by $1/\sqrt{T} = 0.024$.

cross-autocovariances and the second term only the own-autocovariances. If the own-autocovariances are generally negative, and index autocovariance is positive, then the cross-autocovariances must be positive. Moreover, the cross-autocovariances must be large, so large as to exceed the sum of the negative own-autocovariances.

Table 2.8 reports autocorrelation matrices $\hat{\Upsilon}(k)$ of the vector of weekly returns of five size-sorted portfolios, formed from the sample of stocks using weekly returns from July 10, 1962, to December 27, 1994 (1,695 observations). Let $\mathbf{X}_t$ denote the vector $[\ R_{1t}\ \ R_{2t}\ \ R_{3t}\ \ R_{4t}\ \ R_{5t}\ ]'$, where R_{it} is the return on the equal-weighted portfolio of stocks in the ith quintile. Then the kth order autocorrelation *matrix* of $\mathbf{X}_t$ is given by $\Upsilon(k) \equiv \mathbf{D}^{-1/2}\mathrm{E}[(\mathbf{X}_{t-k} - \boldsymbol{\mu})(\mathbf{X}_t - \boldsymbol{\mu})']\mathbf{D}^{-1/2}$, where $\mathbf{D} \equiv \mathrm{diag}(\sigma_1^2, \ldots, \sigma_5^2)$ and $\boldsymbol{\mu} \equiv \mathrm{E}[\mathbf{X}_t]$. By this convention, the i, jth element of $\Upsilon(k)$ is the correlation of R_{it-k} with R_{jt}. The estimator $\hat{\Upsilon}(k)$ is the usual sample autocorrelation matrix.

An interesting pattern emerges from Table 2.8: The entries below the diagonals of $\hat{\Upsilon}(k)$ are almost always larger than those above the diagonals. For example, the first-order autocorrelation between last week's return on large stocks (R_{5t-1}) with this week's return on small stocks (R_{1t}) is 26.5%, whereas the first-order autocorrelation between last week's return on small stocks (R_{1t-1}) with this week's return on large stocks (R_{5t}) is only 2.4%. Similar patterns may be seen in the higher-order autocorrelation matrices, although the magnitudes are smaller since the higher-order cross-autocorrelations decay. The asymmetry of the $\hat{\Upsilon}(k)$ matrices implies that the autocovariance matrix estimators $\hat{\Gamma}(k)$ are also asymmetric.

This intriguing *lead-lag* pattern, where larger capitalization stocks lead and smaller capitalization stocks lag, is more apparent in Table 2.9 which reports the difference of the autocorrelation matrices and their transposes. Every lower-diagonal entry is positive (hence every upper-diagonal entry is negative), implying that the correlation between current returns of smaller stocks and past returns of larger stocks is always larger than the correlation between current returns of larger stocks and past returns of smaller stocks.

Of course, the nontrading model of Chapter 3 also yields an asymmetric autocorrelation matrix. However, we shall see in that chapter that unrealistically high probabilities of nontrading are required to generate cross-autocorrelations of the magnitude reported in Table 2.8.

The results in Tables 2.8 and 2.9 point to the complex patterns of cross-effects among securities as significant sources of positive index autocorrelation. Indeed, Lo and MacKinlay (1990c) show that over half of the positive index autocorrelation is attributable to positive cross-effects. They also observe that positive cross-effects can explain the apparent profitability of *contrarian* investment strategies, strategies that are contrary to the general market direction. These strategies, predicated on the notion that investors tend to overreact to information, consist of selling "winners" and buying "losers." Selling the winners and buying the losers will earn positive expected profits in the presence of negative serial correlation because current losers are likely to become future winners and current winners are likely to become future losers.

Table 2.9. *Asymmetry of cross-autocorrelation matrices.*

$$\widehat{\Upsilon}(1) - \widehat{\Upsilon}'(1) = \begin{array}{c} \\ R_1 \\ R_2 \\ R_3 \\ R_4 \\ R_5 \end{array} \begin{array}{c} \begin{array}{ccccc} R_1 & R_2 & R_3 & R_4 & R_5 \end{array} \\ \begin{pmatrix} 0.000 & -0.104 & -0.153 & -0.195 & -0.241 \\ 0.104 & 0.000 & -0.061 & -0.113 & -0.181 \\ 0.153 & 0.061 & 0.000 & -0.054 & -0.134 \\ 0.195 & 0.113 & 0.054 & 0.000 & -0.088 \\ 0.241 & 0.181 & 0.134 & 0.088 & 0.000 \end{pmatrix} \end{array}$$

$$\widehat{\Upsilon}(2) - \widehat{\Upsilon}'(2) = \begin{array}{c} \\ R_1 \\ R_2 \\ R_3 \\ R_4 \\ R_5 \end{array} \begin{array}{c} \begin{array}{ccccc} R_1 & R_2 & R_3 & R_4 & R_5 \end{array} \\ \begin{pmatrix} 0.000 & -0.052 & -0.079 & -0.089 & -0.094 \\ 0.052 & 0.000 & -0.029 & -0.042 & -0.055 \\ 0.079 & 0.029 & 0.000 & -0.014 & -0.029 \\ 0.089 & 0.042 & 0.014 & 0.000 & -0.018 \\ 0.094 & 0.055 & 0.029 & 0.018 & 0.000 \end{pmatrix} \end{array}$$

$$\widehat{\Upsilon}(3) - \widehat{\Upsilon}'(3) = \begin{array}{c} \\ R_1 \\ R_2 \\ R_3 \\ R_4 \\ R_5 \end{array} \begin{array}{c} \begin{array}{ccccc} R_1 & R_2 & R_3 & R_4 & R_5 \end{array} \\ \begin{pmatrix} 0.000 & -0.035 & -0.069 & -0.087 & -0.093 \\ 0.035 & 0.000 & -0.024 & -0.054 & -0.062 \\ 0.069 & 0.034 & 0.000 & -0.022 & -0.035 \\ 0.087 & 0.054 & 0.022 & 0.000 & -0.018 \\ 0.093 & 0.062 & 0.035 & 0.018 & 0.000 \end{pmatrix} \end{array}$$

$$\widehat{\Upsilon}(4) - \widehat{\Upsilon}'(4) = \begin{array}{c} \\ R_1 \\ R_2 \\ R_3 \\ R_4 \\ R_5 \end{array} \begin{array}{c} \begin{array}{ccccc} R_1 & R_2 & R_3 & R_4 & R_5 \end{array} \\ \begin{pmatrix} 0.000 & -0.033 & -0.059 & -0.084 & -0.102 \\ 0.033 & 0.000 & -0.024 & -0.050 & -0.070 \\ 0.059 & 0.024 & 0.000 & -0.023 & -0.049 \\ 0.084 & 0.050 & 0.023 & 0.000 & -0.030 \\ 0.102 & 0.070 & 0.049 & 0.030 & 0.000 \end{pmatrix} \end{array}$$

Differences between autocorrelation matrices and their transposes for the vector of size-sorted portfolio returns $\mathbf{X}_t \equiv [\, R_{1t} \;\; R_{2t} \;\; R_{3t} \;\; R_{4t} \;\; R_{5t} \,]'$ where R_{it} is the week-t return on the equal-weighted portfolio of stocks in the ith quintile, i=1, ..., 5 (quintile 1 contains the smallest stocks), for the sample of NYSE-AMEX stocks from July 10, 1962 to December 27, 1994 (1,695 observations). Note that $\Upsilon(k) \equiv \mathbf{D}^{-1/2}\mathrm{E}[(\mathbf{X}_{t-k} - \mu)(\mathbf{X}_t - \mu)']\mathbf{D}^{-1/2}$, where $\mathbf{D} \equiv \mathrm{diag}[\sigma_1^2, \ldots, \sigma_5^2]$.

But the presence of positive cross-effects provides another channel through which contrarian strategies can be profitable. If, for example, a high return for security A today implies that security B's return will probably be high tomorrow, then a contrarian investment strategy will be profitable even if each security's returns are unforecastable using past returns of that security alone. To see how, suppose the market consists of only the two stocks, A and B; if A's return is higher than the market today, a contrarian sells it and buys B. But if A and B are positively cross-autocorrelated, a higher return for A today implies a higher return for B tomorrow on average, and thus the contrarian will have profited from his long position in B on average.

Nowhere is it required that the stock market overreacts, i.e., that individual returns are negatively autocorrelated. Therefore, the fact that some contrarian strategies have positive expected profits need not imply stock market overreaction. In fact, for the particular contrarian strategy that Lo and MacKinlay (1990c) examine, over half of the expected profits is due to cross-effects and not to negative autocorrelation in individual security returns.

These cross-effects may also explain the apparent profitability of several other trading strategies that have recently become popular in the financial community. For example, *long/short* or *market-neutral* strategies in which long positions are offset dollar-for-dollar by short positions can earn superior returns in exactly the fashion described above, despite the fact that they are designed to take advantage of own-effects, i.e., positive and negative forecasts of individual securities' expected returns. The performance of *matched-book* or *pairs* trading strategies can also be attributed to cross-effects as well as own-effects.

Although several studies have attempted to explain these striking lead-lag effects (see, for example, Badrinath, Kale, and Noe [1995], Boudoukh, Richardson, and Whitelaw [1994], Jegadeesh and Swaminathan [1993], Conrad, Kaul, and Nimalendran [1991], Brennan, Jegadeesh, and Swaminathan [1993], Jegadeesh and Titman [1995], and Mech [1993]), we are still far from having a complete understanding of their nature and sources.

2.8.4 Tests Using Long-Horizon Returns

Several recent studies have employed longer-horizon returns—multi-year returns in most cases—in examining the random walk hypothesis, predictability, and the profitability of contrarian strategies, with some surprising results. Distinguishing between short and long return-horizons can be important because it is now well known that weekly fluctuations in stock returns differ in many ways from movements in three- to five-year returns. We consider the econometric trade-offs between short- and long-horizon returns in more detail in Chapter 7, and provide only a brief discussion here of the long-horizon implications for the random walk hypotheses.

In contrast to the positive serial correlation in daily, weekly, and monthly index returns documented by Lo and MacKinlay (1988) and others, Fama and French (1988b) and Poterba and Summers (1988) find *negative* serial correlation in multi-year index returns. For example, Poterba and Summers (1988) report a variance ratio of 0.575 for 96-month returns of the value-weighted CRSP NYSE index from 1926 to 1985, implying negative serial correlation at some return horizons (recall that the variance ratio is a specific linear combination of autocorrelation coefficients). Both Fama and French (1988b) and Poterba and Summers (1988) conclude that there is substantial mean-reversion in stock market prices at longer horizons, which they attribute to the presence of a "transitory" component such as the y_t component in (2.5.1).

There is, however, good reason to be wary of such inferences when they are based on long-horizon returns. Perhaps the most obvious concern is the extremely small sample size: From 1926 to 1985, there are only 12 nonoverlapping five-year returns. While overlapping returns do provide some incremental information, the results in Boudoukh and Richardson (1994), Lo and MacKinlay (1989), Richardson and Smith (1991), and Richardson and Stock (1989) suggest that this increment is modest at best and misleading at worst. In particular, Richardson and Stock (1989) propose an asymptotic approximation which captures the spirit of overlapping long-horizon return calculations—they allow the return horizon q to increase with the sample size T so that q/T converges to a finite value δ between zero and one— which shows that variance ratios can be severely biased when the return horizon is a significant fraction of the total sample period. For example, using their asymptotic approximation (2.5.10), discussed in Section 2.5.1, the expected value for the variance ratio with overlapping returns is given by (2.5.12) under RW1. This expression implies that with a return horizon of 96 months and a sample period of 60 years, $\delta=8/60=0.133$ hence the expected variance ratio is $(1-\delta)^2=0.751$, despite the fact that RW1 is assumed to hold. Under RW2 and RW3, even more dramatic biases can occur (see, for example, Romano and Thombs [1996]).

These difficulties are reflected in the magnitudes of the standard errors associated with long-horizon return autocorrelations and variance ratios (see, for example, Richardson and Stock (1989, Table 5), which are typically so large as to yield z-statistics close to zero regardless of the point estimates. Richardson (1993) and Richardson and Stock (1989) show that properly adjusting for the small sample sizes, and for other statistical issues associated with long-horizon returns, reverses many of the inferences of Fama and French (1988b) and Poterba and Summers (1988).

Moreover, the point estimates of autocorrelation coefficients and other time series parameters tend to exhibit considerable sampling variation for long-horizon returns. For example, simple bias adjustments can change the signs of the autocorrelations, as Kim, Nelson, and Startz (1988) and Richardson and Stock (1989) demonstrate. This is not surprising given the extremely small sample sizes that long-horizon returns produce (see, for example, the magnitude of the bias adjustments in Section 2.4.1).

Finally, Kim, Nelson, and Startz (1988) show that the negative serial correlation in long-horizon returns is extremely sensitive to the sample period and may be largely due to the first ten years of the 1926 to 1985 sample. Although ten years is a very significant portion of the data and cannot be excluded without careful consideration, nevertheless it is troubling that the sign of the serial correlation coefficient hinges on data from the Great Depression. This conundrum—whether to omit data influenced by a single cataclysmic event, or to include it and argue that such an event is representative of the economic system—underscores the fragility of small-sample statistical inference. Overall, there is little evidence for mean reversion in long-horizon returns, though this may be more of a symptom of small sample sizes rather than conclusive evidence against mean reversion—we simply cannot tell.

These considerations point to short-horizon returns as the more immediate source from which evidence of predictability might be culled. This is not to say that a careful investigation of returns over longer time spans will be uninformative. Indeed, it may be only at these lower frequencies that the impact of economic factors such as the business cycle is detectable. Moreover, to the extent that transaction costs are greater for strategies exploiting short-horizon predictability, long-horizon predictability may be a more genuine form of unexploited profit opportunity. Nevertheless, the econometric challenges posed by long-horizon returns are considerable, and the need for additional economic structure is particularly great in such cases.

2.9 Conclusion

Recent econometric advances and empirical evidence seem to suggest that financial asset returns are predictable to some degree. Thirty years ago this would have been tantamount to an outright rejection of market efficiency. However, modern financial economics teaches us that other, perfectly rational, factors may account for such predictability. The fine structure of securities markets and frictions in the trading process can generate predictability. Time-varying expected returns due to changing business conditions can generate predictability. A certain degree of predictability may be necessary to reward investors for bearing certain dynamic risks. Motivated by these considerations, we shall develop many models and techniques to address these and other related issues in the coming chapters.

Problems—Chapter 2

2.1 If $\{P_t\}$ is a martingale, show that: (1) the minimum mean-squared error forecast of P_{t+1}, conditioned on the entire history $\{P_t, P_{t-1}, \ldots\}$, is simply P_t; (2) nonoverlapping kth differences are uncorrelated at all leads and lags for all $k > 0$.

2.2 How are the RW1, RW2, RW3, and martingale hypotheses related (include a Venn diagram to illustrate the relations among the four models)? Provide specific examples of each.

2.3 Characterize the set of all two-state Markov chains (2.2.9) that do not satisfy RW1 and for which the CJ statistic is one. What are the general properties of such Markov chains, e.g., do they generate sequences, reversals, etc.?

2.4 Derive (2.4.19) for processes with stationary increments. Why do the weights decline linearly? Using this expression, construct examples of non-random-walk processes for which the variance ratio test has very low power.

2.5 Using daily and monthly returns data for ten individual stocks and the equal- and value-weighted CRSP market indexes (EWRETD and VWRETD), perform the following statistical analysis using any statistical package of your choice. Note that some of the stocks do not have complete return histories, so be sure to use only valid observations. Also, for subsample analyses, split the *available* observations into equal subsamples.

2.5.1 Compute the sample mean $\hat{\mu}$, standard deviation $\hat{\sigma}$, and first-order autocorrelation coefficient $\hat{\rho}(1)$ for daily simple returns over the entire 1962 to 1994 sample period for the ten stocks and the two indexes. Split the sample into four equal subperiods and compute the same statistics in each subperiod—are they stable over time?

2.5.2 Compute the sample mean $\hat{\mu}$, standard deviation $\hat{\sigma}$, and first-order autocorrelation coefficient $\hat{\rho}(1)$ for continuously compounded daily returns over the entire 1962 to 1994 period, and for each of the four equal subperiods. Compare these to the results for simple returns—can continuous compounding change inferences substantially?

2.5.3 Plot histograms of daily simple returns for VWRETD and EWRETD over the entire 1962 to 1994 sample period. Plot another histogram of the normal distribution with mean and variance equal to the sample mean and variance of the returns plotted in the first histograms. Do daily simple returns look approximately normal? Which looks closer to normal: VWRETD or EWRETD? Perform the same analysis for continuously compounded daily returns and compare these results to those for simple returns.

2.5.4 Using daily simple returns for the entire 1962 to 1994 sample period, construct 99% confidence intervals for $\hat{\mu}$ for VWRETD, EWRETD, and the ten individual stock return series. Divide the sample into four equal subperiods and construct 99% confidence intervals in each of the four subperiods for the twelve series—do they shift a great deal?

2.5.5 Compute the skewness, kurtosis, and studentized range of daily simple returns of VWRETD, EWRETD, and the ten individual stocks over the entire 1962 to 1994 sample period, and in each of the four equal subperiods. Which of the skewness, kurtosis, and studentized range estimates are statistically different from the skewness, kurtosis, and studentized range of a normal random variable at the 5% level? For these twelve series, perform the same calculations using monthly data. What do you conclude about the normality of these return series, and why?

3

Market Microstructure

WHILE IT IS ALWAYS the case that some features of the data will be lost in the process of modeling economic phenomena, determining which features to focus on requires some care and judgment. In exploring the dynamic properties of financial asset prices in Chapter 2, we have taken prices and returns as the principal objects of interest without explicit reference to the institutional structures in which they are determined. We have ignored the fact that security prices are generally denominated in fixed increments, typically eighths of a dollar or *ticks* for stock prices. Also, securities do not trade at evenly spaced intervals throughout the day, and on some days they do not trade at all. Indeed, the very process of trading can have an important impact on the statistical properties of financial asset prices: In markets with designated marketmakers, the existence of a *spread* between the price at which the marketmaker is willing to buy (the *bid* price) and the price at which the marketmaker is willing to sell (the *offer* or *ask* price) can have a nontrivial impact on the serial correlation of price changes.

For some purposes, such aspects of the market's *microstructure* can be safely ignored, particularly when longer investment horizons are involved. For example, it is unlikely that bid-ask bounce (to be defined in Section 3.2) is responsible for the negative autocorrelation in the five-year returns of US stock indexes such as the Standard and Poor's 500,[1] even though the existence of a bid-ask spread does induce negative autocorrelation in returns (see Section 3.2.1).

However, for other purposes—the measurement of execution costs and market liquidity, the comparison of alternative marketmaking mechanisms, the impact of competition and the potential for collusion among marketmakers—market microstructure is central. Indeed, market microstructure is now one of the most active research areas in economics and finance, span-

---

[1]See Section 2.5 in Chapter 2 and Section 7.2.1 in Chapter 7 for further discussion of long-horizon returns.

ning many markets and many models.[2] To test some of these models, and to determine the importance of market microstructure effects for other research areas, we require some empirical measures of market microstructure effects. We shall construct such measures in this chapter.

In Section 3.1, we present a simple model of the trading process to capture the effects of nonsynchronous trading. In Section 3.2, we consider the effects of the bid-ask spread on the time-series properties of price changes, and in Section 3.3 we explore several techniques for modeling transactions data which pose several unique challenges including price discreteness and irregular sampling intervals.

3.1 Nonsynchronous Trading

The *nonsynchronous trading* or *nontrading* effect arises when time series, usually asset prices, are taken to be recorded at time intervals of one length when in fact they are recorded at time intervals of other, possibly irregular, lengths. For example, the daily prices of securities quoted in the financial press are usually *closing* prices, prices at which the last transaction in each of those securities occurred on the previous business day. These closing prices generally do not occur at the same time each day, but by referring to them as "daily" prices, we have implicitly and incorrectly assumed that they are equally spaced at 24-hour intervals. As we shall see below, such an assumption can create a false impression of predictability in price changes and returns even if true price changes or returns are statistically independent.

In particular, the nontrading effect induces potentially serious biases in the moments and co-moments of asset returns such as their means, variances, covariances, betas, and autocorrelation and cross-autocorrelation coefficients. For example, suppose that the returns to stocks A and B are temporally independent but A trades less frequently than B. If news affecting the aggregate stock market arrives near the close of the market on one day, it is more likely that B's end-of-day price will reflect this information than A's, simply because A may not trade after the news arrives. Of course, A will respond to this information eventually but the fact that it responds with a lag induces spurious cross-autocorrelation between the daily returns of A and B when calculated with *closing* prices. This lagged response will

---

[2]The literature is far too vast to give a complete citation list here. In addition to the citations listed in each of the sections below, readers interested in an introduction to market microstructure are encouraged to consult the following excellent monographs and conference volumes that, together, provide a fairly complete treatment of the major issues and models in this literature: Cohen, Maier, Schwartz, and Whitcomb (1986), Davis and Holt (1993), Frankel, Galli, and Giovannini (1996), Kagel and Roth (1995), Lo (1995), O'Hara (1995), and SEC (1994).

also induce spurious own-autocorrelation in the daily returns of A: During periods of nontrading, A's observed return is zero and when A does trade, its observed return reverts to the cumulated mean return, and this mean-reversion creates negative serial correlation in A's returns. These effects have obvious implications for tests of predictability and nonlinearity in asset returns (see Chapters 2 and 12), as well as for quantifying the trade-offs between risk and expected return (see Chapters 4–6).

Perhaps the first to recognize the importance of nonsynchronous prices was Fisher (1966). More recently, explicit models of nontrading have been developed by Atchison, Butler, and Simonds (1987), Cohen, Maier, Schwartz, and Whitcomb (1978, 1979), Cohen, Hawawini, Maier, Schwartz, and Whitcomb (1983b), Dimson (1979), Lo and MacKinlay (1988, 1990a, 1990c), and Scholes and Williams (1977). Whereas earlier studies considered the effects of nontrading on empirical applications of the Capital Asset Pricing Model and the Arbitrage Pricing Theory,[3] more recent attention has been focused on spurious autocorrelations induced by nonsynchronous trading.[4] Although the various models of nontrading may differ in their specifics, they all have the common theme of modeling the behavior of asset returns that are mistakenly assumed to be measured at evenly spaced time intervals when in fact they are not.

3.1.1 A Model of Nonsynchronous Trading

Since most empirical investigations of stock price behavior focus on returns or price changes, we take as primitive the (unobservable) return-generating process of a collection of N securities. To capture the effects of nontrading, we shall follow the nonsynchronous trading model of Lo and MacKinlay (1990a) which associates with each security i in each period t an unobserved or *virtual* continuously compounded return r_{it}. These virtual returns represent changes in the underlying value of the security in the absence of any trading frictions or other institutional rigidities. They reflect both company-specific information and economy-wide effects, and in a frictionless market these returns would be identical to the observed returns of the security.

To model the nontrading phenomenon as a purely spurious statistical artifact—not an economic phenomenon motivated by private information and strategic considerations—suppose in each period t there is some probability π_i that security i does not trade and whether the security trades or not is independent of the virtual returns $\{r_{it}\}$ (and all other random variables

---

[3]See, for example, Cohen, Hawawini, Maier, Schwartz, and Whitcomb (1983a, b), Dimson (1979), Scholes and Williams (1977), and Shanken (1987b).

[4]See Atchison, Butler, and Simonds (1987), Cohen, Maier, Schwartz, and Whitcomb (1979, 1986), and Lo and MacKinlay (1988, 1988b, 1990a, 1990c).

in this model).[5] Therefore, this nontrading process can be viewed as an IID sequence of coin tosses,[6] with different nontrading probabilities across securities. By allowing cross-sectional differences in the random nontrading processes, we shall be able to capture the effects of nontrading on the returns of portfolios of securities.

The *observed* return of security i, r_{it}^o, depends on whether security i trades in period t. If security i does not trade in period t, let its observed return be zero—if no trades occur, then the closing price is set to the previous period's closing price, and hence $r_{it}^o = \log(p_{it}/p_{it-1}) = \log 1 = 0$. If, on the other hand, security i does trade in period t, let its observed return be the sum of the virtual returns in period t and in all prior *consecutive* periods in which i did not trade.

For example, consider a sequence of five consecutive periods in which security i trades in periods 1, 2, and 5, and does not trade in periods 3 and 4. The above nontrading mechanism implies that: the observed return in period 2 is simply the virtual return ($r_{i2}^o = r_{i2}$); the observed returns in period 3 and 4 are both zero ($r_{i3}^o = r_{i4}^o = 0$); and the observed return in period 5 is the sum of the virtual returns from periods 3 to 5 ($r_{i5}^o = r_{i3} + r_{i4} + r_{i5}$).[7] This captures the essential feature of nontrading as a source of spurious autocorrelation: News affects those stocks that trade more frequently first and influences the returns of more thinly traded securities with a lag. In this framework the impact of news on returns is captured by the virtual returns process and the impact of the lag induced by nontrading is captured by the observed returns process r_{it}^o.

To complete the specification of this nontrading model, suppose that virtual returns are governed by a one-factor linear model:

$$r_{it} = \mu_i + \beta_i f_t + \epsilon_{it} \qquad i = 1, \ldots, N \tag{3.1.1}$$

where f_t is some zero-mean common factor and ϵ_{it} is zero-mean idiosyncratic noise that is temporally and cross-sectionally independent at all leads and lags. Since we wish to focus on nontrading as the *sole* source of autocorrelation, we also assume that the common factor f_t is IID and is independent of

---

[5]The case where trading is correlated with virtual returns is not without interest, but it is inconsistent with the spirit of the nontrading as a kind of measurement error. In the presence of private information and strategic behavior, trading activity does typically depend on virtual returns (suitably defined), and strategic trading can induce serial correlation in observed returns, but such correlation can hardly be dismissed as "spurious". See Section 3.1.2 for further discussion.

[6]This assumption may be relaxed to allow for state-dependent probabilities, i.e., autocorrelated nontrading; see the discussion in Section 3.1.2.

[7]Period 1's return obviously depends on how many consecutive periods prior to period 1 that the security did not trade. If it traded in period 0, then the period-1 return is simply equal to its virtual return; if it did not trade in period 0 but did trade in period −1, then period 1's observed return is the sum of period 0's and period 1's virtual returns; etc.

ϵ_{it-k} for all i, t, and k.[8] Each period's virtual return is random and captures movements caused by information arrival as well as idiosyncratic noise. The particular nontrading and return-cumulation process we assume captures the lag with which news and noise is incorporated into security prices due to infrequent trading. The dynamics of such a stylized model are surprisingly rich, and they yield several important empirical implications.

To derive an explicit expression for the observed returns process and to deduce its time-series properties we introduce two related random variables:

$$\delta_{it} \quad = \quad \begin{cases} 1 \text{ (no trade)} & \text{with probability } \pi_i \\ 0 \text{ (trade)} & \text{with probability } 1 - \pi_i \end{cases} \qquad (3.1.2)$$

$$X_{it}(k) \quad \equiv \quad (1-\delta_{it})\delta_{it-1}\delta_{it-2}\cdots\delta_{it-k}, \qquad k > 0$$

$$= \quad \begin{cases} 1 & \text{with probability } (1-\pi_i)\pi_i^k \\ 0 & \text{with probability } 1 - (1-\pi_i)\pi_i^k \end{cases}, \qquad (3.1.3)$$

where $X_{it}(0) \equiv 1 - \delta_{it}$, $\{\delta_{it}\}$ is assumed to be independent of $\{\delta_{jt}\}$ for $i \neq j$ and temporally IID for each $i = 1, 2, \ldots, N$.

The indicator variable δ_{it} takes on the value one when security i does not trade in period t and is zero otherwise. $X_{it}(k)$ is also an indicator variable and takes on the value one when security i trades in period t but has not traded in any of the k previous consecutive periods, and is zero otherwise. Since π_i is within the unit interval, for large k the variable $X_{it}(k)$ will be zero with high probability. This is not surprising since it is highly unlikely that security i should trade today but never in the past.

Having defined the $X_{it}(k)$'s it is now a simple matter to derive an explicit expression for observed returns r_{it}^o:

$$r_{it}^o \quad = \quad \sum_{k=0}^{\infty} X_{it}(k)\, r_{it-k} \qquad i = 1, \ldots, N. \qquad (3.1.4)$$

If security i does not trade in period t, then $\delta_{it}=1$ which implies that $X_{it}(k)=0$ for all k, and thus $r_{it}^o=0$. If i does trade in period t, then its observed return is equal to the sum of today's virtual return r_{it} and its past k_t virtual returns, where the random variable k_t is the number of past *consecutive* periods that i has not traded. We call this the *duration* of nontrading, which may be expressed as

$$k_t \quad \equiv \quad \sum_{k=1}^{\infty} \left\{ \prod_{j=1}^{k} \delta_{it-j} \right\}. \qquad (3.1.5)$$

Although (3.1.4) will prove to be more convenient for subsequent calculations, k_t may be used to give a somewhat more intuitive definition of the

---

[8]These strong assumptions are made primarily for expositional convenience and may be relaxed considerably. See Section 3.1.2 for further discussion.

observed returns process:

$$r_{it}^o = \sum_{k=0}^{k_t} r_{it-k} \qquad i = 1, \dots, N. \tag{3.1.6}$$

Whereas (3.1.4) shows that in the presence of nontrading the observed returns process is a (stochastic) function of *all* past returns, the equivalent relation (3.1.6) reveals that r_{it}^o may also be viewed as a random sum with a random number of terms.[9]

A third and perhaps most natural way to view observed returns is the following:

$$r_{it}^o = \begin{cases} 0 & \text{with probability } \pi_i \\ r_{it} & \text{with probability } (1-\pi_i)^2 \\ r_{it} + r_{it-1} & \text{with probability } (1-\pi_i)^2 \pi_i \\ r_{it} + r_{it-1} + r_{it-2} & \text{with probability } (1-\pi_i)^2 \pi_i^2 \\ \quad \vdots & \qquad \vdots \\ r_{it} + \cdots + r_{it-k} & \text{with probability } (1-\pi_i)^2 \pi_i^k \\ \quad \vdots & \qquad \vdots \end{cases} \tag{3.1.7}$$

Expressed in this way, it is apparent that nontrading can induce spurious serial correlation in observed returns because each r_{it}^o contains within it the sum of past k consecutive virtual returns for every k with some positive probability $(1 - \pi_i)^2 \pi_i^k$.

To see how the nontrading probability π_i is related to the duration of nontrading, consider the mean and variance of k_t:

$$\mathrm{E}[k_t] = \frac{\pi_i}{1 - \pi_i}, \qquad \mathrm{Var}[k_t] = \frac{\pi_i}{(1 - \pi_i)^2}. \tag{3.1.8}$$

If $\pi_i = \frac{1}{2}$ then security i goes without trading for one period at a time on average; if $\pi_i = \frac{3}{4}$ then the average number of consecutive periods of nontrading

---

[9]This is similar in spirit to the Scholes and Williams (1977) subordinated stochastic process representation of observed returns, although we do not restrict the trading times to take values in a fixed finite interval. With suitable normalizations it may be shown that our nontrading model converges weakly to the continuous-time Poisson process of Scholes and Williams (1977). From (3.1.4) the observed returns process may also be considered an infinite-order moving average of virtual returns where the MA coefficients are stochastic. This is in contrast to Cohen, Maier, Schwartz, and Whitcomb (1986, Chapter 6) in which observed returns are assumed to be a finite-order MA process with nonstochastic coefficients. Although our nontrading process is more general, their observed returns process includes a bid-ask spread component; ours does not.

is three. As expected, if the security trades every period so that $\pi_i = 0$, both the mean and variance of k_t are zero.

Implications for Individual Security Returns

To see how nontrading can affect the time-series properties of the observed returns of individual securities, consider the moments of r_{it}^o which, in turn, depend on the moments of $X_{it}(k)$.[10] For the nontrading process (3.1.2)–(3.1.3), the observed returns processes $\{r_{it}^o\}$ $(i = 1, \ldots, N)$ are covariance-stationary with the following first and second moments:

$$E[r_{it}^o] \;=\; \mu_i \tag{3.1.9}$$

$$\text{Var}[r_{it}^o] \;=\; \sigma_i^2 + \frac{2\pi_i}{1 - \pi_i}\,\mu_i^2 \tag{3.1.10}$$

$$\text{Cov}[r_{it}^o, r_{jt+n}^o] \;=\; \begin{cases} -\mu_i^2 \pi_i^n & \text{for } i = j,\; n > 0 \\[2mm] \frac{(1-\pi_i)(1-\pi_j)}{1-\pi_i\pi_j}\,\beta_i\beta_j\sigma_f^2\,\pi_j^n & \text{for } i \neq j,\; n \geq 0 \end{cases} \tag{3.1.11}$$

$$\text{Corr}[r_{it}^o, r_{it+n}^o] \;=\; \frac{-\mu_i^2 \pi_i^n}{\sigma_i^2 + \frac{2\pi_i}{1-\pi_i}\mu_i^2}\,, \qquad n > 0, \tag{3.1.12}$$

where $\sigma_i^2 \equiv \text{Var}[r_{it}]$ and $\sigma_f^2 \equiv \text{Var}[f_t]$.

From (3.1.9) and (3.1.10) it is clear that nontrading does not affect the mean of observed returns but does increase their variance if the security has a nonzero expected return. Moreover, (3.1.12) shows that having a nonzero expected return induces negative serial correlation in individual security returns at all leads and lags which decays geometrically. The intuition for this phenomenon follows from the fact that during nontrading periods the observed return is zero and during trading periods the observed return reverts back to its cumulated mean return, and this mean reversion yields negative serial correlation. When $\mu_i = 0$, there is no mean reversion hence no negative serial correlation in this case.

Maximal Spurious Autocorrelation

These moments also allow us to calculate the maximal negative autocorrelation attributable to nontrading in individual security returns. Since the autocorrelation of observed returns (3.1.12) is a nonpositive continuous function of π_i that is zero at $\pi_i = 0$ and approaches zero as π_i approaches unity, it must attain a minimum for some π_i in $[0,1)$. Determining this lower bound is a straightforward exercise in calculus, and hence we calculate it only for the first-order autocorrelation and leave the higher-order cases to the reader.

---

[10]To conserve space, we summarize the results here and refer readers to Lo and MacKinlay (1990a, 1990c) for further details.

Under (3.1.2)–(3.1.3) the minimum first-order autocorrelation of the observed returns process $\{r_{it}^o\}$ with respect to nontrading probabilities π_i is given by

$$\operatorname*{Min}_{\{\pi_i\}} \operatorname{Corr}[r_{it}^o, r_{it+1}^o] = -\left(\frac{|\xi_i|}{1 + \sqrt{2}\,|\xi_i|}\right)^2, \tag{3.1.13}$$

where $\xi_i \equiv \mu_i/\sigma_i$, and the minimum is attained at

$$\pi_i = \frac{1}{1 + \sqrt{2}\,|\xi_i|}. \tag{3.1.14}$$

Over all values of $\pi_i \in [0, 1)$ and $\xi_i \in (-\infty, +\infty)$, we have

$$\operatorname*{Inf}_{\{\pi_i, \xi_i\}} \operatorname{Corr}[r_{it}^o, r_{it+1}^o] = -\frac{1}{2}, \tag{3.1.15}$$

which is the limit of (3.1.13) as $|\xi_i|$ increases without bound, but is never attained by finite ξ_i.

Although the lower bound of $-\frac{1}{2}$ seems quite significant, it is virtually unattainable for any empirically plausible parameter values. For example, if we consider a period to be one trading day, typical values for μ_i and σ_i are .05% and 2.5%, respectively, implying a typical value of 0.02 for ξ_i. According to (3.1.13), this would induce a spurious autocorrelation of at most -0.037% in individual security returns and would require a nontrading probability of 97.2% to attain, which corresponds to an average nontrading duration of 35.4 days!

These results also imply that nontrading-induced autocorrelation is magnified by taking longer sampling intervals since under the hypothesized virtual returns process, doubling the holding period doubles μ_i but only multiplies σ_i by a factor of $\sqrt{2}$. Therefore more extreme negative autocorrelations are feasible for longer-horizon individual returns. However, this is not of direct empirical relevance since the effects of time aggregation have been ignored. To see how, observe that the nontrading process (3.1.2)–(3.1.3) is not independent of the sampling interval but changes in a nonlinear fashion. For example, if a period is taken to be one week, the possibility of *daily* nontrading and all its concomitant effects on weekly observed returns is eliminated by assumption. A proper comparison of observed returns across distinct sampling intervals must allow for nontrading at the finest time increment, after which the implications for coarser-sampled returns may be developed. We shall postpone further discussion of this and other issues of time aggregation until later in this section.

Asymmetric Cross-Autocovariances
Several other important empirical implications of this nontrading model are captured by (3.1.11). In particular, the sign of the cross-autocovariances

is determined by the sign of $\beta_i \beta_j$. Also, the expression is not symmetric with respect to i and j: If $\pi_i = 0$ and $\pi_j \neq 0$, then there is spurious cross-autocovariance between r_{it}^o and r_{jt+n}^o but no cross-autocovariance between r_{jt}^o and r_{it+n}^o for any $n > 0$.[11] The intuition for this result is simple: When security j exhibits nontrading, the returns to a constantly trading security i can forecast j due to the common factor f_t present in both returns. That j exhibits nontrading implies that future observed returns r_{jt+n}^o will be a weighted average of all past virtual returns r_{jt+n-k} (with the $X_{jt+n}(k)$'s as random weights), of which one term will be the current virtual return r_{jt}. Since the contemporaneous virtual returns r_{it} and r_{jt} are correlated (because of the common factor), r_{it}^o can forecast r_{jt+n}^o. However, r_{it}^o is itself unforecastable because $r_{it}^o = r_{it}$ for all t (since $\pi_i = 0$) and r_{it} is IID by assumption, thus r_{jt}^o is uncorrelated with r_{it+n}^o for any $n > 0$.

The asymmetry of (3.1.11) yields an empirically testable restriction on the cross-autocovariances of returns. Since the only source of asymmetry in (3.1.11) is cross-sectional differences in the probabilities of nontrading, information regarding these probabilities may be extracted from sample moments. Specifically, denote by $\mathbf{r}_t^o$ the vector $[\, r_{1t}^o \ r_{2t}^o \ \cdots \ r_{Nt}^o \,]'$ of observed returns of the N securities and define the autocovariance matrix $\boldsymbol{\Gamma}_n$ as

$$\boldsymbol{\Gamma}_n = \mathrm{E}[(\mathbf{r}_t^o - \boldsymbol{\mu})(\mathbf{r}_{t+n}^o - \boldsymbol{\mu})'], \qquad \boldsymbol{\mu} \equiv \mathrm{E}[\mathbf{r}_t^o]. \tag{3.1.16}$$

Denoting the (i, j)th element of $\boldsymbol{\Gamma}_n$ by $\gamma_{ij}(n)$, we have by definition

$$\gamma_{ij}(n) = \frac{(1 - \pi_i)(1 - \pi_j)}{1 - \pi_i \pi_j} \, \beta_i \, \beta_j \, \sigma_f^2 \, \pi_j^n. \tag{3.1.17}$$

If the nontrading probabilities π_i differ across securities, $\boldsymbol{\Gamma}_n$ is asymmetric. From (3.1.17) it is evident that

$$\frac{\gamma_{ij}(n)}{\gamma_{ji}(n)} = \left(\frac{\pi_j}{\pi_i}\right)^n. \tag{3.1.18}$$

Therefore relative nontrading probabilities may be estimated directly using sample autocovariances $\hat{\boldsymbol{\Gamma}}_n$. To derive estimates of the probabilities π_i themselves we need only estimate one such probability, say π_1, and the remaining probabilities may be obtained from the ratios (3.1.18). A consistent estimator of π_1 is readily constructed with sample means and autocovariances via (3.1.11).

---

[11]An alternative interpretation of this asymmetry may be found in the time-series literature concerning Granger-causality (see Granger [1969]), in which r_{it}^o is said to *Granger-cause* r_{jt}^o if the return to i predicts the return to j. In the above example, security i *Granger-causes* security j when j is subject to nontrading but i is not. Since our nontrading process may be viewed as a form of measurement error, the fact that the returns to one security may be exogenous with respect to the returns of another has been proposed under a different guise in Sims (1974, 1977).

Implications for Portfolio Returns

Suppose securities are grouped by their nontrading probabilities and equal-weighted portfolios are formed based on this grouping so that portfolio A contains N_a securities with identical nontrading probability π_a, and similarly for portfolio B. Denote by r_{at}^o and r_{bt}^o the observed time-t returns on these two portfolios respectively, which are approximately averages of the individual returns:

$$r_{\kappa t}^o \approx \frac{1}{N_\kappa} \sum_{i \in I_\kappa} r_{it}^o, \qquad \kappa = a, b, \tag{3.1.19}$$

where the summation is over all securities i in the set of indices I_κ which comprise portfolio κ. The reason (3.1.19) is not exact is that both observed and virtual returns are assumed to be continuously compounded, and the logarithm of a sum is not the sum of the logarithms.[12] However, if r_{it}^o takes on small values and is not too volatile—plausible assumptions for the short return intervals that nonsynchronous trading models typically focus on—the approximation error in (3.1.19) is negligible.

The time-series properties of (3.1.19) may be derived from a simple asymptotic approximation that exploits the cross-sectional independence of the disturbances ϵ_{it}. Similar asymptotic arguments can be found in the Arbitrage Pricing Theory (APT) literature (see Chapter 6); hence our assumption of independence may be relaxed to the same extent that it may be relaxed in studies of the APT in which portfolios are required to be "well-diversified."[13] In such cases, as the number of securities in portfolios A and B (denoted by N_a and N_b, respectively) increases without bound, the following equalities obtain almost surely:

$$r_\kappa^o \stackrel{a.s.}{=} \mu_\kappa + (1 - \pi_\kappa)\beta_\kappa \sum_{k=0}^{\infty} \pi_\kappa^k f_{t-k}, \tag{3.1.20}$$

where

$$\mu_\kappa \equiv \frac{1}{N_\kappa} \sum_{i \in I_\kappa} \mu_i, \qquad \beta_\kappa \equiv \frac{1}{N_\kappa} \sum_{i \in I_\kappa} \beta_i \tag{3.1.21}$$

---

[12]A precise interpretation of $r_{\kappa t}^o$ is the return to a portfolio whose value is calculated as an unweighted geometric average of the component securities' prices. The expected return of such a portfolio will be lower than that of an equal-weighted portfolio whose returns are calculated as the arithmetic means of the simple returns of the component securities. This issue is examined in greater detail by Modest and Sundaresan (1983) and Eytan and Harpaz (1986) in the context of the Value Line Index which was an unweighted geometric average until 1988.

[13]See, for example, Chamberlain (1983a), Chamberlain and Rothschild (1983), and Wang (1993). The essence of these weaker conditions is simply to allow a Law of Large Numbers to be applied to the average of the disturbances, so that "idiosyncratic risk" vanishes almost surely as the cross section grows.

for $\kappa = a, b$. The first and second moments of the portfolios' returns are then given by

$$\mathrm{E}[r_{\kappa t}^o] = \mu_\kappa = \mathrm{E}[r_{\kappa t}] \tag{3.1.22}$$

$$\mathrm{Var}[r_{\kappa t}^o] \stackrel{a}{=} \beta_\kappa^2 \left(\frac{1 - \pi_\kappa}{1 + \pi_\kappa}\right) \sigma_f^2 \tag{3.1.23}$$

$$\mathrm{Cov}[r_{\kappa t}^o, r_{\kappa t+n}^o] \stackrel{a}{=} \beta_\kappa^2 \left(\frac{1 - \pi_\kappa}{1 + \pi_\kappa}\right) \pi_\kappa^n \sigma_f^2, \qquad n \geq 0 \tag{3.1.24}$$

$$\mathrm{Corr}[r_{\kappa t}^o, r_{\kappa t+n}^o] \stackrel{a}{=} \pi_\kappa^n, \qquad n \geq 0 \tag{3.1.25}$$

$$\mathrm{Cov}[r_{at}^o, r_{bt+n}^o] \stackrel{a}{=} \frac{(1 - \pi_a)(1 - \pi_b)}{1 - \pi_a \pi_b} \beta_a \beta_b \sigma_f^2 \pi_b^n, \tag{3.1.26}$$

where the symbol "$\stackrel{a}{=}$" indicates that the equality obtains only asymptotically.

From (3.1.22) we see that observed portfolio returns have the same mean as the corresponding virtual returns. In contrast to observed individual returns, the variance of r_{at}^o is lower asymptotically than the variance of its virtual counterpart r_{at} since

$$r_{at} \approx \frac{1}{N_a} \sum_{i \in I_a} r_{it} = \mu_a + \beta_a f_t + \frac{1}{N_a} \sum_{i \in I_a} \epsilon_{it} \tag{3.1.27}$$

$$\stackrel{a}{=} \mu_a + \beta_a f_t, \tag{3.1.28}$$

where (3.1.28) follows from the law of large numbers applied to the last term in (3.1.27). Thus $\mathrm{Var}[r_{at}] \stackrel{a}{=} \beta_a^2 \sigma_f^2$, which is greater than or equal to $\mathrm{Var}[r_{at}^o]$.

Since the nontrading-induced autocorrelation (3.1.25) declines geometrically, observed portfolio returns follow a first-order autoregressive process with autoregressive coefficient equal to the nontrading probability. In contrast to expression (3.1.11) for individual securities, the autocorrelations of observed portfolio returns do not depend explicitly on the expected return of the portfolio, yielding a much simpler estimator for π_κ: the nth root of the nth order autocorrelation coefficient. Therefore, we may easily estimate all nontrading probabilities by using only the sample first-order own-autocorrelation coefficients for the portfolio returns.

Comparing (3.1.26) to (3.1.11) shows that the cross-autocovariance between observed portfolio returns takes the same form as that of observed individual returns. If there are differences across portfolios in the nontrading probabilities, the autocovariance matrix for observed portfolio returns will be asymmetric. This may give rise to the types of lead–lag relations empirically documented by Lo and MacKinlay (1988) in size-sorted portfolios. Ratios of the cross-autocovariances may be formed to estimate relative nontrading probabilities for portfolios, since

$$\frac{\text{Cov}[r_{at}^o, r_{bt+n}^o]}{\text{Cov}[r_{bt}^o, r_{at+n}^o]} \stackrel{a}{=} \left(\frac{\pi_b}{\pi_a}\right)^n. \tag{3.1.29}$$

In addition, for purposes of testing the overall specification of the non-trading model, these ratios give rise to many over-identifying restrictions, since

$$\frac{\gamma_{a\kappa_1}(n)\, \gamma_{\kappa_1\kappa_2}(n)\, \gamma_{\kappa_2\kappa_3}(n) \cdots \gamma_{\kappa_{r-1}\kappa_r}(n)\, \gamma_{\kappa_r b}(n)}{\gamma_{\kappa_1 a}(n)\, \gamma_{\kappa_2\kappa_1}(n)\, \gamma_{\kappa_3\kappa_2}(n) \cdots \gamma_{\kappa_r\kappa_{r-1}}(n)\, \gamma_{b\kappa_r}(n)} = \left(\frac{\pi_b}{\pi_a}\right)^n \tag{3.1.30}$$

for any arbitrary sequence of distinct indices $\kappa_1, \kappa_2, \ldots, \kappa_r$, $a \neq b$, $r \leq N_p$, where N_p is the number of distinct portfolios and $\gamma_{\kappa_i\kappa_j}(n) \equiv \text{Cov}[r_{\kappa_i t}^o, r_{\kappa_j t+n}^o]$. Therefore, although there are N_p^2 distinct autocovariances in $\mathbf{\Gamma}_n$, the restrictions implied by the nontrading process yield far fewer degrees of freedom.

Time Aggregation

The discrete-time framework we have adopted so far does not require the specification of the calendar length of a "period." This advantage is more apparent than real since any empirical implementation of the nontrading model (3.1.2)–(3.1.3) must either implicitly or explicitly define a period to be a particular fixed calendar time interval. Once the calendar time interval has been chosen, the stochastic behavior of coarser-sampled data is restricted by the parameters of the most finely sampled process. For example, if the length of a period is taken to be one day, then the moments of observed monthly returns may be expressed as functions of the parameters of the daily observed returns process. We derive such restrictions in this section.

To do this, denote by $r_{i\tau}^o(q)$ the observed return of security i at time τ where one unit of τ-time is equivalent to q units of t-time, thus:

$$r_{i\tau}^o(q) \equiv \sum_{t=(\tau-1)q+1}^{\tau q} r_{it}^o. \tag{3.1.31}$$

Then under the nontrading process (3.1.2)–(3.1.3), it can be shown that the time-aggregated observed returns processes $\{r_{i\tau}^o(q)\}$ $(i = 1, \ldots, N)$ are covariance-stationary with the following first and second moments (see Lo and MacKinlay [1990a]):

$$\text{E}[r_{i\tau}^o(q)] = q\mu_i \tag{3.1.32}$$

$$\text{Var}[r_{i\tau}^o(q)] = q\sigma_i^2 + \frac{2\pi_i(1 - \pi_i^q)}{(1 - \pi_i)^2}\mu_i^2 \tag{3.1.33}$$

$$\text{Cov}[r^o_{i\tau}(q), r^o_{i\tau+n}(q)] = -\mu^2_i \, \pi^{(n-1)q+1}_i \left(\frac{1-\pi^q_i}{1-\pi_i}\right)^2, \quad n > 0 \qquad (3.1.34)$$

$$\text{Corr}[r^o_{i\tau}(q), r^o_{i\tau+n}(q)] = -\frac{\xi^2_i(1-\pi^q_i)^2\pi^{nq-q+1}_i}{q(1-\pi_i)^2 + 2\pi_i(1-\pi^2_i)\xi^2_i}, \quad n > 0 \quad (3.1.35)$$

$$\text{Cov}[r^o_{i\tau}(q), r^o_{j\tau+n}(q)] = \frac{(1-\pi_i)(1-\pi_j)}{1-\pi_i\pi_j} \, \beta_i \, \beta_j \, \sigma^2_f \, \pi^{(n-1)q+1}_j$$

$$\times \left(\frac{1-\pi^q_i}{1-\pi_i}\right)^2, \quad i \neq j, \quad n \geq 0, \qquad (3.1.36)$$

where $\xi_i \equiv \mu_i/\sigma_i$ as before.

Although expected returns time-aggregate linearly, (3.1.33) shows that variances do not. As a result of the negative serial correlation in r^o_{it}, the variance of a sum is less than the sum of the variances. Time aggregation does not affect the sign of the autocorrelations in (3.1.35) although their magnitudes do decline with the aggregation value q. As in (3.1.12), the auto-correlation of time-aggregated returns is a nonpositive continuous function of π_i on $[0, 1)$ which is zero at $\pi_i = 0$ and approaches zero as π_i approaches unity, and hence it attains a minimum.

To explore the behavior of the first-order autocorrelation, we plot it as a function of π_i in Figure 3.1 for a variety of values of q and ξ: q takes on the values 5, 22, 66, and 244 to correspond to weekly, monthly, quarterly, and annual returns, respectively, since $q = 1$ is taken to be one day, and ξ takes on the values 0.09, 0.16, and 0.21 to correspond to daily, weekly, and monthly returns, respectively.[14] Figure 3.1a plots the first-order autocorrelation $\rho_1(p)$ for the four values of q with $\xi = 0.09$. The curve marked "$q = 5$" shows that the weekly first-order autocorrelation induced by nontrading never exceeds -5% and only attains that value with a daily nontrading probability in excess of 90%.

Although the autocorrelation of coarser-sampled returns such as monthly or quarterly have more extreme minima, they are attained only at higher nontrading probabilities. Also, time-aggregation need not always yield a more negative autocorrelation, as is apparent from the portion of the graphs to the left of, say, $\pi = .80$; in that region, an increase in the aggregation value q leads to an autocorrelation closer to zero. Indeed as q increases without bound the autocorrelation (3.1.35) approaches zero for fixed π_i, and thus nontrading has little impact on longer-horizon returns.

---

[14]Values for ξ were obtained by taking the ratio of the sample mean to the sample standard deviation for daily, weekly, and monthly equal-weighted stock returns indexes for the sample period from 1962 to 1987 as reported in Lo and MacKinlay (1988, Tables 1a–c). Although these values may be more representative of stock indexes rather than individual securities, nevertheless for the sake of illustration they should suffice.

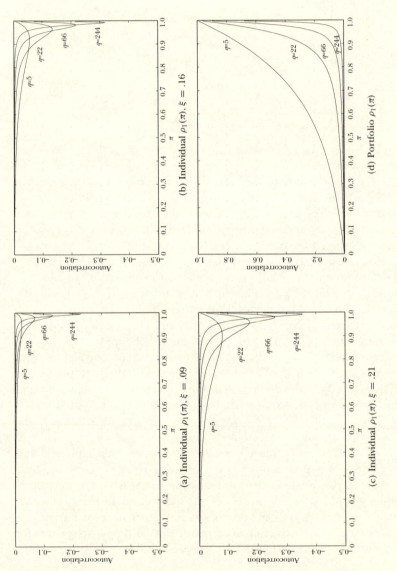

Figure 3.1.   Nontrading-Induced Autocorrelations

The effects of increasing ξ are traced out in Figures 3.1b and 3.1c. Even if we assume $\xi = 0.21$ for daily data, a most extreme value, the nontrading-induced autocorrelation in weekly returns is at most -8% and requires a daily nontrading probability of over 90%. From (3.1.8) we see that when $\pi_i = .90$ the average duration of nontrading is nine days! Since no security listed on the New York or American Stock Exchanges is inactive for two weeks (unless it has been delisted), we infer from Figure 3.1 that the impact of nontrading for individual short-horizon stock returns is negligible.

Time Aggregation For Portfolios
Similar time-aggregated analytical results can be derived for observed portfolio returns. Denote by $r_{a\tau}^o(q)$ the observed return of portfolio A at time τ where one unit of τ-time is equivalent to q units of t-time; thus

$$r_{a\tau}^o(q) \equiv \sum_{t=(\tau-1)q+1}^{\tau q} r_{at}^o, \tag{3.1.37}$$

where r_{at}^o is given by (3.1.19). Then under (3.1.2)–(3.1.3) the observed portfolio returns processes $\{r_{a\tau}^o(q)\}$ and $\{r_{b\tau}^o(q)\}$ are covariance-stationary with the following first and second moments as N_a and N_b increase without bound:

$$\mathrm{E}[r_{\kappa\tau}^o(q)] \overset{a}{=} q\mu_\kappa \tag{3.1.38}$$

$$\mathrm{Var}[r_{\kappa\tau}^o(q)] \overset{a}{=} \left[q - 2\pi_\kappa \frac{1-\pi_\kappa^q}{1-\pi_\kappa} \right] \beta_\kappa^2 \sigma_f^2 \tag{3.1.39}$$

$$\mathrm{Cov}[r_{\kappa\tau}^o(q), r_{\kappa\tau+n}^o(q)] \overset{a}{=} \left[\frac{1-\pi_\kappa}{1+\pi_\kappa} \right] \left[\frac{1-\pi_\kappa^q}{1-\pi_\kappa} \right]^2$$
$$\times \pi_\kappa^{nq-q+1} \beta_\kappa^2 \sigma_f^2, \qquad n > 0 \tag{3.1.40}$$

$$\mathrm{Corr}[r_{\kappa\tau}^o(q), r_{\kappa\tau+n}^o(q)] \overset{a}{=} \frac{(1-\pi_\kappa^q)^2 \, \pi_\kappa^{nq-q+1}}{q(1-\pi_\kappa^2) - 2\pi_\kappa(1-\pi_\kappa^q)}, \qquad n > 0 \tag{3.1.41}$$

$\mathrm{Cov}[r_{a\tau}^o(q), r_{b\tau+n}^o(q)]$

$$\overset{a}{=} \begin{cases} \left[q - \dfrac{\pi_a(1-\pi_a^q)(1-\pi_b)^2 + \pi_b(1-\pi_b^q)(1-\pi_a)^2}{(1-\pi_a)(1-\pi_b)} \right] \dfrac{\beta_a\beta_b\sigma_f^2}{1-\pi_a\pi_b} & \text{for} \quad n = 0 \\[4mm] \dfrac{(1-\pi_a)(1-\pi_b)}{1-\pi_a\pi_b} \left[\dfrac{1-\pi_b^q}{1-\pi_b} \right]^2 \pi_b^{nq-q+1} \beta_a \beta_b \sigma_f^2 & \text{for} \quad n > 0 \end{cases} \tag{3.1.42}$$

for $\kappa = a, b, q > 1$, and arbitrary portfolios a, b, and time τ.

Equation (3.1.40) shows that time aggregation also affects the autocorrelation of observed portfolio returns in a highly nonlinear fashion. In contrast to the autocorrelation for time-aggregated individual securities, (3.1.40) approaches unity for any fixed q as π_κ approaches unity; therefore the maximal autocorrelation is one.

To investigate the behavior of the portfolio autocorrelation we plot it as a function of the portfolio nontrading probability π in Figure 3.1d for $q = 5$, 22, 66, and 244. Besides differing in sign, portfolio and individual autocorrelations also differ in absolute magnitude, the former being much larger than the latter for a given nontrading probability. If the nontrading phenomenon is extant, it will be most evident in portfolio returns. Also, portfolio autocorrelations are monotonically decreasing in q so that time aggregation always decreases nontrading-induced serial dependence in portfolio returns. This implies that we are most likely to find evidence of nontrading in short-horizon returns. We exploit both these implications in the empirical analysis of Section 3.4.1.

3.1.2 Extensions and Generalizations

Despite the simplicity of the model of nonsynchronous trading in Section 3.1.1, its implications for observed time series are surprisingly rich. The framework can be extended and generalized in many directions with little difficulty.

It is a simple matter to relax the assumption that individual virtual returns are IID by allowing the common factor to be autocorrelated and the disturbances to be cross-sectionally correlated. For example, allowing f_t to be a stationary AR(1) is conceptually straightforward, although the calculations become somewhat more involved. This specification will yield a decomposition of observed autocorrelations into two components: one due to the common factor and another due to nontrading.

Allowing cross-sectional dependence in the disturbances also complicates the moment calculations but does not create any intractabilities.[15] Indeed, generalizations to multiple factors, time-series dependence of the disturbances, and correlation between factors and disturbances are only limited by the patience and perseverance of the reader; the necessary moment calculations are not intractable, but merely tedious.

Dependence can be built into the nontrading process itself by assuming that the δ_{it}'s are Markov chains, so that the conditional probability of trading

---

[15]As we discussed earlier, some form of cross-sectional weak dependence must be imposed so that the asymptotic arguments of the portfolio results still obtain. Of course, such an assumption may not always be appropriate as, for example, in the case of companies within the same industry, whose residual risks we might expect to be positively correlated. Therefore, the asymptotic approximation will be most accurate for well-diversified portfolios.

tomorrow depends on whether or not a trade occurs today. Although this specification does admit compact and elegant expressions for the moments of the observed returns process, we shall leave their derivation to the reader (see Problem 3.3). However, a brief summary of the implications for the time-series properties of observed returns may be worthwhile: (1) Individual security returns may be positively autocorrelated and portfolio returns may be negatively autocorrelated, but these possibilities are unlikely given empirically relevant parameter values; (2) It is possible, but unlikely, for autocorrelation matrices to be symmetric; and (3) Spurious index autocorrelation induced by nontrading is higher (or lower) when there is positive (or negative) persistence in nontrading. In principle, property (3) might be sufficient to explain the magnitude of index autocorrelations in recent stock market data. However, several calibration experiments indicate the degree of persistence in nontrading required to yield weekly autocorrelations of 30% is empirically implausible (see Lo and MacKinlay [1990c] for details).

One final direction for further investigation is the possibility of dependence between the nontrading and virtual returns processes. If virtual returns are taken to be new information then the extent to which traders exploit this information in determining when (and what) to trade will show itself as correlation between r_{it} and δ_{jt}. Many strategic considerations are involved in models of information-based trading, and an empirical analysis of such issues promises to be as challenging as it is exciting.[16]

However, if it is indeed the case that return autocorrelation is induced by information-based nontrading, in what sense is this autocorrelation spurious? The premise of the extensive literature on nonsynchronous trading is that nontrading is an outcome of institutional features such as lagged adjustments and nonsynchronously reported prices. But if nonsynchronicity is purposeful and informationally motivated, then the serial dependence it induces in asset returns should be considered genuine, since it is the result of economic forces rather than measurement error. In such cases, purely statistical models of nontrading are clearly inappropriate and an economic model of strategic interactions is needed.

3.2 The Bid-Ask Spread

One of the most important characteristics that investors look for in an organized financial market is liquidity, the ability to buy or sell significant

---

[16]Some good illustrations of the kind of trading behavior that can arise from strategic considerations are contained in Admati and Pfleiderer (1988, 1989), Bertsimas and Lo (1996), Easley and O'Hara (1987, 1990), Kyle (1985), and Wang (1993, 1994).

quantities of a security quickly, anonymously, and with relatively little price impact. To maintain liquidity, many organized exchanges use marketmakers, individuals who stand ready to buy or sell whenever the public wishes to sell or buy. In return for providing liquidity, marketmakers are granted monopoly rights by the exchange to post different prices for purchases and sales: They buy at the *bid* price P_b and sell at a higher *ask* price P_a. This ability to buy low and sell high is the marketmaker's primary source of compensation for providing liquidity, and although the bid-ask spread $P_a - P_b$ is rarely larger than one or two ticks—the *NYSE Fact Book: 1994 Data* reports that the spread was \$0.25 or less in 90.8% of the NYSE bid-ask quotes from 1994—over a large number of trades marketmakers can earn enough to compensate them for their services.

The diminutive size of typical spreads also belies their potential importance in determining the time-series properties of asset returns. For example, Phillips and Smith (1980) show that most of the abnormal returns associated with particular options trading strategies are eliminated when the costs associated with the bid-ask spread are included. Blume and Stambaugh (1983) argue that the bid-ask spread creates a significant upward bias in mean returns calculated with transaction prices. More recently, Keim (1989) shows that a significant portion of the so-called *January* effect—the fact that smaller-capitalization stocks seem to outperform larger capitalization stocks over the few days surrounding the turn of the year— may be attributable to closing prices recorded at the bid price at the end of December and closing prices recorded at the ask price at the beginning of January. Even if the bid-ask spread remains unchanged during this period, the movement from bid to ask is enough to yield large portfolio returns, especially for lower-priced stocks for which the *percentage* bid-ask spread is larger. Since low-priced stocks also tend to be low-capitalization stocks, Keim's (1989) results do offer a partial explanation for the January effect.[17]

The presence of the bid-ask spread complicates matters in several ways. Instead of one price for each security, there are now three: the bid price, the ask price, and the transaction price which need not be either the bid or the ask (although in some cases it is), nor need it lie in between the two (although in most cases it does). How should returns be calculated, from bid-to-bid, ask-to-bid, etc.? Moreover, as random buys and sells arrive at the market, prices can bounce back and forth between the ask and the bid prices, creating spurious volatility and serial correlation in returns, even if the economic value of the security is unchanged.

---

[17]Keim (1989) also documents the relation between other calendar anomalies (the weekend effect, holiday effects, etc.) and systematic movements between the bid and ask prices.

3.2.1 Bid-Ask Bounce

To account for the impact of the bid-ask spread on the time-series properties of asset returns, Roll (1984) proposes the following simple model. Denote by P_t^* the time-t fundamental value of a security in a frictionless economy, and denote by s the bid-ask spread (see Glosten and Milgrom [1985], for example). Then the observed market price P_t may be written as

$$P_t = P_t^* + I_t \frac{s}{2} \qquad (3.2.1)$$

$$I_t \quad \text{IID} \quad \begin{cases} +1 & \text{with probability } \frac{1}{2} \text{ (buyer-initiated)} \\ -1 & \text{with probability } \frac{1}{2} \text{ (seller-initiated)} \end{cases} \qquad (3.2.2)$$

where I_t is an order-type indicator variable, indicating whether the transaction at time t is at the ask (buyer-initiated) or at the bid (seller-initiated) price. The assumption that P_t^* is the fundamental value of the security implies that $\mathrm{E}[I_t] = 0$, hence $\Pr(I_t=1) = \Pr(I_t=-1) = \frac{1}{2}$. Assume for the moment that there are no changes in the fundamentals of the security; hence $P_t^* = P^*$ is fixed through time. Then the process for price changes ΔP_t is given by

$$\Delta P_t = \Delta P_t^* + (I_t - I_{t-1})\frac{s}{2} = (I_t - I_{t-1})\frac{s}{2}, \qquad (3.2.3)$$

and under the assumption that I_t is IID the variance, covariance, and autocorrelation of ΔP_t may be readily computed

$$\mathrm{Var}[\,\Delta P_t\,] = \frac{s^2}{2} \qquad (3.2.4)$$

$$\mathrm{Cov}[\,\Delta P_{t-1}\,,\,\Delta P_t\,] = -\frac{s^2}{4} \qquad (3.2.5)$$

$$\mathrm{Cov}[\,\Delta P_{t-k}\,,\,\Delta P_t\,] = 0, \qquad k > 1 \qquad (3.2.6)$$

$$\mathrm{Corr}[\,\Delta P_{t-1}\,,\,\Delta P_t\,] = -\frac{1}{2}. \qquad (3.2.7)$$

Despite the fact that fundamental value P_t^* is fixed, ΔP_t exhibits volatility and *negative* serial correlation as the result of *bid-ask bounce*. The intuition is clear: If P^* is fixed so that prices take on only two values, the bid and the ask, and if the current price is the ask, then the price change between the current price and the previous price must be either 0 or s and the price change between the next price and the current price must be either 0 or $-s$. The same argument applies if the current price is the bid, hence the serial correlation between adjacent price changes is nonpositive. This intuition applies more generally to cases where the order-type indicator I_t is not IID,[18] hence the model is considerably more general than it may seem.

The larger the spread s, the higher the volatility and the first-order autocovariance, both increasing proportionally so that the first-order auto-correlation remains constant at $-\frac{1}{2}$. Observe from (3.2.6) that the bid-ask spread does not induce any higher-order serial correlation.

Now let the fundamental value P_t^* change through time, but suppose that its increments are serially uncorrelated and independent of I_t.[19] Then (3.2.5) still applies, but the first-order autocorrelation (3.2.7) is no longer $-\frac{1}{2}$ because of the additional variance of ΔP_t^* in the denominator. Specifically if $\sigma^2(\Delta P^*)$ is the variance of ΔP_t^*, then

$$\mathrm{Corr}[\,\Delta P_{t-1}\,,\,\Delta P_t\,] \;=\; -\,\frac{s^2/4}{(s^2/2)+\sigma^2(\Delta P^*)} \;\leq\; 0. \qquad (3.2.8)$$

Although (3.2.5) shows that a given spread s implies a first-order autoco-variance of $-s^2/4$, the logic may be reversed so that a given autocovariance coefficient and value of p imply a particular value for s. Solving for s in (3.2.5) yields

$$s \;=\; 2\sqrt{-\,\mathrm{Cov}[\Delta P_{t-1}, \Delta P_t]}\;, \qquad (3.2.9)$$

hence s may be easily estimated from the sample autocovariances of price changes (see the discussion in Section 3.4.2 regarding the empirical imple-mentation of (3.2.9) for further details).

Estimating the bid-ask spread may seem superfluous given the fact that bid-ask quotes are observable. However, Roll (1984) argues that the quoted spread may often differ from the *effective* spread, i.e., the spread between the actual market prices of a sell order and a buy order. In many instances, transactions occur at prices *within* the bid-ask spread, perhaps because mar-ketmakers do not always update their quotes in a timely fashion, or because they wish to rebalance their own inventory and are willing to "better" their quotes momentarily to achieve this goal, or because they are willing to pro-vide discounts to customers that are trading for reasons other than private information (see Eikeboom [1993], Glosten and Milgrom [1985], Goldstein [1993], and the discussion in the next section for further details). Roll's (1984) model is one measure of this effective spread, and is also a means for

---

[18]For example, serial correlation in I_t (of either sign) does not change the fact that bid-ask bounce induces negative serial correlation in price changes, although it does affect the magnitude. See Choi, Salandro, and Shastri (1988) for an explicit analysis of this case.

[19]Roll (1984) argues that price changes must be serially uncorrelated in an informationally efficient market. However, Leroy (1973), Lucas (1978), and others have shown that this need not be the case. Nevertheless, for short-horizon returns, e.g., daily or intradaily returns, it is difficult to pose an empirically plausible equilibrium model of asset returns that exhibits significant serial correlation.

accounting for the effects of the bid-ask spread on the time-series properties
of asset returns.

3.2.2 Components of the Bid-Ask Spread

Although Roll's model of the bid-ask spread captures one important aspect
of its effect on transaction prices, it is by no means a complete theory of
the economic determinants and the dynamics of the spread. In particular,
Roll (1984) takes *s* as given, but in practice the size of the spread is the
single most important quantity that marketmakers control in their strategic
interactions with other market participants. In fact, Glosten and Milgrom
(1985) argue convincingly that *s* is determined endogenously and is unlikely
to be independent of P^* as we have assumed in Section 3.2.1.

Other theories of the marketmaking process have decomposed the
spread into more fundamental components, and these components often
behave in different ways through time and across securities. Estimating the
separate components of the bid-ask spread is critical for properly implementing these theories with transactions data. In this section we shall turn
to some of the econometric issues surrounding this task.

There are three primary economic sources for the bid-ask spread: order-
processing costs, inventory costs, and adverse-selection costs. The first two
consist of the basic setup and operating costs of trading and recordkeeping,
and the carrying of undesired inventory subject to risk. Although these costs
have been the main focus of earlier literature,[20] it is the adverse-selection
component that has received much recent attention.[21] Adverse selection
costs arise because some investors are better informed about a security's
value than the marketmaker, and trading with such investors will, on average, be a losing proposition for the marketmaker. Since marketmakers
have no way to distinguish the informed from the uninformed, they are
forced to engage in these losing trades and must be rewarded accordingly.
Therefore, a portion of the marketmaker's bid-ask spread may be viewed
as compensation for taking the other side of potential information-based
trades. Because this information component can have very different statistical properties from the order-processing and inventory components, it is
critical to distinguish between them in empirical applications. To do so,
Glosten (1987) provides a simple asymmetric-information model that captures the salient features of adverse selection for the components of the
bid-ask spread, and we shall present an abbreviated version of his elegant
analysis here (see, also, Glosten and Harris [1988] and Stoll [1989]).

[20]See, for example, Amihud and Mendelson (1980), Bagehot (1971), Demsetz (1968), Ho
and Stoll (1981), Stoll (1978), and Tiniç (1972).
[21]See Bagehot (1971), Copeland and Galai (1983), Easley and O'Hara (1987), Glosten
(1987), Glosten and Harris (1988), Glosten and Milgrom (1985), and Stoll (1989).

Glosten's Decomposition

Denote by P_b and P_a the bid and ask prices, respectively, and let P be the "true" or *common-information* market price, the price that all investors without private information (*uninformed* investors) agree upon. Under risk-neutrality, the common-information price is given by $P = E[P^*|\Omega]$ where Ω denotes the common or public information set and P^* denotes the price that would result if everyone had access to all information. The bid and ask prices may then be expressed as the following sums:

$$P_b = P - A_b - C_b \tag{3.2.10}$$

$$P_a = P + A_a + C_a \tag{3.2.11}$$

$$s \equiv P_a - P_b = (A_a + A_b) + (C_a + C_b), \tag{3.2.12}$$

where $A_a + A_b$ is the adverse-selection component of the spread, to be determined below, and $C_a + C_b$ includes the order-processing and inventory components which Glosten calls the *gross profit* component and takes as exogenous.[22] If uninformed investors observe a purchase at the ask, then they will revise their valuation of the asset from P to $P+A_a$ to account for the possibility that the trade was information-motivated, and similarly, if a sale at the bid is observed, then P will be revised to $P-A_b$. But how are A_a and A_b determined?

Glosten assumes that all potential marketmakers have access to common information only, and he defines their updating rule in response to transactions at various possible bid and ask prices as

$$a(x) = E\left[P^* \mid \Omega \cup \{ \text{investor buys at } x\} \right] \tag{3.2.13}$$

$$b(y) = E\left[P^* \mid \Omega \cup \{ \text{investor sells at } y\} \right]. \tag{3.2.14}$$

A_a and A_b are then given by the following relations:

$$A_a = a(P_a) - P, \qquad A_b = P - b(P_b). \tag{3.2.15}$$

Under suitable restrictions for $a(\cdot)$ and $b(\cdot)$, an equilibrium among competing marketmakers will determine bid and ask prices so that the expected profits from marketmaking activities will cover all costs, including $C_a + C_b$ and $A_a + A_b$; hence

$$P_a = a(P_a) + C_a = P + \big(a(P_a) - P\big) + C_a = P + A_a + C_a \tag{3.2.16}$$

$$P_b = b(P_b) - C_b = P - \big(P - b(P_b)\big) - C_b = P - A_b - C_b. \tag{3.2.17}$$

---

[22] See Amihud and Mendelson (1980); Cohen, Maier, Schwartz, and Whitcomb (1981); Ho and Stoll (1981); and Stoll (1978) for models of these costs.

An immediate implication of (3.2.16) and (3.2.17) is that only a portion of the total spread, C_a+C_b, covers the basic costs of marketmaking, so that the quoted spread $A_a+A_b+C_a+C_b$ can be larger than Stoll's (1985) "effective" spread—the spread between purchase and sale prices that occur strictly within the quoted bid-ask spread—the difference being the adverse-selection component A_a+A_b. This accords well with the common practice of marketmakers giving certain customers a better price than the quoted bid or ask on certain occasions, presumably because these customers are perceived to be trading for reasons other than private information, e.g., liquidity needs, index-portfolio rebalancing, etc.

Implications for Transaction Prices

To derive the impact of these two components on transaction prices, denote by $\hat{P}_n$ the price at which the nth transaction is consummated, and let

$$\hat{P}_n = P_a I_a + P_b I_b, \tag{3.2.18}$$

where I_a (I_b) is an indicator function that takes on the value one if the transaction occurs at the ask (bid) and zero otherwise. Substituting (3.2.16)–(3.2.17) into (3.2.18) then yields

$$\hat{P}_n = E[P^*|\Omega \cup A]I_a + E[P^*|\Omega \cup B]I_b + C_a I_a - C_b I_b \tag{3.2.19}$$

$$= P_n + C_n Q_n \tag{3.2.20}$$

$$P_n \equiv E[P^*|\Omega \cup A]I_a + E[P^*|\Omega \cup B]I_b \tag{3.2.21}$$

$$C_n \equiv \begin{cases} C_a & \text{if buyer-initiated trade} \\ C_b & \text{if seller-initiated trade} \end{cases} \tag{3.2.22}$$

$$Q_n \equiv \begin{cases} +1 & \text{if buyer-initiated trade} \\ -1 & \text{if seller-initiated trade} \end{cases} \tag{3.2.23}$$

where A is the event in which the transaction occurs at the ask and B is the event in which the transaction occurs at the bid. Observe that P_n is the common information price *after* the nth transaction.

Although (3.2.20) is a decomposition that is frequently used in this literature, Glosten's model adds an important new feature: correlation between P_n and Q_n. If P is the common information price before the nth transaction and P_n is the common information price afterwards, Glosten shows that

$$\text{Cov}[P_n, Q_n|P] = E[A|P] \quad \text{where} \quad A \equiv \begin{cases} A_a & \text{if } Q_n = +1 \\ A_b & \text{if } Q_n = -1. \end{cases} \tag{3.2.24}$$

That P_n and Q_n must be correlated follows from the existence of adverse selection. If $Q_n=+1$, the possibility that the buyer-initiated trade is information-based will cause an upward revision in P, and for the same reason,

$Q_n = -1$ will cause a downward revision in P. There is only one case in which P_n and Q_n are uncorrelated: when the adverse-selection component of the spread is zero.

Implications for Transaction Price Dynamics

To derive implications for the dynamics of transactions prices, denote by ϵ_n the revisions in P_{n-1} due to the arrival of new public information between trades $n-1$ and n. Then the nth transaction price may be written as

$$P_n = P_{n-1} + \epsilon_n + A_n Q_n. \tag{3.2.25}$$

Taking the first difference of (3.2.20) then yields

$$\hat{P}_n - \hat{P}_{n-1} = \left(P_n - P_{n-1}\right) + \left(C_n Q_n - C_{n-1} Q_{n-1}\right) \tag{3.2.26}$$

$$= A_n Q_n + \epsilon_n + \left(C_n Q_n - C_{n-1} Q_{n-1}\right), \tag{3.2.27}$$

which shows that transaction price changes are comprised of a gross-profits component which, like Roll's (1984) model of the bid-ask spread, exhibits reversals, and an adverse-selection component that tends to be permanent. Therefore, Glosten's attribution of the effective spread to the gross-profits component is not coincidental, but well-motivated by the fact that it is this component that induces negative serial correlation in returns, not the adverse-selection component. Accordingly, Glosten (1987) provides alternative relations between spreads and return covariances which incorporate this distinction between the adverse-selection and gross-profits components. In particular, under certain simplifying assumptions Glosten shows that[23]

$$E[\hat{R}_k] = R(1 + \gamma\beta), \qquad \text{Cov}[\hat{r}_{k-1}, r_k] = -\frac{\gamma s_p^2}{4}, \tag{3.2.28}$$

where

$$s_p \equiv \frac{P_a - P_b}{(P_a + P_b)/2}, \qquad \gamma \equiv \frac{C}{C + A}, \qquad \beta \equiv \frac{s_p^2/4}{1 - (s_p^2/4)},$$

and where $\hat{R}_k$, R, are the per-period market and true returns, respectively, and $\hat{r}_k$ is the continuously compounded per-period market return.

These relations show that the presence of adverse selection ($\gamma < 1$) has an additional impact on means and covariances of returns that is not captured by other models of the bid-ask spread. Whether or not the adverse-selection

---

[23]Specifically, he assumes that: (1) True returns are independent of all past history; (2) The spread is symmetric about the true price; and (3) The gross-profit component does not cause conditional drift in prices.

component is economically important is largely an empirical issue that has yet to be determined decisively,[24] nevertheless Glosten's (1987) model shows that adverse selection can have very different implications for the statistical properties of transactions data than other components of the bid-ask spread.

3.3 Modeling Transactions Data

One of the most exciting recent developments in empirical finance is the availability of low-cost *transactions* databases: historical prices, quantities, bid-ask quotes and sizes, and associated market conditions, transaction by transaction and time-stamped to the nearest second. For example, the NYSE's Trades and Quotes (TAQ) database contains all equity transactions reported on the *Consolidated Tape* from 1992 to the present, which includes all transactions on the NYSE, AMEX, NASDAQ, and the regional exchanges. The Berkeley Options Database provides similar data for options transactions, and transactions databases for many other securities and markets are being developed as interest in market microstructure issues continues to grow.

The advent of such transactions databases has given financial economists the means to address a variety of issues surrounding the fine structure of the trading process or *price discovery*. For example, what are determinants of the bid-ask spread, and is adverse selection a more important factor than inventory costs in explaining marketmaking behavior?[25] Does the very act of trading move prices, and if so, how large is this *price impact* effect and how does it vary with the size of the trade?[26] Why do prices tend to fall more often on whole-dollar multiples than on half-dollar multiples, more often on half-dollar multiples than on quarter-dollar multiples, etc.?[27] What are the benefits and costs of other aspects of a market's microstructure, such as margin requirements, the degree of competition faced by dealers, the frequency that orders are cleared, and intraday volatility?[28] Although none of

---

[24]Recent attempts to quantify the relative contributions of order-processing/inventory costs and adverse selection costs to the bid-ask spread include: Affleck-Graves, Hegde, and Miller (1994), Glosten and Harris (1988),George, Kaul, and Nimalendran (1991), Huang and Stoll (1995a), and Stoll (1989). See Section 3.4.2 for further discussion.

[25]See Amihud and Mendelson (1980), Bagehot (1971), Copeland and Galai (1983), Demsetz (1968), Easley and O'Hara (1987), Glosten (1987), Glosten and Harris (1988), Glosten and Milgrom (1985), Ho and Stoll (1981), Stoll (1978, 1989), and Tiniç (1972).

[26]See Bertsimas and Lo (1996), Chan and Lakonishok (1993b, 1995), and Keim and Madhavan (1995a,b, 1996).

[27]See Ball, Torous, and Tschoegl (1985); Christie, Harris, and Schultz (1994); Christie and Schultz (1994); Goodhart and Curcio (1990); Harris (1991); Niederhoffer (1965, 1966); Niederhoffer and Osborne (1966); and Osborne (1962).

[28]See Cohen, Maier, Schwartz, and Whitcomb (1986), Harris, Sofianos, and Shapiro (1994), Hasbrouck (1991a, b), Madhavan and Smidt (1991), and Stoll and Whaley (1990).

these questions are new to the recent literature, the kind of answers we can provide have changed dramatically, thanks to transactions data. Even the event study, which traditionally employs daily returns data, has been applied recently to transactions data to sift out the impact of news announcements *within* the day (see, for example, Barclay and Litzenberger [1988]).

The richness of these datasets does not come without a price—transactions datasets are considerably more difficult to manipulate and analyze because of their sheer size. For example, in 1994 the NYSE consummated over 49 million transactions, and for each transaction, the NYSE's Trades and Quotes (TAQ) database records several pieces of information: transaction price, time of trade, volume, and various condition codes describing the trade. Bid-ask quotes and depths are also recorded. Even for individual securities, a sample size of 100,000 observations for a single year of transactions data is not unusual.

3.3.1 Motivation

Transactions data pose a number of unique econometric challenges that do not easily fit into the framework we have developed so far. For example, transactions data are sampled at irregularly spaced random intervals—whenever trades occur—and this presents a number of problems for standard econometric models: observations are unlikely to be identically distributed (since some observations are very closely spaced in time while others may be separated by hours or days), it is difficult to capture seasonal effects (such as time-of-day regularities) with simple indicator functions, and forecasting is no longer a straightforward exercise because the transaction times are random.

Also, transaction prices are always quoted in discrete units or *ticks*—currently $0.125 for equities, $0.0625 for equity options, $0.05 for futures contracts on the Standard and Poor's 500 index, $0.03125 for US Treasury bonds and notes, and so on. While there are no *a priori* theoretical reasons to rule out continuous prices, the transactions costs associated with quoting and processing such prices make them highly impractical.[29] Of course,

---

[29]Despite the indivisibilities that accompany price discreteness, there seems to be general agreement among economists and practitioners alike that the efficiency gains from discrete prices far outweigh the potential costs of indivisible trading lots. However, an unresolved issue is the *optimal degree* of discreteness, which balances the costs of indivisibilities against the benefits of discreteness. For example, on the NYSE, the minimum price movement of stocks with prices greater than or equal to $1 is one tick, but this minimum price variation was set years ago before the advent of high-speed digital computers and corresponding electronic trading mechanisms. It is unclear whether or not an eighth of a dollar is the optimal degree of discreteness today. Indeed, recent discussions between the NYSE and the US Securities and Exchange Commission seem to indicate a move towards *decimalization* under which prices and quotes are denominated in cents. See Ball, Torous, and Tschoegl (1985); Brennan and Copeland (1988); Harris (1991); and the SEC's (1994) *Market 2000* study for further discussion.

Table 3.1. *Summary statistics for daily returns of five NYSE stocks.*

Statistic	AAC	APD	CBS	CCB	KAB
P_{max}	5.250	86.750	216.500	629.750	7.250
P_{min}	1.375	40.625	129.000	360.250	2.875
$\overline{P}$	3.353	55.878	173.924	467.844	4.665
$\hat{\sigma}(P)$	0.811	11.380	18.877	53.251	0.816
r_{max} (%)	21.43	6.48	6.58	4.94	16.13
r_{min} (%)	−14.29	−5.49	−7.83	−9.43	−12.50
$\overline{R}$ (%)	0.12	0.11	0.02	−0.00	0.00
$\hat{\sigma}(R)$ (%)	4.88	1.61	1.45	1.46	3.48

Summary statistics for daily returns data from January 2, 1990, to December 31, 1992, for five NYSE stocks: AAC = Anacomp; APD = Air Products and Chemicals; CBS = Columbia Broadcasting System; CCB = Capital Cities ABC; KAB = Kaneb Services.

discreteness is less problematic for coarser-sampled data, which may be well-approximated by a continuous-state process. But it becomes more relevant for transaction price changes, since such finely sampled price changes typically take on only a few distinct values. For example, the *NYSE Fact Book: 1994 Data* reports that in 1994, 97.4% of all transactions on the NYSE occurred with no change or a one-tick price change. Moreover, price changes greater than 4 ticks are extremely rare, as documented in Hausman, Lo, and MacKinlay (1992).

Discreteness and Prices

Discreteness affects both prices and returns, but in somewhat different ways. With respect to prices, several studies have documented the phenomenon of *price clustering*, the tendency for prices to fall more frequently on certain values than on others.[30] For example, Figure 3.2a displays the histograms of the fractional part of the daily closing prices of the following five NYSE stocks during the three-year period from January 2, 1990, to December 31, 1992 (see Table 3.1 for summary statistics): Anacomp (AAC), Air Products and Chemicals (APD), Columbia Broadcasting System (CBS), Capital Cities

---

[30]See, for example, Ball, Torous, and Tschoegl (1985); Goodhart and Curcio (1990); Harris (1991); Niederhoffer (1965, 1966); Niederhoffer and Osborne (1966); and Osborne (1962).

ABC (CCB), and Kaneb Services (KAB). The histogram for CBS is a particularly good illustration of the classic price-clustering pattern: Prices tend
to fall more frequently on whole-dollar multiples than on half-dollar multiples, more frequently on half-dollars than on quarter-dollars, and more
frequently on even eighths than on odd eighths. Price-clustering is even
more pronounced for transactions data.

The importance of these patterns of discreteness has been highlighted
by the recent controversy and litigation surrounding the publication of
two empirical studies by Christie and Schultz (1994) and Christie, Harris,
and Schultz (1994). They argue that the tendency for bid-ask quotes on
NASDAQ stocks to cluster more frequently on even eighths than on odd
eighths is an indication of tacit collusion among NASDAQ dealers to maintain wider spreads. Of course, there are important differences between the
NASDAQ's market structure and those of other organized exchanges, and
more detailed analysis is required to determine if such differences can explain the empirical regularities documented by Christie and Schultz (1994)
and Christie, Harris, and Schultz (1994). Although the outcome of this
controversy is yet to be decided, all parties concerned would agree that
discreteness can have a tremendous impact on securities markets.[31]

Discreteness and Returns

The empirical relevance of discreteness for returns depends to a large extent
on the holding period and the price level, for reasons that we shall discuss
below. For transactions data, discreteness is considerably more problematic
because the price change from one transaction to the next is typically only
one or two ticks. For example, if the minimum price variation is an eighth of
a dollar, a stock currently priced at $10 a share can never yield a transaction
return between zero and $\pm 1.25\%$. In fact, in this case, the transaction return
must fall on a discrete "grid" of integer multiples of 1.25%. For higher-
priced stocks, this grid is considerably finer. For example, the transactions
return for a $50 stock will fall on a grid of integer multiples of 0.25%.
Moreover, as the price level varies through time, the collection of transaction
returns obtained may seem less discrete because the grid corresponding
to the entire dataset will be the superposition of the grids at each price
level. Therefore, if price levels are high and volatile, or if the timespan of
the dataset is long (which implies higher price-variability under a random
walk model for prices), the discreteness of transaction returns will be less
apparent.

Table 3.2 contains a concrete example of this intuition. It reports the
relative frequencies of transaction price changes for the five stocks in Fig-

---

[31] Other contributions to the NASDAQ controversy include Chan, Christie, and Schultz
(1995), Furbush and Smith (1976), Godek (1996), Grossman, Miller, Fischel, Cone, and Ross
(1995), Huang and Stoll (1995b), Kandel and Marx (1996), and Kleidon and Willig (1995).

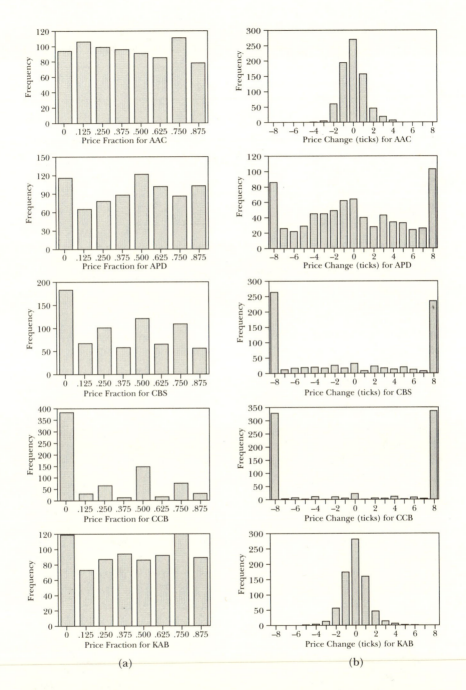

Figure 3.2. *Histogram of Daily Price Fractions and Price Changes for Five NYSE Stocks from January 2, 1990 to December 31, 1992*

Table 3.2.   *Relative frequencies of price changes for tick data of five stocks.*

Stock	Number of Trades	≤ −4	−3	−2	−1	0	+1	+2	+3	≥ +4
AAC	18,056	0.02	0.03	0.17	12.44	74.34	12.58	0.18	0.04	0.18
APD	26,905	0.32	0.41	3.22	13.48	64.40	14.23	3.14	0.41	0.39
CBS	21,315	2.24	6.64	7.35	7.26	52.42	7.93	7.42	6.31	2.43
CCB	23,128	15.72	0.70	1.69	3.90	55.11	4.56	1.89	0.58	15.85
KAB	21,008	0.01	0.00	0.16	11.77	75.79	12.04	0.15	0.00	0.07

Relative frequency count, in percent, for all 1991 transaction price changes in ticks for five NYSE stocks: AAC=Anacomp; APD=Air Products and Chemicals; CBS=Columbia Broadcasting System; CCB=Capital Cities ABC; KAB=Kaneb Services.

ure 3.2 using all of the stocks' transactions during the 1991 calendar year. The lower-priced stocks—KAB and AAC—have very few transaction price changes beyond the −1 tick to +1 tick range; these three values account for 99.6% and 99.3% of all the trades for KAB and AAC, respectively. In contrast, for a higher-priced stock like CCB, with an average price of $468 during 1991, the range from −1 tick to +1 tick accounts for 63.6% of its trades. While discreteness is relatively less pronounced for CCB, it is nevertheless still present. Even when we turn to daily data, the histograms of daily price changes in Figure 3.2b show that discreteness can still be important, especially for lower-priced stocks such as KAB and AAC.

Moreover, discreteness may be more evident in the *conditional* and *joint* distribution of high frequency returns, even if it is difficult to detect in the *unconditional* or *marginal* distributions. For example, consider the graphs in Figure 3.3a in which pairs of adjacent daily simple returns (R_t, R_{t+1}) are plotted for each of the five stocks in Table 3.1 over the three-year sample period. These *m-histories* (here, $m = 2$) are often used to detect structure in nonlinear dynamical systems (see Chapter 12). The scales of the two axes are identical for all five stocks to make cross-stock comparisons meaningful, and range from −5% to 5% in Figure 3.3a, −10% to 10% in Figure 3.3b, and −20% to 20% in Figure 3.3c.

Figure 3.3a shows that there is considerable structure in the returns of the lower-priced stocks, KAB and AAC; this is a radially symmetric structure that is solely attributable to discreteness. In contrast, no structure is evident in the 2-histories of the higher-priced stocks, CBS and CCB. Since APD's initial price is in between those of the other four stocks, it displays less struc-

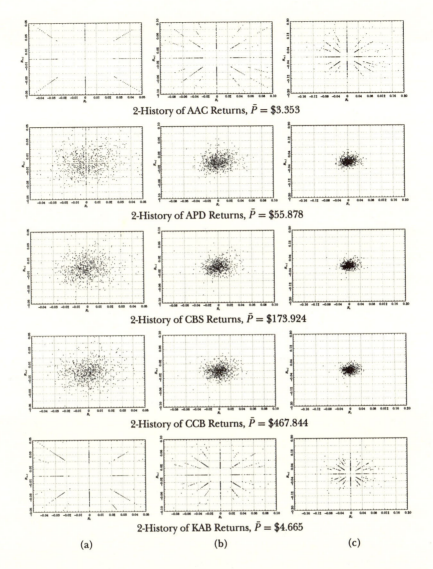

Figure 3.3. *2-Histories of Daily Stock Returns for Five NYSE Stocks from January 2, 1990 to December 31, 1992*

ture than the lower-priced stocks but more than the higher-priced stocks. Figures 3.3b and 3.3c show that changing the scale of the plots can often reduce and, in the case of APD, completely obscure the regularities associated with discreteness. For further discussion of these 2-histories, see Crack and Ledoit (1996).

These empirical observations have motivated several explicit models of price discreteness, and we shall discuss the strengths and weaknesses of each of these models in the following sections.

3.3.2 Rounding and Barrier Models

Several models of price discreteness begin with a "true" but unobserved continuous-state price process P_t, and obtain the observed price process P_t^o by discretizing P_t in some fashion (see, for example, Ball [1988], Cho and Frees [1988], and Gottlieb and Kalay [1985]). Although this may be a convenient starting point, the use of the term "true" price for the continuous-state price process in this literature is an unfortunate choice of terminology—it implies that the discrete observed price is an approximation to the true price when, in fact, the reverse is true: continuous-state models are approximations to actual market prices which are discrete. When the approximation errors inherent in continuous-state models are neglected, this can yield misleading inferences, especially for transactions data.[32]

Rounding Errors

To formalize this notion of approximation error, denote by X_t the gross return of the continuous-state process P_t between $t-1$ and t, i.e., $X_t \equiv P_t/P_{t-1}$. We shall measure the impact of discreteness by comparing X_t to the gross returns process $X_t^o \equiv P_t^o/P_{t-1}^o$ corresponding to a discretized price process P_t^o.

The most common method of discretizing P_t is to round it to a multiple of d, the minimum price variation increment. To formalize this, we shall require the *floor* and *ceiling* functions

$$\lfloor x \rfloor \equiv \text{greatest integer} \leq x \quad \text{(floor function)} \quad (3.3.1)$$

$$\lceil x \rceil \equiv \text{least integer} \geq x \quad \text{(ceiling function)}, \quad (3.3.2)$$

for any real number x.[33] Using (3.3.1) and (3.3.2), we can express the three most common methods of discretizing P_t compactly as

$$P_t^o = \left\lfloor \frac{P_t}{d} \right\rfloor d \quad (3.3.3)$$

---

[32] The question of which price is the "true" price may not be crucial for the statistical aspects of models of discreteness—after all, whether one is an approximation to the other or vice-versa affects only the sign of the approximation error, not its absolute magnitude—but it is central to the motivation and interpretation of the results (see the discussion at the end of Section 3.3.2 for examples). Therefore, although we shall adopt the terminology of this literature for the moment, the reader is asked to keep this ambiguity in mind while reading this section.

[33] For further properties and applications of these integer functions, see Graham, Knuth, and Patashnik (1989, Chapter 3).

$$P_t^o = \left\lfloor \frac{P_t}{d} \right\rfloor d \qquad (3.3.4)$$

$$P_t^o = \left\lfloor \frac{P_t}{d} + \frac{1}{2} \right\rfloor d, \qquad (3.3.5)$$

where the first method rounds *down*, the second rounds *up*, and the third rounds to the *nearest* multiple of d. For simplicity, we shall consider only (3.3.3), although our analysis easily extends to the other two methods.

At the heart of the discreteness issue is the difference between the return X_t based on continuous-state prices and the return X_t^o based on discretized prices. To develop a sense of just how different these two returns can be, we shall construct an upper bound for the quantity $|X_t^o - X_t| = |R_t^o - R_t|$, where R_t and R_t^o denote the simple net return of the continuous-state and discretized price processes, respectively. Let x and y be any two arbitrary nonnegative real numbers such that $y > 1$, and observe that

$$\frac{x-1}{y} < \frac{\lfloor x \rfloor}{\lfloor y \rfloor} < \frac{x}{y-1}. \qquad (3.3.6)$$

Subtracting x/y from (3.3.6) then yields

$$-\frac{1}{y} < \frac{\lfloor x \rfloor}{\lfloor y \rfloor} - \frac{x}{y} < \frac{x}{y(y-1)}, \qquad (3.3.7)$$

which implies the inequality

$$\left| \frac{\lfloor x \rfloor}{\lfloor y \rfloor} - \frac{x}{y} \right| < \frac{1}{y} \, \text{Max} \left[\frac{x}{y-1}, 1 \right]. \qquad (3.3.8)$$

Assuming that $P_t > d$ for all t, we may set $x \equiv P_t/d$, $y \equiv P_{t-1}/d$ and substitute these expressions into (3.3.8) to obtain the following upper bound:

$$|R_t^o - R_t| < \frac{\delta_{t-1}}{1 - \delta_{t-1}} \, \text{Max} \, [\, X_t \, , \, 1 - \delta_{t-1} \,] \equiv L(X_t, \delta_{t-1}), \qquad (3.3.9)$$

where $\delta_{t-1} \equiv d/P_{t-1}$ is defined to be the *grid size* at time $t-1$.

Although the upper bound (3.3.9) is a strict inequality, it is in fact the *least upper bound*, i.e., for any fixed d and any $\epsilon > 0$, there always exists some combination of P_{t-1} and X_t for which $|R_t^o - R_t|$ exceeds $L(\delta, X_t, P_{t-1}) - \epsilon$. Therefore, (3.3.9) measures the worst-case deviation of R_t^o from R_t, and it is the tightest of all such measures.

Note that (3.3.9) does not yield a uniform upper bound in r_t, since L depends on r_t:

$$L(X_t, \delta_{t-1}) = \frac{\delta_{t-1}}{1 - \delta_{t-1}} \left\{ 1 + \text{Max} \, [\, R_t \, , \, -\delta_{t-1} \,] \right\}. \qquad (3.3.10)$$

Nevertheless, it still provides a useful guideline for the impact of discreteness on returns as prices and returns vary. For example, (3.3.9) formalizes the intuition that discreteness is less problematic for higher-priced stocks, since L is an increasing function of δ_{t-1} and, therefore, a decreasing function of P_{t-1}.

It is important to keep in mind that (3.3.9) is only an upper bound, and while it does provide a measure of the *worst-case* discrepancy between R_t and R_t^o, it is not a measure of the discrepancy itself.[34] This distinction is best understood by grappling with the fact that the expected upper bound $E[L(X_t, \delta_{t-1})|\delta_{t-1}]$ is an increasing function of the mean and variance of X_t—the larger the expected return and volatility, the larger is the average value of the upper bound. This seems paradoxical because it is generally presumed that discreteness is less problematic for longer-horizon returns, but these have higher means and variances by construction. The paradox is readily resolved by observing that although the expected upper bound increases as the mean and variance increase, the probability mass of $|R_t^o - R_t|$ near the upper bound may actually decline. Therefore, although the expected worst-case discrepancy increases with the mean and variance, the probability that such discrepancies are realized is smaller. Also, as we shall see below, the expected upper bound seems to be relatively insensitive to changes in the mean and variance of X_t, so that when measured as a percentage of the expected return $E[X_t]$, the expected upper bound does decline for longer-horizon returns.

By specifying a particular process for P_t, we can evaluate the expectation of $L(\cdot)$ to develop some sense for the magnitudes of expected discreteness bias $E[|R_t^o - R_t|]$ that are possible. For example, let P_t follow a geometric random walk with drift μ and diffusion coefficient σ so that $\log P_t/P_{t-1}$ are IID normal random variables with mean μ and variance σ^2. In this case, we have

$$E\left[L(d, X_t, P_{t-1}) \mid P_{t-1} \right]$$

$$= \frac{\delta}{1-\delta} \left\{ e^{\mu + \frac{\sigma^2}{2}} \Phi\left(-\frac{\log(1-\delta) - \mu - \sigma^2}{\sigma} \right) \right.$$

$$\left. + \Phi\left(\frac{\log(1-\delta) - \mu}{\sigma} \right) \right\}, \qquad (3.3.11)$$

where $\Phi(\cdot)$ is the normal CDF.[35]

---

[34] Ideally, we would like to characterize $|R_t^o - R_t|$ directly, but it is surprisingly difficult to do so with any degree of generality. However, see the discussion below regarding the rounding and barrier models—under specific parametric assumptions for X_t, more precise characterizations of the discreteness bias are available.

[35] Note the similarity between (3.3.11) and the Black-Scholes call-option pricing formula.

Tables 3.3a–c report numerical values of (3.3.9) for price levels $P_{t-1} =$ $1, $5, $10, $50, $100, and $200, and for values of μ and σ corresponding to annual means and standard deviations for simple returns ranging from 10% to 50% each, respectively, and then rescaled to represent daily returns in Table 3.3a, monthly returns in Table 3.3b, and annual returns in Table 3.3c.

Table 3.3a shows that for stocks priced at $1, the expected upper bound for the discreteness bias is approximately 14 percentage points, a substantial bias indeed. However, this expected upper bound declines to approximately 0.25 percentage points for a $50 stock and is a negligible 0.06 percentage points for a $200 stock. These upper bounds provide the rationale for the empirical examples of Figures 3.3a–c and the common intuition that discreteness has less of an impact on higher-priced stocks. Table 3.3a also shows that for daily returns, changes in the mean and standard deviation of returns have relatively little impact on the magnitudes of the upper bounds.

Tables 3.3b and 3.3c indicate that the potential magnitudes of discreteness bias are relatively stable, increasing only slightly as the return-horizon increases. Whereas the expected upper bound is about 2.5 percentage points for daily returns when $P_{t-1} = \$5$, it ranges from 2.8% to 3.9% for annual returns. This implies that as a fraction of the typical holding period return, discreteness bias is much less important as the return horizon increases. Not surprisingly, changes in the mean and standard deviation of returns have more impact with an annual return-horizon.

Rounding Models
Even if $\mathrm{E}[|R_t^o - R_t|]$ is small, the statistical properties of P_t^o can still differ in subtle but important ways from those of P_t. If discreteness is an unavoidable aspect of the data at hand, it may be necessary to consider a more explicit statistical model of the discrete price process. As we suggested above, a rounding model can allow us to infer the parameters of the continuous-state process from observations of the rounded process. In particular, in much of the rounding literature it is assumed that P_t follows a geometric Brownian motion $dP = \mu P dt + \sigma P dW$, and the goal is to estimate μ and σ from the observed price process P_t^o. Clearly, the standard volatility estimator $\hat{\sigma}$ based on continuously compounded observed returns will be an inconsistent estimator of σ, converging in probability to $\sqrt{\mathrm{E}[(\log P_{t+1}^o - \log P_t^o)^2]}$ rather than to $\sqrt{\mathrm{E}[(\log P_{t+1} - \log P_t)^2]}$. Moreover, it can be shown that $\hat{\sigma}$ will be an *overestimate* of σ in the presence of price-discreteness (see Ball [1988, Table I] and Gottlieb and Kalay [1985, Table I] for approximate magnitudes of this upward bias). Ball (1988), Cho and Frees (1988), Gottlieb and Kalay

---

This is no accident, since $\mathrm{Max}[X_t, 1-\delta]$ may be rewritten as $\mathrm{Max}[X_t - (1-\delta), 0] + 1-\delta$; hence the upper bound may be recast as the payoff of a call option on X_t with strike price 1.

Table 3.3a. *Expected upper bounds for discreteness bias: daily returns.*

m	$s = 10\%$	$s = 20\%$	$s = 30\%$	$s = 40\%$	$s = 50\%$
$P_{t-1} = \$1$					
10%	14.2895	14.2895	14.2895	14.2895	14.2895
20%	14.2930	14.2930	14.2930	14.2930	14.2930
30%	14.2961	14.2961	14.2961	14.2961	14.2961
40%	14.2991	14.2991	14.2991	14.2991	14.2991
50%	14.3018	14.3018	14.3018	14.3018	14.3018
$P_{t-1} = \$5$					
10%	2.5648	2.5650	2.5676	2.5721	2.5772
20%	2.5654	2.5655	2.5672	2.5709	2.5755
30%	2.5660	2.5660	2.5671	2.5701	2.5741
40%	2.5665	2.5665	2.5672	2.5695	2.5730
50%	2.5670	2.5670	2.5674	2.5692	2.5721
$P_{t-1} = \$50$					
10%	0.2511	0.2516	0.2520	0.2525	0.2529
20%	0.2511	0.2515	0.2520	0.2524	0.2528
30%	0.2511	0.2515	0.2519	0.2523	0.2527
40%	0.2511	0.2515	0.2518	0.2522	0.2526
50%	0.2511	0.2514	0.2518	0.2521	0.2525
$P_{t-1} = \$100$					
10%	0.1254	0.1256	0.1259	0.1261	0.1263
20%	0.1254	0.1256	0.1258	0.1260	0.1262
30%	0.1254	0.1256	0.1258	0.1260	0.1262
40%	0.1254	0.1256	0.1258	0.1260	0.1261
50%	0.1254	0.1256	0.1257	0.1259	0.1261
$P_{t-1} = \$200$					
10%	0.0627	0.0628	0.0629	0.0630	0.0631
20%	0.0627	0.0628	0.0629	0.0630	0.0631
30%	0.0627	0.0628	0.0629	0.0630	0.0631
40%	0.0627	0.0628	0.0628	0.0629	0.0630
50%	0.0627	0.0628	0.0628	0.0629	0.0630

Expected upper bounds for discreteness bias in simple returns $|R_t^o - R_t| \times 100$ under a geometric random walk for prices P_t with drift and diffusion parameters μ and σ calibrated to annual mean and standard deviation of simple returns m and s, respectively, each ranging from 10% to 50%, and then rescaled to match *daily* data, i.e., $\mu/360$, $\sigma/\sqrt{360}$. Discretized prices $P_t^o \equiv \lfloor P_t/d \rfloor d$, $d = 0.125$, are used to calculate returns $R_t^o \equiv (P_t^o/P_{t-1}^o) - 1$.

Table 3.3b. *Expected upper bounds for discreteness bias: monthly returns.*

m	$s = 10\%$	$s = 20\%$	$s = 30\%$	$s = 40\%$	$s = 50\%$
$P_{t-1} = \$1$					
10%	14.3996	14.4067	14.4788	14.6117	14.7626
20%	14.5044	14.5064	14.5462	14.6449	14.7723
30%	14.6015	14.6019	14.6219	14.6907	14.7944
40%	14.6919	14.6920	14.7011	14.7462	14.8272
50%	14.7767	14.7767	14.7804	14.8081	14.8688
$P_{t-1} = \$5$					
10%	2.5945	2.6228	2.6501	2.6759	2.7004
20%	2.6075	2.6300	2.6545	2.6782	2.7010
30%	2.6222	2.6385	2.6599	2.6816	2.7027
40%	2.6374	2.6482	2.6664	2.6859	2.7053
50%	2.6523	2.6589	2.6738	2.6911	2.7088
$P_{t-1} = \$50$					
10%	0.2544	0.2569	0.2594	0.2619	0.2642
20%	0.2554	0.2576	0.2599	0.2621	0.2643
30%	0.2566	0.2584	0.2604	0.2624	0.2645
40%	0.2580	0.2593	0.2610	0.2629	0.2647
50%	0.2593	0.2602	0.2617	0.2634	0.2651
$P_{t-1} = \$100$					
10%	0.1270	0.1283	0.1296	0.1308	0.1319
20%	0.1276	0.1286	0.1298	0.1309	0.1320
30%	0.1282	0.1290	0.1300	0.1311	0.1321
40%	0.1288	0.1295	0.1304	0.1313	0.1322
50%	0.1295	0.1300	0.1307	0.1315	0.1324
$P_{t-1} = \$200$					
10%	0.0635	0.0641	0.0647	0.0653	0.0659
20%	0.0637	0.0643	0.0648	0.0654	0.0659
30%	0.0640	0.0645	0.0650	0.0655	0.0660
40%	0.0644	0.0647	0.0651	0.0656	0.0661
50%	0.0647	0.0649	0.0653	0.0657	0.0661

Expected upper bounds for discreteness bias in simple returns $|R_t^o - R_t| \times 100$ under a geometric random walk for prices P_t with drift and diffusion parameters μ and σ calibrated to annual mean and standard deviation of simple returns m and s, respectively, each ranging from 10% to 50%, and then rescaled to match *monthly* data, i.e., $\mu/12$, $\sigma/\sqrt{12}$. Discretized prices $P_t^o \equiv \lfloor P_t/d \rfloor d$, $d = 0.125$, are used to calculate returns $R_t^o \equiv (P_t^o/P_{t-1}^o) - 1$.

Table 3.3c. *Expected upper bounds for discreteness bias: annual returns.*

m	$s = 10\%$	$s = 20\%$	$s = 30\%$	$s = 40\%$	$s = 50\%$
$P_{t-1} = \$1$					
10%	15.7285	16.0498	16.5424	17.0439	17.5247
20%	17.1430	17.2297	17.5320	17.9288	18.3478
30%	18.5714	18.5857	18.7221	18.9889	19.3203
40%	20.0000	20.0014	20.0464	20.1957	20.4299
50%	21.4286	21.4286	21.4396	21.5080	21.6541
$P_{t-1} = \$5$					
10%	2.8372	2.9105	2.9958	3.0815	3.1644
20%	3.0778	3.1076	3.1677	3.2385	3.3118
30%	3.3333	3.3407	3.3736	3.4248	3.4846
40%	3.5897	3.5909	3.6046	3.6364	3.6807
50%	3.8462	3.8463	3.8506	3.8673	3.8968
$P_{t-1} = \$50$					
10%	0.2775	0.2846	0.2929	0.3013	0.3094
20%	0.3009	0.3039	0.3097	0.3166	0.3238
30%	0.3258	0.3266	0.3298	0.3348	0.3407
40%	0.3509	0.3510	0.3524	0.3555	0.3598
50%	0.3759	0.3760	0.3764	0.3780	0.3809
$P_{t-1} = \$100$					
10%	0.1386	0.1421	0.1463	0.1505	0.1545
20%	0.1502	0.1517	0.1547	0.1581	0.1617
30%	0.1627	0.1631	0.1647	0.1672	0.1701
40%	0.1752	0.1753	0.1760	0.1775	0.1797
50%	0.1877	0.1877	0.1880	0.1888	0.1902
$P_{t-1} = \$200$					
10%	0.0692	0.0710	0.0731	0.0752	0.0772
20%	0.0751	0.0758	0.0773	0.0790	0.0808
30%	0.0813	0.0815	0.0823	0.0836	0.0850
40%	0.0876	0.0876	0.0879	0.0887	0.0898
50%	0.0938	0.0938	0.0939	0.0943	0.0951

Expected upper bounds for discreteness bias in simple returns $|R_t^o - R_t| \times 100$ under a geometric random walk for prices P_t with drift and diffusion parameters μ and σ calibrated to annual mean and standard deviation of simple returns m and s, respectively, each ranging from 10% to 50%. Discretized prices $P_t^o \equiv \lfloor P_t/d \rfloor d$, $d = 0.125$, are used to calculate returns $R_t^o \equiv (P_t^o/P_{t-1}^o) - 1$.

(1985), and Harris (1990) all provide methods for estimating σ consistently from the observed price process P_t^o.[36]

Barrier Models

A slightly different but closely related set of models of price discreteness has been proposed by Cho and Frees (1988) and Marsh and Rosenfeld (1986) which we shall call *barrier* models. In these models, the continuous-state "true" price process P_t is also a continuous-time process, and trades are observed whenever P_t reaches certain levels or *barriers*.

Marsh and Rosenfeld (1986) place these barriers at multiples of an eighth, so that conditional on the most recent trade at, say $40\frac{2}{8}$, the waiting time until the next trade is the first-passage time of P_t to two barriers, one at $40\frac{2}{8}$ and the other at $40\frac{3}{8}$ (assuming that P_t has positive drift).

Cho and Frees (1988) focus on gross returns instead of prices and define stopping times τ_n as

$$\tau_n \equiv \inf_t \left\{ t > \tau_{n-1} : \frac{P_t}{P(\tau_{n-1})} \notin \left(\frac{1}{1+d}, 1+d \right) \right\}. \qquad (3.3.12)$$

Therefore, according to their model a stock which has just traded at time τ_{n-1} at \$10.000 a share will trade next at time τ_n when the unobserved continuous-state gross returns process $P_t/\$10.000$ reaches either 1.125 or 1/1.125, or when P_t reaches either \$10.125 or \$8.888. If P_t reaches \$8.888, the stock will trade next when P_t reaches either \$10.000 or \$7.901, and so on.

This process captures price-discreteness of a very different nature since the price increments defined by the stopping times are not integer multiples of any fixed quantity (for example, the lower barrier 1/1.125 does not correspond to a one-eighth price decline). However, such an unnatural definition of discreteness does greatly simplify the characterization of stopping times and the estimation of the parameters of P_t, since the first-difference of τ_n is IID.

Under the more natural specification of price discreteness, not considered by Cho and Frees (1988), the stopping time becomes

$$\tau_n^* = \inf_t \left\{ t > \tau_{n-1} : \frac{P_t}{P(\tau_{n-1})} \notin \left(1 - \frac{d}{P(\tau_{n-1})}, 1 + \frac{d}{P(\tau_{n-1})} \right) \right\} \qquad (3.3.13)$$

which reduces to the Marsh and Rosenfeld (1986) model in which the increments of stopping times are not IID.

---

[36]However, see the discussion at the end of Section 3.3.2 for some caveats about the motivation for these models.

Limitations

Although all of the previous rounding and barrier models do capture price discreteness and admit consistent estimators of the parameters of the unobserved continuous-state price process, they suffer from at least three important limitations.

First, for unobserved price processes other than geometric Brownian motion, these models and their corresponding parameter estimators become intractable.

Second, the rounding and barrier models focus exclusively on prices and allow no role for other economic variables that might influence price behavior, e.g., bid-ask spreads, volatility, trading volume, etc.

Third, and most importantly, the distinction between the "true" and observed price is artificial at best, and the economic interpretation of the two quantities is unclear. For example, Ball (1988), Cho and Frees (1988), Gottlieb and Kalay (1985), and Harris (1990) all provide methods for estimating the volatility of a continuous-time price process from discrete observed prices, never questioning the motivation of this arduous task. If the continuous-time price process is an approximation to actual market prices, why is the volatility of the approximating process of interest? One might argue that derivative pricing models such as the Black-Scholes/Merton formulas depend on the parameters of such continuous-time processes, but those models are also approximations to market prices, prices which exhibit discreteness as well. Therefore, a case must be made for the economic relevance of the parameters of continuous-state price processes to properly motivate the statistical models of discreteness in Section 3.3.2.

In the absence of a well-articulated model of "true" price, it seems unnatural to argue that the "true" price is continuous, implying that observed discrete market prices are somehow less genuine. After all, the economic definition of price is that quantity of numeraire at which two mutually consenting economic agents are willing to consummate a trade. Despite the fact that institutional restrictions may require prices to fall on discrete values, as long as both buyers and sellers are aware of this discreteness in advance and are still willing to engage in trade, then discrete prices corresponding to market trades are "true" prices in every sense.

3.3.3 The Ordered Probit Model

To address the limitations of the rounding and barrier models, Hausman, Lo, and MacKinlay (1992) propose an alternative in which price *changes* are modeled directly using a statistical model known as *ordered probit*, a technique used most frequently in empirical studies of dependent variables that take on only a finite number of values possessing a natural ordering.[37] Heuristically,

---

[37]For example, the dependent variable might be the level of education, as measured by three categories: less than high school, high school, and college education. The dependent

ordered probit analysis is a generalization of the linear regression model to cases where the dependent variable is discrete. As such, among the existing models of stock price discreteness—e.g., Ball (1988), Cho and Frees (1988), Gottlieb and Kalay (1985), Harris (1990), and Marsh and Rosenfeld (1986)—ordered probit is the only specification that can easily capture the impact of "explanatory" variables on price changes while also accounting for price discreteness and irregular transaction intervals.

The Basic Specification

Specifically, consider a sequence of transaction prices $P(t_0), P(t_1), \ldots, P(t_n)$ sampled at times $t_0, t_1, \ldots, t_n$, and denote by $Y_1, Y_2, \ldots, Y_n$ the corresponding price changes, where $Y_k \equiv P(t_k) - P(t_{k-1})$ is assumed to be an integer multiple of some divisor, e.g., a tick. Let Y_k^* denote an unobservable continuous random variable such that

$$Y_k^* = \mathbf{X}_k'\beta + \epsilon_k, \qquad \mathrm{E}[\epsilon_k|\mathbf{X}_k] = 0, \qquad \epsilon_k \ \mathrm{INID} \ \mathcal{N}(0, \sigma_k^2), \qquad (3.3.14)$$

where the $(q \times 1)$ vector $\mathbf{X}_k \equiv [\ X_{1k} \ \cdots \ X_{qk}\ ]'$ is a vector of explanatory variables that determines the conditional mean of Y_k^* and "INID" indicates that the ϵ_k's are independently but *not* identically distributed, an important difference from standard econometric models which we shall return to shortly. Note that subscripts are used to denote *transaction* time, whereas time arguments t_k denote calendar or *clock* time, a convention we shall follow throughout Section 3.3.3.

The heart of the ordered probit model is the assumption that observed price changes Y_k are related to the continuous variables Y_k^* in the following manner:

$$Y_k = \begin{cases} s_1 & \text{if } Y_k^* \in A_1 \\ s_2 & \text{if } Y_k^* \in A_2 \\ \vdots & \vdots \\ s_m & \text{if } Y_k^* \in A_m, \end{cases} \qquad (3.3.15)$$

where the sets A_j form a *partition* of the state space $\mathcal{S}^*$ of Y_k^*, i.e., $\mathcal{S}^* = \bigcup_{j=1}^m A_j$ and $A_i \cap A_j = \emptyset$ for $i \neq j$, and the s_j's are the discrete values that comprise the state space $\mathcal{S}$ of Y_k.

The motivation for the ordered probit specification is to uncover the mapping between $\mathcal{S}^*$ and $\mathcal{S}$ and relate it to a set of economic variables. In Hausman, Lo, and MacKinlay (1992), the s_j's are defined as: $0, -\frac{1}{8}, +\frac{1}{8}$,

---

variable is discrete and is naturally ordered since college education always follows high school (see Maddala [1983] for further details). The ordered probit model was developed by Aitchison and Silvey (1957) and Ashford (1959), and generalized to nonnormal disturbances by Gurland, Lee, and Dahm (1960). For more recent extensions, see Maddala (1983), McCullagh (1980), and Thisted (1991).

$-\frac{2}{8}$, $+\frac{2}{8}$, and so on. For simplicity, the state-space partition of $\mathcal{S}^*$ is usually defined to be intervals:

$$A_1 \equiv (-\infty, \alpha_1] \qquad\qquad (3.3.16)$$

$$A_2 \equiv (\alpha_1, \alpha_2] \qquad\qquad (3.3.17)$$

$$\vdots$$

$$A_i \equiv (\alpha_{i-1}, \alpha_i] \qquad\qquad (3.3.18)$$

$$\vdots$$

$$A_m \equiv (\alpha_{m-1}, \infty). \qquad\qquad (3.3.19)$$

Although the observed price change can be any number of ticks, positive or negative, we assume that m in (3.3.15) is finite to keep the number of unknown parameters finite. This poses no difficulties since we may always let some states in $\mathcal{S}$ represent a multiple (and possibly countably infinite) number of values for the observed price change. For example, in the empirical application of Hausman, Lo, and MacKinlay (1992), s_1 is defined to be a price change of -4 ticks *or less*, s_9 to be a price change of $+4$ ticks *or more*, and s_2 to s_8 to be price changes of -3 ticks to $+3$ ticks, respectively. This parsimony is obtained at the cost of losing *price resolution*. That is, under this specification the ordered probit model does not distinguish between price changes of $+4$ and price changes greater than $+4$, since the $+4$-tick outcome and the greater than $+4$-tick outcome have been grouped together into a common event. The same is true for price changes of -4 ticks and price changes less than -4. This partitioning is illustrated in Figure 3.4 which superimposes the partition boundaries $\{\alpha_i\}$ on the density function of Y_k^*, and the sizes of the regions enclosed by the partitions determine the probabilities π_i of the discrete events.

Moreover, in principle the resolution may be made arbitrarily finer by simply introducing more states, i.e., by increasing m. As long as (3.3.14) is correctly specified, increasing price resolution will not affect the estimated β asymptotically (although finite-sample properties may differ). However, in practice the data will impose a limit on the fineness of price resolution simply because there will be no observations in the extreme states when m is too large, in which case a subset of the parameters is not identified and cannot be estimated.

The Conditional Distribution of Price Changes

Observe that the ϵ_k's in (3.3.14) are assumed to be nonidentically distributed, conditioned on the $\mathbf{X}_k$'s. The need for this somewhat nonstandard assumption comes from the irregular and random spacing of transactions data. If, for example, transaction prices were determined by the model in Marsh and Rosenfeld (1986) where the Y_k^*'s are increments of arithmetic

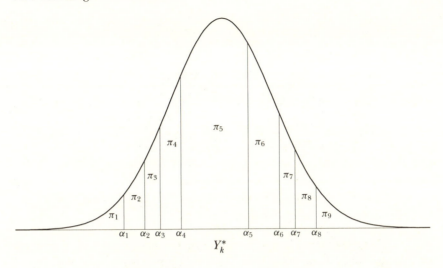

Figure 3.4. *The Ordered Probit Model*

Brownian motion with variance proportional to $\Delta t_k \equiv t_k - t_{k-1}$, σ_k^2 must be a linear function of Δt_k which varies from one transaction to the next.

More generally, to allow for more general forms of conditional heteroskedasticity, let us assume that σ_k^2 is a linear function of a vector of predetermined variables $\mathbf{W}_k \equiv [\ W_{1k} \ \cdots \ W_{Lk}\ ]'$ so that

$$\mathrm{E}[\epsilon_k|\mathbf{X}_k, \mathbf{W}_k] \quad = \quad 0, \qquad \epsilon_k \ \mathrm{INID}\ \mathcal{N}(0, \sigma_k^2) \qquad (3.3.20)$$

$$\sigma_k^2 \quad = \quad \gamma_0^2 + \gamma_1^2 W_{1k} + \cdots + \gamma_L^2 W_{Lk}, \qquad (3.3.21)$$

where (3.3.20) replaces the corresponding hypothesis in (3.3.14) and the conditional volatility coefficients $\{\gamma_j\}$ are squared in (3.3.21) to ensure that the conditional volatility is nonnegative. In this more general framework, the arithmetic Brownian motion model of Marsh and Rosenfeld (1986) can be easily accommodated by setting

$$\mathbf{X}_k'\boldsymbol{\beta} \quad = \quad \mu\Delta t_k \qquad (3.3.22)$$

$$\sigma_k^2 \quad = \quad \gamma^2\Delta t_k. \qquad (3.3.23)$$

In this case, $\mathbf{W}_k$ contains only one variable, Δt_k (which is also the only variable contained in $\mathbf{X}_k$). The fact that the same variable is included in both $\mathbf{X}_k$ and $\mathbf{W}_k$ does not create perfect multicollinearity since one vector affects the conditional mean of Y_k^* while the other affects the conditional variance.

The dependence structure of the observed process Y_k is clearly induced by that of Y_k^* and the definitions of the A_j's, since

$$P(\,Y_k = s_j \mid Y_{k-1} = s_i\,) = P(\,Y_k^* \in A_j \mid Y_{k-1}^* \in A_i\,). \qquad (3.3.24)$$

As a consequence, if $\mathbf{X}_k$ and $\mathbf{W}_k$ are temporally independent, the observed process Y_k is also temporally independent. Of course, these are fairly restrictive assumptions and are certainly not necessary for any of the statistical inferences that follow. We require only that the ϵ_k's be *conditionally* independent, so that all serial dependence is captured by the $\mathbf{X}_k$'s and the $\mathbf{W}_k$'s. Consequently, the independence of the ϵ_k's does not imply that the Y_k^*'s are independently distributed because no restrictions have been placed on the temporal dependence of the $\mathbf{X}_k$'s or $\mathbf{W}_k$'s.

The conditional distribution of observed price changes Y_k, conditioned on $\mathbf{X}_k$ and $\mathbf{W}_k$, is determined by the partition boundaries and the particular distribution of ϵ_k. For normal ϵ_k's, the conditional distribution is

$$
\begin{aligned}
P(Y_k &= s_i | \mathbf{X}_k, \mathbf{W}_k) \\[4pt]
&= P(\,\mathbf{X}_k'\boldsymbol{\beta} + \epsilon_k \in A_i \mid \mathbf{X}_k, \mathbf{W}_k\,) \qquad\qquad\qquad (3.3.25) \\[6pt]
&= \begin{cases}
P(\,\mathbf{X}_k'\boldsymbol{\beta} + \epsilon_k \le \alpha_1 \mid \mathbf{X}_k, \mathbf{W}_k\,) & \text{if } i = 1 \\
P(\,\alpha_{i-1} < \mathbf{X}_k'\boldsymbol{\beta} + \epsilon_k \le \alpha_i \mid \mathbf{X}_k, \mathbf{W}_k\,) & \text{if } 1 < i < m \\
P(\,\alpha_{m-1} < \mathbf{X}_k'\boldsymbol{\beta} + \epsilon_k \mid \mathbf{X}_k, \mathbf{W}_k\,) & \text{if } i = m
\end{cases} \quad (3.3.26) \\[6pt]
&= \begin{cases}
\Phi\left(\frac{\alpha_1 - \mathbf{X}_k'\boldsymbol{\beta}}{\sigma_k(\mathbf{W}_k)}\right) & \text{if } i = 1 \\[6pt]
\Phi\left(\frac{\alpha_i - \mathbf{X}_k'\boldsymbol{\beta}}{\sigma_k(\mathbf{W}_k)}\right) - \Phi\left(\frac{\alpha_{i-1} - \mathbf{X}_k'\boldsymbol{\beta}}{\sigma_k(\mathbf{W}_k)}\right) & \text{if } 1 < i < m \\[6pt]
1 - \Phi\left(\frac{\alpha_{m-1} - \mathbf{X}_k'\boldsymbol{\beta}}{\sigma_k}\right) & \text{if } i = m,
\end{cases} \quad (3.3.27)
\end{aligned}
$$

where $\sigma_k(\mathbf{W}_k)$ is written as an argument of $\mathbf{W}_k$ to show how the conditioning variables enter the conditional distribution, and $\Phi(\cdot)$ is the standard normal cumulative distribution function.

To develop some intuition for the ordered probit model, observe that the probability of any particular observed price change is determined by where the conditional mean lies relative to the partition boundaries. Therefore, for a given conditional mean $\mathbf{X}_k'\boldsymbol{\beta}$, shifting the boundaries will alter the probabilities of observing each state (see Figure 3.4).

In fact, by shifting the boundaries appropriately, ordered probit can fit any arbitrary multinomial distribution. This implies that the assumption of normality underlying ordered probit plays no special role in determining the probabilities of states; a logistic distribution, for example, could have served equally well. However, since it is considerably more difficult to capture conditional heteroskedasticity in the ordered logit model, we have chosen the normal distribution.

Given the partition boundaries, a higher conditional mean $\mathbf{X}'_k\beta$ implies a higher probability of observing a more extreme positive state. Of course, the labeling of states is arbitrary, but the *ordered* probit model makes use of the natural ordering of the states. The regressors allow us to separate the effects of various economic factors that influence the likelihood of one state versus another. For example, suppose that a large positive value of $\mathbf{X}_1$ usually implies a large negative observed price change and vice versa. Then the ordered probit coefficient β_1 will be negative in sign and large in magnitude (relative to σ_k, of course).

By allowing the data to determine the partition boundaries α, the coefficients β of the conditional mean, and the conditional variance σ_k^2, the ordered probit model captures the empirical relation between the unobservable continuous state space $\mathcal{S}^*$ and the observed discrete state space $\mathcal{S}$ as a function of the economic variables $\mathbf{X}_k$ and $\mathbf{W}_k$.

Maximum Likelihood Estimation

Let $I_k(i)$ be an indicator variable which takes on the value one if the realization of the kth observation Y_k is the ith state s_i, and zero otherwise. Then the log-likelihood function $\mathcal{L}$ for the vector of price changes $\mathbf{Y} = [\ Y_1\ \ Y_2\ \ \cdots\ \ Y_n\ ]'$, conditional on the explanatory variables $\mathbf{X} = [\ \mathbf{X}_1\ \mathbf{X}_2\ \cdots\ \mathbf{X}_n\ ]'$ and $\mathbf{W} = [\ \mathbf{W}_1\ \mathbf{W}_2\ \cdots\ \mathbf{W}_n\ ]'$, is given by

$$
\begin{aligned}
\mathcal{L}(\mathbf{Y}|\mathbf{X}, \mathbf{W}) = \sum_{k=1}^{n} \Bigg\{ & I_k(1) \log \Phi\left(\frac{\alpha_1 - \mathbf{X}'_k\beta}{\sigma_k(\mathbf{W}_k)} \right) \\
& + \sum_{i=2}^{m-1} I_k(i) \log \left[\Phi\left(\frac{\alpha_i - \mathbf{X}'_k\beta}{\sigma_k(\mathbf{W}_k)} \right) - \Phi\left(\frac{\alpha_{i-1} - \mathbf{X}'_k\beta}{\sigma_k(\mathbf{W}_k)} \right) \right] \\
& + I_k(m) \log \left[1 - \Phi\left(\frac{\alpha_{m-1} - \mathbf{X}'_k\beta}{\sigma_k(\mathbf{W}_k)} \right) \right] \Bigg\} .
\end{aligned} \tag{3.3.28}
$$

Although σ_k^2 is allowed to vary linearly with $\mathbf{W}_k$, there are some constraints that must be placed on the parameters to achieve identification since, for example, doubling the α's, the β's, and σ_k leaves the likelihood unchanged. A typical identification assumption is to set $\gamma_0 = 1$. We are then left with three issues that must be resolved before estimation is possible: (i) the number of states m; (ii) the specification of the regressors $\mathbf{X}_k$; and (iii) the specification of the conditional variance σ_k^2.

In choosing m, we must balance price resolution against the practical constraint that too large an m will yield no observations in the extreme states s_1 and s_m. For example, if we set m to 101 and define the states s_1 and s_{101}

symmetrically to be price changes of -50 ticks and $+50$ ticks, respectively, we would find no Y_k's among typical NYSE stock transactions falling into either of these states, and it would be impossible to estimate the parameters associated with these two states. Perhaps the easiest method for determining m is to use the empirical frequency distribution of the dataset as a guide, setting m as large as possible, but not so large that the extreme states have no observations in them.[38]

The remaining two issues must be resolved on a case-by-case basis since the specification for the regressors and σ_k^2 are dictated largely by the particular application at hand. For forecasting purposes, lagged price changes and market indexes may be appropriate regressors, but for estimating a structural model of marketmaker monopoly power, other variables might be more appropriate.

3.4 Recent Empirical Findings

The empirical market microstructure literature is an extensive one, straddling both academic and industry publications, and it is difficult if not impossible to provide even a superficial review in a few pages. Instead, we shall present three specific market microstructure applications in this section, each in some depth, to give readers a more concrete illustration of empirical research in this exciting and rapidly growing literature. Section 3.4.1 provides an empirical analysis of nonsynchronous trading in which the magnitude of the nontrading bias is measured using daily, weekly, and monthly stock returns. Section 3.4.2 reviews the empirical analysis of effective bid-ask spreads based on the model in Roll (1984). And Section 3.4.3 presents an application of the ordered probit model to transactions data.

3.4.1 Nonsynchronous Trading

Before considering the empirical evidence for nontrading effects we summarize the qualitative implications of the nontrading model of Section 3.1.1. Although many of these implications are consistent with other models of nonsynchronous trading, the sharp comparative static results and exposi-

---

[38]For example, Hausman, Lo, and MacKinlay (1992) set $m = 9$ for the larger stocks, implying extreme states of -4 ticks or less and $+4$ ticks or more, and set $m = 5$ for the smaller stocks, implying extreme states of -2 ticks or less and $+2$ ticks or more. Note that although the definition of states need not be symmetric (state s_1 can be -6 ticks or less, implying that state s_9 is $+2$ ticks or more), the symmetry of the histogram of price changes in their dataset suggests a symmetric definition of the s_j's.

tional simplicity are unique to this framework. Under the assumptions of Section 3.1.1, the presence of nonsynchronous trading

1. does not affect the mean of either observed individual or portfolio returns.
2. increases the variance of observed individual security returns that have nonzero means. The smaller the mean, the smaller the increase in the variance of observed returns.
3. decreases the variance of observed portfolio returns when portfolios are well-diversified and consist of securities with common nontrading probability.
4. induces geometrically declining *negative* serial correlation in observed individual security returns that have nonzero means. The smaller the absolute value of the mean, the closer is the autocorrelation to zero.
5. induces geometrically declining *positive* serial correlation in observed portfolio returns when portfolios are well-diversified and consist of securities with a common nontrading probability, yielding an AR(1) for the observed returns process.
6. induces geometrically declining cross-autocorrelation between observed returns of securities i and j which is of the same sign as $\beta_i \beta_j$. This cross-autocorrelation is generally *asymmetric*: The covariance of current observed returns to i with future observed returns to j need not be the same as the covariance of current observed returns to j with future observed returns to i. The asymmetry arises from the fact that different securities may have different nontrading probabilities.
7. induces geometrically declining *positive* cross-autocorrelation between observed returns of portfolios A and B when portfolios are well-diversified and consist of securities with common nontrading probabilities. This cross-autocorrelation is also asymmetric and arises from the fact that securities in different portfolios may have different nontrading probabilities.
8. induces *positive* serial dependence in an equal-weighted index if the betas of the securities are generally of the same sign, and if individual returns have small means.
9. and time aggregation increases the maximal nontrading-induced negative autocorrelation in observed individual security returns, but this maximal negative autocorrelation is attained at nontrading probabilities increasingly closer to unity as the degree of aggregation increases.
10. and time aggregation decreases the nontrading-induced autocorrelation in observed portfolio returns for all nontrading probabilities.

Since the effects of nonsynchronous trading are more apparent in securities grouped by nontrading probabilities than in individual stocks, our empirical application uses the returns of ten size-sorted portfolios for daily,

weekly, and monthly data from 1962 to 1994. We use market capitalization to group securities because the relative thinness of the market for
any given stock is highly correlated with the stock's total market value;
hence stocks with similar market values are likely to have similar nontrading
probabilities.[39] We choose to form ten portfolios to maximize the homo-
geneity of nontrading probabilities within each portfolio while still maintaining reasonable diversification so that the asymptotic approximation of
(3.1.20) might still obtain.[40]

Daily Nontrading Probabilities Implicit in Autocorrelations

Table 3.4 reports first-order autocorrelation matrices Γ_1 for the vector of
four of the ten size-sorted portfolio returns using daily, weekly, and monthly
data taken from the Center for Research in Security Prices (CRSP) database.
Portfolio 1 contains stocks with the smallest market values and portfolio 10
contains those with the largest.[41] From casual inspection it is apparent
that these autocorrelation matrices are not symmetric. The second column
of matrices is the autocorrelation matrices minus their transposes, and it
is evident that elements below the diagonal dominate those above it. This
confirms the lead–lag pattern reported in Lo and MacKinlay (1990c).

The fact that the returns of large stocks tend to lead those of smaller
stocks does suggest that nonsynchronous trading may be a source of correlation. However, the magnitudes of the autocorrelations for weekly and
monthly returns imply an implausible level of nontrading. This is most evident in Table 3.5, which reports estimates of daily nontrading probabilities
implicit in the weekly and monthly own-autocorrelations of Table 3.4.

For example, using (3.1.40) the daily nontrading probability implied by
an estimated weekly autocorrelation of 37% for portfolio 1 is estimated to
be 71.7%.[42] Using (3.1.8) we estimate the average time between trades to

---

[39]Only ordinary common shares are included in this analysis. Excluded are American
Depository Receipts (ADRs) and other specialized securities where using market value to characterize nontrading is less meaningful.

[40]The returns to these portfolios are continuously compounded returns of individual simple
returns arithmetically averaged. We have repeated the correlation analysis for continuously
compounded returns of portfolios whose values are calculated as unweighted geometric averages of included securities' prices. The results for these portfolio returns are practically
identical to those for the continuously compounded returns of equal-weighted portfolios.

[41]We report only a subset of four portfolios for the sake of brevity.

[42]Standard errors for autocorrelation-based probability and nontrading duration estimates
are obtained by applying a first-order Taylor expansion (see Section A.4 of the Appendix) to
(3.1.8) and (3.1.40) using heteroskedasticity- and autocorrelation-consistent standard errors
for daily, weekly, and monthly first-order autocorrelation coefficients. These latter standard
errors are computed by regressing returns on a constant and lagged returns, and using Newey
and West's (1987) procedure to calculate heteroskedasticity- and autocorrelation-consistent
standard errors for the slope coefficient (which is simply the first-order autocorrelation coefficient of returns).

Table 3.4. *Autocorrelation matrices for size-sorted portfolio returns.*

Daily

$\hat{\Gamma}_1$

	1	4	7	10
1	.39	.29	.21	.07
4	.41	.34	.29	.11
7	.40	.38	.33	.15
10	.34	.36	.34	.19

$\hat{\Gamma}_1 - \hat{\Gamma}_1'$

	1	4	7	10
1	.00	−.13	−.19	−.27
4	.13	.00	−.09	−.25
7	.19	.09	.00	−.19
10	.27	.25	.19	.00

Weekly

$\hat{\Gamma}_1$

	1	4	7	10
1	.37	.19	.12	−.02
4	.34	.21	.15	−.00
7	.32	.23	.17	.02
10	.24	.19	.15	.01

$\hat{\Gamma}_1 - \hat{\Gamma}_1'$

	1	4	7	10
1	.00	−.15	−.20	−.26
4	.15	.00	−.08	−.19
7	.20	.08	.00	−.14
10	.26	.19	.14	.00

Monthly

$\hat{\Gamma}_1$

	1	4	7	10
1	.21	.10	.06	.01
4	.28	.16	.11	.04
7	.30	.19	.14	.05
10	.27	.18	.14	.03

$\hat{\Gamma}_1 - \hat{\Gamma}_1'$

	1	4	7	10
1	.00	−.20	−.25	−.29
4	.18	.00	−.08	−.14
7	.24	.08	.00	−.09
10	.26	.14	.09	.00

Sample first-order autocorrelation matrix $\hat{\Gamma}_1$ for the (4×1) subvector $[\, r_1^o \; r_4^o \; r_7^o \; r_{10}^o \,]'$ of observed returns to ten equal-weighted size-sorted portfolios using daily, weekly, and monthly NYSE-AMEX common stock returns data from the CRSP files for the time period July 3, 1962 to December 30, 1994. Stocks are assigned to portfolios annually using the market value at the end of the prior year. If this market value is missing the end of year market value is used. If both market values are missing the stock is not included. Only securities with complete daily return histories within a given month are included in the daily returns calculations. r_1^o is the return to the portfolio containing securities with the smallest market values and r_{10}^o is the return to the portfolio of securities with the largest. There are approximately equal numbers of securities in each portfolio. The entry in the ith row and jth column is the correlation between r_{it}^o and r_{jt+1}^o.

To gauge the degree of asymmetry in these autocorrelation matrices, the difference $\hat{\Gamma}_1 - \hat{\Gamma}_1'$ is also reported.

be 2.5 days! The corresponding daily nontrading probability is 86.6% using monthly returns, implying an average nontrading duration of 6.5 days.

For comparison Table 3.5 also reports estimates of the nontrading probabilities using daily data and using trade information from the CRSP files. In the absence of time aggregation own-autocorrelations of portfolio returns are consistent estimators of nontrading probabilities; thus the entries in the column of Table 3.5 labelled "$\hat{\pi}_\kappa (q = 1)$" are simply taken from the diagonal of the autocovariance matrix in Table 3.4.

For the smaller securities, the point estimates yield plausible nontrading durations, but the estimated durations decline only marginally for larger-

Table 3.5.   *Estimates of daily nontrading probabilities.*

κ	$\hat{\pi}_\kappa$	$\hat{\pi}_\kappa(q=1)$	$\hat{E}[k_t]$	$\hat{\pi}_\kappa(q=5)$	$\hat{E}[k_t]$	$\hat{\pi}_\kappa(q=22)$	$\hat{E}[k_t]$
1	.225	.394	0.65	.717	2.54	.866	6.47
	(0.013)	(0.026)	(0.07)	(0.034)	(0.42)	(0.029)	(1.64)
4	.052	.343	0.52	.560	1.28	.837	5.12
	(0.004)	(0.023)	(0.05)	(0.059)	(0.31)	(0.043)	(1.61)
7	.019	.328	0.49	.497	0.99	.819	4.52
	(0.002)	(0.016)	(0.04)	(0.062)	(0.25)	(0.048)	(1.46)
10	.002	.188	0.23	.139	0.16	.515	1.06
	(0.001)	(0.019)	(0.03)	(0.126)	(0.17)	(0.461)	(1.96)

Estimates of daily nontrading probabilities implicit in ten weekly and monthly size-sorted port-folio return autocorrelations. Entries in the column labelled "$\hat{\pi}_\kappa$" are averages of the fraction of securities in portfolio κ that did not trade on each trading day, where the average is computed over all trading days from July 3, 1962 to December 30, 1994. Entries in the "$\hat{\pi}_\kappa(q=1)$" column are the first-order autocorrelation coefficients of daily portfolio returns, which are consistent estimators of daily nontrading probabilities. Entries in the "$\hat{\pi}_\kappa(q=5)$" and "$\hat{\pi}_\kappa(q=22)$" columns are estimates of daily nontrading probabilities obtained from first-order weekly and monthly portfolio return autocorrelation coefficients, using the time aggregation relations of Section 3.2 ($q=5$ for weekly returns and $q=22$ for monthly returns since there are 5 and 22 trading days in a week and a month, respectively). Entries in columns labelled "$\hat{E}[k_t]$" are estimates of the expected number of consecutive days without trading implied by the probability estimates in columns to the immediate left. Standard errors are reported in parentheses; all are heteroskedasticity- and autocorrelation-consistent.

size portfolios. A duration of nearly one fourth of a day is much too large for securities in the largest portfolio. More direct evidence is provided in the column labelled $\hat{\pi}_\kappa$, which reports the average fraction of securities in a given portfolio that do not trade during each trading day.[43] This average is computed over all trading days from July 3, 1962 to December 30, 1994 (8179 observations). Comparing the entries in this column with those in the others shows the limitations of nontrading as an explanation for the autocorrelations in the data. Nontrading may be responsible for some of the time-series properties of stock returns but cannot be the only source of autocorrelation.

[43]This information is provided in the CRSP daily files in which the closing price of a security is reported to be the negative of the average of the bid and ask prices on days when that security did not trade. Standard errors for probability estimates are based on the daily time series of the fraction of no-trades. The standard errors are heteroskedasticity- and autocorrelation-consistent.

Table 3.6. *Nontrading-implied weekly index autocorrelations.*

Estimator of π_i	Implied Index ρ_1 (%) $(\beta_1 = 1, \beta_{10} = 1)$	Implied Index ρ_1 (%) $(\beta_1 = 1.5, \beta_{10} = 0.5)$
Negative Share Price	1.4	1.8
Daily Autocorrelation	4.8	5.9

Implied first-order autocorrelation ρ_1 of weekly returns of an equal-weighted portfolio of ten size-sorted portfolios (which approximates an equal-weighted portfolio of all securities), using two different estimators of daily nontrading probabilities for the portfolios: the average fraction of negative share prices reported by CRSP, and daily nontrading probabilities implied by first-order autocorrelations of daily returns. Since the index autocorrelation depends on the betas of the ten portfolios, it is computed for two sets of betas, one in which all betas are set to 1.0 and another in which the betas decline linearly from $\beta_1 = 1.5$ to $\beta_{10} = 0.5$. The sample weekly autocorrelation for an equal-weighted portfolio of the ten portfolios is 0.21. Results are based on data from July 3, 1962 to December 30, 1994.

Nonsynchronous Trading and Index Autocorrelation

Denote by r_{mt}^o the observed return in period t to an equal-weighted portfolio of all N securities. Its autocovariance and autocorrelation are readily shown to be

$$\text{Cov}[r_{mt}^o, r_{mt+n}^o] = \frac{\iota' \mathbf{\Gamma}(n) \iota}{N^2} , \qquad \text{Corr}[r_{mt}^o, r_{mt+n}^o] = \frac{\iota' \mathbf{\Gamma}(n) \iota}{\iota' \mathbf{\Gamma}(0) \iota} , \quad (3.4.1)$$

where $\mathbf{\Gamma}_o$ is the contemporaneous covariance matrix of r_t^o and ι is an $(N \times 1)$ vector of ones. If the betas of the securities are generally of the same sign and if the mean return of each security is small, then r_{mt}^o is likely to be positively autocorrelated. Alternatively, if the cross-autocovariances are positive and dominate the negative own-autocovariances, the equal-weighted index will exhibit positive serial dependence. Can this explain Lo and MacKinlay's (1988b) strong rejection of the random walk hypothesis for the CRSP weekly equal-weighted index, which exhibits a first-order autocorrelation over 20%?

With little loss in generality we let $N = 10$ and consider the equal-weighted portfolio of the ten size-sorted portfolios, which is an approximately equal-weighted portfolio of all securities. Using (3.1.36) we may calculate the *weekly* autocorrelation of r_{mt}^o induced by particular *daily* non-trading probabilities π_i and beta coefficients β_i. To do this, we need to select empirically plausible values for π_i and β_i, $i = 1, 2, \ldots, 10$. This is done in Table 3.6 using two different methods of estimating the π_i's and two different assumptions for the β_i's.

The first row corresponds to weekly autocorrelations computed with the nontrading probabilities obtained from the fractions of negative share prices reported by CRSP (see Table 3.5). The first entry, 1.4%, is the first-order autocorrelation of the weekly equal-weighted index assuming that all twenty portfolio betas are 1.0, and the second entry, 1.8%, is computed under the alternative assumption that the betas decline linearly from $\beta_1 = 1.5$ for the portfolio of smallest stocks to $\beta_{10} = 0.5$ for the portfolio of the largest. The second row reports similar autocorrelations implied by nontrading probabilities estimated from daily autocorrelations using (3.1.41).

The largest implied first-order autocorrelation for the weekly equal-weighted returns index reported in Table 3.6 is only 5.9%. Using direct estimates of nontrading via negative share prices yields an autocorrelation of less than 2%. These magnitudes are still considerably smaller than the 21% sample autocorrelation of the equal-weighted index return. In summary, the recent empirical evidence provides little support for nontrading as an important source of spurious correlation in the returns of common stock over daily and longer frequencies.[44]

3.4.2 Estimating the Effective Bid-Ask Spread

In implementing the model of Section 3.2.1, Roll (1984) argues that the percentage bid-ask spread s_r may be more easily interpreted than the absolute bid-ask spread s, and he shows that the first-order autocovariance of simple returns is related to s_r in the following way:

$$\text{Cov}[\ R_{t-1}\ ,\ R_t\ ]\quad=\quad -\frac{s_r^2}{4}-\frac{s_r^4}{16}\ \approx\ -\frac{s_r^2}{4} \tag{3.4.2}$$

$$s_r\ \equiv\ \frac{s}{\sqrt{P_a P_b}}, \tag{3.4.3}$$

where s_r is defined as a percentage of the *geometric average* of the average bid and ask prices P_a and P_b. Using the approximation in (3.4.2), the percentage spread may be recovered as

$$s_r\ \approx\ 2\sqrt{-\text{Cov}[R_{t-1}, R_t]}\ . \tag{3.4.4}$$

Note that (3.4.4) and (3.2.9) are only well-defined when the return autocovariance is negative, since by construction the bid-ask bounce can only induce negative first-order serial correlation. However, in practice, positive serial correlation in returns is not uncommon, and in these cases, Roll simply defines the spread to be (see footnotes a and b of his Table I):

$$s_r\ \equiv\ -\,2\sqrt{|\,\text{Cov}[R_{t-1}, R_t]|}\ . \tag{3.4.5}$$

---

[44]Boudoukh, Richardson, and Whitelaw (1995), Mech (1993) and Sias and Starks (1994) present additional empirical results on nontrading as a source of autocorrelation. While the papers do not agree on the level of autocorrelation induced by nontrading, all three papers conclude that nontrading cannot completely account for the observed autocorrelations.

This convention seems difficult to justify on economic grounds—negative spreads are typically associated with marketmaking activity, i.e., the provision of liquidity, yet this seems to have little connection with the presence of positive serial correlation in returns. A more plausible alternative interpretation of cases where (3.4.4) is complex-valued is that the Roll (1984) model is misspecified and that additional structure must be imposed to account for the positive serial correlation (see, for example, George et al. [1991], Glosten and Harris [1988], Huang and Stoll [1995a], and Stoll [1989]).

Roll estimates the effective spreads of NYSE and AMEX stocks year by year using daily returns data from 1963 to 1982, and finds the overall average effective spread to be 0.298% for NYSE stocks and 1.74% for AMEX stocks (recall that AMEX stocks tend to be lower-priced; hence they ought to have larger percentage spreads). However, these figures must be interpreted with caution since 24,358 of the 47,414 estimated effective spreads were negative, suggesting the presence of substantial specification errors. Perhaps another symptom of these specification errors is the fact that estimates of the effective spread based on weekly data differ significantly from those based on daily data. Nevertheless, the magnitudes of these effects are clearly important for empirical applications of transactions data.

Glosten and Harris (1988) refine and estimate Glosten's (1987) decomposition of the bid-ask spread using transactions data for 250 NYSE stocks and conclude that the permanent adverse-selection component is indeed present in the data. Stoll (1989) develops a similar decomposition of the spread, and using transactions data for National Market System securities on the NASDAQ system from October to December of 1984, he concludes that 43% of the quoted spread is due to adverse selection, 10% is due to inventory-holding costs, and the remaining 47% is due to order-processing costs. George, Kaul, and Nimalendran (1991) allow the expected return of the unobservable "true" price (P_t^* in the notation of Section 3.2.1) to vary through time, and using daily and weekly data for NYSE and AMEX stocks from 1963 to 1985 and NASDAQ stocks and from 1983 to 1987, they obtain a much smaller estimate for the portion of the spread attributable to adverse selection—8% to 13%—with the remainder due to order-processing costs, and no evidence of inventory costs. Huang and Stoll (1995a) propose a more general model that contains these other specifications as special cases and estimate the components of the spread to be 21% adverse-selection costs, 14% inventory-holding costs, and 65% order-processing costs using 1992 transactions data for 19 of the 20 stocks in the Major Market Index.

The fact that these estimates vary so much across studies makes it difficult to regard any single study as conclusive. The differences come from two sources: different specifications for the dynamics of the bid-ask spread, and the use of different datasets. There is clearly a need for a more detailed and comprehensive analysis in which all of these specifications are applied to a variety of datasets to gauge the explanatory power and stability of each model.

3.4.3 Transactions Data

In Hausman, Lo, and MacKinlay (1992), three specific aspects of transactions data are examined using the ordered probit model of Section 3.3.3: (1) Does the particular *sequence* of trades affect the conditional distribution of price changes, e.g., does the sequence of three price changes $+1, -1, +1$ have the same effect on the conditional distribution of the next price change as the sequence $-1, +1, +1$? (2) Does trade size affect price changes, and if so, what is the price impact per unit volume of trade from one transaction to the next? (3) Does price discreteness matter? In particular, can the conditional distribution of price changes be modeled as a simple linear regression of price changes on explanatory variables without accounting for discreteness at all?

To address these three questions, Hausman, Lo, and MacKinlay (1992) estimate the ordered probit model for 1988 transactions data of over a hundred stocks. To conserve space, we focus only on their smaller and more detailed sample of six stocks—International Business Machines Corporation (IBM), Quantum Chemical Corporation (CUE), Foster Wheeler Corporation (FWC), Handy and Harman Company (HNH), Navistar International Corporation (NAV), and American Telephone and Telegraph Incorporated (T). For these six stocks, they focus only on *intraday* transaction price changes since it has been well-documented that overnight returns differ substantially from intraday returns (see, for example, Amihud and Mendelson [1987], Stoll and Whaley [1990], and Wood, McInish, and Ord [1985]). They also impose several other filters to eliminate "problem" transactions and quotes, which yielded sample sizes ranging from 3,174 trades for HNH to 206,794 trades for IBM.

They also use bid and ask prices in their analysis, and since bid-ask quotes are reported only when they are revised, some effort is required to match quotes to transactions. A natural algorithm is to match each transaction price to the most recently reported quote *prior* to the transaction; however, Bronfman (1991) and Lee and Ready (1991) have shown that prices of trades that precipitate quote revisions are sometimes reported with a lag, so that the order of quote revision and transaction price is reversed in official records such as the Consolidated Tape. To address this issue, Hausman, Lo, and MacKinlay (1992) match transaction prices to quotes that are set *at least five seconds prior* to the transaction—the evidence in Lee and Ready (1991) suggests that this will account for most of the missequencing. This is only one example of the kind of unique challenges that transactions data pose.

To provide some intuition for this enormous dataset, we report a few summary statistics in Table 3.7. Our sample contains considerable price dispersion, with the low stock price ranging from $3.125 for NAV to $104.250 for IBM, and the high ranging from $7.875 for NAV to $129.500 for IBM. At $219 million, HNH has the smallest market capitalization in our sample, and IBM has the largest with a market value of $69.8 billion.

The empirical analysis also requires some indicator of whether a transaction was buyer-initiated or seller-initiated, otherwise the notion of price impact is ill-defined—a 100,000-share block-purchase has quite a different price impact from a 100,000-share block-sale. Obviously, this is a difficult task because for every trade there is always a buyer and a seller. What we hope to capture is which of the two parties is more anxious to consummate the trade and is therefore willing to pay for it by being closer to the bid price or the ask price. Perhaps the most obvious indicator is whether the transaction occurs at the ask price or at the bid price; if it is the former then the transaction is most likely a "buy" and if it is the latter then the transaction is most likely a "sell." Unfortunately, a large number of transactions occur at prices strictly *within* the bid-ask spread, so that this method for signing trades will leave the majority of trades indeterminate.

Hausman, Lo, and MacKinlay (1992) use the well-known algorithm of signing a transaction as a buy if the transaction price is higher than the mean of the prevailing bid-ask quote (the most recent quote that is set at least five seconds prior to the trade); they classify it as a sell if the price is lower. If the price equals the mean of the prevailing bid-ask quote, they classify the trade as an *indeterminate* trade. This method yields far fewer indeterminate trades than classifying according to transactions at the bid or at the ask. Unfortunately, little is known about the relative merits of this method of classification versus others such as the *tick test* (which classifies a transaction as a buy, a sell, or indeterminate if its price is greater than, less than, or equal to the previous transaction's price, respectively), simply because it is virtually impossible to obtain the data necessary to evaluate these alternatives.

The Empirical Specification

To estimate the parameters of the ordered probit model via maximum likelihood, three specification decisions must be made: (i) the number of states m, (ii) the explanatory variables X_k, and (iii) the parametrization of the variance σ_k^2.

In choosing m, we must balance price resolution against the practical constraint that too large an m will yield no observations in the extreme states s_1 and s_m. For example, if we set m to 101 and define the states s_1 and s_{101} symmetrically to be price changes of -50 ticks and $+50$ ticks, respectively, we would find no Y_k's among our six stocks falling into these two states. Using the empirical distribution of the data as a guide, Hausman, Lo, and

Table 3.7.   *Summary statistics for transactions data of six stocks.*

Variable	IBM	CUE	FWC	HNH	NAV	T
Low Price	104.250	65.500	11.500	14.250	3.125	24.125
High Price	129.500	108.250	17.250	18.500	7.875	30.375
Market Value ($Billions)	69.815	2.167	0.479	0.219	0.998	28.990
% Trades at Prices:						
> Midquote	43.81	43.19	37.13	22.53	40.80	32.37
= Midquote	12.66	18.67	23.58	26.28	18.11	25.92
< Midquote	43.53	38.14	39.29	51.20	41.09	41.71
Price Change, Y_k						
Mean:	−0.0010	0.0016	−0.0017	−0.0028	−0.0002	0.0001
Std. Dev.:	0.7530	1.2353	0.6390	0.7492	0.6445	0.6540
Time Between Trades, Δt_k						
Mean:	27.21	203.52	296.54	1129.37	58.36	31.00
Std. Dev.:	34.13	282.16	416.49	1497.44	76.53	34.39
Bid-Ask Spread, AB_k						
Mean:	1.9470	3.2909	2.0830	2.4707	1.4616	1.6564
Std. Dev.:	1.4625	1.6203	1.1682	0.8994	0.6713	0.7936
S&P500 Futures Return						
Mean:	−0.0000	−0.0004	−0.0017	−0.0064	0.0001	−0.0001
Std. Dev.:	0.0716	0.1387	0.1475	0.1963	0.1038	0.0765
Buy-Sell Indicator, IBS_k						
Mean:	0.0028	0.0505	−0.0216	−0.2867	−0.0028	−0.0933
Std. Dev.:	0.9346	0.9005	0.8739	0.8095	0.9049	0.8556
Signed Transformed Volume						
Mean:	0.1059	0.3574	−0.0523	−1.9543	0.0332	−0.4256
Std. Dev.:	6.1474	5.6643	6.2798	6.0890	6.9705	7.5846
Median Trading Volume ($)	57,375	40,900	6,150	5,363	3,000	7,950

Summary statistics for transaction prices and corresponding ordered probit explanatory variables of International Business Machines Corporation (IBM, 206,794 trades), Quantum Chemical Corporation (CUE, 26,927 trades), Foster Wheeler Corporation (FWC, 18,199 trades), Handy and Harman Company (HNH, 3,174 trades), Navistar International Corporation (NAV, 96,127 trades), and American Telephone and Telegraph Company (T, 180,726 trades), for the period from January 4, 1988 to December 30, 1988.

MacKinlay (1992) set $m = 9$ for the larger stocks, implying extreme states of −4 ticks or less and +4 ticks or more, and set $m = 5$ for the two smaller stocks, FWC and HNH, implying extreme states of −2 ticks or less and +2 ticks or more.

The explanatory variables X_k are selected to capture several aspects of transaction price changes: clock-time effects (such as the arithmetic Brownian motion model), the effects of bid-ask bounce (since many transactions are merely movements from the bid price to the ask price or vice versa), the size of the transaction (so price impact can be determined as a function of the quantity traded), and the impact of "systematic" or marketwide movements on the conditional distribution of an individual stock's price changes. These aspects call for the following explanatory variables:

Δt_k: The time elapsed between transactions $k-1$ and k, in seconds.

AB_{k-1}: The bid-ask spread prevailing at time t_{k-1}, in ticks.

Y_{k-l}: Three lags [$l = 1, 2, 3$] of the dependent variable Y_k. Recall that for $m = 9$, price changes less than -4 ticks are set equal to -4 ticks (state s_1), and price changes greater than $+4$ ticks are set equal to $+4$ ticks (state s_9), and similarly for $m = 5$.

V_{k-l}: Three lags [$l = 1, 2, 3$] of the dollar volume of the $(k-l)$th transaction, defined as the price of the $(k-l)$th transaction (in dollars, not ticks) times the number of shares traded (denominated in hundreds of shares); hence dollar volume is denominated in hundreds of dollars. To reduce the influence of outliers, if the share volume of a trade exceeds the 99.5 percentile of the empirical distribution of share volume for that stock, it is set *equal* to the 99.5 percentile.

$SP500_{k-l}$: Three lags [$l = 1, 2, 3$] of five-minute continuously compounded returns of the Standard and Poor's (S&P) 500 index futures price, for the contract maturing in the closest month beyond the month in which transaction $k - l$ occurred, where the return is computed with the futures price recorded one minute before the nearest round minute *prior* to t_{k-l} and the price recorded five minutes before this.

IBS_{k-l}: Three lags [$l = 1, 2, 3$] of an indicator variable that takes the value $+1$ if the $(k - l)$th transaction price is greater than the average of the quoted bid and ask prices at time t_{k-l}, the value -1 if the $(k-l)$th transaction price is less than the average of the bid and ask prices at time t_{k-1}, and zero otherwise, i.e.,

$$IBS_{k-l} \equiv \begin{cases} 1 & \text{if} \quad P_{k-l} > \frac{1}{2}(P^a_{k-l} + P^b_{k-l}) \\ 0 & \text{if} \quad P_{k-l} = \frac{1}{2}(P^a_{k-l} + P^b_{k-l}) \\ -1 & \text{if} \quad P_{k-l} < \frac{1}{2}(P^a_{k-l} + P^b_{k-l}). \end{cases}$$

The specification of $X'_k\beta$ is then given by the following expression:

$$\begin{aligned} X'_k\beta &= \beta_1\Delta t_k + \beta_2 Y_{k-1} + \beta_3 Y_{k-2} + \beta_4 Y_{k-3} + \beta_5 SP500_{k-1} + \beta_6 SP500_{k-2} \\ &\quad + \beta_7 SP500_{k-3} + \beta_8 IBS_{k-1} + \beta_9 IBS_{k-2} + \beta_{10} IBS_{k-3} \\ &\quad + \beta_{11}\{ T_\lambda(V_{k-1}) \cdot IBS_{k-1} \} + \beta_{12}\{ T_\lambda(V_{k-2}) \cdot IBS_{k-2} \} \\ &\quad + \beta_{13}\{ T_\lambda(V_{k-3}) \cdot IBS_{k-3} \}. \end{aligned}$$

The variable Δt_k is included in X_k to allow for clock-time effects on the conditional mean of Y_k^*. If prices are stable in transaction time rather than clock time, this coefficient should be zero. Lagged price changes are included to account for serial dependencies, and lagged returns of the S&P500 index futures price are included to account for market-wide effects on price changes.

To measure the price impact of a trade per unit volume, the term $T_\nu(V_{k-l})$ is included, which is dollar volume transformed according to the Box and Cox (1964) transformation $T_\nu(\cdot)$:

$$T_\nu(x) \equiv \frac{x^\nu - 1}{\nu},$$

where $\nu \in [0, 1]$ is also a parameter to be estimated. The Box-Cox transformation allows dollar volume to enter into the conditional mean nonlinearly, a particularly important innovation since common intuition suggests that price impact may exhibit economies of scale with respect to dollar volume; i.e., although total price impact is likely to increase with volume, the marginal price impact probably does not. The Box-Cox transformation captures the linear specification ($\nu = 1$) and concave specifications up to and including the logarithmic function ($\nu = 0$). The estimated curvature of this transformation will play an important role in the measurement of price impact.

The transformed dollar volume variable is interacted with IBS_{k-l}, an indicator of whether the trade was buyer-initiated ($\text{IBS}_k=1$), seller-initiated [$\text{IBS}_k = -1$], or indeterminate ($\text{IBS}_k=0$). A positive β_{11} would imply that buyer-initiated trades tend to push prices up and seller-initiated trades tend to drive prices down. Such a relation is predicted by several information-based models of trading, e.g., Easley and O'Hara (1987). Moreover, the magnitude of β_{11} is the per-unit volume impact on the conditional mean of Y_k^*, which may be readily translated into the impact on the conditional probabilities of observed price changes. The sign and magnitudes of β_{12} and β_{13} measure the persistence of price impact.

Finally, to complete the specification the conditional variance $\sigma_k^2 \equiv \gamma_0^2 + \sum \gamma_i^2 W_{ik}$ must be parametrized. To allow for clock-time effects Δt_k is included, and since there is some evidence linking bid-ask spreads to the information content and volatility of price changes (see, for example, Glosten [1987], Hasbrouck [1988, 1991a,b], and Petersen and Umlauf [1990]), the lagged spread AB_{k-1} is also included. And since the parameter vectors α, β, and γ are unidentified without additional restrictions, γ_0^2 is set to one. This yields the specification

$$\sigma_k^2 \equiv 1 + \gamma_1^2 \Delta t_k + \gamma_2^2 \text{AB}_{k-1}.$$

In summary, the 9-state specification requires the estimation of 24 parameters: the partition boundaries $\alpha_1, \ldots, \alpha_8$, the variance parameters γ_1 and γ_2,

Table 3.8a. *Estimates of ordered probit partition boundaries.*

Parameter	IBM	CUE	FWC	HNH	NAV	T
α_1	−4.670	−6.213	−4.378	−4.456	−7.263	−8.073
	(−145.65)	(−18.92)	(−25.24)	(−5.98)	(−39.23)	(−56.95)
α_2	−4.157	−5.447	−1.712	−1.801	−7.010	−7.270
	(−157.75)	(−18.99)	(−25.96)	(−5.92)	(−36.53)	(−62.40)
α_3	−3.109	−2.795	1.679	1.923	−6.251	−5.472
	(−171.59)	(−19.14)	(26.32)	(5.97)	(−37.22)	(−63.43)
α_4	−1.344	−1.764	4.334	4.477	−1.972	−1.850
	(−155.47)	(−18.95)	(25.26)	(5.85)	(−34.59)	(−61.41)
α_5	1.326	1.605	—	—	1.938	1.977
	(154.91)	(18.81)			(34.66)	(62.82)
α_6	3.126	2.774	—	—	6.301	5.378
	(167.81)	(19.11)			(36.36)	(62.43)
α_7	4.205	5.502	—	—	7.742	7.294
	(152.17)	(19.10)			(31.63)	(57.63)
α_8	4.732	6.150	—	—	8.638	8.156
	(138.75)	(18.94)			(30.26)	(56.23)

Maximum likelihood estimates of the partition boundaries of the ordered probit model for transaction price changes of International Business Machines Corporation (IBM, 206,794 trades), Quantum Chemical Corporation (CUE, 26,927 trades), Foster Wheeler Corporation (FWC, 18,199 trades), Handy and Harman Company (HNH, 3,174 trades), Navistar International Corporation (NAV, 96,127 trades), and American Telephone and Telegraph Company (T, 180,726 trades), for the period from January 4, 1988 to December 30, 1988.

the coefficients of the explanatory variables $\beta_1, \dots, \beta_{13}$, and the Box-Cox parameter ν. The 5-state specification requires the estimation of only 20 parameters.

The Maximum Likelihood Estimates
Tables 3.8a and 3.10b report the maximum likelihood estimates of the ordered probit model for the six stocks. Table 3.8a contains the estimates of the boundary partitions α, and Table 3.8b contains the estimates of the "slope" coefficients β. Entries in each of the columns labeled with ticker symbols are the parameter estimates for that stock; z-statistics, which are asymptotically standard normal under the null hypothesis that the corresponding coefficient is zero, are contained in parentheses below each estimate.

Table 3.8a shows that the partition boundaries are estimated with high precision for all stocks and, as expected, the z-statistics are much larger for those stocks with many more observations. Note that the partition bound-

Table 3.8b. *Estimates of ordered probit "slope" coefficients.*

Parameter	IBM	CUE	FWC	HNH	NAV	T
γ_1 : $\Delta t/100$	0.399	0.499	0.275	0.187	0.428	0.387
	(15.57)	(11.62)	(11.26)	(4.07)	(10.01)	(8.89)
γ_2 : AB_{-1}	0.515	1.110	0.723	1.109	0.869	0.868
	(71.08)	(15.39)	(14.54)	(4.48)	(19.93)	(38.16)
β_1 : $\Delta t/100$	−0.115	−0.014	−0.013	−0.010	−0.032	−0.127
	(−11.42)	(−2.14)	(−3.50)	(−2.69)	(−3.82)	(−9.51)
β_2 : Y_{-1}	−1.012	−0.333	−1.325	−0.740	−2.609	−2.346
	(−135.57)	(−13.46)	(−24.49)	(−5.18)	(−36.32)	(−62.74)
β_3 : Y_{-2}	−0.532	−0.000	−0.638	−0.406	−1.521	−1.412
	(−85.00)	(−0.03)	(−16.45)	(−4.06)	(−34.13)	(−56.52)
β_4 : Y_{-3}	−0.211	−0.020	−0.223	−0.116	−0.536	−0.501
	(−47.15)	(−1.42)	(−9.23)	(−1.84)	(−31.63)	(−47.91)
β_5 : $SP500_{-1}$	1.120	2.292	1.359	0.472	0.419	0.625
	(54.22)	(13.54)	(13.49)	(1.36)	(8.05)	(17.12)
β_6 : $SP500_{-2}$	−0.257	1.373	0.302	0.448	0.150	0.177
	(−12.06)	(9.61)	(2.93)	(1.20)	(2.87)	(4.96)
β_7 : $SP500_{-3}$	0.006	0.677	0.204	0.388	0.159	0.141
	(0.26)	(5.15)	(1.97)	(1.13)	(3.02)	(3.93)
β_8 : IBS_{-1}	−1.137	−1.915	−0.791	−0.803	−0.501	−0.740
	(−63.64)	(−15.36)	(−7.81)	(−2.89)	(−17.38)	(−23.01)
β_9 : IBS_{-2}	−0.369	−0.279	−0.184	−0.184	−0.370	−0.340
	(−21.55)	(−3.37)	(−3.66)	(−0.75)	(−15.38)	(−18.11)
β_{10} : IBS_{-3}	−0.174	0.079	−0.177	−0.022	−0.301	−0.299
	(−10.29)	(0.98)	(−3.64)	(−0.17)	(−15.37)	(−19.78)
β_{11} : $T_v(V_{-1})IBS_{-1}$	0.122	0.217	0.050	0.038	0.013	0.032
	(47.37)	(12.97)	(1.80)	(0.55)	(2.56)	(4.51)
β_{12} : $T_v(V_{-2})IBS_{-2}$	0.047	0.036	0.015	0.036	0.011	0.014
	(18.57)	(2.83)	(1.54)	(0.55)	(2.54)	(4.22)
β_{13} : $T_v(V_{-3})IBS_{-3}$	0.019	0.007	0.015	−0.006	0.005	0.005
	(7.70)	(0.59)	(1.56)	(−0.34)	(2.09)	(3.02)

Maximum likelihood estimates of the "slope" coefficients of the ordered probit model for transaction price changes of International Business Machines Corporation (IBM, 206,794 trades), Quantum Chemical Corporation (CUE, 26,927 trades), Foster Wheeler Corporation (FWC, 18,199 trades), Handy and Harman Company (HNH, 3,174 trades), Navistar International Corporation (NAV, 96,127 trades), and American Telephone and Telegraph Company (T, 180,726 trades), for the period from January 4, 1988 to December 30, 1988.

aries are not evenly spaced, e.g., $|\alpha_3-\alpha_4| = 1.765$, whereas $|\alpha_4-\alpha_5| = 2.670$ (it can be shown that these two values are statistically different). One implication is that the eighths-barrier model of discrete prices, e.g., that of Marsh and Rosenfeld (1986), is not consistent with these transactions data. Another implication is that the estimated *conditional* probabilities of price changes need not look normal, but may (and do) display a clustering phenomenon similar to the clustering of the *unconditional* distribution of price changes on even eighths.

Table 3.8b shows that the conditional means of the Y_k^*'s for all six stocks are only marginally affected by Δt_k. Moreover, the z-statistics are minuscule, especially in light of the large sample sizes. However, Δt does enter into the σ_k^2 expression significantly—in fact, since all the parameters for σ_k^2 are significant, homoskedasticity may be rejected—and hence clock-time is important for the conditional variances, but not for the conditional means of Y_k^*. Note that this does not necessarily imply the same for the conditional distribution of the Y_k's, which is *nonlinearly* related to the conditional distribution of the Y_k^*'s. For example, the conditional mean of the Y_k's may well depend on the conditional variance of the Y_k^*'s, so that clock-time can still affect the conditional mean of observed price changes even though it does not affect the conditional mean of Y_k^*.

Order Flow, Discreteness, and Price Impact

More striking is the significance and sign of the lagged price change coefficients $\hat{\beta}_2$, $\hat{\beta}_3$, and $\hat{\beta}_4$, which are negative for all stocks, implying a tendency towards price reversals. For example, if the past three price changes were each one tick, the conditional mean of Y_k^* changes by $\hat{\beta}_2+\hat{\beta}_3+\hat{\beta}_4$. However, if the sequence of price changes was $1/-1/1$, then the effect on the conditional mean is $\hat{\beta}_2-\hat{\beta}_3+\hat{\beta}_4$, a quantity closer to zero for each of the security's parameter estimates.

Note that these coefficients measure reversal tendencies *beyond* that induced by the presence of a constant bid-ask spread as in Roll (1984). The effect of bid-ask bounce on the conditional mean should be captured by the indicator variables IBS_{k-1}, IBS_{k-2}, and IBS_{k-3}. In the absence of all other information (such as market movements or past price changes), these variables pick up any price effects that buys and sells might have on the conditional mean. As expected, the estimated coefficients are generally negative, indicating the presence of reversals due to movements from bid to ask or ask to bid prices. Hausman, Lo, and MacKinlay (1992) compare their magnitudes formally and conclude that the conditional mean of price changes is *path-dependent* with respect to past price changes—the *sequence* of price changes or *order flow* matters.

Using these parameter estimates, Hausman, Lo, and MacKinlay (1992) are also able to address the second two questions they put forward. Price impact—the effect of a trade on the market price—can be quantified with relatively high precision, it does increase with trade size although not linearly, and it differs from stock to stock. The more liquid stocks such as IBM tend to have relatively flat price-impact functions, whereas less liquid stocks such as HNH are more sensitive to trade size (see, in particular, Hausman, Lo, and MacKinlay [1992, Figure 4]).

Also, discreteness does matter, in the sense that the conditional distribution of price changes implied by the ordered probit specification can capture certain nonlinearities—price-clustering on even eighths versus odd eighths, for example—that other techniques such as ordinary least squares cannot.

While it is still too early to say whether the ordered probit model will have broader applications in market microstructure studies, it is currently the only model that can capture discreteness, irregular trade intervals, and the effects of economic variables on transaction prices in a relatively parsimonious fashion.

3.5 Conclusion

There are many outstanding economic and econometric issues that can now be resolved in the market microstructure literature thanks to the plethora of newly available transactions databases. In this chapter we have touched on only three of the issues that are part of the burgeoning market microstructure literature: nonsynchronous trading, the bid-ask spread, and modeling transactions data. However, the combination of transactions databases and ever-increasing computing power is sure to create many new directions of research. For example, the measurement and control of trading costs has been of primary concern to large institutional investors, but there has been relatively little academic research devoted to this important topic because the necessary data were unavailable until recently. Similarly, measures of market transparency, liquidity, and competitiveness all figure prominently in recent theoretical models of security prices, but it has been virtually impossible to implement any of these theories until recently because of a lack of data. The experimental markets literature has also contributed many insights into market microstructure issues but its enormous potential is only beginning to be realized. Given the growing interest in market microstructure by academics, investment professionals and, most recently, policymakers involved in rewriting securities markets regulations, the next few years are sure to be an extremely exciting and fertile period for this area.

Problems—Chapter 3

3.1 Derive the mean, variance, autocovariance, and autocorrelation functions (3.1.9)–(3.1.12) of the observed returns process $\{r_{it}^o\}$ for the nontrading model of Section 3.1. Hint: Use the representation (3.1.4).

3.2   Under the nontrading process defined by (3.1.2)–(3.1.3), and assuming that virtual returns have a linear one-factor structure (3.1.1), show how nontrading affects the estimated beta of a typical security. Recall that a security's beta is defined as the slope coefficient of a regression of the security's returns on the return of the market portfolio.

3.3   Suppose that the trading process $\{\delta_{it}\}$ defined in (3.1.2) were not IID, but followed a two-state Markov chain instead, with transition probabilities given by

$$
\begin{array}{c}
 & \delta_{it} \\
 & \begin{array}{cc} 0 & \quad 1 \end{array} \\
\delta_{it-1} \quad \begin{array}{c} 0 \\ 1 \end{array} & \left(\begin{array}{cc} \pi_i & 1 - \pi_i \\ 1 - \pi_i' & \pi_i' \end{array} \right).
\end{array}
\tag{3.5.1}
$$

3.3.1   Derive the unconditional mean, variance, first-order autocovariance, and steady-state distribution of δ_{it} as functions of π_i and π_i'.

3.3.2   Calculate the mean, variance, and autocorrelation function of the observed returns process r_{it}^o under (3.5.1). How does serial correlation in δ_{it} affect the moments of observed returns?

3.3.3   Using daily returns for any individual security, estimate the parameters π_i and π_i' assuming that the virtual returns process is IID. Are the estimates empirically plausible?

3.4   Extend the Roll (1984) model to allow for a serially correlated order-type indicator variable. In particular, let I_t be a two-state Markov with -1 and 1 as the two states, and derive expressions for the moments of ΔP_t in terms of s and the transition probabilities of I_t. How do these results differ from the IID case? How would you reinterpret Roll's (1984) findings in light of this more general model of bid-ask bounce?

3.5   How does price discreteness affect the *sampling* properties of the mean, standard deviation, and first-order autocorrelation estimators, if at all? Hint: Simulate continuous-state prices with various starting price levels, round to the nearest eighth, calculate the statistics of interest, and tabulate the relevant sampling distributions.

3.6   The following questions refer to an extract of the NYSE's *TAQ Database* which consists of all transactions for IBM stock that occurred on January 4th and 5th, 1988 (2,748 trades).

3.6.1   Construct a histogram for IBM's stock price. Do you see any evidence of price clustering? Construct a histogram for IBM's stock price *changes*. Is there any price-change clustering? Construct the following two histograms and compare and contrast: the histogram of price changes conditional on prices falling on an even eighth, and the histogram of price changes conditional on prices falling on an odd eighth. Using these histograms, comment on the importance or unimportance of discrete prices for statistical inference.

3.6.2 What is the average time between trades for IBM? Construct a 95% confidence interval about this average. Using these quantities and the central limit theorem, what is the probability that IBM does *not* trade in any given one-minute interval? Divide the trading day into one-minute intervals, and estimate directly the *unconditional* and *conditional* probabilities of nontrading, where the conditional probabilities are conditioned on whether a trade occurred during the previous minute (hint: think about Markov chains). Is the nontrading process independent?

3.6.3 Plot price and volume on the same graph, with time-of-day as the horizontal axis. Are there any discernible patterns? Propose and perform statistical tests of such patterns and other patterns that might not be visible to the naked eye but are motivated by economic considerations; e.g., block trades are followed by larger price changes than nonblock trades, etc.[45]

3.6.4 Devise and estimate a model that measures price impact, i.e., the actual cost of trading *n* shares of IBM. Feel free to use *any* statistical methods at your disposal—there is no single right answer (in particular, ordered probit is not necessarily the best way to do this). Think carefully about the underlying economic motivation for measuring price impact.

3.7 The following questions refer to an extract of the NYSE's *TAQ Database* which consists of bid-ask quote revisions and depths for IBM stock that were displayed during January 4th and 5th, 1988 (1,327 quote revisions).

3.7.1 Construct a histogram for IBM's bid-ask spread. Can you conclude from this that the dynamics of the bid-ask spread are unimportant? Why or why not? You may wish to construct various conditional histograms to properly answer this question.

3.7.2 Are there any discernible relations between revisions in the bid-ask quotes and transactions? That is, do revisions in bid-ask quotes "cause" trades to occur, or do trades motivate revisions in the quotes? Propose and estimate a model to answer this question.

3.7.3 How are changes in the bid and ask prices related to volume, if at all? For example, do quote revisions cause trades to occur, or do trades motivate revisions in the quotes? Propose and estimate a model to answer this question.

3.7.4 Consider an asset allocation rule in which an investor invests fully in stocks until experiencing a sequence of three *consecutive* declines, after

---

[45]The NYSE defines a block trade as any trade consisting of 10,000 shares or more.

which he will switch completely into bonds until experiencing a sequence of six *consecutive* advances. Implement this rule for an initial investment of $100,000 with the transactions data, but do it two ways: (1) use the average of the bid-ask spread for purchases or sales; (2) use the ask price for purchases and the bid price for sales. How much do you have left at the end of two days of trading? You may assume a zero riskfree rate for this exercise.

4
Event-Study Analysis

ECONOMISTS ARE FREQUENTLY ASKED to measure the effect of an economic event on the value of a firm. On the surface this seems like a difficult task, but a measure can be constructed easily using financial market data in an event study. The usefulness of such a study comes from the fact that, given rationality in the marketplace, the effect of an event will be reflected immediately in asset prices. Thus the event's economic impact can be measured using asset prices observed over a relatively short time period. In contrast, direct measures may require many months or even years of observation.

The general applicability of the event-study methodology has led to its wide use. In the academic accounting and finance field, event-study methodology has been applied to a variety of firm-specific and economy-wide events. Some examples include mergers and acquisitions, earnings announcements, issues of new debt or equity, and announcements of macroeconomic variables such as the trade deficit.[1] However, applications in other fields are also abundant. For example, event studies are used in the field of law and economics to measure the impact on the value of a firm of a change in the regulatory environment,[2] and in legal-liability cases event studies are used to assess damages.[3] In most applications, the focus is the effect of an event on the price of a particular class of securities of the firm, most often common equity. In this chapter the methodology will be discussed in terms of common stock applications. However, the methodology can be applied to debt securities with little modification.

Event studies have a long history. Perhaps the first published study is Dolley (1933). Dolley examined the price effects of stock splits, studying nominal price changes at the time of the split. Using a sample of 95 splits

---

[1] We will further discuss the first three examples later in the chapter. McQueen and Roley (1993) provide an illustration using macroeconomic news announcements.

[2] See Schwert (1981).

[3] See Mitchell and Netter (1994).

from 1921 to 1931, he found that the price increased in 57 of the cases and
the price declined in only 26 instances. There was no effect in the other 12
cases. Over the decades from the early 1930s until the late 1960s the level of
sophistication of event studies increased. Myers and Bakay (1948), Barker
(1956, 1957, 1958), and Ashley (1962) are examples of studies during this
time period. The improvements include removing general stock market
price movements and separating out confounding events. In the late 1960s
seminal studies by Ball and Brown (1968) and Fama, Fisher, Jensen, and
Roll (1969) introduced the methodology that is essentially still in use today.
Ball and Brown considered the information content of earnings, and Fama,
Fisher, Jensen, and Roll studied the effects of stock splits after removing the
effects of simultaneous dividend increases.

In the years since these pioneering studies, several modifications of the
basic methodology have been suggested. These modifications handle complications arising from violations of the statistical assumptions used in the
early work, and they can accommodate more specific hypotheses. Brown
and Warner (1980, 1985) are useful papers that discuss the practical importance of many of these modifications. The 1980 paper considers implementation issues for data sampled at a monthly interval and the 1985 paper
deals with issues for daily data.

This chapter explains the econometric methodology of event studies.
Section 4.1 briefly outlines the procedure for conducting an event study.
Section 4.2 sets up an illustrative example of an event study. Central to
any event study is the measurement of the abnormal return. Section 4.3
details the first step—measuring the normal performance—and Section 4.4
follows with the necessary tools for calculating the abnormal return, making statistical inferences about these returns, and aggregating over many
event observations. In Sections 4.3 and 4.4 the discussion maintains the
null hypothesis that the event has no impact on the distribution of returns.
Section 4.5 discusses modifying the null hypothesis to focus only on the
mean of the return distribution. Section 4.6 analyzes of the power of an
event study. Section 4.7 presents a nonparametric approach to event studies which eliminates the need for parametric structure. In some cases theory
provides hypotheses concerning the relation between the magnitude of the
event abnormal return and firm characteristics. In Section 4.8 we consider
cross-sectional regression models which are useful to investigate such hypotheses. Section 4.9 considers some further issues in event-study design
and Section 4.10 concludes.

4.1 Outline of an Event Study

At the outset it is useful to give a brief outline of the structure of an event
study. While there is no unique structure, the analysis can be viewed

as having seven steps:

1. *Event definition.* The initial task of conducting an event study is to define the event of interest and identify the period over which the security prices of the firms involved in this event will be examined—the *event window*. For example, if one is looking at the information content of an earnings announcement with daily data, the event will be the earnings announcement and the event window might be the one day of the announcement. In practice, the event window is often expanded to two days, the day of the announcement and the day after the announcement. This is done to capture the price effects of announcements which occur after the stock market closes on the announcement day. The period prior to or after the event may also be of interest and included separately in the analysis. For example, in the earnings-announcement case, the market may acquire information about the earnings prior to the actual announcement and one can investigate this possibility by examining pre-event returns.

2. *Selection criteria.* After identifying the event of interest, it is necessary to determine the selection criteria for the inclusion of a given firm in the study. The criteria may involve restrictions imposed by data availability such as listing on the NYSE or AMEX or may involve restrictions such as membership in a specific industry. At this stage it is useful to summarize some characteristics of the data sample (e.g., firm market capitalization, industry representation, distribution of events through time) and note any potential biases which may have been introduced through the sample selection.

3. *Normal and abnormal returns.* To appraise the event's impact we require a measure of the abnormal return. The abnormal return is the actual *ex post* return of the security over the event window minus the normal return of the firm over the event window. The normal return is defined as the return that would be expected if the event did not take place. For each firm i and event date τ we have

$$\epsilon_{it}^* = R_{it} - \mathrm{E}[R_{it} \mid X_t], \qquad (4.1.1)$$

where ϵ_{it}^*, R_{it}, and $\mathrm{E}(R_{it})$ are the abnormal, actual, and normal returns, respectively, for time period t. X_t is the conditioning information for the normal performance model. There are two common choices for modeling the normal return—the *constant-mean-return model* where X_t is a constant, and the *market model* where X_t is the market return. The constant-mean-return model, as the name implies, assumes that the mean return of a given security is constant through time. The market model assumes a stable linear relation between the market return and the security return.

4. *Estimation procedure.* Once a normal performance model has been selected, the parameters of the model must be estimated using a subset
of the data known as the *estimation window.* The most common choice,
when feasible, is to use the period prior to the event window for the estimation window. For example, in an event study using daily data and the
market model, the market-model parameters could be estimated over
the 120 days prior to the event. Generally the event period itself is not
included in the estimation period to prevent the event from influencing
the normal performance model parameter estimates.

5. *Testing procedure.* With the parameter estimates for the normal performance model, the abnormal returns can be calculated. Next, we need
to design the testing framework for the abnormal returns. Important
considerations are defining the null hypothesis and determining the
techniques for aggregating the abnormal returns of individual firms.

6. *Empirical results.* The presentation of the empirical results follows the
formulation of the econometric design. In addition to presenting the
basic empirical results, the presentation of diagnostics can be fruitful.
Occasionally, especially in studies with a limited number of event observations, the empirical results can be heavily influenced by one or two
firms. Knowledge of this is important for gauging the importance of
the results.

7. *Interpretation and conclusions.* Ideally the empirical results will lead to
insights about the mechanisms by which the event affects security prices.
Additional analysis may be included to distinguish between competing
explanations.

4.2 An Example of an Event Study

The Financial Accounting Standards Board (FASB) and the Securities Exchange Commission strive to set reporting regulations so that financial statements and related information releases are informative about the value of
the firm. In setting standards, the information content of the financial disclosures is of interest. Event studies provide an ideal tool for examining the
information content of the disclosures.

In this section we describe an example selected to illustrate the event-
study methodology. One particular type of disclosure—quarterly earnings
announcements—is considered. We investigate the information content of
quarterly earnings announcements for the thirty firms in the Dow Jones
Industrial Index over the five-year period from January 1989 to December
1993. These announcements correspond to the quarterly earnings for the
last quarter of 1988 through the third quarter of 1993. The five years of
data for thirty firms provide a total sample of 600 announcements. For

each firm and quarter, three pieces of information are compiled: the date of the announcement, the actual announced earnings, and a measure of the expected earnings. The source of the date of the announcement is Datastream, and the source of the actual earnings is Compustat.

If earnings announcements convey information to investors, one would expect the announcement impact on the market's valuation of the firm's equity to depend on the magnitude of the unexpected component of the announcement. Thus a measure of the deviation of the actual announced earnings from the market's prior expectation is required. We use the mean quarterly earnings forecast from the Institutional Brokers Estimate System (I/B/E/S) to proxy for the market's expectation of earnings. I/B/E/S compiles forecasts from analysts for a large number of companies and reports summary statistics each month. The mean forecast is taken from the last month of the quarter. For example, the mean third-quarter forecast from September 1990 is used as the measure of expected earnings for the third quarter of 1990.

In order to examine the impact of the earnings announcement on the value of the firm's equity, we assign each announcement to one of three categories: good news, no news, or bad news. We categorize each announcement using the deviation of the actual earnings from the expected earnings. If the actual exceeds expected by more than 2.5% the announcement is designated as good news, and if the actual is more than 2.5% less than expected the announcement is designated as bad news. Those announcements where the actual earnings is in the 5% range centered about the expected earnings are designated as no news. Of the 600 announcements, 189 are good news, 173 are no news, and the remaining 238 are bad news.

With the announcements categorized, the next step is to specify the sampling interval, event window, and estimation window that will be used to analyze the behavior of firms' equity returns. For this example we set the sampling interval to one day; thus daily stock returns are used. We choose a 41-day event window, comprised of 20 pre-event days, the event day, and 20 post-event days. For each announcement we use the 250-trading-day period prior to the event window as the estimation window. After we present the methodology of an event study, we use this example as an illustration.

4.3 Models for Measuring Normal Performance

A number of approaches are available to calculate the normal return of a given security. The approaches can be loosely grouped into two categories—statistical and economic. Models in the first category follow from statistical assumptions concerning the behavior of asset returns and do not depend on any economic arguments. In contrast, models in the second category rely on assumptions concerning investors' behavior and are not based solely on statistical assumptions. It should, however, be noted that to use economic models in practice it is necessary to add statistical assumptions. Thus the potential advantage of economic models is not the absence of statistical assumptions, but the opportunity to calculate more precise measures of the normal return using economic restrictions.

For the statistical models, it is conventional to assume that asset returns are jointly multivariate normal and independently and identically distributed through time. Formally, we have:

(A1) Let $\mathbf{R}_t$ be an $(N \times 1)$ vector of asset returns for calendar time period t. $\mathbf{R}_t$ is independently multivariate normally distributed with mean $\boldsymbol{\mu}$ and covariance matrix $\boldsymbol{\Omega}$ for all t.

This distributional assumption is sufficient for the constant-mean-return model and the market model to be correctly specified and permits the development of exact finite-sample distributional results for the estimators and statistics. Inferences using the normal return models are robust to deviations from the assumption. Further, we can explicitly accommodate deviations using a generalized method of moments framework.

4.3.1 Constant-Mean-Return Model

Let μ_i, the ith element of $\boldsymbol{\mu}$, be the mean return for asset i. Then the constant-mean-return model is

$$R_{it} = \mu_i + \xi_{it} \tag{4.3.1}$$
$$\mathrm{E}[\xi_{it}] = 0 \qquad \mathrm{Var}[\xi_{it}] = \sigma_{\xi_i}^2,$$

where R_{it}, the ith element of $\mathbf{R}_t$, is the period-t return on security i, ξ_{it} is the disturbance term, and $\sigma_{\xi_i}^2$ is the (i, i) element of $\boldsymbol{\Omega}$.

Although the constant-mean-return model is perhaps the simplest model, Brown and Warner (1980, 1985) find it often yields results similar to those of more sophisticated models. This lack of sensitivity to the model choice can be attributed to the fact that the variance of the abnormal return is frequently not reduced much by choosing a more sophisticated model. When using daily data the model is typically applied to nominal returns. With monthly data the model can be applied to real returns or excess returns (the return in excess of the nominal riskfree return generally measured using the US Treasury bill) as well as nominal returns.

4.3.2 Market Model

The market model is a statistical model which relates the return of any given security to the return of the market portfolio. The model's linear specification follows from the assumed joint normality of asset returns.[4] For any security i we have

$$R_{it} = \alpha_i + \beta_i R_{mt} + \epsilon_{it} \qquad (4.3.2)$$
$$\mathrm{E}[\epsilon_{it}] = 0 \qquad \mathrm{Var}[\epsilon_{it}] = \sigma^2_{\epsilon_i},$$

where R_{it} and R_{mt} are the period-t returns on security i and the market portfolio, respectively, and ϵ_{it} is the zero mean disturbance term. α_i, β_i, and $\sigma^2_{\epsilon_i}$ are the parameters of the market model. In applications a broad-based stock index is used for the market portfolio, with the S&P500 index, the CRSP value-weighted index, and the CRSP equal-weighted index being popular choices.

The market model represents a potential improvement over the constant-mean-return model. By removing the portion of the return that is related to variation in the market's return, the variance of the abnormal return is reduced. This can lead to increased ability to detect event effects. The benefit from using the market model will depend upon the R^2 of the market-model regression. The higher the R^2, the greater is the variance reduction of the abnormal return, and the larger is the gain. See Section 4.4.4 for more discussion of this point.

4.3.3 Other Statistical Models

A number of other statistical models have been proposed for modeling the normal return. A general type of statistical model is the *factor model.* Factor models potentially provide the benefit of reducing the variance of the abnormal return by explaining more of the variation in the normal return. Typically the factors are portfolios of traded securities. The market model is an example of a one-factor model, but in a multifactor model one might include industry indexes in addition to the market. Sharpe (1970) and Sharpe, Alexander, and Bailey (1995) discuss index models with factors based on industry classification. Another variant of a factor model is a procedure which calculates the abnormal return by taking the difference between the actual return and a portfolio of firms of similar size, where size is measured by market value of equity. In this approach typically ten size groups are considered and the loading on the size portfolios is restricted

---

[4]The specification actually requires the asset weights in the market portfolio to remain constant. However, changes over time in the market portfolio weights are small enough that they have little effect on empirical work.

to unity. This procedure implicitly assumes that expected return is directly related to the market value of equity.

In practice the gains from employing multifactor models for event studies are limited. The reason for this is that the marginal explanatory power of additional factors beyond the market factor is small, and hence there is little reduction in the variance of the abnormal return. The variance reduction will typically be greatest in cases where the sample firms have a common characteristic, for example they are all members of one industry or they are all firms concentrated in one market capitalization group. In these cases the use of a multifactor model warrants consideration.

Sometimes limited data availability may dictate the use of a restricted model such as the *market-adjusted-return model*. For some events it is not feasible to have a pre-event estimation period for the normal model parameters, and a market-adjusted abnormal return is used. The market-adjusted-return model can be viewed as a restricted market model with α_i constrained to be 0 and β_i constrained to be 1. Since the model coefficients are prespecified, an estimation period is not required to obtain parameter estimates. This model is often used to study the underpricing of initial public offerings.[5] A general recommendation is to use such restricted models only as a last resort, and to keep in mind that biases may arise if the restrictions are false.

4.3.4 Economic Models

Economic models restrict the parameters of statistical models to provide more constrained normal return models. Two common economic models which provide restrictions are the Capital Asset Pricing Model (CAPM) and exact versions of the Arbitrage Pricing Theory (APT). The CAPM, due to Sharpe (1964) and Lintner (1965b), is an equilibrium theory where the expected return of a given asset is a linear function of its covariance with the return of the market portfolio. The APT, due to Ross (1976), is an asset pricing theory where in the absence of asymptotic arbitrage the expected return of a given asset is determined by its covariances with multiple factors. Chapters 5 and 6 provide extensive treatments of these two theories.

The Capital Asset Pricing Model was commonly used in event studies during the 1970s. During the last ten years, however, deviations from the CAPM have been discovered, and this casts doubt on the validity of the restrictions imposed by the CAPM on the market model. Since these restrictions can be relaxed at little cost by using the market model, the use of the CAPM in event studies has almost ceased.

Some studies have used multifactor normal performance models motivated by the Arbitrage Pricing Theory. The APT can be made to fit the

---

[5]See Ritter (1990) for an example.

Time Line:

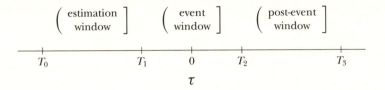

Figure 4.1. *Time Line for an Event Study*

cross-section of mean returns, as shown by Fama and French (1996a) and others, so a properly chosen APT model does not impose false restrictions on mean returns. On the other hand the use of the APT complicates the implementation of an event study and has little practical advantage relative to the unrestricted market model. See, for example, Brown and Weinstein (1985). There seems to be no good reason to use an economic model rather than a statistical model in an event study.

4.4 Measuring and Analyzing Abnormal Returns

In this section we consider the problem of measuring and analyzing abnormal returns. We use the market model as the normal performance return model, but the analysis is virtually identical for the constant-mean-return model.

We first define some notation. We index returns in event time using τ. Defining $\tau = 0$ as the event date, $\tau = T_1 + 1$ to $\tau = T_2$ represents the event window, and $\tau = T_0 + 1$ to $\tau = T_1$ constitutes the estimation window. Let $L_1 = T_1 - T_0$ and $L_2 = T_2 - T_1$ be the length of the estimation window and the event window, respectively. If the event being considered is an announcement on a given date then $T_2 = T_1 + 1$ and $L_2 = 1$. If applicable, the post-event window will be from $\tau = T_2 + 1$ to $\tau = T_3$ and its length is $L_3 = T_3 - T_2$. The timing sequence is illustrated on the time line in Figure 4.1.

We interpret the abnormal return over the event window as a measure of the impact of the event on the value of the firm (or its equity). Thus, the methodology implicitly assumes that the event is exogenous with respect to the change in market value of the security. In other words, the revision in value of the firm is caused by the event. In most cases this methodology is appropriate, but there are exceptions. There are examples where an event is triggered by the change in the market value of a security, in which case the event is endogenous. For these cases, the usual interpretation will be incorrect.

It is typical for the estimation window and the event window not to overlap. This design provides estimators for the parameters of the normal return model which are not influenced by the event-related returns. Including the event window in the estimation of the normal model parameters could lead to the event returns having a large influence on the normal return measure. In this situation both the normal returns and the abnormal returns would reflect the impact of the event. This would be problematic since the methodology is built around the assumption that the event impact is captured by the abnormal returns. In Section 4.5 we consider expanding the null hypothesis to accommodate changes in the risk of a firm around the event. In this case an estimation framework which uses the event window returns will be required.

4.4.1 Estimation of the Market Model

Recall that the market model for security i and observation τ in event time is

$$R_{i\tau} = \alpha_i + \beta_i R_{m\tau} + \epsilon_{i\tau}. \tag{4.4.1}$$

The estimation-window observations can be expressed as a regression system,

$$\mathbf{R}_i = \mathbf{X}_i \boldsymbol{\theta}_i + \boldsymbol{\epsilon}_i, \tag{4.4.2}$$

where $\mathbf{R}_i = [R_{iT_0+1} \cdots R_{iT_1}]'$ is an $(L_1 \times 1)$ vector of estimation-window returns, $\mathbf{X}_i = [\boldsymbol{\iota}\ \mathbf{R}_m]$ is an $(L_1 \times 2)$ matrix with a vector of ones in the first column and the vector of market return observations $\mathbf{R}_m = [R_{mT_0+1} \cdots R_{mT_1}]'$ in the second column, and $\boldsymbol{\theta}_i = [\alpha_i\ \beta_i]'$ is the (2×1) parameter vector. $\mathbf{X}$ has a subscript because the estimation window may have timing that is specific to firm i. Under general conditions ordinary least squares (OLS) is a consistent estimation procedure for the market-model parameters. Further, given the assumptions of Section 4.3, OLS is efficient. The OLS estimators of the market-model parameters using an estimation window of L_1 observations are

$$\hat{\boldsymbol{\theta}}_i = (\mathbf{X}_i'\mathbf{X}_i)^{-1}\mathbf{X}_i'\mathbf{R}_i \tag{4.4.3}$$

$$\hat{\sigma}^2_{\epsilon_i} = \frac{1}{L_1 - 2}\hat{\boldsymbol{\epsilon}}_i'\hat{\boldsymbol{\epsilon}}_i \tag{4.4.4}$$

$$\hat{\boldsymbol{\epsilon}}_i = \mathbf{R}_i - \mathbf{X}_i\hat{\boldsymbol{\theta}}_i \tag{4.4.5}$$

$$\text{Var}[\hat{\boldsymbol{\theta}}_i] = (\mathbf{X}_i'\mathbf{X}_i)^{-1}\sigma^2_{\epsilon_i}. \tag{4.4.6}$$

We next show how to use these OLS estimators to measure the statistical properties of abnormal returns. First we consider the abnormal return properties of a given security and then we aggregate across securities.

4.4.2 Statistical Properties of Abnormal Returns

Given the market-model parameter estimates, we can measure and analyze the abnormal returns. Let $\hat{\epsilon}_i^*$ be the $(L_2 \times 1)$ sample vector of abnormal returns for firm i from the event window, $T_1 + 1$ to T_2. Then using the market model to measure the normal return and the OLS estimators from (4.4.3), we have for the abnormal return vector:

$$
\begin{aligned}
\hat{\epsilon}_i^* &= \mathbf{R}_i^* - \hat{\alpha}_i \iota - \hat{\beta}_i \mathbf{R}_m^* \\
&= \mathbf{R}_i^* - \mathbf{X}_i^* \hat{\theta}_i,
\end{aligned}
\tag{4.4.7}
$$

where $\mathbf{R}_i^* = [R_{iT_1+1} \cdots R_{iT_2}]'$ is an $(L_2 \times 1)$ vector of event-window returns, $\mathbf{X}_i^* = [\iota \ \mathbf{R}_m^*]$ is an $(L_2 \times 2)$ matrix with a vector of ones in the first column and the vector of market return observations $\mathbf{R}_m^* = [R_{mT_1+1} \cdots R_{mT_2}]'$ in the second column, and $\hat{\theta}_i = [\hat{\alpha}_i \ \hat{\beta}_i]'$ is the (2×1) parameter vector estimate. Conditional on the market return over the event window, the abnormal returns will be jointly normally distributed with a zero conditional mean and conditional covariance matrix $\mathbf{V}_i$ as shown in (4.4.8) and (4.4.9), respectively.

$$
\begin{aligned}
\mathrm{E}[\hat{\epsilon}_i^* \mid \mathbf{X}_i^*] &= \mathrm{E}[\mathbf{R}_i^* - \mathbf{X}_i^* \hat{\theta}_i \mid \mathbf{X}_i^*] \\
&= \mathrm{E}[(\mathbf{R}_i^* - \mathbf{X}_i^* \theta_i) - \mathbf{X}_i^* (\hat{\theta}_i - \theta_i) \mid \mathbf{X}_i^*] \\
&= 0.
\end{aligned}
\tag{4.4.8}
$$

$$
\begin{aligned}
\mathbf{V}_i &= \mathrm{E}[\hat{\epsilon}_i^* \hat{\epsilon}_i^{*\prime} \mid \dot{\mathbf{X}}_i^*] \\
&= \mathrm{E}\big[[\epsilon_i^* - \mathbf{X}_i^* (\hat{\theta}_i - \theta_i)][\epsilon_i^* - \mathbf{X}_i^* (\hat{\theta}_i - \theta_i)]' \mid \mathbf{X}_i^*\big] \\
&= \mathrm{E}[\epsilon_i^* \epsilon_i^{*\prime} - \epsilon_i^* (\hat{\theta}_i - \theta_i)' \mathbf{X}_i^{*\prime} - \mathbf{X}_i^* (\hat{\theta}_i - \theta_i) \epsilon_i^{*\prime} \\
&\qquad + \mathbf{X}_i^* (\hat{\theta}_i - \theta_i)(\hat{\theta}_i - \theta_i)' \mathbf{X}_i^{*\prime} \mid \mathbf{X}_i^*] \\
&= \mathbf{I} \sigma_{\epsilon_i}^2 + \mathbf{X}_i^* (\mathbf{X}_i' \mathbf{X}_i)^{-1} \mathbf{X}_i^{*\prime} \sigma_{\epsilon_i}^2.
\end{aligned}
\tag{4.4.9}
$$

$\mathbf{I}$ is the $(L_2 \times L_2)$ identity matrix.

From (4.4.8) we see that the abnormal return vector, with an expectation of zero, is unbiased. The covariance matrix of the abnormal return vector from (4.4.9) has two parts. The first term in the sum is the variance due to the future disturbances and the second term is the additional variance due to the sampling error in $\hat{\theta}_i$. This sampling error, which is common for all the elements of the abnormal return vector, will lead to serial correlation of the abnormal returns despite the fact that the true disturbances are independent through time. As the length of the estimation window L_1 becomes large, the second term will approach zero as the sampling error of the parameters vanishes, and the abnormal returns across time periods will become independent asymptotically.

Under the null hypothesis, H_0, that the given event has no impact on the mean or variance of returns, we can use (4.4.8) and (4.4.9) and the joint normality of the abnormal returns to draw inferences. Under H_0, for the vector of event-window sample abnormal returns we have

$$\hat{\epsilon}_i^* \sim \mathcal{N}(0, \mathbf{V}_i). \qquad (4.4.10)$$

Equation (4.4.10) gives us the distribution for any single abnormal return observation. We next build on this result and consider the aggregation of abnormal returns.

4.4.3 Aggregation of Abnormal Returns

The abnormal return observations must be aggregated in order to draw overall inferences for the event of interest. The aggregation is along two dimensions—through time and across securities. We will first consider aggregation through time for an individual security and then will consider aggregation both across securities and through time.

We introduce the cumulative abnormal return to accommodate multiple sampling intervals within the event window. Define $\text{CAR}_i(\tau_1, \tau_2)$ as the cumulative abnormal return for security i from τ_1 to τ_2 where $T_1 < \tau_1 \le \tau_2 \le T_2$. Let γ be an $(L_2 \times 1)$ vector with ones in positions $\tau_1 - T_1$ to $\tau_2 - T_1$ and zeroes elsewhere. Then we have

$$\widehat{\text{CAR}}_i(\tau_1, \tau_2) \equiv \gamma' \hat{\epsilon}_i^* \qquad (4.4.11)$$

$$\text{Var}[\widehat{\text{CAR}}_i(\tau_1, \tau_2)] = \sigma_i^2(\tau_1, \tau_2) = \gamma' \mathbf{V}_i \gamma. \qquad (4.4.12)$$

It follows from (4.4.10) that under H_0,

$$\widehat{\text{CAR}}_i(\tau_1, \tau_2) \sim \mathcal{N}(0, \sigma_i^2(\tau_1, \tau_2)). \qquad (4.4.13)$$

We can construct a test of H_0 for security i from (4.4.13) using the standardized cumulative abnormal return,

$$\widehat{\text{SCAR}}_i(\tau_1, \tau_2) = \frac{\widehat{\text{CAR}}_i(\tau_1, \tau_2)}{\hat{\sigma}_i(\tau_1, \tau_2)}, \qquad (4.4.14)$$

where $\hat{\sigma}_i^2(\tau_1, \tau_2)$ is calculated with $\hat{\sigma}_{\epsilon_i}^2$ from (4.4.4) substituted for $\sigma_{\epsilon_i}^2$. Under the null hypothesis the distribution of $\widehat{\text{SCAR}}_i(\tau_1, \tau_2)$ is Student t with $L_1 - 2$

degrees of freedom. From the properties of the Student t distribution, the expectation of $\widehat{\text{SCAR}}_i(\tau_1, \tau_2)$ is 0 and the variance is $(\frac{L_1-2}{L_1-4})$. For a large estimation window (for example, $L_1 > 30$), the distribution of $\widehat{\text{SCAR}}_i(\tau_1, \tau_2)$ will be well approximated by the standard normal.

The above result applies to a sample of one event and must be extended for the usual case where a sample of many event observations is aggregated. To aggregate across securities and through time, we assume that there is not any correlation across the abnormal returns of different securities. This will generally be the case if there is not any clustering, that is, there is not any overlap in the event windows of the included securities. The absence of any overlap and the maintained distributional assumptions imply that the abnormal returns and the cumulative abnormal returns will be independent across securities. Inferences with clustering will be discussed later.

The individual securities' abnormal returns can be averaged using $\hat{\epsilon}_i^*$ from (4.4.7). Given a sample of N events, defining $\bar{\epsilon}^*$ as the sample average of the N abnormal return vectors, we have

$$\bar{\epsilon}^* = \frac{1}{N} \sum_{i=1}^{N} \hat{\epsilon}_i^* \qquad (4.4.15)$$

$$\text{Var}\left[\bar{\epsilon}^*\right] = \mathbf{V} = \frac{1}{N^2} \sum_{i=1}^{N} \mathbf{V}_i. \qquad (4.4.16)$$

We can aggregate the elements of this average abnormal returns vector through time using the same approach as we did for an individual security's vector. Define $\overline{\text{CAR}}(\tau_1, \tau_2)$ as the cumulative average abnormal return from τ_1 to τ_2 where $T_1 < \tau_1 \leq \tau_2 \leq T_2$ and γ again represents an $(L_2 \times 1)$ vector with ones in positions $\tau_1 - T_1$ to $\tau_2 - T_1$ and zeroes elsewhere. For the cumulative average abnormal return we have

$$\overline{\text{CAR}}(\tau_1, \tau_2) \equiv \gamma'\bar{\epsilon}^* \qquad (4.4.17)$$

$$\text{Var}[\overline{\text{CAR}}(\tau_1, \tau_2)] = \bar{\sigma}^2(\tau_1, \tau_2) = \gamma'\mathbf{V}\gamma. \qquad (4.4.18)$$

Equivalently, to obtain $\overline{\text{CAR}}(\tau_1, \tau_2)$, we can aggregate using the sample cumulative abnormal return for each security i. For N events we have

$$\overline{\text{CAR}}(\tau_1, \tau_2) = \frac{1}{N} \sum_{i=1}^{N} \widehat{\text{CAR}}_i(\tau_1, \tau_2) \qquad (4.4.19)$$

$$\text{Var}\left[\overline{\text{CAR}}(\tau_1, \tau_2)\right] = \bar{\sigma}^2(\tau_1, \tau_2) = \frac{1}{N^2} \sum_{i=1}^{N} \sigma_i^2(\tau_1, \tau_2). \qquad (4.4.20)$$

In (4.4.16), (4.4.18), and (4.4.20) we use the assumption that the event windows of the N securities do not overlap to set the covariance terms to zero. Inferences about the cumulative abnormal returns can be drawn using

$$\overline{\text{CAR}}(\tau_1, \tau_2) \sim \mathcal{N}\left(0, \bar{\sigma}^2(\tau_1, \tau_2)\right), \tag{4.4.21}$$

since under the null hypothesis the expectation of the abnormal returns is zero. In practice, since $\bar{\sigma}^2(\tau_1, \tau_2)$ is unknown, we can use $\hat{\bar{\sigma}}^2(\tau_1, \tau_2) = \frac{1}{N^2} \sum_{i=1}^{N} \hat{\sigma}_i^2(\tau_1, \tau_2)$ as a consistent estimator and proceed to test H_0 using

$$J_1 = \frac{\overline{\text{CAR}}(\tau_1, \tau_2)}{\left[\hat{\bar{\sigma}}^2(\tau_1, \tau_2)\right]^{\frac{1}{2}}} \overset{a}{\sim} \mathcal{N}(0, 1). \tag{4.4.22}$$

This distributional result is for large samples of events and is not exact because an estimator of the variance appears in the denominator.

A second method of aggregation is to give equal weighting to the individual SCAR_i's. Defining $\overline{\text{SCAR}}(\tau_1, \tau_2)$ as the average over N securities from event time τ_1 to τ_2, we have

$$\overline{\text{SCAR}}(\tau_1, \tau_2) = \frac{1}{N} \sum_{i=1}^{N} \widehat{\text{SCAR}}_i(\tau_1, \tau_2). \tag{4.4.23}$$

Assuming that the event windows of the N securities do not overlap in calendar time, under H_0, $\overline{\text{SCAR}}(\tau_1, \tau_2)$ will be normally distributed in large samples with a mean of zero and variance $(\frac{L_1-2}{N(L_1-4)})$. We can test the null hypothesis using

$$J_2 = \left(\frac{N(L_1 - 4)}{L_1 - 2}\right)^{\frac{1}{2}} \overline{\text{SCAR}}(\tau_1, \tau_2) \overset{a}{\sim} \mathcal{N}(0, 1). \tag{4.4.24}$$

When doing an event study one will have to choose between using J_1 or J_2 for the test statistic. One would like to choose the statistic with higher power, and this will depend on the alternative hypothesis. If the true abnormal return is constant across securities then the better choice will give more weight to the securities with the lower abnormal return variance, which is what J_2 does. On the other hand if the true abnormal return is larger for securities with higher variance, then the better choice will give equal weight to the realized cumulative abnormal return of each security, which is what J_1 does. In most studies, the results are not likely to be sensitive to the choice of J_1 versus J_2 because the variance of the CAR is of a similar magnitude across securities.

4.4.4 Sensitivity to Normal Return Model

We have developed results using the market model as the normal return model. As previously noted, using the market model as opposed to the constant-mean-return model will lead to a reduction in the abnormal return variance. This point can be shown by comparing the abnormal return variances. For this illustration we take the normal return model parameters as given.

The variance of the abnormal return for the market model is

$$
\begin{aligned}
\sigma^2_{\epsilon_i} &= \mathrm{Var}[R_{it} - \alpha_i - \beta_i R_{mt}] \\
&= \mathrm{Var}[R_{it}] - \beta_i^2 \mathrm{Var}[R_{mt}] \\
&= (1 - R_i^2) \mathrm{Var}[R_{it}], \qquad (4.4.25)
\end{aligned}
$$

where R_i^2 is the R^2 of the market-model regression for security i.

For the constant-mean-return model, the variance of the abnormal return ξ_{it} is the variance of the unconditional return, $\mathrm{Var}[R_{it}]$, that is,

$$
\sigma^2_{\xi_i} = \mathrm{Var}[R_{it} - \mu_i] = \mathrm{Var}[R_{it}]. \qquad (4.4.26)
$$

Combining (4.4.25) and (4.4.26) we have

$$
\sigma^2_{\epsilon_i} = (1 - R_i^2) \sigma^2_{\xi_i}. \qquad (4.4.27)
$$

Since R_i^2 lies between zero and one, the variance of the abnormal return using the market model will be less than or equal to the abnormal return variance using the constant-mean-return model. This lower variance for the market model will carry over into all the aggregate abnormal return measures. As a result, using the market model can lead to more precise inferences. The gains will be greatest for a sample of securities with high market-model R^2 statistics.

In principle further increases in R^2 could be achieved by using a multi-factor model. In practice, however, the gains in R^2 from adding additional factors are usually small.

4.4.5 CARs for the Earnings-Announcement Example

The earnings-announcement example illustrates the use of sample abnormal returns and sample cumulative abnormal returns. Table 4.1 presents the abnormal returns averaged across the 30 firms as well as the averaged cumulative abnormal return for each of the three earnings news categories. Two normal return models are considered: the market model and, for comparison, the constant-mean-return model. Plots of the cumulative abnormal returns are also included, with the CARs from the market model in Figure 4.2a and the CARs from the constant-mean-return model in Figure 4.2b.

The results of this example are largely consistent with the existing literature on the information content of earnings. The evidence strongly

Table 4.1. *Abnormal returns for an event study of the information content of earnings announcements.*

Event Day	Market Model						Constant-Mean-Return Model					
	Good News		No News		Bad News		Good News		No News		Bad News	
	$\bar{\epsilon}^*$	CAR	$\bar{\epsilon}^*$	CAR	$\bar{\epsilon}^*$	CAR	$\bar{\epsilon}^*$	CAR	$\bar{\epsilon}^*$	CAR	$\bar{\epsilon}^*$	CAR
−20	.093	.093	.080	.080	−.107	−.107	.105	.105	.019	.019	−.077	−.077
−19	−.177	−.084	.018	.098	−.180	−.286	−.235	−.129	−.048	−.029	−.142	−.219
−18	.088	.004	.012	.110	.029	−.258	.069	−.060	−.086	−.115	−.043	−.262
−17	.024	.029	−.151	−.041	−.079	−.337	−.026	−.086	−.140	−.255	−.057	−.319
−16	−.018	.011	−.019	−.060	−.010	−.346	−.086	−.172	.039	−.216	−.075	−.394
−15	−.040	−.029	.013	−.047	−.054	−.401	−.183	−.355	.099	−.117	−.037	−.431
−14	.038	.008	.040	−.007	−.021	−.421	−.020	−.375	−.150	−.266	−.101	−.532
−13	.056	.064	−.057	−.065	.007	−.414	−.025	−.399	−.191	−.458	−.069	−.601
−12	.065	.129	.146	.081	−.090	−.504	.101	−.298	.133	−.325	−.106	−.707
−11	.069	.199	−.020	.061	−.088	−.592	.126	−.172	.006	−.319	−.169	−.876
−10	.028	.227	.025	.087	−.092	−.683	.134	−.038	.103	−.216	−.009	−.885
−9	.155	.382	.115	.202	−.040	−.724	.210	.172	.022	−.194	.011	−.874
−8	.057	.438	.070	.272	.072	−.652	.106	.278	.163	−.031	.135	−.738
−7	−.010	.428	−.106	.166	−.026	−.677	−.002	.277	.009	−.022	−.027	−.765
−6	.104	.532	.026	.192	−.013	−.690	.011	.288	−.029	−.051	.030	−.735
−5	.085	.616	−.085	.107	.164	−.527	.061	.349	−.068	−.120	.320	−.415
−4	.099	.715	.040	.147	−.139	−.666	.031	.379	.089	−.031	−.205	−.620
−3	.117	.832	.036	.183	.098	−.568	.067	.447	.013	−.018	.085	−.536
−2	.006	.838	.226	.409	−.112	−.680	.010	.456	.311	.294	−.256	−.791
−1	.164	1.001	−.168	.241	−.180	−.860	.198	.654	−.170	.124	−.227	−1.018
0	.965	1.966	−.091	.150	−.679	−1.539	1.034	1.688	−.164	−.040	−.643	−1.661
1	.251	2.217	−.008	.142	−.204	−1.743	.357	2.045	−.170	−.210	−.212	−1.873
2	−.014	2.203	.007	.148	.072	−1.672	−.013	2.033	.054	−.156	.078	−1.795
3	−.164	2.039	.042	.190	.083	−1.589	−.088	1.944	−.121	−.277	.146	−1.648
4	−.014	2.024	.000	.190	.106	−1.483	.041	1.985	.023	−.253	.149	−1.499
5	.135	2.160	−.038	.152	.194	−1.289	.248	2.233	−.003	−.256	.286	−1.214
6	−.052	2.107	−.302	−.150	.076	−1.213	−.035	2.198	−.319	−.575	.070	−1.143
7	.060	2.167	−.199	−.349	.120	−1.093	.017	2.215	−.112	−.687	.102	−1.041
8	.155	2.323	−.108	−.457	−.041	−1.134	.112	2.326	−.187	−.874	.056	−.986
9	−.008	2.315	−.146	−.603	−.069	−1.203	−.052	2.274	−.057	−.931	−.071	−1.056
10	.164	2.479	.082	−.521	.130	−1.073	.147	2.421	.203	−.728	.267	−.789
11	−.081	2.398	.040	−.481	−.009	−1.082	−.013	2.407	.045	−.683	.006	−.783
12	−.058	2.341	.246	−.235	−.038	−1.119	−.054	2.354	.299	−.384	.017	−.766
13	−.165	2.176	.014	−.222	.071	−1.048	−.246	2.107	−.067	−.451	.114	−.652
14	−.081	2.095	−.091	−.312	.019	−1.029	−.011	2.096	−.024	−.475	.089	−.564
15	−.007	2.088	−.001	−.314	−.043	−1.072	−.027	2.068	−.059	−.534	−.022	−.585
16	.065	2.153	−.020	−.334	−.086	−1.159	.103	2.171	−.046	−.580	−.084	−.670
17	.081	2.234	.017	−.317	−.050	−1.208	.066	2.237	−.098	−.677	−.054	−.724
18	.172	2.406	.054	−.263	.066	−1.142	.110	2.347	.021	−.656	−.071	−.795
19	−.043	2.363	.119	−.144	−.088	−1.230	−.055	2.292	.088	−.568	.026	−.769
20	.013	2.377	.094	−.050	−.028	−1.258	.019	2.311	.013	−.554	−.115	−.884

The sample consists of a total of 600 quarterly announcements for the thirty companies in the Dow Jones Industrial Index for the five-year period January 1989 to December 1993. Two models are considered for the normal returns, the market model using the CRSP value-weighted index and the constant-mean-return model. The announcements are categorized into three groups, good news, no news, and bad news. $\bar{\epsilon}^*$ is the sample average abnormal return for the specified day in event time and $\overline{\text{CAR}}$ is the sample average cumulative abnormal return for day −20 to the specified day. Event time is measured in days relative to the announcement date.

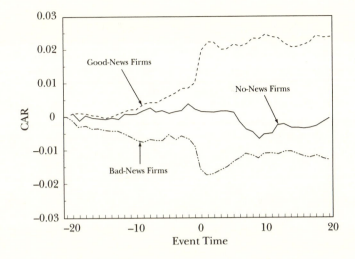

Figure 4.2a.   *Plot of Cumulative Market-Model Abnormal Return for Earning Announcements*

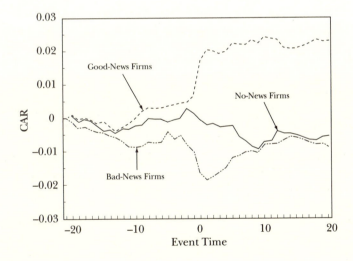

Figure 4.2b.   *Plot of Cumulative Constant-Mean-Return-Model Abnormal Return for Earning Announcements*

supports the hypothesis that earnings announcements do indeed convey information useful for the valuation of firms. Focusing on the announcement day (day zero) the sample average abnormal return for the good-news firm using the market model is 0.965%. Since the standard error of the one-day good-news average abnormal return is 0.104%, the value of J_1 is 9.28 and the null hypothesis that the event has no impact is strongly rejected. The story is the same for the bad-news firms. The event day sample abnormal return is −0.679%, with a standard error of 0.098%, leading to J_1 equal to −6.93 and again strong evidence against the null hypothesis. As would be expected, the abnormal return of the no-news firms is small at −0.091% and, with a standard error of 0.098%, is less than one standard error from zero. There is also some evidence of the announcement effect on day one. The average abnormal returns are 0.251% and −0.204% for the good-news and the bad-news firms respectively. Both these values are more than two standard errors from zero. The source of these day-one effects is likely to be that some of the earnings announcements are made on event day zero after the close of the stock market. In these cases the effects will be captured in the return on day one.

The conclusions using the abnormal returns from the constant-mean-return model are consistent with those from the market model. However, there is some loss of precision using the constant-mean-return model, as the variance of the average abnormal return increases for all three categories. When measuring abnormal returns with the constant-mean-return model the standard errors increase from 0.104% to 0.130% for good-news firms, from 0.098% to 0.124% for no-news firms, and from 0.098% to 0.131% for bad-news firms. These increases are to be expected when considering a sample of large firms such as those in the Dow Index since these stocks tend to have an important market component whose variability is eliminated using the market model.

The CAR plots show that to some extent the market gradually learns about the forthcoming announcement. The average CAR of the good-news firms gradually drifts up in days −20 to −1, and the average CAR of the bad-news firms gradually drifts down over this period. In the days after the announcement the CAR is relatively stable, as would be expected, although there does tend to be a slight (but statistically insignificant) increase for the bad-news firms in days two through eight.

4.4.6 Inferences with Clustering

In analyzing aggregated abnormal returns, we have thus far assumed that the abnormal returns on individual securities are uncorrelated in the cross section. This will generally be a reasonable assumption if the event windows of the included securities do not overlap in calendar time. The assumption allows us to calculate the variance of the aggregated sample cumulative abnormal returns without concern about covariances between individual sample CARs, since they are zero. However, when the event windows do overlap, the covariances between the abnormal returns may differ from zero, and the distributional results presented for the aggregated abnormal returns are not applicable. Bernard (1987) discusses some of the problems related to clustering.

When there is one event date in calendar time, clustering can be accommodated in two different ways. First, the abnormal returns can be aggregated into a portfolio dated using event time, and the security level analysis of Section 4.4 can be applied to the portfolio. This approach allows for cross correlation of the abnormal returns.

A second way to handle clustering is to analyze the abnormal returns without aggregation. One can test the null hypothesis that the event has no impact using unaggregated security-by-security data. The basic approach is an application of a multivariate regression model with dummy variables for the event date; it is closely related to the multivariate F-test of the CAPM presented in Chapter 5. The approach is developed in the papers of Schipper and Thompson (1983, 1985), Malatesta and Thompson (1985), and Collins and Dent (1984). It has some advantages relative to the portfolio approach. First, it can accommodate an alternative hypothesis where some of the firms have positive abnormal returns and some of the firms have negative abnormal returns. Second, it can handle cases where there is partial clustering, that is, where the event date is not the same across firms but there is overlap in the event windows. This approach also has some drawbacks, however. In many cases the test statistic has poor finite-sample properties, and often it has little power against economically reasonable alternatives.

4.5 Modifying the Null Hypothesis

Thus far we have focused on a single null hypothesis—that the given event has no impact on the behavior of security returns. With this null hypothesis either a mean effect or a variance effect represents a violation. However, in some applications we may be interested in testing only for a mean effect. In these cases, we need to expand the null hypothesis to allow for changing (usually increasing) variances.

To accomplish this, we need to eliminate any reliance on past returns in estimating the variance of the aggregated cumulative abnormal returns. Instead, we use the cross section of cumulative abnormal returns to form an estimator of the variance. Boehmer, Musumeci, and Poulsen (1991) discuss this methodology, which is best applied using the constant-mean-return model to measure the abnormal return.

The cross-sectional approach to estimating the variance can be applied to both the average cumulative abnormal return $(\overline{CAR}(\tau_1, \tau_2))$ and the average standardized cumulative abnormal return $(\overline{SCAR}(\tau_1, \tau_2))$. Using the cross section to form estimators of the variances we have

$$\widehat{\text{Var}}\big[\overline{\text{CAR}}(\tau_1, \tau_2)\big] \;=\; \frac{1}{N^2} \sum_{i=1}^{N} \big(\text{CAR}_i(\tau_1, \tau_2) - \overline{\text{CAR}}(\tau_1, \tau_2)\big)^2 \qquad (4.5.1)$$

$$\widehat{\text{Var}}\big[\overline{\text{SCAR}}(\tau_1, \tau_2)\big] \;=\; \frac{1}{N^2} \sum_{i=1}^{N} \big(\text{SCAR}_i(\tau_1, \tau_2) - \overline{\text{SCAR}}(\tau_1, \tau_2)\big)^2. \qquad (4.5.2)$$

For these estimators of the variances to be consistent we require the abnormal returns to be uncorrelated in the cross section. An absence of clustering is sufficient for this requirement. Note that cross-sectional homoskedasticity is not required for consistency. Given these variance estimators, the null hypothesis that the cumulative abnormal returns are zero can then be tested using large sample theory given the consistent estimators of the variances in (4.5.2) and (4.5.1).

One may also be interested in the impact of an event on the risk of a firm. The relevant measure of risk must be defined before this issue can be addressed. One choice as a risk measure is the market-model beta as implied by the Capital Asset Pricing Model. Given this choice, the market model can be formulated to allow the beta to change over the event window and the stability of the beta can be examined. See Kane and Unal (1988) for an application of this idea.

4.6 Analysis of Power

To interpret an event study, we need to know what is our ability to detect the presence of a nonzero abnormal return. In this section we ask what is the likelihood that an event-study test rejects the null hypothesis for a given level of abnormal return associated with an event, that is, we evaluate the power of the test.

We consider a two-sided test of the null hypothesis using the cumulative-abnormal-return-based statistic J_1 from (4.4.22). We assume that the abnormal returns are uncorrelated across securities; thus the variance of $\overline{\text{CAR}}$ is $\bar{\sigma}^2(\tau_1, \tau_2)$, where $\bar{\sigma}^2(\tau_1, \tau_2) = 1/N^2 \sum_{i=1}^{N} \sigma_i^2(\tau_1, \tau_2)$ and N is the sample size. Under the null hypothesis the distribution of J_1 is standard normal. For a two-sided test of size α we reject the null hypothesis if $J_1 < \Phi^{-1}(\alpha/2)$ or if $J_1 > \Phi^{-1}(1-\alpha/2)$ where $\Phi(\cdot)$ is the standard normal cumulative distribution function (CDF).

Given an alternative hypothesis H_A and the CDF of J_1 for this hypothesis, we can tabulate the power of a test of size α using

$$
\begin{aligned}
P(\alpha, H_A) \;=\;\; & \Pr\left(J_1 \; < \; \Phi^{-1}\left(\tfrac{\alpha}{2}\right) \;\mid\; H_A\right) \\
& + \Pr\left(J_1 \; > \; \Phi^{-1}\left(1 - \tfrac{\alpha}{2}\right) \;\mid\; H_A\right).
\end{aligned}
\qquad (4.6.1)
$$

With this framework in place, we need to posit specific alternative hypotheses. Alternatives are constructed to be consistent with event studies using data sampled at a daily interval. We build eight alternative hypotheses using four levels of abnormal returns, 0.5%, 1.0%, 1.5%, and 2.0%, and two levels for the average variance of the cumulative abnormal return of a given security over the sampling interval, 0.0004 and 0.0016. These variances correspond to standard deviations of 2% and 4%, respectively. The sample size, that is the number of securities for which the event occurs, is varied from 1 to 200. We document the power for a test with a size of 5% ($\alpha = 0.05$) giving values of -1.96 and 1.96 for $\Phi^{-1}(\alpha/2)$ and $\Phi^{-1}(1-\alpha/2)$, respectively. In applications, of course, the power of the test should be considered when selecting the size.

The power results are presented in Table 4.2 and are plotted in Figures 4.3a and 4.3b. The results in the left panel of Table 4.2 and in Figure 4.3a are for the case where the average variance is 0.0004, corresponding to a standard deviation of 2%. This is an appropriate value for an event which does not lead to increased variance and can be examined using a one-day event window. Such a case is likely to give the event-study methodology its highest power. The results illustrate that when the abnormal return is only 0.5% the power can be low. For example, with a sample size of 20 the power of a 5% test is only 0.20. One needs a sample of over 60 firms before the power reaches 0.50. However, for a given sample size, increases in power are substantial when the abnormal return is larger. For example, when the abnormal return is 2.0% the power of a 5% test with 20 firms is almost 1.00 with a value of 0.99. The general results for a variance of 0.0004 is that when the abnormal return is larger than 1% the power is quite high even for small sample sizes. When the abnormal return is small a larger sample size is necessary to achieve high power.

In the right panel of Table 4.2 and in Figure 4.3b the power results are presented for the case where the average variance of the cumulative abnormal return is 0.0016, corresponding to a standard deviation of 4%. This case corresponds roughly to either a multi-day event window or to a one-day event window with the event leading to increased variance which is accommodated as part of the null hypothesis. Here we see a dramatic decline in the power of a 5% test. When the CAR is 0.5% the power is only 0.09 with 20 firms and only 0.42 with a sample of 200 firms. This magnitude

Table 4.2. *Power of event-study test statistic* J_1 *to reject the null hypothesis that the abnormal return is zero.*

Sample Size	Abnormal Return				Abnormal Return			
	0.5%	1.0%	1.5%	2.0%	0.5%	1.0%	1.5%	2.0%
	$\sigma = 2\%$				$\sigma = 4\%$			
1	0.06	0.08	0.12	0.17	0.05	0.06	0.07	0.08
2	0.06	0.11	0.19	0.29	0.05	0.06	0.08	0.11
3	0.07	0.14	0.25	0.41	0.06	0.07	0.10	0.14
4	0.08	0.17	0.32	0.52	0.06	0.08	0.12	0.17
5	0.09	0.20	0.39	0.61	0.06	0.09	0.13	0.20
6	0.09	0.23	0.45	0.69	0.06	0.09	0.15	0.23
7	0.10	0.26	0.51	0.75	0.06	0.10	0.17	0.26
8	0.11	0.29	0.56	0.81	0.06	0.11	0.19	0.29
9	0.12	0.32	0.61	0.85	0.07	0.12	0.20	0.32
10	0.12	0.35	0.66	0.89	0.07	0.12	0.22	0.35
11	0.13	0.38	0.70	0.91	0.07	0.13	0.24	0.38
12	0.14	0.41	0.74	0.93	0.07	0.14	0.25	0.41
13	0.15	0.44	0.77	0.95	0.07	0.15	0.27	0.44
14	0.15	0.46	0.80	0.96	0.08	0.15	0.29	0.46
15	0.16	0.49	0.83	0.97	0.08	0.16	0.31	0.49
16	0.17	0.52	0.85	0.98	0.08	0.17	0.32	0.52
17	0.18	0.54	0.87	0.98	0.08	0.18	0.34	0.54
18	0.19	0.56	0.89	0.99	0.08	0.19	0.36	0.56
19	0.19	0.59	0.90	0.99	0.08	0.19	0.37	0.59
20	0.20	0.61	0.92	0.99	0.09	0.20	0.39	0.61
25	0.24	0.71	0.96	1.00	0.10	0.24	0.47	0.71
30	0.28	0.78	0.98	1.00	0.11	0.28	0.54	0.78
35	0.32	0.84	0.99	1.00	0.11	0.32	0.60	0.84
40	0.35	0.89	1.00	1.00	0.12	0.35	0.66	0.89
45	0.39	0.92	1.00	1.00	0.13	0.39	0.71	0.92
50	0.42	0.94	1.00	1.00	0.14	0.42	0.76	0.94
60	0.49	0.97	1.00	1.00	0.16	0.49	0.83	0.97
70	0.55	0.99	1.00	1.00	0.18	0.55	0.88	0.99
80	0.61	0.99	1.00	1.00	0.20	0.61	0.92	0.99
90	0.66	1.00	1.00	1.00	0.22	0.66	0.94	1.00
100	0.71	1.00	1.00	1.00	0.24	0.71	0.96	1.00
120	0.78	1.00	1.00	1.00	0.28	0.78	0.98	1.00
140	0.84	1.00	1.00	1.00	0.32	0.84	0.99	1.00
160	0.89	1.00	1.00	1.00	0.35	0.89	1.00	1.00
180	0.92	1.00	1.00	1.00	0.39	0.92	1.00	1.00
200	0.94	1.00	1.00	1.00	0.42	0.94	1.00	1.00

The power is reported for a test with a size of 5%. The sample size is the number of event observations included in the study, and σ is the square root of the average variance of the abnormal return across firms.

of abnormal return is difficult to detect with the larger variance of 0.0016. In contrast, when the CAR is as large as 1.5% or 2.0% the 5% test still has reasonable power. For example, when the abnormal return is 1.5% and

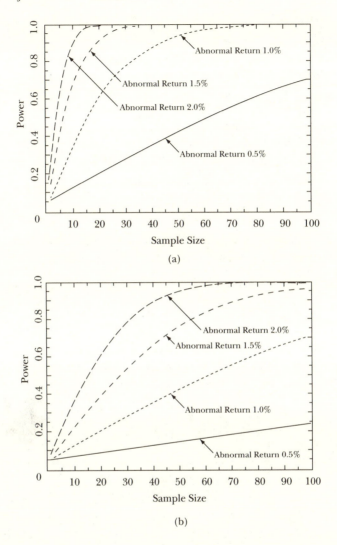

Figure 4.3. *Power of Event-Study Test Statistic J_1 to Reject the Null Hypothesis that the Abnormal Return Is Zero, When the Square Root of the Average Variance of the Abnormal Return Across Firms is (a) 2% and (b) 4%*

there is a sample size of 30, the power is 0.54. Generally if the abnormal return is large one will have little difficulty rejecting the null hypothesis of no abnormal return.

We have calculated power analytically using distributional assumptions. If these distributional assumptions are inappropriate then our power calculations may be inaccurate. However, Brown and Warner (1985) explore this issue and find that the analytical computations and the empirical power are very close.

It is difficult to reach general conclusions concerning the the ability of event-study methodology to detect nonzero abnormal returns. When conducting an event study it is necessary to evaluate the power given the parameters and objectives of the study. If the power seems sufficient then one can proceed, otherwise one should search for ways of increasing the power. This can be done by increasing the sample size, shortening the event window, or by developing more specific predictions of the null hypothesis.

4.7 Nonparametric Tests

The methods discussed to this point are parametric in nature, in that specific assumptions have been made about the distribution of abnormal returns. Alternative nonparametric approaches are available which are free of specific assumptions concerning the distribution of returns. In this section we discuss two common nonparametric tests for event studies, the sign test and the rank test.

The sign test, which is based on the sign of the abnormal return, requires that the abnormal returns (or more generally cumulative abnormal returns) are independent across securities and that the expected proportion of positive abnormal returns under the null hypothesis is 0.5. The basis of the test is that under the null hypothesis it is equally probable that the CAR will be positive or negative. If, for example, the alternative hypothesis is that there is a positive abnormal return associated with a given event, the null hypothesis is $H_0 \colon p \leq 0.5$ and the alternative is $H_A \colon p > 0.5$ where $p = \Pr(\text{CAR}_i \geq 0.0)$. To calculate the test statistic we need the number of cases where the abnormal return is positive, N^+, and the total number of cases, N. Letting J_3 be the test statistic, then asymptotically as N increases we have

$$ J_3 \; = \; \left[\frac{N^+}{N} - 0.5 \right] \frac{N^{1/2}}{0.5} \; \sim \; \mathcal{N}(0, 1) \, . $$

For a test of size $(1 - \alpha)$, H_0 is rejected if $J_3 > \Phi^{-1}(\alpha)$.

A weakness of the sign test is that it may not be well specified if the distribution of abnormal returns is skewed, as can be the case with daily data. With skewed abnormal returns, the expected proportion of positive abnormal returns can differ from one half even under the null hypothesis. In response to this possible shortcoming, Corrado (1989) proposes a nonparametric rank test for abnormal performance in event studies. We briefly describe his test of the null hypothesis that there is no abnormal return on event day zero. The framework can be easily altered for events occurring over multiple days.

Drawing on notation previously introduced, consider a sample of L_2 abnormal returns for each of N securities. To implement the rank test it is necessary for each security to rank the abnormal returns from 1 to L_2. Define $K_{i\tau}$ as the rank of the abnormal return of security i for event time period τ. Recall that τ ranges from $T_1 + 1$ to T_2 and $\tau = 0$ is the event day. The rank test uses the fact that the expected rank under the null hypothesis is $\frac{L_2+1}{2}$. The test statistic for the null hypothesis of no abnormal return on event day zero is:

$$J_4 = \frac{1}{N} \sum_{i=1}^{N} \left(K_{i0} - \frac{L_2 + 1}{2} \right) / s(L_2) \tag{4.7.1}$$

$$s(L_2) = \sqrt{\frac{1}{L_2} \sum_{\tau=T_1+1}^{T_2} \left(\frac{1}{N} \sum_{i=1}^{N} \left(K_{i\tau} - \frac{L_2 + 1}{2} \right) \right)^2} \tag{4.7.2}$$

Tests of the null hypothesis can be implemented using the result that the asymptotic null distribution of J_4 is standard normal. Corrado (1989) gives further details.

Typically, these nonparametric tests are not used in isolation but in conjunction with their parametric counterparts. The nonparametric tests enable one to check the robustness of conclusions based on parametric tests. Such a check can be worthwhile as illustrated by the work of Campbell and Wasley (1993). They find that for daily returns on NASDAQ stocks the nonparametric rank test provides more reliable inferences than do the standard parametric tests.

4.8 Cross-Sectional Models

Theoretical models often suggest that there should be an association between the magnitude of abnormal returns and characteristics specific to the event observation. To investigate this association, an appropriate tool is a cross-sectional regression of abnormal returns on the characteristics of interest. To set up the model, define $\mathbf{y}$ as an ($N \times 1$) vector of cumulative abnormal return observations and $\mathbf{X}$ as an ($N \times K$) matrix of characteristics. The first column of $\mathbf{X}$ is a vector of ones and each of the remaining ($K - 1$) columns is a vector consisting of the characteristic for each event observation. Then, for the model, we have the regression equation

$$\mathbf{y} = \mathbf{X}\theta + \eta, \tag{4.8.1}$$

where θ is the ($K \times 1$) coefficient vector and η is the ($N \times 1$) disturbance vector. Assuming $E[\mathbf{X}'\eta] = 0$, we can consistently estimate θ using OLS.

For the *OLS* estimator we have

$$\hat{\theta} = (\mathbf{X'X})^{-1}\mathbf{X'y}. \tag{4.8.2}$$

Assuming the elements of η are cross-sectionally uncorrelated and homoskedastic, inferences can be derived using the usual OLS standard errors. Defining σ_η^2 as the variance of the elements of η we have

$$\text{Var}[\hat{\theta}] = (\mathbf{X'X})^{-1}\sigma_\eta^2. \tag{4.8.3}$$

Using the unbiased estimator for σ_η^2,

$$\hat{\sigma}_\eta^2 = \frac{1}{(N-K)}\hat{\eta}'\hat{\eta}, \tag{4.8.4}$$

where $\hat{\eta} = \mathbf{y} - \mathbf{X}\hat{\theta}$, we can construct t-statistics to assess the statistical significance of the elements of $\hat{\theta}$. Alternatively, without assuming homoskedasticity, we can construct heteroskedasticity-consistent z-statistics using

$$\text{Var}[\hat{\theta}] = \frac{1}{N}(\mathbf{X'X})^{-1}\left[\sum_{i=1}^{N}\mathbf{x}_i\mathbf{x}_i'\hat{\eta}_i^2\right](\mathbf{X'X})^{-1}, \tag{4.8.5}$$

where $\mathbf{x}_i'$ is the ith row of $\mathbf{X}$ and $\hat{\eta}_i$ is the ith element of $\hat{\eta}$. This expression for the standard errors can be derived using the Generalized Method of Moments framework in Section A.2 of the Appendix and also follows from the results of White (1980). The use of heteroskedasticity-consistent standard errors is advised since there is no reason to expect the residuals of (4.8.1) to be homoskedastic.

Asquith and Mullins (1986) provide an example of this approach. The two-day cumulative abnormal return for the announcement of an equity offering is regressed on the size of the offering as a percentage of the value of the total equity of the firm and on the cumulative abnormal return in the eleven months prior to the announcement month. They find that the magnitude of the (negative) abnormal return associated with the announcement of equity offerings is related to both these variables. Larger pre-event cumulative abnormal returns are associated with less negative abnormal returns, and larger offerings are associated with more negative abnormal returns. These findings are consistent with theoretical predictions which they discuss.

One must be careful in interpreting the results of the cross-sectional regression approach. In many situations, the event-window abnormal return will be related to firm characteristics not only through the valuation effects of the event but also through a relation between the firm characteristics and the extent to which the event is anticipated. This can happen when investors rationally use firm characteristics to forecast the likelihood of the event occurring. In these cases, a linear relation between the firm characteristics and the valuation effect of the event can be hidden. Malatesta and Thompson (1985) and Lanen and Thompson (1988) provide examples of this situation.

Technically, the relation between the firm characteristics and the degree of anticipation of the event introduces a selection bias. The assumption that the regression residual is uncorrelated with the regressors, $E[\mathbf{X}'\boldsymbol{\eta}] = 0$, breaks down and the OLS estimators are inconsistent. Consistent estimators can be derived by explicitly allowing for the selection bias. Acharya (1988, 1993) and Eckbo, Maksimovic, and Williams (1990) provide examples of this. Prabhala (1995) provides a good discussion of this problem and the possible solutions. He argues that, despite misspecification, under weak conditions, the OLS approach can be used for inferences and the t-statistics can be interpreted as lower bounds on the true significance level of the estimates.

4.9 Further Issues

A number of further issues often arise when conducting an event study. We discuss some of these in this section.

4.9.1 Role of the Sampling Interval

If the timing of an event is known precisely, then the ability to statistically identify the effect of the event will be higher for a shorter sampling interval. The increase results from reducing the variance of the abnormal return without changing the mean. We evaluate the empirical importance of this issue by comparing the analytical formula for the power of the test statistic J_1 with a daily sampling interval to the power with a weekly and a monthly interval. We assume that a week consists of five days and a month is 22 days. The variance of the abnormal return for an individual event observation is assumed to be $(4\%)^2$ on a daily basis and linear in time.

In Figure 4.4, we plot the power of the test of no event-effect against the alternative of an abnormal return of 1% for 1 to 200 securities. As one would expect given the analysis of Section 4.6, the decrease in power going from a daily interval to a monthly interval is severe. For example, with 50 securities the power for a 5% test using daily data is 0.94, whereas the power using weekly and monthly data is only 0.35 and 0.12, respectively. The clear message is that there is a substantial payoff in terms of increased power from reducing the length of the event window. Morse (1984) presents detailed analysis of the choice of daily versus monthly data and draws the same conclusion.

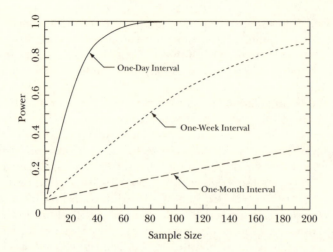

Figure 4.4. *Power of Event-Study Test Statistic J_1 to Reject the Null Hypothesis that the Abnormal Return is Zero, for Different Sampling Intervals, When the Square Root of the Average Variance of the Abnormal Return Across Firms Is 4% for the Daily Interval*

A sampling interval of one day is not the shortest interval possible. With the increased availability of transaction data, recent studies have used observation intervals of duration shorter than one day. The use of intra-daily data involves some complications, however, of the sort discussed in Chapter 3, and so the net benefit of very short intervals is unclear. Barclay and Litzenberger (1988) discuss the use of intra-daily data in event studies.

4.9.2 Inferences with Event-Date Uncertainty

Thus far we have assumed that the event date can be identified with certainty. However, in some studies it may be difficult to identify the exact date. A common example is when collecting event dates from financial publications such as the *Wall Street Journal.* When the event announcement appears in the newspaper one can not be certain if the market was informed before the close of the market the prior trading day. If this is the case then the prior day is the event day; if not, then the current day is the event day. The usual method of handling this problem is to expand the event window to two days—day 0 and day +1. While there is a cost to expanding the event window, the results in Section 4.6 indicate that the power properties of two-day event windows are still good, suggesting that it is worth bearing the cost to avoid the risk of missing the event.

Ball and Torous (1988) investigate this issue. They develop a maximum-likelihood estimation procedure which accommodates event-date uncertainty and examine results of their explicit procedure versus the informal procedure of expanding the event window. The results indicate that the informal procedure works well and there is little to gain from the more elaborate estimation framework.

4.9.3 Possible Biases

Event studies are subject to a number of possible biases. Nonsynchronous trading can introduce a bias. The nontrading or nonsynchronous trading effect arises when prices are taken to be recorded at time intervals of one length when in fact they are recorded at time intervals of other possibly irregular lengths. For example, the daily prices of securities usually employed in event studies are generally "closing" prices, prices at which the last transaction in each of those securities occurred during the trading day. These closing prices generally do not occur at the same time each day, but by calling them "daily" prices, we have implicitly and incorrectly assumed that they are equally spaced at 24-hour intervals. As we showed in Section 3.1 of Chapter 3, this nontrading effect induces biases in the moments and co-moments of returns.

The influence of the nontrading effect on the variances and covariances of individual stocks and portfolios naturally feeds into a bias for the market-model beta. Scholes and Williams (1977) present a consistent estimator of beta in the presence of nontrading based on the assumption that the true return process is uncorrelated through time. They also present some empirical evidence showing the nontrading-adjusted beta estimates of thinly traded securities to be approximately 10 to 20% larger than the unadjusted estimates. However, for actively traded securities, the adjustments are generally small and unimportant.

Jain (1986) considers the influence of thin trading on the distribution of the abnormal returns from the market model with the beta estimated using the Scholes-Williams approach. He compares the distribution of these abnormal returns to the distribution of the abnormal returns using the usual OLS betas and finds that the differences are minimal. This suggests that in general the adjustment for thin trading is not important.

The statistical analysis of Sections 4.3, 4.4, and 4.5 is based on the assumption that returns are jointly normal and temporally IID. Departures from this assumption can lead to biases. The normality assumption is important for the exact finite-sample results. Without assuming normality, all results would be asymptotic. However, this is generally not a problem for event studies since the test statistics converge to their asymptotic distributions rather quickly. Brown and Warner (1985) discuss this issue.

There can also be an upward bias in cumulative abnormal returns when these are calculated in the usual way. The bias arises from the observation-by-observation rebalancing to equal weights implicit in the calculation of the aggregate cumulative abnormal return combined with the use of trans-action prices which can represent both the bid and the ask side of the market. Blume and Stambaugh (1983) analyze this bias and show that it can be important for studies using low-market-capitalization firms which have, in percentage terms, wide bid-ask spreads. In these cases the bias can be eliminated by considering cumulative abnormal returns that represent buy-and-hold strategies.

4.10 Conclusion

In closing, we briefly discuss examples of event-study successes and limita-tions. Perhaps the most successful applications have been in the area of corporate finance. Event studies dominate the empirical research in this area. Important examples include the wealth effects of mergers and acqui-sitions and the price effects of financing decisions by firms. Studies of these events typically focus on the abnormal return around the date of the first announcement.

In the 1960s there was a paucity of empirical evidence on the wealth effects of mergers and acquisitions. For example, Manne (1965) discusses the various arguments for and against mergers. At that time the debate cen-tered on the extent to which mergers should be regulated in order to foster competition in the product markets. Manne argues that mergers represent a natural outcome in an efficiently operating market for corporate control and consequently provide protection for shareholders. He downplays the importance of the argument that mergers reduce competition. At the con-clusion of his article Manne suggests that the two competing hypotheses for mergers could be separated by studying the price effects of the involved corporations. He hypothesizes that if mergers created market power one would observe price increases for both the target and acquirer. In contrast if the merger represented the acquiring corporation paying for control of the target, one would observe a price increase for the target only and not for the acquirer. However, at that time Manne concludes in reference to the price effects of mergers that "... no data are presently available on this subject."

Since that time an enormous body of empirical evidence on mergers and acquisitions has developed which is dominated by the use of event studies. The general result is that, given a successful takeover, the abnormal returns of the targets are large and positive and the abnormal returns of the acquirer are close to zero. Jarrell and Poulsen (1989) find that the average abnormal return for target shareholders exceeds 20% for a sample of 663 successful takeovers from 1960 to 1985. In contrast the abnormal return for acquirers is close to zero at 1.14%, and even negative at −1.10% in the 1980's.

Eckbo (1983) explicitly addresses the role of increased market power in explaining merger-related abnormal returns. He separates mergers of competing firms from other mergers and finds no evidence that the wealth effects for competing firms are different. Further, he finds no evidence that rivals of firms merging horizontally experience negative abnormal returns. From this he concludes that reduced competition in the product market is not an important explanation for merger gains. This leaves competition for corporate control a more likely explanation. Much additional empirical work in the area of mergers and acquisitions has been conducted. Jensen and Ruback (1983) and Jarrell, Brickley, and Netter (1988) provide detailed surveys of this work.

A number of robust results have been developed from event studies of financing decisions by corporations. When a corporation announces that it will raise capital in external markets there is on average a negative abnormal return. The magnitude of the abnormal return depends on the source of external financing. Asquith and Mullins (1986) study a sample of 266 firms announcing an equity issue in the period 1963 to 1981 and find that the two-day average abnormal return is −2.7%, while on a sample of 80 firms for the period 1972 to 1982 Mikkelson and Partch (1986) find that the two-day average abnormal return is −3.56%. In contrast, when firms decide to use straight debt financing, the average abnormal return is closer to zero. Mikkelson and Partch (1986) find the average abnormal return for debt issues to be −0.23% for a sample of 171 issues. Findings such as these provide the fuel for the development of new theories. For example, these external financing results motivate the pecking order theory of capital structure developed by Myers and Majluf (1984).

A major success related to those in the corporate finance area is the implicit acceptance of event-study methodology by the U.S. Supreme Court for determining materiality in insider trading cases and for determining appropriate disgorgement amounts in cases of fraud. This implicit acceptance in the 1988 Basic, Incorporated v. Levinson case and its importance for securities law is discussed in Mitchell and Netter (1994).

There have also been less successful applications of event-study methodology. An important characteristic of a successful event study is the ability to identify precisely the date of the event. In cases where the date is difficult to identify or the event is partially anticipated, event studies have been less useful. For example, the wealth effects of regulatory changes for affected entities can be difficult to detect using event-study methodology. The problem is that regulatory changes are often debated in the political arena over time and any accompanying wealth effects will be incorporated gradually into the value of a corporation as the probability of the change being adopted increases.

Dann and James (1982) discuss this issue in their study of the impact of deposit interest rate ceilings on thrift institutions. They look at changes in rate ceilings, but decide not to consider a change in 1973 because it was due to legislative action and hence was likely to have been anticipated by the market. Schipper and Thompson (1983, 1985) also encounter this problem in a study of merger-related regulations. They attempt to circumvent the problem of anticipated regulatory changes by identifying dates when the probability of a regulatory change increases or decreases. However, they find largely insignificant results, leaving open the possibility that the absence of distinct event dates accounts for the lack of wealth effects.

Much has been learned from the body of research that uses event-study methodology. Most generally, event studies have shown that, as we would expect in a rational marketplace, prices do respond to new information. We expect that event studies will continue to be a valuable and widely used tool in economics and finance.

Problems—Chapter 4

4.1   Show that when using the market model to measure abnormal returns, the sample abnormal returns from equation (4.4.7) are asymptotically independent as the length of the estimation window (L_1) increases to infinity.

4.2   You are given the following information for an event. Abnormal returns are sampled at an interval of one day. The event-window length is three days. The mean abnormal return over the event window is 0.3% per day. You have a sample of 50 event observations. The abnormal returns are independent across the event observations as well as across event days for a given event observation. For 25 of the event observations the daily standard deviation of the abnormal return is 3% and for the remaining 25 observations the daily standard deviation is 6%. Given this information, what would be the power of the test for an event study using the cumulative abnormal return test statistic in equation (4.4.22)? What would be the power using the standardized cumulative abnormal return test statistic in equation (4.4.24)? For the power calculations, assume the standard deviation of the abnormal returns is known.

4.3   What would be the answers to question 4.2 if the mean abnormal return is 0.6% per day for the 25 firms with the larger standard deviation?

5

The Capital Asset Pricing Model

ONE OF THE IMPORTANT PROBLEMS of modern financial economics is the quantification of the tradeoff between risk and expected return. Although common sense suggests that risky investments such as the stock market will generally yield higher returns than investments free of risk, it was only with the development of the Capital Asset Pricing Model (CAPM) that economists were able to quantify risk and the reward for bearing it. The CAPM implies that the expected return of an asset must be linearly related to the covariance of its return with the return of the market portfolio. In this chapter we discuss the econometric analysis of this model.

The chapter is organized as follows. In Section 5.1 we briefly review the CAPM. Section 5.2 presents some results from efficient-set mathematics, including those that are important for understanding the intuition of econometric tests of the CAPM. The methodology for estimation and testing is presented in Section 5.3. Some tests are based on large-sample statistical theory making the size of the test an issue, as we discuss in Section 5.4. Section 5.5 considers the power of the tests, and Section 5.6 considers testing with weaker distributional assumptions. Implementation issues are covered in Section 5.7, and Section 5.8 considers alternative approaches to testing based on cross-sectional regressions.

5.1 Review of the CAPM

Markowitz (1959) laid the groundwork for the CAPM. In this seminal research, he cast the investor's portfolio selection problem in terms of expected return and variance of return. He argued that investors would optimally hold a mean-variance efficient portfolio, that is, a portfolio with the highest expected return for a given level of variance. Sharpe (1964) and Lintner (1965b) built on Markowitz's work to develop economy-wide implications. They showed that if investors have homogeneous expectations and optimally hold mean-variance efficient portfolios then, in the absence of market frictions, the portfolio of all invested wealth, or the market portfolio, will itself be a mean-variance efficient portfolio. The usual CAPM equation is a direct implication of the mean-variance efficiency of the market portfolio.

The Sharpe and Lintner derivations of the CAPM assume the existence of lending and borrowing at a riskfree rate of interest. For this version of the CAPM we have for the expected return of asset i,

$$E[R_i] = R_f + \beta_{im}(E[R_m] - R_f) \tag{5.1.1}$$

$$\beta_{im} = \frac{\text{Cov}[R_i, R_m]}{\text{Var}[R_m]}, \tag{5.1.2}$$

where R_m is the return on the market portfolio, and R_f is the return on the riskfree asset. The Sharpe-Lintner version can be most compactly expressed in terms of returns in excess of this riskfree rate or in terms of *excess returns*. Let Z_i represent the return on the ith asset in excess of the riskfree rate, $Z_i \equiv R_i - R_f$. Then for the Sharpe-Lintner CAPM we have

$$E[Z_i] = \beta_{im} E[Z_m] \tag{5.1.3}$$

$$\beta_{im} = \frac{\text{Cov}[Z_i, Z_m]}{\text{Var}[Z_m]}, \tag{5.1.4}$$

where Z_m is the excess return on the market portfolio of assets. Because the riskfree rate is treated as being nonstochastic, equations (5.1.2) and (5.1.4) are equivalent. In empirical implementations, proxies for the riskfree rate are stochastic and thus the betas can differ. Most empirical work relating to the Sharpe-Lintner version employs excess returns and thus uses (5.1.4).

Empirical tests of the Sharpe-Lintner CAPM have focused on three implications of (5.1.3): (1) The intercept is zero; (2) Beta completely captures the cross-sectional variation of expected excess returns; and (3) The market risk premium, $E[Z_m]$ is positive. In much of this chapter we will focus on the first implication; the last two implications will be considered later, in Section 5.8.

In the absence of a riskfree asset, Black (1972) derived a more general version of the CAPM. In this version, known as the Black version, the expected return of asset i in excess of the zero-beta return is linearly related to its beta. Specifically, for the expected return of asset i, $E[R_i]$, we have

$$E[R_i] = E[R_{om}] + \beta_{im}(E[R_m] - E[R_{om}]). \tag{5.1.5}$$

R_m is the return on the market portfolio, and R_{om} is the return on the *zero-beta portfolio* associated with m. This portfolio is defined to be the portfolio that has the minimum variance of all portfolios uncorrelated with m. (Any other uncorrelated portfolio would have the same expected return, but a higher variance.) Since it is wealth in real terms that is relevant, for the Black model, returns are generally stated on an inflation-adjusted basis and β_{im} is defined in terms of real returns,

$$\beta_{im} = \frac{\text{Cov}[R_i, R_m]}{\text{Var}[R_m]}. \tag{5.1.6}$$

Econometric analysis of the Black version of the CAPM treats the zero-beta portfolio return as an unobserved quantity, making the analysis more complicated than that of the Sharpe-Lintner version. The Black version can be tested as a restriction on the real-return market model. For the real-return market model we have

$$E[R_i] = \alpha_{im} + \beta_{im}E[R_m], \tag{5.1.7}$$

and the implication of the Black version is

$$\alpha_{im} = E[R_{om}](1 - \beta_{im}) \quad \forall\, i. \tag{5.1.8}$$

In words, the Black model restricts the asset-specific intercept of the real-return market model to be equal to the expected zero-beta portfolio return times one minus the asset's beta.

The CAPM is a single-period model; hence (5.1.3) and (5.1.5) do not have a time dimension. For econometric analysis of the model, it is necessary to add an assumption concerning the time-series behavior of returns and estimate the model over time. We assume that returns are independently and identically distributed (IID) through time and jointly multivariate normal. This assumption applies to excess returns for the Sharpe-Lintner version and to real returns for the Black version. While the assumption is strong, it has the benefit of being theoretically consistent with the CAPM holding period by period; it is also a good empirical approximation for a monthly observation interval. We will discuss relaxing this assumption in Section 5.6.

The CAPM can be useful for applications requiring a measure of expected stock returns. Some applications include cost of capital estimation, portfolio performance evaluation, and event-study analysis. As an example, we briefly discuss its use for estimating the cost of capital. The cost of equity capital is required for use in corporate capital budgeting decisions and in the determination of a fair rate of return for regulated utilities. Implementation of the model requires three inputs: the stock's beta, the market risk premium, and the riskfree return. The usual estimator of beta of the equity is the OLS estimator of the slope coefficient in the excess-return market model, that is, the beta in the regression equation

$$Z_{it} = \alpha_{im} + \beta_{im} Z_{mt} + \epsilon_{it}, \tag{5.1.9}$$

where i denotes the asset and t denotes the time period, $t = 1, \ldots, T$. Z_{it} and Z_{mt} are the realized excess returns in time period t for asset i and the market portfolio, respectively. Typically the Standard and Poor's 500 Index serves as a proxy for the market portfolio, and the US Treasury bill rate proxies for the riskfree return. The equation is most commonly estimated using 5 years of monthly data ($T = 60$). Given an estimate of the beta, the cost of capital is calculated using a historical average for the excess return on the S&P 500 over Treasury bills. This sort of application is only justified if the CAPM provides a good description of the data.

5.2 Results from Efficient-Set Mathematics

In this section we review the mathematics of mean-variance efficient sets. The interested reader is referred to Merton (1972) and Roll (1977) for detailed treatments. An understanding of this topic is useful for interpreting much of the empirical research relating to the CAPM, because the key testable implication of the CAPM is that the market portfolio of risky assets is a mean-variance efficient portfolio. Efficient-set mathematics also plays a role in the analysis of multifactor pricing models in Chapter 6.

We start with some notation. Let there be N risky assets with mean vector μ and covariance matrix Ω. Assume that the expected returns of at least two assets differ and that the covariance matrix is of full rank. Define ω_a as the ($N \times 1$) vector of portfolio weights for an arbitrary portfolio a with weights summing to unity. Portfolio a has mean return $\mu_a = \omega_a{'}\mu$ and variance $\sigma_a^2 = \omega_a{'}\Omega\omega_a$. The covariance between any two portfolios a and b is $\omega_a{'}\Omega\omega_b$. Given the population of assets we next consider minimum-variance portfolios in the absence of a riskfree asset.

Definition. Portfolio p is the minimum-variance portfolio of all portfolios with mean return μ_p if its portfolio weight vector is the solution to the following constrained optimization:

$$\min_{\omega} \omega{'}\Omega\omega \tag{5.2.1}$$

subject to

$$\omega{'}\mu = \mu_p \tag{5.2.2}$$

$$\omega{'}\iota = 1. \tag{5.2.3}$$

To solve this problem, we form the Lagrangian function L, differentiate with respect to ω, set the resulting equations to zero, and then solve for ω. For the Lagrangian function we have

$$L = \omega{'}\Omega\omega + \delta_1(\mu_p - \omega{'}\mu) + \delta_2(1 - \omega{'}\iota), \tag{5.2.4}$$

where ι is a conforming vector of ones and δ_1 and δ_2 are Lagrange multipliers. Differentiating L with respect to ω and setting the result equal to zero, we have

$$2\Omega\omega - \delta_1\mu - \delta_2\iota = 0. \tag{5.2.5}$$

Combining (5.2.5) with (5.2.2) and (5.2.3) we find the solution

$$\omega_p = \mathbf{g} + \mathbf{h}\mu_p, \tag{5.2.6}$$

where $\mathbf{g}$ and $\mathbf{h}$ are $(N \times 1)$ vectors,

$$\mathbf{g} = \frac{1}{D}[B(\Omega^{-1}\iota) - A(\Omega^{-1}\mu)] \tag{5.2.7}$$

$$\mathbf{h} = \frac{1}{D}[C(\Omega^{-1}\mu) - A(\Omega^{-1}\iota)], \tag{5.2.8}$$

and $A = \iota'\Omega^{-1}\mu$, $B = \mu'\Omega^{-1}\mu$, $C = \iota'\Omega^{-1}\iota$, and $D = BC - A^2$.

Next we summarize a number of results from efficient-set mathematics for minimum-variance portfolios. These results follow from the form of the solution for the minimum-variance portfolio weights in (5.2.6).

Result 1: The minimum-variance frontier can be generated from any two distinct minimum-variance portfolios.

Result 1': Any portfolio of minimum-variance portfolios is also a minimum-variance portfolio.

Result 2: Let p and r be any two minimum-variance portfolios. The covariance of the return of p with the return of r is

$$\text{Cov}[R_p, R_r] = \frac{C}{D}\left(\mu_p - \frac{A}{C}\right)\left(\mu_r - \frac{A}{C}\right) + \frac{1}{C}. \tag{5.2.9}$$

Result 3: Define portfolio g as the global minimum-variance portfolio. For portfolio g, we have

$$\omega_g = \frac{1}{C}\Omega^{-1}\iota \tag{5.2.10}$$

$$\mu_g = \frac{A}{C} \tag{5.2.11}$$

$$\sigma_g^2 = \frac{1}{C}. \tag{5.2.12}$$

Result 4: For each minimum-variance portfolio p, except the global minimum-variance portfolio g, there exists a unique minimum-variance portfolio that has zero covariance with p. This portfolio is called the zero-beta portfolio with respect to p.

Result 4′: The covariance of the return of the global minimum-variance portfolio g with any asset or portfolio of assets a is

$$\text{Cov}[R_g, R_a] = \frac{1}{C}. \tag{5.2.13}$$

Figure 5.1 illustrates the set of minimum-variance portfolios in the absence of a riskfree asset in mean-standard deviation space. Minimum-variance portfolios with an expected return greater than or equal to the expected return of the global minimum-variance portfolio are efficient portfolios. These portfolios have the highest expected return of all portfolios with an equal or lower variance of return. In Figure 5.1 the minimum-variance portfolio is g. Portfolio p is an efficient portfolio. Portfolio op is the zero-beta portfolio with respect to p. It can be shown that it plots in the location shown in Figure 5.1, that is, the expected return on the zero-beta portfolio is the expected return on portfolio p, less the slope of the minimum-variance frontier at p times the standard deviation of portfolio p.

Result 5: Consider a multiple regression of the return on any asset or portfolio R_a on the return of any minimum-variance portfolio R_p (except for the global minimum-variance portfolio) and the return of its associated zero-beta portfolio R_{op}.

$$R_a = \beta_0 + \beta_1 R_{op} + \beta_2 R_p + \epsilon_p \tag{5.2.14}$$

$$\text{E}[\epsilon_p \mid R_p, R_{op}] = 0. \tag{5.2.15}$$

For the regression coefficients we have

$$\beta_2 = \frac{\text{Cov}[R_a, R_p]}{\sigma_p^2} = \beta_{ap} \tag{5.2.16}$$

$$\beta_1 = \frac{\text{Cov}[R_a, R_{op}]}{\sigma_{op}^2} = 1 - \beta_{ap} \tag{5.2.17}$$

$$\beta_0 = 0 \tag{5.2.18}$$

where β_{ap} is the beta of asset a with respect to portfolio p.

Result 5′: For the expected return of a we have

$$\mu_a = (1 - \beta_{ap})\mu_{op} + \beta_{ap}\mu_p. \tag{5.2.19}$$

We next introduce a riskfree asset into the analysis and consider portfolios composed of a combination of the N risky assets and the riskfree asset. With a riskfree asset the portfolio weights of the risky assets are not constrained to sum to 1, since $(1 - \omega'\iota)$ can be invested in the riskfree asset.

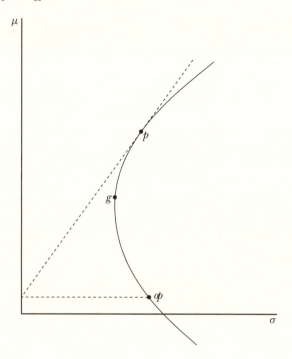

Figure 5.1. *Minimum-Variance Portfolios Without Riskfree Asset*

Given a riskfree asset with return R_f the minimum-variance portfolio with expected return μ_p will be the solution to the constrained optimization

$$\min_{\omega} \omega'\Omega\omega \qquad (5.2.20)$$

subject to

$$\omega'\mu + (1 - \omega'\iota)R_f = \mu_p. \qquad (5.2.21)$$

As in the prior problem, we form the Lagrangian function L, differentiate it with respect to ω, set the resulting equations to zero, and then solve for ω. For the Lagrangian function we have

$$L = \omega'\Omega\omega + \delta\left(\mu_p - \omega'\mu - (1 - \omega'\iota)R_f\right). \qquad (5.2.22)$$

Differentiating L with respect to ω and setting the result equal to zero, we have

$$2\,\Omega\omega - \delta(\mu - R_f\iota) = 0. \qquad (5.2.23)$$

Combining (5.2.23) with (5.2.21) we have

$$\omega_p = \frac{(\mu_p - R_f)}{(\mu - R_f\iota)'\Omega^{-1}(\mu - R_f\iota)}\,\Omega^{-1}(\mu - R_f\iota). \qquad (5.2.24)$$

Note that we can express ω_p as a scalar which depends on the mean of p times a portfolio weight vector which does not depend on p,

$$\omega_p = c_p\overline{\omega}, \qquad (5.2.25)$$

where

$$c_p = \frac{(\mu_p - R_f)}{(\mu - R_f\iota)'\Omega^{-1}(\mu - R_f\iota)} \qquad (5.2.26)$$

and

$$\overline{\omega} = \Omega^{-1}(\mu - R_f\iota). \qquad (5.2.27)$$

Thus with a riskfree asset all minimum-variance portfolios are a combination of a given risky asset portfolio with weights proportional to $\overline{\omega}$ and the riskfree asset. This portfolio of risky assets is called the tangency portfolio and has weight vector

$$\omega_q = \frac{1}{\iota'\Omega^{-1}(\mu - R_f\iota)}\,\Omega^{-1}(\mu - R_f\iota). \qquad (5.2.28)$$

We use the subscript q to identify the tangency portfolio. Equation (5.2.28) divides the elements of $\overline{\omega}$ by their sum to get a vector whose elements sum to one, that is, a portfolio weight vector. Figure 5.2 illustrates the set of minimum-variance portfolios in the presence of a riskfree asset. With a riskfree asset all efficient portfolios lie along the line from the riskfree asset through portfolio q.

The expected excess return per unit risk is useful to provide a basis for economic interpretation of tests of the CAPM. The *Sharpe ratio* measures this quantity. For any asset or portfolio a, the Sharpe ratio is defined as the mean excess return divided by the standard deviation of return,

$$sr_a = \frac{\mu_a - R_f}{\sigma_a}. \qquad (5.2.29)$$

In Figure 5.2 the Sharpe ratio is the slope of the line from the riskfree return $(R_f, 0)$ to the portfolio (μ_a, σ_a). The tangency portfolio q can be characterized as the portfolio with the maximum Sharpe ratio of all portfolios of risky assets. Testing the mean-variance efficiency of a given portfolio is equivalent to testing whether the Sharpe ratio of that portfolio is the maximum of the set of Sharpe ratios of all possible portfolios.

5.3 Statistical Framework for Estimation and Testing

Initially we use the assumption that investors can borrow and lend at a riskfree rate of return, and we consider the Sharpe-Lintner version of the CAPM. Then, we eliminate this assumption and analyze the Black version.

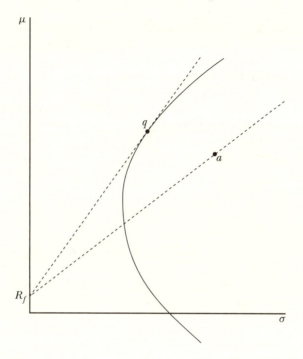

Figure 5.2. *Minimum-Variance Portfolios With Riskfree Asset*

5.3.1 Sharpe-Lintner Version

Define $\mathbf{Z}_t$ as an $(N \times 1)$ vector of excess returns for N assets (or portfolios of assets). For these N assets, the excess returns can be described using the excess-return market model:

$$\mathbf{Z}_t = \boldsymbol{\alpha} + \boldsymbol{\beta} Z_{mt} + \boldsymbol{\epsilon}_t \tag{5.3.1}$$

$$\mathrm{E}[\boldsymbol{\epsilon}_t] = 0 \tag{5.3.2}$$

$$\mathrm{E}[\boldsymbol{\epsilon}_t \boldsymbol{\epsilon}_t'] = \boldsymbol{\Sigma} \tag{5.3.3}$$

$$\mathrm{E}[Z_{mt}] = \mu_m, \qquad \mathrm{E}[(Z_{mt} - \mu_m)^2] = \sigma_m^2 \tag{5.3.4}$$

$$\mathrm{Cov}[Z_{mt}, \boldsymbol{\epsilon}_t] = 0. \tag{5.3.5}$$

$\boldsymbol{\beta}$ is the $(N \times 1)$ vector of betas, Z_{mt} is the time period t market portfolio excess return, and $\boldsymbol{\alpha}$ and $\boldsymbol{\epsilon}_t$ are $(N \times 1)$ vectors of asset return intercepts and disturbances, respectively. As will be the case throughout this chapter we have suppressed the dependence of $\boldsymbol{\alpha}$, $\boldsymbol{\beta}$, and $\boldsymbol{\epsilon}_t$ on the market portfolio or its proxy. For convenience, with the Sharpe-Lintner version, we redefine μ to refer to the expected excess return.

The implication of the Sharpe-Lintner version of the CAPM for (5.3.1) is that all of the elements of the vector α are zero. This implication follows from comparing the unconditional expectation of (5.3.1) to (5.1.3) and forms the principal hypothesis for tests of the model. If all elements of α are zero then m is the tangency portfolio.

We use the maximum likelihood approach to develop estimators of the unconstrained model. Ordinary least squares (OLS) regressions asset by asset lead to the same estimators for α and β. To start, we consider the probability density function (pdf) of excess returns conditional on the excess return of the market. Given the assumed joint normality of excess returns for the pdf of $\mathbf{Z}_t$, we have

$$
f(\mathbf{Z}_t \mid Z_{mt}) = (2\pi)^{-\frac{N}{2}} |\mathbf{\Sigma}|^{-\frac{1}{2}}
$$
$$
\times \exp\left[-\tfrac{1}{2}(\mathbf{Z}_t - \alpha - \beta Z_{mt})'\mathbf{\Sigma}^{-1}(\mathbf{Z}_t - \alpha - \beta Z_{mt})\right], \quad (5.3.6)
$$

and since excess returns are temporally IID, given T observations, the joint probability density function is

$$
f(\mathbf{Z}_1, \mathbf{Z}_2, \ldots, \mathbf{Z}_T \mid Z_{m1}, Z_{m2}, \ldots, Z_{mT})
$$
$$
= \prod_{t=1}^{T} p(\mathbf{Z}_t \mid Z_{mt}) \qquad\qquad\qquad\qquad (5.3.7)
$$
$$
= \prod_{t=1}^{T} (2\pi)^{-\frac{N}{2}} |\mathbf{\Sigma}|^{-\frac{1}{2}}
$$
$$
\times \exp\left[-\tfrac{1}{2}(\mathbf{Z}_t - \alpha - \beta Z_{mt})'\mathbf{\Sigma}^{-1}(\mathbf{Z}_t - \alpha - \beta Z_{mt})\right]. \quad (5.3.8)
$$

Given (5.3.8) and the excess-return observations, the parameters of the excess-return market model can be estimated using *maximum likelihood*. This approach is desirable because, given certain regularity conditions, maximum likelihood estimators are consistent, asymptotically efficient, and asymptotically normal. To define the maximum likelihood estimator, we form the *log-likelihood function*, that is, the logarithm of the joint probability density function viewed as a function of the unknown parameters, α, β, and $\mathbf{\Sigma}$. Denoting $\mathcal{L}$ as the log-likelihood function we have:

$$
\mathcal{L}(\alpha, \beta, \mathbf{\Sigma}) = -\frac{NT}{2}\log(2\pi) - \frac{T}{2}\log|\mathbf{\Sigma}|
$$
$$
-\frac{1}{2}\sum_{t=1}^{T}(\mathbf{Z}_t - \alpha - \beta Z_{mt})'\mathbf{\Sigma}^{-1}(\mathbf{Z}_t - \alpha - \beta Z_{mt}). \quad (5.3.9)
$$

The maximum likelihood estimators are the values of the parameters which maximize $\mathcal{L}$. To find these estimators, we differentiate $\mathcal{L}$ with respect to α, β, and Σ, and set the resulting equations to zero. The partial derivatives are

$$\frac{\partial \mathcal{L}}{\partial \alpha} = \Sigma^{-1} \left[\sum_{t=1}^{T} (\mathbf{Z}_t - \alpha - \beta Z_{mt}) \right] \tag{5.3.10}$$

$$\frac{\partial \mathcal{L}}{\partial \beta} = \Sigma^{-1} \left[\sum_{t=1}^{T} (\mathbf{Z}_t - \alpha - \beta Z_{mt}) Z_{mt} \right] \tag{5.3.11}$$

$$\frac{\partial \mathcal{L}}{\partial \Sigma} = -\frac{T}{2} \Sigma^{-1}$$
$$+ \frac{1}{2} \Sigma^{-1} \left[\sum_{t=1}^{T} (\mathbf{Z}_t - \alpha - \beta Z_{mt})(\mathbf{Z}_t - \alpha - \beta Z_{mt})' \right] \Sigma^{-1}. \tag{5.3.12}$$

Setting (5.3.10), (5.3.11), and (5.3.12) to zero, we can solve for the maximum likelihood estimators. These are

$$\hat{\alpha} = \hat{\mu} - \hat{\beta}\hat{\mu}_m \tag{5.3.13}$$

$$\hat{\beta} = \frac{\sum_{t=1}^{T} (\mathbf{Z}_t - \hat{\mu})(Z_{mt} - \hat{\mu}_m)}{\sum_{t=1}^{T} (Z_{mt} - \hat{\mu}_m)^2} \tag{5.3.14}$$

$$\hat{\Sigma} = \frac{1}{T} \sum_{t=1}^{T} (\mathbf{Z}_t - \hat{\alpha} - \hat{\beta}Z_{mt})(\mathbf{Z}_t - \hat{\alpha} - \hat{\beta}Z_{mt})', \tag{5.3.15}$$

where

$$\hat{\mu} = \frac{1}{T} \sum_{t=1}^{T} \mathbf{Z}_t \quad \text{and} \quad \hat{\mu}_m = \frac{1}{T} \sum_{t=1}^{T} Z_{mt}.$$

As already noted, these are just the formulas for OLS estimators of the parameters.

The distributions of the maximum likelihood estimators conditional on the excess return of the market, $Z_{m1}, Z_{m2}, \ldots, Z_{mT}$, follow from the assumed joint normality of excess returns and the IID assumption. The variances and covariances of the estimators can be derived using the inverse of the *Fisher information matrix*. As discussed in the Appendix, the Fisher information matrix is minus the expectation of the second order derivative of the log-likelihood function with respect to the vector of the parameters.

The conditional distributions are

$$\hat{\alpha} \sim \mathcal{N}\left(\alpha, \frac{1}{T}\left[1 + \frac{\hat{\mu}_m^2}{\hat{\sigma}_m^2}\right]\Sigma\right) \qquad (5.3.16)$$

$$\hat{\beta} \sim \mathcal{N}\left(\beta, \frac{1}{T}\left[\frac{1}{\hat{\sigma}_m^2}\right]\Sigma\right) \qquad (5.3.17)$$

$$T\hat{\Sigma} \sim \mathcal{W}_N(T - 2, \Sigma), \qquad (5.3.18)$$

where $\hat{\mu}_m$ is as previously defined and

$$\hat{\sigma}_m^2 = \frac{1}{T}\sum_{t=1}^{T}(Z_{mt} - \hat{\mu}_m)^2.$$

The notation $\mathcal{W}_N(T - 2, \Sigma)$ indicates that the $(N \times N)$ matrix $T\hat{\Sigma}$ has a Wishart distribution with $(T - 2)$ degrees of freedom and covariance matrix Σ. This distribution is a multivariate generalization of the chi-square distribution. Anderson (1984) and Muirhead (1983) provide discussions of its properties.

The covariance of $\hat{\alpha}$ and $\hat{\beta}$ is

$$\text{Cov}[\hat{\alpha}, \hat{\beta}'] = -\frac{1}{T}\left[\frac{\hat{\mu}_m}{\hat{\sigma}_m^2}\right]\Sigma. \qquad (5.3.19)$$

$\hat{\Sigma}$ is independent of both $\hat{\alpha}$ and $\hat{\beta}$.

Using the unconstrained estimators, we can form a Wald test statistic of the null hypothesis,

$$H_0: \quad \alpha = 0 \qquad (5.3.20)$$

against the alternative hypothesis,

$$H_A: \quad \alpha \neq 0. \qquad (5.3.21)$$

The Wald test statistic is

$$\begin{aligned} J_0 &= \hat{\alpha}'\left[\text{Var}[\hat{\alpha}]\right]^{-1}\hat{\alpha} \\ &= T\left[1 + \frac{\hat{\mu}_m^2}{\hat{\sigma}_m^2}\right]^{-1}\hat{\alpha}'\Sigma^{-1}\hat{\alpha}, \qquad (5.3.22) \end{aligned}$$

where we have substituted from (5.3.16) for $\text{Var}[\hat{\alpha}]$. Under the null hypothesis J_0 will have a chi-square distribution with N degrees of freedom. Since Σ is unknown, to use J_0 for testing H_0, we substitute a consistent estimator for Σ in (5.3.22) and then asymptotically the null distribution will be chi-square with N degrees of freedom. The maximum likelihood estimator of Σ can serve as a consistent estimator.

However, in this case we need not resort to large-sample distribution theory to draw inferences using a Wald-type test. The finite-sample distribution, which is developed in MacKinlay (1987) and Gibbons, Ross, and Shanken (1989), can be determined by applying the following theorem presented in Muirhead (1983):

Theorem. *Let the m-vector* $\mathbf{x}$ *be distributed* $\mathcal{N}(0, \Omega)$, *let the* $(m \times m)$ *matrix* $\mathbf{A}$ *be distributed* $\mathcal{W}_m(n, \Omega)$ *with* $(n \geq m)$, *and let* $\mathbf{x}$ *and* $\mathbf{A}$ *be independent. Then:*

$$\frac{(n - m + 1)}{m} \mathbf{x}'\mathbf{A}^{-1}\mathbf{x} \sim F_{m, n-m+1}.$$

To apply this theorem we set $\mathbf{x} = \sqrt{T}[1 + \hat{\mu}_m^2/\hat{\sigma}_m^2]^{-1/2}\hat{\alpha}$, $\mathbf{A} = T\hat{\Sigma}$, $m = N$, and $n = (T - 2)$. Then defining J_1 as the test statistic we have:

$$J_1 = \frac{(T - N - 1)}{N} \left[1 + \frac{\hat{\mu}_m^2}{\hat{\sigma}_m^2}\right]^{-1} \hat{\alpha}'\hat{\Sigma}^{-1}\hat{\alpha}. \qquad (5.3.23)$$

Under the null hypothesis, J_1 is unconditionally distributed central F with N degrees of freedom in the numerator and $(T - N - 1)$ degrees of freedom in the denominator.

We can construct the Wald test J_0 and the finite-sample F-test J_1 using only the estimators from the unconstrained model, that is, the excess-return market model. To consider a third test, the likelihood ratio test, we need the estimators of the constrained model. For the constrained model, the Sharpe-Lintner CAPM, the estimators follow from solving for β and Σ from (5.3.11) and (5.3.12) with α constrained to be zero. The constrained estimators are

$$\hat{\beta}^* = \frac{\sum_{t=1}^{T} \mathbf{Z}_t Z_{mt}}{\sum_{t=1}^{T} Z_{mt}^2} \qquad (5.3.24)$$

$$\hat{\Sigma}^* = \frac{1}{T} \sum_{t=1}^{T} (\mathbf{Z}_t - \hat{\beta}^* Z_{mt})(\mathbf{Z}_t - \hat{\beta}^* Z_{mt})'. \qquad (5.3.25)$$

The distributions of the constrained estimators under the null hypothesis are

$$\hat{\beta}^* \sim \mathcal{N}\left(\beta, \frac{1}{T}\left[\frac{1}{\hat{\mu}_m^2 + \hat{\sigma}_m^2}\right]\Sigma\right) \qquad (5.3.26)$$

$$T\hat{\Sigma}^* \sim \mathcal{W}_N(T - 1, \Sigma). \qquad (5.3.27)$$

Given both the unconstrained and constrained maximum likelihood estimators, we can test the restrictions implied by the Sharpe-Lintner version using the likelihood ratio test. This test is based on the logarithm of the likelihood ratio, which is the value of the constrained log-likelihood function minus the unconstrained log-likelihood function evaluated at the maximum likelihood estimators. Denoting $\mathcal{LR}$ as the log-likelihood ratio, we have

$$
\begin{aligned}
\mathcal{LR} &= \mathcal{L}^* - \mathcal{L} \\
&= -\frac{T}{2}\big[\log|\hat{\Sigma}^*| - \log|\hat{\Sigma}|\big],
\end{aligned}
\tag{5.3.28}
$$

where $\mathcal{L}^*$ represents the constrained log-likelihood function. To derive (5.3.28) we have used the fact that summation in the last term in both the unconstrained and constrained likelihood function evaluated at the maximum likelihood estimators simplifies to NT. We now show this for the unconstrained function. For the summation of the last term in (5.3.9), evaluated at the maximum likelihood estimators, we have

$$
\sum_{t=1}^{T}(\mathbf{Z}_t - \hat{\alpha} - \hat{\beta}Z_{mt})'\hat{\Sigma}^{-1}(\mathbf{Z}_t - \hat{\alpha} - \hat{\beta}Z_{mt})
\tag{5.3.29}
$$

$$
= \sum_{t=1}^{T}\mathrm{trace}\big[\hat{\Sigma}^{-1}(\mathbf{Z}_t - \hat{\alpha} - \hat{\beta}Z_{mt})(\mathbf{Z}_t - \hat{\alpha} - \hat{\beta}Z_{mt})'\big]
\tag{5.3.30}
$$

$$
= \mathrm{trace}\left[\hat{\Sigma}^{-1}\sum_{t=1}^{T}(\mathbf{Z}_t - \hat{\alpha} - \hat{\beta}Z_{mt})(\mathbf{Z}_t - \hat{\alpha} - \hat{\beta}Z_{mt})'\right]
\tag{5.3.31}
$$

$$
= \mathrm{trace}[\hat{\Sigma}^{-1}(T\hat{\Sigma})] = T\,\mathrm{trace}[I] = NT.
\tag{5.3.32}
$$

The step from (5.3.29) to (5.3.30) uses the result that trace $AB =$ trace BA, and the step to (5.3.31) uses the result that the trace of a sum is equal to the sum of a trace. In (5.3.32) we use the result that the trace of the identity matrix is equal to its dimension.

The test is based on the asymptotic result that, under the null hypothesis, -2 times the logarithm of the likelihood ratio is distributed chi-square with degrees of freedom equal to the number of restrictions under H_0. That is, we can test H_0 using

$$
\begin{aligned}
J_2 &= -2\mathcal{LR} \\
&= T\big[\log|\hat{\Sigma}^*| - \log|\hat{\Sigma}|\big] \overset{a}{\sim} \chi_N^2.
\end{aligned}
\tag{5.3.33}
$$

Interestingly, here we need not resort to large-sample theory to conduct a likelihood ratio test. J_1 in (5.3.23) is itself a likelihood ratio test statistic. This result, which we next develop, follows from the fact that J_1 is a monotonic transformation of J_2. The constrained maximum likelihood estimators can be expressed in terms of the unconstrained estimators. For $\hat{\beta}^*$ we have

$$\hat{\beta}^* = \hat{\beta} + \frac{\hat{\mu}_m}{\hat{\mu}_m^2 + \hat{\sigma}_m^2} \hat{\alpha}, \tag{5.3.34}$$

and for $\hat{\Sigma}^*$ we have

$$
\begin{aligned}
\hat{\Sigma}^* &= \frac{1}{T} \sum_{t=1}^{T} (\mathbf{Z}_t - \hat{\beta}^* Z_{mt})(\mathbf{Z}_t - \hat{\beta}^* Z_{mt})' \\
&= \frac{1}{T} \sum_{t=1}^{T} \left[(\mathbf{Z}_t - \hat{\alpha} - \hat{\beta} Z_{mt}) + \left(1 - \frac{\hat{\mu}_m Z_{mt}}{\hat{\mu}_m^2 + \hat{\sigma}_m^2} \right) \hat{\alpha} \right] \\
&\quad \times \left[(\mathbf{Z}_t - \hat{\alpha} - \hat{\beta} Z_{mt}) + \left(1 - \frac{\hat{\mu}_m Z_{mt}}{\hat{\mu}_m^2 + \hat{\sigma}_m^2} \right) \hat{\alpha} \right]'. \tag{5.3.35}
\end{aligned}
$$

Noting that

$$\sum_{t=1}^{T} (\mathbf{Z}_t - \hat{\alpha} - \hat{\beta} Z_{mt})' \left(1 - \frac{\hat{\mu}_m Z_{mt}}{\hat{\mu}_m^2 + \hat{\sigma}_m^2} \right) \hat{\alpha} = 0, \tag{5.3.36}$$

we have

$$\hat{\Sigma}^* = \hat{\Sigma} + \left(\frac{\hat{\sigma}_m^2}{\hat{\mu}_m^2 + \hat{\sigma}_m^2} \right) \hat{\alpha} \hat{\alpha}'. \tag{5.3.37}$$

Taking the determinant of both sides we have

$$|\hat{\Sigma}^*| = |\hat{\Sigma}| \left[\left(\frac{\hat{\sigma}_m^2}{\hat{\mu}_m^2 + \hat{\sigma}_m^2} \right) \hat{\alpha}' \hat{\Sigma}^{-1} \hat{\alpha} + 1 \right], \tag{5.3.38}$$

where to go from (5.3.37) to (5.3.38) we factorize $\hat{\Sigma}$ and use the result that $|\mathbf{I} + \mathbf{xx}'| = (1 + \mathbf{x}'\mathbf{x})$ for the identity matrix $\mathbf{I}$ and a vector $\mathbf{x}$. Substituting (5.3.38) into (5.3.28) gives

$$\mathcal{LR} = -\frac{T}{2} \log \left[\left(\frac{\hat{\sigma}_m^2}{\hat{\mu}_m^2 + \hat{\sigma}_m^2} \right) \hat{\alpha}' \hat{\Sigma}^{-1} \hat{\alpha} + 1 \right], \tag{5.3.39}$$

and for J_1 we have

$$J_1 = \frac{(T - N - 1)}{N} \left(\exp\left[\tfrac{J_2}{T} \right] - 1 \right) \tag{5.3.40}$$

which is a monotonic transformation of J_2. This shows that J_1 can be interpreted as a likelihood ratio test.

Since the finite-sample distribution of J_1 is known, equation (5.3.40) can also be used to derive the finite-sample distribution of J_2. As we shall see, under the null hypothesis the finite-sample distribution of J_2 can differ from its large-sample distribution. Jobson and Korkie (1982) suggest an adjustment to J_2 which has better finite-sample properties. Defining J_3 as the modified statistic, we have

$$
\begin{aligned}
J_3 &= \frac{(T - \frac{N}{2} - 2)}{T} J_2 \\
&= (T - \tfrac{N}{2} - 2) \left[\log |\hat{\boldsymbol{\Sigma}}^*| - \log |\hat{\boldsymbol{\Sigma}}| \right] \overset{a}{\sim} \chi_N^2.
\end{aligned} \tag{5.3.41}
$$

We will visit the issue of the finite-sample properties of J_2 and J_3 in Section 5.4.

A useful economic interpretation can be made of the test statistic J_1 using results from efficient-set mathematics. Gibbons, Ross, and Shanken (1989) show that

$$
J_1 = \frac{(T - N - 1)}{N} \left(\frac{\frac{\hat{\mu}_q^2}{\hat{\sigma}_q^2} - \frac{\hat{\mu}_m^2}{\hat{\sigma}_m^2}}{1 + \frac{\hat{\mu}_m^2}{\hat{\sigma}_m^2}} \right), \tag{5.3.42}
$$

where the portfolio denoted by q represents the *ex post* tangency portfolio constructed as in (5.2.28) from the N included assets *plus* the market portfolio. Recall from Section 5.2 that the portfolio with the maximum squared Sharpe ratio of all portfolios is the tangency portfolio. Thus when *ex post* the market portfolio is the tangency portfolio J_1 will be equal to zero, and as the squared Sharpe ratio of the market decreases, J_1 will increase, indicating stronger evidence against the efficiency of the market portfolio. In Section 5.7.2 we present an empirical example using J_1 after considering the Black version of the CAPM in the next section.

5.3.2 Black Version

In the absence of a riskfree asset we consider the Black version of the CAPM in (5.1.5). The expected return on the zero-beta portfolio $E[R_{om}]$ is treated as an unobservable and hence becomes an unknown model parameter. Defining the zero-beta portfolio expected return as γ, the Black version is

$$
\begin{aligned}
E[\mathbf{R}_t] &= \iota\gamma + \beta(E[R_{mt}] - \gamma) \\
&= (\iota - \beta)\gamma + \beta E[R_{mt}].
\end{aligned} \tag{5.3.43}
$$

With the Black model, the unconstrained model is the real-return market model. Define $\mathbf{R}_t$ as an ($N \times 1$) vector of real returns for N assets (or portfolios of assets). For these N assets, the real-return market model is

$$\mathbf{R}_t = \alpha + \beta R_{mt} + \epsilon_t \tag{5.3.44}$$

$$\mathrm{E}[\epsilon_t] = 0 \tag{5.3.45}$$

$$\mathrm{E}[\epsilon_t \epsilon_t'] = \Sigma \tag{5.3.46}$$

$$\mathrm{E}[R_{mt}] = \mu_m, \qquad \mathrm{E}[(R_{mt} - \mu_m)^2] = \sigma_m^2 \tag{5.3.47}$$

$$\mathrm{Cov}[R_{mt}, \epsilon_t] = 0. \tag{5.3.48}$$

β is the ($N \times 1$) vector of asset betas, R_{mt} is the time period t market portfolio return, and α and ϵ_t are ($N \times 1$) vectors of asset return intercepts and disturbances, respectively.

The testable implication of the Black version is apparent from comparing the unconditional expectation of (5.3.44) with (5.3.43). The implication is

$$\alpha = (\iota - \beta)\gamma. \tag{5.3.49}$$

This implication is more complicated to test than the zero-intercept restriction of the Sharpe-Lintner version because the parameters β and γ enter in a nonlinear fashion.

Given the IID assumption and the joint normality of returns, the Black version of the CAPM can be estimated and tested using the maximum likelihood approach. The maximum likelihood estimators of the unrestricted model, that is, the real-return market model in (5.3.44), are identical to the estimators of the excess-return market model except that real returns are substituted for excess returns. Thus $\hat{\mu}$, for example, is now the vector of sample mean real returns. For the maximum likelihood estimators of the parameters we have

$$\hat{\alpha} = \hat{\mu} - \hat{\beta}\hat{\mu}_m \tag{5.3.50}$$

$$\hat{\beta} = \frac{\sum_{t=1}^{T}(\mathbf{R}_t - \hat{\mu})(R_{mt} - \hat{\mu}_m)}{\sum_{t=1}^{T}(R_{mt} - \hat{\mu}_m)^2} \tag{5.3.51}$$

$$\hat{\Sigma} = \frac{1}{T}\sum_{t=1}^{T}(\mathbf{R}_t - \hat{\alpha} - \hat{\beta}R_{mt})(\mathbf{R}_t - \hat{\alpha} - \hat{\beta}R_{mt})', \tag{5.3.52}$$

where

$$\hat{\mu} = \frac{1}{T}\sum_{t=1}^{T}\mathbf{R}_t \quad \text{and} \quad \hat{\mu}_m = \frac{1}{T}\sum_{t=1}^{T}R_{mt}.$$

Conditional on the real return of the market, $R_{m1}, R_{m2}, \ldots, R_{mT}$, the distributions are

$$\hat{\alpha} \sim \mathcal{N}\left(\alpha, \frac{1}{T}\left[1 + \frac{\hat{\mu}_m^2}{\hat{\sigma}_m^2}\right]\Sigma\right) \tag{5.3.53}$$

$$\hat{\beta} \sim \mathcal{N}\left(\beta, \frac{1}{T}\left[\frac{1}{\hat{\sigma}_m^2}\right]\Sigma\right) \tag{5.3.54}$$

$$T\hat{\Sigma} \sim \mathcal{W}_N(T - 2, \Sigma), \tag{5.3.55}$$

where

$$\hat{\sigma}_m^2 = \frac{1}{T}\sum_{t=1}^{T}(R_{mt} - \hat{\mu}_m)^2.$$

The covariance of $\hat{\alpha}$ and $\hat{\beta}$ is

$$\text{Cov}[\hat{\alpha}, \hat{\beta}'] = -\left[\frac{\hat{\mu}_m}{\hat{\sigma}_m^2}\right]\Sigma. \tag{5.3.56}$$

For the constrained model, that is, the Black version of the CAPM, the log-likelihood function is

$$\mathcal{L}(\gamma, \beta, \Sigma) = -\frac{NT}{2}\log(2\pi) - \frac{T}{2}\log|\Sigma|$$

$$-\frac{1}{2}\sum_{t=1}^{T}(\mathbf{R}_t - \gamma(\iota - \beta) - \beta R_{mt})'\Sigma^{-1}$$

$$\times (\mathbf{R}_t - \gamma(\iota - \beta) - \beta R_{mt}). \tag{5.3.57}$$

Differentiating with respect to γ, β, and Σ, we have

$$\frac{\partial \mathcal{L}}{\partial \gamma} = (\iota - \beta)'\Sigma^{-1}\left[\sum_{t=1}^{T}(\mathbf{R}_t - \gamma(\iota - \beta) - \beta R_{mt})\right] \tag{5.3.58}$$

$$\frac{\partial \mathcal{L}}{\partial \beta} = \Sigma^{-1}\left[\sum_{t=1}^{T}(\mathbf{R}_t - \gamma(\iota - \beta) - \beta R_{mt})(R_{mt} - \gamma)\right] \tag{5.3.59}$$

$$\frac{\partial \mathcal{L}}{\partial \Sigma} = -\frac{T}{2}\Sigma^{-1} + \frac{1}{2}\Sigma^{-1}\left[\sum_{t=1}^{T}(\mathbf{R}_t - \gamma(\iota - \beta) - \beta R_{mt})\right.$$

$$\left.\times (\mathbf{R}_t - \gamma(\iota - \beta) - \beta R_{mt})'\right]\Sigma^{-1}. \tag{5.3.60}$$

Setting (5.3.59), (5.3.59), and (5.3.60) to zero, we can solve for the maximum likelihood estimators. These are:

$$\hat{\gamma}^* = \frac{(\iota - \hat{\beta}^*)'\hat{\Sigma}^{*-1}(\hat{\mu} - \hat{\beta}^*\hat{\mu}_m)}{(\iota - \hat{\beta}^*)'\hat{\Sigma}^{*-1}(\iota - \hat{\beta}^*)} \tag{5.3.61}$$

$$\hat{\beta}^* = \frac{\sum_{t=1}^{T}(\mathbf{R}_t - \hat{\gamma}^*\iota)(R_{mt} - \hat{\gamma}^*)}{\sum_{t=1}^{T}(R_{mt} - \hat{\gamma}^*)^2} \tag{5.3.62}$$

$$\hat{\Sigma}^* = \frac{1}{T}\sum_{t=1}^{T}(\mathbf{R}_t - \hat{\gamma}^*(\iota - \hat{\beta}^*) - \hat{\beta}^* R_{mt})(\mathbf{R}_t - \hat{\gamma}^*(\iota - \hat{\beta}^*) - \hat{\beta}^* R_{mt})'. \tag{5.3.63}$$

Equations (5.3.61), (5.3.62), and (5.3.63) do not allow us to solve explicitly for the maximum likelihood estimators. The maximum likelihood estimators can be obtained, given initial consistent estimators of β and Σ, by iterating over (5.3.61), (5.3.62), and (5.3.63) until convergence. The unconstrained estimators $\hat{\beta}$ and $\hat{\Sigma}$ can serve as the initial consistent estimators of β and Σ, respectively.

Given both the constrained and unconstrained maximum likelihood estimators, we can construct an asymptotic likelihood ratio test of the null hypothesis.[1] The null and alternative hypotheses are

$$H_0: \quad \alpha = (\iota - \beta)\gamma \tag{5.3.64}$$

$$H_A: \quad \alpha \neq (\iota - \beta)\gamma. \tag{5.3.65}$$

A likelihood ratio test can be constructed in a manner analogous to the test constructed for the Sharpe-Lintner version in (5.3.33). Defining J_4 as the test statistic, we have

$$J_4 = T\left[\log|\hat{\Sigma}^*| - \log|\hat{\Sigma}|\right] \overset{a}{\sim} \chi^2_{N-1}. \tag{5.3.66}$$

Notice that the degrees of freedom of the null distribution is $N-1$. Relative to the Sharpe-Lintner version of the model, the Black version loses one degree of freedom because the zero-beta expected return is a free parameter. In addition to the $N(N-1)/2$ parameters in the residual covariance matrix, the unconstrained model has $2N$ parameters, N parameters comprising the vector α and N comprising the vector β. The constrained model has, in addition to the same number of covariance matrix parameters, N parameters comprising the vector β and the parameter for the expected zero-beta portfolio return γ. Thus the unconstrained model has $(N-1)$ more free parameters than the constrained model.

---

[1]In the context of the Black version of the CAPM, Gibbons (1982) first developed this test. Shanken (1985b) provides detailed analysis.

We can also adjust J_4 to improve the finite-sample properties. Defining J_5 as the adjusted test statistic we have

$$J_5 = \left(T - \tfrac{N}{2} - 2\right)\left[\log|\hat{\Sigma}^*| - \log|\hat{\Sigma}|\right] \overset{a}{\sim} \chi^2_{N-1}. \qquad (5.3.67)$$

In finite samples, the null distribution of J_5 will more closely match the chi-square distribution. (See Section 5.4 for a comparison in the context of the Sharpe-Lintner version.)

There are two drawbacks to the methods we have just discussed. First, the estimation is somewhat tedious since one must iterate over the first-order conditions. Second, the test is based on large-sample theory and can have very poor finite-sample properties. We can use the results of Kandel (1984) and Shanken (1986) to overcome these drawbacks. These authors show how to calculate exact maximum likelihood estimators and how to implement an approximate test with good finite-sample performance.

For the unconstrained model, consider the market model expressed in terms of returns in excess of the expected zero-beta return γ:

$$\mathbf{R}_t - \gamma\iota = \alpha + \beta(R_{mt} - \gamma) + \epsilon_t. \qquad (5.3.68)$$

Assume γ is known. Then the maximum likelihood estimators for the unconstrained model are

$$\hat{\alpha}(\gamma) = \hat{\mu} - \gamma\iota - \hat{\beta}(\hat{\mu}_m - \gamma), \qquad (5.3.69)$$

$$\hat{\beta} = \frac{\sum_{t=1}^{T}(\mathbf{R}_t - \hat{\mu})(R_{mt} - \hat{\mu}_m)}{\sum_{t=1}^{T}(R_{mt} - \hat{\mu}_m)^2}, \qquad (5.3.70)$$

and

$$\hat{\Sigma} = \frac{1}{T}\sum_{t=1}^{T}[\mathbf{R}_t - \hat{\mu} - \hat{\beta}(R_{mt} - \hat{\mu}_m)][\mathbf{R}_t - \hat{\mu} - \hat{\beta}(R_{mt} - \hat{\mu}_m)]'. \qquad (5.3.71)$$

The unconstrained estimators of β and Σ do not depend on the value of γ but, as indicated, the estimator of α does. The value of the unconstrained log-likelihood function evaluated at the maximum likelihood estimators is

$$\mathcal{L} = -\frac{NT}{2}\log(2\pi) - \frac{T}{2}\log|\hat{\Sigma}| - \frac{NT}{2} \qquad (5.3.72)$$

which does not depend on γ.

Constraining $\boldsymbol{\alpha}$ to be zero, the constrained estimators are

$$\hat{\boldsymbol{\beta}}^* = \frac{\sum_{t=1}^{T}(\mathbf{R}_t - \gamma \iota)(R_{mt} - \gamma)}{\sum_{t=1}^{T}(R_{mt} - \gamma)^2} \tag{5.3.73}$$

$$\hat{\boldsymbol{\Sigma}}^* = \frac{1}{T}\sum_{t=1}^{T}\left(\mathbf{R}_t - \gamma(\iota - \hat{\boldsymbol{\beta}}^*) - \hat{\boldsymbol{\beta}}^* R_{mt}\right)$$

$$\times \left(\mathbf{R}_t - \gamma(\iota - \hat{\boldsymbol{\beta}}^*) - \hat{\boldsymbol{\beta}}^* R_{mt}\right)', \tag{5.3.74}$$

and the value of the constrained likelihood function is

$$\mathcal{L}^*(\gamma) = -\frac{NT}{2}\log(2\pi) - \frac{T}{2}\log|\hat{\boldsymbol{\Sigma}}^*(\gamma)| - \frac{NT}{2}. \tag{5.3.75}$$

Note that the constrained function does depend on γ. Forming the logarithm of the likelihood ratio we have

$$\mathcal{LR}(\gamma) = \mathcal{L}^*(\gamma) - \mathcal{L}$$

$$= -\frac{T}{2}\left[\log|\hat{\boldsymbol{\Sigma}}^*(\gamma)| - \log|\hat{\boldsymbol{\Sigma}}|\right]. \tag{5.3.76}$$

The value of γ that minimizes the value of the logarithm of the likelihood ratio will be the value which maximizes the constrained log-likelihood function and thus is the maximum likelihood estimator of γ.

Using the same development as for the Sharpe-Lintner version, the log-likelihood ratio can be simplified to

$$\mathcal{LR}(\gamma) = -\frac{T}{2}\log\left[\left(\frac{\hat{\sigma}_m^2}{(\hat{\mu}_m - \gamma)^2 + \hat{\sigma}_m^2}\right)\hat{\boldsymbol{\alpha}}(\gamma)'\hat{\boldsymbol{\Sigma}}^{-1}\hat{\boldsymbol{\alpha}}(\gamma) + 1\right]$$

$$= -\frac{T}{2}\log\left[\left(\frac{\hat{\sigma}_m^2}{(\hat{\mu}_m - \gamma)^2 + \hat{\sigma}_m^2}\right)[\hat{\boldsymbol{\mu}} - \gamma\iota - \hat{\boldsymbol{\beta}}(\hat{\mu}_m - \gamma)]'\hat{\boldsymbol{\Sigma}}^{-1}\right.$$

$$\left. \times [\hat{\boldsymbol{\mu}} - \gamma\iota - \hat{\boldsymbol{\beta}}(\hat{\mu}_m - \gamma)] + 1\right]. \tag{5.3.77}$$

Minimizing $\mathcal{LR}$ with respect to γ is equivalent to maximizing G where

$$G = \left(\frac{\hat{\sigma}_m^2}{(\hat{\mu}_m - \gamma)^2 + \hat{\sigma}_m^2}\right)[\hat{\boldsymbol{\mu}} - \gamma\iota - \hat{\boldsymbol{\beta}}(\hat{\mu}_m - \gamma)]'\hat{\boldsymbol{\Sigma}}^{-1}[\hat{\boldsymbol{\mu}} - \gamma\iota - \hat{\boldsymbol{\beta}}(\hat{\mu}_m - \gamma)]. \tag{5.3.78}$$

Thus the value of γ which maximizes G will be the maximum likelihood estimator. There are two solutions of $\partial G/\partial\gamma = 0$, and these are the real roots of the quadratic equation

$$H(\gamma) = A\gamma^2 + B\gamma + C, \tag{5.3.79}$$

where

$$A \equiv \frac{1}{\hat{\sigma}_m^2} (\iota - \hat{\beta})' \hat{\Sigma}^{-1} (\hat{\mu} - \hat{\beta}\hat{\mu}_m) - \frac{\hat{\mu}_m}{\hat{\sigma}_m^2} (\iota - \hat{\beta})' \hat{\Sigma}^{-1} (\iota - \hat{\beta})$$

$$B \equiv \left(1 + \frac{\hat{\mu}_m^2}{\hat{\sigma}_m^2}\right) (\iota - \hat{\beta})' \hat{\Sigma}^{-1} (\iota - \hat{\beta}) - \frac{1}{\hat{\sigma}_m^2} (\hat{\mu} - \hat{\beta}\hat{\mu}_m)' \hat{\Sigma}^{-1} (\hat{\mu} - \hat{\beta}\hat{\mu}_m)$$

$$C \equiv -\left(1 + \frac{\hat{\mu}_m^2}{\hat{\sigma}_m^2}\right) (\iota - \hat{\beta})' \hat{\Sigma}^{-1} (\hat{\mu} - \hat{\beta}\hat{\mu}_m)$$

$$+ \frac{\hat{\mu}_m}{\hat{\sigma}_m^2} (\hat{\mu} - \hat{\beta}\hat{\mu}_m)' \hat{\Sigma}^{-1} (\hat{\mu} - \hat{\beta}\hat{\mu}_m).$$

If A is greater than zero, the maximum likelihood estimator $\hat{\gamma}^*$ is the largest root, and if A is less than zero, then $\hat{\gamma}^*$ is the smallest root. A will be greater than zero if $\hat{\mu}_m$ is greater than the mean return on the sample global minimum-variance portfolio; that is, the market portfolio is on the efficient part of the constrained mean-variance frontier. We can substitute $\hat{\gamma}^*$ into (5.3.62) and (5.3.63) to obtain $\hat{\beta}^*$ and $\hat{\Sigma}^*$ without resorting to an iterative procedure.

We can construct an approximate test of the Black version using returns in excess of γ as in (5.3.68). If γ is known then the same methodology used to construct the Sharpe-Lintner version F-test in (5.3.23) applies to testing the null hypothesis that the zero-beta excess-return market-model intercept is zero. The test statistic is

$$J_6(\gamma) = \frac{(T-N-1)}{N} \left[1 + \frac{(\hat{\mu}_m - \gamma)^2}{\hat{\sigma}_m^2}\right]^{-1} \hat{\alpha}(\gamma)' \hat{\Sigma}^{-1} \hat{\alpha}(\gamma) \sim F_{N,T-N-1}.$$

$$(5.3.80)$$

Because γ is unknown, the test in (5.3.80) cannot be directly implemented. But an approximate test can be implemented with $J_6(\hat{\gamma}^*)$. Because $\gamma = \hat{\gamma}^*$ minimizes the log-likelihood ratio, it minimizes $J_6(\gamma)$. Hence $J_6(\hat{\gamma}^*) \leq J_6(\gamma_o)$, where γ_o is the unknown true value of γ. Therefore a test using $J_6(\hat{\gamma}^*)$ will accept too often. If the null hypothesis is rejected using $\hat{\gamma}^*$ it will be rejected for any value of γ_o. This testing approach can provide a useful check because the usual asymptotic likelihood ratio test in (5.3.77) has been found to reject too often.

Finally, we consider inferences for the expected zero-beta portfolio return. Given the maximum likelihood estimator of γ, we require its asymptotic variance to make inferences. Using the Fisher information matrix, the asymptotic variance of the maximum likelihood of γ is

$$\text{Var}[\hat{\gamma}^*] \stackrel{a}{=} \frac{1}{T} \left(1 + \frac{(\mu_m - \gamma)^2}{\sigma_m^2}\right) [(\iota - \beta)'\Sigma^{-1}(\iota - \beta)]^{-1}. \qquad (5.3.81)$$

This estimator can be evaluated at the maximum likelihood estimates, and then inferences concerning the value of γ are possible given the asymptotic normality of $\hat{\gamma}^*$.

5.4 Size of Tests

In some econometric models there are no analytical results on the finite-sample properties of estimators. In such cases, it is common to rely on large-sample statistics to draw inferences. This reliance opens up the possibility that the size of the test will be incorrect if the sample size is not large enough for the asymptotic results to provide a good approximation. Because there is no standard sample size for which large-sample theory can be applied, it is good practice to investigate the appropriateness of the theory.

The multivariate F-test we have developed provides an ideal framework for illustrating the problems that can arise if one relies on asymptotic distribution theory for inference. Using the known finite-sample distribution of the F-test statistic J_1, we can calculate the finite-sample size for the various asymptotic tests. Such calculations are possible because the asymptotic test statistics are monotonic transformations of J_1.

We draw on the relations of J_1 to the large-sample test statistics. Comparing equations (5.3.22) and (5.3.23) for J_0 we have

$$J_1 = \frac{(T - N - 1)}{NT} J_0. \tag{5.4.1}$$

Recall in (5.3.40) for J_2 we have

$$J_1 = \frac{(T - N - 1)}{N} \left(\exp\left[\frac{J_2}{T} \right] - 1 \right), \tag{5.4.2}$$

and for J_3 from (5.4.2) and (5.3.41),

$$J_1 = \frac{(T - N - 1)}{N} \left(\exp\left[\frac{J_3}{(T - \frac{N}{2} - 2)} \right] - 1 \right). \tag{5.4.3}$$

Under the null hypothesis, J_0, J_2, and J_3 are all asymptotically distributed chi-square with N degrees of freedom. The exact null distribution of J_1 is central F with N degrees of freedom in the numerator and $T - N - 1$ degrees of freedom in the denominator.

We calculate the exact size of a test based on a given large-sample statistic and its asymptotic 5% critical value. For example, consider a test using J_0 with 10 portfolios and 60 months of data. In this case, under the null hypothesis J_0 is asymptotically distributed as a chi-square random variate with 10 degrees of freedom. Given this distribution, the critical value for a test with an asymptotic size of 5% is 18.31. From (5.4.1) this value of 18.31

for J_0 corresponds to a critical value of 1.495 for J_1. Given that the exact null distribution of J_1 is F with 10 degrees of freedom in the numerator and 49 degrees of freedom in the denominator, a test using this critical value for J_1 has a size of 17.0%. Thus, the asymptotic 5% test has a size of 17.0% in a sample of 60 months; it rejects the null hypothesis more than three times too often.

Table 5.1 presents this calculation for J_0, J_2, and J_3 using 10, 20, and 40 for values of N and using 60, 120, 180, 240, and 360 for values of T. It is apparent that the finite-sample size of the tests is larger than the asymptotic size of 5%. Thus the large-sample tests will reject the null hypothesis too often. This problem is severe for the asymptotic tests based on J_0 and J_2. When $N = 10$ the problem is mostly important for the low values of T. For example, the finite-sample size of a test with an asymptotic size of 5% is 17.0% and 9.6% for J_0 and J_2, respectively. As N increases the severity of the problem increases. When $N = 40$ and $T = 60$ the finite-sample size of an asymptotic 5% test is 98.5% for J_0 and 80.5% for J_2. In these cases, the null hypothesis will be rejected most of the time even when it is true. With $N = 40$, the size of a 5% asymptotic test is still overstated considerably even when $T = 360$.

The asymptotic test with a finite-sample adjustment based on J_3 performs much better in finite samples than does its unadjusted counterpart. Only in the case of $N = 40$ and $T = 60$ is the exact size significantly overstated. This shows that finite-sample adjustments of asymptotic test statistics can play an important role.

5.5 Power of Tests

When drawing inferences using a given test statistic it is important to consider its power. The power is the probability that the null hypothesis will be rejected given that an alternative hypothesis is true. Low power against an interesting alternative suggests that the test is not useful to discriminate between the alternative and the null hypothesis. On the other hand, if the power is high, then the test can be very informative but it may also reject the null hypothesis against alternatives that are close to the null in economic terms. In this case a rejection may be due to small, economically unimportant deviations from the null.

To document the power of a test, it is necessary to specify the alternative data-generating process and the size of the test. The power for a given size of test is the probability that the test statistic is greater than the critical value under the null hypothesis, given that the alternative hypothesis is true.

To illustrate the power of tests of the CAPM, we will focus on the test of the Sharpe-Lintner version using J_1 from (5.3.23). The power of this test

Table 5.1. *Finite-sample size of tests of the Sharpe-Lintner CAPM using large-sample test statistics.*

N	T	J_0	J_2	J_3
10	60	0.170	0.096	0.051
	120	0.099	0.070	0.050
	180	0.080	0.062	0.050
	240	0.072	0.059	0.050
	360	0.064	0.056	0.050
20	60	0.462	0.211	0.057
	120	0.200	0.105	0.051
	180	0.136	0.082	0.051
	240	0.109	0.073	0.050
	360	0.086	0.064	0.050
40	60	0.985	0.805	0.141
	120	0.610	0.275	0.059
	180	0.368	0.164	0.053
	240	0.257	0.124	0.052
	360	0.165	0.092	0.051

The exact finite-sample size is presented for tests with a size of 5% asymptotically. The finite-sample size uses the distribution of J_1 and the relation between J_1 and the large-sample test statistics, J_0, J_2, and J_3. N is the number of dependent portfolios, and T is the number of time-series observations.

should be representative, and it is convenient to document since the exact finite-sample distribution of J_1 is known under both the null and alternative hypotheses. Conditional on the excess return of the market portfolio, for the distribution of J_1 as defined in (5.3.23), we have

$$J_1 \sim F_{N,T-N-1}(\delta), \tag{5.5.1}$$

where δ is the noncentrality parameter of the F distribution and

$$\delta = T \left[1 + \frac{\hat{\mu}_m^2}{\hat{\sigma}_m^2} \right]^{-1} \alpha' \Sigma^{-1} \alpha. \tag{5.5.2}$$

To specify the distribution of J_1 under both the null and the alternative hypotheses, we need to specify δ, N, and T.

Under the null hypothesis α is zero, so in this case δ is zero and we have the previous result that the distribution is central F with N and $T - N - 1$ degrees of freedom in the numerator and denominator, respectively. Under the alternative hypothesis, to specify δ we need to condition on a value of $\hat{\mu}_m^2/\hat{\sigma}_m^2$ and specify the value of $\alpha'\Sigma^{-1}\alpha$. For the value of $\hat{\mu}_m^2/\hat{\sigma}_m^2$, given a monthly observation interval, we choose 0.013 which corresponds to an *ex post* annualized mean excess return of 8% and a sample annualized standard deviation of 20%.

For the quadratic term $\alpha'\Sigma^{-1}\alpha$, rather than separately specifying α and Σ, we can use the following result of Gibbons, Ross, and Shanken (1989).[2] Recalling that q is the tangency portfolio and that m is the market portfolio, we have

$$\alpha'\Sigma^{-1}\alpha \;=\; \frac{\mu_q^2}{\sigma_q^2} - \frac{\mu_m^2}{\sigma_m^2} \;=\; sr_q^2 - sr_m^2. \qquad (5.5.3)$$

Using this relation, we need only specify the difference in the squared Sharpe ratio for the tangency portfolio and the market portfolio. The tangency portfolio is for the universe composed of the N included portfolios and the market portfolio. We consider four sets of values for the tangency portfolio parameters. For all cases the annualized standard deviation of the tangency portfolio is set to 16%. The annualized expected excess return then takes on four values, 8.5%, 10.2%, 11.6%, and 13.0%. Using an annualized expected excess return of 8% for the market and an annualized standard deviation of 20% for the market's excess return, these four values correspond to values of 0.01, 0.02, 0.03, and 0.04 for δ/T.

We consider five values for N: 1, 5, 10, 20, and 40. For T we consider four values—60, 120, 240, and 360—which are chosen to correspond to 5, 10, 20, and 30 years of monthly data. The power is tabulated for a test with a size of 5%. The results are presented in Table 5.2.

Substantial variation in the power of the test for different experimental designs and alternatives is apparent in Table 5.2. For a fixed value of N, considerable increases in power are possible with larger values of T. For example, under alternative 2 for N equal to 10, the power increases from 0.082 to 0.380 as T increases from 60 to 360.

The power gain is substantial when N is reduced for a fixed alternative. For example, under alternative 3, for T equal to 120, the power increases from 0.093 to 0.475 as N decreases from 40 to 1. However, such gains would not be feasible in practice. As N is reduced, the Sharpe ratio of the tangency portfolio (and the noncentrality parameter of the F distribution) will decline unless the portfolios are combined in proportion to their weightings in that portfolio. The choice of N which maximizes the power will depend on the

---

[2]We discuss this result further in Chapter 6.

Table 5.2. Power of F-test of Sharpe-Lintner CAPM using statistic J_1.

	$N = 1$	$N = 5$	$N = 10$	$N = 20$	$N = 40$
Alternative 1: $\mu_q = 8.5\%$ $\sigma_q = 16\%$					
$T = 60$	0.117	0.075	0.065	0.059	0.053
$T = 120$	0.191	0.106	0.086	0.072	0.062
$T = 240$	0.341	0.178	0.134	0.103	0.082
$T = 360$	0.480	0.259	0.190	0.139	0.105
Alternative 2: $\mu_q = 10.2\%$ $\sigma_q = 16\%$					
$T = 60$	0.189	0.103	0.082	0.068	0.057
$T = 120$	0.339	0.174	0.130	0.098	0.077
$T = 240$	0.597	0.340	0.247	0.174	0.124
$T = 360$	0.770	0.508	0.380	0.267	0.183
Alternative 3: $\mu_q = 11.6\%$ $\sigma_q = 16\%$					
$T = 60$	0.262	0.134	0.101	0.078	0.061
$T = 120$	0.475	0.251	0.180	0.128	0.093
$T = 240$	0.769	0.504	0.374	0.261	0.175
$T = 360$	0.908	0.711	0.570	0.416	0.280
Alternative 4: $\mu_q = 13.0\%$ $\sigma_q = 16\%$					
$T = 60$	0.334	0.167	0.121	0.089	0.065
$T = 120$	0.593	0.332	0.237	0.163	0.110
$T = 240$	0.873	0.647	0.502	0.356	0.234
$T = 360$	0.965	0.845	0.726	0.563	0.389

The alternative hypothesis is characterized by the value of the expected excess return and the value of the standard deviation of the tangency portfolio. The tangency portfolio is with respect to the N included portfolios and the market portfolio. μ_q is the expected excess return of the tangency portfolio, and σ_q is the annualized standard deviation of the excess return of the tangency portfolio. The market portfolio is assumed to have an expected excess return of 8.0% and a standard deviation of 20%. Under the null hypothesis the market portfolio is the tangency portfolio. N is the number of portfolios included in the test and T is the number of months of data included.

rate at which the Sharpe ratio of the tangency portfolio declines as assets are grouped together.

While we do not have general results about the optimal design of a multivariate test, we can draw some insights from this power analysis. Increasing the length of the time series can lead to a significant payoff in terms of power. Further, the power is very sensitive to the value of N. The analysis suggests that the value of N should be kept small, perhaps no larger than about ten.

5.6 Nonnormal and Non-IID Returns

In this section we are concerned with inferences when there are deviations
from the assumption that returns are jointly normal and IID through time.
We consider tests which accommodate non-normality, heteroskedasticity,
and temporal dependence of returns. Such tests are of interest for two reasons. First, while the normality assumption is sufficient, it is not necessary to
derive the CAPM as a theoretical model. Rather, the normality assumption
is adopted for statistical purposes. Without this assumption, finite-sample
properties of asset pricing model tests are difficult to derive. Second, departures of monthly security returns from normality have been documented.[3]
There is also abundant evidence of heteroskedasticity and temporal dependence in stock returns.[4] Even though temporal dependence makes the
CAPM unlikely to hold as an exact theoretical model, it is still of interest to
examine the empirical performance of the model. It is therefore desirable
to consider the effects of relaxing these statistical assumptions.

Robust tests of the CAPM can be constructed using a Generalized
Method of Moments (GMM) framework. We focus on tests of the Sharpe-
Lintner version; however, robust tests of the Black version can be constructed
in the same manner. Within the GMM framework, the distribution of returns
conditional on the market return can be both serially dependent and conditionally heteroskedastic. We need only assume that excess asset returns
are stationary and ergodic with finite fourth moments. The subsequent
analysis draws on Section A.2 of the Appendix which contains a general
development of the GMM methodology. We continue with a sample of T
time-series observations and N assets. Following the Appendix, we need to
set up the vector of moment conditions with zero expectation. The required
moment conditions follow from the excess-return market model. The residual vector provides N moment conditions, and the product of the excess
return of the market and the residual vector provides another N moment
conditions. Using the notation of the Appendix, for $\mathbf{f}_t(\boldsymbol{\theta})$ we have

$$\mathbf{f}_t(\boldsymbol{\theta}) \; = \; \mathbf{h}_t \otimes \epsilon_t, \tag{5.6.1}$$

where $\mathbf{h}_t' = [1 \; Z_{mt}]$, $\epsilon_t = \mathbf{Z}_t - \alpha - \beta \, Z_{mt}$, and $\boldsymbol{\theta}' = [\alpha' \; \beta']$.

The specification of the excess-return market model implies the mo-
ment condition $\mathrm{E}[\mathbf{f}_t(\boldsymbol{\theta}_0)] = 0$, where $\boldsymbol{\theta}_0$ is the true parameter vector. This
moment condition forms the basis for estimation and testing using a GMM
approach. GMM chooses the estimator so that linear combinations of the
sample average of this moment condition are zero. For the sample average,

---

[3]See Fama (1965, 1976), Blattberg and Gonedes (1974), Affleck-Graves and McDonald
(1989), and Table 1.1 in Chapter 1.

[4]See Chapters 2 and 12, and the references given in those chapters.

we have

$$\mathbf{g}_T(\boldsymbol{\theta}) = \frac{1}{T}\sum_{t=1}^{T}\mathbf{f}_t(\boldsymbol{\theta}). \qquad (5.6.2)$$

The GMM estimator $\hat{\boldsymbol{\theta}}$ is chosen to minimize the quadratic form

$$\mathbf{Q}_T(\boldsymbol{\theta}) = \mathbf{g}_T(\boldsymbol{\theta})'\mathbf{W}\mathbf{g}_T(\boldsymbol{\theta}), \qquad (5.6.3)$$

where $\mathbf{W}$ is a positive definite $(2N \times 2N)$ weighting matrix. Since in this case we have $2N$ moment condition equations and $2N$ unknown parameters, the system is exactly identified and $\hat{\boldsymbol{\theta}}$ can be chosen to set the average of the sample moments $\mathbf{g}_T(\boldsymbol{\theta})$ equal to zero. The GMM estimator will not depend on $\mathbf{W}$ since $\mathbf{Q}_T(\hat{\boldsymbol{\theta}})$ will attain its minimum of zero for any weighting matrix. The estimators from this GMM procedure are equivalent to the maximum likelihood estimators in (5.3.13) and (5.3.14). The estimators are

$$\hat{\alpha} = \hat{\mu} - \hat{\beta}\hat{\mu}_m \qquad (5.6.4)$$

$$\hat{\beta} = \frac{\sum_{t=1}^{T}(\mathbf{Z}_t - \hat{\mu})(Z_{mt} - \hat{\mu}_m)}{\sum_{t=1}^{T}(Z_{mt} - \hat{\mu}_m)^2}. \qquad (5.6.5)$$

The importance of the GMM approach for this application is that a robust covariance matrix of the estimators can be formed. The variances of $\hat{\alpha}$ and $\hat{\beta}$ will differ from the variances in the maximum likelihood approach. The covariance matrix of the GMM estimator $\hat{\boldsymbol{\theta}}$ follows from equation (A.2.8) in the Appendix. It is

$$\mathbf{V} = [\mathbf{D}_0'\mathbf{S}_0^{-1}\mathbf{D}_0]^{-1}, \qquad (5.6.6)$$

where

$$\mathbf{D}_0 = E\left[\frac{\partial \mathbf{g}_T(\boldsymbol{\theta})}{\partial \boldsymbol{\theta}'}\right] \qquad (5.6.7)$$

and

$$\mathbf{S}_0 = \sum_{l=-\infty}^{+\infty} E[\mathbf{f}_t(\boldsymbol{\theta})\mathbf{f}_{t-l}(\boldsymbol{\theta})']. \qquad (5.6.8)$$

The asymptotic distribution of $\hat{\boldsymbol{\theta}}$ is normal. Thus we have

$$\hat{\boldsymbol{\theta}} \overset{a}{\sim} \mathcal{N}\left(\boldsymbol{\theta}, \frac{1}{T}[\mathbf{D}_0'\mathbf{S}_0^{-1}\mathbf{D}_0]^{-1}\right). \qquad (5.6.9)$$

The application of the distributional result in (5.6.9) requires consistent estimators of $\mathbf{D}_0$ and $\mathbf{S}_0$ since they are unknown. In this case, for $\mathbf{D}_0$ we have

$$\mathbf{D}_0 = -\begin{bmatrix} 1 & \mu_m \\ \mu_m & (\sigma_m^2 + \mu_m^2) \end{bmatrix} \otimes \mathbf{I}_N. \qquad (5.6.10)$$

A consistent estimator $\mathbf{D}_T$ can easily be constructed using the maximum likelihood estimators of μ_m and σ_m^2. To compute a consistent estimator of $\mathbf{S}_0$, an assumption is necessary to reduce the summation in (5.6.8) to a finite number of terms. Section A.3 in the Appendix discusses possible assumptions. Defining $\mathbf{S}_T$ as a consistent estimator of $\mathbf{S}_0$, $(1/T)[\mathbf{D}_T'\mathbf{S}_T^{-1}\mathbf{D}_T]^{-1}$ is a consistent estimator of the covariance matrix of $\hat{\boldsymbol{\theta}}$. Noting that $\hat{\boldsymbol{\alpha}} = \mathbf{R}\hat{\boldsymbol{\theta}}$ where $\mathbf{R} = (1\ \ 0) \otimes \mathbf{I}_N$, a robust estimator of $\mathrm{Var}(\hat{\boldsymbol{\alpha}})$ is $(1/T)\mathbf{R}[\mathbf{D}_T'\mathbf{S}_T^{-1}\mathbf{D}_T]^{-1}\mathbf{R}'$. Using this we can construct a chi-square test of the Sharpe-Lintner model as in (5.3.22). The test statistic is

$$J_7 = T\hat{\boldsymbol{\alpha}}' \left[\mathbf{R}[\mathbf{D}_T'\mathbf{S}_T^{-1}\mathbf{D}_T]^{-1}\mathbf{R}'\right]^{-1} \hat{\boldsymbol{\alpha}}. \qquad (5.6.11)$$

Under the null hypothesis $\boldsymbol{\alpha} = 0$,

$$J_7 \overset{a}{\sim} \chi_N^2. \qquad (5.6.12)$$

MacKinlay and Richardson (1991) illustrate the bias in standard CAPM test statistics that can result from violations of the standard distributional assumptions. Specifically, they consider the case of contemporaneous conditional heteroskedasticity. With contemporaneous conditional heteroskedasticity, the variance of the market-model residuals of equation (5.3.3) depends on the contemporaneous market return. In their example, the assumption that excess returns are IID and jointly multivariate Student t leads to conditional heteroskedasticity. The multivariate Student t assumption for excess returns can be motivated both empirically and theoretically. One empirical stylized fact from the distribution of returns literature is that returns have fatter tails and are more peaked than one would expect from a normal distribution. This is consistent with returns coming from a multivariate Student t. Further, the multivariate Student t is a return distribution for which mean-variance analysis is consistent with expected utility maximization, making the choice theoretically appealing.[5]

The bias in the size of the standard CAPM test for the Student t case depends on the Sharpe ratio of the market portfolio and the degrees of freedom of the Student t. MacKinlay and Richardson (1991) present some estimates of the potential bias for various Sharpe ratios and for Student t degrees of freedom equal to 5 and 10. They find that in general the bias is small, but if the Sharpe ratio is high and the degrees of freedom small, the bias can be substantial and lead to incorrect inferences. Calculation of the test statistic J_7 based on the GMM framework provides a simple check for the possibility that the rejection of the model is the result of heteroskedasticity in the data.

---

[5] See Ingersoll (1987), p. 104.

5.7 Implementation of Tests

In this section we consider issues relating to empirical implementation of the test methodology. A summary of empirical results, an illustrative implementation, and discussion of the observability of the market portfolio are included.

5.7.1 Summary of Empirical Evidence

An enormous amount of literature presenting empirical evidence on the CAPM has evolved since the development of the model in the 1960s. The early evidence was largely positive, with Black, Jensen, and Scholes (1972), Fama and MacBeth (1973), and Blume and Friend (1973) all reporting evidence consistent with the mean-variance efficiency of the market portfolio. There was some evidence against the Sharpe-Lintner version of the CAPM as the estimated mean return on the zero-beta portfolio was higher than the riskfree return, but this could be accounted for by the Black version of the model.

In the late 1970s less favorable evidence for the CAPM began to appear in the so-called anomalies literature. In the context of the tests discussed in this chapter, the anomalies can be thought of as firm characteristics which can be used to group assets together so that the tangency portfolio of the included portfolios has a high *ex post* Sharpe ratio relative to the Sharpe ratio of the market proxy. Alternatively, contrary to the prediction of the CAPM, the firm characteristics provide explanatory power for the cross section of sample mean returns beyond the beta of the CAPM.

Early anomalies included the price-earnings-ratio effect and the size effect. Basu (1977) first reported the price-earnings-ratio effect. Basu's finding is that the market portfolio appears not to be mean-variance efficient relative to portfolios formed on the basis of the price-earnings ratios of firms. Firms with low price-earnings ratios have higher sample returns, and firms with high price-earnings ratios have lower mean returns than would be the case if the market portfolio was mean-variance efficient. The size effect, which was first documented by Banz (1981), is the result that low market capitalization firms have higher sample mean returns than would be expected if the market portfolio was mean-variance efficient. These two anomalies are at least partially related, as the low price-earnings-ratio firms tend to be small.

A number of other anomalies have been discovered more recently. Fama and French (1992, 1993) find that beta cannot explain the difference in return between portfolios formed on the basis of the ratio of book value of equity to market value of equity. Firms with high book-market ratios have higher average returns than is predicted by the CAPM. Similarly,

DeBondt and Thaler (1985) and Jegadeesh and Titman (1995) find that a portfolio formed by buying stocks whose value has declined in the past (*losers*) and selling stocks whose value has risen in the past (*winners*) has a higher average return than the CAPM predicts. Fama (1991) provides a good discussion of these and other anomalies.

Although the results in the anomalies literature may signal economically important deviations from the CAPM, there is little theoretical motivation for the firm characteristics studied in this literature. This opens up the possibility that the evidence against the CAPM is overstated because of data-snooping and sample selection biases. We briefly discuss these possibilities.

Data-snooping biases refer to the biases in statistical inference that result from using information from data to guide subsequent research with the same or related data. These biases are almost impossible to avoid due to the nonexperimental nature of economics. We do not have the luxury of running another experiment to create a new data set. Lo and MacKinlay (1990b) illustrate the potential magnitude of data-snooping biases in a test of the Sharpe-Lintner version of the CAPM. They consider the case where the characteristic used to group stocks into portfolios (e.g. size or price-earnings ratio) is selected not from theory but from previous observations of mean stock returns using related data. Comparisons of the null distribution of the test statistic with and without data-snooping suggests that the magnitude of the biases can be immense. However, in practice, it is difficult to specify the adjustment that should be made for data-snooping. Thus, the main message is a warning that the biases should at least be considered as a potential explanation for model deviations.

Sample selection biases can arise when data availability leads to certain subsets of stocks being excluded from the analysis. For example, Kothari, Shanken, and Sloan (1995) argue that data requirements for studies looking at book-market ratios lead to failing stocks being excluded and a resulting survivorship bias. Since the failing stocks would be expected to have low returns and high book-market ratios, the average return of the included high book-market-ratio stocks would have an upward bias. Kothari, Shanken, and Sloan (1995) argue that this bias is largely responsible for the previously cited result of Fama and French (1992, 1993). However, the importance of this particular survivorship bias is not fully resolved as Fama and French (1996b) dispute the conclusions of Kothari, Shanken, and Sloan. In any event, it is clear that researchers should be aware of the potential problems that can arise from sample selection biases.

5.7.2 Illustrative Implementation

We present tests of the Sharpe-Lintner model to illustrate the testing methodology. We consider four test statistics: J_1 from (5.3.23), J_2 from (5.3.33), J_3

from (5.3.41), and J_7 from (5.6.11). The tests are conducted using a thirty-year sample of monthly returns on ten portfolios. Stocks listed on the New York Stock Exchange and on the American Stock Exchange are allocated to the portfolios based on the market value of equity and are value-weighted within the portfolios. The CRSP value-weighted index is used as a proxy for the market portfolio, and the one-month US Treasury bill return is used for the riskfree return. The sample extends from January 1965 through December 1994.

Tests are conducted for the overall period, three ten-year subperiods, and six five-year subperiods. The subperiods are also used to form overall aggregate test statistics by assuming that the subperiod statistics are independent. The aggregate statistics for J_2, J_3, and J_7 are the sum of the individual statistics. The distribution of the sum under the null hypothesis will be chi-square with degrees of freedom equal to the number of subperiods times the degrees of freedom for each subperiod. The aggregate statistic for J_1 is calculated by scaling and summing the F statistics. The scale factor is calculated by approximating the F distribution with a scaled chi-square distribution. The approximation matches the first two moments. The degrees of freedom of the null distribution of the scaled sum of the subperiod J_1's is the number of subperiods times the degrees of freedom of the chi-square approximation.

The empirical results are reported in Table 5.3. The results present evidence against the Sharpe-Lintner CAPM. Using J_1, the p-value for the overall thirty-year period is 0.020, indicating that the null hypothesis is rejected at the 5% significance level. The five- and ten-year subperiod results suggest that the strongest evidence against the restrictions imposed by the model is in the first ten years of the sample from January 1965 to December 1974.

Comparisons of the results across test statistics reveal that in finite samples inferences can differ. A comparison of the results for J_1 versus J_2 illustrates the previously discussed fact that the asymptotic likelihood ratio test tends to reject too often. The finite-sample adjustment to J_2 works well as inferences with J_3 are almost identical to those with J_1.

5.7.3 Unobservability of the Market Portfolio

In the preceding analysis, we have not addressed the problem that the return on the market portfolio is unobserved and a proxy is used in the tests. Most tests use a value- or equal-weighted basket of NYSE and AMEX stocks as the market proxy, whereas theoretically the market portfolio contains all assets. Roll (1977) emphasizes that tests of the CAPM really only reject the mean-variance efficiency of the proxy and that the model might not be rejected if the return on the true market portfolio were used. Several approaches have

Table 5.3.   *Empirical results for tests of the Sharpe-Lintner version of the CAPM.*

Time	J_1	p-value	J_2	p-value	J_3	p-value	J_7	p-value
Five-year subperiods								
1/65–12/69	2.038	0.049	20.867	0.022	18.432	0.048	22.105	0.015
1/70–12/74	2.136	0.039	21.712	0.017	19.179	0.038	21.397	0.018
1/75–12/79	1.914	0.066	19.784	0.031	17.476	0.064	27.922	0.002
1/80–12/84	1.224	0.300	13.378	0.203	11.818	0.297	13.066	0.220
1/85–12/89	1.732	0.100	18.164	0.052	16.045	0.098	16.915	0.076
1/90–12/94	1.153	0.344	12.680	0.242	11.200	0.342	12.379	0.260
Overall	77.224	0.004	106.586	**	94.151	0.003	113.785	**
Ten-year subperiods								
1/65–12/74	2.400	0.013	23.883	0.008	22.490	0.013	24.649	0.006
1/75–12/84	2.248	0.020	22.503	0.013	21.190	0.020	27.192	0.002
1/85–12/94	1.900	0.053	19.281	0.037	18.157	0.052	16.373	0.089
Overall	57.690	0.001	65.667	**	61.837	0.001	68.215	**
Thirty-year period								
1/65–12/94	2.159	0.020	21.612	0.017	21.192	0.020	22.176	0.014

**Less than 0.0005.

Results are for ten value-weighted portfolios ($N = 10$) with stocks assigned to the portfolios based on market value of equity. The CRSP value-weighted index is used as a measure of the market portfolio and a one-month Treasury bill is used as a measure of the riskfree rate. The tests are based on monthly data from January 1965 to December 1994.

been suggested to consider if inferences are sensitive to the use of a proxy in place of the market portfolio.

One approach is advanced in Stambaugh (1982). He examines the sensitivity of tests to the exclusion of assets by considering a number of broader proxies for the market portfolio.[6] He shows that inferences are similar whether one uses a stock-based proxy, a stock- and bond-based proxy, or a stock-, bond-, and real-estate-based proxy. This suggests that inferences are not sensitive to the error in the proxy when viewed as a measure of the market portfolio and thus Roll's concern is not an empirical problem.

[6]Related work considers the possibility of accounting for the return on human capital. See Mayers (1972), Campbell (1996a), and Jagannathan and Wang (1996).

A second approach to the problem is presented by Kandel and Stambaugh (1987) and Shanken (1987a). Their papers estimate an upper bound on the correlation between the market proxy return and the true market return necessary to overturn the rejection of the CAPM. The basic finding is that if the correlation between the proxy and the true market exceeds about 0.70, then the rejection of the CAPM with a market proxy would also imply the rejection of the CAPM with the true market portfolio. Thus, as long as we believe there is a high correlation between the true market return and the proxies used, the rejections remain intact.

5.8 Cross-Sectional Regressions

So far in this chapter we have focused on the mean-variance efficiency of the market portfolio. Another view of the CAPM is that it implies a linear relation between expected returns and market betas which completely explain the cross section of expected returns. These implications can be tested using a cross-sectional regression methodology.

Fama and MacBeth (1973) first developed the cross-sectional regression approach. The basic idea is, for each cross section, to project the returns on the betas and then aggregate the estimates in the time dimension. Assuming that the betas are known, the regression model for the tth cross section of N assets is

$$Z_t = \gamma_{0t}\, \iota + \gamma_{1t}\, \beta_m + \eta_t,\qquad (5.8.1)$$

where Z_t is the $(N \times 1)$ vector of excess asset returns for time period t, ι is an $(N \times 1)$ vector of ones, and β_m is the $(N \times 1)$ vector of CAPM betas.

Implementation of the Fama-MacBeth approach involves two steps. First, given T periods of data, (5.8.1) is estimated using OLS for each t, $t = 1, \ldots, T$, giving the T estimates of γ_{0t} and γ_{1t}. Then in the second step, the time series of $\hat{\gamma}_{0t}$'s and $\hat{\gamma}_{1t}$'s are analyzed. Defining $\gamma_0 = E[\gamma_{0t}]$ and $\gamma_1 = E[\gamma_{1t}]$, the implications of the Sharpe-Lintner CAPM are $\gamma_0 = 0$ (zero intercept) and $\gamma_1 > 0$ (positive market risk premium). Because the returns are normally distributed and temporally IID, the gammas will also be normally distributed and IID. Hence, given time series of γ_{0t} and γ_{1t}, $t = 1, \ldots, T$, we can test these implications using the usual t-test. Defining $w(\hat{\gamma}_j)$ as the t-statistic, we have

$$w(\hat{\gamma}_j) = \frac{\hat{\gamma}_j}{\hat{\sigma}_{\gamma_j}},\qquad (5.8.2)$$

where

$$\hat{\gamma}_j = \frac{1}{T}\sum_{t=1}^{T}\hat{\gamma}_{jt}\qquad (5.8.3)$$

and

$$\hat{\sigma}_{\gamma_j}^2 = \frac{1}{T(T-1)} \sum_{t=1}^{T} (\hat{\gamma}_{jt} - \hat{\gamma}_j)^2. \tag{5.8.4}$$

The distribution of $w(\hat{\gamma}_j)$ is Student t with $(T-1)$ degrees of freedom and asymptotically is standard normal. Given the test statistics, inferences can be made in the usual fashion.

The Fama-MacBeth approach is particularly useful because it can easily be modified to accommodate additional risk measures beyond the CAPM beta. By adding additional risk measures, we can examine the hypothesis that beta completely describes the cross-sectional variation in expected returns. For example, we can consider if firm size has explanatory power for the cross-section of expected returns where firm size is defined as the logarithm of the market value of equity. Defining ς_t as the $(N \times 1)$ vector with elements corresponding to firm size at the beginning of period t, we can augment (5.8.1) to investigate if firm size has explanatory power not captured by the market beta:

$$Z_t = \gamma_{0t} \iota + \gamma_{1t} \beta_m + \gamma_{2t} \varsigma_t + \eta_t. \tag{5.8.5}$$

Using the $\hat{\gamma}_{2t}$'s from (5.8.5), we can test the hypothesis that size does not have any explanatory power beyond beta, that is, $\gamma_2 = 0$, by setting $j = 2$ in (5.8.2)–(5.8.4).

The Fama-MacBeth methodology, while useful, does have several problems. First, it cannot be directly applied because the market betas are not known. Thus the regressions are conducted using betas estimated from the data, which introduces an errors-in-variables complication. The errors-in-variables problem can be addressed in two ways. One approach, adopted by Fama and MacBeth, is to minimize the errors-in-variables problem by grouping the stocks into portfolios and increasing the precision of the beta estimates. A second approach, developed by Litzenberger and Ramaswamy (1979) and refined by Shanken (1992b), is to explicitly adjust the standard errors to correct for the biases introduced by the errors-in-variables. Shanken suggests multiplying $\hat{\sigma}_{\gamma_j}^2$ in (5.8.4) by an adjustment factor $(1 + (\hat{\mu}_m - \hat{\gamma}_o)^2 / \hat{\sigma}_m^2)$. While this approach eliminates the errors-in-variables bias in the t-statistic in (5.8.2), it does not eliminate the possibility that other variables might enter spuriously in (5.8.5) as a result of the unobservability of the true betas.

The unobservability of the market portfolio is also a potential problem for the cross-sectional regression approach. Roll and Ross (1994) show that if the true market portfolio is efficient, the cross-sectional relation between expected returns and betas can be very sensitive to even small deviations of the market portfolio proxy from the true market portfolio. Thus evidence of the lack of a relation between expected return and beta could be the result of the fact that empirical work is forced to work with proxies for the market portfolio. Kandel and Stambaugh (1995) show that this extreme sensitivity can potentially be mitigated by using a generalized-least-squares (GLS) estimation approach in place of ordinary least squares. However their result depends on knowing the true covariance matrix of returns. The gains from using GLS with an estimated covariance matrix are as yet uncertain.

5.9 Conclusion

In this chapter we have concentrated on the classical approach to testing the unconditional CAPM. Other lines of research are also of interest. One important topic is the extension of the framework to test conditional versions of the CAPM, in which the model holds conditional on state variables that describe the state of the economy. This is useful because the CAPM can hold conditionally, period by period, and yet not hold unconditionally. Chapter 8 discusses the circumstances under which the conditional CAPM might hold in a dynamic equilibrium setting, and Chapter 12 discusses econometric methods for testing the conditional CAPM.

Another important subject is Bayesian analysis of mean-variance efficiency and the CAPM. Bayesian analysis allows the introduction of prior information and addresses some of the shortcomings of the classical approach such as the stark dichotomy between acceptance and rejection of the model. Harvey and Zhou (1990), Kandel, McCulloch, and Stambaugh (1995), and Shanken (1987c) are examples of work with this perspective.

We have shown that there is some statistical evidence against the CAPM in the past 30 years of US stock-market data. Despite this evidence, the CAPM remains a widely used tool in finance. There is controversy about how the evidence against the model should be interpreted. Some authors argue that the CAPM should be replaced by multifactor models with several sources of risk; others argue that the evidence against the CAPM is overstated because of mismeasurement of the market portfolio, improper neglect of conditioning information, data-snooping, or sample-selection bias; and yet others claim that no risk-based model can explain the anomalies of stock-market behavior. In the next chapter we explore multifactor asset pricing models and then return to this debate in Section 6.6.

Problems—Chapter 5

5.1   Result 5 states that for a multiple regression of the return on any asset or portfolio R_a on the return of any minimum-variance portfolio R_p (except for the global minimum-variance portfolio) and the return of its associated zero-beta portfolio R_{op}, $R_a = \beta_0 + \beta_1 R_{op} + \beta_2 R_p + \epsilon_p$, the regression coefficients are $\beta_2 = \beta_{ap}$, $\beta_1 = 1 - \beta_{ap}$, and $\beta_0 = 0$. Show this.

5.2 Show that the intercept of the excess-return market model, α, is zero if the market portfolio is the tangency portfolio.

5.3 Using monthly returns from the 10-year period January 1985 to December 1994 for three individual stocks of your choice, a value-weighted market index, and a Treasury bill with one month to maturity, perform the following tests of the Sharpe-Lintner Capital Asset Pricing Model.

5.3.1 Using the entire 10-year sample, regress excess returns of each stock on the excess (value-weighted) market return, and perform tests with a size of 5% that the intercept is zero. Report the point estimates, t-statistics, and whether or not you reject the CAPM. Perform regression diagnostics to check your specification.

5.3.2 For each stock, perform the same test over each of the two equi-partitioned subsamples and report the point estimates, t-statistics, and whether or not you reject the CAPM in each subperiod. Also include the same diagnostics as above.

5.3.3 Combine all three stocks into a single equal-weighted portfolio and re-do the tests for the entire sample and for each of the two subsamples, and report the point estimates, t-statistics, and whether or not you reject the CAPM for the whole sample and in each subsample. Include diagnostics.

5.3.4 Jointly test that the intercepts for all three stocks are zero using the F-test statistic J_1 in (5.3.23) for the whole sample and for each subsample.

5.4 Derive the Gibbons, Ross, and Shanken result in equation (5.5.3).

6

Multifactor Pricing Models

AT THE END OF CHAPTER 5 we summarized empirical evidence indicating that the CAPM beta does not completely explain the cross section of expected asset returns. This evidence suggests that one or more additional factors may be required to characterize the behavior of expected returns and naturally leads to consideration of multifactor pricing models. Theoretical arguments also suggest that more than one factor is required, since only under strong assumptions will the CAPM apply period by period. Two main theoretical approaches exist. The Arbitrage Pricing Theory (APT) developed by Ross (1976) is based on arbitrage arguments and the Intertemporal Capital Asset Pricing Model (ICAPM) developed by Merton (1973a) is based on equilibrium arguments. In this chapter we will consider the econometric analysis of multifactor models.

The chapter proceeds as follows. Section 6.1 briefly discusses the theoretical background of the multifactor approaches. In Section 6.2 we consider estimation and testing of the models with known factors, while in Section 6.3 we develop estimators for risk premia and expected returns. Since the factors are not always provided by theory, we discuss ways to construct them in Section 6.4. Section 6.5 presents empirical results. Because of the lack of specificity of the models, deviations can always be explained by additional factors. This raises an issue of interpreting model violations which we discuss in Section 6.6.

6.1 Theoretical Background

The Arbitrage Pricing Theory (APT) was introduced by Ross (1976) as an alternative to the Capital Asset Pricing Model. The APT can be more general than the CAPM in that it allows for multiple risk factors. Also, unlike the CAPM, the APT does not require the identification of the market portfolio. However, this generality is not without costs. In its most general form the APT provides an *approximate* relation for expected asset returns with an unknown number of unidentified factors. At this level rejection of the theory is impossible (unless arbitrage opportunities exist) and as a consequence testability of the model depends on the introduction of additional assumptions.[1]

The Arbitrage Pricing Theory assumes that markets are competitive and frictionless and that the return generating process for asset returns being considered is

$$R_i = a_i + \mathbf{b}'_i \mathbf{f} + \epsilon_i \tag{6.1.1}$$

$$\mathrm{E}[\epsilon_i \mid \mathbf{f}] = 0 \tag{6.1.2}$$

$$\mathrm{E}[\epsilon_i^2] = \sigma_i^2 \leq \sigma^2 < \infty, \tag{6.1.3}$$

where R_i is the return for asset i, a_i is the intercept of the factor model, $\mathbf{b}_i$ is a $(K \times 1)$ vector of factor sensitivities for asset i, $\mathbf{f}$ is a $(K \times 1)$ vector of common factor realizations, and ϵ_i is the disturbance term. For the system of N assets,

$$\mathbf{R} = \mathbf{a} + \mathbf{B}\mathbf{f} + \epsilon \tag{6.1.4}$$

$$\mathrm{E}[\epsilon \mid \mathbf{f}] = 0 \tag{6.1.5}$$

$$\mathrm{E}[\epsilon \epsilon' \mid \mathbf{f}] = \Sigma. \tag{6.1.6}$$

In the system equation, $\mathbf{R}$ is an $(N \times 1)$ vector with $\mathbf{R} = [R_1 \ R_2 \ \cdots \ R_N]'$, $\mathbf{a}$ is an $(N \times 1)$ vector with $\mathbf{a} = [a_1 \ a_2 \ \cdots \ a_N]'$, $\mathbf{B}$ is an $(N \times K)$ matrix with $\mathbf{B} = [\mathbf{b}_1 \ \mathbf{b}_2 \ \cdots \ \mathbf{b}_N]'$, and ϵ is an $(N \times 1)$ vector with $\epsilon = [\epsilon_1 \ \epsilon_2 \ \cdots \ \epsilon_N]'$. We further assume that the factors account for the common variation in asset returns so that the disturbance term for large well-diversified portfolios vanishes.[2] This requires that the disturbance terms be sufficiently uncorrelated across assets.

Given this structure, Ross (1976) shows that the absence of arbitrage in large economies implies that

$$\mu \approx \iota \lambda_0 + \mathbf{B} \lambda_K, \tag{6.1.7}$$

where μ is the $(N \times 1)$ expected return vector, λ_0 is the model zero-beta parameter and is equal to the riskfree return if such an asset exists, and λ_K is a $(K \times 1)$ vector of factor risk premia. Here, and throughout the chapter,

---

[1]There has been substantial debate on the testability of the APT. Shanken (1982) and Dybvig and Ross (1985) provide one interesting exchange. Dhrymes, Friend, Gultekin, and Gultekin (1984) also question the empirical relevance of the model.

[2]A large well-diversified portfolio is a portfolio with a large number of stocks with weightings of order $\frac{1}{N}$.

let ι represent a conforming vector of ones. The relation in (6.1.7) is approximate as a finite number of assets can be arbitrarily mispriced. Because (6.1.7) is only an approximation, it does not produce directly testable restrictions for asset returns. To obtain restrictions we need to impose additional structure so that the approximation becomes exact.

Connor (1984) presents a competitive equilibrium version of the APT which has exact factor pricing as a feature. In Connor's model the additional requirements are that the market portfolio be well-diversified and that the factors be pervasive. The market portfolio will be well-diversified if no single asset in the economy accounts for a significant proportion of aggregate wealth. The requirement that the factors be pervasive permits investors to diversify away idiosyncratic risk without restricting their choice of factor risk exposure.

Dybvig (1985) and Grinblatt and Titman (1985) take a different approach. They investigate the potential magnitudes of the deviations from exact factor pricing given structure on the preferences of a representative agent. Both papers conclude that given a reasonable specification of the parameters of the economy, theoretical deviations from exact factor pricing are likely to be negligible. As a consequence empirical work based on the exact pricing relation is justified.

Exact factor pricing can also be derived in an intertemporal asset pricing framework. The Intertemporal Capital Asset Pricing Model developed in Merton (1973a) combined with assumptions on the conditional distribution of returns delivers a multifactor model. In this model, the market portfolio serves as one factor and state variables serve as additional factors. The additional factors arise from investors' demand to hedge uncertainty about future investment opportunities. Breeden (1979), Campbell (1993a, 1996), and Fama (1993) explore this model, and we discuss it in Chapter 8.

In this chapter, we will generally not differentiate the APT from the ICAPM. We will analyze models where we have exact factor pricing, that is,

$$\boldsymbol{\mu} = \iota \lambda_0 + \mathbf{B}\,\boldsymbol{\lambda}_K. \tag{6.1.8}$$

There is some flexibility in the specification of the factors. Most empirical implementations choose a proxy for the market portfolio as one factor. However, different techniques are available for handling the additional factors. We will consider several cases. In one case, the factors of the APT and the state variables of the ICAPM need not be traded portfolios. In other cases the factors are returns on portfolios. These factor portfolios are called mimicking portfolios because jointly they are maximally correlated with the factors. Exact factor pricing will hold with such portfolios. Huberman, Kandel, and Stambaugh (1987) and Breeden (1979) discuss this issue in the context of the APT and ICAPM, respectively.

6.2 Estimation and Testing

In this section we consider the estimation and testing of various forms of the exact factor pricing relation. The starting point for the econometric analysis of the model is an assumption about the time-series behavior of returns. We will assume that returns conditional on the factor realizations are IID through time and jointly multivariate normal. This is a strong assumption, but it does allow for limited dependence in returns through the time-series behavior of the factors. Furthermore, this assumption can be relaxed by casting the estimation and testing problem in a Generalized Method of Moments framework as outlined in the Appendix. The GMM approach for multifactor models is just a generalization of the GMM approach to testing the CAPM presented in Chapter 5.

As previously mentioned, the multifactor models specify neither the number of factors nor the identification of the factors. Thus to estimate and test the model we need to determine the factors—an issue we will address in Section 6.4. In this section we will proceed by taking the number of factors and their identification as given.

We consider four versions of the exact factor pricing model: (1) Factors are portfolios of traded assets and a riskfree asset exists; (2) Factors are portfolios of traded assets and there is not a riskfree asset; (3) Factors are not portfolios of traded assets; and (4) Factors are portfolios of traded assets and the factor portfolios span the mean-variance frontier of risky assets. We use maximum likelihood estimation to handle all four cases. See Shanken (1992b) for a treatment of the same four cases using a cross-sectional regression approach.

Given the joint normality assumption for the returns conditional on the factors, we can construct a test of any of the four cases using the likelihood ratio. Since derivation of the test statistic parallels the derivation of the likelihood ratio test of the CAPM presented in Chapter 5, we will not repeat it here. The likelihood ratio test statistic for all cases takes the same general form. Defining J as the test statistic we have

$$J = -\left(T - \frac{N}{2} - K - 1\right)[\log|\hat{\Sigma}| - \log|\hat{\Sigma}^*|], \qquad (6.2.1)$$

where $\hat{\Sigma}$ and $\hat{\Sigma}^*$ are the maximum likelihood estimators of the residual covariance matrix for the unconstrained model and constrained model, respectively. T is the number of time-series observations, N is the number of included portfolios, and K is the number of factors. As discussed in Chapter 5, the statistic has been scaled by $(T - \frac{N}{2} - K - 1)$ rather than the usual T to improve the convergence of the finite-sample null distribution to the large sample distribution.[3] The large sample distribution of J under the null hypothesis will be chi-square with the degrees of freedom equal to the number of restrictions imposed by the null hypothesis.

6.2.1 Portfolios as Factors with a Riskfree Asset

We first consider the case where the factors are traded portfolios and there exists a riskfree asset. The unconstrained model will be a K-factor model expressed in excess returns. Define $\mathbf{Z}_t$ as an $(N \times 1)$ vector of excess returns for N assets (or portfolios of assets). For excess returns, the K-factor linear model is:

$$\mathbf{Z}_t = \mathbf{a} + \mathbf{B}\mathbf{Z}_{Kt} + \epsilon_t \tag{6.2.2}$$

$$E[\epsilon_t] = 0 \tag{6.2.3}$$

$$E[\epsilon_t \epsilon_t'] = \mathbf{\Sigma} \tag{6.2.4}$$

$$E[\mathbf{Z}_{Kt}] = \boldsymbol{\mu}_K, \qquad E[(\mathbf{Z}_{Kt} - \boldsymbol{\mu}_K)(\mathbf{Z}_{Kt} - \boldsymbol{\mu}_K)'] = \mathbf{\Omega}_K \tag{6.2.5}$$

$$\mathrm{Cov}[\mathbf{Z}_{Kt}, \epsilon_t'] = \mathbf{O}. \tag{6.2.6}$$

$\mathbf{B}$ is the $(N \times K)$ matrix of factor sensitivities, $\mathbf{Z}_{Kt}$ is the $(K \times 1)$ vector of factor portfolio excess returns, and $\mathbf{a}$ and ϵ_t are $(N \times 1)$ vectors of asset return intercepts and disturbances, respectively. $\mathbf{\Sigma}$ is the variance-covariance matrix of the disturbances, and $\mathbf{\Omega}_K$ is the variance-covariance matrix of the factor portfolio excess returns, while $\mathbf{O}$ is a $(K \times N)$ matrix of zeroes. Exact factor pricing implies that the elements of the vector $\mathbf{a}$ in (6.2.2) will be zero.

For the unconstrained model in (6.2.2) the maximum likelihood estimators are just the OLS estimators:

$$\hat{\mathbf{a}} = \hat{\boldsymbol{\mu}} - \hat{\mathbf{B}}\hat{\boldsymbol{\mu}}_K \tag{6.2.7}$$

$$\hat{\mathbf{B}} = \left[\sum_{t=1}^{T} (\mathbf{Z}_t - \hat{\boldsymbol{\mu}})(\mathbf{Z}_{Kt} - \hat{\boldsymbol{\mu}}_K)' \right] \left[\sum_{t=1}^{T} (\mathbf{Z}_{Kt} - \hat{\boldsymbol{\mu}}_K)(\mathbf{Z}_{Kt} - \hat{\boldsymbol{\mu}}_K)' \right]^{-1} \tag{6.2.8}$$

$$\hat{\mathbf{\Sigma}} = \frac{1}{T} \sum_{t=1}^{T} (\mathbf{Z}_t - \hat{\mathbf{a}} - \hat{\mathbf{B}}\mathbf{Z}_{Kt})(\mathbf{Z}_t - \hat{\mathbf{a}} - \hat{\mathbf{B}}\mathbf{Z}_{Kt})', \tag{6.2.9}$$

where

$$\hat{\boldsymbol{\mu}} = \frac{1}{T} \sum_{t=1}^{T} \mathbf{Z}_t \quad \text{and} \quad \hat{\boldsymbol{\mu}}_K = \frac{1}{T} \sum_{t=1}^{T} \mathbf{Z}_{Kt}.$$

[3]See equation (5.3.41) and Jobson and Korkie (1982).

For the constrained model, with **a** constrained to be zero, the maximum likelihood estimators are

$$\hat{\mathbf{B}}^* = \left[\sum_{t=1}^{T} \mathbf{Z}_t \mathbf{Z}'_{Kt} \right] \left[\sum_{t=1}^{T} \mathbf{Z}_{Kt} \mathbf{Z}'_{Kt} \right]^{-1} \tag{6.2.10}$$

$$\hat{\mathbf{\Sigma}}^* = \frac{1}{T} \sum_{t=1}^{T} (\mathbf{Z}_t - \hat{\mathbf{B}}^* \mathbf{Z}_{Kt})(\mathbf{Z}_t - \hat{\mathbf{B}}^* \mathbf{Z}_{Kt})'. \tag{6.2.11}$$

The null hypothesis **a** equals zero can be tested using the likelihood ratio statistic J in (6.2.1). Under the null hypothesis the degrees of freedom of the null distribution will be N since the null hypothesis imposes N restrictions.

In this case we can also construct an exact multivariate F-test of the null hypothesis. Defining J_1 as the test statistic we have

$$J_1 = \frac{(T - N - K)}{N} [1 + \hat{\mu}'_K \hat{\mathbf{\Omega}}_K^{-1} \hat{\mu}_K]^{-1} \hat{\mathbf{a}}' \hat{\mathbf{\Sigma}}^{-1} \hat{\mathbf{a}}, \tag{6.2.12}$$

where $\hat{\mathbf{\Omega}}_K$ is the maximum likelihood estimator of $\mathbf{\Omega}_K$,

$$\hat{\mathbf{\Omega}}_K = \frac{1}{T} \sum_{t=1}^{T} (\mathbf{Z}_{Kt} - \hat{\mu}_K)(\mathbf{Z}_{Kt} - \hat{\mu}_K)'. \tag{6.2.13}$$

Under the null hypothesis, J_1 is unconditionally distributed central F with N degrees of freedom in the numerator and $(T - N - K)$ degrees of freedom in the denominator. This test can be very useful since it can eliminate the problems that can accompany the use of asymptotic distribution theory. Jobson and Korkie (1985) provide a derivation of J_1.

6.2.2 Portfolios as Factors without a Riskfree Asset

In the absence of a riskfree asset, there is a zero-beta model that is a multi-factor equivalent of the Black version of the CAPM. In a multifactor context, the zero-beta portfolio is a portfolio with no sensitivity to any of the factors, and expected returns in excess of the zero-beta return are linearly related to the columns of the matrix of factor sensitivities. The factors are assumed to be portfolio returns in excess of the zero-beta return.

Define $\mathbf{R}_t$ as an $(N \times 1)$ vector of real returns for N assets (or portfolios of assets). For the unconstrained model, we have a K-factor linear model:

$$\mathbf{R}_t = \mathbf{a} + \mathbf{B} \mathbf{R}_{Kt} + \epsilon_t \tag{6.2.14}$$

$$E[\epsilon_t] = 0 \tag{6.2.15}$$

$$E[\epsilon_t \epsilon_t'] = \mathbf{\Sigma} \tag{6.2.16}$$

$$E[\mathbf{R}_{Kt}] = \mu_K, \qquad E[(\mathbf{R}_{Kt} - \mu_K)(\mathbf{R}_{Kt} - \mu_K)'] = \mathbf{\Omega}_K \qquad (6.2.17)$$

$$\text{Cov}[\mathbf{R}_{Kt}, \epsilon_t'] = \mathbf{O}. \qquad (6.2.18)$$

$\mathbf{B}$ is the $(N \times K)$ matrix of factor sensitivities, $\mathbf{R}_{Kt}$ is the $(K \times 1)$ vector of factor portfolio real returns, and $\mathbf{a}$ and ϵ_t are $(N \times 1)$ vectors of asset return intercepts and disturbances, respectively. $\mathbf{O}$ is a $(K \times N)$ matrix of zeroes.

For the unconstrained model in (6.2.14) the maximum likelihood estimators are

$$\hat{\mathbf{a}} = \hat{\mu} - \hat{\mathbf{B}}\hat{\mu}_K \qquad (6.2.19)$$

$$\hat{\mathbf{B}} = \left[\sum_{t=1}^{T} (\mathbf{R}_t - \hat{\mu})(\mathbf{R}_{Kt} - \hat{\mu}_K)' \right] \left[\sum_{t=1}^{T} (\mathbf{R}_{Kt} - \hat{\mu}_K)(\mathbf{R}_{Kt} - \hat{\mu}_K)' \right]^{-1} \qquad (6.2.20)$$

$$\hat{\mathbf{\Sigma}} = \frac{1}{T} \sum_{t=1}^{T} (\mathbf{R}_t - \hat{\mathbf{a}} - \hat{\mathbf{B}}\mathbf{R}_{Kt})(\mathbf{R}_t - \hat{\mathbf{a}} - \hat{\mathbf{B}}\mathbf{R}_{Kt})', \qquad (6.2.21)$$

where

$$\hat{\mu} = \frac{1}{T} \sum_{t=1}^{T} \mathbf{R}_t \quad \text{and} \quad \hat{\mu}_K = \frac{1}{T} \sum_{t=1}^{T} \mathbf{R}_{Kt}.$$

In the constrained model real returns enter in excess of the expected zero-beta portfolio return γ_0. For the constrained model, we have

$$\mathbf{R}_t = \iota\gamma_0 + \mathbf{B}(\mathbf{R}_{Kt} - \iota\gamma_0) + \epsilon_t \qquad (6.2.22)$$

$$= (\iota - \mathbf{B}\iota)\gamma_0 + \mathbf{B}\mathbf{R}_{Kt} + \epsilon_t.$$

The constrained model estimators are:

$$\hat{\mathbf{B}}^* = \left[\sum_{t=1}^{T} (\mathbf{R}_t - \iota\hat{\gamma}_0)(\mathbf{R}_{Kt} - \iota\hat{\gamma}_0)' \right]$$

$$\times \left[\sum_{t=1}^{T} (\mathbf{R}_{Kt} - \iota\hat{\gamma}_0)(\mathbf{R}_{Kt} - \iota\hat{\gamma}_0)' \right]^{-1} \qquad (6.2.23)$$

$$\hat{\mathbf{\Sigma}}^* = \frac{1}{T} \sum_{t=1}^{T} [\mathbf{R}_t - \iota\hat{\gamma}_0 - \hat{\mathbf{B}}^*(\mathbf{R}_{Kt} - \iota\hat{\gamma}_0)]$$

$$\times [\mathbf{R}_t - \iota\hat{\gamma}_0 - \hat{\mathbf{B}}^*(\mathbf{R}_{Kt} - \iota\hat{\gamma}_0)]' \qquad (6.2.24)$$

$$\hat{\gamma}_0 = [(\iota - \hat{\mathbf{B}}^*\iota)'\hat{\mathbf{\Sigma}}^{*-1}(\iota - \hat{\mathbf{B}}^*\iota)]^{-1}$$

$$\times [(\iota - \hat{\mathbf{B}}^*\iota)'\hat{\mathbf{\Sigma}}^{*-1}(\hat{\mu} - \hat{\mathbf{B}}^*\hat{\mu}_K)]. \qquad (6.2.25)$$

The maximum likelihood estimates can be obtained by iterating over (6.2.23) to (6.2.25). $\hat{\mathbf{B}}$ from (6.2.20) and $\hat{\Sigma}$ from (6.2.21) can be used as starting values for $\mathbf{B}$ and Σ in (6.2.25).

Exact maximum likelihood estimators can also be calculated without iteration for this case. The methodology is a generalization of the approach outlined for the Black version of the CAPM in Chapter 5; it is presented by Shanken (1985a). The estimator of γ_0 is the solution of a quadratic equation. Given γ_0, the constrained maximum likelihood estimators of $\mathbf{B}$ and Σ follow from (6.2.23) and (6.2.24).

The restrictions of the constrained model in (6.2.22) on the unconstrained model in (6.2.14) are

$$\mathbf{a} = (\iota - \mathbf{B}\iota)\gamma_0. \qquad (6.2.26)$$

These restrictions can be tested using the likelihood ratio statistic J in (6.2.1). Under the null hypothesis the degrees of freedom of the null distribution will be $N-1$. There is a reduction of one degree of freedom in comparison to the case with a riskfree asset. A degree of freedom is used up in estimating the zero-beta expected return.

For use in Section 6.3, we note that the asymptotic variance of $\hat{\gamma}_0$ evaluated at the maximum likelihood estimators is

$$\mathrm{Var}[\hat{\gamma}_0] = \frac{1}{T}\left(1 + (\hat{\mu}_K - \hat{\gamma}_0\iota)'\hat{\Omega}_K^{-1}(\hat{\mu}_K - \hat{\gamma}_0\iota)\right)$$
$$\times\,[(\iota - \hat{\mathbf{B}}^*\iota)'\hat{\Sigma}^{*-1}(\iota - \hat{\mathbf{B}}^*\iota)]^{-1}. \qquad (6.2.27)$$

6.2.3 Macroeconomic Variables as Factors

Factors need not be traded portfolios of assets; in some cases proposed factors include macroeconomic variables such as innovations in GNP, changes in bond yields, or unanticipated inflation. We now consider estimating and testing exact factor pricing models with such factors.

Again define $\mathbf{R}_t$ as an $(N \times 1)$ vector of real returns for N assets (or portfolios of assets). For the unconstrained model we have a K-factor linear model:

$$\mathbf{R}_t = \mathbf{a} + \mathbf{B}\mathbf{f}_{Kt} + \epsilon_t \qquad (6.2.28)$$

$$\mathrm{E}[\epsilon_t] = 0 \qquad (6.2.29)$$

$$\mathrm{E}[\epsilon_t\epsilon_t'] = \Sigma \qquad (6.2.30)$$

$$\mathrm{E}[\mathbf{f}_{Kt}] = \mu_{fK}, \qquad \mathrm{E}[(\mathbf{f}_{Kt} - \mu_{fK})(\mathbf{f}_{Kt} - \mu_{fK})'] = \Omega_K \qquad (6.2.31)$$

$$\mathrm{Cov}[\mathbf{f}_{Kt}, \epsilon_t'] = \mathbf{O}. \qquad (6.2.32)$$

B is the ($N \times K$) matrix of factor sensitivities, $\mathbf{f}_{Kt}$ is the ($K \times 1$) vector of factor realizations, and **a** and $\boldsymbol{\epsilon}_t$ are ($N \times 1$) vectors of asset return intercepts and disturbances, respectively. **O** is a ($K \times N$) matrix of zeroes.

For the unconstrained model in (6.2.14) the maximum likelihood estimators are

$$\hat{\mathbf{a}} = \hat{\boldsymbol{\mu}} - \hat{\mathbf{B}}\hat{\boldsymbol{\mu}}_{fK} \tag{6.2.33}$$

$$\hat{\mathbf{B}} = \left[\sum_{t=1}^{T} (\mathbf{R}_t - \hat{\boldsymbol{\mu}})(\mathbf{f}_{Kt} - \hat{\boldsymbol{\mu}}_{fK})' \right]$$

$$\times \left[\sum_{t=1}^{T} (\mathbf{f}_{Kt} - \hat{\boldsymbol{\mu}}_{fK})(\mathbf{f}_{Kt} - \hat{\boldsymbol{\mu}}_{fK})' \right]^{-1} \tag{6.2.34}$$

$$\hat{\boldsymbol{\Sigma}} = \frac{1}{T} \sum_{t=1}^{T} (\mathbf{R}_t - \hat{\mathbf{a}} - \hat{\mathbf{B}}\mathbf{f}_{Kt})(\mathbf{R}_t - \hat{\mathbf{a}} - \hat{\mathbf{B}}\mathbf{f}_{Kt})', \tag{6.2.35}$$

where

$$\hat{\boldsymbol{\mu}} = \frac{1}{T} \sum_{t=1}^{T} \mathbf{R}_t \quad \text{and} \quad \hat{\boldsymbol{\mu}}_{fK} = \frac{1}{T} \sum_{t=1}^{T} \mathbf{f}_{Kt}.$$

The constrained model is most conveniently formulated by comparing the unconditional expectation of (6.2.28) with (6.1.8). The unconditional expectation of (6.2.28) is

$$\boldsymbol{\mu} = \mathbf{a} + \mathbf{B}\boldsymbol{\mu}_{fK}, \tag{6.2.36}$$

where $\boldsymbol{\mu}_{fK} = \mathrm{E}[\mathbf{f}_{Kt}]$. Equating the right hand sides of (6.1.8) and (6.2.36) we have

$$\mathbf{a} = \iota\lambda_0 + \mathbf{B}(\boldsymbol{\lambda}_K - \boldsymbol{\mu}_{fK}). \tag{6.2.37}$$

Defining γ_0 as the zero-beta parameter λ_0 and defining $\boldsymbol{\gamma}_1$ as $(\boldsymbol{\lambda}_K - \boldsymbol{\mu}_{fK})$ where $\boldsymbol{\lambda}_K$ is the ($K \times 1$) vector of factor risk premia, for the constrained model, we have

$$\mathbf{R}_t = \iota\gamma_0 + \mathbf{B}\boldsymbol{\gamma}_1 + \mathbf{B}\mathbf{f}_{Kt} + \boldsymbol{\epsilon}_t. \tag{6.2.38}$$

The constrained model estimators are

$$\hat{\mathbf{B}}^* = \left[\sum_{t=1}^{T} (\mathbf{R}_t - \iota\hat{\gamma}_0)(\mathbf{f}_{Kt} + \hat{\boldsymbol{\gamma}}_1)' \right]$$

$$\times \left[\sum_{t=1}^{T} (\mathbf{f}_{Kt} + \hat{\boldsymbol{\gamma}}_1)(\mathbf{f}_{Kt} + \hat{\boldsymbol{\gamma}}_1)' \right]^{-1} \tag{6.2.39}$$

$$\hat{\boldsymbol{\Sigma}}^* = \frac{1}{T} \sum_{t=1}^{T} [(\mathbf{R}_t - \iota\hat{\gamma}_0) - \hat{\mathbf{B}}^*(\mathbf{f}_{Kt} + \hat{\gamma}_1)]$$

$$\times [(\mathbf{R}_t - \iota\hat{\gamma}_0) - \hat{\mathbf{B}}^*(\mathbf{f}_{Kt} + \hat{\gamma}_1)]' \quad\quad (6.2.40)$$

$$\hat{\boldsymbol{\gamma}} = [\mathbf{X}'\hat{\boldsymbol{\Sigma}}^{*-1}\mathbf{X}]^{-1} [\mathbf{X}'\hat{\boldsymbol{\Sigma}}^{*-1}(\hat{\boldsymbol{\mu}} - \hat{\mathbf{B}}^*\hat{\boldsymbol{\mu}}_{fK})], \quad\quad (6.2.41)$$

where in (6.2.41) $\mathbf{X} \equiv [\iota \, \hat{\mathbf{B}}^*]$ and $\boldsymbol{\gamma} \equiv [\gamma_0 \, \boldsymbol{\gamma}_1']'$.

The maximum likelihood estimates can be obtained by iterating over (6.2.39) to (6.2.41). $\hat{\mathbf{B}}$ from (6.2.34) and $\hat{\boldsymbol{\Sigma}}$ from (6.2.35) can be used as starting values for $\mathbf{B}$ and $\boldsymbol{\Sigma}$ in (6.2.41).

The restrictions of (6.2.38) on (6.2.28) are

$$\mathbf{a} = \iota\gamma_0 + \mathbf{B}\boldsymbol{\gamma}_1. \quad\quad (6.2.42)$$

These restrictions can be tested using the likelihood ratio statistic J in (6.2.1). Under the null hypothesis the degrees of freedom of the null distribution is $N - K - 1$. There are N restrictions but one degree of freedom is lost estimating γ_0, and K degrees of freedom are used estimating the K elements of $\boldsymbol{\lambda}_K$.

The asymptotic variance of $\hat{\boldsymbol{\gamma}}$ follows from the maximum likelihood approach. The variance evaluated at the maximum likelihood estimators is

$$\widehat{\text{Var}}[\hat{\boldsymbol{\gamma}}] = \frac{1}{T}\left(1 + (\hat{\boldsymbol{\gamma}}_1 + \hat{\boldsymbol{\mu}}_{fK})'\hat{\boldsymbol{\Omega}}_K^{-1}(\hat{\boldsymbol{\gamma}}_1 + \hat{\boldsymbol{\mu}}_{fK})\right) [\mathbf{X}'\hat{\boldsymbol{\Sigma}}^{*-1}\mathbf{X}]^{-1}. \quad (6.2.43)$$

Applying the partitioned inverse rule to (6.2.43), for the variances of the components of $\hat{\boldsymbol{\gamma}}$ we have estimators

$$\widehat{\text{Var}}[\hat{\gamma}_0] = \frac{1}{T}\left(1 + (\hat{\boldsymbol{\gamma}}_1 + \hat{\boldsymbol{\mu}}_{fK})'\hat{\boldsymbol{\Omega}}_K^{-1}(\hat{\boldsymbol{\gamma}}_1 + \hat{\boldsymbol{\mu}}_{fK})\right)$$

$$[\iota'\hat{\boldsymbol{\Sigma}}^{*-1}\iota - \iota'\hat{\boldsymbol{\Sigma}}^{*-1}\hat{\mathbf{B}}^*(\hat{\mathbf{B}}^{*'}\hat{\boldsymbol{\Sigma}}^{*-1}\hat{\mathbf{B}}^*)^{-1}\hat{\mathbf{B}}^{*'}\hat{\boldsymbol{\Sigma}}^{*-1}\iota]^{-1} \quad (6.2.44)$$

$$\widehat{\text{Var}}[\hat{\boldsymbol{\gamma}}_1] = \frac{1}{T}\left(1 + (\hat{\boldsymbol{\gamma}}_1 + \hat{\boldsymbol{\mu}}_{fK})'\hat{\boldsymbol{\Omega}}_K^{-1}(\hat{\boldsymbol{\gamma}}_1 + \hat{\boldsymbol{\mu}}_{fK})\right)(\hat{\mathbf{B}}^{*'}\hat{\boldsymbol{\Sigma}}^{*-1}\hat{\mathbf{B}}^*)^{-1}$$

$$+ (\hat{\mathbf{B}}^{*'}\hat{\boldsymbol{\Sigma}}^{*-1}\hat{\mathbf{B}}^*)^{-1}\hat{\mathbf{B}}^{*'}\hat{\boldsymbol{\Sigma}}^{*-1}\iota(\widehat{\text{Var}}[\hat{\gamma}_0])$$

$$\times \iota'\hat{\boldsymbol{\Sigma}}^{*-1}\hat{\mathbf{B}}^*(\hat{\mathbf{B}}^{*'}\hat{\boldsymbol{\Sigma}}^{*-1}\hat{\mathbf{B}}^*)^{-1}. \quad\quad (6.2.45)$$

We will use these variance results for inferences concerning the factor risk premia in Section 6.3.

6.2.4 Factor Portfolios Spanning the Mean-Variance Frontier

When factor portfolios span the mean-variance frontier, the intercept term of the exact pricing relation λ_0 is zero without the need for a riskfree asset.

Thus this case retains the simplicity of the first case with the riskfree asset. In the context of the APT, spanning occurs when two well-diversified portfolios are on the minimum-variance boundary. Chamberlain (1983a) provides discussion of this case.

The unconstrained model will be a K-factor model expressed in real returns. Define $\mathbf{R}_t$ as an ($N \times 1$) vector of real returns for N assets (or portfolios of assets). Then for real returns we have a K-factor linear model:

$$\mathbf{R}_t = \mathbf{a} + \mathbf{B}\mathbf{R}_{Kt} + \epsilon_t \tag{6.2.46}$$

$$E[\epsilon_t] = 0 \tag{6.2.47}$$

$$E[\epsilon_t\epsilon_t'] = \Sigma \tag{6.2.48}$$

$$E[\mathbf{R}_{Kt}] = \mu_K, \qquad E[(\mathbf{R}_{Kt} - \mu_K)(\mathbf{R}_{Kt} - \mu_K)'] = \Omega_K \tag{6.2.49}$$

$$\mathrm{Cov}[\mathbf{R}_{Kt}, \epsilon_t'] = \mathbf{O}. \tag{6.2.50}$$

$\mathbf{B}$ is the ($N \times K$) matrix of factor sensitivities, $\mathbf{R}_{Kt}$ is the ($K \times 1$) vector of factor portfolio real returns, and $\mathbf{a}$ and ϵ_t are ($N \times 1$) vectors of asset return intercepts and disturbances, respectively. $\mathbf{O}$ is a ($K \times N$) matrix of zeroes. The restrictions on (6.2.46) imposed by the included factor portfolios spanning the mean-variance frontier are:

$$\mathbf{a} = 0 \quad \text{and} \quad \mathbf{B}\iota = \iota. \tag{6.2.51}$$

To understand the intuition behind these restrictions, we can return to the Black version of the CAPM from Chapter 5 and can construct a spanning example. The theory underlying the model differs but empirically the restrictions are the same as those on a two-factor APT model with spanning. The unconstrained Black model can be written as

$$\mathbf{R}_t = \mathbf{a} + \beta_{om}\mathbf{R}_{ot} + \beta_m\mathbf{R}_{mt} + \epsilon_t, \tag{6.2.52}$$

where $\mathbf{R}_{mt}$ and $\mathbf{R}_{ot}$ are the return on the market portfolio and the associated zero-beta portfolio, respectively. The restrictions on the Black model are $\mathbf{a} = 0$ and $\beta_{om} + \beta_m = \iota$ as shown in Chapter 5. These restrictions correspond to those in (6.2.51).

For the unconstrained model in (6.2.46) the maximum likelihood estimators are

$$\hat{\mathbf{a}} = \hat{\mu} - \hat{\mathbf{B}}\hat{\mu}_K \tag{6.2.53}$$

$$\hat{\mathbf{B}} = \left[\sum_{t=1}^{T} (\mathbf{R}_t - \hat{\boldsymbol{\mu}})(\mathbf{R}_{Kt} - \hat{\boldsymbol{\mu}}_K)' \right]$$

$$\times \left[\sum_{t=1}^{T} (\mathbf{R}_{Kt} - \hat{\boldsymbol{\mu}}_K)(\mathbf{R}_{Kt} - \hat{\boldsymbol{\mu}}_K)' \right]^{-1} \qquad (6.2.54)$$

$$\hat{\boldsymbol{\Sigma}} = \frac{1}{T} \sum_{t=1}^{T} (\mathbf{R}_t - \hat{\mathbf{a}} - \hat{\mathbf{B}}\mathbf{R}_{Kt})(\mathbf{R}_t - \hat{\mathbf{a}} - \hat{\mathbf{B}}\mathbf{R}_{Kt})', \qquad (6.2.55)$$

where

$$\hat{\boldsymbol{\mu}} = \frac{1}{T} \sum_{t=1}^{T} \mathbf{R}_t \quad \text{and} \quad \hat{\boldsymbol{\mu}}_K = \frac{1}{T} \sum_{t=1}^{T} \mathbf{R}_{Kt}.$$

To estimate the constrained model, we consider the unconstrained model in (6.2.46) with the matrix $\mathbf{B}$ partitioned into an $(N \times 1)$ column vector $\mathbf{b}_1$ and an $(N \times (K-1))$ matrix $\mathbf{B}_1$ and the factor portfolio vector partitioned into the first row $\mathbf{R}_{1t}$ and the last $(K-1)$ rows $\mathbf{R}_{K^*t}$. With this partitioning the constraint $\mathbf{B}\boldsymbol{\iota} = \boldsymbol{\iota}$ can be written $\mathbf{b}_1 + \mathbf{B}_1\boldsymbol{\iota} = \boldsymbol{\iota}$. For the unconstrained model we have

$$\mathbf{R}_t = \mathbf{a} + \mathbf{b}_1 \mathbf{R}_{1t} + \mathbf{B}_1 \mathbf{R}_{K^*t} + \boldsymbol{\epsilon}_t. \qquad (6.2.56)$$

Substituting $\mathbf{a} = 0$ and $\mathbf{b}_1 = \boldsymbol{\iota} - \mathbf{B}_1\boldsymbol{\iota}$ into (6.2.56) gives the constrained model,

$$\mathbf{R}_t - \boldsymbol{\iota}\mathbf{R}_{1t} = \mathbf{B}_1 (\mathbf{R}_{K^*t} - \boldsymbol{\iota}\mathbf{R}_{1t}) + \boldsymbol{\epsilon}_t. \qquad (6.2.57)$$

Using (6.2.57) the maximum likelihood estimators are

$$\hat{\mathbf{B}}_1^* = \left[\sum_{t=1}^{T} (\mathbf{R}_t - \boldsymbol{\iota}\mathbf{R}_{1t})(\mathbf{R}_{K^*t} - \boldsymbol{\iota}\mathbf{R}_{1t})' \right]$$

$$\times \left[\sum_{t=1}^{T} (\mathbf{R}_{Kt} - \boldsymbol{\iota}\mathbf{R}_{1t})(\mathbf{R}_{K^*t} - \boldsymbol{\iota}\mathbf{R}_{1t})' \right]^{-1} \qquad (6.2.58)$$

$$\hat{\mathbf{b}}_1^* = \boldsymbol{\iota} - \hat{\mathbf{B}}_1^*\boldsymbol{\iota} \qquad (6.2.59)$$

$$\hat{\boldsymbol{\Sigma}}^* = \frac{1}{T} \sum_{t=1}^{T} (\mathbf{R}_t - \hat{\mathbf{B}}^*\mathbf{R}_{Kt})(\mathbf{R}_t - \hat{\mathbf{B}}^*\mathbf{R}_{Kt})'. \qquad (6.2.60)$$

The null hypothesis $\mathbf{a}$ equals zero can be tested using the likelihood ratio statistic J in (6.2.1). Under the null hypothesis the degrees of freedom of the null distribution will be $2N$ since $\mathbf{a} = 0$ is N restrictions and $\mathbf{B}\boldsymbol{\iota} = \boldsymbol{\iota}$ is N additional restrictions.

We can also construct an exact test of the null hypothesis given the linearity of the restrictions in (6.2.51) and the multivariate normality assumption.

Defining J_2 as the test statistic we have

$$J_2 = \frac{(T-N-K)}{N}\left[\frac{|\hat{\Sigma}^*|}{|\hat{\Sigma}|} - 1\right]. \qquad (6.2.61)$$

Under the null hypothesis, J_2 is unconditionally distributed central F with $2N$ degrees of freedom in the numerator and $2(T-N-K)$ degrees of freedom in the denominator. Huberman and Kandel (1987) present a derivation of this test.

6.3 Estimation of Risk Premia and Expected Returns

All the exact factor pricing models allow one to estimate the expected return on a given asset. Since the expected return relation is $\mu = \iota\lambda_0 + \mathbf{B}\lambda_K$, one needs measures of the factor sensitivity matrix $\mathbf{B}$, the riskfree rate or the zero-beta expected return λ_0, and the factor risk premia λ_K. Obtaining measures of $\mathbf{B}$ and the riskfree rate or the expected zero-beta return is straightforward. For the given case the constrained maximum likelihood estimator $\hat{\mathbf{B}}^*$ can be used for $\mathbf{B}$. The observed riskfree rate is appropriate for the riskfree asset or, in the cases without a riskfree asset, the maximum likelihood estimator $\hat{\gamma}_0$ can be used for the expected zero-beta return.

Further estimation is necessary to form estimates of the factor risk premia. The appropriate procedure varies across the four cases of exact factor pricing. In the case where the factors are the excess returns on traded portfolios, the risk premia can be estimated directly from the sample means of the excess returns on the portfolios. For this case we have

$$\hat{\lambda}_K = \hat{\mu}_K = \frac{1}{T}\sum_{t=1}^{T}\mathbf{Z}_{Kt}. \qquad (6.3.1)$$

An estimator of the variance of $\hat{\lambda}_K$ is

$$\widehat{\text{Var}}[\hat{\lambda}_K] = \frac{1}{T}\hat{\Omega}_K = \frac{1}{T^2}\sum_{t=1}^{T}(\mathbf{Z}_{Kt} - \hat{\mu}_K)(\mathbf{Z}_{Kt} - \hat{\mu}_K)'. \qquad (6.3.2)$$

In the case where portfolios are factors but there is no riskfree asset, the factor risk premia can be estimated using the difference between the sample mean of the factor portfolios and the estimated zero-beta return:

$$\hat{\lambda}_K = \hat{\mu}_K - \iota\hat{\gamma}_0. \qquad (6.3.3)$$

In this case, an estimator of the variance of $\hat{\lambda}_K$ is

$$\widehat{\text{Var}}[\hat{\lambda}_K] = \frac{1}{T}\hat{\Omega}_K + \widehat{\text{Var}}[\hat{\gamma}_0]\iota\iota', \qquad (6.3.4)$$

where $\widehat{\text{Var}}[\hat{\gamma}_0]$ is from (6.2.27). The fact that $\hat{\mu}_K$ and $\hat{\gamma}_0$ are independent has been utilized to set the covariance term in (6.3.4) to zero.

In the case where the factors are not traded portfolios, an estimator of the vector of factor risk premia λ_K is the sum of the estimator of the mean of the factor realizations and the estimator of γ_1,

$$\hat{\lambda}_K = \hat{\mu}_{fK} + \hat{\gamma}_1. \tag{6.3.5}$$

An estimator of the variance of $\hat{\lambda}_K$ is

$$\widehat{\text{Var}}[\hat{\lambda}_K] = \frac{1}{T}\hat{\Omega}_K + \widehat{\text{Var}}[\hat{\gamma}_1], \tag{6.3.6}$$

where $\widehat{\text{Var}}[\hat{\gamma}_1]$ is from (6.2.45). Because $\hat{\mu}_{fK}$ and $\hat{\gamma}_1$ are independent the covariance term in (6.3.6) is zero.

The fourth case, where the factor portfolios span the mean-variance frontier, is the same as the first case except that real returns are substituted for excess returns. Here $\hat{\lambda}_K$ is the vector of factor portfolio sample means and λ_0 is zero.

For any asset the expected return can be estimated by substituting the estimates of $\mathbf{B}$, λ_0, and λ_K into (6.1.8). Since (6.1.8) is nonlinear in the parameters, calculating a standard error requires using a linear approximation and estimates of the covariances of the parameter estimates.

It is also of interest to ask if the factors are jointly priced. Given the vector of risk premia estimates and its covariance matrix, tests of the null hypothesis that the factors are jointly not priced can be conducted using the following test statistic:

$$J_3 = \frac{(T-K)}{TK}\hat{\lambda}_K' \widehat{\text{Var}}[\hat{\lambda}_K]^{-1}\hat{\lambda}_K. \tag{6.3.7}$$

Asymptotically, under the null hypothesis that $\lambda_K = 0$, J_3 has an F distribution with K and $T-K$ degrees of freedom. This distributional result is an application of the Hotelling T^2 statistic and will be exact in finite samples for the cases where the estimator of λ_K is based only on the sample means of the factors. We can also test the significance of any individual factor using

$$J_4 = \frac{\hat{\lambda}_{jK}}{\sqrt{\upsilon_{jj}}} \stackrel{a}{\sim} \mathcal{N}(0, 1), \tag{6.3.8}$$

where $\hat{\lambda}_{jK}$ is the jth element of $\hat{\lambda}_K$ and υ_{jj} is the (j, j)th element of $\widehat{\text{Var}}[\hat{\lambda}_K]$. Testing if individual factors are priced is sensible for cases where the factors have been theoretically specified. With empirically derived factors, such tests are not useful because, as we explain in Section 6.4.1, factors are identified only up to an orthogonal transformation; hence individual factors do not have clear-cut economic interpretations.

Shanken (1992b) shows that factor risk premia can also be estimated using a two-pass cross-sectional regression approach. In the first pass the factor sensitivities are estimated asset-by-asset using OLS. These estimators represent a measure of the factor loading matrix $\mathbf{B}$ which we denote $\tilde{\mathbf{B}}$. This estimator of $\mathbf{B}$ will be identical to the unconstrained maximum likelihood estimators previously presented for jointly normal and IID residuals.

Using this estimator of $\mathbf{B}$ and the $(N \times 1)$ vector of asset returns for each time period, the *ex post* factor risk premia can be estimated time-period-by-time-period in the second pass. The second-pass regression is

$$\mathbf{Z}_t = \iota\lambda_{0t} + \tilde{\mathbf{B}}\lambda_{Kt} + \boldsymbol{\eta}_t. \tag{6.3.9}$$

The regression can be consistently estimated using OLS; however, GLS can also be used. The output of the regression is a time series of *ex post* risk premia, $\hat{\lambda}_{Kt}$, $t = 1, \ldots, T$, and an *ex post* measure of the zero-beta portfolio return, $\hat{\lambda}_{0t}$, $t = 1, \ldots, T$.

Common practice is then to conduct inferences about the risk premia using the means and standard deviations of these *ex post* series. While this approach is a reasonable approximation, Shanken (1992b) shows that the calculated standard errors of the means will understate the true standard errors because they do not account for the estimation error in $\tilde{\mathbf{B}}$. Shanken derives an adjustment which gives consistent standard errors. No adjustment is needed when a maximum likelihood approach is used, because the maximum likelihood estimators already incorporate the adjustment.

6.4 Selection of Factors

The estimation and testing results in Section 6.2 assume that the identity of the factors is known. In this section we address the issue of specifying the factors. The approaches fall into two basic categories, statistical and theoretical. The statistical approaches, largely motivated by the APT, involve building factors from a comprehensive set of asset returns (usually much larger than the set of returns used to estimate and test the model). Sample data on these returns are used to construct portfolios that represent factors. The theoretical approaches involve specifying factors based on arguments that the factors capture economy-wide systematic risks.

6.4.1 Statistical Approaches

Our starting point for the statistical construction of factors is the linear factor model. We present the analysis in terms of real returns. The same analysis will apply to excess returns in cases with a riskfree asset. Recall that for the linear model we have

$$\mathbf{R}_t = \mathbf{a} + \mathbf{B}\mathbf{f}_t + \epsilon_t \tag{6.4.1}$$

$$E[\epsilon_t \epsilon_t' \mid \mathbf{f}_t] = \Sigma, \tag{6.4.2}$$

where $\mathbf{R}_t$ is the $(N \times 1)$ vector of asset returns for time period t, $\mathbf{f}_t$ is the $(K \times 1)$ vector of factor realizations for time period t, and ϵ_t is the $(N \times 1)$ vector of model disturbances for time period t. The number of assets, N, is now very large and usually much larger than the number of time periods, T. There are two primary statistical approaches, factor analysis and principal components.

Factor Analysis
Estimation using factor analysis involves a two-step procedure. First the factor sensitivity matrix $\mathbf{B}$ and the disturbance covariance matrix Σ are estimated and then these estimates are used to construct measures of the factor realizations. For standard factor analysis it is assumed that there is a *strict factor structure*. With this structure K factors account for all the cross covariance of asset returns and hence Σ is diagonal. (Ross imposes this structure in his original development of the APT.)

Given a strict factor structure and K factors, we can express the $(N \times N)$ covariance matrix of asset returns as the sum of two components, the variation from the factors plus the residual variation,

$$\Omega = \mathbf{B}\,\Omega_K\,\mathbf{B}' + \mathbf{D}, \tag{6.4.3}$$

where $E[\mathbf{f}_t \mathbf{f}_t'] = \Omega_K$ and $\Sigma = \mathbf{D}$ to indicate it is diagonal. With the factors unknown, a rotational indeterminacy exists and $\mathbf{B}$ is identified only up to a nonsingular transformation. This rotational indeterminacy can be eliminated by restricting the factors to be orthogonal to each other and to have unit variance. In this case we have $\Omega_K = \mathbf{I}$ and $\mathbf{B}$ is unique up to an orthogonal transformation. All transforms $\mathbf{BG}$ are equivalent for any $(K \times K)$ orthogonal transformation matrix $\mathbf{G}$, i.e., $\mathbf{GG}' = \mathbf{I}$. With these restrictions in place we can express the return covariance matrix as

$$\Omega = \mathbf{B}\mathbf{B}' + \mathbf{D}. \tag{6.4.4}$$

With the structure in (6.4.4) and the assumption that asset returns are jointly normal and temporally IID, estimators of $\mathbf{B}$ and $\mathbf{D}$ can be formulated using maximum likelihood factor analysis. Because the first-order conditions for maximum likelihood are highly nonlinear in the parameters, solving for the estimators with the usual iterative procedure can be slow and convergence difficult. Alternative algorithms have been developed by Jöreskog (1967) and Rubin and Thayer (1982) which facilitate quick convergence to the maximum likelihood estimators.

One interpretation of the maximum likelihood estimator of $\mathbf{B}$ given the maximum likelihood estimator of $\mathbf{D}$ is that $\mathbf{D}^{-1}$ times the estimator of $\mathbf{B}$ has the eigenvectors of $\hat{\mathbf{D}}^{-1}\hat{\mathbf{\Omega}}$ associated with the K largest eigenvalues as its columns. For details of the estimation the interested reader can see these papers, or Morrison (1990, chapter 9) and references therein.

The second step in the estimation procedure is to estimate the factors given $\mathbf{B}$ and $\mathbf{\Sigma}$. Since the factors are derived from the covariance structure, the means are not specified in (6.4.1). Without loss of generality, we can restrict the factors to have zero means and express the factor model in terms of deviations about the means,

$$(\mathbf{R}_t - \mu) = \mathbf{B}\mathbf{f}_t + \epsilon_t. \tag{6.4.5}$$

Given (6.4.5), a candidate to proxy for the factor realizations for time period t is the cross-sectional generalized least squares (GLS) regression estimator. Using the maximum likelihood estimators of $\mathbf{B}$ and $\mathbf{D}$ we have for each t

$$\hat{\mathbf{f}}_t = (\hat{\mathbf{B}}'\hat{\mathbf{D}}^{-1}\hat{\mathbf{B}})^{-1}\hat{\mathbf{B}}'\hat{\mathbf{D}}^{-1}(\mathbf{R}_t - \hat{\mu}). \tag{6.4.6}$$

Here we are estimating $\mathbf{f}_t$ by regressing $(\mathbf{R}_t - \hat{\mu})$ onto $\hat{\mathbf{B}}$. The factor realization series, $\hat{\mathbf{f}}_t$, $t = 1, \dots, T$, can be employed to test the model using the approach in Section 6.2.3.

Since the factors are linear combinations of returns we can construct portfolios which are perfectly correlated with the factors. Denoting $\mathbf{R}_{Kt}$ as the $(K \times 1)$ vector of factor portfolio returns for time period t, we have

$$\hat{\mathbf{R}}_{Kt} = \mathbf{A}\mathbf{W}\mathbf{R}_t, \tag{6.4.7}$$

where

$$\mathbf{W} = (\hat{\mathbf{B}}'\hat{\mathbf{D}}^{-1}\hat{\mathbf{B}})^{-1}\hat{\mathbf{B}}'\hat{\mathbf{D}}^{-1},$$

and $\mathbf{A}$ is defined as a diagonal matrix with $1/W_j$ as the jth diagonal element, where W_j is the jth element of $\mathbf{W}\iota$.

The factor portfolio weights obtained for the jth factor from this procedure are equivalent to the weights that would result from solving the following optimization problem and then normalizing the weights to sum to one:

$$\operatorname*{Min}_{\omega_j} \omega_j'\hat{\mathbf{D}}\omega_j \tag{6.4.8}$$

subject to

$$\omega_j'\hat{\mathbf{b}}_k = 0 \qquad \forall k \neq j \tag{6.4.9}$$

$$\omega_j'\hat{\mathbf{b}}_k = 1 \qquad \forall k = j. \tag{6.4.10}$$

That is, the factor portfolio weights minimize the residual variance subject to the constraints that each factor portfolio has a unit loading on its own factor and zero loadings on other factors. The resulting factor portfolio returns can be used in all the approaches discussed in Section 6.2.

If **B** and **D** are known, then the factor estimators based on GLS with the population values of **B** and **D** will have the maximum correlation with the population factors. This follows from the minimum-variance unbiased estimator property of generalized least squares given the assumed normality of the disturbance vector. But in practice the factors in (6.4.6) and (6.4.7) need not have the maximum correlation with the population common factors since they are based on estimates of **B** and **D**. Lehmann and Modest (1988) present an alternative to GLS. In the presence of measurement error, they find this alternative can produce factor portfolios with a higher population correlation with the common factors. They suggest for the jth factor to use $\hat{\omega}_j' \mathbf{R}_t$ where the $(N \times 1)$ vector $\hat{\omega}_j$ is the solution to the following problem:

$$\underset{\boldsymbol{\omega}_j}{\text{Min}}\, \omega_j' \hat{\mathbf{D}}\, \omega_j \qquad\qquad (6.4.11)$$

subject to

$$\omega_j' \hat{\mathbf{b}}_k \;=\; 0 \qquad \forall k \neq j \qquad\qquad (6.4.12)$$

$$\omega_j' \iota \;=\; 1. \qquad\qquad\qquad\qquad (6.4.13)$$

This approach finds the portfolio which has the minimum residual variance of all portfolios orthogonal to the other $(K-1)$ factors. Unlike the GLS procedure, this procedure ignores the information in the factor loadings of the jth factor. It is possible that this is beneficial because of the measurement error in the loadings. Indeed, Lehmann and Modest find that this method of forming factor portfolios results in factors with less extreme weightings on the assets and a resulting higher correlation with the underlying common factors.

Principal Components

Factor analysis represents only one statistical method of forming factor portfolios. An alternative approach is principal components analysis. Principal components is a technique to reduce the number of variables being studied without losing too much information in the covariance matrix. In the present application, the objective is to reduce the dimension from N asset returns to K factors. The principal components serve as the factors. The first principal component is the (normalized) linear combination of asset returns with maximum variance. The second principal component is the (normalized) linear combination of asset returns with maximum variance of all combinations orthogonal to the first principal component. And so on.

The first sample principal component is $\mathbf{x}_1^{*\prime}\mathbf{R}_t$ where the $(N \times 1)$ vector $\mathbf{x}_1^*$ is the solution to the following problem:

$$\underset{\mathbf{x}_1}{\text{Max}}\, \mathbf{x}_1' \hat{\boldsymbol{\Omega}}\, \mathbf{x}_1 \qquad (6.4.14)$$

subject to

$$\mathbf{x}_1'\mathbf{x}_1 = 1. \qquad (6.4.15)$$

$\hat{\boldsymbol{\Omega}}$ is the sample covariance matrix of returns. The solution $\mathbf{x}_1^*$ is the eigenvector associated with the largest eigenvalue of $\hat{\boldsymbol{\Omega}}$. To facilitate the portfolio interpretation of the factors we can define the first factor as $\boldsymbol{\omega}_1'\mathbf{R}_t$ where $\boldsymbol{\omega}_1$ is $\mathbf{x}_1^*$ scaled by the reciprocal of $\boldsymbol{\iota}'\mathbf{x}_1^*$ so that its elements sum to one. The second sample principal component solves the above problem for $\mathbf{x}_2$ in the place of $\mathbf{x}_1$ with the additional restriction $\mathbf{x}_1^{*\prime}\mathbf{x}_2 = 0$. The solution $\mathbf{x}_2^*$ is the eigenvector associated with the second largest eigenvalue of $\hat{\boldsymbol{\Omega}}$. $\mathbf{x}_2^*$ can be scaled by the reciprocal of $\boldsymbol{\iota}'\mathbf{x}_2^*$ giving $\boldsymbol{\omega}_2$, and then the second factor portfolio will be $\boldsymbol{\omega}_2'\mathbf{R}_t$. In general the jth factor will be $\boldsymbol{\omega}_j'\mathbf{R}_t$ where $\boldsymbol{\omega}_j$ is the rescaled eigenvector associated with the jth largest eigenvalue of $\hat{\boldsymbol{\Omega}}$. The factor portfolios derived from the first K principal components analysis can then be employed as factors for all the tests outlined in Section 6.2.

Another principal components approach has been developed by Connor and Korajczyk (1986, 1988).[4] They propose using the eigenvectors associated with the K largest eigenvalues of the $(T \times T)$ centered returns cross-product matrix rather than the standard approach which uses the principal components of the $(N \times N)$ sample covariance matrix. They show that as the cross section becomes large the $(K \times T)$ matrix with the rows consisting of the K eigenvectors of the cross-product matrix will converge to the matrix of factor realizations (up to a nonsingular linear transformation reflecting the rotational indeterminancy of factor models). The potential advantages of this approach are that it allows for time-varying factor risk premia and that it is computationally convenient. Because it is typical to have a cross section of assets much larger than the number of time-series observations, analyzing a $(T \times T)$ matrix can be less burdensome than working with an $(N \times N)$ sample covariance matrix.

Factor Analysis or Principal Components?
We have discussed two statistical primary approaches for constructing the model factors—factor analysis and principal components. Within each approach there are possible variations in the process of estimating the factors. A question arises as to which technique is optimal in the sense of providing the most precise measures of the population factors given a fixed sample of returns. Unfortunately the answer in finite samples is not clear although all procedures can be justified in large samples.

[4]See also Mei (1993).

Chamberlain and Rothschild (1983) show that consistent estimates of the factor loading matrix $\mathbf{B}$ can be obtained from the eigenvectors associated with the largest eigenvalues of $\mathbf{\Upsilon}^{-1}\mathbf{\Omega}$, where $\mathbf{\Upsilon}$ is any arbitrary positive definite matrix with eigenvalues bounded away from zero and infinity. Both standard factor analysis and principal components fit into this category, for factor analysis $\mathbf{\Upsilon} = \mathbf{D}$ and for principal components $\mathbf{\Upsilon} = \mathbf{I}$. However, the finite-sample applicability of the result is unclear since it is required that both the number of assets N and the number of time periods T go to infinity.

The Connor and Korajczyk principal components approach is also consistent as N increases. It has the further potential advantage that it only requires $T \geq K$ and does not require T to increase to infinity. However, whether in finite samples it dominates factor analysis or standard principal components is an open question.

6.4.2 Number of Factors

The underlying theory of the multifactor models does not specify the number of factors that are required, that is, the value of K. While, for the theory to be useful, K should be reasonably small, the researcher still has significant latitude in the choice. In empirical work this lack of specification has been handled in several ways. One approach is to repeat the estimation and testing of the model for a variety of values of K and observe if the tests are sensitive to increasing the number of factors. For example Lehmann and Modest (1988) present empirical results for five, ten, and fifteen factors. Their results display minimal sensitivity when the number of factors increases from five to ten to fifteen. Similarly Connor and Korajczyk (1988) consider five and ten factors with little sensitivity to the additional five factors. These results suggest that five factors are adequate.

A second approach is to test explicitly for the adequacy of K factors. An asymptotic likelihood ratio test of the adequacy of K factors can be constructed using -2 times the difference of the value of the log-likelihood function of the covariance matrix evaluated at the constrained and unconstrained estimators. Morrison (1990, p. 362) presents this test. The likelihood ratio test statistic is

$$J_5 = -\left(T - 1 - \tfrac{1}{6}(2N + 5) - \frac{2}{3}K\right) [\log |\hat{\mathbf{\Omega}}| - \log |\hat{\mathbf{B}}\hat{\mathbf{B}}' + \hat{\mathbf{D}}|], \quad (6.4.16)$$

where $\hat{\mathbf{\Omega}}$ is the maximum likelihood estimator of $\mathbf{\Omega}$ and $\hat{\mathbf{B}}$ and $\hat{\mathbf{D}}$ are the maximum likelihood estimators of $\mathbf{B}$ and $\mathbf{D}$, respectively. The leading term is an adjustment to improve the convergence of the finite-sample null distribution to the large-sample distribution. Under the null hypothesis that K factors are adequate, J_5 will be asymptotically distributed ($T \to \infty$) as a chi-square variate with $\frac{1}{2}[(N - K)^2 - N - K]$ degrees of freedom. Roll and

Ross (1980) use this approach and conclude that three or four factors are adequate.

A potential drawback of using the test from maximum likelihood factor analysis is that the constrained model assumes a strict factor structure—an assumption which is not theoretically necessary. Connor and Korajczyk (1993) develop an asymptotic test ($N \to \infty$) for the adequacy of K factors under the assumption of an approximate factor structure. Their test uses the result that with an approximate factor structure the average cross-sectional variation explained by the $K+1$'st factor approaches zero as N increases,

$$\lim_{N \to \infty} \frac{1}{N} \mathbf{b}'_{K+1} \mathbf{b}_{K+1} = 0, \qquad (6.4.17)$$

where the dependence of $\mathbf{b}_{K+1}$ on N is implicit. This implies that in a large cross section generated by a K-factor model, the average residual variance in a linear factor model estimated with $K+1$ factors should converge to the average residual variance with K factors. This is the implication Connor and Korajczyk test. Examining returns from stocks listed on the New York Stock Exchange and the American Stock Exchange they conclude that there are up to six pervasive factors.

6.4.3 Theoretical Approaches

Theoretically based approaches for selecting factors fall into two main categories. One approach is to specify macroeconomic and financial market variables that are thought to capture the systematic risks of the economy. A second approach is to specify characteristics of firms which are likely to explain differential sensitivity to the systematic risks and then form portfolios of stocks based on the characteristics.

Chen, Roll, and Ross (1986) is a good example of the first approach. The authors argue that in selecting factors we should consider forces which will explain changes in the discount rate used to discount future expected cash flows and forces which influence expected cash flows themselves. Based on intuitive analysis and empirical investigation a five-factor model is proposed. The factors include the yield spread between long and short interest rates for US government bonds (maturity premium), expected inflation, unexpected inflation, industrial production growth, and the yield spread between corporate high- and low-grade bonds (default premium). Aggregate consumption growth and oil prices are found not to have incremental effects beyond the five factors.[5]

---

[5]An alternative implementation of the first approach is given by Campbell (1996a) and is discussed in Chapter 8.

The second approach of creating factor portfolios based on firm characteristics has been used in a number of studies. These characteristics have mostly surfaced from the literature of CAPM violations discussed in Chapter 5. Characteristics which have been found to be empirically important include market value of equity, price-to-earnings ratio, and ratio of book value of equity to market value of equity. The general finding is that factor models which include a broad based market portfolio (such as an equal-weighted index) and factor portfolios created using these characteristics do a good job in explaining the cross section of returns. However, because the important characteristics have been identified largely through empirical analysis, their importance may be overstated because of data-snooping biases. We will discuss this issue in Section 6.6.

6.5 Empirical Results

Many empirical studies of multifactor models exist. We will review four of the studies which nicely illustrate the estimation and testing methodology we have discussed. Two comprehensive studies using statistical approaches to select the factors are Lehmann and Modest (1988) and Connor and Korajczyk (1988). Lehmann and Modest [LM] use factor analysis and Connor and Korajczyk [CK] use $(T \times T)$ principal components. Two studies using the theoretical approach to factor identification are Fama and French (1993) and Chen, Roll, and Ross (1986). Fama and French [FF] use firm characteristics to form factor portfolios and Chen, Roll, and Ross [CRR] specify macroeconomic variables as factors. The first three studies include tests of the implications of exact factor pricing, while Chen, Roll, and Ross focus on whether or not the factors are priced. The evidence supporting exact factor pricing is mixed. Table 6.1 summarizes the main results from LM, CK, and FF.

A number of general points emerge from this table. The strongest evidence against exact factor pricing comes from tests using dependent portfolios based on market value of equity and book-to-market ratios. Even multifactor models have difficulty explaining the "size" effect and "book to market" effect. Portfolios which are formed based on dividend yield and based on own variance provide little evidence against exact factor pricing. The CK results for January and non-January months suggest that the evidence against exact factor pricing does not arise from the January effect.

Using the statistical approaches, CK and LM find little sensitivity to increasing the number of factors beyond five. On the other hand FF find some improvement going from two factors to five factors. In results not included, FF find that with stocks only three factors are necessary and that when bond portfolios are included then five factors are needed. These

Table 6.1. *Summary of results for tests of exact factor pricing using zero-intercept F-test.*

Study	Time period	Portfolio characteristic	N	K	p-value
CK	64:01–83:12	market value of equity	10	5	0.002
CK			10	10	0.002
CK^J			10	5	0.236
CK^J			10	10	0.171
CK^{NJ}			10	5	0.011
CK^{NJ}			10	10	0.019
LM	63:01–82:12	market value of equity	5	5	**
LM			5	10	**
LM			5	15	**
LM			20	5	0.11
LM			20	10	0.14
LM			20	15	0.42
LM	63:01–82:12	dividend yield	5	5	0.17
LM			5	10	0.18
LM			5	15	0.17
LM			20	5	0.94
LM			20	10	0.97
LM			20	15	0.98
LM	63:01–82:12	own variance	5	5	0.29
LM			5	10	0.57
LM			5	15	0.55
LM			20	5	0.83
LM			20	10	0.97
LM			20	15	0.98
FF	63:07–91:12	stocks and bonds	32	2	0.010
FF			32	3	0.039
FF			32	5	0.025

**Less than 0.001.

CK refers to Connor and Korajczyk (1988), LM refers to Lehmann and Modest (1988), and FF refers to Fama and French (1993). The CK factors are derived using $(T \times T)$ principal components, the LM factors are derived using maximum likelihood factor analysis, and the FF factors are prespecified factor portfolios. For the FF two-factor case the factors are the return on a portfolio of low market value of equity firms minus a portfolio of high market value of equity firms and the return on a portfolio of high book-to-market value firms minus a portfolio of low book-to-market value firms. For the three-factor case the factors are those in the two-factor case plus the return on the CRSP value-weighted stock index. For the five-factor case the returns on a term structure factor and a default risk factor are added. CK include tests separating the intercept for January from the intercept for other months. CK^J are results of tests of the hypothesis that the January intercept is zero and CK^{NJ} are results of tests of the hypothesis that the non-January intercept is zero. CK and FF work with a monthly sampling interval. LM use a daily interval to estimate the factors and a weekly interval for testing. The test results from CK and LM are based on tests from four five-year periods aggregated together. The portfolio characteristic represents the firm characteristic used to allocate stocks into the dependent portfolios. FF use 25 stock portfolios and 7 bond portfolios. The stock portfolios are created using a two way sort based on market value of equity and book-value-to-market-value ratios. The bond portfolios include five US government bond portfolios and two corporate bond portfolios. The government bond portfolios are created based on maturity and the corporate bond portfolios are created based on the level of default risk. N is the number of dependent portfolios and K is the number of factors. The p-values are reported for the zero-intercept F-test.

results are generally consistent with direct tests for the number of factors discussed in Section 6.4.2.

The LM results display considerable sensitivity to the number of dependent portfolios included. The p-values are considerably lower with fewer portfolios. This is most likely an issue of the power of the test. For these tests with an unspecified alternative hypothesis, reducing the number of portfolios without eliminating the deviations from the null hypothesis can lead to substantial increases in power, because fewer restrictions must be tested.

The CRR paper focuses on the pricing of the factors. They use a cross-sectional regression methodology which is similar to the approach presented in Section 6.3. As previously noted they find evidence of five priced factors. The factors include the yield spread between long and short interest rates for US government bonds (maturity premium), expected inflation, unexpected inflation, industrial production growth, and the yield spread between corporate high- and low-grade bonds (default premium).

6.6 Interpreting Deviations from Exact Factor Pricing

We have just reviewed empirical evidence which suggests that, while multifactor models do a reasonable job of describing the cross section of returns, deviations from the models do exist. Given this, it is important to consider the possible sources of deviations from exact factor pricing. This issue is important because in a given finite sample it is always possible to find an additional factor that will make the deviations vanish. However the procedure of adding an extra factor implicitly assumes that the source of the deviations is a missing risk factor and does not consider other possible explanations.

In this section we analyze the deviations from exact factor pricing for a given model with the objective of exploring the source of the deviations. For the analysis the potential sources of deviations are categorized into two groups—risk-based and nonrisk-based. The objective is to evaluate the plausibility of the argument that the deviations from the given factor model can be explained by additional risk factors.

The analysis relies on an important distinction between the two categories, namely, a difference in the behavior of the maximum squared Sharpe ratio as the cross section of securities is increased. (Recall that the Sharpe ratio is the ratio of the mean excess return to the standard deviation of the excess return.) For the risk-based alternatives the maximum squared Sharpe ratio is bounded and for the nonrisk-based alternatives the maximum squared Sharpe ratio is a less useful construct and can, in principle, be unbounded.

6.6.1 Exact Factor Pricing Models, Mean-Variance Analysis, and the Optimal Orthogonal Portfolio

For the initial analysis we drop back to the level of the primary assets in the economy. Let N be the number of primary assets. Assume that a riskfree asset exists. Let $\mathbf{Z}_t$ represent the $(N \times 1)$ vector of excess returns for period t. Assume $\mathbf{Z}_t$ is stationary and ergodic with mean $\boldsymbol{\mu}$ and covariance matrix $\boldsymbol{\Omega}$ that is full rank. We also take as given a set of K factor portfolios and analyze the deviations from exact factor pricing. For the factor model, as in (6.2.2), we have

$$\mathbf{Z}_t = \mathbf{a} + \mathbf{B}\mathbf{Z}_{Kt} + \boldsymbol{\epsilon}_t. \tag{6.6.1}$$

Here $\mathbf{B}$ is the $(N \times K)$ matrix of factor loadings, $\mathbf{Z}_{Kt}$ is the $(K \times 1)$ vector of time-t factor portfolio excess returns, and $\mathbf{a}$ and $\boldsymbol{\epsilon}_t$ are $(N \times 1)$ vectors of asset return intercepts and disturbances, respectively. The variance-covariance matrix of the disturbances is $\boldsymbol{\Sigma}$ and the variance-covariance matrix of the factors is $\boldsymbol{\Omega}_K$, as in (6.2.3)–(6.2.6). The values of $\mathbf{a}$, $\mathbf{B}$, and $\boldsymbol{\Sigma}$ will depend on the factor portfolios, but this dependence is suppressed for notational convenience.

If we have exact factor pricing relative to the K factors, all the elements of the vector $\mathbf{a}$ will be zero; equivalently, a linear combination of the factor portfolios forms the tangency portfolio (the mean-variance efficient portfolio of risky assets given the presence of a riskfree asset). Let Z_{qt} be the excess return of the (*ex ante*) tangency portfolio and let ω_q be the $(N \times 1)$ vector of portfolio weights. From mean-variance analysis (see Chapter 5),

$$\omega_q = (\boldsymbol{\iota}'\boldsymbol{\Omega}^{-1}\boldsymbol{\mu})^{-1}\boldsymbol{\Omega}^{-1}\boldsymbol{\mu}. \tag{6.6.2}$$

In the context of the K-factor model in (6.6.1), we have exact factor pricing when the tangency portfolio in (6.6.2) can be formed from a linear combination of the K factor portfolios.

Now consider the case where we do not have exact factor pricing, so the tangency portfolio cannot be formed from a linear combination of the factor portfolios. Our interest is in developing the relation between the deviations from the asset pricing model, $\mathbf{a}$, and the residual covariance matrix, $\boldsymbol{\Sigma}$. To facilitate this, we define the *optimal orthogonal portfolio*,[6] which is the unique portfolio that can be combined with the K factor portfolios to form the tangency portfolio and is orthogonal to the factor portfolios.

Definition (optimal orthogonal portfolio). *Take as given K factor portfolios which cannot be combined to form the tangency portfolio or the global minimum-variance portfolio. A portfolio h will be defined as the optimal orthogonal portfolio with respect to these K factor portfolios if*

$$\omega_q = \mathbf{W}_p\omega + \omega_h(1 - \boldsymbol{\iota}'\omega) \tag{6.6.3}$$

---

[6]See Roll (1980) for general properties of orthogonal portfolios.

and

$$\omega'_h \Omega W_p = 0 \qquad (6.6.4)$$

for a $(K \times 1)$ vector ω where W_p is the $(N \times K)$ matrix of asset weights for the factor portfolios, ω_h is the $(N \times 1)$ vector of asset weights for the optimal orthogonal portfolio, and ω_q is the $(N \times 1)$ vector of asset weights for the tangency portfolio. If one considers a model without any factor portfolios $(K = 0)$ then the optimal orthogonal portfolio will be the tangency portfolio.

The weights of portfolio h can be expressed in terms of the parameters of the K-factor model. The vector of weights is

$$\begin{aligned}
\omega_h &= (\iota' \Omega^{-1} a)^{-1} \Omega^{-1} a \\
&= (\iota' \Sigma^\dagger a)^{-1} \Sigma^\dagger a,
\end{aligned} \qquad (6.6.5)$$

where the $\dagger$ superscript indicates the generalized inverse. The usefulness of this portfolio comes from the fact that when added to (6.6.1) the intercept will vanish and the factor loading matrix $\mathbf{B}$ will not be altered. The optimality restriction in (6.6.3) leads to the intercept vanishing, and the orthogonality condition in (6.6.4) leads to $\mathbf{B}$ being unchanged. Adding in Z_{ht}:

$$Z_t = \mathbf{B} Z_{Kt} + \beta_h Z_{ht} + \mathbf{u}_t \qquad (6.6.6)$$

$$E[\mathbf{u}_t] = 0 \qquad (6.6.7)$$

$$E[\mathbf{u}_t \mathbf{u}'_t] = \Phi \qquad (6.6.8)$$

$$E[Z_{ht}] = \mu_h, \qquad E[(Z_{ht} - \mu_h)^2] = \sigma_h^2 \qquad (6.6.9)$$

$$\mathrm{Cov}[\mathbf{Z}_{Kt}, \mathbf{u}_t] = 0 \qquad (6.6.10)$$

$$\mathrm{Cov}[Z_{ht}, \mathbf{u}_t] = 0. \qquad (6.6.11)$$

We can relate the optimal orthogonal portfolio parameters to the factor model deviations by comparing (6.6.1) and (6.6.6). Taking the unconditional expectations of both sides,

$$a = \beta_h \mu_h, \qquad (6.6.12)$$

and by equating the variance of ϵ_t with the variance of $\beta_h Z_{ht} + \mathbf{u}_t$,

$$\Sigma = \beta_h \beta'_h \sigma_h^2 + \Phi = aa' \frac{\sigma_h^2}{\mu_h^2} + \Phi. \qquad (6.6.13)$$

The key link between the model deviations and the residual variances and covariances emerges from (6.6.13). The intuition for the link is straightforward. Deviations from the model must be accompanied by a common component in the residual variance to prevent the formation of a portfolio with a positive deviation and a residual variance that decreases to zero as the number of securities in the portfolio grows, that is, an asymptotic arbitrage opportunity.

6.6.2 Squared Sharpe Ratios

The squared Sharpe ratio is a useful construct for interpreting much of the ensuing analysis. The tangency portfolio q has the maximum squared Sharpe measure of all portfolios. The squared Sharpe ratio of q, s_q^2, is

$$s_q^2 = \mu' \Omega^{-1} \mu. \tag{6.6.14}$$

Given that the K factor portfolios and the optimal orthogonal portfolio h can be combined to form the tangency portfolio, the maximum squared Sharpe ratio of these $K+1$ portfolios will be s_q^2. Since h is orthogonal to the portfolios K, MacKinlay (1995) shows that one can express s_q^2 as the sum of the squared Sharpe ratio of the orthogonal portfolio and the squared maximum Sharpe ratio of the factor portfolios,

$$s_q^2 = s_h^2 + s_K^2, \tag{6.6.15}$$

where $s_h^2 = \mu_h^2 / \sigma_h^2$ and $s_K^2 = \mu_K' \Omega_K^{-1} \mu_K$.[7]

Empirical tests of multifactor models employ subsets of the N assets. The factor portfolios need not be linear combinations of the subset of assets. Results similar to those above will hold within a subset of N assets. For subset analysis when considering the tangency portfolio (of the subset), the maximum squared Sharpe ratio of the assets and factor portfolios, and the optimal orthogonal portfolio for the subset, it is necessary to augment the N assets with the factor portfolios K. Defining $\mathbf{Z}_{t_s}^*$ as the $(N+K \times 1)$ vector $[\mathbf{Z}_t' \ \mathbf{Z}_{Kt}']'$ with mean $\mu_s^{*'}$ and covariance matrix Ω_s^*, for the tangency portfolio of these $N+K$ assets we have

$$s_{q_s}^2 = \mu_s^{*'} \Omega_s^{*-1} \mu_s^*. \tag{6.6.16}$$

The subscript s indicates that a subset of the assets is being considered. If any of the factor portfolios is a linear combination of the N assets, it will be necessary to use the generalized inverse in (6.6.16).

---

[7] This result is related to the work of Gibbons, Ross, and Shanken (1989).

The analysis (with a subset of assets) involves the quadratic $\mathbf{a}'\Sigma^{-1}\mathbf{a}$ computed using the parameters for the N assets. Gibbons, Ross, and Shanken (1989) and Lehmann (1987, 1992) provide interpretations of this quadratic term using Sharpe ratios. Assuming Σ is of full rank, they show

$$\mathbf{a}'_s\Sigma^{-1}_s\mathbf{a}_s = s^2_{q_s} - s^2_K. \tag{6.6.17}$$

Consistent with (6.6.15), for the subset of assets $\mathbf{a}'\Sigma^{-1}\mathbf{a}$ is the squared Sharpe ratio of the subset's optimal orthogonal portfolio h_s. Therefore, for a given subset of assets:

$$s^2_{h_s} = \mathbf{a}'_s\Sigma^{-1}_s\mathbf{a}_s \tag{6.6.18}$$

and

$$s^2_{q_s} = s^2_{h_s} + s^2_K. \tag{6.6.19}$$

Note that the squared Sharpe ratio of the subset's optimal orthogonal portfolio is less than or equal to that of the population optimal orthogonal portfolio, that is,

$$s^2_{h_s} \leq s^2_h. \tag{6.6.20}$$

Next we use the optimal orthogonal portfolio and the Sharpe ratios results together with the model deviation residual variance link to develop implications for distinguishing among asset pricing models. Hereafter the s subscript is suppressed. No ambiguity will result since, in the subsequent analysis, we will be working only with subsets of the assets.

6.6.3 Implications for Separating Alternative Theories

If a given factor model is rejected a common interpretation is that more (or different) risk factors are required to explain the risk-return relation. This interpretation suggests that one should include additional factors so that the null hypothesis will be accepted. A shortcoming of this popular approach is that there are multiple potential interpretations of why the hypothesis is accepted. One view is that genuine progress in terms of identifying the "right" asset pricing model has been made. But it could also be the case that the apparent success in identifying a better model has come from finding a good within-sample fit through data-snooping. The likelihood of this possibility is increased by the fact that the additional factors lack theoretical motivation.

This section attempts to discriminate between the two interpretations. To do this, we compare the distribution of the test statistic under the null hypothesis with the distribution under each of the alternatives.

We reconsider the zero-intercept F-test of the null hypothesis that the intercept vector $\mathbf{a}$ from (6.6.1) is 0. Let H_0 be the null hypothesis and H_A

be the alternative:

$$H_0: \quad \mathbf{a} \;=\; 0$$

$$H_A: \quad \mathbf{a} \;\neq\; 0.$$

H_0 can be tested using the test statistic J_1 from (6.2.12):

$$J_1 \;=\; \frac{(T-N-K)}{N}\,[1+\hat{\boldsymbol{\mu}}_K'\hat{\boldsymbol{\Omega}}_K^{-1}\hat{\boldsymbol{\mu}}_K]^{-1}\hat{\mathbf{a}}'\hat{\boldsymbol{\Sigma}}^{-1}\hat{\mathbf{a}}, \tag{6.6.21}$$

where T is the number of time-series observations, N is the number of assets or portfolios of assets included, and K is the number of factor portfolios. The hat superscripts indicate the maximum likelihood estimators. Under the null hypothesis, J_1 is unconditionally distributed central F with N degrees of freedom in the numerator and $(T-N-K)$ degrees of freedom in the denominator.

To interpret deviations from the null hypothesis, we require a general representation for the distribution of J_1. Conditional on the factor portfolio returns the distribution of J_1 is

$$J_1 \;\sim\; F_{N,T-N-K}(\delta), \tag{6.6.22}$$

$$\delta \;=\; T[1+\hat{\boldsymbol{\mu}}_K'\hat{\boldsymbol{\Omega}}_K^{-1}\hat{\boldsymbol{\mu}}_K]^{-1}\mathbf{a}'\boldsymbol{\Sigma}^{-1}\mathbf{a}, \tag{6.6.23}$$

where δ is the noncentrality parameter of the F distribution. If $K=0$ then the term $[1+\hat{\boldsymbol{\mu}}_K'\hat{\boldsymbol{\Omega}}_K^{-1}\hat{\boldsymbol{\mu}}_K]^{-1}$ will not appear in (6.6.21) or in (6.6.23), and J_1 will be unconditionally distributed non-central F.

We consider the distribution of J_1 under two different alternatives, which are separated by their implications for the maximum value of the squared Sharpe ratio. With the risk-based multifactor alternative there will be an upper bound on the squared Sharpe ratio, whereas with the nonrisk-based alternatives the maximum squared Sharpe ratio is unbounded as the number of assets increases.

First consider the distribution of J_1 under the alternative hypothesis that deviations are due to missing factors. Drawing on the results for the squared Sharpe ratios, the noncentrality parameter of the F distribution is

$$\delta \;=\; T[1+\hat{\boldsymbol{\mu}}_K'\hat{\boldsymbol{\Omega}}_K^{-1}\hat{\boldsymbol{\mu}}_K]^{-1}s_{h_s}^2. \tag{6.6.24}$$

From (6.6.20), the third term in (6.6.24) is bounded above by s_h^2 and positive. The second term is bounded between zero and one. Thus there is an upper bound for δ,

$$\delta \;<\; Ts_h^2 \;\leq\; Ts_q^2. \tag{6.6.25}$$

The second inequality follows from the fact that the tangency portfolio q has the maximum Sharpe ratio of any asset or portfolio.

Given a maximum value for the squared Sharpe ratio, the upper bound on the noncentrality parameter can be important. With this bound, independent of how one arranges the assets to be included as dependent variables in the pricing model regression and for any value of N,[8] there is a limit on the distance between the null distribution and the distribution of the test statistic under the missing-factor alternative. All the assets can be mispriced and yet the bound will still apply.

In contrast, when the alternative one has in mind is that the source of deviations is nonrisk-based, such as data snooping, market frictions, or market irrationalities, the notion of a maximum squared Sharpe ratio is not useful. The squared Sharpe ratio (and the noncentrality parameter) are in principle unbounded because the theory linking the deviations and the residual variances and covariances does not apply. When comparing alternatives with the intercepts of about the same magnitude, in general, one would expect to see larger test statistics in this nonrisk-based case.

We examine the informativeness of the above analysis by considering alternatives with realistic parameter values. We consider the distribution of the test statistic for three cases: the null hypothesis, the missing risk factors alternative, and the nonrisk-based alternative. For the risk-based alternative, the framework is designed to be similar to that in Fama and French (1993). For the nonrisk-based alternative we use a setup that is consistent with the analysis of Lo and MacKinlay (1990b) and the work of Lakonishok, Shleifer, and Vishny (1994).

Consider a one-factor asset pricing model using a time series of the excess returns for 32 portfolios as the dependent variable. The one factor (independent variable) is the excess return of the market so that the zero-intercept null hypothesis is the CAPM. The length of the time series is 342 months. This setup corresponds to that of Fama and French (1993, Table 9, regression (ii)). The null distribution of the test statistic J_1 is

$$J_1 \sim F_{32,309}(0). \tag{6.6.26}$$

To define the distribution of J_1 under the alternatives of interest one needs to specify the parameters necessary to calculate the noncentrality parameter. For the risk-based alternative, given a value for the squared Sharpe ratio of the optimal orthogonal portfolio, the distribution corresponding to the upper bound of the noncentrality parameter from (6.6.25) can be considered. The Sharpe ratio of the optimal orthogonal portfolio can be obtained using (6.6.15) given the squared Sharpe ratios of the tangency portfolio and of the included factor portfolio.

---

[8] In practice when using the F-test it will be necessary for N to be less than $T-K$ so that $\hat{\Sigma}$ will be of full rank.

MacKinlay (1995) argues that in a perfect capital markets setting, a reasonable value for the Sharpe ratio squared of the tangency portfolio for an observation interval of one month is 0.031 (or approximately 0.6 for the Sharpe ratio on an annualized basis). This value, for example, corresponds to a portfolio with an annual expected excess return of 10% and a standard deviation of 16%. If the maximum squared Sharpe ratio of the included factor portfolios is the *ex post* squared Sharpe ratio of the CRSP value-weighted index, the implied maximum squared Sharpe ratio for the optimal orthogonal portfolio is 0.021. This monthly value of 0.021 would be consistent with a portfolio which has an annualized mean excess return of 8% and annualized standard deviation of 16%. We work through the analysis using this value.

Using this squared Sharpe ratio for the optimal orthogonal portfolio to calculate δ, the distribution of J_1 from equation (6.2.1) is

$$J_1 \sim F_{32,309}(7.1). \tag{6.6.27}$$

This distribution will be used to characterize the risk-based alternative.

One can specify the distribution for two nonrisk-based alternatives by specifying values of $\mathbf{a}$, Σ, and $\hat{\mu}_K' \hat{\Omega}_K^{-1} \hat{\mu}_K$, and then calculating δ from (6.6.23). To specify the intercepts we assume that the elements of $\mathbf{a}$ are normally distributed with a mean of zero. We consider two values for the standard deviation, 0.0007 and 0.001. When the standard deviation of the elements of $\mathbf{a}$ is 0.001 about 95% of deviations will lie between -0.002 and $+0.002$, an annualized spread of about 4.8%. A standard deviation of 0.0007 for the deviations would correspond to an annual spread of about 3.4%. These spreads are consistent with spreads that could arise from data-snooping.[9] They are plausible and even somewhat conservative given the contrarian strategy returns presented in papers such as Lakonishok, Shleifer, and Vishny (1993). For Σ we use a sample estimate based on portfolios sorted by market capitalization for the Fama and French (1993) sample period 1963 to 1991. The effect of $\hat{\mu}_K' \hat{\Omega}_K^{-1} \hat{\mu}_K$ on δ will typically be small, so it is set to zero. To get an idea of a reasonable value for the noncentrality parameter given this alternative, the expected value of δ given the distributional assumption for the elements of $\mathbf{a}$ conditional upon $\Sigma = \hat{\Sigma}$ is considered. The expected value of the noncentrality parameter is 39.4 for a standard deviation of 0.0007 and 80.3 for a standard deviation of 0.001. Using these values for the noncentrality parameter, the distribution of J_1 is

$$J_1 \sim F_{32,309}(39.4) \tag{6.6.28}$$

---

[9]With data-snooping the distribution of J_1 is not exactly a noncentral F (see Lo and MacKinlay [1990b]). However, for the purposes of this analysis, the noncentral F will be a good approximation.

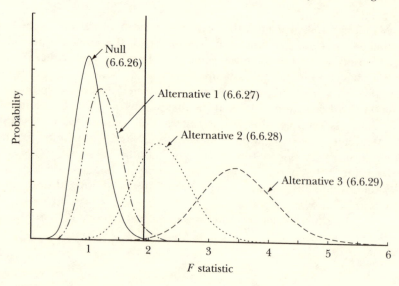

Figure 6.1. *Distributions for the CAPM Zero-Intercept Test Statistic for Four Hypotheses*

when $\sigma_a = 0.0007$ and

$$\mathcal{J}_1 \sim F_{32,309}(80.3) \tag{6.6.29}$$

when $\sigma_a = 0.001$.

A plot of the four distributions from (6.6.26), (6.6.27), (6.6.28), and (6.6.29) is in Figure 6.1. The vertical bar on the plot represents the value 1.91 which Fama and French calculate for the test statistic. From this figure, notice that the distributions under the null hypothesis and the risk-based alternative hypothesis are quite close together.[10] This reflects the impact of the upper bound on the noncentrality parameter. In contrast, the nonrisk-based alternatives' distributions are far to the right of the other two distributions, consistent with the unboundedness of the noncentrality parameter for these alternatives.

Given that Fama and French find a test statistic of 1.91, these results suggest that the missing-risk-factors argument is not the whole story. From Figure 6.1 one can see that 1.91 is still in the upper tail when the distribution of $\mathcal{J}_1$ in the presence of missing risk factors is tabulated. The p-value using this distribution is 0.03 for the monthly data. Hence it seems unlikely that missing factors completely explain the deviations.

The data offer some support for the nonrisk-based alternative views. The test statistic falls almost in the middle of the nonrisk-based alterna-

---

[10]See MacKinlay (1987) for detailed analysis of the risk-based alternative.

tive with the lower standard deviation of the elements of **a**. Several of the nonrisk-based alternatives could equally well explain the results. Different nonrisk-based views can give the same noncentrality parameter and test-statistic distribution. The results are consistent with the data-snooping alternative of Lo and MacKinlay (1990b), with the related sample selection biases discussed by Breen and Korajczyk (1993) and Kothari, Shanken, and Sloan (1995), and with the presence of market inefficiencies.

6.7 Conclusion

In this chapter we have developed the econometrics for estimating and testing multifactor pricing models. These models provide an attractive alternative to the single-factor CAPM, but users of such models should be aware of two serious dangers that arise when factors are chosen to fit existing data without regard to economic theory. First, the models may overfit the data because of data-snooping bias; in this case they will not be able to predict asset returns in the future. Second, the models may capture empirical regularities that are due to market inefficiency or investor irrationality; in this case they may continue to fit the data but they will imply Sharpe ratios for factor portfolios that are too high to be consistent with a reasonable underlying model of market equilibrium. Both these problems can be mitigated if one derives a factor structure from an equilibrium model, along the lines discussed in Chapter 8. In the end, however, the usefulness of multifactor models will not be fully known until sufficient new data become available to provide a true out-of-sample check on their performance.

Problems—Chapter 6

6.1 Consider a multiple regression of the return on any asset or portfolio R_a on the returns of any set of portfolios from which the entire minimum-variance boundary can be generated. Show that the intercept of this regression will be zero and that the factor regression coefficients for any asset will sum to unity.

6.2 Consider two economies, economy A and economy B. The mean excess-return vector and the covariance matrix is specified below for each of the economies. Assume there exist a riskfree asset, N risky assets with mean excess return μ and nonsingular covariance matrix Ω, and a risky factor portfolio with mean excess return μ_p and variance σ_p^2. The factor portfolio is not a linear combination of the N assets. (This criterion can be met by eliminating one of the assets which is included in the factor portfolio if necessary.) For both economies A and B:

$$\mu = \mathbf{a} + \beta \mu_p \tag{6.7.1}$$

$$\Omega = \beta \beta' \sigma_p^2 + \delta \delta' \sigma_h^2 + I \sigma_\epsilon^2. \tag{6.7.2}$$

Given the above mean and covariance matrix and the assumption that the factor portfolio p is a traded asset, what is the maximum squared Sharpe ratio for the given economies?

6.3 Returning to the above problem, the economies are further specified. Assume the elements of $\mathbf{a}$ are cross-sectionally independent and identically distributed,

$$a_i \sim \text{IID}(0, \sigma_a^2) \qquad i = 1, \dots, N. \tag{6.7.3}$$

The specification of the distribution of the elements of δ conditional on $\mathbf{a}$ differentiates economies A and B. For economy A:

$$\delta_i \mid \mathbf{a} \sim \text{IID}(a_i, 0) \qquad i = 1, \dots, N, \tag{6.7.4}$$

and for economy B:

$$\delta_i \mid \mathbf{a} \sim \text{IID}(0, \sigma_a^2) \qquad i = 1, \dots, N. \tag{6.7.5}$$

Unconditionally the cross-sectional distribution of the elements of δ will be the same for both economies, but for economy A conditional on $\mathbf{a}$, δ is fixed. What is the maximum squared Sharpe ratio for each economy? What is the maximum squared Sharpe ratio for each economy as the N increases to infinity?

7

Present-Value Relations

THE FIRST PART of this book has examined the behavior of stock returns in some detail. The exclusive focus on returns is traditional in empirical research on asset pricing; yet it belies the name of the field to study only returns and not to say anything about asset prices themselves. Many of the most important applications of financial economics involve valuing assets, and for these applications it is essential to be able to calculate the prices that are implied by models of returns. In this chapter we discuss recent research that tries to bring attention back to price behavior. We deal with common stock prices throughout, but of course the concepts developed in this chapter are applicable to other assets as well.

The basic framework for our analysis is the *discounted-cash-flow* or *present-value* model. This model relates the price of a stock to its expected future cash flows—its dividends—discounted to the present using a constant or time-varying discount rate. Since dividends in all future periods enter the present-value formula, the dividend in any one period is only a small component of the price. Therefore long-lasting or *persistent* movements in dividends have much larger effects on prices than temporary movements do. A similar insight applies to variation in discount rates. The discount rate between any one period and the next is only a small component of the long-horizon discount rate applied to a distant future cash flow; therefore persistent movements in discount rates have much larger effects on prices than temporary movements do. For this reason the study of asset prices is intimately related to the study of long-horizon asset returns. Section 7.1 uses the present-value model to discuss these links between movements in prices, dividends, and returns.

We mentioned at the end of Chapter 2 that there is some evidence for predictability of stock returns at long horizons. This evidence is statistically weak when only past returns are used to forecast future returns, as in Chapter 2, but it becomes considerably stronger when other variables, such as the dividend-price ratio or the level of interest rates, are brought into the analysis. In Section 7.2, we use the formulas of Section 7.1 to help interpret these findings. We show how various test statistics will behave, both under the null hypothesis and under the simple alternative hypothesis that the expected stock return is time-varying and follows a persistent first-order autoregressive (AR(1)) process. A major theme of the section is that recent empirical findings using longer-horizon data are roughly consistent with this persistent AR(1) alternative model. We also develop the implications of the AR(1) model for price behavior. Persistent movements in expected returns have dramatic effects on stock prices, making them much more volatile than they would be if expected returns were constant.

The source of this persistent variation in expected stock returns is an important unresolved issue. One view is that the time-variation in expected returns and the associated volatility of stock prices are evidence against the Efficient Markets Hypothesis (EMH). But as we argued in Chapter 1, the EMH can only be tested in conjunction with a model of equilibrium returns. This chapter describes evidence against the joint hypothesis that the EMH holds and that equilibrium stock returns are constant, but it leaves open the possibility that a model with time-varying equilibrium stock returns can be constructed to fit the data. We explore this possibility further in Chapter 8.

7.1 The Relation between Prices, Dividends, and Returns

In this section we discuss the present-value model of stock prices. Using the identity that relates stock prices, dividends, and returns, Section 7.1.1 presents the expected-present-value formula for a stock with constant expected returns. Section 7.1.1 assumes away the possibility that there are so-called rational bubbles in stock prices, but this possibility is considered in Section 7.1.2. Section 7.1.3 studies the general case where expected stock returns vary through time. The exact present-value formula is nonlinear in this case, but a loglinear approximation yields some useful insights. Section 7.1.4 develops a simple example in which the expected stock return is time-varying and follows an AR(1) process.

We first recall the definition of the return on a stock given in Chapter 1. The net simple return is

$$R_{t+1} \equiv \frac{P_{t+1} + D_{t+1}}{P_t} - 1. \qquad (7.1.1)$$

This definition is straightforward, but it does use two notational conventions that deserve emphasis. First, R_{t+1} denotes the return on the stock held from time t to time $t + 1$. The subscript $t + 1$ is used because the return only becomes known at time $t + 1$. Second, P_t denotes the price of a share of stock measured at the *end* of period t, or equivalently an ex-dividend price:

Purchase of the stock at price P_t today gives one a claim to next period's dividend per share D_{t+1} but not to this period's dividend D_t.[1]

An alternative measure of return is the log or continuously compounded return, defined in Chapter 1 as

$$r_{t+1} \equiv \log(1 + R_{t+1}). \tag{7.1.2}$$

Here, as throughout this chapter, we use lowercase letters to denote log variables.

7.1.1 The Linear Present-Value Relation with Constant Expected Returns

In this section we explore the consequences of the assumption that the expected stock return is equal to a constant R:

$$E_t[R_{t+1}] = R. \tag{7.1.3}$$

Taking expectations of the identity (7.1.1), imposing (7.1.3), and rearranging, we obtain an equation relating the current stock price to the next period's expected stock price and dividend:

$$P_t = E_t\left[\frac{P_{t+1} + D_{t+1}}{1 + R}\right]. \tag{7.1.4}$$

This expectational difference equation can be solved forward by repeatedly substituting out future prices and using the Law of Iterated Expectations—the result that $E_t[E_{t+1}[X]] = E_t[X]$, discussed in Chapter 1—to eliminate future-dated expectations. After solving forward K periods we have

$$P_t = E_t\left[\sum_{i=1}^{K}\left(\frac{1}{1+R}\right)^i D_{t+i}\right] + E_t\left[\left(\frac{1}{1+R}\right)^K P_{t+K}\right]. \tag{7.1.5}$$

The second term on the right-hand side of (7.1.5) is the expected discounted value of the stock price K periods from the present. For now, we assume that this term shrinks to zero as the horizon K increases:

$$\lim_{K \to \infty} E_t\left[\left(\frac{1}{1+R}\right)^K P_{t+K}\right] = 0. \tag{7.1.6}$$

---

[1] These timing assumptions are standard in the finance literature. However some of the literature on volatility tests, for example Shiller (1981) and Campbell and Shiller (1987, 1988a,b), uses the alternative timing convention that the stock price is measured at the beginning of the period or traded cum-dividend. Differences between the formulas given in this chapter and those in the original volatility papers are due to this difference in timing conventions.

Assumption (7.1.6) will be satisfied unless the stock price is expected to grow forever at rate R or faster. In Section 7.1.2 below, we discuss models of *rational bubbles* that relax this assumption.

Letting K increase in (7.1.5) and assuming (7.1.6), we obtain a formula expressing the stock price as the expected present value of future dividends out to the infinite future, discounted at a constant rate. For future convenience we write this expected present value as P_{Dt}:

$$P_t = P_{Dt} \equiv \mathrm{E}_t\left[\sum_{i=1}^{\infty}\left(\frac{1}{1+R}\right)^i D_{t+i}\right]. \tag{7.1.7}$$

An unrealistic special case that nevertheless provides some useful intuition occurs when dividends are expected to grow at a constant rate G (which must be smaller than R to keep the stock price finite):

$$\mathrm{E}_t[D_{t+i}] = (1+G)\,\mathrm{E}_t[D_{t+i-1}] = (1+G)^i D_t. \tag{7.1.8}$$

Substituting (7.1.8) into (7.1.7), we obtain the well-known "Gordon growth model" (Gordon [1962]) for the price of a stock with a constant discount rate R and dividend growth rate G, where $G < R$:

$$P_t = \frac{\mathrm{E}_t[D_{t+1}]}{R-G} = \frac{(1+G)D_t}{R-G}. \tag{7.1.9}$$

The Gordon growth model shows that the stock price is extremely sensitive to a permanent change in the discount rate R when R is close to G, since the elasticity of the price with respect to the discount rate is $(dP/dR)(R/P) = -R/(R-G)$.

It is important to avoid two common errors in interpreting these formulas. First, note that we have made no assumptions about equity repurchases by firms. Equity repurchases affect the time pattern of expected future dividends per share in (7.1.7), but they do not affect the validity of the formula itself. Problem 7.1 explores this point in more detail.

Second, the hypothesis that the expected stock return is constant through time is sometimes known as the *martingale model* of stock prices.[2] But a constant expected stock return does not imply a martingale for the stock price itself. Recall that a martingale for the price requires $\mathrm{E}_t[P_{t+1}] = P_t$, whereas (7.1.4) implies that

$$\mathrm{E}_t[P_{t+1}] = (1+R)\,P_t - \mathrm{E}_t[D_{t+1}]. \tag{7.1.10}$$

---

[2]See Chapter 2 for a careful discussion of the martingale hypothesis. LeRoy (1989) surveys the martingale literature from Samuelson (1965) on. More general martingale results for risk-neutralized price processes are discussed in Chapter 9.

The expected stock price next period does not equal the stock price today as would be required if the stock price were a martingale; rather, the expected future stock price equals one plus the constant required return, $(1 + R)$, times the current stock price, less an adjustment for dividend payments.[3] To obtain a martingale, we must construct a portfolio for which all dividend payments are reinvested in the stock. At time t, this portfolio will have N_t shares of the stock, where

$$N_{t+1} = N_t \left(1 + \frac{D_{t+1}}{P_{t+1}}\right). \tag{7.1.11}$$

The value of this portfolio at time t, discounted to time 0 at rate R, is

$$M_t = \frac{N_t P_t}{(1 + R)^t}. \tag{7.1.12}$$

It is straightforward to show that M_t is a martingale.

Even though the stock price P_t is not generally a martingale, it will follow a linear process with a *unit root* if the dividend D_t follows a linear process with a unit root.[4] In this case the expected present-value formula (7.1.7) relates two unit-root processes for P_t and D_t. It can be transformed to a relation between stationary variables, however, by subtracting a multiple of the dividend from both sides of the equation. We get

$$P_t - \frac{D_t}{R} = \left(\frac{1}{R}\right) E_t \left[\sum_{i=0}^{\infty} \left(\frac{1}{1+R}\right)^i \Delta D_{t+1+i}\right]. \tag{7.1.13}$$

Equation (7.1.13) relates the difference between the stock price and $1/R$ times the dividend to the expectation of the discounted value of future changes in dividends, which is stationary if changes in dividends are stationary. In this case, even though the dividend process is nonstationary and the price process is nonstationary, there is a stationary linear combination of prices and dividends, so that prices and dividends are *cointegrated*.[5]

---

[3] In the special case where dividends are expected to grow at a constant rate G, this simplifies to $E_t P_{t+1} = (1 + G)P_t$. The stock price is expected to grow at the same rate as the dividend, because the dividend-price ratio is constant in this case.

[4] Loosely, a variable follows a stationary time-series process if shocks to the variable have temporary but not permanent effects. A variable follows a process with a unit root, also known as an *integrated* process, if shocks have permanent effects on the level of the variable, but not on the change in the variable. In this case the first difference of the variable is stationary, but the level is not. A martingale is a unit-root process where the immediate effect of a shock is the same as the permanent effect. See Chapter 2 or a textbook in time-series analysis such as Hamilton (1994) for precise definitions of these concepts.

[5] Two variables with unit roots are cointegrated if some linear combination of the variables is stationary. See Engle and Granger (1987) or Hamilton (1994) for general discussion, or Campbell and Shiller (1987) for this application of the concept. Note that here the stationary linear combination of the variables involves the constant discount rate R, which generally is not known *a priori*.

Although this formulation of the expected present-value model has been explored empirically by Campbell and Shiller (1987), West (1988b), and others, stock prices and dividends are like many other macroeconomic time series in that they appear to grow exponentially over time rather than linearly. This means that a linear model, even one that allows for a unit root, is less appropriate than a loglinear model. Below we develop a present-value framework that is appropriate when dividends follow a loglinear process.

7.1.2 Rational Bubbles

In the previous section we obtained an expectational difference equation, (7.1.4), and solved it forward to show that the stock price must equal P_{Dt}, the expected present value of future dividends. The argument relied on the assumption (7.1.5) that the expected discounted stock price, K periods in the future, converges to zero as the horizon K increases. In this section we discuss models that relax this assumption.

The convergence assumption (7.1.5) is essential for obtaining a unique solution P_{Dt} to (7.1.4). Once we drop the assumption, there is an infinite number of solutions to (7.1.4). Any solution can be written in the form

$$P_t = P_{Dt} + B_t, \tag{7.1.14}$$

where

$$B_t = \mathrm{E}_t\left[\frac{B_{t+1}}{1+R}\right]. \tag{7.1.15}$$

The additional term B_t in (7.1.14) appears in the price only because it is expected to be present next period, with an expected value $(1 + R)$ times its current value.

The term P_{Dt} is sometimes called *fundamental value*, and the term B_t is often called a *rational bubble*. The word "bubble" recalls some of the famous episodes in financial history in which asset prices rose far higher than could easily be explained by fundamentals, and in which investors appeared to be betting that other investors would drive prices even higher in the future.[6] The adjective "rational" is used because the presence of B_t in (7.1.14) is entirely consistent with rational expectations and constant expected returns.

---

[6]Mackay (1852) is a classic reference on early episodes such as the Dutch tulipmania in the 17th Century and the London South Sea Bubble and Paris Mississippi Bubble in the 18th Century. Kindleberger (1989) describes these and other more recent episodes, while Garber (1989) argues that Dutch tulip prices were more closely related to fundamentals than is commonly realized.

It is easiest to illustrate the idea of a rational bubble with an example. Blanchard and Watson (1982) suggest a bubble of the form

$$B_{t+1} = \begin{cases} \left(\frac{1+R}{\pi}\right) B_t + \zeta_{t+1}, & \text{with probability } \pi; \\ \zeta_{t+1}, & \text{with probability } 1 - \pi. \end{cases} \qquad (7.1.16)$$

This obeys the restriction (7.1.15), provided that the shock ζ_{t+1} satisfies $E_t\zeta_{t+1} = 0$. The Blanchard and Watson bubble has a constant probability, $1 - \pi$, of bursting in any period. If it does not burst, it grows at a rate $\frac{1+R}{\pi} - 1$, faster than R, in order to compensate for the probability of bursting. Many other bubble examples can be constructed; Problem 7.2 explores an example suggested by Froot and Obstfeld (1991), in which the bubble is a nonlinear function of the stock's dividend.

Although rational bubbles have attracted considerable attention, there are both theoretical and empirical arguments that can be used to rule out bubble solutions to the difference equation (7.1.4). Theoretical arguments may be divided into partial-equilibrium arguments and general-equilibrium arguments.

In partial equilibrium, the first point to note is that there can never be a negative bubble on an asset with limited liability. If a negative bubble were to exist, it would imply a negative expected asset price at some date in the future, and this would be inconsistent with limited liability. A second important point follows from this: A bubble on a limited-liability asset cannot start within an asset pricing model. It must have existed since asset trading began if it exists today. The reason is that if the bubble ever has a zero value, its expected future value is also zero by condition (7.1.15). But since the bubble can never be negative, it can only have a zero expectation if it is zero in the future with probability one (Diba and Grossman (1988)).

Third, a bubble cannot exist if there is any upper limit on the price of an asset. Thus a commodity-price bubble is ruled out by the existence of some high-priced substitute in infinitely elastic supply (for example, solar energy in the case of oil). Stock-price bubbles may be ruled out if firms impose an upper limit on stock prices by issuing stock in response to price increases. Finally, bubbles cannot exist on assets such as bonds which have a fixed value on a terminal date.

General-equilibrium considerations also limit the possibilities for rational bubbles. Tirole (1982) has shown that bubbles cannot exist in a model with a finite number of infinite-lived rational agents. The argument is easiest to see when short sales are allowed, although it does not in fact depend on the possibility of short sales. If a positive bubble existed in an asset infinite-lived agents could sell the asset short, invest some of the proceeds to pay the dividend stream, and have positive wealth left over. This arbitrage opportunity rules out bubbles.

Tirole (1985) has studied the possibility of bubbles within the Diamond (1965) overlapping-generations model. In this model there is an infinite number of finite-lived agents, but Tirole shows that even here a bubble cannot arise when the interest rate exceeds the growth rate of the economy, because the bubble would eventually become infinitely large relative to the wealth of the economy. This would violate some agent's budget constraint. Thus bubbles can only exist in *dynamically inefficient* overlapping-generations economies that have overaccumulated private capital, driving the interest rate down below the growth rate of the economy. Many economists feel that dynamic inefficiency is unlikely to occur in practice, and Abel, Mankiw, Summers, and Zeckhauser (1989) present empirical evidence that it does not describe the US economy.

There are also some empirical arguments against the existence of bubbles. The most important point is that bubbles imply explosive behavior of various series. In the absence of bubbles, if the dividend D_t follows a linear process with a unit root then the stock price P_t has a unit root while the change in the price ΔP_t and the spread between price and a multiple of dividends $P_t - D_t/R$ are stationary. With bubbles, these variables all have an explosive conditional expectation: $\lim_{K \to \infty}(1/(1 + R)^K)\mathrm{E}_t[X_{t+K}] \neq 0$ for $X_t = P_t$, ΔP_t, or $P_t - D_t/R$. Empirically, there is little evidence of explosive behavior in these series. A caveat is that stochastic bubbles are nonlinear, so standard linear methods may fail to detect the explosive behavior of the conditional expectation in these models.

Finally, we note that rational bubbles cannot explain the observed predictability of stock returns. Bubbles create volatility in prices without creating predictability in returns. To the extent that price volatility can be explained by return predictability, the bubble hypothesis is superfluous.

Although rational bubbles may be implausible, there is much to be learned from studying them. An important theme of this chapter is that small movements in expected returns can have large effects on prices if they are persistent. Conversely, large persistent swings in prices can have small effects on expected returns in any one period. A rational bubble can be seen as the extreme case where price movements are so persistent—indeed, explosive—that they have no effects on expected returns at all.

7.1.3 An Approximate Present-Value Relation with Time-Varying Expected Returns

So far we have assumed that expected stock returns are constant. This assumption is analytically convenient, but it contradicts the evidence in Chapter 2 and in Section 7.2 that stock returns are predictable.

It is much more difficult to work with present-value relations when expected stock returns are time-varying, for then the relation between prices and returns becomes nonlinear. One approach is to use a loglinear approximation, as suggested by Campbell and Shiller (1988a,b). The loglinear relation between prices, dividends, and returns provides an accounting framework: High prices must eventually be followed by high future dividends, low future returns, or some combination of the two, and investors' expectations must be consistent with this, so high prices must be associated with high expected future dividends, low expected future returns, or some combination of the two. Similarly, high returns must be associated with upward revisions in expected future dividends, downward revisions in expected future returns, or some combination of the two (Campbell [1991]).

Thus the loglinear framework enables us to calculate asset price behavior under any model of expected returns, rather than just the model with constant expected returns. The loglinear framework has the additional advantage that it is tractable under the empirically plausible assumption that dividends and returns follow loglinear driving processes. Later in this chapter we use the loglinear framework to interpret the large empirical literature on predictability in long-horizon stock returns.

The loglinear approximation starts with the definition of the log stock return r_{t+1}. Using (7.1.1), (7.1.2), and the convention that logs of variables are denoted by lowercase letters, we have

$$r_{t+1} \equiv \log(P_{t+1} + D_{t+1}) - \log(P_t)$$

$$= p_{t+1} - p_t + \log(1 + \exp(d_{t+1} - p_{t+1})). \qquad (7.1.17)$$

The last term on the right-hand side of (7.1.17) is a nonlinear function of the log dividend-price ratio, $f(d_{t+1} - p_{t+1})$. Like any nonlinear function $f(x_{t+1})$, it can be approximated around the mean of x_{t+1}, $\overline{x}$, using a first-order Taylor expansion:

$$f(x_{t+1}) \approx f(\overline{x}) + f'(\overline{x})(x_{t+1} - \overline{x}). \qquad (7.1.18)$$

Substituting this approximation into (7.1.17), we obtain

$$r_{t+1} \approx k + \rho \, p_{t+1} + (1 - \rho)d_{t+1} - p_t, \qquad (7.1.19)$$

where ρ and k are parameters of linearization defined by $\rho \equiv 1/(1 + \exp(\overline{d - p}))$, where $(\overline{d - p})$ is the average log dividend-price ratio, and $k \equiv -\log(\rho) - (1 - \rho)\log(1/\rho - 1)$. When the dividend-price ratio is constant, then $\rho = 1/(1 + D/P)$, the reciprocal of one plus the dividend-price ratio. Empirically, in US data over the period 1926 to 1994 the average dividend-price ratio has been about 4% annually, implying that ρ should be about 0.96 in annual data, or about 0.997 in monthly data. The Taylor approximation (7.1.18) replaces the log of the sum of the stock price and the dividend in (7.1.17) with a weighted average of the log stock price and the log dividend in (7.1.19). The log stock price gets a weight ρ close to one, while the log dividend gets a weight $1 - \rho$ close to zero because the dividend is on average much smaller than the stock price, so a given proportional change in the dividend has a much smaller effect on the return than the same proportional change in the price.

Approximation Accuracy

The approximation (7.1.19) holds exactly when the log dividend-price ratio is constant, for then d_{t+1} and p_{t+1} move together one-for-one and equation (7.1.19) is equivalent to equation (7.1.17). Like any other Taylor expansion, the approximation (7.1.19) will be accurate provided that the variation in the log dividend-price ratio is not too great. One can get a sense for the accuracy of the approximation by comparing the exact return (7.1.17) with the approximate return (7.1.19) in actual data. Using monthly nominal dividends and prices on the CRSP value-weighted stock index over the period 1926:1 to 1994:12, for example, the exact and approximate returns have means of 0.78% and 0.72% per month, standard deviations of 5.55% and 5.56% per month, and a correlation of 0.99991. The approximation error—the difference between the approximate and the exact return—has a mean of -0.06%, a standard deviation of 0.08%, and a correlation of 0.08 with the exact return. Using annual nominal dividends and prices on the CRSP value-weighted stock index over the period 1926 to 1994, the exact and approximate returns have means of 9.20% and 9.03% per year, standard deviations of 19.29% and 19.42% per year, and a correlation of 0.99993. The approximation error has a mean of -0.17%, a standard deviation of 0.26%, and a correlation of 0.51 with the exact return. Thus the approximation misstates the average stock return but captures the dynamics of stock returns well, especially when it is applied to monthly data.[7]

Implications for Prices

Equation (7.1.19) is a linear difference equation for the log stock price, analogous to the linear difference equation for the level of the stock price that we obtained in (7.1.4) under the assumption of constant expected returns. Solving forward and imposing the condition that

$$\lim_{j \to \infty} \rho^j p_{t+j} = 0, \qquad (7.1.20)$$

we obtain

$$p_t = \frac{k}{1-\rho} + \sum_{j=0}^{\infty} \rho^j [(1-\rho)d_{t+1+j} - r_{t+1+j}]. \qquad (7.1.21)$$

[7]One can also compare exact and approximate real returns. The correction for inflation has no important effects on the comparison. See Campbell and Shiller (1988a) for a more detailed evaluation of approximation accuracy at short and long horizons.

Equation (7.1.21) is a dynamic accounting identity; it has been obtained merely by approximating an identity and solving forward subject to a terminal condition. The terminal condition (7.1.20) rules out rational bubbles that would cause the log stock price to grow exponentially forever at rate $1/\rho$ or faster. Equation (7.1.21) shows that if the stock price is high today, then there must be some combination of high dividends and low stock returns in the future.[8]

Equation (7.1.21) holds *ex post*, but it also holds *ex ante*. Taking expectations of (7.1.21), and noting that $p_t = E_t[p_t]$ because p_t is known at time t, we obtain

$$p_t = \frac{k}{1-\rho} + E_t\left[\sum_{j=0}^{\infty} \rho^j[(1-\rho)d_{t+1+j} - r_{t+1+j}]\right]. \tag{7.1.22}$$

This should be thought of as a consistency condition for expectations, analogous to the statement that the expectations of random variables X and Y should add up to the expectation of the sum $X + Y$. If the stock price is high today, then investors must be expecting some combination of high future dividends and low future returns. Equation (7.1.22) is a dynamic generalization of the Gordon formula for a stock price with constant required returns and dividend growth. Campbell and Shiller (1988a,b) call (7.1.22)—and (7.1.24) below—the *dynamic Gordon growth model* or the *dividend-ratio model*.

Like the original Gordon growth model, the dynamic Gordon growth model says that stock prices are high when dividends are expected to grow rapidly or when dividends are discounted at a low rate; but the effect on the stock price of a high dividend growth rate (or a low discount rate) now depends on how long the dividend growth rate is expected to be high (or how long the discount rate is expected to be low), whereas in the original model these rates are assumed to be constant at their initial levels forever. One can use the definitions of ρ and k to show that the dynamic Gordon growth model reduces to the original Gordon growth model when dividend growth rates and discount rates are constant.

For future convenience, we can simplify the notation in (7.1.22), rewriting it as

$$p_t = \frac{k}{1-\rho} + p_{dt} - p_{rt}, \tag{7.1.23}$$

where p_{dt} is the expected discounted value of $(1 - \rho)$ times future log dividends in (7.1.22) and p_{rt} is the expected discounted value of future log stock returns. This parallels the notation we used for the constant-expected-return case in Section 7.1.1.

---

[8]Campbell and Shiller (1988a) evaluate the accuracy of the approximation in (7.1.21).

Equation (7.1.22) can be rewritten in terms of the log dividend-price ratio rather than the log stock price:

$$d_t - p_t = -\frac{k}{1-\rho} + E_t \left[\sum_{j=0}^{\infty} \rho^j [-\Delta d_{t+1+j} + r_{t+1+j}] \right]. \qquad (7.1.24)$$

The log dividend-price ratio is high when dividends are expected to grow only slowly, or when stock returns are expected to be high. This equation is useful when the dividend follows a loglinear unit-root process, so that log dividends and log prices are nonstationary. In this case changes in log dividends are stationary, so from (7.1.24) the log dividend-price ratio is stationary provided that the expected stock return is stationary. Thus log stock prices and dividends are cointegrated, and the stationary linear combination of these variables involves no unknown parameters since it is just the log ratio. This simple structure makes the loglinear model easier to use in empirical work than the linear cointegrated model (7.1.13).

So far we have written asset prices as linear combinations of expected future dividends and returns. We can use the same approach to write asset returns as linear combinations of revisions in expected future dividends and returns (Campbell [1991]). Substituting (7.1.22) into (7.1.19), we obtain

$$r_{t+1} - E_t[r_{t+1}] = E_{t+1} \left[\sum_{j=0}^{\infty} \rho^j \Delta d_{t+1+j} \right] - E_t \left[\sum_{j=0}^{\infty} \rho^j \Delta d_{t+1+j} \right]$$

$$- \left(E_{t+1} \left[\sum_{j=1}^{\infty} \rho^j r_{t+1+j} \right] - E_t \left[\sum_{j=1}^{\infty} \rho^j r_{t+1+j} \right] \right). \quad (7.1.25)$$

This equation shows that unexpected stock returns must be associated with changes in expectations of future dividends or real returns. An increase in expected future dividends is associated with a capital gain today, while an increase in expected future returns is associated with a capital loss today. The reason is that with a given dividend stream, higher future returns can only be generated by future price appreciation from a lower current price. For convenience, we can simplify the notation of (7.1.25) to

$$r_{t+1} - E_t[r_{t+1}] = \eta_{t+1} = \eta_{d,t+1} - \eta_{r,t+1}, \qquad (7.1.26)$$

where η_{t+1} is the unexpected stock return, $\eta_{d,t+1}$ is the change in expectations of future dividends in (7.1.25), and $\eta_{r,t+1}$ is the change in expectations of future returns.

7.1.4 Prices and Returns in a Simple Example

The formulas developed in the previous section may be easier to understand in the context of a simple example. Later we will argue that the example is not only simple, but also empirically relevant. Suppose that the expected log stock return is a constant r plus an observable zero-mean variable x_t:

$$E_t[r_{t+1}] = r + x_t. \tag{7.1.27}$$

We further assume that x_t follows the first-order autoregressive (AR(1)) process

$$x_{t+1} = \phi x_t + \xi_{t+1}, \qquad -1 < \phi < 1. \tag{7.1.28}$$

When the AR coefficient ϕ is close to one, we will say that the x_t process is highly *persistent*. Equation (7.1.28) implies that the variance of x_t and its innovation ξ_t, which we write as σ_x^2 and σ_ξ^2 respectively, are related by $\sigma_\xi^2 = (1 - \phi^2)\sigma_x^2$.

Under these assumptions, it is straightforward to show that

$$p_{rt} \equiv E_t\left[\sum_{j=0}^{\infty} \rho^j r_{t+1+j}\right] = \frac{r}{1-\rho} + \frac{x_t}{1-\rho\phi}. \tag{7.1.29}$$

Equation (7.1.29) gives the effect on the stock price of variation through time in the expected stock return. The equation shows that a change in the expected return has a greater effect on the stock price when the expected return is persistent: Since ρ is close to one, a 1% increase in the expected return today reduces the stock price by about 2% if $\phi = 0.5$, by about 4% if $\phi = 0.75$, and by about 10% if $\phi = 0.9$.

This example illustrates an important point. The variability of expected stock returns is measured by the standard deviation of x_t. If this standard deviation is small, it is tempting to conclude that changing expected returns have little influence on stock prices, in other words, that variability in p_{rt} is small. Equation (7.1.29) shows that this conclusion is too hasty: The standard deviation of p_{rt} is the standard deviation of x_t divided by $(1 - \rho\phi)$, so if expected returns vary in a persistent fashion, p_{rt} can be very variable even when x_t itself is not. This point was stated by Summers (1986), and particularly forcefully by Shiller (1984):

> Returns on speculative assets are nearly unforecastable; this fact is the basis of the most important argument in the oral tradition against a role for mass psychology in speculative markets. One form of this argument claims that because real returns are nearly unforecastable, the real price of stocks is close to the intrinsic value, that is, the present value with constant discount rate of optimally forecasted future real dividends. This argument ... is one of the most remarkable errors in the history of economic thought.

In our example the stock price can be written as the sum of two terms. The first term is the expected discounted value of future dividends, p_{dt}; this is not quite a random walk for the reasons given in Section 7.1.1 above, but it is close to a random walk when the dividend stream is not too large or variable. The second term is a stationary AR(1) process, $-p_{rt}$. This two-component description of stock prices is often found in the literature (see Summers [1986], Fama and French [1988b], Poterba and Summers [1988], and Jegadeesh [1991]).

The AR(1) example also yields a particularly simple formula for the one-period stock return r_{t+1}. The general stock-return equation (7.1.25) simplifies because the innovation in expected future stock returns, $\eta_{r,t+1}$, is given by $\rho\xi_{t+1}/(1-\rho\phi)$. Thus we have

$$r_{t+1} = r + x_t + \eta_{d,t+1} - \frac{\rho\xi_{t+1}}{1-\rho\phi}. \tag{7.1.30}$$

To understand the implications of this expression, assume for simplicity that news about dividends and about future returns, $\eta_{d,t+1}$ and ξ_{t+1}, are uncorrelated.[9] Then using the notation $\mathrm{Var}[\eta_{d,t+1}] = \sigma_d^2$ (so σ_d^2 represents the variance of news about all future dividends, not the variance of the current dividend), and using the fact that $\sigma_\xi^2 = (1-\phi^2)\sigma_x^2$, we can calculate the variance of r_{t+1} as

$$\mathrm{Var}[r_{t+1}] = \sigma_d^2 + \sigma_x^2 \left[\frac{1+\rho^2-2\rho\phi}{(1-\phi\rho)^2}\right] \approx \sigma_d^2 + \frac{2\sigma_x^2}{1-\phi}, \tag{7.1.31}$$

where the approximate equality holds when $\phi \ll \rho$ and ρ is close to one. Persistence in the expected return process increases the variability of realized returns, for small but persistent changes in expected returns have large effects on prices and thus on realized returns.

Equations (7.1.28) and (7.1.30) can also be used to show that realized stock returns follow an ARMA(1,1) process and to calculate the autocorrelations of this process. There are offsetting effects: The positive autocorrelations of expected returns in (7.1.28) appear in realized returns as well, but a positive innovation to future expected returns causes a contemporaneous capital loss, and this introduces negative autocorrelation into realized returns. In the ARMA(1,1) representation the AR coefficient is the positive persistence parameter ϕ, but the MA coefficient is negative. Problem 7.3 explores these effects in detail, showing that the latter effect dominates provided that $\phi < \rho$. Thus there is some presumption that changing expected returns create negative autocorrelations in realized returns.

Problem 7.3 also generalizes the example to allow for a nonzero covariance between dividend news and expected-return news. Stock returns can

[9]This might be the case, for example, if expected returns are determined by the volatility of the dividend growth process, and dividend volatility is driven by a GARCH model of the type discussed in Chapter 12 so that shocks to volatility are uncorrelated with shocks to the level of dividends.

be positively autocorrelated if dividend news and expected-return news have a sufficiently large positive covariance. The covariance between dividend news and expected-return news can also be chosen to make stock returns serially uncorrelated. This case, in which stock returns follow a serially uncorrelated white noise process while expected stock returns follow a persistent AR(1) process, illustrates the possibility that an asset market may be weak-form efficient (returns are unforecastable from the history of returns themselves) but not semistrong-form efficient (returns are forecastable from the information variable x_t).

This possibility seems to be empirically relevant for the US stock market. The statistically insignificant long-horizon autocorrelations reported at the end of Chapter 2 imply that there is only weak evidence for predictability of long-horizon stock returns given past stock returns; but in the next section we show that there is stronger evidence for predictability of long-horizon returns given other information variables.

7.2 Present-Value Relations and US Stock Price Behavior

We now use the identities discussed in the previous section to interpret recent empirical findings on the time-series behavior of US stock prices. Section 7.2.1 discusses empirical work that predicts stock returns over long horizons, using forecasting variables other than past returns themselves. We present illustrative empirical results when dividend-price ratios and interest rate variables are used to forecast stock returns. Section 7.2.2 relates long-horizon return behavior to price behavior, in particular stock price volatility. Section 7.2.3 shows how time-series models can be used to calculate the long-horizon implications of short-horizon asset market behavior.

7.2.1 Long-Horizon Regressions

Recently there has been much interest in regressions of returns, measured over various horizons, onto forecasting variables. Popular forecasting variables include ratios of price to dividends or earnings (see Campbell and Shiller [1988a,b], Fama and French [1988a], Hodrick [1992], and Shiller [1984]), and various interest rate measures such as the yield spread between long- and short-term rates, the quality yield spread between low- and high-grade corporate bonds or commercial paper, and measures of recent changes in the level of short rates (see Campbell [1987], Fama and French [1989], Hodrick [1992], and Keim and Stambaugh [1986]).

Here we concentrate on the dividend-price ratio, which in US data is the most successful forecasting variable for long-horizon returns, and on a short-term nominal interest-rate variable. We start with prices and dividends on the value-weighted CRSP index of stocks traded on the NYSE, the AMEX, and the NASDAQ. The dividend-price ratio is measured as the sum of dividends paid on the index over the previous year, divided by the current level of the index; summing dividends over a full year removes any seasonal patterns in dividend payments, but the current stock index is used to incorporate the most recent information in stock prices.[10]

The interest-rate variable is a transformation of the one-month nominal US Treasury bill rate motivated by the fact that unit-root tests often fail to reject the hypothesis that the bill rate has a unit root. We subtract a backward one-year moving average of past bill rates from the current bill rate to get a *stochastically detrended* interest rate that is equivalent to a triangularly weighted moving average of past changes in bill rates, where the weights decline as one moves back in time. Accordingly the detrended interest rate is stationary if changes in bill rates are stationary. This stochastic detrending method has been used by Campbell (1991) and Hodrick (1992).

Table 7.1 shows a typical set of results when the dividend-price ratio is used to forecast returns. The table reports monthly regressions of log real stock returns onto the log of the dividend-price ratio at the start of the holding period. Returns are measured over a holding period of K months, which ranges from one month to 48 months (four years); whenever $K > 1$, the regressions use overlapping monthly data. Results are reported for the period 1927 to 1994 and also for subsamples 1927 to 1951 and 1952 to 1994. For each regression Table 7.1 reports the R^2 statistic and the t-statistic for the hypothesis that the coefficient on the log dividend-price ratio is zero. The t-statistic is corrected for heteroskedasticity and serial correlation in the equation error using the asymptotic theory discussed in the Appendix. Table 7.1 follows Fama and French (1988a) except that the regressor is the log dividend-price ratio rather than the level of the dividend-price ratio (a change which makes very little difference to the results), overlapping monthly data are used for all horizons, and the sample periods are updated. Although the results in the table are for real stock returns, almost identical results are obtained for excess returns over the one-month Treasury bill rate.

At a horizon of one month, the regression results in Table 7.1 are rather unimpressive: The R^2 statistics never exceed 2%, and the t-statistics exceed 2 only in the post-World War II subsample. The striking fact about the table is how much stronger the results become when one increases the horizon K. At a two-year horizon the R^2 statistic is 14% for the full sample, 22% for the prewar subsample, and 32% for the postwar subsample; at a four-year horizon the R^2 statistic is 26% for the full sample and 42% for each of the subsamples. In the full sample and the prewar subsample the regression t-

[10]This way of measuring the dividend-price ratio is standard in the academic literature, and it is also commonly used in the financial industry.

Table 7.1. *Long-horizon regressions of log stock returns on the log dividend-price ratio.*

$$r_{t+1} + \cdots + r_{t+K} = \beta(K)(d_t - p_t) + \eta_{t+K,K}$$

	Forecast Horizon (K)					
	1	3	12	24	36	48
1927 to 1994						
$\hat{\beta}(K)$	0.012	0.044	0.191	0.383	0.528	0.654
$R^2(K)$	0.004	0.015	0.068	0.144	0.209	0.267
$t(\hat{\beta}(K))$	1.221	1.400	2.079	4.113	4.631	3.943
1927 to 1951						
$\hat{\beta}(K)$	0.015	0.059	0.274	0.629	0.880	1.050
$R^2(K)$	0.003	0.014	0.074	0.207	0.322	0.424
$t(\hat{\beta}(K))$	0.660	0.844	1.677	4.521	2.967	3.783
1952 to 1994						
$\hat{\beta}(K)$	0.024	0.079	0.329	0.601	0.776	0.863
$R^2(K)$	0.015	0.047	0.190	0.344	0.428	0.432
$t(\hat{\beta}(K))$	2.733	3.055	3.228	3.225	3.315	3.561

r is the log real return on a value-weighted index of NYSE, AMEX, and NASDAQ stocks. $(d-p)$ is the log ratio of dividends over the last year to the current price. Regressions are estimated by OLS, with Hansen and Hodrick (1980) standard errors, calculated from equation (A.3.3) in the Appendix setting autocovariances beyond lag $K - 1$ to zero. Newey and West (1987) standard errors with $q = K - 1$ or $q = 2(K - 1)$ are very similar and typically are slightly smaller than those reported in the table.

statistics also increase dramatically with the forecast horizon, although they are fairly stable within the range 3.0 to 3.5 in the postwar subsample.

It is interesting to compare the results in Table 7.1 with those obtained when stock returns are regressed onto the stochastically detrended short-term interest rate in Table 7.2. The regressions reported in Table 7.2 are run in just the same way as those in Table 7.1. Once again almost identical results are obtained if real returns are replaced by excess returns over the one-month Treasury bill rate.

Table 7.2 shows that, like the dividend-price ratio, the stochastically detrended short rate has some ability to forecast stock returns. However this forecasting power is very different in two respects. First, it is concentrated in the postwar subsample; this is not surprising since short-term interest rates were pegged by the Federal Reserve during much of the 1930s and 1940s, and so the detrended short rate hardly varies in these years. Second, the forecasting power of the short rate is at much shorter horizons than the

Table 7.2.   *Long-horizon regressions of log stock returns on the stochastically detrended short-term interest rate.*

$$r_{t+1} + \cdots + r_{t+K} = \beta(K)(y_{1,t} - \textstyle\sum_{i=0}^{11} y_{1,t-i}/12) + \eta_{t+K,K}$$

	\multicolumn{6}{c}{Forecast Horizon (K)}					
	1	3	12	24	36	48
1927 to 1994						
$\hat{\beta}(K)$	−5.468	−17.181	−41.663	−4.492	−26.148	−20.129
$R^2(K)$	0.005	0.016	0.023	0.000	0.004	0.002
$t(\hat{\beta}(K))$	−2.292	−2.582	−1.564	−0.164	−1.341*	−0.838*
1927 to 1951						
$\hat{\beta}(K)$	3.144	−6.183	73.712	158.989	−67.505	−50.900
$R^2(K)$	0.000	0.000	0.012	0.031	0.005	0.002
$t(\hat{\beta}(K))$	0.222	−0.165	0.520	1.662	−0.637*	−0.580*
1952 to 1994						
$\hat{\beta}(K)$	−6.547	−18.621	−56.406	−26.115	−26.573	−25.894
$R^2(K)$	0.019	0.047	0.103	0.013	0.010	0.008
$t(\hat{\beta}(K))$	−3.263	−3.206	−2.741	−1.354	−1.555*	−1.092*

r is the log real return on a value-weighted index of NYSE, AMEX, and NASDAQ stocks. $y_{1,t}$ is the 1-month nominal Treasury bill rate. Regressions are estimated by OLS, with Hansen and Hodrick (1980) standard errors, calculated from equation (A.3.3) in the Appendix setting autocovariances beyond lag $K-1$ to zero. Newey and West (1987) standard errors, with $q = (K-1)$, are used when the Hansen and Hodrick (1980) covariance matrix estimator is not positive definite. The cases where this occurs are marked ∗.

forecasting power of the dividend-price ratio. The postwar R^2 statistics are comparable to those in Table 7.1 at horizons of one or three months, but they peak at 0.10 at a horizon of one year and then rapidly decline. The regression t-statistics are likewise insignificant beyond a one-year horizon.

How can we understand the hump-shaped pattern of R^2 statistics and t-statistics in Table 7.2 and the strongly increasing pattern in Table 7.1? At one level, the results in Table 7.1 can be understood by recalling the formula relating the log dividend-price ratio to expectations of future returns and dividend growth rates, given above as (7.1.24):

$$d_t - p_t = \mathrm{E}_t \left[\sum_{j=0}^{\infty} \rho^j \left[-\Delta d_{t+1+j} + r_{t+1+j} \right] \right].$$

This expression shows that the log dividend-price ratio will be a good proxy for market expectations of future stock returns, provided that expectations of future dividend growth rates are not too variable. Moreover, in general the log dividend-price ratio will be a better proxy for expectations of long-horizon returns than for expectations of short-horizon returns, because the expectations on the right-hand side of (7.1.24) are of a discounted value of all returns into the infinite future. This may help to explain the improvement in forecast power as the horizon increases in Table 7.1.

Even in the absence of this effect, however, it is possible to obtain results like those in Tables 7.1 and 7.2. To see this we now return to our AR(1) example in which the variable x_t, a perfect proxy for the expected stock return at any horizon, is observable and can be used as a regressor by the econometrician. Problem 7.4 develops a structural model of stock prices and dividends in which a multiple of the log dividend-price ratio has the properties of the variable x_t in the AR(1) example.

We use the AR(1) example to show that when x_t is persistent, the R^2 of a return regression on x_t is very small at a short horizon; as the horizon increases, the R^2 first increases and then eventually decreases. We also discuss finite-sample difficulties with statistical inference in long-horizon regressions.

R^2 Statistics

First consider regressing the one-period return r_{t+1} on the variable x_t. For simplicity, we will ignore constant terms since these are not the objects of interest; constants could be included in the regression, or we could simply work with demeaned data. In population, $\beta(1) = 1$, so the fitted value is just x_t itself, with variance σ_x^2, while the variance of the return is given by equation (7.1.31) above. It follows that the one-period regression R^2 statistic, which we write as $R^2(1)$, is

$$R^2(1) \equiv \frac{\text{Var}\left[E_t[r_{t+1}]\right]}{\text{Var}[r_{t+1}]} \approx \left(\frac{\sigma_d^2}{\sigma_x^2} + \frac{2}{1-\phi}\right)^{-1}, \qquad (7.2.1)$$

where for simplicity we are using the approximate version of (7.1.31) that holds when $\phi \ll \rho$ and ρ is close to one. $R^2(1)$ reaches an upper bound of $(1 - \phi)/2$ when the variability of dividend news, σ_d^2, is zero. Thus even when a stock is effectively a real consol bond with known real dividends, so that all variation in its price is due to changing expected returns, the one-period R^2 statistic will be small when ϕ is large. The reason is that innovations to expected returns cause large unforecastable changes in stock prices when expected returns are persistent.

The behavior of the R^2 statistic in a long-horizon regression is somewhat more complicated. A regression with horizon K takes the form

$$r_{t+1} + \cdots + r_{t+K} = \beta(K)x_t + \eta_{t+K,K}. \qquad (7.2.2)$$

In the AR(1) example, the best forecast of the one-period return j periods ahead is always $E_t[x_{t+j-1}] = \phi^{j-1} x_t$. The best forecast of the cumulative return over K months is found by summing the forecasts of one-period returns up to horizon K, so $\beta(K) = (1+\phi+\cdots+\phi^{K-1}) = (1-\phi^K)/(1-\phi)$.

The R^2 statistic for the K-period regression is given by

$$R^2(K) \equiv \frac{\text{Var}\,[E_t[r_{t+1}] + \cdots + E_t[r_{t+K}]]}{\text{Var}[r_{t+1} + \cdots + r_{t+K}]}. \tag{7.2.3}$$

Dividing by the one-period R^2 statistic and rearranging, we obtain

$$\frac{R^2(K)}{R^2(1)} = \left(\frac{\text{Var}\,[E_t[r_{t+1}] + \cdots + E_t[r_{t+K}]]}{\text{Var}\,[E_t[r_{t+1}]]}\right)$$
$$\times \left(\frac{\text{Var}[r_{t+1}]}{\text{Var}[r_{t+1} + \cdots + r_{t+K}]}\right). \tag{7.2.4}$$

The first ratio on the right-hand side of (7.2.4) is just the square of the K-period regression coefficient divided by the square of the one-period regression coefficient. In the AR(1) example this is $(1-\phi^K)^2/(1-\phi)^2$, which is approximately equal to K^2 for large ϕ and small K. The second ratio on the right-hand side of (7.2.4) is closely related to the variance ratio discussed in Chapter 2. In fact, it can be rewritten as $1/(KV(K))$, where $V(K)$ is the K-period variance ratio for stock returns. In the AR(1) example, Problem 7.3 shows that the autocorrelations of stock returns are all negative. It follows that $V(K) < 1$, so $1/(KV(K)) > 1/K$.

Putting the two terms on the right-hand side of (7.2.4) together, we find that if expected stock returns are very persistent, the multiperiod R^2 statistic grows at first approximately in proportion to the horizon K. This behavior is well illustrated by the results in Table 7.1. Intuitively, it occurs because forecasts of expected returns several periods ahead are only slightly less variable than the forecast of the next period's expected return, and they are perfectly correlated with it. Successive realized returns, on the other hand, are slightly negatively correlated with one another. Thus at first the variance of the multiperiod fitted value grows more rapidly than the variance of the multiperiod realized return, increasing the multiperiod R^2 statistic. Eventually, of course, forecasts of returns in the distant future die out so the first ratio on the right-hand side of (7.2.4) converges to a fixed limit; but the variability of realized multiperiod returns continues to increase, so the second ratio on the right-hand side of (7.2.4) becomes proportional to $1/K$. Thus eventually multiperiod R^2 statistics go to zero as the horizon increases.

It may be helpful to give an even more explicit formula for the AR(1) example in the case where the long horizon is just two periods, that is where $K = 2$. In this case tedious but straightforward calculations and the simplifying approximation that holds when $\phi \ll \rho$ and ρ is close to one yield

$$\frac{R^2(2)}{R^2(1)} \approx (1+\phi)^2 \left[\frac{2 + (1-\phi)(\sigma_d^2/\sigma_x^2)}{2(1+\phi) + 2(1-\phi)(\sigma_d^2/\sigma_x^2)} \right]. \qquad (7.2.5)$$

The ratio in (7.2.5) approaches $(1+\phi)$ as σ_d^2/σ_x^2 approaches zero, so a two-period regression may have an R^2 statistic almost twice that of a one-period regression if expected returns are persistent and highly variable. On the other hand the ratio approaches $(1+\phi)^2/2$ as σ_d^2/σ_x^2 approaches infinity, so a two-period regression may have an R^2 statistic only half that of a one-period regression if expected returns have only small and transitory variation.

Calculations for horizons beyond two periods become very messy, but Campbell (1993b) reports some numerical results. When $\phi = 0.98$, $\rho = 0.995$, and $\sigma_d^2/\sigma_x^2 = 0$, for example, a one-period regression has an R^2 statistic of only 1.5%, but the maximum R^2 is 63% for a 152-period regression. When the forecasting variable is highly persistent, the R^2 statistic can continue to rise out to extremely long horizons.

Difficulties with Inference in Finite Samples
The t-statistics reported in Tables 7.1 and 7.2 are based on the asymptotic theory summarized in the Appendix. There are however a number of pitfalls in applying this theory to regressions of returns onto the information variable x_t.

A first problem arises from the fact that in the regression of the one-period return r_{t+1} on x_t, $r_{t+1} = \beta(1)x_t + \eta_{t+1}$, the regressor x_t is correlated with past error terms η_{t-i} for $i \geq 0$, even though it is not correlated with contemporaneous or future error terms η_{t+1+i}. These correlations exist because shocks to the state variable x_t are correlated with shocks to returns, and the variable x_t is persistent. In the language of econometrics, the regressor x_t is *predetermined*, but it is not *exogenous*. This leads to finite-sample bias in the coefficient of a regression of returns on x_t. In the AR(1) example, there is a simple formula for the bias when the regression horizon is one period:

$$E[\hat{\beta}(1) - \beta(1)] = -\left(\frac{1+3\phi}{T}\right)\frac{\sigma_{\eta\xi}}{\sigma_\xi^2} = \frac{\rho(1+3\phi)}{(1-\rho\phi)T}. \qquad (7.2.6)$$

The term $-(1+3\phi)/T$ is the Kendall (1954) expression for the bias in the OLS estimate of the persistence parameter ϕ obtained by regressing x_{t+1} on x_t. As Stambaugh (1986) has shown, this bias leads to a bias in the OLS estimate of the coefficient $\beta(1)$ when the return innovation η_{t+1} covaries with the innovation in the forecasting variable ξ_{t+1}. In our simple example with uncorrelated news about dividends and future returns driving current returns, the ratio $\sigma_{\eta\xi}/\sigma_\xi^2 = -\rho/(1-\rho\phi)$, which produces the second equality in (7.2.6). This bias can be substantial: With $\rho = 0.997$, for example, it equals $36/T$ when $\phi = 0.9$, $73/T$ when $\phi = 0.95$, and $171/T$ when $\phi = 0.98$.[11]

A second problem is that the asymptotic theory given in the Appendix may be misleading in finite samples when the horizon K is large relative to the sample size. Hodrick (1992) and Nelson and Kim (1993) use Monte Carlo methods to illustrate this for the case where stock returns are regressed on dividend-price ratios. Richardson and Stock (1989) show that the finite-sample properties of regressions with large K can be accounted for using an alternative asymptotic theory in which K increases asymptotically at the same rate as the sample size. Section 2.5.1 of Chapter 2 discusses the application of their theory to univariate regressions of returns on past returns.

One way to avoid this problem is to transform the basic regression so that it no longer has overlapping residuals. This has been proposed by Jegadeesh (1991) for the Fama and French (1988b) regression of returns on lagged returns, and it has been advocated more generally by Cochrane (1991). For example, we might estimate

$$r_{t+1} = \gamma(K)(x_t + \cdots + x_{t+1-K}) + v_{t+1,K}, \qquad (7.2.7)$$

where the error term $v_{t+1,K}$ is now serially uncorrelated. The numerator of the regression coefficient $\gamma(K)$ in (7.2.7) is the same as the numerator of the regression coefficient $\beta(K)$ in (7.2.2), because the covariance of x measured at one date and r measured at another date depends only on the difference between the two dates. Hence $\gamma(K) = 0$ in (7.2.7) if and only if $\beta(K) = 0$ in (7.2.2). However it does not necessarily follow that tests of $\gamma(K) = 0$ and $\beta(K) = 0$ have the same asymptotic properties under the null or general alternative hypotheses. Hodrick (1992) presents Monte Carlo evidence on the distributions of both kinds of test statistics; he finds that they both tend to reject the null too often if asymptotic critical values are used, so that the long-horizon t-statistics reported in Tables 7.1 and 7.2 should be treated with caution. However he also finds that these biases are not strong enough to account for the evidence of return predictability reported in the tables.

An important unresolved question is whether there are circumstances under which long-horizon regressions have greater power to detect deviations from the null hypothesis than do short-horizon regressions. Hodrick (1992) and Mark (1995) present some suggestive Monte Carlo evidence that this may be the case, and Campbell (1993b) also studies the issue, but the literature has not reached any firm conclusion at this stage.

---

[11]Similar biases afflict the regression when the horizon is greater than one period. See Hodrick (1992) and Mark (1995) for Monte Carlo evidence on this point.

7.2.2 Volatility Tests

In the previous section we have explored regressions whose dependent variables are returns measured over long horizons. One motivation for such regressions is that asset prices are influenced by expectations of returns into the distant future, so long-horizon procedures are necessary if we are to understand price behavior. We now turn to empirical work that looks at price variability more directly.

LeRoy and Porter (1981) and Shiller (1981) started a heated debate in the early 1980s by arguing that stock prices are too volatile to be rational forecasts of future dividends discounted at a constant rate. This controversy has since died down, partly because it is now more clearly understood that a rejection of constant-discount-rate models is not the same as a rejection of the Efficient Markets Hypothesis, and partly because regression tests have convinced many financial economists that expected stock returns are time-varying rather than constant. Nonetheless the volatility literature has introduced some important ideas that are closely connected with the work on multiperiod return regressions discussed in the previous section. Useful surveys of this literature include Gilles and LeRoy (1991), LeRoy (1989), Shiller (1989, Chapter 4), and West (1988a).

The early papers in the volatility literature used levels of stock prices and dividends, but here we restate the ideas in logarithmic form. This is consistent with the more recent literature and with the exposition in the rest of this chapter. We begin by defining a log *perfect-foresight stock price,*

$$p_t^* \equiv \sum_{j=0}^{\infty} \rho^j \left[(1-\rho)d_{t+1+j} + k - r \right]. \tag{7.2.8}$$

The perfect-foresight price p_t^* is so named because from the *ex post* stock price identity (7.1.21) it is the price that would prevail if *realized* returns were constant at some level r, that is, if there were no revisions in expectations driving unexpected returns. Equivalently, from the *ex ante* stock price identity (7.1.22) it is the price that would prevail if expected returns were constant and investors had perfect knowledge of future dividends. Substituting (7.2.8) into (7.1.21), we find that

$$p_t^* - p_t = \sum_{j=0}^{\infty} \rho^j (r_{t+1+j} - r). \tag{7.2.9}$$

The difference between p_t^* and p_t is just a discounted sum of future demeaned stock returns.

If we now take expectations and use the definition given in (7.1.22) and (7.1.23) of the price component p_{rt}, we find that

$$E_t[p_t^*] - p_t = p_{rt} - \frac{r}{1-\rho} = p_{rt} - E[p_{rt}]. \tag{7.2.10}$$

Recall that p_{rt} can be interpreted as that component of the stock price which is associated with changing expectations of future stock returns. Thus the conditional expectation of $p_t^* - p_t$ measures the effect of changing expected stock returns on the current stock price. In the AR(1) example developed earlier, the conditional expectation of $p_t^* - p_t$ is just $x_t/(1-\rho\phi)$ from (7.1.29).

If expected stock returns are constant through time, then the right-hand side of (7.2.10) is zero. The constant-expected-return hypothesis implies that $p_t^* - p_t$ is a forecast error uncorrelated with information known at time t. Equivalently, it implies that the stock price is a rational expectation of the perfect-foresight stock price:

$$p_t = \mathrm{E}_t[p_t^*]. \qquad (7.2.11)$$

How can these ideas be used to test the hypothesis that expected stock returns are constant? For simplicity of exposition, we begin by making two unrealistic assumptions: first, that log stock prices and dividends follow stationary stochastic processes, so that they have well-defined first and second moments; and second, that log dividends are observable into the infinite future, so that the perfect-foresight price p_t^* is observable to the econometrician. Below we discuss how these assumptions are relaxed.

Orthogonality and Variance-Bounds Tests

Equation (7.2.11) implies that $p_t^* - p_t$ is *orthogonal* to information variables known at time t. An orthogonality test of (7.2.11) regresses $p_t^* - p_t$ onto information variables and tests for zero coefficients. If the information variables include the stock price p_t itself, this is equivalent to a regression of p_t^* onto p_t and other variables, where the hypothesis to be tested is now that p_t has a unit coefficient and the other variables have zero coefficients. These regressions are variants of the long-horizon return regressions discussed in the previous section. Equation (7.2.9) shows that $p_t^* - p_t$ is just a discounted sum of future demeaned stock returns, so an orthogonality test of (7.2.11) is a return regression with an infinite horizon, where more distant returns are geometrically downweighted.[12]

Instead of testing orthogonality directly, much of the literature tests the implications of orthogonality for the volatility of stock prices. The most famous such implication, derived by LeRoy and Porter (1981) and Shiller (1981), is the *variance inequality* for the stock price:

$$\mathrm{Var}[p_t^*] = \mathrm{Var}[p_t] + \mathrm{Var}[p_t^* - p_t] \geq \mathrm{Var}[p_t]. \qquad (7.2.12)$$

---

[12]The downweighting allows the R^2 statistic in the regression to be positive, whereas we showed in Section 7.2.1 that the R^2 statistic in an unweighted finite-horizon return regression converges to zero as the horizon increases. Durlauf and Hall (1989), Scott (1985), and Shiller (1989, Chapter 11) have run regressions of this sort.

The equality in (7.2.12) holds because under the null hypothesis (7.2.11) $p_t^* - p_t$ must be uncorrelated with p_t so no covariance term appears in the variance of p_t^*; the variance inequality follows directly. Equation (7.2.12) can also be understood by noting that an optimal forecast cannot be more variable than the quantity it is forecasting. With constant expected returns the stock price forecasts only the present value of future dividends, so it cannot be more variable than the realized present value of future dividends. Tests of this and related propositions are known as *variance-bounds tests*.

As Durlauf and Phillips (1988) point out, variance-bounds tests can be restated as orthogonality tests. To see this, consider a regression of p_t on $p_t^* - p_t$. This is the reverse of the regression considered above, but it too should have a zero coefficient under the null hypothesis. The reverse regression coefficient is always $\theta \equiv \text{Cov}[p_t^* - p_t, p_t] / \text{Var}[p_t^* - p_t]$. It is straightforward to show that

$$\frac{\text{Var}[p_t^*] - \text{Var}[p_t]}{\text{Var}[p_t^* - p_t]} = 1 + 2\theta, \tag{7.2.13}$$

so the variance inequality (7.2.12) will be satisfied whenever the reverse regression coefficient $\theta > -1/2$. This is a weaker restriction than the orthogonality condition $\theta = 0$, so the orthogonality test clearly has power in some situations where the variance-bounds test has none. The justification for using a variance-bounds test is not increased power; rather it is that a variance-bounds test helps one to describe the way in which the null hypothesis fails.

Unit Roots

Our analysis so far has assumed that the population variances of log prices and dividends exist. This will not be the case if log dividends follow a unit-root process; then, as Kleidon (1986) points out, the sample variances of prices and dividends can be very misleading. Marsh and Merton (1986) provide a particularly neat example. Suppose that expected stock returns are constant, so the null hypothesis is true. Suppose also that a firm's managers use its stock price as an indicator of "permanent earnings," setting the firm's dividend equal to a constant fraction of its stock price last period. In log form, we have

$$d_{t+1} = \bar{\delta} + p_t, \tag{7.2.14}$$

where there is a unique constant $\bar{\delta}$ that satisfies the null hypothesis (7.2.11). It can be shown that both log dividends and log prices follow unit-root processes in this example. Substituting (7.2.14) into (7.2.8), we find that the perfect-foresight stock price is related to the actual stock price by

$$p_t^* = (1 - \rho) \sum_{j=0}^{\infty} \rho^j p_{t+j}. \tag{7.2.15}$$

This is just a smoothed version of the actual stock price p_t, so its variance depends on the variance and autocorrelations of p_t. Since autocorrelations can never be greater than one, p_t^* must have a lower variance than p_t. The importance of this result is not that it applies to population variances (which are not well defined in this example because both log prices and log dividends have unit roots), but that it applies to sample variances in every sample. Thus the variance inequality (7.2.12) will always be violated in the Marsh-Merton example.

This unit-root problem is important, but it is also easy to circumvent. The variable $p_t^* - p_t$ is always stationary provided that stock returns are stationary, so any test that $p_t^* - p_t$ is orthogonal to stationary variables will be well-behaved. The problems pointed out by Kleidon (1986) and Marsh and Merton (1986) arise when $p_t^* - p_t$ is regressed on the stock price p_t, which has a unit root. These problems can be avoided by using unit-root regression theory or by choosing a stationary regressor, such as the log dividend-price ratio. Some other ways to deal with the unit-root problem are explored in Problem 7.5.[13]

Finite-Sample Considerations

So far we have treated the perfect-foresight stock price as if it were an observable variable. But as defined in (7.2.8), the perfect-foresight price is unobservable in a finite sample because it is a discounted sum of dividends out to the infinite future. The definition of p_t^* implies that

$$p_t^* = (1 - \rho) \sum_{j=0}^{T-t-1} \rho^j (d_{t+1+j} + k - r) + \rho^{T-t-1} p_T^*. \qquad (7.2.16)$$

Given data up through time T the first term on the right-hand side of (7.2.16) is observable but the second term is not.

Following Shiller (1981), one standard response to this difficulty is to replace the unobservable p_t^* by an observable proxy $p_{t,T}^*$ that uses only in-sample information:

$$p_{t,T}^* \equiv (1 - \rho) \sum_{j=0}^{T-t-1} \rho^j (d_{t+1+j} + k - r) + \rho^{T-t-1} p_T. \qquad (7.2.17)$$

Here the terminal value of the actual stock price, p_T, is used in place of the terminal value of the perfect-foresight stock price, p_T^*.[14] Several points are

---

[13]Durlauf and Hall (1989) apply unit-root regression theory, while Campbell and Shiller (1988a,b) replace the log stock price with the log dividend-price ratio. Problem 7.5 is based on the work of Mankiw, Romer, and Shapiro (1985) and West (1988b).

[14]Shiller (1981) used the sample average price instead of the end-of-sample price in his terminal condition, but later work, including Shiller (1989), follows the approach discussed here.

worth noting about the variable $p^*_{t,T}$. First, if expected returns are constant, (7.2.11) continues to hold when $p^*_{t,T}$ is substituted for p^*_t. Thus tests of the constant-expected-return model can use $p^*_{t,T}$. Second, a rational bubble in the stock price will affect both p_t and $p^*_{t,T}$. Thus tests using $p^*_{t,T}$ include bubbles in the null rather than the alternative hypothesis. Third, the difference $p^*_{t,T} - p_t$ can be written as a discounted sum of demeaned stock returns, with the sum terminating at the end of the sample period T rather than at some fixed horizon from the present date t. Thus orthogonality tests using $p^*_{t,T} - p_t$ are just long-horizon return regressions, where future returns are geometrically discounted and the horizon is the end of the sample period.

As one might expect, the asymptotic theory for statistical inference in orthogonality and variance-bounds tests is essentially the same as the theory used to conduct statistical inference in long-horizon return regressions.[15] As always, in finite samples it is important to look at the effective order of overlap (that is, the number of periods in (7.2.9) during which discounted future returns make a nonnegligible contribution to today's value of $p^*_{t,T} - p_t$). If this is large relative to the sample size, then asymptotic theory is unlikely to be a reliable guide for statistical inference.

Flavin (1983) gives a particularly clear intuition for why this might be a problem in the context of variance-bounds tests. She points out that whenever a sample variance around a sample mean is used to estimate a population variance, there is some downward bias caused by the fact that the true mean of the process is unknown. When the process is white noise, it is well-known that this bias can be corrected by dividing the sum of squares by $T - 1$ instead of T. Unfortunately, the downward bias is more severe for serially correlated processes (intuitively, there is a smaller number of effective observations for these processes), so this correction becomes inadequate in the presence of serial correlation. Now $p^*_{t,T}$ is more highly serially correlated than p_t, since $p^*_{t,T}$ changes only as dividends drop out of the present-value formula and discount factors are updated, while p_t is affected by new information about dividends. Thus the ratio of the sample variance of $p^*_{t,T}$ to the sample variance of p_t is downward-biased, and this can cause the variance inequality in (7.2.12) to be violated too often in finite samples. From the equivalence of variance-bounds and orthogonality tests, the same problem arises in a regression context.

7.2.3 Vector Autoregressive Methods

The methods discussed in the previous two sections have the common feature that they try to look directly at long-horizon properties of the data. This

---

[15]LeRoy and Steigerwald (1992) use Monte Carlo methods to study the power of orthogonality and variance-bounds tests.

can lead to statistical difficulties in finite samples. An alternative approach
is to assume that the dynamics of the data are well described by a simple
time-series model; long-horizon properties can then be imputed from the
short-run model rather than estimated directly. In the variance-bounds literature, this is the approach of LeRoy and Porter (1981). These authors note
that a variance-bounds test does not require observations of the perfect-
foresight price p_t^* itself; it merely requires an estimate of the variance of p_t^*,
which can be obtained from a univariate time-series model for dividends.
West (1988b) develops a variant of this procedure.

To see how this approach can work, suppose that one observes the
complete vector of state variables $\mathbf{x}_t$ used by market participants, and that
$\mathbf{x}_t$ follows a vector autoregressive (VAR) process. Any VAR model can be
written in first-order form by augmenting the state vector with suitable lags
of the original variables, so without loss of generality we write:

$$\mathbf{x}_{t+1} = \mathbf{A}\mathbf{x}_t + \epsilon_{t+1}. \tag{7.2.18}$$

Here $\mathbf{A}$ is a matrix of VAR coefficients, and ϵ_{t+1} is a vector of shocks to the
VAR. We have dropped constants for simplicity; one can think of the state
vector as including demeaned variables.

Equation (7.2.18) implies that multiperiod forecasts of the state vector
$\mathbf{x}_t$ can be formed by matrix multiplication:

$$\mathrm{E}_t[\mathbf{x}_{t+1+j}] = \mathbf{A}^{j+1}\mathbf{x}_t. \tag{7.2.19}$$

This makes it easy to calculate the long-horizon forecasts that determine
prices in (7.1.22) and (7.1.23), or the revisions of long-horizon forecasts
that determine returns in (7.1.25) and (7.1.26).

Vector Autoregressions and Price Volatility

As a first example, suppose that the state vector includes the stock price
p_t as its first element and the dividend d_t as its second element, while the
remaining elements are other relevant forecasting variables. We define
vectors $e\mathbf{1}' = [1\ 0\ 0\ \dots\ 0]$ and $e\mathbf{2}' = [0\ 1\ 0\ \dots\ 0]$. These vectors pick
out the first element (p_t) and the second element (d_t) from the state vector
$\mathbf{x}_t$. Using these definitions and equations (7.1.22), (7.1.23), and (7.2.19),
the dividend component of the stock price is

$$p_{dt} = (1-\rho)\sum_{j=0}^{\infty}\rho^j e\mathbf{2}'\mathbf{A}^{j+1}\mathbf{x}_t = (1-\rho)e\mathbf{2}'\mathbf{A}(\mathbf{I}-\rho\mathbf{A})^{-1}\mathbf{x}_t. \tag{7.2.20}$$

The stock price itself is $p_t = e\mathbf{1}'\mathbf{x}_t$, so the expected-return component of
the stock price is the difference between the two. If expected returns are

constant, then $p_t = p_{dt}$, which imposes the restriction

$$e\mathbf{1}' = (1 - \rho)e\mathbf{2}'\mathbf{A}(\mathbf{I} - \rho\mathbf{A})^{-1} \qquad (7.2.21)$$

on the VAR system. This can be tested using a nonlinear Wald test.[16]

So far we have assumed that the vector $\mathbf{x}_t$ includes all the relevant variables observed by market participants. Fortunately this very strong assumption can be relaxed. Even if $\mathbf{x}_t$ includes only a subset of the relevant information, under the constant-expected-return null hypothesis the stock price p_t should still equal the best VAR forecast of the discounted value of future dividends as given on the right-hand side of (7.2.21). Intuitively, when the null hypothesis is true the stock price perfectly reveals investors' information about the discounted value of future dividends. Another way to see the same point is to interpret the restriction (7.2.21) as enforcing the unforecastability of multiperiod stock returns. If multiperiod returns are unforecastable given investors' information, they will also be unforecastable given any smaller set of information variables, and thus the VAR test of (7.2.21) is a valid test of the null hypothesis.

One can also show that (7.2.21) is a nonlinear transformation of the restrictions implied by the unforecastability of single-period stock returns. In the VAR system the single-period stock return is unforecastable if and only if

$$e\mathbf{1}'(\mathbf{I} - \rho\mathbf{A}) = (1 - \rho)e\mathbf{2}'\mathbf{A}, \qquad (7.2.22)$$

which is obtained from (7.2.21) by postmultiplying each side by $(\mathbf{I} - \rho\mathbf{A})$. The economic meaning of this is that multiperiod returns are unforecastable if and only if one-period returns are unforecastable. However Wald test statistics are sensitive to nonlinear transformations of hypotheses; thus Wald tests of the VAR coefficient restrictions may behave differently when the restrictions are stated in the infinite-horizon form (7.2.21) than when they are stated in the single-period form (7.2.22). An interesting question for future research is how alternative VAR test statistics behave in simple models of time-varying expected returns such as the AR(1) example developed in this chapter.

An important caveat is that when the constant-expected-return null hypothesis is false, the VAR estimate of p_{dt} will in general depend on the information included in the VAR. Thus one should be cautious in interpreting VAR estimates that reject the null hypothesis. As an example, consider an updated version of the VAR system used by Campbell and Shiller (1988a) which includes the log dividend-price ratio and the real log dividend growth rate. These variables are used in place of the real log price and log dividend

---

[16]For details see Campbell and Shiller (1987, 1988a,b). Campbell and Shiller also show how to test other models of expected stock returns in the VAR framework.

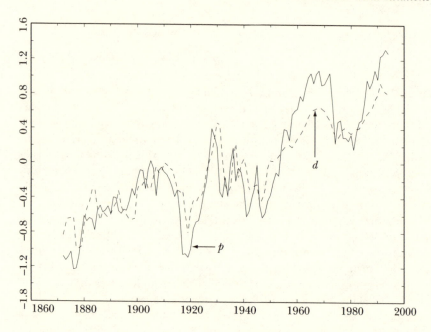

Figure 7.1. *Log Real Stock Price and Dividend Series, Annual US Data, 1872 to 1994*

in order to ensure that the VAR system is stationary. The system is estimated with four lags using annual data from 1871 to 1994. Figure 7.1 shows the real log stock price as a solid line and the real log dividend as a dashed line. Both series have been demeaned so that the sample mean in the Figure is zero. The two lines tend to move together, but the movements of the log stock price are larger than those of the log dividend; thus the price-dividend ratio is procyclical and the dividend-price ratio is countercyclical. Figure 7.2 again shows the demeaned real log stock price as a solid line, but now the dashed line is the demeaned VAR estimate of p_{dt}, the present value of future dividends. Because the real log dividend is close to a random walk, the VAR estimate of p_{dt} is close to d_t itself and thus the variation in p_t is larger than that in p_{dt}. Figure 7.3 shows the log dividend-price ratio as a solid line and the log ratio of dividend to p_{dt} as a dashed line.[17] The present-value model with constant discount rates explains very little of the variation in stock prices relative to dividends.

While this general conclusion is robust, the smoothness of p_{dt} is sensitive to the specification of the VAR system. In a low-order system with four lags

[17]These series have not been demeaned; the level of the dividend-price ratio can be recovered from the figure by exponentiating the plotted solid line.

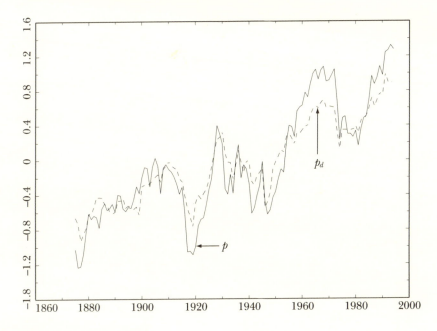

Figure 7.2. *Log Real Stock Price and Estimated Dividend Component, Annual US Data, 1876 to 1994*

or fewer, p_{dt} moves closely with d_t. As one increases the lag length towards ten lags, p_{dt} becomes much smoother and more like a trend line. The same thing happens if one adds to the VAR system a ratio of price to a 10-year or 30-year moving average of earnings, as suggested by Campbell and Shiller (1988b). There appears to be some long-run mean-reversion in dividend growth which is captured by these expanded VAR systems.

In conclusion, the VAR approach strongly suggests that the stock market is too volatile to be consistent with the view that stock prices are optimal forecasts of future dividends discounted at a constant rate. Some VAR systems suggest that the optimal dividend forecast is close to the current dividend, others that the optimal dividend forecast is even smoother than the current dividend; neither type of system can account for the tendency of stock prices to move more than one-for-one with dividends.[18] Strictly speaking, however, once the null hypothesis $p_t = p_{dt}$ is rejected, any interpretation

---

[18]Barsky and De Long (1993) point out that stock price behavior could be rationalized if there were a unit-root component in dividend growth, but they do not present any direct econometric evidence for such a component. Donaldson and Kamstra (1996) argue that a nonlinear dividend forecasting model delivers more volatile forecasts of long-run future dividends. This remains an active research area.

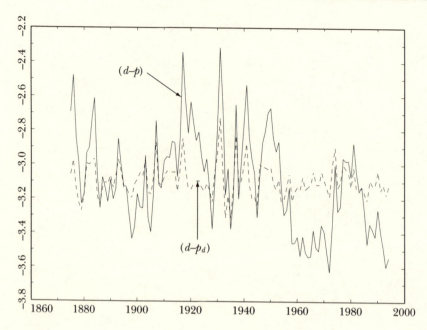

Figure 7.3. *Log Dividend-Price Ratio and Estimated Dividend Component, Annual US data, 1876 to 1994*

of the behavior of p_{dt} is conditional on the information variables included in the VAR.

Vector Autoregressions and Return Volatility

A common criticism of volatility tests, which applies equally to VAR systems including prices and dividends, is that the time-series process driving dividends may not be stable through time.[19] Fortunately it is possible to analyze the variability of stock returns without modeling the dividend process. Consider a state vector $\mathbf{x}_t$ whose first element is the one-period stock return and whose other elements are relevant forecasting variables for returns. With this system the unexpected stock return becomes

$$r_{t+1} - \mathrm{E}_t[r_{t+1}] = \mathbf{e}\mathbf{1}'\epsilon_{t+1}. \tag{7.2.23}$$

---

[19] The Modigliani-Miller theorem says that firm-value maximization by managers does not constrain the form of dividend policy. Lehmann (1991) uses this to argue that the stochastic process describing dividends is unlikely to be stable.

Recall that the revision in expectations of all future stock returns, $\eta_{r,t+1}$, is defined as

$$\eta_{r,t+1} \equiv E_{t+1}\left[\sum_{j=1}^{\infty} \rho^j r_{t+1+j}\right] - E_t\left[\sum_{j=1}^{\infty} \rho^j r_{t+1+j}\right].$$

This becomes

$$\eta_{r,t+1} = e\mathbf{1}'\sum_{j=1}^{\infty} \rho^j \mathbf{A}^j \epsilon_{t+1} = e\mathbf{1}'\rho\mathbf{A}(\mathbf{I} - \rho\mathbf{A})^{-1}\epsilon_{t+1}. \tag{7.2.24}$$

From (7.1.26) the revision in expectations of future dividends, $\eta_{d,t+1}$, can be treated as a residual:

$$\eta_{d,t+1} = (r_{t+1} - E_t[r_{t+1}]) + \eta_{r,t+1} = e\mathbf{1}'\left(\mathbf{I} + \rho\mathbf{A}(\mathbf{I} - \rho\mathbf{A})^{-1}\right)\epsilon_{t+1}.$$

As a concrete example, consider an updated version of the system estimated by Campbell (1991) in which the state vector has three elements; the real stock return (r_t), the log dividend-price ratio (x_{2t}), and the level of the stochastically detrended short-term interest rate (x_{3t}). Using monthly data over the period 1952:1 to 1994:12, the estimated first-order VAR for these variables, with asymptotic standard errors in parentheses, is

$$\begin{pmatrix} r_{t+1} \\ x_{2,t+1} \\ x_{3,t+1} \end{pmatrix} = \begin{pmatrix} \begin{array}{ccc} 0.055 & 0.655 & -0.520 \\ (0.053) & (0.230) & (0.166) \\ -0.038 & 0.999 & -0.000 \\ (0.001) & (0.003) & (0.002) \\ -0.032 & -0.040 & 0.707 \\ (0.011) & (0.046) & (0.050) \end{array} \end{pmatrix} \begin{pmatrix} r_t \\ x_{2t} \\ x_{3t} \end{pmatrix}$$

$$+ \begin{pmatrix} \epsilon_{1,t+1} \\ \epsilon_{2,t+1} \\ \epsilon_{3,t+1} \end{pmatrix}. \tag{7.2.25}$$

The matrix in (7.2.25) is a numerical example of the VAR coefficient matrix **A**. The R^2 statistics for the three regressions summarized in (7.2.25) are 0.040, 0.996, and 0.537, respectively, indicating a modest degree of forecastability for monthly stock returns.[20]

---

[20] As the coefficient estimates suggest, the log dividend-price ratio has a root extremely close to unity in this sample period. Although there are theoretical reasons for believing that the log dividend-price ratio is stationary, and unit-root tests reject a unit root over long sample periods in US data, the persistence of the log dividend-price ratio does lead to inference problems in the VAR system. Hodrick (1992) is a careful Monte Carlo study of these problems.

We can substitute the estimated **A** matrix into the formula (7.2.24) and use the estimated variance-covariance matrix of the error vector ϵ_{t+1} to calculate the sample variances and covariance of the expected-return and dividend components of stock returns. The estimated expected-return component has a sample variance equal to 0.75 times the variance of realized returns, while the estimated dividend component has a sample variance only 0.12 times the variance of realized returns. The remaining variance of realized returns (0.13 of the total) is attributed to covariance between the expected-return and dividend components.[21]

The reason for this result is that the log dividend-price ratio forecasts stock returns, and it is itself a highly persistent process. Thus revisions in the log dividend-price ratio are associated with persistent changes in expected future returns, and this can justify large changes in stock prices. The estimated VAR process is somewhat more complicated than the simple AR(1) example developed earlier in this chapter, for it includes two forecasting variables, each of which is close to a univariate AR(1). However the main effect of the interest-rate variable is to increase the forecastability of one-period stock returns; it has a rather modest effect on the long-run behavior of the system, which is dominated by the persistent movements of the log dividend-price ratio. Thus the long-run properties of the VAR system are similar to those of the AR(1) example. From this and our previous analysis, one would expect that VAR systems like (7.2.25) could account for the pattern of long-horizon regression results, and this indeed seems to be the case as shown by Campbell (1991), Hodrick (1992), and Kandel and Stambaugh (1989). Of course, VAR systems impose more structure on the data; but Hodrick (1992) presents some Monte Carlo evidence that when the structure is correct, the finite-sample behavior of VAR systems is correspondingly better than that of long-horizon regressions with a large horizon relative to the sample size.

7.3 Conclusion

The research described in this chapter has helped to transform the way financial economists view asset markets. It used to be thought that expected asset returns were approximately constant and that movements in prices could be attributed to news about future cash payments to investors. Today the importance of time-variation in expected returns is widely recognized,

---

[21]Over a longer period 1926 to 1988, the two variances and the covariance have roughly equal shares of the overall variance of realized stock returns. Asymptotic standard errors for the variance decomposition can be calculated using the delta method explained in Section A.4 of the Appendix. As in the price-dividend VAR discussed above, the decomposition is conditional on the information variables included in the VAR system.

and this has broad implications for both academics and investment professionals.

At the academic level, there is an explosion of research on the determinants of time-varying expected returns. Economists are exploring a great variety of ideas, from macroeconomic models of real business cycles to more heterodox models of investor psychology. We discuss some of these ideas in Chapter 8. At a more practical level, dynamic asset-allocation models are becoming increasingly popular. The techniques discussed here can provide quantitative inputs for these investment strategies. In this context long-horizon return regressions may be attractive not only for their potential statistical advantages, but also because investment strategies based on long-horizon return forecasts are likely to incur lower transactions costs.

Problems—Chapter 7

7.1 In the late 1980s corporations began to repurchase shares on a large scale. In this problem you are asked to analyze the effect of repurchases on the relation between stock prices and dividends.

Consider a firm with fixed cash flow per period, X. The total market value of the firm (including the current cash flow X) is V. This is the present value of current and future cash flow, discounted at a constant rate R: $V = (1 + R)X/R$. Each period, the firm uses a fraction λ of its cash flow to repurchase shares at cum-dividend prices, and then uses a fraction $(1 - \lambda)$ of its cash flow to pay dividends on the remaining shares. The firm has N_t shares outstanding at the beginning of period t (before it repurchases shares).

7.1.1 What are the cum-dividend price per share and dividend per share at time t?

7.1.2 Derive a relation between the dividend-price ratio, the growth rate of dividends per share G, and the discount rate R.

7.1.3 Show that the price per share equals the expected present value of dividends per share, discounted at rate R. Explain intuitively why this formula is correct, even though the firm is devoting only a portion of its cash flow to dividends.

7.2 Consider a stock whose log dividend d_t follows a random walk with drift:

$$d_{t+1} = \mu + d_t + \epsilon_{t+1},$$

where $\epsilon_{t+1} \sim \mathcal{N}(0, \sigma^2)$. Assume that the required log rate of return on the stock is a constant r.

7.2.1 We use the notation F_t (for "fundamental value") to denote the expected present value of dividends, discounted using the required rate of return. Show that F_t is a constant multiple of the dividend D_t. Write the ratio F_t/D_t as a function of the parameters of the model.

7.2.2 Show that another formula for the stock price which gives the same expected rate of return is

$$P_t = F_t + cD_t^\lambda,$$

where $\lambda > 0$ is a function of the other parameters of the model. Solve for λ.

7.2.3 Discuss the strengths and weaknesses of this model of a rational bubble as compared with the Blanchard-Watson bubble, (7.1.16) in the text.

Note: This problem is based on Froot and Obstfeld (1991).

7.3 Consider a stock whose expected return obeys

$$E_t[r_{t+1}] = r + x_t. \tag{7.1.27}$$

Assume that x_t follows an AR(1) process,

$$x_{t+1} = \phi x_t + \xi_{t+1}, \qquad 0 < \phi < 1. \tag{7.1.28}$$

7.3.1 Assume that ξ_{t+1} is uncorrelated with news about future dividend payments on the stock. Using the loglinear approximate framework developed in Section 7.1.3, derive the autocovariance function of realized stock returns. Assume that $\phi < \rho$, where ρ is the parameter of linearization in the loglinear framework. Show that the autocovariances of stock returns are all negative and die off at rate ϕ. Give an economic interpretation of your formula for return autocovariances.

7.3.2 Now allow ξ_{t+1} to be correlated with news about future dividend payments. Show that the autocovariances of stock returns can be positive if ξ_{t+1} and dividend news have a sufficiently large positive covariance.

7.4 Suppose that the log "fundamental value" of a stock, v_t, obeys the process

$$v_t = \mu - \left(\frac{1-\rho}{\rho}\right)(d_t - v_{t-1}) + v_{t-1} + \epsilon_t,$$

where μ is a constant, ρ is the parameter of linearization defined in Section 7.1.3, d_t is the log dividend on the asset, and ϵ_t is a white noise error term.

7.4.1 Show that if the price of the stock equals its fundamental value, then the approximate log stock return defined in Section 7.1.3 is unforecastable.

7.4.2 Now suppose that the managers of the company pay dividends according to the rule

$$d_t = c + \lambda v_{t-1} + (1 - \lambda)d_{t-1} + \eta_t,$$

where c and λ are constants ($0 < \lambda < 1$), and η_t is a white noise error uncorrelated with ϵ_t. Managers partially adjust dividends towards fundamental value, where the speed of adjustment is given by λ. Marsh and Merton (1986) have argued for the empirical relevance of this dividend policy. Show that if the price of the stock equals its fundamental value, the log dividend-price ratio follows an AR(1) process. What is the persistence of this process as a function of λ and ρ?

7.4.3 Now suppose that the stock price does not equal fundamental value, but rather satisfies $p_t = v_t - \gamma(d_t - v_t)$, where $\gamma > 0$. That is, price exceeds fundamental value whenever fundamental value is high relative to dividends. Show that the approximate log stock return and the log dividend-price ratio satisfy the AR(1) model (7.1.27) and (7.1.28), where the optimal forecaster of the log stock return, x_t, is a positive multiple of the log dividend-price ratio.

7.4.4 Show that in this example innovations in stock returns are negatively correlated with innovations in x_t.

7.5 Recall the definition of the perfect-foresight stock price:

$$p_t^* \equiv \sum_{j=0}^{\infty} \rho^j \left[(1 - \rho)d_{t+1+j} + k - r \right]. \tag{7.2.8}$$

The hypothesis that expected returns are constant implies that the actual stock price p_t is a rational expectation of p_t^*, given investors' information. Now consider forecasting dividends using a smaller information set J_t. Define $\hat{p}_t \equiv E[p_t^* \mid J_t]$.

7.5.1 Show that $\text{Var}(p_t) \geq \text{Var}(\hat{p}_t)$. Give some economic intuition for this result.

7.5.2 Show that $\text{Var}(p_t^* - \hat{p}_t) \geq \text{Var}(p_t^* - p_t)$ and that $\text{Var}(p_t^* - \hat{p}_t) \geq \text{Var}(p_t - \hat{p}_t)$. Give some economic intuition for these results. Discuss circumstances where these variance inequalities can be more useful than the inequality in part 7.5.1.

7.5.3 Now define $\hat{r}_{t+1} \equiv k + \rho \hat{p}_{t+1} + (1-\rho)d_{t+1} - \hat{p}_t$. $\hat{r}_{t+1}$ is the return that would prevail under the constant-expected-return model if dividends were forecast using the information set J_t. Show that $\text{Var}(r_{t+1}) \leq \text{Var}(\hat{r}_{t+1})$. Give some economic intuition for this result and discuss circumstances where it can be more useful than the inequality in part 7.5.1.

Note: This problem is based on Mankiw, Romer, and Shapiro (1985) and West (1988b).

8

Intertemporal Equilibrium Models

THIS CHAPTER RELATES asset prices to the consumption and savings decisions of investors. The static asset pricing models discussed in Chapters 5 and 6 ignore consumption decisions. They treat asset prices as being determined by the portfolio choices of investors who have preferences defined over wealth one period in the future. Implicitly these models assume that investors consume all their wealth after one period, or at least that wealth uniquely determines consumption so that preferences defined over consumption are equivalent to preferences defined over wealth. This simplification is ultimately unsatisfactory. In the real world investors consider many periods in making their portfolio decisions, and in this intertemporal setting one must model consumption and portfolio choices simultaneously.

Intertemporal equilibrium models of asset pricing have the potential to answer two questions that have been left unresolved in earlier chapters. First, what forces determine the riskless interest rate (or more generally the rate of return on a zero-beta asset) and the rewards that investors demand for bearing risk? In the CAPM the riskless interest rate or zero-beta return and the reward for bearing market risk are exogenous parameters; the model gives no account of where they come from. In the APT the single price of market risk is replaced by a vector of factor risk prices, but again the risk prices are determined outside the model. We shall see in this chapter that intertemporal models can yield insights into the determinants of these parameters.

A second, related question has to do with predictable variations in asset returns. The riskless real interest rate moves over time, and in Chapter 7 we presented evidence that forecasts of stock returns also move over time. Importantly, excess stock returns appear to be just as forecastable as real stock returns, suggesting that the reward for bearing stock market risk changes over time. Are these phenomena consistent with market efficiency? Is it possible to construct a model with rational, utility-maximizing investors in which the equilibrium return on risky assets varies over time in the way described in Chapter 7? We shall use intertemporal equilibrium models to explore these questions.

Section 8.1 begins by stating the proposition that there exists a *stochastic discount factor* such that the expected product of any asset return with the stochastic discount factor equals one. This proposition holds very generally in models that rule out arbitrage opportunities in financial markets. Equilibrium models with optimizing investors imply tight links between the stochastic discount factor and the marginal utilities of investors' consumption. Thus by studying the stochastic discount factor one can relate asset prices to the underlying preferences of investors.

In Section 8.1 we show how the behavior of asset prices can be used to reach conclusions about the behavior of the stochastic discount factor. In particular we describe Hansen and Jagannathan's (1991) procedure for calculating a lower bound on the volatility of the stochastic discount factor, given any set of asset returns. Using long-run annual data on US short-term interest rates and stock returns over the period 1889 to 1994, we estimate the standard deviation of the stochastic discount factor to be 30% per year or more.

Consumption-based asset pricing models aggregate investors into a single representative agent, who is assumed to derive utility from the aggregate consumption of the economy. In these models the stochastic discount factor is the *intertemporal marginal rate of substitution*—the discounted ratio of marginal utilities in two successive periods—for the representative agent. The *Euler equations*—the first-order conditions for optimal consumption and portfolio choices of the representative agent—can be used to link asset returns and consumption.

Section 8.2 discusses a commonly used consumption-based model in which the representative agent has time-separable power utility. In this model a single parameter governs both *risk aversion* and the *elasticity of intertemporal substitution*—the willingness of the representative agent to adjust planned consumption growth in response to investment opportunities. In fact, the elasticity of intertemporal substitution is the reciprocal of risk aversion, so in this model risk-averse investors must also be unwilling to adjust their consumption growth rates to changes in interest rates. The model explains the risk premia on assets by their covariances with aggregate consumption growth, multiplied by the risk-aversion coefficient for the representative investor.

Using long-run annual US data, we emphasize four stylized facts. First, the average excess return on US stocks over short-term debt—the *equity premium*—is about 6% per year. Second, aggregate consumption is very smooth, so covariances with consumption growth are small. Putting these facts together, the power utility model can only fit the equity premium if the coefficient of relative risk aversion is very large. This is the *equity premium puzzle* of Mehra and Prescott (1985). Third, there are some predictable movements in short-term real interest rates, but there is little evidence of accompanying predictable movements in consumption growth. This suggests that the elasticity of intertemporal substitution is small, which in the power utility model again implies a large coefficient of relative risk aversion. Finally, there are predictable variations in excess returns on stocks over short-term debt which do not seem to be related to changing covariances of stock returns with consumption growth. These lead formal statistical tests to reject the power-utility model.

In Sections 8.3 and 8.4 we explore some ways in which the basic model can be modified to fit these facts. In Section 8.3 we discuss the effects of market frictions such as transactions costs, limits on investors' ability to borrow or sell assets short, exogenous variation in the asset demands of some investors, and income risks that investors are unable to insure. We argue that many plausible frictions make aggregate consumption an inadequate proxy for the consumption of stock market investors, and we discuss ways to get testable restrictions on asset prices even when consumption is not measured. We also discuss a generalization of power utility that breaks the tight link between risk aversion and the elasticity of intertemporal substitution.

In Section 8.4 we explore the possibility that investors have more complicated preferences than generalized power utility. For example, the utility function of the representative agent may be nonseparable between consumption and some other good such as leisure. We emphasize models in which utility is nonseparable over time because investors derive utility from the level of consumption relative to a time-varying habit or subsistence level. Finally, we consider some unorthodox models that draw inspiration from experimental and psychological research.

8.1 The Stochastic Discount Factor

We begin our analysis of the stochastic discount factor in the simplest possible way, by considering the intertemporal choice problem of an investor who can trade freely in asset i and who maximizes the expectation of a time-separable utility function:

$$\text{Max } E_t \left[\sum_{j=0}^{\infty} \delta^j \, U(C_{t+j}) \right], \tag{8.1.1}$$

where δ is the time discount factor, C_{t+j} is the investor's consumption in period $t + j$, and $U(C_{t+j})$ is the period utility of consumption at $t + j$. One of the first-order conditions or *Euler equations* describing the investor's optimal consumption and portfolio plan is

$$U'(C_t) = \delta E_t [(1 + R_{i,t+1}) U'(C_{t+1})]. \qquad (8.1.2)$$

The left-hand side of (8.1.2) is the marginal utility cost of consuming one real dollar less at time t; the right-hand side is the expected marginal utility benefit from investing the dollar in asset i at time t, selling it at time $t+1$ for $(1 + R_{i,t+1})$ dollars, and consuming the proceeds. The investor equates marginal cost and marginal benefit, so (8.1.2) describes the optimum.

If we divide both the left- and right-hand sides of (8.1.2) by $U'(C_t)$, we get

$$1 = E_t[(1 + R_{i,t+1}) M_{t+1}], \qquad (8.1.3)$$

where $M_{t+1} = \delta U'(C_{t+1}) / U'(C_t)$. The variable M_{t+1} in (8.1.3) is known as the *stochastic discount factor*, or *pricing kernel*. In the present model it is equivalent to the discounted ratio of marginal utilities $\delta U'(C_{t+1}) / U'(C_t)$, which is called the *intertemporal marginal rate of substitution*. Note that the intertemporal marginal rate of substitution, and hence the stochastic discount factor, are always positive since marginal utilities are positive.

Expectations in (8.1.3) are taken conditional on information available at time t; however, by taking unconditional expectations of the left- and right-hand sides of (8.1.3) and lagging one period to simplify notation, we obtain an unconditional version:

$$1 = E[(1 + R_{it}) M_t]. \qquad (8.1.4)$$

These relationships can be rearranged so that they explicitly determine expected asset returns. Working with the unconditional form for convenience, we have $E[(1 + R_{it}) M_t] = E[1 + R_{it}] E[M_t] + Cov[R_{it}, M_t]$, so

$$E[1 + R_{it}] = \frac{1}{E[M_t]} \left(1 - Cov[R_{it}, M_t]\right). \qquad (8.1.5)$$

If there is an asset whose unconditional covariance with the stochastic discount factor is zero—an "unconditional zero-beta" asset—then (8.1.5) implies that this asset's expected gross return $E[1 + R_{0t}] = 1/E[M_t]$. This can be substituted into (8.1.5) to obtain an expression for the excess return Z_{it} on asset i over the zero-beta return:

$$E[Z_{it}] \equiv E[R_{it} - R_{0t}] = -E[1 + R_{0t}] Cov[R_{it}, M_t]. \qquad (8.1.6)$$

This shows that an asset's expected return is greater, the smaller its covariance with the stochastic discount factor. The intuition behind this result is that an asset whose covariance with M_{t+1} is small tends to have low returns when the investor's marginal utility of consumption is high—that is, when consumption itself is low. Such an asset is risky in that it fails to deliver wealth precisely when wealth is most valuable to the investor. The investor therefore demands a large risk premium to hold it.

Although it is easiest to understand (8.1.3) by reference to the intertemporal choice problem of an investor, the equation can be derived merely from the absence of arbitrage, without assuming that investors maximize well-behaved utility functions.[1] We show this in a discrete-state setting with states $s = 1 \ldots S$ and assets $i = 1 \ldots N$. Define q_i as the price of asset i and $\mathbf{q}$ as the $(N \times 1)$ vector of asset prices, and define X_{si} as the payoff of asset i in state s and $\mathbf{X}$ as an $(S \times N)$ matrix giving the payoffs of each asset in each state. Provided that all asset prices are nonzero, we can further define $\mathbf{G}$ as an $(S \times N)$ matrix giving the gross return on each asset in each state. That is, the typical element of $\mathbf{G}$ is $G_{si} = 1 + R_{si} = X_{si}/q_i$.

Now define an $(S \times 1)$ vector $\mathbf{p}$, with typical element p_s, to be a *state price vector* if it satisfies $\mathbf{X}'\mathbf{p} = \mathbf{q}$. An asset can be thought of as a bundle of state-contingent payoffs, one for each state; the sth element of the state price vector, p_s, gives the price of one dollar to be paid in state s, and we represent each asset price as the sum of its state-contingent payoffs times the appropriate state prices: $q_i = \sum_s p_s X_{si}$. Equivalently, if we divide through by q_i, we get $1 = \sum_s p_s(1 + R_{si})$ or $\mathbf{G}'\mathbf{p} = \iota$, where ι is an $(S \times 1)$ vector of ones.

An important result is that there exists a positive state price vector if and only if there are no arbitrage opportunities (that is, no available assets or combinations of assets with nonpositive cost today, nonnegative payoffs tomorrow, and a strictly positive payoff in at least one state). Furthermore, if there exists a positive state price vector, then (8.1.3) is satisfied for some positive random variable M. To see this, define $M_s = p_s/\pi_s$, where π_s is the probability of state s. For any asset i the relationship $\mathbf{G}'\mathbf{p} = \iota$ implies

$$1 = \sum_{s=1}^{S} p_s(1 + R_{si}) = \sum_{s=1}^{S} \pi_s M_s(1 + R_{si}) = \mathrm{E}[(1 + R_i)M], \qquad (8.1.7)$$

which is the static discrete-state equivalent of (8.1.3). M_s is the ratio of the state price of state s to the probability of state s; hence it is positive because state prices and probabilities are both positive.

If M_s is small, then state s is "cheap" in the sense that investors are unwilling to pay a high price to receive wealth in state s. An asset that tends to deliver wealth in cheap states has a return that covaries negatively with M. Such an asset is itself cheap and has a high return on average. This is the intuition for (8.1.6) within a discrete-state framework.

In the discrete-state model, asset markets are complete if for each state s, one can combine available assets to get a nonzero payoff in s and zero

---

[1] The theory underlying equation (8.1.3) is discussed at length in textbooks such as Ingersoll (1987). The role of conditioning information has been explored by Hansen and Richard (1987).

payoffs in all other states. A further important result is that the state price vector is unique if and only if asset markets are complete. In this case M is unique, but with incomplete markets there may exist many M's satisfying equation (8.1.3). This result can be understood by considering an economy with several utility-maximizing investors. The first-order condition (8.1.2) holds for each investor, so each investor's marginal utilities can be used to construct a stochastic discount factor that prices the assets in the economy. With complete markets, the investors' marginal utilities are perfectly correlated so they all yield the same, unique stochastic discount factor; with incomplete markets there may be idiosyncratic variation in marginal utilities and hence multiple stochastic discount factors that satisfy (8.1.3).

8.1.1 Volatility Bounds

Any model of expected asset returns may be viewed as a model of the stochastic discount factor. Before we discuss methods of testing particular models, we ask more generally what asset return data may be able to tell us about the behavior of the stochastic discount factor. Hansen and Jagannathan (1991) have developed a lower bound on the volatility of stochastic discount factors that could be consistent with a given set of asset return data. They begin with the unconditional equation (8.1.4) and rewrite it in vector form as

$$\iota = \mathrm{E}[(\iota + \mathbf{R}_t)M_t], \tag{8.1.8}$$

where ι is an N-vector of ones and $\mathbf{R}_t$ is the N-vector of time-t asset returns, with typical element R_{it}.

Hansen and Jagannathan assume that $\mathbf{R}_t$ has a nonsingular variance-covariance matrix Ω, in other words, that no asset or combination of assets is unconditionally riskless. There may still exist an unconditional zero-beta asset with gross mean return equal to the reciprocal of the unconditional mean of the stochastic discount factor, but Hansen and Jagannathan assume that if there is such an asset, its identity is not known *a priori*. Hence they treat the unconditional mean of the stochastic discount factor as an unknown parameter $\overline{M}$. For each possible $\overline{M}$, Hansen and Jagannathan form a candidate stochastic discount factor $M_t^*(\overline{M})$ as a linear combination of asset returns. They show that the variance of $M_t^*(\overline{M})$ places a lower bound on the variance of any stochastic discount factor that has mean $\overline{M}$ and satisfies (8.1.8).

Hansen and Jagannathan first show how asset pricing theory determines the coefficients $\beta_{\overline{M}}$ in

$$M_t^*(\overline{M}) = \overline{M} + (\mathbf{R}_t - \mathrm{E}[\mathbf{R}_t])'\beta_{\overline{M}}. \tag{8.1.9}$$

If $M_t^*(\overline{M})$ is to be a stochastic discount factor it must satisfy (8.1.8),

$$\iota = \mathrm{E}[(\iota + \mathbf{R}_t)M_t^*(\overline{M})].$$

Expanding the expectation of the product $\mathrm{E}[(\iota + \mathbf{R}_t)M_t^*(\overline{M})]$, we have

$$
\begin{aligned}
\iota &= \overline{M}\mathrm{E}[\iota + \mathbf{R}_t] + \mathrm{Cov}[\mathbf{R}_t, M_t^*(\overline{M})] \\
&= \overline{M}\mathrm{E}[\iota + \mathbf{R}_t] + \mathrm{E}[(\mathbf{R}_t - \mathrm{E}[\mathbf{R}_t])(M_t^*(\overline{M}) - \overline{M})] \\
&= \overline{M}\mathrm{E}[\iota + \mathbf{R}_t] + \mathrm{E}[(\mathbf{R}_t - \mathrm{E}[\mathbf{R}_t])(\mathbf{R}_t - \mathrm{E}[\mathbf{R}_t])'\beta_{\overline{M}}] \\
&= \overline{M}\mathrm{E}[\iota + \mathbf{R}_t] + \Omega\beta_{\overline{M}}, \quad\quad (8.1.10)
\end{aligned}
$$

where Ω is the unconditional variance-covariance matrix of asset returns. It follows then that

$$
\beta_{\overline{M}} = \Omega^{-1}(\iota - \overline{M}\mathrm{E}[\iota + \mathbf{R}_t]), \quad\quad (8.1.11)
$$

and the variance of the implied stochastic discount factor is

$$
\begin{aligned}
\mathrm{Var}[M_t^*(\overline{M})] &= \beta'_{\overline{M}}\Omega\beta_{\overline{M}} \\
&= (\iota - \overline{M}\mathrm{E}[\iota + \mathbf{R}_t])'\Omega^{-1}(\iota - \overline{M}\mathrm{E}[\iota + \mathbf{R}_t]). \quad (8.1.12)
\end{aligned}
$$

The right-hand side of (8.1.12) is a lower bound on the volatility of any stochastic discount factor with mean $\overline{M}$. To see this, note that any other $M_t(\overline{M})$ satisfying (8.1.8) must have the property

$$
\mathrm{E}[(\iota + \mathbf{R}_t)(M_t(\overline{M}) - M_t^*(\overline{M}))] = \mathrm{Cov}[\mathbf{R}_t, M_t(\overline{M}) - M_t^*(\overline{M})] = 0. \quad (8.1.13)
$$

Since $M_t^*(\overline{M})$ is just a linear combination of asset returns, it follows that $\mathrm{Cov}[M_t^*(\overline{M}), M_t(\overline{M}) - M_t^*(\overline{M})] = 0$. Thus

$$
\begin{aligned}
\mathrm{Var}[M_t(\overline{M})] &= \mathrm{Var}[M_t^*(\overline{M})] + \mathrm{Var}[M_t(\overline{M}) - M_t^*(\overline{M})] \\
&\quad + \mathrm{Cov}[M_t^*(\overline{M}), M_t(\overline{M}) - M_t^*(\overline{M})] \\
&= \mathrm{Var}[M_t^*(\overline{M})] + \mathrm{Var}[M_t(\overline{M}) - M_t^*(\overline{M})] \\
&\geq \mathrm{Var}[M_t^*(\overline{M})]. \quad\quad (8.1.14)
\end{aligned}
$$

In fact, we can go beyond this inequality to show that

$$
\mathrm{Var}[M_t(\overline{M})] = \frac{\mathrm{Var}[M_t^*(\overline{M})]}{(\mathrm{Corr}[M_t(\overline{M}), M_t^*(\overline{M})])^2}, \quad\quad (8.1.15)
$$

so a stochastic discount factor can only have a variance close to the lower bound if it is highly correlated with the combination of asset returns $M_t^*(\overline{M})$.

The Benchmark Portfolio

We can restate these results in a more familiar way by introducing the idea of a *benchmark portfolio*. We first augment the vector of risky assets with an artificial unconditionally riskless asset whose return is $1/\overline{M} - 1$. Recall that we have proceeded under the assumption that no unconditionally riskless asset exists; but if it were to exist, its return would have to be $1/\overline{M} - 1$. We then define the benchmark portfolio return as

$$R_{bt}(\overline{M}) \equiv \frac{M_t^*(\overline{M})}{\mathrm{E}[M_t^*(\overline{M})^2]} - 1. \qquad (8.1.16)$$

It is straightforward to check that this return can be obtained by forming a portfolio of the risky assets and the artificial riskless asset, and that it satisfies the condition (8.1.8) on returns. Problem 8.1 is to prove that R_{bt} has the following properties:

(P1) R_{bt} is mean-variance efficient. That is, no other portfolio has smaller variance and the same mean.

(P2) Any stochastic discount factor $M_t(\overline{M})$ has a greater correlation with R_{bt} than with any other portfolio. For this reason R_{bt} is sometimes referred to as a *maximum-correlation portfolio* (see Breeden, Gibbons, and Litzenberger [1989]).

(P3) All asset returns obey a beta-pricing relation with the benchmark portfolio. That is,

$$\mathrm{E}\left[R_{it} - \left(\frac{1}{\overline{M}} - 1\right)\right] = \beta_{ib}\left(\mathrm{E}[R_{bt}] - \left(\frac{1}{\overline{M}} - 1\right)\right), \qquad (8.1.17)$$

where $\beta_{ib} \equiv \mathrm{Cov}[R_{it}, R_{bt}]/\mathrm{Var}[R_{bt}]$. When an unconditional zero-beta asset exists, then it can be substituted into (8.1.17) to get a conventional beta-pricing equation.

Two further properties are useful for a geometric interpretation of the Hansen-Jagannathan bounds. Consider Figure 8.1. Panel (a) is the familiar mean-standard deviation diagram for asset returns, with the mean gross return plotted on the vertical axis and the standard deviation of return on the horizontal. Panel (b) is a similar diagram for stochastic discount factors, with the axes rotated; standard deviation is now on the vertical axis and mean on the horizontal. This convention is natural because in panel (a) we think of assets' second moments determining their mean returns, while in panel (b) we vary the mean stochastic discount factor exogenously and trace out the consequences for the standard deviation of the stochastic

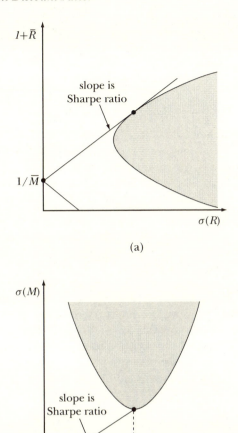

Figure 8.1. *(a) Mean-Standard Deviation Diagram for Asset Returns; (b) Implied Standard Deviation-Mean Diagram for Stochastic Discount Factors*

discount factor. In panel (a), the feasible set of risky asset returns is shown. We augment this with a riskless gross return $1/\overline{M}$ on the vertical axis; the minimum-variance set is then the tangent line from $1/\overline{M}$ to the feasible set of risky assets, and the reflection of the tangent in the vertical axis. Property (P1) means that the benchmark portfolio return is in the minimum-variance set. It plots on the lower branch because its positive correlation with the stochastic discount factor gives it a lower mean gross return than $1/\overline{M}$.

We can now state two more properties:

(P4)   The ratio of standard deviation to gross mean for the benchmark portfolio satisfies

$$\frac{\sigma[R_{bt}]}{\mathrm{E}[1 + R_{bt}]} = \frac{1/\overline{M} - \mathrm{E}[1 + R_{bt}]}{\sigma[R_{bt}]}. \tag{8.1.18}$$

But the right-hand side of this equation is just the slope of the tangent line in panel (a) of Figure 8.1. As explained in Chapter 5, this slope is the maximum Sharpe ratio for the set of assets.

(P5)   The ratio of standard deviation to mean for the benchmark portfolio gross return is a lower bound on the same ratio for the stochastic discount factor. That is,

$$\frac{\sigma[1 + R_{bt}]}{\mathrm{E}[1 + R_{bt}]} \leq \frac{\sigma[M_t(\overline{M})]}{\mathrm{E}[M_t(\overline{M})]}. \tag{8.1.19}$$

Properties (P4) and (P5) establish that the stochastic discount factor in panel (b) must lie above the point where a ray from the origin, with slope equal to the maximum Sharpe ratio in panel (a), passes through the vertical line at $\overline{M}$. As we vary $\overline{M}$, we trace out a feasible region for the stochastic discount factor in panel (b). This region is higher, and thus more restrictive, when the maximum Sharpe ratio in panel (a) is large for a variety of mean stochastic discount factors $\overline{M}$. A set of asset return data with a high maximum Sharpe ratio over a wide range of $\overline{M}$ is challenging for asset pricing theory in the sense that it requires the stochastic discount factor to be highly variable. By looking at panel (a) one can see that such a data set will contain portfolios with very different mean returns and similar, small standard deviations. A leading example is the set of returns on US Treasury bills, which have differences in mean returns that are absolutely small, but large relative to the standard deviations of bill returns.

The above analysis applies to returns themselves; the calculations are somewhat simpler if excess returns are used. Writing the excess return on asset i over some reference asset k (not necessarily riskless) as $Z_{it} = R_{it} - R_{kt}$, and the vector of excess returns as $\mathbf{Z}_t$, the basic condition (8.1.4) becomes

$$0 = \mathrm{E}[\mathbf{Z}_t M_t]. \tag{8.1.20}$$

Proceeding as before, we form $M_t^*(\overline{M}) = \overline{M} + (\mathbf{Z}_t - \mathrm{E}[\mathbf{Z}_t])'\tilde{\beta}_{\overline{M}}$, where the tilde is used to indicate that $\tilde{\beta}$ is defined with excess returns. We find that $\tilde{\beta}_{\overline{M}} = \tilde{\Omega}^{-1}(-\overline{M}\mathrm{E}[\mathbf{Z}_t])$, where $\tilde{\Omega}$ is the variance-covariance matrix of excess returns. It follows that the lower bound on the variance of the stochastic discount factor is now

$$\mathrm{Var}[M_t^*(\overline{M})] = \overline{M}^2 \mathrm{E}[\mathbf{Z}_t]'\tilde{\Omega}^{-1}\mathrm{E}[\mathbf{Z}_t]. \tag{8.1.21}$$

If we have only a single excess return Z_t, then this condition simplifies to $\mathrm{Var}[M_t^*(\overline{M})] = \overline{M}^2 (\mathrm{E}[Z_t])^2 / \mathrm{Var}[Z_t]$, or

$$\frac{\sigma[M_t^*(\overline{M})]}{\overline{M}} = \frac{\mathrm{E}[Z_t]}{\sigma[Z_t]}. \tag{8.1.22}$$

This is illustrated in Figure 8.2, which has the same structure as Figure 8.1. Now the restriction on the stochastic discount factor in panel (b) is that it should lie above a ray from the origin with the same slope as a ray from the origin through the single risky excess return in panel (a).

Implications of Nonnegativity
So far we have ignored the restriction that M_t must be nonnegative. Hansen and Jagannathan (1991) show that this can be handled fairly straightforwardly when an unconditionally riskless asset exists. In this case the mean of M_t is known, and the problem can be restated as finding coefficients α that define a random variable

$$M_t^{*+} \equiv ((\iota + \mathbf{R}_t)'\alpha)^+, \tag{8.1.23}$$

where $X^+ \equiv \max(X, 0)$ is the nonnegative part of X, subject to the constraint

$$\mathrm{E}[(\iota + \mathbf{R}_t)M_t^{*+}] = \mathrm{E}[(\iota + \mathbf{R}_t)((\iota + \mathbf{R}_t)'\alpha)^+] = \iota. \tag{8.1.24}$$

In the absence of the nonnegativity constraint, this yields the previous solution for the case where there is an unconditionally riskless asset. With the nonnegativity constraint, it is much harder to find a coefficient vector α that satisfies (8.1.24); Hansen and Jagannathan (1991) discuss strategies for transforming the problem to make the solution easier. Once a coefficient vector is found, however, it is easy to show that M_t^{*+} has minimum variance among all nonnegative random variables M_t satisfying (8.1.8). To see this, consider any other M_t and note that

$$
\begin{aligned}
\mathrm{E}[M_t M_t^{*+}] &= \mathrm{E}[M_t((\iota + \mathbf{R}_t)'\alpha)^+] \\
&\geq \alpha' \mathrm{E}[(\iota + \mathbf{R}_t)M_t] \\
&= \alpha' \mathrm{E}[(\iota + \mathbf{R}_t)M_t^{*+}] = \mathrm{E}[(M_t^{*+})^2]. \tag{8.1.25}
\end{aligned}
$$

But if $\mathrm{E}[M_t M_t^{*+}] \geq \mathrm{E}[(M_t^{*+})^2]$, then $\mathrm{E}[M_t^2] \geq \mathrm{E}[(M_t^{*+})^2]$ since the correlation between these variables cannot be greater than one.

The above analysis can be generalized to deal with the more realistic case in which there is no unconditionally riskless asset, by augmenting the return vector with a hypothetical riskless asset and varying the return on this asset. This introduces some technical complications which are discussed by Hansen and Jagannathan (1991).

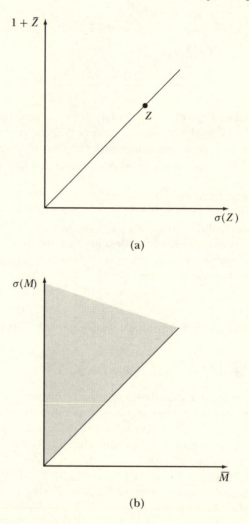

Figure 8.2. *(a) Mean-Standard Deviation Diagram for a Single Excess Asset Return; (b) Implied Standard Deviation-Mean Diagram for Stochastic Discount Factors*

A First Look at the Equity Premium Puzzle

The Hansen-Jagannathan approach can be used to understand the well-known equity premium puzzle of Mehra and Prescott (1985).[2] Mehra and Prescott argue that the average excess return on the US stock market—the

---

[2]Cochrane and Hansen (1992) approach the equity premium puzzle from this point of view. Kocherlakota (1996) surveys the large literature on the puzzle.

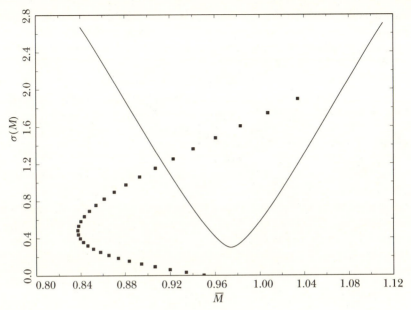

Figure 8.3. *Feasible Region for Stochastic Discount Factors Implied by Annual US Data, 1891 to 1994*

equity premium—is too high to be easily explained by standard asset pricing models. They make this point in the context of a tightly parametrized consumption-based model, but it can be made more generally using the excess-return restriction (8.1.22). Over the period 1889 to 1994, the annual excess simple return on the Standard and Poors stock index over commercial paper has a standard deviation of 18% and a mean of 6%.[3] Thus the slope of the rays from the origin in Figure 8.2 should be 0.06/0.18 = 0.33, meaning that the standard deviation of the stochastic discount factor must be at least 33% if it has a mean of one. As we shall see in the next section, the standard consumption-based model with a risk-aversion coefficient in the conventional range implies that the stochastic discount factor has a mean near one, but an annual standard deviation much less than 33%.

[3]The return on six-month commercial paper, rolled over in January and July, is used instead of a Treasury bill return because Treasury bill data are not available in the early part of this long sample period. Mehra and Prescott (1985) splice together commercial paper and Treasury bill rates, whereas here we use commercial paper rates throughout the sample period for consistency. The choice of short-term rates makes little difference to the results. Table 8.1 below gives some sample moments for log asset returns, but the moments stated here are for simple returns.

Figure 8.3, whose format follows Hansen and Jagannathan (1991), also illustrates the equity premium puzzle. The figure shows the feasible region for the stochastic discount factor implied by equation (8.1.12) and the annual data on real stock and commercial paper returns over the period 1891 to 1994. The figure does not use the nonnegativity restriction discussed in the previous section. The global minimum standard deviation for the stochastic discount factor is about 0.33, corresponding to a mean stochastic discount factor of about 0.98 and an unconditional riskless return of about 2%. As the mean moves away from 0.98, the standard-deviation bound rapidly increases. The difference between the feasible region in Figure 8.3 and the region above a ray from the origin with slope 0.33 is caused by the fact that Figure 8.3 uses bond and stock returns separately rather than merely the excess return on stocks over bonds. The figure also shows mean-standard deviation points corresponding to various degrees of risk aversion and a fixed time discount rate in a consumption-based representative agent asset pricing model of the type discussed in the next section. The first point above the horizontal axis has relative risk aversion of one; successive points have risk aversion of two, three, and so on. The points do not enter the feasible region until relative risk aversion reaches a value of 25.

In interpreting Figure 8.3 and similar figures, one should keep in mind that both the volatility bound for the stochastic discount factor and the points implied by particular asset pricing models are estimated with error. Statistical methods are available to test whether a particular model satisfies the volatility bound (see for example Burnside [1994], Cecchetti, Lam, and Mark [1994], and Hansen, Heaton, and Luttmer [1995]). These methods use the Generalized Method of Moments of Hansen (1982), discussed in the Appendix.

8.2 Consumption-Based Asset Pricing with Power Utility

In Section 8.1 we showed how an equation relating asset returns to the stochastic discount factor, (8.1.3), could be derived from the first-order condition of a single investor's intertemporal consumption and portfolio choice problem. This equation is restated here for convenience:

$$1 = E_t[(1 + R_{i,t+1})M_{t+1}]. \tag{8.2.1}$$

It is common in empirical research to assume that individuals can be aggregated into a single representative investor, so that aggregate consumption can be used in place of the consumption of any particular individual. Equation (8.2.1) with $M_{t+1} = \delta U'(C_{t+1})/U'(C_t)$, where C_t is aggregate consumption, is known as the *consumption CAPM*, or CCAPM.

In this section we examine the empirical implications of the CCAPM. We begin by assuming that there is a representative agent who maximizes a time-separable power utility function, so that

$$U(C_t) = \frac{C_t^{1-\gamma} - 1}{1 - \gamma}, \qquad (8.2.2)$$

where γ is the coefficient of relative risk aversion. As γ approaches one, the utility function in (8.2.2) approaches the log utility function $U(C_t) = \log(C_t)$.

The power utility function has several important properties. First, it is scale-invariant: With constant return distributions, risk premia do not change over time as aggregate wealth and the scale of the economy increase. A related property is that if different investors in the economy have the same power utility function and can freely trade all the risks they face, then even if they have different wealth levels they can be aggregated into a single representative investor with the same utility function as the individual investors.[4] This provides some justification for the use of aggregate consumption, rather than individual consumption, in the CCAPM.

A property of power utility that may be less desirable is that it rigidly links two important concepts. When utility has the power form the *elasticity of intertemporal substitution* (the derivative of planned log consumption growth with respect to the log interest rate), which we write as ψ, is the reciprocal of the coefficient of relative risk aversion γ. Hall (1988) has argued that this linkage is inappropriate because the elasticity of intertemporal substitution concerns the willingness of an investor to move consumption between time periods—it is well-defined even if there is no uncertainty—whereas the coefficient of relative risk aversion concerns the willingness of an investor to move consumption between states of the world—it is well-defined even in a one-period model with no time dimension. In Section 8.3.2 below we discuss a more general utility specification, due to Epstein and Zin (1991) and Weil (1989), that preserves the scale-invariance of power utility but breaks the tight link between the coefficient of relative risk aversion and the elasticity of intertemporal substitution.

Taking the derivative of (8.2.2) with respect to consumption, we find that marginal utility $U'(C_t) = C_t^{-\gamma}$. Substituting into (8.2.1) we get

$$1 = E_t \left[(1 + R_{i,t+1}) \delta \left(\frac{C_{t+1}}{C_t} \right)^{-\gamma} \right], \qquad (8.2.3)$$

---

[4]Grossman and Shiller (1982) show that this result generalizes to a model with nontraded assets (uninsurable idiosyncratic risks) if consumption and asset prices follow diffusion processes in a continuous-time model.

which was first derived by Grossman and Shiller (1981), following the closely related continuous-time model of Breeden (1979). A typical objective of empirical research is to estimate the coefficient of relative risk aversion γ (or its reciprocal ψ) and to test the restrictions imposed by (8.2.3). It is easiest to do this if one assumes that asset returns and aggregate consumption are jointly homoskedastic and lognormal. Although this implies constant expected excess log returns, and thus cannot fit the data, it is useful for building intuition and understanding methods that can be applied to more realistic models. Accordingly we make this assumption in Section 8.2.1 and relax it in Section 8.2.2, where we discuss the use of Hansen's (1982) Generalized Method of Moments (GMM) to test the power utility model without making distributional assumptions on returns and consumption. Our discussion follows closely the seminal work of Hansen and Singleton (1982, 1983).

8.2.1 Power Utility in a Lognormal Model

When a random variable X is conditionally lognormally distributed, it has the convenient property (mentioned in Chapter 1) that

$$\log E_t[X] = E_t[\log X] + \tfrac{1}{2} \text{Var}_t[\log X], \tag{8.2.4}$$

where $\text{Var}_t[\log X] \equiv E_t[(\log X - E_t[\log X])^2]$. If in addition X is conditionally homoskedastic, then $\text{Var}_t[\log X] = E[(\log X - E_t[\log X])^2] = \text{Var}[\log X - E_t[\log X]]$. Thus with joint conditional lognormality and homoskedasticity of asset returns and consumption, we can take logs of (8.2.3), use the notational convention that lowercase letters denote logs, and obtain

$$0 = E_t[r_{i,t+1}] + \log \delta - \gamma E_t[\Delta c_{t+1}] + \left(\tfrac{1}{2}\right)[\sigma_i^2 + \gamma^2 \sigma_c^2 - 2\gamma \sigma_{ic}]. \tag{8.2.5}$$

Here the notation σ_{xy} denotes the unconditional covariance of innovations $\text{Cov}[x_{t+1} - E_t[x_{t+1}], y_{t+1} - E_t[y_{t+1}]]$, and $\sigma_x^2 \equiv \sigma_{xx}$.

Equation (8.2.5), which was first derived by Hansen and Singleton (1983), has both time-series and cross-sectional implications. In the time series, the riskless real interest rate obeys

$$r_{f,t+1} = -\log \delta - \frac{\gamma^2 \sigma_c^2}{2} + \gamma E_t[\Delta c_{t+1}]. \tag{8.2.6}$$

The riskless real rate is linear in expected consumption growth, with slope coefficient equal to the coefficient of relative risk aversion. The equation can be reversed to express expected consumption growth as a linear function of the riskless real interest rate, with slope coefficient $\psi = 1/\gamma$; in fact this relation between expected consumption growth and the interest rate is what defines the elasticity of intertemporal substitution.

The assumption of homoskedasticity makes the log risk premium on any asset over the riskless real rate constant, so expected real returns on other assets are also linear in expected consumption growth with slope coefficient γ. We have

$$\mathrm{E}_t[r_{i,t+1} - r_{f,t+1}] + \frac{\sigma_i^2}{2} = \gamma\sigma_{ic}. \tag{8.2.7}$$

The variance term on the left-hand side of (8.2.7) is a Jensen's Inequality adjustment arising from the fact that we are describing expectations of log returns. We can eliminate the need for this adjustment by rewriting the equation in terms of the log of the expected ratio of gross returns:

$$\log \mathrm{E}_t[(1 + R_{i,t+1})/(1 + R_{f,t+1})] = \gamma\sigma_{ic}.$$

Equation (8.2.7) shows that risk premia are determined by the coefficient of relative risk aversion times covariance with consumption growth. Of course, we have already presented evidence against the implication of this model that risk premia are constant. Nevertheless we explore the model as a useful way to develop intuition and understand econometric techniques used in more general models.

A Second Look at the Equity Premium Puzzle

Equation (8.2.7) clarifies the argument of Mehra and Prescott (1985) that the equity premium is too high to be consistent with observed consumption behavior unless investors are extremely risk averse. Mehra and Prescott's analysis is complicated by the fact that they do not use observed stock returns, but instead calculate stock returns implied by the (counterfactual) assumption that stock dividends equal consumption. Problem 8.2 carries out a loglinear version of this calculation.

One can appreciate the equity premium puzzle more directly by examining the moments of log real stock and commercial paper returns and consumption growth shown in Table 8.1. The asset returns are measured annually over the period 1889 to 1994. The mean excess log return of stocks over commercial paper is 4.2% with a standard deviation of 17.7%; using the formula for the mean of a lognormal random variable, this implies that the mean excess simple return is 6% as stated earlier.

As is conventional in the literature, the consumption measure used in Table 8.1 is consumption of nondurables and services.[5] The covariance of the excess log stock return with log consumption growth is the correlation of the two series, times the standard deviation of the log stock return, times the standard deviation of log consumption growth. Because consumption of nondurables and services is a smooth series, log consumption growth has

---

[5] This implicitly assumes that utility is separable across this form of consumption and other sources of utility. In Section 8.4 we discuss ways in which this assumption can be relaxed.

Table 8.1.   *Moments of consumption growth and asset returns.*

Variable	Mean	Standard deviation	Correlation with consumption growth	Covariance with consumption growth
Consumption growth	0.0172	0.0328	1.0000	0.0011
Stock return	0.0601	0.1674	0.4902	0.0027
CP return	0.0183	0.0544	−0.1157	−0.0002
Stock–CP return	0.0418	0.1774	0.4979	0.0029

Consumption growth is the change in log real consumption of nondurables and services. The stock return is the log real return on the S&P 500 index since 1926, and the return on a comparable index from Grossman and Shiller (1981) before 1926. CP is the real return on 6-month commercial paper, bought in January and rolled over in July. All data are annual, 1889 to 1994.

a small standard deviation of only 3.3%; hence the excess stock return has a covariance with log consumption growth of only 0.003 despite the fact that the correlation of the two series is about 0.5. Substituting the moments in Table 8.1 into (8.2.7) shows that a risk-aversion coefficient of 19 is required to fit the equity premium.[6] This is much greater than 10, the maximum value considered plausible by Mehra and Prescott.

It is worth noting that the implied risk-aversion coefficient is sensitive to the timing convention used for consumption. While asset prices are measured at the end of each period, consumption is measured as a flow during a period. In correlating asset returns with consumption growth one can assume that measured consumption represents beginning-of-period consumption or end-of-period consumption. The former assumption leads one to correlate the return over a period with the ratio of the next period's consumption to this period's consumption, while the latter assumption leads one to correlate the return over a period with the ratio of this period's consumption to last period's consumption. The former assumption, which we use here, gives a much higher correlation between asset returns and consumption growth and hence a lower risk-aversion coefficient than the latter assumption.[7]

---

[6]Table 8.1 reports the moments of asset returns and consumption growth whereas equation (8.2.7) requires the moments of innovations in these series. However the variation in conditional expected returns and consumption growth seems to be small enough that the moments of innovations are similar to the moments of the raw series.

[7]Grossman, Melino, and Shiller (1987) handle this problem more carefully by assuming an underlying continuous-time model and deriving its implications for time-averaged data.

These calculations can be related to the work of Hansen and Jagannathan (1991) in the following way. In the representative-agent model with power utility, the stochastic discount factor $M_{t+1} = \delta(C_{t+1}/C_t)^{-\gamma}$, and the log stochastic discount factor $m_{t+1} = \log(\delta) - \gamma \Delta c_{t+1}$. If we are willing to make the approximation $m_{t+1} \approx M_{t+1} - 1$, which will be accurate if M_{t+1} has a mean close to one and is not too variable, then we have $\mathrm{Var}[M_{t+1}] \approx \mathrm{Var}[m_{t+1}] = \gamma^2 \mathrm{Var}[\Delta c_{t+1}]$. Equivalently, the standard deviation of the stochastic discount factor must be approximately the coefficient of relative risk aversion times the standard deviation of consumption growth. Using the Hansen-Jagannathan methodology we found that the standard deviation of the stochastic discount factor must be at least 0.33 to fit our annual stock market data. Since the standard deviation of consumption growth is 0.033, this by itself implies a coefficient of risk aversion of at least 0.33/0.033 = 10. But a coefficient of risk aversion this low is consistent with the data only if stock returns and consumption are perfectly correlated. If we use the fact that the empirical correlation is about 0.5, we can use the tighter volatility bound in equation (8.1.15) to double the required standard deviation of the stochastic discount factor and hence double the risk-aversion coefficient to about 20.

The Riskfree Rate Puzzle

One response to the equity premium puzzle is to consider larger values for the coefficient of relative risk aversion γ. Kandel and Stambaugh (1991) have advocated this.[8] However this leads to a second puzzle. Equation (8.2.5) implies that the unconditional mean riskless interest rate is

$$\mathrm{E}[r_{ft}] = -\log \delta + \gamma g - \frac{\gamma^2 \sigma_c^2}{2}, \tag{8.2.8}$$

where g is the mean growth rate of consumption. The average riskless interest rate is determined by three factors. First, the riskless rate is high if the time preference rate $-\log \delta$ is high. Second, the riskless rate is high if the average consumption growth rate g is high, for then the representative agent has an incentive to try to borrow to reduce the discrepancy between consumption today and in the future. The strength of this effect is inversely proportional to the elasticity of intertemporal substitution in consumption; in a power utility model where risk aversion equals the reciprocal of intertemporal substitution, the strength of the effect is directly proportional to γ. Finally, the riskless rate is low if the variance of consumption growth is high, for then the representative agent has a precautionary motive for

---

[8]One might think that introspection would be sufficient to rule out very large values of γ. However Kandel and Stambaugh (1991) point out that introspection can deliver very different estimates of risk aversion depending on the size of the gamble considered. This suggests that introspection can be misleading or that some more general model of utility is needed.

saving. The strength of this precautionary saving effect is proportional to the square of risk aversion, γ^2.

Given the historical average short-term real interest rate of 1.8%, the historical average consumption growth rate of 1.8%, and the historical average standard deviation of consumption growth of 3.3% shown in Table 8.1, a γ of 19 implies a discount factor δ of 1.12; this is greater than one, corresponding to a negative rate of time preference. Weil (1989) calls this the *riskfree rate puzzle*. Intuitively, the puzzle is that if investors are extremely risk-averse (γ is large), then with power utility they must also be extremely unwilling to substitute intertemporally (ψ is small). Given positive average consumption growth, a low riskless interest rate and a positive rate of time preference, such investors would have a strong desire to borrow from the future. A low riskless interest rate is possible in equilibrium only if investors have a negative rate of time preference that reduces their desire to borrow.

Of course, these calculations depend on the exact moments given in Table 8.1. In some data sets an even larger coefficient of relative risk aversion is needed to fit the equity premium: Kandel and Stambaugh (1991), for example, consider a risk-aversion coefficient of 29. With risk aversion this large, the precautionary savings term $-\gamma^2\sigma_c^2/2$ in equation (8.2.8) reduces the equilibrium riskfree rate and so Kandel and Stambaugh do not need a negative rate of time preference to fit the riskfree rate. A visual impression of this effect is given in Figure 8.3, which shows the mean stochastic discount factor first decreasing and then increasing as γ increases with a fixed δ. Since the riskless interest rate is the reciprocal of the mean stochastic discount factor, this implies that the riskless interest rate first increases and then decreases with γ. The behavior of the riskless interest rate is always a problem for models with high γ, however, as the interest rate is extremely sensitive to the parameters g and σ^2 and reasonable values of the interest rate are achieved only as a knife-edge case when the effects of g and σ^2 almost exactly offset each other.

Is the Equity Premium Puzzle a Robust Phenomenon?

Another response to the equity premium puzzle is to argue that it is an artefact of the particular data set on US stock returns. While we have not reported standard errors for risk-aversion estimates, careful empirical research by Cecchetti, Lam, and Mark (1994), Kocherlakota (1996), and others shows that the data can reject risk-aversion coefficients lower than about 10 using standard statistical methods. However, the validity of these tests depends on the characteristics of the data set in which they are used.

Rietz (1988) has argued that there may be a *peso problem* in these data. A peso problem arises when there is a small positive probability of an important event, and investors take this probability into account when setting market prices. If the event does not occur in a particular sample period, investors may appear to be irrational in the sample. While it may seem implausible that this could be an important problem in 100 years of data, Rietz (1988) argues that an economic catastrophe that destroys almost all stock-market value can be extremely unlikely and yet have a major depressing effect on stock prices.

A related point has been made by Brown, Goetzmann, and Ross (1995). These authors argue that financial economists concentrate on the US stock market precisely because it has survived and grown to become the world's largest market. In some other markets, such as those of Russia, investors have had all their wealth expropriated during the last 100 years and so there is no continuous record of market prices; in others, such as the Argentine market, returns have been so poor that today these markets are regarded as comparatively less important emerging markets. If this survivorship effect is important, estimates of average US stock returns are biased upwards.

Although these points have some validity, they are unlikely to be the whole explanation for the equity premium puzzle. The difficulty with the Rietz (1988) argument is that it requires not only an economic catastrophe, but one which affects stock market investors more seriously than investors in short-term debt instruments. The Russian example suggests that a catastrophe causes very low returns on debt as well as on equity, in which case the peso problem affects estimates of the average levels of returns but not estimates of the equity premium. Also, there seems to be a surprisingly large equity premium not only in the last 100 years of US data, but also in US data from earlier in the 19th Century as shown by Siegel (1994) and in data from other countries as shown by Campbell (1996b).

Time-Variation in Expected Asset Returns and Consumption Growth
Equation (8.2.5) gives a relation between rational expectations of asset returns and rational expectations of consumption growth. It implies that expected asset returns are perfectly correlated with expected consumption growth, but the standard deviation of expected asset returns is γ times as large as the standard deviation of expected consumption growth. Equivalently, the standard deviation of expected consumption growth is $\psi = 1/\gamma$ times as large as the standard deviation of expected asset returns.

This suggests an alternative way to estimate γ or ψ. Hansen and Singleton (1983), followed by Hall (1988) and others, have proposed instrumental variables (IV) regression as a way to approach the problem. If we define an error term $\eta_{i,t+1} \equiv r_{i,t+1} - E_t[r_{i,t+1}] - \gamma(\Delta c_{t+1} - E_t[\Delta c_{t+1}])$, then we can rewrite equation (8.2.5) as a regression equation,

$$r_{i,t+1} = \mu_i + \gamma \Delta c_{t+1} + \eta_{i,t+1}. \tag{8.2.9}$$

In general the error term $\eta_{i,t+1}$ will be correlated with realized consumption growth so OLS is not an appropriate estimation method. However $\eta_{i,t+1}$ is

Table 8.2.　*Instrumental variables regressions for returns and consumption growth.*

$$(8.2.9)\ r_{i,t+1} = \mu_i + \gamma \Delta c_{t+1} + \eta_{i,t+1}$$

$$(8.2.10)\ \Delta c_{t+1} = \tau_i + \psi r_{i,t+1} + \zeta_{i,t+1}$$

Return	First-stage regressions		$\hat{\gamma}$	$\hat{\psi}$	Test	Test
(instruments)	r	Δc	(s.e.)	(s.e.)	(8.2.9)	(8.2.10)
Commercial paper	0.275	0.034	−1.984	−0.088	0.106	0.028
(1)	(0.000)	(0.485)	(1.318)	(0.113)	(0.004)	(0.234)
Stock index	0.080	0.034	−6.365	−0.100	0.008	0.007
(1)	(0.071)	(0.485)	(5.428)	(0.091)	(0.673)	(0.705)
Commercial paper	0.297	0.102	−0.953	−0.118	0.221	0.091
(1 and 2)	(0.000)	(0.145)	(0.567)	(0.109)	(0.000)	(0.096)
Stock index	0.110	0.102	−0.235	−0.008	0.105	0.097
(1 and 2)	(0.105)	(0.145)	(1.650)	(0.059)	(0.056)	(0.075)

Log real consumption growth rates and asset returns are measured in annual US data, 1889 to 1994. The columns headed "First-stage regressions" report the R^2 statistics and joint significance levels of the explanatory variables in regressions of returns and consumption growth on the instruments. The columns headed $\hat{\gamma}$ and $\hat{\psi}$ report two-stage least squares instrumental-variables (IV) estimates of the parameters γ and ψ in regressions (8.2.9) and (8.2.10) respectively. The columns headed "Test (8.2.9)" and "Test (8.2.10)" report the R^2 statistics and joint significance levels of the explanatory variables in regressions of IV regression residuals (8.2.9) and (8.2.10) on the instruments. The instruments include either one lag (in rows marked 1), or one and two lags (in rows marked 1 and 2) of the real commercial paper rate, the real consumption growth rate, and the log dividend-price ratio.

uncorrelated with any variables in the information set at time t. Hence any lagged variables correlated with asset returns can be used as instruments in an IV regression to estimate the coefficient of relative risk aversion γ.

Table 8.2 illustrates two-stage least squares estimation of (8.2.9). In this table the asset returns are the real commercial paper rate and real stock return from Table 8.1, and consumption growth is the annual growth rate of real nondurables and services consumption. The instruments are either one lag, or one and two lags, of the real commercial paper rate, the real consumption growth rate, and the log dividend-price ratio.

For each asset and set of instruments, the table first reports the R^2 statistics and significance levels for first-stage regressions of the asset return and consumption growth rate onto the instruments. The table then shows the IV estimate of γ with its standard error, and—in the column headed

"Test (8.2.9)"—the R^2 statistic for a regression of the residual on the instruments together with the associated significance level of a test of the over-identifying restrictions of the model. This test is discussed at the end of Section A.1 of the Appendix.

Table 8.2 shows strong evidence that the real commercial paper rate is forecastable, and weaker evidence that the real stock return is forecastable. There is very little evidence that consumption growth is forecastable.[9] The IV estimates of γ are negative rather than positive as implied by the underlying theory, but they are not significantly different from zero. The overidentifying restrictions of the model are strongly rejected when the commercial paper rate is used as the asset.

One problem with IV estimation of (8.2.9) is that the instruments are only very weakly correlated with the regressor because consumption growth is hard to forecast in this data set. Nelson and Startz (1990) have shown that in this situation asymptotic theory can be a poor guide to inference in finite samples; the asymptotic standard error of the coefficient tends to be too small and the overidentifying restrictions of the model may be rejected even when it is true. To circumvent this problem, one can reverse the regression (8.2.9) and estimate

$$\Delta c_{t+1} = \tau_i + \psi r_{i,t+1} + \zeta_{i,t+1}. \tag{8.2.10}$$

If the orthogonality conditions hold, then as we have already discussed the estimate of ψ in (8.2.10) will asymptotically be the reciprocal of the estimate of γ in (8.2.9). In a finite sample, however, if γ is large and ψ is small then IV estimates of (8.2.10) will be better behaved than IV estimates of (8.2.9).

In Table 8.2 ψ is estimated to be negative, like γ, but is small and insignificantly different from zero. The overidentifying restrictions of the model ("Test (8.2.10)") are not rejected when only 1 lag of the instruments is used, and they are rejected at the 10% level when 2 lags of the instruments are used. Table 8.2 also shows that the residual from the IV regression is only marginally less forecastable than consumption growth itself. These results are not particularly encouraging for the consumption model, but equally they do not provide strong evidence against the view that investors have power utility with a very high γ (which would explain the equity premium puzzle) and a correspondingly small ψ (which would explain the unpredictability of consumption growth in the face of predictable asset returns).

---

[9]In postwar quarterly data there is stronger evidence of predictable variation in consumption growth. Campbell and Mankiw (1990) show that this variation is associated with predictable income growth.

8.2.2 Power Utility and Generalized Method of Moments

So far we have worked with a restrictive loglinear specification and have discussed cross-sectional and time-series aspects of the data separately. The Generalized Method of Moments (GMM) of Hansen (1982), applied to the consumption CAPM by Hansen and Singleton (1982), allows us to estimate and test the power utility model without making distributional assumptions and without ignoring either dimension of the data. Section A.2 of the Appendix summarizes the GMM approach, and explains its relation to linear instrumental variables.

When GMM is used to estimate the consumption CAPM with power utility, using the same asset returns and instruments as in Table 8.2 and assuming white noise errors, the overidentifying restrictions of the model are strongly rejected whenever stocks and commercial paper are included together in the system. The weak evidence against the model in Table 8.2 becomes much stronger. This occurs because there is predictable variation in *excess* returns on stocks over commercial paper.[10] Such predictable variation is ruled out by the loglinear homoskedastic model (8.2.5) but could in principle be explained by a heteroskedastic model in which conditional covariances of asset returns with consumption are correlated with the forecasting variables.[11] The GMM system allows for this possibility, without linearizing the model or imposing distributional assumptions, so the GMM rejection is powerful evidence against the standard consumption CAPM with power utility.

Faced with this evidence, economists have explored two main directions for research. A first possibility is that market frictions invalidate the standard consumption CAPM. The measured returns used to test the model may not actually be available to investors, who may face transactions costs and constraints on their ability to borrow or shortsell assets. Market frictions may also make aggregate consumption an inadequate proxy for the consumption of stock market investors. A second possibility is that investors have more complicated preferences than the simple power specification. We explore each of these possibilities in the next two sections.

8.3 Market Frictions

We now consider various market frictions that may be relevant for asset pricing. If investors face transactions costs or limits on their ability to borrow

---

[10]Recall that in Chapter 7 we presented evidence that the dividend-price ratio forecasts excess stock returns. The dividend-price ratio is one of the instruments used here.

[11]One can understand this by considering a heteroskedastic version of the linearized model (8.2.5) in which the variances have time subscripts. Campbell (1987) and Harvey (1989) apply GMM to models of this type which impose the restriction that asset returns' conditional means are linear functions of their conditional second moments. We discuss this work further in Chapter 12.

or sell assets short, then they may have only a limited ability to exploit the empirical patterns in returns. In Section 8.3.1 we show how this can alter the basic Hansen and Jagannathan (1991) analysis of the volatility of the stochastic discount factor.

The same sorts of frictions may make aggregate consumption an inadequate proxy for the consumption of stock market investors. In Section 8.3.2 we discuss some of the evidence on this point, and then follow Campbell (1993a, 1996) in developing a representative-agent asset pricing theory in which the consumption of the representative investor need not be observed. The theory uses a generalization of power utility, due to Epstein and Zin (1989, 1991) and Weil (1989), that breaks the link between risk aversion and intertemporal substitution. The resulting model, in the spirit of Merton (1973a), is a multifactor model with restrictions on the risk prices of the factors; hence it can be tested using the econometric methods discussed in Chapter 6.

8.3.1 Market Frictions and Hansen-Jagannathan Bounds

The volatility bounds of Hansen and Jagannathan (1991), discussed in Section 8.1.1, assume that investors can freely trade in all assets without incurring transactions costs and without limitations on borrowing or short sales. These assumptions are obviously rather extreme, but they have been relaxed by He and Modest (1995) and Luttmer (1994). To understand the approach, note that if asset i cannot be sold short, then the standard equality restriction $E[(1 + R_{it})M_t] = 1$ must be replaced by an inequality restriction

$$E[(1 + R_{it})M_t] \leq 1. \tag{8.3.1}$$

If the inequality is strict, then an investor would like to sell the asset but is prevented from doing so by the shortsales constraint. Instead, the investor holds a zero position in the asset.

Shortsales constraints may apply to some assets but not others; if they apply to all assets, then they can be interpreted as a *solvency constraint*, in that they ensure that an investor cannot make investments today that deliver negative wealth tomorrow. Assuming limited liability for all risky assets, so that the minimum value of each asset tomorrow is zero, a portfolio with nonnegative weights in every asset also has a minimum value of zero tomorrow.

Investors may also face borrowing constraints that limit their ability to sell assets to finance consumption today. Such constraints deliver inequality restrictions of the form (8.3.1) for all raw asset returns, but the standard equality constraint holds for excess returns since the investor is free to short one asset in order to take a long position in another asset.

Shortsales constraints can also be used to model proportional transactions costs of the type that might result from a bid-ask spread that does not depend on the size of a trade. When there are transactions costs, the after-transaction-cost return on an asset bought today and sold tomorrow is not the negative of the after-transaction-cost return on the same asset sold today and bought back tomorrow. These two returns can be measured separately and can both be included in the set of returns if they are made subject to shortsales constraints.

In the presence of shortsales constraints, the vector equality (8.1.8) is replaced by another vector equality

$$\boldsymbol{\theta} = \mathrm{E}[(\iota + \mathbf{R}_t)M_t], \tag{8.3.2}$$

where $\boldsymbol{\theta}$ is an unknown vector. The model implies various restrictions on $\boldsymbol{\theta}$ such as the restriction that $\theta_i \leq 1$ for all i. Volatility bounds can now be found for each $\overline{M}$ by choosing, subject to the restrictions, the value of $\boldsymbol{\theta}$ that delivers the lowest variance for $M_t^*(\overline{M})$. He and Modest (1995) find that by combining borrowing constraints, a restriction on the short sale of Treasury bills, and asset-specific transaction costs they can greatly reduce the volatility bound on the stochastic discount factor.

This analysis is extremely conservative in that $\boldsymbol{\theta}$ is chosen to minimize the volatility bound without asking what underlying equilibrium would support this choice for $\boldsymbol{\theta}$. If there are substantial transactions costs, for example, then even risk-neutral traders will not sell one asset to buy another asset with a higher return unless the return difference exceeds the transactions costs. But the one-period transaction costs will not be relevant if traders can buy the high-return asset and hold it for many periods, or if a trader has new wealth to invest and must pay the cost of purchasing one asset or the other. Thus the work of He and Modest (1995) and Luttmer (1994) is exploratory, a way to get a sense for the extent to which market frictions loosen the bounds implied by a frictionless market.

Some authors have tried to solve explicitly for the asset prices that are implied by equilibrium models with transactions costs. This is a difficult task because transactions costs make the investor's decision problem comparatively intractable except in very special cases (see Davis and Norman (1990)). Aiyagari and Gertler (1991), Amihud and Mendelson (1986), Constantinides (1986), Heaton and Lucas (1996), and Vayanos (1995) have begun to make some progress on this topic.

8.3.2 Market Frictions and Aggregate Consumption Data

The rejection of the standard consumption CAPM may be due in part to difficulties in measuring aggregate consumption. The consumption CAPM applies to true consumption measured at a point in time, but the available data are time-aggregated and measured with error. Wilcox (1992) describes the sampling procedures used to construct consumption data, while Grossman,

Melino, and Shiller (1987) and Wheatley (1988) have tested the model allowing for time-aggregation and measurement error, respectively. Roughly speaking, these data problems can cause asset returns weighted by measured marginal utility of consumption, $(1 + R_{i,t+1}) \delta (C_{t+1} / C_t)^{-\gamma}$, to be forecastable in the short run but not the long run. Thus one can allow for such problems by lagging the instruments more than one period when testing the model.[12] Doing this naturally weakens the evidence against the consumption CAPM, but the model is still rejected at conventional significance levels unless very long lags are used.

A more radical suggestion is that aggregate consumption is not an adequate proxy for the consumption of stock market investors even in the long run. One simple explanation is that there are two types of agents in the economy: constrained agents who are prevented from trading in asset markets and simply consume their labor income each period, and unconstrained agents. The consumption of the constrained agents is irrelevant to the determination of equilibrium asset prices, but it may be a large fraction of aggregate consumption. Campbell and Mankiw (1990) argue that predictable variation in consumption growth, correlated with predictable variation in income growth, suggests an important role for constrained agents, while Mankiw and Zeldes (1991) use panel data to show that the consumption of stockholders is more volatile and more highly correlated with the stock market than the consumption of nonstockholders.

The constrained agents in the above model do not directly influence asset prices, because they are assumed not to hold or trade financial assets. Another strand of the literature argues that there may be some investors who buy and sell stocks for exogenous, perhaps psychological reasons. These *noise traders* can influence stock prices because other investors, who are rational utility-maximizers, must be induced to accommodate their shifts in demand. If utility-maximizing investors are risk-averse, then they will only buy stocks from noise traders who wish to sell if stock prices fall and expected stock returns rise; conversely they will only sell stocks to noise traders who wish to buy if stock prices rise and expected stock returns fall. Campbell and Kyle (1993), Cutler, Poterba, and Summers (1991), DeLong et al. (1990a, 1990b), and Shiller (1984) develop this model in some detail. The model implies that rational investors do not hold the market portfolio—instead they shift in and out of the stock market in response to changing demand from noise traders—and do not consume aggregate consumption since some consumption is accounted for by noise traders. This makes the

---

[12]Campbell and Mankiw (1990) discuss this in the context of a linearized model. Breeden, Gibbons, and Litzenberger (1989) make a related point, arguing that at short horizons one should replace consumption with the return on a portfolio constructed to be highly correlated with longer-run movements in consumption. Brainard, Nelson, and Shapiro (1991) find that the consumption CAPM works better at long horizons than at short horizons.

model hard to test without having detailed information on the investment strategies of different market participants.

It is also possible that utility-maximizing stock market investors are heterogeneous in important ways. If investors are subject to large idiosyncratic risks in their labor income and can share these risks only indirectly by trading a few assets such as stocks and Treasury bills, their individual consumption paths may be much more volatile than aggregate consumption. Even if individual investors have the same power utility function, so that any individual's consumption growth rate raised to the power $-\gamma$ would be a valid stochastic discount factor, the aggregate consumption growth rate raised to the power $-\gamma$ may not be a valid stochastic discount factor.[13] Problem 8.3, based on Mankiw (1986), explores this effect in a simple two-period model.

Recent research has begun to explore the empirical relevance of imperfect risk-sharing for asset pricing. Heaton and Lucas (1996) calibrate individual income processes to micro data from the Panel Study of Income Dynamics (PSID). Because the PSID data show that idiosyncratic income variation is largely transitory, Heaton and Lucas find that investors can minimize its effects on their consumption by borrowing and lending. Thus they find only limited effects on asset pricing unless they restrict borrowing or assume the presence of large transactions costs. Constantinides and Duffie (1996) construct a theoretical model in which idiosyncratic shocks have permanent effects on income; they show that this type of income risk can have large effects on asset pricing.

Given this evidence, it seems important to develop empirically testable intertemporal asset pricing models that do not rely so heavily on aggregate consumption data. One approach is to substitute consumption out of the consumption CAPM to obtain an asset pricing model that relates mean returns to covariances with the underlying state variables that determine consumption. The strategy is to try to characterize the preferences that an investor would have to have in order to be willing to buy and hold the aggregate wealth portfolio, without necessarily assuming that this investor also consumes aggregate consumption.

There are several classic asset pricing models of this type set in continuous time, most notably Cox, Ingersoll, and Ross (1985a) and Merton (1973a). But those models are hard to work with empirically. Campbell (1993a) suggests a simple way to get an empirically tractable discrete-time

----

[13]This is an example of Jensen's Inequality. Since marginal utility is nonlinear, the average of investors' marginal utilities of consumption is not generally the same as the marginal utility of average consumption. This problem disappears when investors' individual consumption streams are perfectly correlated with one another as they will be in a complete markets setting. Grossman and Shiller (1982) point out that it also disappears in a continuous-time model when the processes for individual consumption streams and asset prices are diffusions.

model using the utility specification developed by Epstein and Zin (1989, 1991) and Weil (1989), which we now summarize.

Separating Risk Aversion and Intertemporal Substitution

Epstein, Zin, and Weil build on the approach of Kreps and Porteus (1978) to develop a more flexible version of the basic power utility model. That model is restrictive in that it makes the elasticity of intertemporal substitution, ψ, the reciprocal of the coefficient of relative risk aversion, γ. Yet it is not clear that these two concepts should be linked so tightly. Risk aversion describes the consumer's reluctance to substitute consumption across states of the world and is meaningful even in an atemporal setting, whereas the elasticity of intertemporal substitution describes the consumer's willingness to substitute consumption over time and is meaningful even in a deterministic setting. The Epstein-Zin-Weil model retains many of the attractive features of power utility but breaks the link between the parameters γ and ψ.

The Epstein-Zin-Weil objective function is defined recursively by

$$U_t = \left\{ (1-\delta) C_t^{\frac{1-\gamma}{\theta}} + \delta \left(E_t [U_{t+1}^{1-\gamma}] \right)^{\frac{1}{\theta}} \right\}^{\frac{\theta}{1-\gamma}}, \tag{8.3.3}$$

where $\theta \equiv (1-\gamma)/(1-1/\psi)$. When $\theta = 1$ the recursion (8.3.3) becomes linear; it can then be solved forward to yield the familiar time-separable power utility model.

The intertemporal budget constraint for a representative agent can be written as

$$W_{t+1} = (1 + R_{m,t+1})(W_t - C_t), \tag{8.3.4}$$

where W_{t+1} is the representative agent's wealth, and $(1 + R_{m,t+1})$ is the return on the "market" portfolio of all invested wealth. This form of the budget constraint is appropriate for a complete-markets model in which wealth includes human capital as well as financial assets. Epstein and Zin use a complicated dynamic programming argument to show that (8.3.3) and (8.3.4) together imply an Euler equation of the form[14]

$$1 = E_t \left[\left[\left\{ \delta \left(\frac{C_{t+1}}{C_t} \right)^{-\frac{1}{\psi}} \right\}^{\theta} \left\{ \frac{1}{(1 + R_{m,t+1})} \right\}^{1-\theta} (1 + R_{i,t+1}) \right] \right]. \tag{8.3.5}$$

If we assume that asset returns and consumption are homoskedastic and jointly lognormal, then this implies that the riskless real interest rate is

$$r_{f,t+1} = -\log \delta + \frac{\theta - 1}{2} \sigma_m^2 - \frac{\theta}{2\psi^2} \sigma_c^2 + \frac{1}{\psi} E_t[\Delta c_{t+1}]. \tag{8.3.6}$$

---

[14]There are in fact typos in equations (10) through (12) of Epstein and Zin (1991) which give intermediate steps in the derivation.

The premium on risky assets, including the market portfolio itself, is

$$E_t[r_{i,t+1}] - r_{f,t+1} + \frac{\sigma_i^2}{2} = \theta \frac{\sigma_{ic}}{\psi} + (1 - \theta)\sigma_{im}. \tag{8.3.7}$$

This says that the risk premium on asset i is a weighted combination of asset i's covariance with consumption growth (divided by the elasticity of intertemporal substitution ψ) and asset i's covariance with the market return. The weights are θ and $1 - \theta$ respectively. The Epstein-Zin-Weil model thus nests the consumption CAPM with power utility ($\theta = 1$) and the traditional static CAPM ($\theta = 0$).

It is tempting to use (8.3.7) together with observed data on aggregate consumption and stock market returns to estimate and test the Epstein-Zin-Weil model. Epstein and Zin (1991) report results of this type. In a similar spirit, Giovannini and Weil (1989) use the model to reinterpret the results of Mankiw and Shapiro (1986), who found that betas with the market have greater explanatory power for the cross-sectional pattern of returns than do betas with consumption; this is consistent with a value of θ close to zero. However this procedure ignores the fact that the intertemporal budget constraint (8.3.4) also links consumption and market returns. We now show that the budget constraint can be used to substitute consumption out of the asset pricing model.

Substituting Consumption Out of the Model
Campbell (1993a) points out that one can loglinearize the intertemporal budget constraint (8.3.4) around the mean log consumption-wealth ratio to obtain

$$\Delta w_{t+1} \approx r_{m,t+1} + k + \left(1 - \frac{1}{\rho}\right)(c_t - w_t), \tag{8.3.8}$$

where $\rho \equiv 1 - \exp(\overline{c - w})$ and k is a constant that plays no role in what follows. Combining this with the trivial equality $\Delta w_{t+1} = \Delta c_{t+1} - \Delta(c_{t+1} - w_{t+1})$, solving the resulting difference equation forward, and taking expectations, we can write the budget constraint in the form

$$c_t - w_t = E_t\left[\sum_{j=1}^{\infty} \rho^j (r_{m,t+j} - \Delta c_{t+j})\right] + \frac{\rho k}{1 - \rho}. \tag{8.3.9}$$

This equation says that if the consumption-wealth ratio is high, then the agent must expect either high returns on wealth in the future or low consumption growth rates. This follows just from the approximate budget constraint without imposing any behavioral assumptions. It is directly analogous to the linearized formula for the log dividend-price ratio in Chapter 7. Here wealth can be thought of as an asset that pays consumption as its dividend.[15]

If we now combine the budget constraint (8.3.9) with the loglinear Euler equations for the Epstein-Zin-Weil model, (8.3.6) and (8.3.7), we obtain a closed-form solution for consumption relative to wealth:

$$c_t - w_t = (1 - \psi)\mathrm{E}_t\left[\sum_{j=1}^{\infty} \rho^j r_{m,t+j}\right] + \frac{\rho(k - \mu_m)}{1 - \rho}. \tag{8.3.10}$$

Here μ_m is a constant related to the conditional variances of consumption growth and the market portfolio return. The log consumption-wealth ratio is a constant, plus $(1 - \psi)$ times the discounted value of expected future returns on invested wealth. If ψ is less than one, the consumer is reluctant to substitute intertemporally and the income effect of higher returns dominates the substitution effect, raising today's consumption relative to wealth. If ψ is greater than one, the substitution effect dominates and the consumption-wealth ratio falls when expected returns rise. Thus (8.3.10) extends to a dynamic context the classic comparative statics results of Samuelson (1969).

(8.3.10) implies that the innovation in consumption is

$$c_{t+1} - \mathrm{E}_t[c_{t+1}] = r_{m,t+1} - \mathrm{E}_t[r_{m,t+1}] \tag{8.3.11}$$

$$+ (1-\psi)\left(\mathrm{E}_{t+1}\left[\sum_{j=1}^{\infty} \rho^j r_{m,t+1+j}\right] - \mathrm{E}_t\left[\sum_{j=1}^{\infty} \rho^j r_{m,t+1+j}\right]\right).$$

An unexpected return on invested wealth has a one-for-one effect on consumption, no matter what the parameters of the utility function: This follows from the scale independence of the objective function (8.3.3). An increase in expected future returns raises or lowers consumption depending on whether ψ is greater or less than one. Equation (8.3.11) also shows when consumption will be smoother than the return on the market. When the market return is mean-reverting, there is a negative correlation between current returns and revisions in expectations of future returns. This reduces the variability of consumption growth if the elasticity of intertemporal substitution ψ is less than one but amplifies it if ψ is greater than one.

Equation (8.3.11) implies that the covariance of any asset return with consumption growth can be rewritten in terms of covariances with the re-

---

[15]Campbell (1993a) and Campbell and Koo (1996) explore the accuracy of the loglinear approximation in this context by comparing the approximate analytical solution for optimal consumption with a numerical solution. In an example calibrated to US stock market data, the two solutions are close together provided that the investor's elasticity of intertemporal substitution is less than about 3.

turn on the market and revisions in expectations of future returns on the market:

$$\mathrm{Cov}_t\left[r_{i,t+1}, \Delta c_{t+1}\right] \equiv \sigma_{ic} = \sigma_{im} + (1 - \psi)\sigma_{ih}, \tag{8.3.12}$$

where

$$\sigma_{ih} \equiv \mathrm{Cov}_t\left[r_{i,t+1}, \mathrm{E}_{t+1}\left[\sum_{j=1}^{\infty}\rho^j\, r_{m,t+1+j}\right] - \mathrm{E}_t\left[\sum_{j=1}^{\infty}\rho^j\, r_{m,t+1+j}\right]\right]. \tag{8.3.13}$$

σ_{ih} is defined to be the covariance of the return on asset i with "news" about future returns on the market, i.e., revisions in expected future returns.

Substituting (8.3.12) into (8.3.7) and using the definition of θ in terms of the underlying parameters σ and γ, we obtain a cross-sectional asset pricing formula that makes no reference to consumption:

$$\mathrm{E}_t[r_{i,t+1}] - r_{f,t+1} + \frac{\sigma_i^2}{2} = \gamma\sigma_{im} + (\gamma - 1)\sigma_{ih}. \tag{8.3.14}$$

Equation (8.3.14) has several striking features. First, assets can be priced without direct reference to their covariance with consumption growth, using instead their covariances with the return on invested wealth and with news about future returns on invested wealth. This is a discrete-time analogue of Merton's (1973a) continuous-time model in which assets are priced using their covariances with certain *hedge portfolios* that index changes in the investment opportunity set.

Second, the only parameter of the utility function that enters (8.3.14) is the coefficient of relative risk aversion γ. The elasticity of intertemporal substitution ψ does not appear once consumption has been substituted out of the model. This is in striking contrast with the important role played by ψ in the consumption-based Euler equation (8.3.7). Intuitively, this result comes from the fact that ψ plays two roles in the theory. A low value of ψ reduces anticipated fluctuations in consumption, but it also increases the risk premium required to compensate for any contribution to these fluctuations. These offsetting effects lead ψ to cancel out of the asset-based pricing formula (8.3.14).

Third, (8.3.14) expresses the risk premium, net of the Jensen's Inequality adjustment, as a weighted sum of two terms. The first term is the asset's covariance with the market portfolio; the weight on this term is the coefficient of relative risk aversion γ. The second term is the asset's covariance with news about future returns on the market; this receives a weight of $\gamma - 1$. When γ is less than one, assets that do well when there is good news about future returns on the market have lower mean returns, but when γ is greater than one, such assets have higher mean returns. The intuitive explanation is that such assets are desirable because they enable the consumer to profit from improved investment opportunities, but undesirable because they reduce the consumer's ability to hedge against a deterioration in investment opportunities. When $\gamma < 1$ the former effect dominates, and consumers are willing to accept a lower return in order to hold assets that pay off when wealth is most productive. When $\gamma > 1$ the latter effect dominates, and consumers require a higher return to hold such assets.

There are several possible circumstances under which assets can be priced using only their covariances with the return on the market portfolio, as in the logarithmic version of the static CAPM. These cases have been discussed in the literature on intertemporal asset pricing, but (8.3.14) makes it particularly easy to understand them. First, if the coefficient of relative risk aversion $\gamma = 1$, then the opposing effects of covariance with investment opportunities cancel out so that only covariance with the market return is relevant for asset pricing. Second, if the investment opportunity set is constant, then σ_{ih} is zero for all assets, so again assets can be priced using only their covariances with the market return. Third, if the return on the market follows a univariate stochastic process, then news about future returns is perfectly correlated with the current return; thus, covariance with the current return is a sufficient statistic for covariance with news about future returns and can be used to price all assets. Campbell (1996a) argues that the first two cases do not describe US data even approximately, but that the third case is empirically relevant.

A Third Look at the Equity Premium Puzzle
(8.3.14) can be applied to the risk premium on the market itself. When $i = m$, we get

$$E_t[r_{m,t+1}] - r_{f,t+1} + \frac{\sigma_m^2}{2} = \gamma \sigma_m^2 + (\gamma - 1)\sigma_{mh}. \tag{8.3.15}$$

When the market return is unforecastable, there are no revisions of expectations in future returns, so $\sigma_{mh} = 0$. In this case the equity premium with the Jensen's Inequality adjustment is just $\gamma \sigma_m^2$, and the coefficient of relative risk aversion can be estimated in the manner of Friend and Blume (1975) by taking the ratio of the equity premium to the variance of the market return. Using the numbers from Table 8.1, the estimate of risk aversion is $0.0575/0.0315 = 1.828$. This is the risk-aversion coefficient of an investor with power utility whose wealth is entirely invested in a portfolio with an unforecastable return, a risk premium of 5.75% per year, and a variance of 0.0315 (standard deviation of 17.74% per year). The consumption of such an investor would also have a standard deviation of 17.74% per year. This is far greater than the volatility of measured aggregate consumption in

Table 8.1, which explains why the risk-aversion estimate is much lower than the consumption-based estimates discussed earlier.

The Friend and Blume (1975) procedure can be seriously misleading if the market return is serially correlated. If high stock returns are associated with downward revisions of future returns, for example, then σ_{mh} is negative in (8.3.15). With $\gamma > 1$, this reduces the equity risk premium associated with any level of γ and increases the risk-aversion coefficient needed to explain a given equity premium. Intuitively, when $\sigma_{mh} < 0$ the long-run risk of stock market investment is less than the short-run risk because the market tends to mean-revert. Investors with high γ care about long-run risk rather than short-run risk, so the Friend and Blume calculation overstates risk and correspondingly understates the risk aversion needed to justify the equity premium.

Campbell (1996a) shows that the estimated coefficient of relative risk aversion rises by a factor of ten or more if one allows for the empirically estimated degree of mean-reversion in postwar monthly US data. In long-run annual US data the effect is less dramatic but still goes in the same direction. Campbell also shows that risk-aversion estimates increase if one allows for human capital as a component of wealth. In this sense one can derive the equity premium puzzle without any direct reference to consumption data.

An Equilibrium Multifactor Asset Pricing Model

With a few more assumptions, (8.3.14) can be used to derive an equilibrium multifactor asset pricing model of the type discussed in Chapter 6. We write the return on the market as the first element of a K-element state vector $\mathbf{x}_{t+1}$. The other elements are variables that are known to the market by the end of period $t+1$ and are relevant for forecasting future returns on the market. We assume that the vector $\mathbf{x}_{t+1}$ follows a first-order vector autoregression (VAR):

$$\mathbf{x}_{t+1} = \mathbf{A}\mathbf{x}_t + \epsilon_{t+1}. \tag{8.3.16}$$

The assumption that the VAR is first-order is not restrictive, since a higher-order VAR can always be stacked into first-order form.

Next we define a K-element vector $\mathbf{e1}$, whose first element is one and whose other elements are all zero. This vector picks out the real stock return $r_{m,t+1}$ from the vector $\mathbf{x}_{t+1}$: $r_{m,t+1} = \mathbf{e1}'\mathbf{x}_{t+1}$, and $r_{m,t+1} - \mathrm{E}_t\, r_{m,t+1} = \mathbf{e1}'\epsilon_{t+1}$. The first-order VAR generates simple multiperiod forecasts of future returns:

$$\mathrm{E}_t[r_{m,t+1+j}] = \mathbf{e1}'\mathbf{A}^{j+1}\mathbf{x}_t. \tag{8.3.17}$$

It follows that the discounted sum of revisions in forecast returns can be written as

$$
\begin{aligned}
\mathrm{E}_{t+1}\left[\sum_{j=1}^{\infty}\rho^{j}\,r_{m,t+1+j}\right] - \mathrm{E}_{t}\left[\sum_{j=1}^{\infty}\rho^{j}\,r_{m,t+1+j}\right] &= \boldsymbol{e}\mathbf{1}'\sum_{j=1}^{\infty}\rho^{j}\mathbf{A}^{j}\boldsymbol{\epsilon}_{t+1} \\
&= \boldsymbol{e}\mathbf{1}'\rho\mathbf{A}(\mathbf{I}-\rho\mathbf{A})^{-1}\boldsymbol{\epsilon}_{t+1} \\
&= \boldsymbol{\varphi}'\boldsymbol{\epsilon}_{t+1}, \qquad (8.3.18)
\end{aligned}
$$

where $\boldsymbol{\varphi}'$ is defined to equal $\boldsymbol{e}\mathbf{1}'\rho\mathbf{A}(\mathbf{I}-\rho\mathbf{A})^{-1}$, a nonlinear function of the VAR coefficients. The elements of the vector $\boldsymbol{\varphi}$ measure the importance of each state variable in forecasting future returns on the market. If a particular element φ_k is large and positive, then a shock to variable k is an important piece of good news about future investment opportunities.

We now define

$$
\sigma_{ik} \equiv \mathrm{Cov}_t[r_{i,t+1},\epsilon_{k,t+1}], \qquad (8.3.19)
$$

where $\epsilon_{k,t+1}$ is the kth element of $\boldsymbol{\epsilon}_{t+1}$. Since the first element of the state vector is the return on the market, $\sigma_{i1} = \sigma_{im}$. Then (8.3.14) implies that

$$
\mathrm{E}_t[r_{i,t+1}] - r_{f,t+1} = -\frac{\sigma_i^2}{2} + \gamma\sigma_{i1} + (\gamma-1)\sum_{k=1}^{K}\varphi_k\sigma_{ik}, \qquad (8.3.20)
$$

where φ_k is the kth element of $\boldsymbol{\varphi}$. This is a standard K-factor asset pricing model of the type discussed in Chapter 6. The contribution of the intertemporal optimization problem is a set of restrictions on the risk prices of the factors. The first factor (the innovation in the market return) has a risk price of $\lambda_1 = \gamma + (\gamma-1)\varphi_1$. The sign of φ_1 is the sign of the correlation between market return innovations and revisions in expected future market returns. As we have already discussed, this sign affects the risk price of the market factor; with a negative φ_1, for example, the market factor risk price is reduced if γ is greater than one.

The other factors in this model have risk prices of $\lambda_k = (\gamma-1)\varphi_k$ for $k > 1$. Factors here are innovations in variables that help to forecast the return on the market, and their risk prices are proportional to their forecasting importance as measured by the elements of the vector $\boldsymbol{\varphi}$. If a particular variable has a positive value of φ_k, this means that innovations in that variable are associated with good news about future investment opportunities. Such a variable will have a negative risk price if the coefficient of relative risk aversion γ is less than one, and a positive risk price if γ is greater than one.

Campbell (1996a) estimates this model on long-term annual and post-World War II monthly US stock market data. He estimates φ_1 to be negative and large in absolute value, so that the price of stock market risk λ_1 is much smaller than the coefficient of risk aversion γ. The other factors in the model have imprecisely estimated risk prices. Although some of these risk prices are substantial in magnitude, the other factors have minor effects on the mean returns of the assets in the study, because these assets typically have small covariances with the other factors.

8.4 More General Utility Functions

One straightforward response to the difficulties of the standard consumption CAPM is to generalize the utility function. We have already discussed the Epstein-Zin-Weil model, but there are other plausible ways to vary the utility specification while retaining the attractive scale-independence property of power utility.

For example, the utility function may be nonseparable in consumption and some other good. This is easy to handle in a loglinear model if utility is Cobb-Douglas, so that the marginal utility of consumption can be written as

$$U_C(C_t, X_t) = C_t^{-\gamma_1} X_t^{-\gamma_2} \tag{8.4.1}$$

for some good X_t and parameter γ_2. The Euler equation now becomes

$$1 = E_t \left[(1 + R_{i,t+1}) \delta \left(\frac{C_{t+1}}{C_t} \right)^{-\gamma_1} \left(\frac{X_{t+1}}{X_t} \right)^{-\gamma_2} \right]. \tag{8.4.2}$$

Assuming joint lognormality and homoskedasticity, this can be written as

$$E_t[r_{i,t+1}] = \mu_i + \gamma_1 E_t[\Delta c_{t+1}] + \gamma_2 E_t[\Delta x_{t+1}]. \tag{8.4.3}$$

Eichenbaum, Hansen, and Singleton (1988) have considered a model of this form where X_t is leisure. Aschauer (1985) and Startz (1989) have developed models in which X_t is government spending and the stock of durable goods, respectively. Unfortunately, none of these extra variables greatly improve the ability of the consumption CAPM to fit the data. The difficulty is that, at least in data since World War II, these variables are not noisy enough to have much effect on the intertemporal marginal rate of substitution.[16]

8.4.1 Habit Formation

A more promising variation of the basic model is to allow for nonseparability in utility over time. Constantinides (1990) and Sundaresan (1989) have

---

[16]Also, as Campbell and Mankiw (1990) point out, in postwar data there is predictable variation in consumption growth that is uncorrelated with predictable variation in real interest rates even after one allows for predictable variation in leisure, government spending, or durable goods.

argued for the importance of *habit formation*, a positive effect of today's consumption on tomorrow's marginal utility of consumption. Here we discuss some simple ways to implement this idea.

Several modeling issues arise at the outset. We write the period utility function as $U(C_t, X_t)$, where X_t is the time-varying habit or subsistence level. The first issue is the functional form for $U(\cdot)$. Abel (1990, 1996) has proposed that $U(\cdot)$ should be a power function of the ratio C_t/X_t, while Campbell and Cochrane (1995), Constantinides (1990), and Sundaresan (1989) have used a power function of the difference $C_t - X_t$. The second issue is the effect of an agent's own decisions on future levels of habit. In standard *internal-habit* models such as those in Constantinides (1990) and Sundaresan (1989), habit depends on an agent's own consumption and the agent takes account of this when choosing how much to consume. In *external-habit* models such as those in Abel (1990, 1996) and Campbell and Cochrane (1995), habit depends on aggregate consumption which is unaffected by any one agent's decisions. Abel calls this *catching up with the Joneses*. The third issue is the speed with which habit reacts to individual or aggregate consumption. Abel (1990, 1996), Dunn and Singleton (1986), and Ferson and Constantinides (1991) make habit depend on one lag of consumption, whereas Constantinides (1990), Sundaresan (1989), Campbell and Cochrane (1995), and Heaton (1995) make habit react only gradually to changes in consumption.

Ratio Models

Following Abel (1990, 1996), suppose that an agent's utility can be written as a power function of the ratio C_t/X_t,

$$U_t = E_t \sum_{j=0}^{\infty} \delta^j \frac{(C_{t+j}/X_{t+j})^{1-\gamma} - 1}{1-\gamma}, \tag{8.4.4}$$

where X_t summarizes the influence of past consumption levels on today's utility. X_t can be specified as an internal habit or as an external habit. Using one lag of consumption for simplicity, we may have

$$X_t = C_{t-1}^{\kappa}, \tag{8.4.5}$$

the internal-habit specification where an agent's own past consumption matters, or

$$X_t = \overline{C}_{t-1}^{\kappa}, \tag{8.4.6}$$

the external-habit specification where aggregate past consumption $\overline{C}_{t-1}$ matters. Since there is a representative agent, in equilibrium the agent's consumption must of course equal aggregate consumption, but the two formulations yield different Euler equations. In both equations the parameter κ governs the degree of time-nonseparability.

In the internal-habit specification, the derivation of the Euler equation is complicated by the fact that time-t consumption affects the summation in (8.4.4) through the term dated $t + 1$ as well as the term dated t. We have

$$\partial U_t / \partial C_t = \left[1 - \delta \kappa (C_{t+1} / C_t)^{1-\gamma} (X_{t+1} / X_t)^{\gamma-1} \right] (C_t / X_t)^{1-\gamma} (1/C_t). \quad (8.4.7)$$

This is random at time t because it depends on consumption at time $t+1$. Substituting in for X_t and imposing the condition that the agent's own consumption equals aggregate consumption, this becomes

$$\partial U_t / \partial C_t = C_{t-1}^{\kappa(\gamma-1)} C_t^{-\gamma} - \delta \kappa C_t^{\kappa(\gamma-1)} C_{t+1}^{-\gamma} (C_{t+1} / C_t). \quad (8.4.8)$$

If this model is to capture the idea of habit formation, then we need $\kappa(\gamma - 1) \geq 0$ to ensure that an increase in yesterday's consumption increases the marginal utility of consumption today. The Euler equation can now be written as

$$E_t[\partial U / \partial C_t] = \delta E_t[(1 + R_{t+1}) \partial U_{t+1} / \partial C_{t+1}], \quad (8.4.9)$$

where the expectations operator on the left-hand side is necessary because of the randomness of $\partial U / \partial C_t$.

The analysis simplifies considerably in the external-habit specification. In this case (8.4.8) and (8.4.9) can be combined to give

$$1 = \delta E_t \left[(1 + R_{i,t+1})(C_t / C_{t-1})^{\kappa(\gamma-1)} (C_{t+1} / C_t)^{-\gamma} \right]. \quad (8.4.10)$$

If we assume homoskedasticity and joint lognormality of asset returns and consumption growth, this implies the following restrictions on risk premia and the riskless real interest rate:

$$r_{f,t+1} = -\log \delta - \gamma^2 \sigma_c^2 / 2 + \gamma E_t[\Delta c_{t+1}] - \kappa(\gamma - 1)\Delta c_t, \quad (8.4.11)$$

$$E_t[r_{i,t+1} - r_{f,t+1}] + \sigma_i^2 / 2 = \gamma \sigma_{ic}. \quad (8.4.12)$$

Equation (8.4.11) says that the riskless real interest rate equals its value under power utility, less $\kappa(\gamma - 1)\Delta c_t$. Holding consumption today and expected consumption tomorrow constant, an increase in consumption yesterday increases the marginal utility of consumption today. This makes the representative agent want to borrow from the future, driving up the real interest rate. Equation (8.4.12) describing the risk premium is exactly the same as (8.2.7), the risk premium formula for the power utility model. The external habit simply adds a term to the Euler equation (8.4.10) which is known at time t, and this does not affect the risk premium.

Abel (1990, 1996) nevertheless argues that catching up with the Joneses can help to explain the equity premium puzzle. This argument is based on two considerations. First, the average level of the riskless rate in (8.4.11) is

$-\log\delta-\gamma^2\sigma_c^2/2+(\gamma-\kappa(\gamma-1))g$, where g is the average consumption growth rate. When risk aversion γ is very large, a positive κ reduces the average riskless rate. Thus catching up with the Joneses enables one to increase risk aversion to solve the equity premium puzzle without encountering the riskfree rate puzzle. Second, a positive κ is likely to make the riskless real interest rate more variable because of the term $-\kappa(\gamma-1)\Delta c_t$ in (8.4.11). If one solves for the stock returns implied by the assumption that stock dividends equal consumption, a more variable real interest rate increases the covariance of stock returns and consumption σ_{ic} and drives up the equity premium.

The second of these points can be regarded as a weakness rather than a strength of the model. The equity premium puzzle shown in Table 8.1 is that the ratio of the measured equity premium to the measured covariance σ_{ic} is large; increasing the value σ_{ic} implied by a model that equates stock dividends with consumption does not improve matters. Also the real interest rate does not vary greatly in the short run; the standard deviation of the *ex post* real commercial paper return in Table 8.1 is 5.5%, and Table 8.2 shows that about a third of the variance of this return is forecastable, implying a standard deviation for the expected real interest rate of only 3%. Since the standard deviation of consumption growth is also about 3%, large values of κ and γ in equation (8.4.11) tend to produce counterfactual volatility in the expected real interest rate. Similar problems arise in the internal-habit model.

This difficulty with the riskless real interest rate is a fundamental problem for habit-formation models. Time-nonseparable preferences make marginal utility volatile even when consumption is smooth, because consumers derive utility from consumption relative to its recent history rather than from the absolute level of consumption. But unless the consumption and habit processes take particular forms, time-nonseparability also creates large swings in expected marginal utility at successive dates, and this implies large movements in the real interest rate. We now present an alternative specification in which it is possible to solve this problem.

Difference Models

Consider a model in which the utility function is

$$U_t = E_t\left[\sum_{j=0}^{\infty}\delta^j\frac{(C_{t+j}-X_{t+j})^{1-\gamma}-1}{1-\gamma}\right], \tag{8.4.13}$$

and for simplicity treat the habit level X_t as external. This model differs from the ratio model in two important ways. First, in the difference model the agent's risk aversion varies with the level of consumption relative to habit, whereas risk aversion is constant in the ratio model. Second, in the difference model consumption must always be above habit for utility to be well-defined, whereas this is not required in the ratio model.

To understand the first point, it is convenient to work with the surplus consumption ratio S_t, defined by

$$S_t \equiv \frac{C_t - X_t}{C_t}. \qquad (8.4.14)$$

The surplus consumption ratio gives the fraction of total consumption that is surplus to subsistence or habit requirements. If habit X_t is held fixed as consumption C_t varies, the normalized curvature of the utility function, which would equal the coefficient of relative risk aversion and would be a constant γ in the conventional power utility model, is

$$\frac{-Cu_{CC}}{u_C} = \frac{\gamma}{S_t}. \qquad (8.4.15)$$

This measure of risk aversion rises as the the surplus consumption ratio S_t declines, that is, as consumption declines toward habit.[17]

The requirement that consumption always be above habit is satisfied automatically in microeconomic models with exogenous asset returns and endogenous consumption, as in Constantinides (1990) and Sundaresan (1989). It presents a more serious problem in models with exogenous consumption processes. To handle this problem Campbell and Cochrane (1995) specify a nonlinear process by which habit adjusts to consumption, remaining below consumption at all times. Campbell and Cochrane write down a process for the log surplus consumption ratio $s_t \equiv \log(S_t)$. They assume that log consumption follows a random walk with drift g and innovation v_{t+1}, $\Delta c_{t+1} = g + v_{t+1}$. They propose an AR(1) model for s_t:

$$s_{t+1} = (1 - \phi)\bar{s} + \phi s_t + \lambda(s_t) v_{t+1}. \qquad (8.4.16)$$

Here $\bar{s}$ is the steady-state surplus consumption ratio. The parameter ϕ governs the persistence of the log surplus consumption ratio, while the sensitivity function $\lambda(s_t)$ controls the sensitivity of s_{t+1} and thus of log habit x_{t+1} to innovations in consumption growth v_{t+1}.

Equation (8.4.16) specifies that today's habit is a complex nonlinear function of current and past consumption. By taking a linear approximation around the steady state, however, it may be shown that (8.4.16) is ap-

---

[17]Risk aversion may also be measured by the normalized curvature of the value function (maximized utility expressed as a function of wealth), or by the volatility of the stochastic discount factor, or by the maximum Sharpe ratio available in asset markets. While these measures of risk aversion are different from each other in this model, they all move inversely with S_t. Note that γ, the curvature parameter in utility, is no longer a measure of risk aversion in this model.

proximately a traditional habit-formation model in which log habit responds slowly to log consumption,

$$
\begin{aligned}
x_{t+1} &\approx \left[(1-\phi)h + g\right] + \phi x_t + (1-\phi)c_t \\
&= \left[h + \frac{g}{1-\phi}\right] + (1-\phi)\sum_{j=0}^{\infty} \phi^j c_{t-j},
\end{aligned}
\tag{8.4.17}
$$

where $h = \ln(1 - \bar{S})$ is the steady state value of $x-c$. The problem with the traditional model (8.4.17) is that it allows consumption to fall below habit, resulting in infinite or negative marginal utility. A process for s_t defined over the real line implies that consumption can never fall below habit.

Since habit is external, the marginal utility of consumption is $u'(C_t) = (C_t - X_t)^{-\gamma} = S_t^{-\gamma} C_t^{-\gamma}$. The stochastic discount factor is then

$$
M_{t+1} \equiv \delta \frac{u'(C_{t+1})}{u'(C_t)} = \delta \left(\frac{S_{t+1}}{S_t} \frac{C_{t+1}}{C_t} \right)^{-\gamma}.
\tag{8.4.18}
$$

In the standard power utility model $S_t = 1$, so the stochastic discount factor is just consumption growth raised to the power $-\gamma$. To get a volatile stochastic discount factor one needs a large value of γ. In the habit-formation model one can instead get a volatile stochastic discount factor from a volatile surplus consumption ratio S_t.

The riskless real interest rate is related to the stochastic discount factor by $(1 + R_{t+1}^f) = 1/E_t(M_{t+1})$. Taking logs, and using (8.4.16) and (8.4.18), the log riskless real interest rate is

$$
r_{t+1}^f = -\log(\delta) + \gamma g - \gamma(1-\phi)(s_t - \bar{s}) - \frac{\gamma^2 \sigma_v^2}{2}\left[\lambda(s_t) + 1\right]^2.
\tag{8.4.19}
$$

The first two terms on the right-hand side of (8.4.19) are familiar from the power utility model (8.2.6), while the last two terms are new. The third term (linear in $(s_t - \bar{s})$) reflects intertemporal substitution, or mean-reversion in marginal utility. If the surplus consumption ratio is low, the marginal utility of consumption is high. However, the surplus consumption ratio is expected to revert to its mean, so marginal utility is expected to fall in the future. Therefore, the consumer would like to borrow and this drives up the equilibrium risk free interest rate. The fourth term (linear in $[\lambda(s_t)+1]^2$) reflects precautionary savings. As uncertainty increases, consumers become more willing to save and this drives down the equilibrium riskless interest rate.

If this model is to generate stable real interest rates like those observed in the data, the serial correlation parameter ϕ must be near one. Also, the sensitivity function $\lambda(s_t)$ must decline with s_t so that uncertainty is high when

s_t is low and the precautionary saving term offsets the intertemporal substitution term. In fact, Campbell and Cochrane parametrize the $\lambda(s_t)$ function so that these two terms exactly offset each other everywhere, implying a constant riskless interest rate.

Even with a constant riskless interest rate and random-walk consumption, the external-habit model can produce a large equity premium, volatile stock prices, and predictable excess stock returns. The basic mechanism is time-variation in risk aversion. When consumption falls relative to habit, the resulting increase in risk aversion drives up the risk premium on risky assets such as stocks. This also drives down the prices of stocks, helping to explain why stock returns are so much more volatile than consumption growth or riskless real interest rates.

Campbell and Cochrane (1995) calibrate their model to US data on consumption and dividends, solving for equilibrium stock prices in the tradition of Mehra and Prescott (1985). There is also some work on habit formation that uses actual stock return data in the tradition of Hansen and Singleton (1982, 1983). Heaton (1995), for example, estimates an internal-habit model allowing for time-aggregation of the data and for some durability of those goods formally described as nondurable in the national income accounts. Durability can be thought of as the opposite of habit formation, in that consumption expenditure today lowers the marginal utility of consumption expenditure tomorrow. Heaton finds that durability predominates at high frequencies, and habit formation at lower frequencies. However his habit-formation model, like the simple power utility model, is rejected statistically.

Both these approaches assume that aggregate consumption is the driving process for marginal utility. An alternative view is that, for reasons discussed in Section 8.3.2, the consumption of stock market investors may not be adequately proxied by macroeconomic data on aggregate consumption. Under this view the driving process for a habit-formation model should be a process with a reasonable mean and standard deviation, but need not be highly correlated with aggregate consumption.

8.4.2 Psychological Models of Preferences

Psychologists and experimental economists have found that in experimental settings, people make choices that differ in several respects from the standard model of expected utility. In response to these findings unorthodox "psychological" models of preferences have been suggested, and some recent research has begun to apply these models to asset pricing.[18]

---

[18] Useful general references include Hogarth and Reder (1987) and Kreps (1988).

Psychological models may best be understood by comparing them to the standard time-separable specification (8.1.1) in which an investor maximizes

$$\mathrm{E}_t \left[\sum_{j=0}^{\infty} \delta^j \, U(C_{t+j}) \right]. \tag{8.4.20}$$

This specification has three main components: the period utility function $U(C_t)$, the geometric discounting with discount factor δ, and the mathematical expectations operator E_t. Psychological models alter one or more of these components.

The best-known psychological model of decision-making is probably the *prospect theory* of Kahneman and Tversky (1979) and Tversky and Kahneman (1992). Prospect theory was originally formulated in a static context, so it does not emphasize discounting, but it does alter the other two elements of the standard framework. Instead of defining preferences over consumption, preferences are defined over gains and losses relative to some benchmark outcome. A key feature of the theory is that losses are given greater weight than gains. Thus if x is a random variable that is positive for gains and negative for losses, utility might depend on

$$v(x) \;=\; \begin{cases} \frac{x^{1-\gamma_1}-1}{1-\gamma_1} & \text{if } x \ge 0 \\[2mm] -\lambda \frac{x^{1-\gamma_2}-1}{1-\gamma_2} & \text{if } x < 0. \end{cases} \tag{8.4.21}$$

Here γ_1 and γ_2 are curvature parameters for gains and losses, which may differ from one another, and $\lambda > 1$ measures the extent of *loss aversion*, the greater weight given to losses than gains.

Prospect theory also changes the mathematical expectations operator in (8.4.20). The expectations operator weights each possible outcome by its probability; prospect theory allows outcomes to be weighted by nonlinear functions of their probabilities (see Kahneman and Tversky (1979)) or by nonlinear functions of the probabilities of a better or worse outcome. Other, more general models of investor psychology also replace the mathematical expectations operator with a model of subjective expectations. See for example Barberis, Shleifer, and Vishny (1996) DeLong, Shleifer, Summers, and Waldmann (1990b), and Froot (1989).

In applying prospect theory to asset pricing, a key question is how the benchmark outcome defining gains and losses evolves over time. Benartzi and Thaler (1995) assume that investors have preferences defined over returns, where a zero return marks the boundary between a gain and a loss. Returns may be measured over different horizons; a K-month return is relevant if investors update their benchmark outcomes every K months. Benartzi and Thaler consider values of K ranging from one to 18. They show that loss aversion combined with a short horizon can rationalize investors' unwillingness to hold stocks even in the face of a large equity premium. Bonomo and Garcia (1993) obtain similar results in a consumption-based model with loss aversion.

In related work, Epstein and Zin (1990) have developed a parametric version of the choice theory of Yaari (1987). Their specification for period utility displays *first-order risk aversion*—the risk premium required to induce an investor to take a small gamble is proportional to the standard deviation of the gamble rather than the variance as in standard theory. This feature increases the risk premia predicted by the model, but in a calibration exercise in the style of Mehra and Prescott (1985), Epstein and Zin find that they can fit only about one third of the historical equity premium.

Another strand of the literature alters the specification of discounting in (8.4.20). Ainslie (1992) and Loewenstein and Prelec (1992) have argued that experimental evidence suggests not geometric discounting but *hyperbolic discounting*: The discount factor for horizon K is not δ^K but a function of the form $(1 + \delta_1 K)^{-\delta_2/\delta_1}$, where both δ_1 and δ_2 are positive as in the standard theory. This functional form implies that a lower discount rate is used for periods further in the future. Laibson (1996) argues that hyperbolic discounting is well approximated by a utility specification

$$U(C_t) + \beta \mathrm{E}_t \left[\sum_{j=1}^{\infty} \delta^j \, U(C_{t+j}) \right], \tag{8.4.22}$$

where the additional parameter $\beta < 1$ implies greater discounting over the next period than between any periods further in the future.

Hyperbolic discounting leads to *time-inconsistent* choices: Because the discount rate between any two dates shifts as the dates draw nearer, the optimal plan for those dates changes over time even if no new information arrives. The implications for consumption and portfolio choice depend on the way in which this time-consistency problem is resolved. Laibson (1996) derives the Euler equations for consumption choice assuming that the individual chooses each period's consumption in that period without being able to constrain future consumption choices. Interestingly, he shows that with hyperbolic discounting the elasticity of intertemporal substitution is less than the reciprocal of the coefficient of relative risk aversion even when the period utility function has the power form.

8.5 Conclusion

Financial economists have not yet produced a generally accepted model of the stochastic discount factor. Nonetheless substantial progress has been made. We know that the stochastic discount factor must be extremely volatile if it is to explain the cross-sectional pattern of asset returns. We also know that the conditional expectation of the stochastic discount factor must be comparatively stable in order to explain the stability of the riskless real interest rate. These properties put severe restrictions on the kinds of asset pricing models that can be considered.

There is increasing interest in the idea that risk aversion may vary over time with the state of the economy. Time-varying risk aversion can explain the large body of evidence that excess returns on stocks and other risky assets are predictable. One mechanism that can produce time-varying risk aversion is habit formation in the utility function of a representative agent. But it is also possible that investors appear to have time-varying risk aversion because they trade on the basis of irrational expectations, or that time-varying risk aversion arises from the interactions of heterogeneous agents. Grossman and Zhou (1996), for example, present a model in which two agents with different risk-aversion coefficients trade with each other. One of the agents has an exogenous lower bound on wealth, and the resulting equilibrium has a time-varying price of risk. This is likely to be an active area for future research.

Problems—Chapter 8

8.1   Prove that the benchmark portfolio has the properties (P1) through (P5) stated on pages 298 and 300 of this chapter.

8.2   Consider an economy with a representative agent who has power utility with coefficient of relative risk aversion γ. The agent receives a nonstorable endowment. The process for the log endowment, or equivalently the log of consumption c_t, is

$$\Delta c_{t+1} = \mu + \phi \Delta c_t + u_{t+1},$$

where the coefficient ϕ may be either positive or negative. If ϕ is positive then endowment fluctuations are highly persistent; if it is negative then they have an important transitory component.

8.2.1   Assume that consumption and asset returns are jointly lognormal, with constant variances and covariances.

   i.   Use the representative agent's Euler equations to show that the expected log return on any asset is a linear function of the expected growth rate of the endowment. What is the slope coefficient in this relationship?

   ii.   Use the representative agent's Euler equations to show that the difference between the expected log return on any asset and the log riskfree interest rate, plus one-half the own variance of the log asset return (call this sum the "premium" on the asset), is proportional to the conditional covariance of the log asset return with consumption growth. What is the slope coefficient in this relationship?

8.2.2 To a close approximation, the unexpected return on any asset i can be written as

$$
r_{i,t+1} - E_t\, r_{i,t+1} = E_{t+1}\left[\sum_{j=0}^{\infty} \rho^j \Delta d_{i,t+1+j}\right] - E_t\left[\sum_{j=0}^{\infty} \rho^j \Delta d_{i,t+1+j}\right]
$$
$$
- \left(E_{t+1}\left[\sum_{j=1}^{\infty} \rho^j r_{i,t+1+j}\right] - E_t\left[\sum_{j=1}^{\infty} \rho^j r_{i,t+1+j}\right]\right),
$$

where $d_{i,t}$ is the dividend paid on asset i at time t. This approximation was developed as (7.1.25) in Chapter 7.

i.   Use this expression to calculate the unexpected return on an equity which pays aggregate consumption as its dividend.

ii.   Use this expression to calculate the unexpected return on a real consol bond which has a fixed real dividend each period.

8.2.3

i.   Calculate the equity premium and the consol bond premium.

ii.   Show that the bond premium has the opposite sign to ϕ and is proportional to the square of γ. Give an economic interpretation of this result.

iii.   Show that the equity premium is always larger than the bond premium, and the difference between them is proportional to γ. Give an economic interpretation of this result.

iv.   Relate your discussion to the empirical literature on the "equity premium puzzle."

8.3   Consider a two-period world with a continuum of consumers. Each consumer has a random endowment in the second period and consumes only in the second period. In the first period, securities are traded but no money changes hands until the second period. All consumers have log utility over second-period consumption.

8.3.1   Suppose that all consumers' endowments are the same. They are m with probability $1/2$ and $(1-a)m$ with probability $1/2$, where $0 < a < 1$. Suppose that a claim to the second-period aggregate endowment is traded and that it costs p in either state, payable in the second period. Compute the equilibrium price p and the expected return on the claim.

8.3.2   Now suppose that in the second period, with probability 1/2 all consumers receive m; with probability 1/2, a fraction $(1-b)$ of consumers receive m and a fraction b receive $(1-a/b)m$. In the first period, all consumers face the same probability of being in the latter group, but no insurance markets exist through which they can hedge this risk. Compute the expected return on the claim defined above. Is it higher or lower than before? Is it bounded by a function of a and m?

8.3.3   Relate your answer to the recent empirical literature on the determination of stock returns in representative-agent models. To what extent do your results in parts 8.3.1 and 8.3.2 depend on the details of the model, and to what extent might they hold more generally?
Note: This problem is based on Mankiw (1986).

9
Derivative Pricing Models

THE PRICING OF OPTIONS, warrants, and other *derivative* securities—financial securities whose payoffs depend on the prices of other securities—is one of the great successes of modern financial economics. Based on the well-known Law of One Price or no-arbitrage condition, the option pricing models of Black and Scholes (1973) and Merton (1973b) gained an almost immediate acceptance among academics and investment professionals that is unparalleled in the history of economic science.[1]

The fundamental insight of the Black-Scholes and Merton models is that under certain conditions an option's payoff can be exactly replicated by a particular dynamic investment strategy involving only the underlying stock and riskless debt. This particular strategy may be constructed to be *self-financing*, i.e., requiring no cash infusions except at the start and allowing no cash withdrawals until the option expires; since the strategy replicates the option's payoff at expiration, the initial cost of this self-financing investment strategy must be identical to the option's price, otherwise an arbitrage opportunity will arise. This no-arbitrage condition yields not only the option's price but also the means to replicate the option synthetically—via the dynamic investment strategy of stocks and riskless debt—if it does not exist.

This method of pricing options has since been used to price literally hundreds of other types of derivative securities, some considerably more complex than a simple option. In the majority of these cases, the pricing formula can only be expressed implicitly as the solution of a parabolic partial differential equation (PDE) with boundary conditions and initial values determined by the contractual terms of each security. To obtain actual prices, the PDE must be solved numerically, which might have been problematic in 1973 when Black and Scholes and Merton first published their papers but is now commonplace thanks to the breakthroughs in computer

---

[1]See Bernstein (1992, Chapter 11) for a lively account of the intellectual history of the Black-Scholes/Merton option pricing formula.

technology over the past three decades. Although a detailed discussion of
derivative pricing models is beyond the scope of this text—there are many
other excellent sources such as Cox and Rubinstein (1985), Hull (1993),
and Merton (1990)—we do provide brief reviews of Brownian motion in
Section 9.1 and Merton's derivation of the Black-Scholes formula in Section
9.2 for convenience.

Ironically, although pricing derivative securities is often highly computa-
tion-intensive, in principle it leaves very little room for traditional statistical
inference since, by the very nature of the no-arbitrage pricing paradigm,
there exists no "error term" to be minimized and no corresponding statistical fluctuations to contend with. After all, if an option's price is determined
exactly—without error—as some (possibly time-varying) combination of
prices of other traded assets, where is the need for statistical inference?
Methods such as regression analysis do not seem to play a role even in the
application of option pricing models to data.

However, there are at least two aspects of the *implementation* of derivative pricing models that do involve statistical inference and we shall focus
on them in this chapter. The first aspect is the problem of estimating the parameters of continuous-time price processes which are inputs for parametric
derivative pricing formulas. We use the qualifier *parametric* in describing the
derivative pricing formulas considered in this chapter because several *nonparametric* approaches to pricing derivatives have recently been proposed
(see, for example, Aït-Sahalia [1992], Aït-Sahalia and Lo [1995], Hutchinson, Lo, and Poggio [1994], and Rubinstein [1994]).[2] We shall consider
nonparametric derivative pricing models in Chapter 12, and focus on issues
surrounding parametric models in Section 9.3.

The second aspect involves the pricing of path-dependent derivatives
by Monte Carlo simulation. A derivative security is said to be *path-dependent*
if its payoff depends in some way on the entire *path* of the underlying asset's
price during the derivative's life. For example, a put option which gives
the holder the right to sell the underlying asset at its average price—where
the average is calculated over the life of the option—is path-dependent
because the average price is a function of the underlying asset's entire price
path. Although a few analytical approximations for pricing path-dependent
derivatives do exist, by far the most effective method for pricing them is
by Monte Carlo simulation. This raises several issues such as measuring
the accuracy of simulated prices, determining the number of simulations
required for a desired level of accuracy, and designing the simulations to

---

[2]In contrast to the traditional parametric approach in which the price process of the
underlying asset is fully specified up to a finite number of unknown parameters, e.g., a lognormal diffusion with unknown drift and volatility parameters, a nonparametric approach does
not specify the price process explicitly and attempts to infer it from the data under suitable
regularity conditions.

make the most economical use of computational resources. We turn to these issues in Section 9.4.

9.1 Brownian Motion

For certain financial applications it is often more convenient to model prices as evolving continuously through time rather than discretely at fixed dates. For example, Merton's derivation of the Black-Scholes option-pricing formula relies heavily on the ability to adjust portfolio holdings continuously in time so as to replicate an option's payoff exactly. Such a replicating portfolio strategy is often impossible to construct in a discrete-time setting; hence pricing formulas for options and other derivative securities are almost always derived in continuous time (see Section 9.2 for a more detailed discussion).[3]

9.1.1 Constructing Brownian Motion

The first formal mathematical model of financial asset prices—developed by Bachelier (1900) for the larger purpose of pricing warrants trading on the Paris Bourse—was the continuous-time random walk, or Brownian motion. Therefore, it should not be surprising that Brownian motion plays such a central role in modern derivative pricing models. This continuous-time process is closely related to the discrete-time versions of the random walk described in Section 2.1 of Chapter 2, and we shall take the discrete-time random walk as a starting point in our heuristic construction of the Brownian motion.[4] Our goal is to use the discrete-time random walk to define a sequence of continuous-time processes which will converge to a continuous-time analog of the random walk in the limit.

The Discrete-Time Random Walk
Denote by $\{p_k\}$ a discrete-time random walk with increments that take on only two values, Δ and $-\Delta$:

$$p_k = p_{k-1} + \epsilon_k, \qquad \epsilon_k = \begin{cases} \Delta & \text{with probability } \pi \\ -\Delta & \text{with probability } \pi' \equiv 1 - \pi, \end{cases} \qquad (9.1.1)$$

where ϵ_k is IID (hence p_k follows the *Random Walk 1* model of Section 2.1.1 of Chapter 2), and p_0 is fixed. Consider the following continuous-time process $p_n(t)$, $t \in [0, T]$, which can be constructed from the discrete-time process

---

[3]There are two notable exceptions: the equilibrium approach of Rubinstein (1976), and the binomial option-pricing model of Cox, Ross, and Rubinstein (1979).

[4]For a more rigorous derivation, see Billingsley (1968, Section 37).

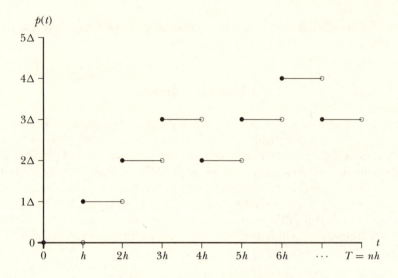

Figure 9.1.   *Sample Path of a Discrete-Time Random Walk*

$\{p_k\}$, $k = 1, \ldots, n$ as follows: Partition the time interval $[0, T]$ into n pieces, each of length $h = T/n$, and define the process

$$p_n(t) = p_{[t/h]} = p_{[nt/T]}, \qquad t \in [0, T], \tag{9.1.2}$$

where $[x]$ denotes the greatest integer less than or equal to x. $p_n(t)$ is a rather simple continuous-time process, constant except at times $t = kh$, $k = 1, \ldots, n$ (see Figure 9.1).

Although $p_n(t)$ is indeed a well-defined continuous-time process, it is still essentially the same as the discrete-time process p_k since it only varies at discrete points in time. However, if we allow n to increase without bound while holding T fixed (hence forcing h to approach 0), then the number of points in $[0, T]$ at which $p_n(t)$ varies will also increase without bound. If, at the same time, we adjust the step size Δ and the probabilities π and π' appropriately as n increases, then $p_n(t)$ converges in distribution to a well-defined nondegenerate continuous-time process $p(t)$ with continuous sample paths on $[0, T]$.

To see why adjustments to Δ, π, and π' are necessary, consider the mean and variance of $p_n(T)$:

$$\mathrm{E}[p_n(T)] = n(\pi - \pi')\Delta \tag{9.1.3}$$

$$\mathrm{Var}[p_n(T)] = 4n\pi\,\pi'\Delta^2. \tag{9.1.4}$$

As n increases without bound, the mean and variance of $p_n(T)$ will also increase without bound if Δ, π, and π' are held fixed. To obtain a well-defined and nondegenerate limiting process, we must maintain finite moments for $p_n(T)$ as n approaches infinity. In particular, since we wish to obtain a continuous-time version of the random walk, we should expect the mean and variance of the limiting process $p(T)$ to be linear in T, as in (2.1.5) and (2.1.6) for the discrete-time random walk. Therefore, we must adjust Δ, π, and π' so that:

$$n(\pi - \pi')\Delta \;=\; \frac{T}{h}(\pi - \pi')\Delta \;\to\; \mu T \qquad (9.1.5)$$

$$4n\pi\,\pi'\Delta^2 \;=\; \frac{T}{h}\,4\pi\,\pi'\Delta^2 \;\to\; \sigma^2 T, \qquad (9.1.6)$$

and this is accomplished by setting:

$$\pi \;=\; \frac{1}{2}\left(1 + \frac{\mu\sqrt{h}}{\sigma}\right),$$

$$\pi' \;=\; \frac{1}{2}\left(1 - \frac{\mu\sqrt{h}}{\sigma}\right), \qquad \Delta \;=\; \sigma\sqrt{h}. \qquad (9.1.7)$$

The adjustments (9.1.7) imply that the step size decreases as n increases, but at the slower rate of $1/\sqrt{n}$ or $\sqrt{h}$. The probabilities converge to $\frac{1}{2}$, also at the rate of $\sqrt{h}$, and hence we write:

$$\pi \;=\; \frac{1}{2} + O(\sqrt{h}), \qquad \pi' \;=\; \frac{1}{2} + O(\sqrt{h}), \qquad \Delta \;=\; O(\sqrt{h}). \quad (9.1.8)$$

where $O(\sqrt{h})$ denotes terms that are of the same *asymptotic order* as $\sqrt{h}$.[5] Therefore, as n increases, the random walk $p_n(T)$ varies more frequently on $[0, T]$, but with smaller step size Δ and with up-step and down-step probabilities approaching $\frac{1}{2}$.

---

[5]A function $f(h)$ is said to be of the same asymptotic order as $g(h)$—denoted by $f(h) \sim O(g(h))$—if the following relation is satisfied:

$$0 \;<\; \lim_{h\to 0}\frac{f(h)}{g(h)} \;<\; \infty.$$

A function $f(h)$ is said to be of smaller asymptotic order as $g(h)$—denoted by $f(h) \sim o(g(h))$—if

$$\lim_{h\to 0}\frac{f(h)}{g(h)} \;=\; 0.$$

Some examples of asymptotic order relations are

$$h \;\sim\; o(\sqrt{h}), \qquad 3h^2 \;\sim\; o(\sqrt{h}), \qquad 5\sqrt{h} + h^2 \;\sim\; O(\sqrt{h}), \qquad h - 8h^2 \;\sim\; O(h).$$

The Continuous-Time Limit

By calculating the moment-generating function of $p_n(T)$ and taking its limit as n approaches infinity, it may be shown that the distribution of $p(T)$ is normal with mean μT and variance $\sigma^2 T$; thus $p_n(T)$ converges in distribution to a $\mathcal{N}(\mu T, \sigma^2 T)$ random variable.

In fact, a much stronger notion of convergence relates $p_n(T)$ to $p(T)$, which involves the *finite-dimensional distributions* (FDDs) of the two stochastic processes. An FDD of a stochastic process $p(t)$ is the joint distribution of any finite number of observations of the stochastic process, i.e., $f(p(t_1), p(t_2), \ldots, p(t_m))$, where $0 \le t_1 < \cdots < t_m \le T$. It can be shown that *all* the FDDs of the stochastic process $p_n(t)$ (not just the random variable $p_n(T)$) converge to the FDDs of a well-defined stochastic process $p(t)$.[6] This implies, for example, that the distribution of $p_n(t)$ converges to the distribution of $p(t)$ for all $t \in [0, T]$ (not just at T), that the joint distribution of $\{p_n(0), p_n(3), p_n(7)\}$ converges to the joint distribution of $\{p(0), p(3), p(7)\}$, and so on.

In addition to the normality of $p(T)$, the *stochastic process* $p(t)$ possesses the following three properties:

(B1) For any t_1 and t_2 such that $0 \le t_1 < t_2 \le T$:

$$p(t_2) - p(t_1) \sim \mathcal{N}\big(\mu(t_2 - t_1), \sigma^2(t_2 - t_1)\big). \qquad (9.1.9)$$

(B2) For any t_1, t_2, t_3, and t_4 such that $0 \le t_1 < t_2 \le t_3 < t_4 \le T$, the increment $p(t_2) - p(t_1)$ is statistically independent of the increment $p(t_4) - p(t_3)$.

(B3) The sample paths of $p(t)$ are continuous.

It is a remarkable fact that $p(t)$, which is the celebrated *arithmetic Brownian motion* or *Wiener process*, is completely characterized by these three properties. If we set $\mu = 0$ and $\sigma = 1$, we obtain *standard Brownian motion* which we shall denote by $B(t)$. Accordingly, we may re-express $p(t)$ as

$$p(t) = \mu t + \sigma B(t), \qquad t \in [0, T]. \qquad (9.1.10)$$

To develop further intuition for $p(t)$, consider the following conditional moments:

$$\mathrm{E}[p(t) \mid p(t_0)] = p(t_0) + \mu(t - t_0) \qquad (9.1.11)$$

$$\mathrm{Var}[p(t) \mid p(t_0)] = \sigma^2(t - t_0) \qquad (9.1.12)$$

---

[6]The convergence of FDDs, coupled with a technical conditional called *tightness*, is called *weak* convergence, a powerful tool in deriving asymptotic approximations for the statistical laws of many nonlinear estimators. See Billingsley (1968) for further details.

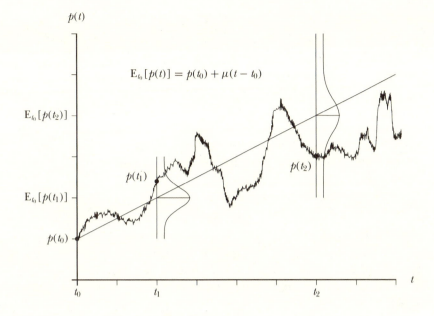

Figure 9.2. *Sample Path and Conditional Expectation of a Brownian Motion with Drift*

$$\text{Cov}[p(t_1), p(t_2)] \quad = \quad \text{Cov}[p(t_1), p(t_2) - p(t_1) + p(t_1)] \quad (9.1.13)$$

$$= \quad \text{Cov}[p(t_1), p(t_2) - p(t_1)]$$

$$+ \text{Cov}[p(t_1), p(t_1)] \qquad\qquad (9.1.14)$$

$$= \quad \text{Var}[p(t_1)] \ = \ \sigma^2 t_1. \qquad\qquad (9.1.15)$$

As for the discrete-time random walk, the conditional mean and variance of $p(t)$ are linear in t (see Figure 9.2). Properties (B2) and (B3) of Brownian motion imply that its sample paths are very erratic and jagged—if they were smooth, the infinitesimal increment $B(t+h)-B(t)$ would be predictable by $B(t)-B(t-h)$, violating independence. In fact, observe that the ratio $\big(B(t+h)-B(t)\big)/h$ does not converge to a well-defined random variable as h approaches 0, since

$$\text{Var}\left[\frac{B(t+h) - B(t)}{h}\right] \ = \ \frac{1}{h}. \qquad\qquad (9.1.16)$$

Therefore, the derivative of Brownian motion, $B'(t)$, does not exist in the ordinary sense, and although the sample paths of Brownian motion are everywhere continuous, they are nowhere differentiable.

9.1.2 Stochastic Differential Equations

Despite this fact, the infinitesimal increment of Brownian motion, i.e., the limit of $B(t+h)-B(t)$ as h approaches an infinitesimal of time (dt), has earned the notation $dB(t)$ with its own unique interpretation because it has become a fundamental building block for constructing other continuous-time processes.[7] Heuristically, $B(t+h)-B(t)$ can be viewed as Gaussian white noise (see Chapter 2) and in the limit as h becomes infinitesimally small, $dB(t)$ is the "continuous-time version" of white noise.

It is understood that $dB(t)$ is a special kind of differential, a *stochastic differential*, not to be confused with the differentials dx and dy of the calculus. Nevertheless, $dB(t)$ does obey some of the mechanical relations that ordinary differentials satisfy. For example, (9.1.10) is often expressed in differential form as:

$$dp(t) \; = \; \mu\, dt + \sigma\, dB(t). \tag{9.1.17}$$

However, (9.1.17) cannot be treated as an ordinary differential equation, and is called a *stochastic differential equation* to emphasize this fact. For example, the natural transformation $dp(t)/dt = \mu + dB(t)/dt$ does not make sense because $dB(t)/dt$ is not a well-defined mathematical object (although $dB(t)$ is, by definition).

Indeed, thus far the symbols in (9.1.17) have little formal content beyond their relation to (9.1.10)—one set of symbols has been defined to be equivalent to another. To give (9.1.17) independent meaning, we must develop a more complete understanding of the properties of the stochastic differential $dB(t)$. For example, since dB is a random variable, what are its moments? How do $(dB)^2$ and $(dB)(dt)$ behave? To answer these questions, consider the definition of $dB(t)$:

$$dB(t) \; \equiv \; \lim_{h \to dt} B(t + h) - B(t) \tag{9.1.18}$$

and recall from (B1) that increments of Brownian motion are normally distributed with zero mean (since $\mu = 0$) and variance equal to the differencing interval h (since $\sigma = 1$). Therefore, we have

$$\mathrm{E}[dB] \; = \; \lim_{h \to dt} \mathrm{E}[B(t + h) - B(t)] \; = \; 0 \tag{9.1.19}$$

$$\mathrm{Var}[dB] \; = \; \lim_{h \to dt} \mathrm{E}[(B(t + h) - B(t))^2] \; = \; dt \tag{9.1.20}$$

$$\mathrm{E}[(dB)(dB)] \; = \; \lim_{h \to dt} \mathrm{E}[(B(t + h) - B(t))^2] \; = \; dt \tag{9.1.21}$$

---

[7] A complete and rigorous exposition of Brownian motion and stochastic differential equations is beyond the scope of this text. Hoel, Port, and Stone (1972, Chapters 4–6), Merton (1990, Chapter 3), and Schuss (1980) provide excellent coverage of this material.

$$\text{Var}[(dB)(dB)] = \lim_{h \to dt} \left\{ \text{E}[(B(t+h) - B(t))^4] - h^2 \right\}$$

$$= o(dt) \tag{9.1.22}$$

$$\text{E}[(dB)(dt)] = \lim_{h \to dt} \text{E}[(B(t+h) - B(t))h] = 0 \tag{9.1.23}$$

$$\text{Var}[(dB)(dt)] = \lim_{h \to dt} \text{E}[(B(t+h) - B(t))^2 h^2] = o(dt). \tag{9.1.24}$$

From (B1) and (9.1.19)–(9.1.20) and we see that $dB(t)$ may be viewed as a normally distributed random variable with zero mean and infinitesimal variance dt. Although a variance of dt may seem like no variance at all, recall that we are in a world of infinitesimals—after all, according to (9.1.17) the expected value of $dp(t)$ is μdt—so a variance of dt is not negligible in a relative sense.

However, a variance of $(dt)^2$ *is* negligible in a relative sense—relative to dt—since the square of an infinitesimal is much smaller than the infinitesimal itself. If we treat terms of order $o(dt)$ as essentially zero, then (9.1.21)–(9.1.24) shows that $(dB)^2$ and $(dB)(dt)$ are both non-stochastic (since the variances of the right-hand sides are of order $o(dt)$) hence the relations $(dB)^2 = dt$ and $(dB)(dt) = 0$ are satisfied not just in expectation but exactly. This yields the well-known multiplication rules for stochastic differentials summarized in Table 9.1. To see why these rules are useful, observe that we

Table 9.1. *Multiplication rules for stochastic differentials.*

$\times$	dB	dt
dB	dt	0
dt	0	0

can now calculate $(dp)^2$:

$$(dp)^2 = (\mu dt + \sigma dB)^2 \tag{9.1.25}$$

$$= \mu^2 (dt)^2 + \sigma^2 (dB)^2 + 2\mu\sigma (dB)(dt)$$

$$= \sigma^2 dt. \tag{9.1.26}$$

This simple calculation shows that although dp is a random variable, $(dp)^2$ is not. It also shows that dp does behave like a random walk increment in that the variance of dp is proportional to the differencing interval dt.

Geometric Brownian Motion

If the arithmetic Brownian motion $p(t)$ is taken to be the price of some asset, Property (B1) shows that price changes over any interval will be normally distributed. But since the support of the normal distribution is the entire real line, normally distributed price changes imply that prices can be negative with positive probability. Because virtually all financial assets enjoy limited liability—the maximum loss is capped at -100% of the total investment—negative prices are empirically implausible.

As in Sections 1.4.2 of Chapter 1 and 2.1.1 of Chapter 2, we may eliminate this problem by defining $p(t)$ to be the natural logarithm of price $P(t)$. Under this definition, $p(t)$ can be an arithmetic Brownian motion without violating limited liability, since the price $P(t) = e^{p(t)}$ is always non-negative. The price process $P(t) \equiv e^{p(t)}$ is said to be a *geometric Brownian motion* or *lognormal diffusion*. We shall examine the statistical properties of both arithmetic and geometric Brownian motion in considerably more detail in Section 9.3.

Itô's Lemma

Although the first complete mathematical theory of Brownian motion is due to Wiener (1923),[8] it is the seminal contribution of Itô (1951) that is largely responsible for the enormous number of applications of Brownian motion to problems in mathematics, statistics, physics, chemistry, biology, engineering, and of course, financial economics. In particular, Itô constructs a broad class of continuous-time stochastic processes based on Brownian motion—now known as *Itô processes* or *Itô stochastic differential equations*—which is *closed* under general nonlinear transformations; that is, an arbitrary nonlinear function $f(p, t)$ of an Itô process p and time t is itself an Itô process.

More importantly, Itô (1951) provides a formula—*Itô's Lemma*—for calculating explicitly the stochastic differential equation that governs the dynamics of $f(p, t)$:

$$df(p, t) \;=\; \frac{\partial f}{\partial p} dp + \frac{\partial f}{\partial t} dt + \tfrac{1}{2} \frac{\partial^2 f}{\partial p^2} (dp)^2. \tag{9.1.27}$$

The modest term "lemma" hardly does justice to the wide-ranging impact (9.1.27) has had; this powerful tool allows us to quantify the evolution of complex stochastic systems in a single step. For example, let p denote the log-price process of an asset and suppose it satisfies (9.1.17); what are the dynamics of the price process $P(t) = e^{p(t)}$? Itô's Lemma provides us with an immediate answer:

$$dP \;=\; \frac{\partial P}{\partial p} dp + \tfrac{1}{2} \frac{\partial^2 P}{\partial p^2} (dp)^2 \tag{9.1.28}$$

---

[8]See Jerison, Singer, and Stroock (1996) for an excellent historical retrospective of Wiener's research which includes several articles about Wiener's influence on modern financial economics.

$$
\begin{aligned}
&= e^p\, dp + \tfrac{1}{2} e^p (dp)^2 \\
&= P(\mu\, dt + \sigma\, dB) + \tfrac{1}{2} P(\sigma^2\, dt) \\
dP &= (\mu + \tfrac{1}{2}\sigma^2) P\, dt + \sigma P\, dB.
\end{aligned}
\tag{9.1.29}
$$

In contrast to arithmetic Brownian motion (9.1.17), we see from (9.1.29) that the instantaneous mean and standard deviation of the geometric Brownian motion are proportional to P. Alternatively (9.1.29) implies that the instantaneous *percentage* price change dP/P behaves like an arithmetic Brownian motion or random walk, which of course is precisely the case given the exponential transformation.

We provide a considerably less trivial example of the power of Itô's Lemma in Section 9.2: Merton's derivation of the Black-Scholes formula.

9.2 A Brief Review of Derivative Pricing Methods

Although we assume that readers are already familiar with the theoretical aspects of pricing options and other derivative securities, we shall provide a very brief review here, primarily to develop terminology and define notation. Our derivation is deliberately terse and we urge readers unfamiliar with these models to spend some time with Merton's (1990, Chapter 8) definitive treatment of the subject. Also, for expositional economy we shall confine our attention to *plain vanilla* options in this chapter, i.e., simple call and put options with no special features, and the underlying asset is assumed to be common stock.[9]

Denote by $G(P(t), t)$ the price at time t of a European call option with strike price X and expiration date $T > t$ on a stock with price $P(t)$ at time t.[10] Of course, G also depends on other quantities such as the maturity date T, the strike price X, and other parameters but we shall usually suppress these arguments except when we wish to focus on them specifically.

However, expressing G as a function of the *current* stock price $P(t)$, and not of past prices, is an important restriction that greatly simplifies the task of finding G (in Section 9.4 we shall consider options that do not satisfy

---

[9]However, the techniques reviewed in this section have been applied in similar fashion to literally hundreds of other types of derivative securities, hence they are considerably more general than they may appear to be.

[10]Recall that a *call* option gives the holder the right to purchase the underlying asset for X and a *put* option gives the holder the right to sell the underlying asset for X. A *European* option is one that can be exercised only on the maturity date. An *American* option is one that can be exercised on or *before* the maturity date. For simplicity we shall deal only with European options in this chapter. See Cox and Rubinstein (1985), Hull (1993), and Merton (1990) for institutional details and differences between the pricing of American and European options.

this restriction). In addition, Black and Scholes (1973) make the following assumptions:

(A1) *There are no market imperfections, e.g., taxes, transactions costs, shortsales constraints, and trading is continuous and frictionless.*

(A2) *There is unlimited riskless borrowing and lending at the continuously compounded rate of return r; hence a $1 investment in such an asset over the time interval τ grows to $1 \cdot e^{r\tau}$. Alternatively, if $D(t)$ is the date t price of a discount bond maturing at date T with face value $1, then for $t \in [0, T]$ the bond price dynamics are given by*

$$dD(t) = rD(t)\,dt. \tag{9.2.1}$$

(A3) *The stock price dynamics are given by a geometric Brownian motion, the solution to the following Itô stochastic differential equation on $t \in [0, T]$:*

$$dP(t) = \mu P(t)\,dt + \sigma P(t)\,dB(t), \qquad P(0) = P_o > 0, \tag{9.2.2}$$

where $B(t)$ is a standard Brownian motion, and at least one investor observes σ without error.

(A4) *There is no arbitrage.*

9.2.1 The Black-Scholes and Merton Approach

The goal is to narrow down the possible expressions for G, with the hope of obtaining a specific formula for it. Black and Scholes (1973) and Merton (1973b) accomplish this by considering relations among the dynamics of the option price G, the stock price P, and the riskless bond D. To do this, we first derive the dynamics of the option price by assuming that G is only a function of the current stock price P and t itself and applying Itô's Lemma (see Section 9.1.2 and Merton [1990, Chapter 3]) to the function $G(P(t), t)$, which yields the dynamics of the option price:

$$dG = \mu_g G\,dt + \sigma_g G\,dB(t), \tag{9.2.3}$$

where

$$\mu_g \equiv \frac{1}{G}\left[\mu P \frac{\partial G}{\partial P} + \frac{\partial G}{\partial t} + \frac{\sigma^2 P^2}{2}\frac{\partial^2 G}{\partial P^2}\right] \tag{9.2.4}$$

$$\sigma_g \equiv \frac{1}{G}\left[\sigma P \frac{\partial G}{\partial P}\right]. \tag{9.2.5}$$

Unfortunately, this expression does not seem to provide any obvious restrictions that might allow us to narrow down the choices for G. One possibility is to set μ_g equal to some "required" rate of return r_o, one that comes from equilibrium considerations of the corresponding risk of the option, much like the CAPM (see Chapter 5). If such an r_o can be identified, the condition $\mu_g = r_o$ reduces to a PDE which, under some regularity and boundary conditions, possesses a unique solution. This is the approach taken by Black and Scholes (1973).[11] However, this approach requires more structure than we have imposed in (A1)–(A4)—a fully articulated dynamic model of economic equilibrium in which r_o can be determined explicitly must be specified.

Merton (1973b) presents an alternative to the equilibrium approach of Black and Scholes (1973) in which the same option-pricing formula is obtained but without any additional assumptions beyond (A1)–(A4). He does this by constructing a portfolio of stocks, options and riskless bonds that requires no initial net investment and no additional funds between 0 and T, a *self-financing* portfolio where long positions are completely financed by short positions. Specifically, denote by $I_p(t)$ the dollar amount invested in the stock at date t, $I_d(t)$ the dollar amount invested in riskless bonds at date t which mature at date T, and $I_g(t)$ the dollar amount invested in the call option at date t. Then the zero net investment condition may be expressed as:

$$I_p(t) + I_d(t) + I_g(t) = 0, \qquad \forall t \in [0, T]. \qquad (9.2.6)$$

Portfolios satisfying (9.2.6) are called *arbitrage* portfolios. Merton (1969) shows that the instantaneous dollar return dI to this arbitrage portfolio is:

$$dI = \frac{I_p}{P} dP + \frac{I_d}{D} dD + \frac{I_g}{G} dG. \qquad (9.2.7)$$

where the stochastic differentials dP and dD are given in (9.2.2) and (9.2.1) respectively, and dG follows from Itô's Lemma:

$$dG = \mu_g G dt + \sigma_g G dB \qquad (9.2.8)$$

$$\mu_g \equiv \frac{\mu P \partial G/\partial P + \partial G/\partial t + \frac{\sigma^2 P^2}{2} \partial^2 G/\partial P^2}{G} \qquad (9.2.9)$$

$$\sigma_g \equiv \frac{\sigma P \partial G/\partial P}{G}. \qquad (9.2.10)$$

Substituting the dynamics of $P(t)$, $B(t)$, and $G(t)$ into (9.2.7) and imposing (9.2.6) yields

$$dI = \big[(\mu - r)I_p + (\mu_g - r)I_g\big]dt + \big[\sigma I_p + \sigma_g I_g\big]dB(t). \qquad (9.2.11)$$

---

[11] In particular, Black and Scholes (1973) assume that the CAPM holds, and obtain r_o by appealing to the security-market-line relation which links expected returns to beta. However, the CAPM is not a dynamic model of equilibrium returns and there are some subtle but significant inconsistencies between the CAPM and continuous-time option-pricing models (see, for example, Dybvig and Ingersoll [1982]). Nevertheless, Rubinstein (1976) provides a dynamic equilibrium model in which the Black-Scholes formula holds.

Now let us further restrict this arbitrage portfolio to be completely riskless in the sense that its return is nonstochastic on $[0, T]$. This may be guaranteed by choosing $I_g = I_g^*$ and $I_p = I_p^*$ so that

$$\sigma I_p^* + \sigma_g I_g^* = 0, \qquad \forall t \in [0, T], \tag{9.2.12}$$

implying that

$$\frac{n_p^*(t)}{n_g^*(t)} = -\frac{\partial G(t)}{\partial P} \tag{9.2.13}$$

for every $t \in [0, T]$, where $n_p^*(t)$ and $n_g^*(t)$ are the number of shares of the stock and the option, respectively, held in the self-financing zero-risk portfolio. Note that unless $\partial G(t)/\partial P$ is constant through time, both $n_p^*(t)$ and $n_g^*(t)$ must be time-varying to ensure that this portfolio is riskless at all times. Such a portfolio is said to be *perfectly hedged* and $-\partial G(t)/\partial P$ is known as the *hedge ratio*.

Imposing (9.2.6) and (9.2.13) for all $t \in [0, T]$ yields a *dynamic* portfolio strategy that is riskless and requires no net investment. But then surely its nonstochastic return dI must be zero, otherwise there would exist a costless, riskless dynamic portfolio strategy that yields a positive return. Therefore, to avoid arbitrage, it must be the case that

$$(\mu - r)I_p^*(t) + (\mu_g(t) - r)I_g^*(t) = 0, \tag{9.2.14}$$

where a time argument has been added to $\mu_g(\cdot)$ to emphasize the fact that it varies through time as well.

Surprisingly, this simple no-arbitrage condition reduces the possible choices of G to just one expression which is a second-order linear parabolic PDE for G:

$$\frac{1}{2}\sigma^2 P^2 \frac{\partial^2 G}{\partial P^2} + rP\frac{\partial G}{\partial P} + \frac{\partial G}{\partial t} - rG = 0, \tag{9.2.15}$$

subject to the following two boundary conditions: $G(P(T), T) = \text{Max}[P(T) - X, 0]$, and $G(0, t) = 0$. The unique solution is, of course, the Black-Scholes formula:

$$G(P(t), t) = P(t)\,\Phi(d_1) - Xe^{-r(T-t)}\,\Phi(d_2) \tag{9.2.16}$$

$$d_1 \equiv \frac{\log(P(t)/X) + (r + \frac{1}{2}\sigma^2)(T-t)}{\sigma\sqrt{T-t}} \tag{9.2.17}$$

$$d_2 \equiv \frac{\log(P(t)/X) + (r - \frac{1}{2}\sigma^2)(T-t)}{\sigma\sqrt{T-t}}, \tag{9.2.18}$$

where $\Phi(\cdot)$ is the standard normal cumulative distribution function, and $T-t$ is the time-to-maturity of the option.

The importance of assumptions (A1) and (A3) should now be apparent: it is the combination of Brownian motion (with its continuous sample paths) and the ability to trade continuously that enables us to construct a perfectly hedged portfolio. If either of these assumptions failed, there would be occasions when the return to the arbitrage portfolio is nonzero and stochastic, i.e., risky. If so, the arbitrage argument no longer applies.

Merton's derivation of the Black-Scholes formula also showcases the power of Itô's Lemma, which gives us the dynamics (9.2.8) of the option price G that led to the PDE (9.2.15). In a discrete-time setting, obtaining the dynamics of a nonlinear function of even the simplest linear stochastic process is generally hopeless, and yet this is precisely what is required to construct a perfectly hedged portfolio.

More importantly, the existence of a self-financing perfectly hedged portfolio of options, stocks, and bonds implies that the option may be synthetically replicated by a self-financing dynamic trading strategy consisting of only stocks and bonds. The initial cost of setting up this replicating portfolio of stocks and bonds must then equal the option's price to rule out arbitrage because the replicating portfolio is self-financing and duplicates the option's payoff at maturity. The hedge ratio (9.2.13) provides the recipe for implementing the replicating strategy.

Option Sensitivities

The sensitivities of G to its other arguments also play crucial roles in trading and managing portfolios of options, so much so that the partial derivatives[12] of G with respect to its arguments have been assigned specific Greek letters in the parlance of investment professionals and are now known collectively as *option sensitivities* or, less formally, as the "Greeks":[13]

$$\text{Delta} \quad \Delta \equiv \frac{\partial G}{\partial P} \quad\quad (9.2.19)$$

$$\text{Gamma} \quad \Gamma \equiv \frac{\partial^2 G}{\partial P^2} \quad\quad (9.2.20)$$

$$\text{Theta} \quad \Theta \equiv \frac{\partial G}{\partial t} \quad\quad (9.2.21)$$

---

[12]The term "partial derivatives" in this context refers, of course, to instantaneous rates of change. This is unfortunate coincidence of terminology is usually not a source of confusion, but readers should beware.

[13]Of course, "vega" is not a Greek letter and $\mathcal{V}$ is simply a script V.

$$\text{Rho} \quad R \; \equiv \; \frac{\partial G}{\partial r} \tag{9.2.22}$$

$$\text{Vega} \quad \mathcal{V} \; \equiv \; \frac{\partial G}{\partial \sigma}. \tag{9.2.23}$$

For the Black-Scholes formula (9.2.16), these option sensitivities can be evaluated explicitly:

$$\Delta \; \equiv \; \Phi(d_1) \tag{9.2.24}$$

$$\Gamma \; \equiv \; \frac{\phi(d_1)}{P\sigma\sqrt{T-t}} \tag{9.2.25}$$

$$\Theta \; \equiv \; -\frac{P\sigma}{2\sqrt{T-t}}\phi(d_1) - Xre^{-r(T-t)}\Phi(d_2) \tag{9.2.26}$$

$$R \; \equiv \; (T-t)Xe^{-r(T-t)}\Phi(d_2) \tag{9.2.27}$$

$$\mathcal{V} \; \equiv \; P\sqrt{T-t}\,\phi(d_1) \tag{9.2.28}$$

where $\phi(\cdot)$ is the standard normal probability density function. We shall have occasion to consider these measures again once we have developed methods for estimating option prices in Section 9.3.3.

9.2.2 The Martingale Approach

Once Black and Scholes (1973) and Merton (1973b) presented their option-pricing models, it quickly became apparent that their approach could be used to price a variety of other securities whose payoffs depend on the prices of other securities: Find some dynamic, costless self-financing portfolio strategy that can replicate the payoff of the derivative, and impose the no-arbitrage condition. This condition usually reduces to a PDE like (9.2.15), subject to boundary conditions that are determined by the specific terms of the derivative security.

It is an interesting fact that pricing derivative securities along these lines does not require any restrictions on agents' preferences other than nonsatiation, i.e., agents prefer more to less, which rules out arbitrage opportunities. Therefore, the pricing formula for any derivative security that can be priced in this fashion must be identical for *all* preferences that do not admit arbitrage. In particular, the pricing formula must be the same regardless of agents' risk tolerances, so that an economy composed of risk-neutral investors must yield the same option price as an economy composed of risk-averse investors. But under risk-neutrality, all assets must earn the same expected rate of return which, under assumption (A2), must equal the riskless rate r. This fundamental insight, due to Cox and Ross (1976), simplifies the computation of option-pricing formulas enormously because in a risk-neutral economy the option's price is simply the expected value of its payoff discounted at the riskless rate:

$$G(t) = e^{-r(T-t)} \, \mathrm{E}_t \big[\mathrm{Max}[P^*(T) - X, 0] \big]. \tag{9.2.29}$$

However, the conditional expectation in (9.2.29) must be evaluated with respect to the random variable $P^*(T)$, not $P(T)$, where $P^*(T)$ is the terminal stock price *adjusted for risk-neutrality*.

Specifically, under assumption (A3), the conditional distribution of $P(T)$ given $P(t)$ is simply a lognormal distribution with $\mathrm{E}[\log P(T) \mid P(t)] = \log P(t) + (\mu - \frac{\sigma^2}{2})(T-t)$ and $\mathrm{Var}[\log P(T) \mid P(t)] = \sigma^2(T-t)$. Under risk-neutrality, the expected rate of return for all assets must be r, and hence the conditional distribution of the *risk-neutralized* terminal stock price $P^*(T)$ is also lognormal, but with $\mathrm{E}[\log P(T) \mid P(t)] = \log P(t) + (r - \frac{\sigma^2}{2})(T-t)$ and $\mathrm{Var}[\log P(T) \mid P(t)] = \sigma^2(T-t)$.

For obvious reasons, this procedure is called the *risk-neutral pricing* method and under assumptions (A1) through (A4), the expectation in (9.2.29) may be evaluated explicitly as a function of the standard normal CDF and yields the Black-Scholes formula (9.2.16).

To emphasize the generality of the risk-neutral pricing method in valuing arbitrary payoff streams, (9.2.29) is often rewritten as

$$G(t) = e^{-r(T-t)} \, \mathrm{E}_t^* \big[\mathrm{Max}[P(T) - X, 0] \big], \tag{9.2.30}$$

where the asterisk in E_t^* indicates that the expectation is to be taken with respect to an adjusted probability distribution, adjusted to be consistent with risk-neutrality. In a more formal setting, Harrison and Kreps (1979) have shown that the adjusted probability distribution is precisely the distribution under which the stock price follows a martingale; thus they call the adjusted distribution the *equivalent martingale measure*. Accordingly, the risk-neutral pricing method is also known as the *martingale pricing technique*. We shall exploit this procedure extensively in Section 9.4 where we propose to evaluate expectations like (9.2.30) by Monte Carlo simulation.

9.3 Implementing Parametric Option Pricing Models

Because there are so many different types of options and other derivative securities, it is virtually impossible to describe a completely general method for implementing all derivative-pricing formulas. The particular features of each derivative security will often play a central role in how its pricing formula is to be applied most effectively. But there are several common aspects to every implementation of a *parametric* option-pricing model—a model in which the price dynamics of the underlying security, called the *fundamental asset*, is specified up to a finite number of parameters—and we shall focus on these common aspects in this section.

To simplify terminology, unless otherwise stated we shall use the term *option* to mean any general derivative security, and the term *stock* to mean the derivative security's underlying fundamental asset. Although there are certainly aspects of some derivative securities that differ dramatically from those of standard equity options and cannot be described in analogous terms, they need not concern us at the current level of generality. After developing a coherent framework for implementing general pricing formulas, we shall turn to modifications tailored to particular derivative securities.

9.3.1 Parameter Estimation of Asset Price Dynamics

The term "parametric" in this section's title is meant to emphasize the reliance of a class of option-pricing formulas on the particular assumptions concerning the fundamental asset's price dynamics. Although these rather strong assumptions often yield elegant and tractable expressions for the option's price, they are typically contradicted by the data, which does not bode well for the pricing formula's success. In fact, perhaps the most important aspect of a successful empirical implementation of any option-pricing model is correctly identifying the dynamics of the stock price, and uncertainty regarding these price dynamics will lead us to consider *nonparametric* alternatives in Chapter 12.

But for the moment, let us assert that the specific form of the stock price process $P(t)$ is known up to a vector of unknown parameters θ which lies in some parameter space Θ, and that it satisfies the following stochastic differential equation:

$$dP(t) \;=\; a(P, t; \alpha)\, dt + b(P, t; \beta)\, dB(t), \qquad t \in [0, T], \quad (9.3.1)$$

where $B(t)$ is a standard Wiener process and $\theta \equiv [\, \alpha'\; \beta'\,]'$ is a $(k \times 1)$ vector of unknown parameters. The functions $a(P, t; \alpha)$ and $b(P, t; \beta)$ are called the *drift* and *diffusion* functions, respectively, or the *coefficient functions* collectively. For example, the lognormal diffusion assumed by Black and Scholes (1973) is given by the following coefficient functions:

$$a(P, t; \alpha) \;=\; \mu P \qquad\qquad\qquad (9.3.2)$$

$$b(P, t; \beta) \;=\; \sigma P \qquad\qquad\qquad (9.3.3)$$

In this case, the parameter vector $\boldsymbol{\theta}$ consists of only two elements, the constants α and β.[14]

In the more general case the functions $a(P, t; \boldsymbol{\alpha})$ and $b(P, t; \boldsymbol{\beta})$ must be restricted in some fashion so as to ensure the existence of a solution to the stochastic differential equation (9.3.1) (see Arnold [1974], for example). Also, for tractability we assume that the coefficient functions only depend on the most recent price $P(t)$; hence the solution to (9.3.1) is a Markov process. This assumption is not as restrictive as it seems, since non-Markov processes can often be re-expressed as a vector Markov process by *expansion of the states*, i.e., by increasing the number of state variables so that the collection of prices and state variables is a vector-Markov process. In practice, however, expanding the states can also create intractabilities that may be more difficult to overcome than the non-Markovian nature of the original price process.

For option-pricing purposes, what concerns us is estimating $\boldsymbol{\theta}$, since pricing formulas for options on $P(t)$ will invariably be functions of some or all of the parameters in $\boldsymbol{\theta}$. In particular, suppose that an explicit expression for the option-pricing function exists and is given by $G(P(t), \boldsymbol{\theta})$ where other dependencies on observable constants such as strike price, time-to-maturity, and the interest rate have been suppressed for notational convenience.[15] An estimator of the option price $\hat{G}$ may then be written as $\hat{G} = G(P(t), \hat{\boldsymbol{\theta}})$, where $\hat{\boldsymbol{\theta}}$ is some estimator of the parameter vector $\boldsymbol{\theta}$. Naturally, the properties of $\hat{G}$ are closely related to the properties of $\hat{\boldsymbol{\theta}}$, so that imprecise estimators of the parameter vector will yield imprecise option prices and vice versa. To quantify this relation between the precision of $\hat{G}$ and of $\hat{\boldsymbol{\theta}}$, we must first consider the procedure for obtaining $\hat{\boldsymbol{\theta}}$.

Maximum Likelihood Estimation

The most direct method for obtaining $\hat{\boldsymbol{\theta}}$ is to estimate it from historical data. Suppose we have a sequence of $n+1$ historical observations of $P(t)$ sampled at non-stochastic dates $t_0 < t_1 < \cdots < t_n$ which are *not necessarily equally spaced*. This is an important feature of financial time series since markets are generally closed on weekends and holidays, yielding irregular sampling intervals. Since $P(t)$ is a continuous-time Markov process by assumption, irregular sampling poses no conceptual problems; the joint density function f of the sample is given by the following product:

$$f(P_0, \ldots, P_n; \boldsymbol{\theta}) \;=\; f_0(P_0; \boldsymbol{\theta}) \prod_{k=1}^{n} f(P_k, t_k \mid P_{k-1}, t_{k-1}; \boldsymbol{\theta}), \qquad (9.3.4)$$

---

[14]Note that although the drift and diffusion functions depend on distinct parameter vectors α and β, these two vectors may contain some parameters in common.

[15]Even if G cannot be obtained in closed-form, θ is a necessary input for numerical solutions of G and must still be estimated.

where $P_k \equiv P(t_k)$, $f_0(P_0)$ is the marginal density function of P_0, and $f(P_k, t_k \mid P_{k-1}, t_{k-1}; \boldsymbol{\theta})$ is the conditional density function of P_k given P_{k-1}, also called the *transition density function*. For notational simplicity, we will write $f(P_k, t_k \mid P_{k-1}, t_{k-1}; \boldsymbol{\theta})$ simply as f_k.

Given (9.3.4) and the observations $P_0, \ldots, P_n$, the parameter vector may be estimated by the method of *maximum likelihood* (see Section A.4 of the Appendix and Silvey [1975, Chapter 4]). To define the maximum likelihood estimator $\hat{\boldsymbol{\theta}}$, let $\mathcal{L}(\boldsymbol{\theta})$ denote the *log-likelihood function*, the natural logarithm of the joint density function of $P_0, \ldots, P_n$ viewed as a function of $\boldsymbol{\theta}$:

$$\mathcal{L}(\boldsymbol{\theta}) \equiv \sum_{k=0}^{n} \log f_k. \tag{9.3.5}$$

The maximum likelihood estimator is then given by

$$\hat{\boldsymbol{\theta}} \equiv \underset{\boldsymbol{\theta} \in \Theta}{\operatorname{argmax}} \, \mathcal{L}(\boldsymbol{\theta}). \tag{9.3.6}$$

Under suitable regularity conditions, $\hat{\boldsymbol{\theta}}$ is consistent and has the following normal limiting distribution:

$$\sqrt{n}(\hat{\boldsymbol{\theta}} - \boldsymbol{\theta}) \overset{a}{\sim} \mathcal{N}\big(0, \mathcal{I}^{-1}(\boldsymbol{\theta})\big), \qquad \mathcal{I}(\boldsymbol{\theta}) \equiv \lim_{n \to \infty} -\mathrm{E}\left[\frac{1}{n} \frac{\partial^2 \mathcal{L}(\boldsymbol{\theta})}{\partial \boldsymbol{\theta} \, \partial \boldsymbol{\theta}'}\right], \tag{9.3.7}$$

where $\mathcal{I}(\boldsymbol{\theta})$ is called the *information matrix*. When n is large, the asymptotic distribution in (9.3.7) allows us to approximate the variance of $\hat{\boldsymbol{\theta}}$ as

$$\mathrm{Var}[\hat{\boldsymbol{\theta}}] \approx \frac{1}{n} \mathcal{I}^{-1}(\hat{\boldsymbol{\theta}}), \tag{9.3.8}$$

and the information matrix $\mathcal{I}(\boldsymbol{\theta})$ may also be estimated in the natural way:

$$\hat{\mathcal{I}} = \frac{1}{n} \frac{\partial^2 \mathcal{L}(\hat{\boldsymbol{\theta}})}{\partial \boldsymbol{\theta} \, \partial \boldsymbol{\theta}'}. \tag{9.3.9}$$

Moreover, $\hat{\boldsymbol{\theta}}$ has been shown to be asymptotically efficient in the class of all consistent and uniformly asymptotically normal (CUAN) estimators; that is, it has the smallest asymptotic variance of all estimators that are CUAN, hence it is the preferred method of estimation whenever feasible. Of course, maximum likelihood estimation is only feasible when the likelihood function can be obtained in closed form which, in our case, requires obtaining the transition density functions f_k in closed form. Unfortunately, a closed-form expression for f_k for arbitrary drift and diffusion functions cannot be obtained in general.

However, it is possible to characterize f_k implicitly as the solution to a PDE. In particular, fix the conditioning variables P_{k-1} and t_{k-1} and let f_k be a function of P_k and t_k; to emphasize this, we drop the subscript k from the arguments and write $f_k(P, t \mid P_{k-1}, t_{k-1})$. Then it follows from the Fokker-Planck or *forward* equation that f_k must satisfy the following (see Lo [1988] for a derivation):

$$\frac{\partial f_k}{\partial t} = -\frac{\partial(a f_k)}{\partial P} + \frac{1}{2}\frac{\partial^2(b^2 f_k)}{\partial P^2} \tag{9.3.10}$$

with initial condition

$$f_k(P, t_{k-1} \mid P_{k-1}, t_{k-1}) = \delta(P - P_{k-1}), \tag{9.3.11}$$

where $\delta(P - P_{k-1})$ is the Dirac-delta function centered at P_{k-1}. Maximum likelihood estimation is feasible whenever (9.3.10) can be solved explicitly and this depends on how complicated the coefficient functions a and b are.

Once f_k is obtained, $\hat{\theta}$ can be computed numerically given the data $P_0, \dots, P_n$. To interpret this estimator, we must check that the regularity conditions for the consistency and asymptotic normality of $\hat{\theta}$ are satisfied. In some cases of interest they are not. For example, a lognormal diffusion $dP = \mu P \, dt + \sigma P \, dB$ violates the stationarity requirement. But in this case, a simple log-transformation of the data does satisfy the regularity conditions: $r_1, r_2, \dots, r_n$, where $r_k \equiv \log P_k/P_{k-1}$, is a stationary sequence. Maximum likelihood estimation of θ may then be performed with $\{r_k\}$. We shall return to this example in Section 9.3.2.

GMM Estimation

For many combinations of coefficient functions a and b, (9.3.10) cannot be solved explicitly, hence for these cases maximum likelihood estimation is infeasible. An alternative proposed by Hansen and Scheinkman (1995) is to apply Hansen's (1982) generalized method of moments (GMM) estimator, which they extend to the case of strictly stationary continuous-time Markov processes (see the Appendix for an exposition of GMM).

The focus of any GMM procedure is, of course, the moment conditions in which the parameter vector θ is implicitly defined. The GMM estimator is that parameter vector $\hat{\theta}$ that minimizes the "distance" between the sample moment conditions and their population counterparts.

The properties of a GMM estimator depend critically on the choice of moment conditions and the distance metric, and for standard discrete-time GMM applications, these two issues have been studied quite thoroughly. Moment conditions are typically suggested by the interaction of conditioning information and optimality or equilibrium conditions such as Euler equations, e.g., the *orthogonality conditions* of linear instrumental variables estimation (see the Appendix, Section A.1). In some cases, the optimal (in an asymptotic sense) distance metric can be deduced explicitly (see, for example, Hamilton [1994, Chapter 14]), and efficiency bounds can be obtained (see Hansen (1985) and Hansen, Heaton, and Ogaki (1988)).

But for continuous-time applications in finance, especially those involving derivative securities, much less is known about the properties of GMM estimators. Indeed, one of Hansen and Scheinkman's (1995) main contributions is to show how to generate moment conditions for continuous-time Markov processes with discretely sampled data. Although a complete exposition of GMM estimation for continuous-time processes is beyond the scope of this text, the central thrust of their approach can be illustrated through a simple example.

Suppose we wish to estimate the parameters of the following stationary diffusion process:

$$dp = -\gamma(p - \mu)\, dt + \sigma\, dB, \qquad p(0) = p_o > 0, \qquad \gamma > 0. \quad (9.3.12)$$

This is a continuous-time version of a stationary $AR(1)$ process with unconditional mean μ (see Section 9.3.4 for further discussion), and hence it satisfies the hypotheses of Hansen and Scheinkman (1995).

To generate moment conditions for $\{p(t)\}$, Hansen and Scheinkman (1995) use the *infinitesimal generator* $\mathcal{D}_o$, also known as the *Dynkin operator*, which is the time-derivative of a conditional expectation. Specifically,

$$\mathcal{D}_o[\cdot] \equiv \frac{d}{dt}\, \mathrm{E}_o[\cdot], \qquad\qquad (9.3.13)$$

where the expectations operator $\mathrm{E}_o[\cdot]$ is a conditional expectation, conditioned on $p(0) = p_o$.

This operator has several important applications for deriving moment conditions of diffusions. For example, consider the following heuristic calculation of the expectation of dp:

$$\mathrm{E}_o[dp] = \mathrm{E}_o[-\gamma(p - \mu)\, dt] + \mathrm{E}_o[\sigma\, dB] \qquad (9.3.14)$$

$$= -\gamma(\mathrm{E}_o[p] - \mu)\, dt + \sigma \mathrm{E}_o[dB] \qquad (9.3.15)$$

$$d\mathrm{E}_o[p] = -\gamma(\mathrm{E}_o[p] - \mu)\, dt \qquad (9.3.16)$$

$$\frac{d}{dt}\mathrm{E}_o[p] = -\gamma(\mathrm{E}_o[p] - \mu) \qquad (9.3.17)$$

$$\mathcal{D}_o[p] = -\gamma(\mathrm{E}_o[p] - \mu), \qquad (9.3.18)$$

where (9.3.14) and (9.3.15) follow from the fact the expectation of a linear function is the linear functions of the expectation, (9.3.16) follows from the same property for the differential operator and from the fact that increments of Brownian motion have zero expectation, and (9.3.17) is another way of expressing (9.3.16).

Before considering the importance of (9.3.18), observe that (9.3.17) is a first-order linear ordinary differential equation in $E_o[p]$ which can easily be solved to yield a closed-form expression for $E_o[p]$ (note the initial condition $E_o[p(0)] = p_o$):

$$E_o[p] = p_o\, e^{-\gamma t} + \mu.$$

By applying similar arguments to the stochastic differential equations of p^2, p^3, and so on—which may be obtained explicitly via Itô's Lemma—all higher moments of p may be computed in the same way.

Now consider the unconditional version of the infinitesimal generator $\mathcal{D}[\cdot] \equiv d E[\cdot]/dt$. A series of calculations similar to (9.3.14)–(9.3.18) follows, but with one important difference: the time derivative of the unconditional expectation is zero, since p is a strictly stationary process, hence we have the restriction:

$$\mathcal{D}[p] = -\gamma(E[p] - \mu) = 0 \qquad (9.3.19)$$

which implies

$$E[p] = \mu \qquad (9.3.20)$$

and this yields a first-moment condition: The unconditional expectation of p must equal the steady-state mean μ.

More importantly, we can apply the infinitesimal generator to any well-behaved transformation $f(\cdot)$ of p and by Itô's Lemma we have:

$$\mathcal{D}[f(p)] = E\left[-f'(p)\,\gamma(p - \mu) + \frac{\sigma^2}{2} f''(p)\right] = 0 \qquad (9.3.21)$$

which yields an infinite number of moment conditions—one for each f—related to the marginal distribution of $f(p)$. From these moment conditions, and under the regularity conditions specified by Hansen and Scheinkman (1995), GMM estimation may be performed in the usual way.

Hansen and Scheinkman (1995) also generate *multipoint* moment conditions—conditions which exploit information contained in the conditional and joint distributions of $f(p)$—making creative use of the properties of time-reversed diffusions along the way, and they provide asymptotic approximations for statistical inference. Although it is too early to say how their approach will perform in practice, it seems quite promising and, for many Itô processes of practical interest, the GMM estimator is currently the only one that is both computationally feasible and consistent.

9.3.2 Estimating σ in the Black-Scholes Model

To illustrate the techniques described in Section 9.3.1, we consider the implementation of the Black-Scholes model (9.2.16) in which the parameter σ must be estimated.

A common misunderstanding about σ is that it is the standard deviation of simple returns R_t of the stock. If, for example, the annual standard deviation of IBM's stock return is 30%, it is often assumed that $\sigma = 0.30$. To see why this is incorrect, let prices $P(t)$ follow a lognormal diffusion (9.2.2) as required by the Black-Scholes model (see Section 9.2.1) and assume, for expositional simplicity, that prices are sampled at equally spaced intervals of length h in the interval $[0, T]$, hence $P_k \equiv P(kh)$, $k = 0, 1, \ldots, n$ and $T = nh$. Then simple returns $R_k(h) \equiv (P_k/P_{k-1}) - 1$ are lognormally distributed with mean and variance:

$$E[R_k(h)] = e^{\mu h} - 1 \tag{9.3.22}$$

$$\text{Var}[R_k(h)] = e^{2\mu h} \cdot \left[e^{\sigma^2 h} - 1\right]. \tag{9.3.23}$$

Therefore, the magnitude of IBM's σ cannot be gauged solely by the 30% estimate since this is an estimate of $\sqrt{\text{Var}[R_k(h)]}$ and not of σ. In particular, solving (9.3.22) and (9.3.23) for σ yields the following:

$$\sigma = \left[\frac{1}{h} \log\left(1 + \frac{\text{Var}[R_k(h)]}{(1 + E[R_k(h)])^2}\right)\right]^{1/2}. \tag{9.3.24}$$

Therefore, a mean and standard deviation of 10% and 30%, respectively, for IBM's annual simple returns implies a value of 26.8% for σ. While 30% and 26.8% may seem almost identical for most practical purposes, the former value implies a Black-Scholes price of $8.48 for a one-year call option with a $35 strike price on a $40 stock, whereas the latter value implies a Black-Scholes price of $8.10 on the same option, an economically significant difference.

Since most published statistics for equity returns are based on simple returns, (9.3.24) is a useful formula to obtain a quick "ballpark" estimate of σ when historical data is not readily available. If historical data *are* available, it is a simple matter to compute the maximum likelihood estimator of σ using continuously compounded returns, as discussed in Sections 9.3.1 and 9.3.3. In particular, applying Itô's Lemma to $\log P(t)$ and substituting (9.2.2) for dP yields

$$d\log P = (\mu - \tfrac{1}{2}\sigma^2)dt + \sigma dB = \alpha dt + \sigma dB \tag{9.3.25}$$

where $\alpha \equiv \mu - \tfrac{1}{2}\sigma^2$. Therefore, continuously compounded returns $r_k(h) \equiv \log(P_k/P_{k-1})$ are IID normal random variables with mean αh and variance $\sigma^2 h$ hence the sample variance of $r_k(h)/\sqrt{h}$ should be a good estimator of σ^2; in fact, the sample variance of $r_k(h)/\sqrt{h}$ is the maximum likelihood estimator of σ. More formally, under (9.3.25) the likelihood function of a sample of continuously compounded returns $r_1(h), \ldots, r_n(h)$ is

$$\mathcal{L}(\alpha, \sigma) = -\frac{n}{2}\log(2\pi\sigma^2 h) - \frac{1}{2\sigma^2 h}\sum_{k=1}^{n}(r_k(h) - \alpha h)^2 \tag{9.3.26}$$

and in this case the maximum likelihood estimators for α and σ^2 can be obtained in closed form:

$$\hat{\alpha} \;=\; \frac{1}{nh} \sum_{k=1}^{n} r_k(h) \tag{9.3.27}$$

$$\hat{\sigma}^2 \;=\; \frac{1}{nh} \sum_{k=1}^{n} (r_k(h) - \hat{\alpha}h)^2. \tag{9.3.28}$$

Moreover, because the $r_k(h)$'s are IID normal random variables under the dynamics (9.2.2), the regularity conditions for the consistency and asymptotic normality of the estimator $\hat{\sigma}^2$ are satisfied (see the Appendix, Section A.4). Therefore, we are assured that $\hat{\alpha}$ and $\hat{\sigma}^2$ are asymptotically efficient in the class of CUAN estimators, with asymptotic covariance matrix given by (9.3.8).

Irregularly Sampled Data
To see why irregularly sampled data poses no problems for continuous-time processes, observe that the sampling interval h is arbitrary and can change mid-sample without affecting the functional form of the likelihood function (9.3.26). Suppose, for example, we measure returns annually for the first n_1 observations and then monthly for the next n_2 observations. If h is measured in units of one year, so that $h = 1$ indicates a one-year holding period, the maximum likelihood estimator of σ^2 for the $n_1 + n_2$ observations is given by

$$\hat{\sigma}^2 \;=\; \frac{1}{n_1} \sum_{k=1}^{n_1} \Big(r_k(1) - \overline{r(1)} \Big)^2$$

$$+\; \frac{1}{n_2} \sum_{k=n_1+1}^{n_2} \left(\frac{r_k(1/12) - \overline{r(1/12)}}{\sqrt{1/12}} \right)^2, \tag{9.3.29}$$

where

$$\overline{r(1)} \;=\; \frac{1}{n_1} \sum_{k=1}^{n_1} r_k(1), \qquad \overline{r(1/12)} \;=\; \frac{1}{n_2} \sum_{k=1}^{n_2} r_k(1/12).$$

Observe that the second term of (9.3.29) may be rewritten as

$$\frac{12}{n_2} \sum_{k=n_1+1}^{n_2} \Big(r_k(1/12) - \overline{r(1/12)} \Big)^2,$$

which is simply the variance estimator of monthly continuously compounded returns, rescaled to an annual frequency.

The ease with which irregularly sampled data can be accommodated is one of the greatest advantages of continuous-time stochastic processes.

However, this advantage comes at some cost: this great flexibility is the result of strong parametric restrictions that each continuous-time process imposes on *all* its finite-dimensional distributions (see Section 9.1.1 for the definition of a finite-dimensional distribution). In particular, the stochastic differential equation (9.3.25) imposes independence and normality on *all* increments of $\log P(t)$ and linearity of the mean and variance in the increment interval, hence the continuously compounded return between a Friday and a Monday must have three times the mean and three times the variance of the continuously compounded return between a Tuesday and a Wednesday, the Tuesday/Thursday return must have the same distribution as the Saturday/Monday return, and so on. In fact, the specification of a continuous-time stochastic process such as (9.3.25) includes an infinity of parametric assumptions. Therefore, the convenience that continuous-time stochastic processes affords in dealing with irregular sampling should be weighed carefully against the many implicit assumptions that come with it.

Continuous-Record Asymptotics

Since we can estimate α and σ from arbitrarily sampled data, a natural question to consider is how to sample returns so as to obtain the "best" estimator? Are 10 annual observations preferable to 100 daily observations, or should we match the sampling interval to the horizon we are ultimately interested in, e.g., the time-to-maturity of the option we wish to value?

To address these issues, consider again a sample of $n+1$ prices $P_0, P_1, \ldots,$ P_n equally spaced at intervals of length h over the fixed time span $[0, T]$ so that $P_k \equiv P(kh)$, $k = 0, \ldots, n$, and $T \equiv nh$. The asymptotic variance of the maximum likelihood estimator of $[\alpha\ \sigma^2]'$ is then given by (9.3.7), which may be evaluated explicitly in this case as:

$$\text{Var}[\hat{\alpha}] \overset{a}{\approx} \frac{\sigma^2}{T} \tag{9.3.30}$$

$$\text{Var}[\hat{\sigma}^2] \overset{a}{\approx} \frac{2\sigma^4}{n}. \tag{9.3.31}$$

Observe that (9.3.31) does not depend on the sampling interval h. As n increases without bound while T is fixed (hence h decreases to 0), $\hat{\sigma}^2$ becomes more precise. This suggests that the "best" estimator for σ^2, the one with smallest asymptotic variance, is the one based on as many observations as possible, regardless of what their sampling interval is.

Interestingly, this result does not hold for the estimator of α, whose asymptotic variance depends on T and not n. More frequent sampling within a fixed time span—often called *continuous-record* asymptotics—will not increase the precision of $\hat{\alpha}$, and the "best" estimator for α is one based on as long a time span as possible.

Table 9.2a. *Asymptotic standard errors for $\hat{\alpha}$.*

n	$\frac{1}{2}$	$\frac{1}{4}$	$\frac{1}{8}$	$\frac{1}{16}$	$\frac{1}{32}$	$\frac{1}{64}$	$\frac{1}{128}$	$\frac{1}{256}$	$\frac{1}{512}$	$\frac{1}{1,024}$
						h				
2	0.2000	0.2828	0.4000	0.5657	0.8000	1.1314	1.6000	2.2627	3.2000	4.5255
4	0.1414	0.2000	0.2828	0.4000	0.5657	0.8000	1.1314	1.6000	2.2627	3.2000
8	0.1000	0.1414	0.2000	0.2828	0.4000	0.5657	0.8000	1.1314	1.6000	2.2627
16	0.0707	0.1000	0.1414	0.2000	0.2828	0.4000	0.5657	0.8000	1.1314	1.6000
32	0.0500	0.0707	0.1000	0.1414	0.2000	0.2828	0.4000	0.5657	0.8000	1.1314
64	0.0354	0.0500	0.0707	0.1000	0.1414	0.2000	0.2828	0.4000	0.5657	0.8000
128	0.0250	0.0354	0.0500	0.0707	0.1000	0.1414	0.2000	0.2828	0.4000	0.5657
256	0.0177	0.0250	0.0354	0.0500	0.0707	0.1000	0.1414	0.2000	0.2828	0.4000
512	0.0125	0.0177	0.0250	0.0354	0.0500	0.0707	0.1000	0.1414	0.2000	0.2828
1,024	0.0088	0.0125	0.0177	0.0250	0.0354	0.0500	0.0707	0.1000	0.1414	0.2000

Asymptotic standard error of $\hat{\alpha}$ for various values of n and h, assuming a base interval of $h = 1$ year and $\sigma = 0.20$. Recall that $T \equiv nh$; hence the values $n = 64$ and $h = 1/16$ imply a sample of 64 observations equally spaced over 4 years.

Tables 9.2a and 9.2b illustrate the sharp differences between $\hat{\alpha}$ and $\hat{\sigma}^2$ by reporting asymptotic standard errors for the two estimators for various values of n and h, assuming a base interval of $h=1$ year and $\sigma=0.20$. Recall that $T \equiv nh$, hence the values $n=64$ and $h=\frac{1}{16}$ imply a sample of 64 observations equally spaced over 4 years.

In Table 9.2a the standard error of $\hat{\alpha}$ declines as we move down the table (corresponding to increasing T), increases as we move left (corresponding to decreasing T), and remains the same along the diagonals (corresponding to a fixed T). For purposes of estimating α, having 2 observations measured at 6-month intervals yields as accurate an estimator as having 1,024 observations measured four times per day.

In Table 9.2b the pattern is quite different. The entries are identical across the columns—only the number of observations n matters for determining the standard error of $\hat{\sigma}^2$. In this case, a sample of 1,024 observations measured four times a day is an order of magnitude more accurate than a sample of 2 observations measured at six-month intervals.

The consistency of $\hat{\sigma}^2$ and the inconsistency of $\hat{\alpha}$ under continuous-record asymptotics, first observed by Merton (1980) for the case of geometric Brownian motion, is true for general diffusion processes and is an artifact of the non-differentiability of diffusion sample paths (see Bertsimas, Kogan, and Lo [1996] for further discussion). In fact, if we observe a continuous record of $P(t)$ over any finite interval, we can recover *without error* the diffusion coefficient $\sigma(\cdot)$, even in cases where it is time-varying. Of course, in

Table 9.2b. *Asymptotic standard errors for $\hat{\sigma}^2$.*

n	$\frac{1}{2}$	$\frac{1}{4}$	$\frac{1}{8}$	$\frac{1}{16}$	$\frac{1}{32}$	$\frac{1}{64}$	$\frac{1}{128}$	$\frac{1}{256}$	$\frac{1}{512}$	$\frac{1}{1,024}$
					h					
2	0.0400	0.0400	0.0400	0.0400	0.0400	0.0400	0.0400	0.0400	0.0400	0.0400
4	0.0283	0.0283	0.0283	0.0283	0.0283	0.0283	0.0283	0.0283	0.0283	0.0283
8	0.0200	0.0200	0.0200	0.0200	0.0200	0.0200	0.0200	0.0200	0.0200	0.0200
16	0.0141	0.0141	0.0141	0.0141	0.0141	0.0141	0.0141	0.0141	0.0141	0.0141
32	0.0100	0.0100	0.0100	0.0100	0.0100	0.0100	0.0100	0.0100	0.0100	0.0100
64	0.0071	0.0071	0.0071	0.0071	0.0071	0.0071	0.0071	0.0071	0.0071	0.0071
128	0.0050	0.0050	0.0050	0.0050	0.0050	0.0050	0.0050	0.0050	0.0050	0.0050
256	0.0035	0.0035	0.0035	0.0035	0.0035	0.0035	0.0035	0.0035	0.0035	0.0035
512	0.0025	0.0025	0.0025	0.0025	0.0025	0.0025	0.0025	0.0025	0.0025	0.0025
1,024	0.0018	0.0018	0.0018	0.0018	0.0018	0.0018	0.0018	0.0018	0.0018	0.0018

Asymptotic standard error of $\hat{\sigma}^2$ for various values of n and h, assuming a base interval of $h = 1$ year and $\sigma = 0.20$. Recall that $T \equiv nh$; hence the values $n = 64$ and $h = 1/16$ imply a sample of 64 observations equally spaced over 4 years.

practice we never observe continuous sample paths—the notion of continuous time is an approximation, and the magnitude of the approximation error varies from one application to the next.

As the sampling interval becomes finer, other problems may arise such as the effects of the bid-ask spread, nonsynchronous trading, and related market microstructure issues (see Chapter 3). For example, suppose we decide to use daily data to estimate σ—how should weekends and holidays be treated? Some choose to ignore them altogether, which is tantamount to assuming that prices exhibit *no* volatility when markets are closed, with the counterfactual implication that Friday's closing price is always equal to Monday's opening price. Alternatively, we may use (9.3.29) in accounting for weekends, but such a procedure implicitly assumes that the price process exhibits the *same* volatility when markets are closed, implying that the Friday-to-Monday return is three times more volatile than the Monday-to-Tuesday return. This is also counterfactual, as French and Roll (1986) have shown.

The benefits of more frequent sampling must be weighed against the costs, as measured by the types of biases associated with more finely sampled data. Unfortunately, there are no general guidelines as to how to make such a tradeoff—it must be made on an individual basis with the particular application and data at hand.[16]

---

[16]See Bertsimas, Kogan, and Lo (1996), Lo and MacKinlay (1989), Perron (1991), and Shiller and Perron (1985) for a more detailed analysis of the interactions between sampling interval and sample size.

9.3.3 Quantifying the Precision of Option Price Estimators

Once the maximum likelihood estimator $\hat{\boldsymbol{\theta}}$ of the underlying asset's parameters is obtained, the maximum likelihood estimator of the option price G may be constructed by inserting $\hat{\boldsymbol{\theta}}$ into the option-pricing formula (or into the numerical algorithm that generates the price).[17] Since $\hat{\boldsymbol{\theta}}$ contains estimation error, $\hat{G} \equiv G(P(t), \hat{\boldsymbol{\theta}})$ will also contain estimation error, and for trading and hedging applications it is imperative that we have some measure of its precision. This can be constructed by applying a first-order Taylor expansion to $G(\hat{\boldsymbol{\theta}})$ to calculate its asymptotic distribution (see Section A.4 of the Appendix)

$$\sqrt{n}(\hat{G} - G) \overset{a}{\sim} \mathcal{N}(0, V_f(\boldsymbol{\theta})) \tag{9.3.32}$$

$$V_f(\boldsymbol{\theta}) \equiv \frac{\partial G(P(t), \boldsymbol{\theta})'}{\partial \boldsymbol{\theta}} \mathcal{I}^{-1}(\boldsymbol{\theta}) \frac{\partial G(P(t), \boldsymbol{\theta})}{\partial \boldsymbol{\theta}}, \tag{9.3.33}$$

where $G \equiv G(P(t), \boldsymbol{\theta})$ and $\mathcal{I}(\boldsymbol{\theta})$ is the information matrix defined in (9.3.7). Therefore, for large n the variance of $\hat{G}$ may be approximated by:

$$\text{Var}[\hat{G}] \approx \frac{1}{n} V_f(\boldsymbol{\theta}), \tag{9.3.34}$$

and V_f may be estimated in the natural way:

$$\hat{V}_f = V_f(\hat{\boldsymbol{\theta}}) = \frac{\partial G(P(t), \hat{\boldsymbol{\theta}})'}{\partial \boldsymbol{\theta}} \mathcal{I}^{-1}(\hat{\boldsymbol{\theta}}) \frac{\partial G(P(t), \hat{\boldsymbol{\theta}})}{\partial \boldsymbol{\theta}}. \tag{9.3.35}$$

In much the same way, the precision of the estimators of an option's sensitivity to its arguments—the option's delta, gamma, theta, rho, and vega (see Section 9.2.1)—may also be readily quantified.

The Black-Scholes Case
As an illustration of these results, consider the case of Black and Scholes (1973) in which $P(t)$ follows a geometric Brownian motion,

$$dP(t) = \mu P(t)\, dt + \sigma P(t)\, dB(t) \tag{9.3.36}$$

and in which the only parameter of interest is σ. Since the maximum likelihood estimator $\hat{\sigma}^2$ of σ^2 has an asymptotic distribution given by

---

[17]This follows from the principle of invariance: The maximum likelihood estimator of a nonlinear function of a parameter vector is the nonlinear function of the parameter vector's maximum likelihood estimator. See, for example, Zehna (1966).

$\sqrt{n}(\hat{\sigma}^2 - \sigma^2) \overset{a}{\sim} \mathcal{N}(0, 2\sigma^4)$ (see Section 9.3.2), the asymptotic distribution of the Black-Scholes call-option price estimator $\hat{G}$ is

$$\sqrt{n}(\hat{G} - G) \overset{a}{\sim} \mathcal{N}(0, V_f), \qquad V_f \equiv \frac{T-t}{2} P^2(t)\,\sigma^2\,\phi^2(d_1), \qquad (9.3.37)$$

where $\phi(\cdot)$ is the standard normal probability density function and d_1 is given in (9.2.17).

From the asymptotic variance V_f given in (9.3.37), some simple comparative static results may be derived:

$$\frac{\partial V_f}{\partial P} = -P\sigma\sqrt{T-t}\,\phi^2(d_1)\,d_2, \qquad \frac{\partial V_f}{\partial X} = \frac{P^2}{X}\sigma\sqrt{T-t}\,\phi^2(d_1)\,d_1 \quad (9.3.38)$$

$$\frac{\partial V_f}{\partial(T-t)} = \tfrac{1}{2}P^2\,\sigma^2\,\phi^2(d_1)$$

$$\times \left[1 - \left(\frac{(r + \tfrac{1}{2}\sigma^2)(T-t)}{\sigma\sqrt{T-t}}\right)^2 \left(\frac{\log(P/X)}{\sigma\sqrt{T-t}}\right)^2\right]. \qquad (9.3.39)$$

The following inequalities may then be established:

$$\frac{\partial V_f}{\partial P} \overset{\geq}{\underset{<}{}} 0 \quad \text{iff} \quad \frac{P}{X} \overset{\leq}{\underset{>}{}} c_1 \qquad (9.3.40)$$

$$\frac{\partial V_f}{\partial X} \overset{\geq}{\underset{<}{}} 0 \quad \text{iff} \quad \frac{P}{X} \overset{\geq}{\underset{<}{}} c_2 \qquad (9.3.41)$$

$$\frac{\partial V_f}{\partial(T-t)} > 0 \quad \text{if} \quad \frac{P}{X} \notin \left(c_2, \frac{1}{c_2}\right) \qquad (9.3.42)$$

$$\frac{\partial V_f}{\partial(T-t)} > 0 \quad \text{if} \quad c_3 < 1, \qquad (9.3.43)$$

where

$$c_1 \equiv e^{-\left(r - \frac{\sigma^2}{2}\right)(T-t)}$$

$$c_2 \equiv e^{-\left(r + \frac{\sigma^2}{2}\right)(T-t)}$$

$$c_3 \equiv \frac{\sqrt{T-t}}{\sigma}\left(r + \frac{\sigma^2}{2}\right).$$

Inequality (9.3.40) shows that the accuracy of $\hat{G}$ decreases with the level of the stock price as long as the ratio of the stock price to the strike price is less than c_1. However, as the stock price increases beyond Xc_1, the accuracy of

Table 9.3. *Cutoff values for comparative statics of* V_f.

$T-t$	c_1	c_2	$1/c_2$	c_3
1	1.0015	0.9967	1.0033	0.0482
2	1.0029	0.9933	1.0067	0.0682
4	1.0059	0.9867	1.0135	0.0964
8	1.0118	0.9736	1.0271	0.1363
12	1.0177	0.9607	1.0409	0.1670
24	1.0358	0.9229	1.0835	0.2361
48	1.0729	0.8518	1.1740	0.3339

$\hat{G}$ begins to increase. Inequality (9.3.41) shows a similar pattern for V_f with respect to the strike price.

Interestingly, inequality (9.3.43) does not depend on either the stock or strike prices, and hence for shorter maturity options the accuracy of $\hat{G}$ will increase with the time-to-maturity $T-t$. But even if (9.3.43) is not satisfied, the accuracy of $\hat{G}$ may still decline with $T-t$ if (9.3.42) holds.

Table 9.3 reports values of c_1 through c_3 for various values of $T-t$ assuming an annual interest rate of 5% and an annual standard deviation of 50%, corresponding to weekly values of $r = \log(1.05)/52$ and $\sigma = 0.50/\sqrt{52}$. Given the numerical values of c_2 and $1/c_2$, (9.3.42) will be satisfied by options that are far enough in- or out-of-the-money. For example, if the stock price is $40, then options maturing in 24 weeks with strike prices greater than $42.09 or less than $38.02 will be more precisely estimated as the time-to-maturity declines. This is consistent with the finding of MacBeth and Merville (1979, 1980) that biases of in- and out-of-the-money options decrease as the time-to-maturity declines, and also supports the observation by Gultekin, Rogalski, and Tiniç (1982) that the Black-Scholes formula is more accurate for short-lived options.[18]

Through first-order Taylor expansions (see Section A.4 of the Appendix), the accuracy of the option's sensitivities (9.2.24)–(9.2.28) can also be readily derived, and thus the accuracy of dynamic hedging strategies can be measured. For convenience, we report the asymptotic variances of these quantities in Table 9.4.

9.3.4 The Effects of Asset Return Predictability

The martingale pricing method described in Section 9.2.2 exploits the fact that the pricing equation (9.2.15) is independent of the drift of $P(t)$. Since

---

[18]There are, of course, other possible explanations for such empirical regularities, such as the presence of stochastic volatility or a misspecification of the stock price dynamics.

Table 9.4. *Asymptotic variances of Black-Scholes call price sensitivity estimators.*

Estimator	Asymptotic Variance
$\hat{\Delta}$	$\frac{1}{2}\phi^2(d_1)\, d_2^2$
$\hat{\Gamma}$	$\frac{1}{2}\Gamma^2(d_1 d_2 - 1)^2$
$\hat{\Theta}$	$2\sigma^4\left[-\dfrac{P\phi(d_1)(1+d_1 d_2)}{4\sigma\sqrt{T-t}} + \dfrac{Xre^{-r(T-t)}\phi(d_2)d_1}{2\sigma^2}\right]^2$
$\hat{R}$	$\frac{1}{2}\left(X(T-t)e^{-r(T-t)}d_1\phi(d_2)\right)^2$
$\hat{V}$	$\frac{1}{2}(Vd_1 d_2)^2$

These asymptotic variances are based on the assumption that the variance estimator $\hat{\sigma}^2$ is the maximum likelihood estimator which has asymptotic distribution $\sqrt{n}(\hat{\sigma}^2 - \sigma^2) \overset{a}{\sim} \mathcal{N}(0, 2\sigma^4)$, hence $\sqrt{n}(F(\hat{\sigma}^2) - F(\sigma^2)) \overset{a}{\sim} \mathcal{N}(0, 2\sigma^4(\partial F(\sigma^2)/\partial \sigma^2)^2)$ where $F(\sigma^2)$ is the option sensitivity. Following standard conventions, the expressions reported in the table are the asymptotic variances of $\sqrt{n}(F(\hat{\sigma}^2) - F(\sigma^2))$ and must be divided by the sample size n to obtain the asymptotic variances of the (unnormalized) sensitivities $F(\hat{\sigma}^2)$.

the drift does not enter into the PDE (9.2.15), for purposes of pricing options it may be set to any arbitrary function or constant without loss of generality (subject to some regularity conditions). In particular, under the equivalent martingale measure in which all asset prices follow martingales, the option's price is simply the present discounted value of its expected payoff at maturity, where the expectation is computed with respect to the *risk-neutralized process* $P^*(t)$:

$$dP^*(t) \;\; = \;\; rP^*(t)\, dt + \sigma P^*(t)\, dB \tag{9.3.44}$$

$$d\log P^*(t) \;\; \equiv \;\; dp^*(t) \;\; = \;\; \left(r - \frac{\sigma^2}{2}\right) dt + \sigma\, dB. \tag{9.3.45}$$

Although the risk-neutralized process is not empirically observable,[19] it is nevertheless an extremely convenient tool for evaluating the price of an option on the stock with a data-generating process given by $P(t)$.

Moreover, the risk-neutral pricing approach yields the following implication: as long as the diffusion coefficient for the log-price process is a fixed

---

[19]However, under certain conditions it can be estimated: see, for example, Aït-Sahalia and Lo (1996), Jackwerth and Rubinstein (1995), Rubinstein (1994), Shimko (1993), and Section 12.3.4 of Chapter 12.

constant σ, then the Black-Scholes formula yields the correct option price regardless of the specification and arguments of the drift. This holds more generally for any derivative asset which can be priced purely by arbitrage, and where the underlying asset's log-price dynamics is described by an Itô diffusion with constant diffusion coefficient: the derivative-pricing formula is functionally independent of the drift and is determined purely by the diffusion coefficient and the contract specifications of the derivative asset.

This may seem paradoxical since two stocks with the same σ but different drifts will yield the same Black-Scholes price, yet the stock with the larger drift has a larger expected return, implying that a call option on that stock is more likely to be in-the-money at maturity than a call option on the stock with the smaller drift. The resolution of this paradox lies in the observation that although the expected payoff of the call option on the larger-drift stock is indeed larger, it must be discounted at a higher rate of return—one that is commensurate with the risk and expected return of its underlying stock—and this higher discount rate exactly offsets the larger expected payoff so that the present value is the same as the price of the call on the stock with the smaller drift. Therefore, the fact that the drift plays no direct role in the Black-Scholes formula belies its importance. The same economic forces that determine the expected returns of stocks, bonds, and other financial assets are also at work in pricing options.

These considerations are less important when the drift is assumed to be constant through time, but if expected returns are time-varying so that stock returns are predictable to some degree, this predictability must be taken into account in estimating σ.

The Trending Ornstein-Uhlenbeck Process

To see how a time-varying drift can influence option prices, we follow Lo and Wang's (1995) analysis by replacing the geometric Brownian motion assumption (A3) of the Black-Scholes model with the following stochastic differential equation for the log-price process $p(t)$:

$$dp(t) = \left(-\gamma(p(t) - \mu t) + \mu\right)dt + \sigma\, dB, \qquad (9.3.46)$$

where

$$\gamma \geq 0, \qquad p(0) = p_0, \qquad t \in [0, \infty).$$

Unlike the geometric Brownian motion dynamics of the original Black-Scholes model, which implies that log-prices follow an arithmetic random walk with IID normal increments, this log-price process is the sum of a zero-mean stationary autoregressive Gaussian process—an Ornstein-Uhlenbeck process—and a deterministic linear trend, so we call this the *trending O-U* process. Rewriting (9.3.46) as

$$d\left(p(t) - \mu t\right) = -\gamma\left(p(t) - \mu t\right)dt + \sigma\, dB \qquad (9.3.47)$$

shows that when $p(t)$ deviates from its trend μt, it is pulled back at a rate proportional to its deviation, where γ is the *speed of adjustment*. This reversion to the trend induces predictability in the returns of this asset.

To develop further intuition for the properties of (9.3.46), consider its explicit solution:

$$p(t) = \mu t + e^{-\gamma t} p_0 + \sigma \int_0^t e^{-\gamma(t-s)} \, dB(s), \qquad (9.3.48)$$

from which we can obtain the unconditional moments and co-moments of continuously compounded τ-period returns $r_t(\tau) \equiv p(t) - p(t-\tau)$:[20]

$$\mathrm{E}[r_t(\tau)] \;=\; \mu\tau \qquad\qquad\qquad\qquad\qquad (9.3.49)$$

$$\mathrm{Var}[r_t(\tau)] \;=\; \frac{\sigma^2}{\gamma}\bigl[1 - e^{-\gamma\tau}\bigr], \qquad \tau \geq 0 \qquad (9.3.50)$$

$$\mathrm{Cov}[r_{t_1}(\tau), r_{t_2}(\tau)] \;=\; -\frac{\sigma^2}{2\gamma} e^{-\gamma(t_2 - t_1 - \tau)}\bigl[1 - e^{-\gamma\tau}\bigr]^2,$$

$$t_1 + \tau \;\leq\; t_2 \qquad\qquad (9.3.51)$$

$$\mathrm{Corr}[r_t(\tau), r_{t+\tau}(\tau)] \;\equiv\; \rho_1(\tau) \;=\; -\frac{1}{2}\bigl[1 - e^{-\gamma\tau}\bigr]. \qquad (9.3.52)$$

Since (9.3.46) is a Gaussian process, the moments (9.3.49)–(9.3.51) completely characterize the finite-dimensional distributions of $r_\tau(t)$ (see Section 9.1.1 for the definition of a finite-dimensional distribution). Unlike the arithmetic Brownian motion or random walk which is nonstationary and often said to be *difference-stationary* or a *stochastic trend*, the trending O-U process is said to be *trend-stationary* since its deviations from trend follow a stationary process.[21]

---

[20] Since we have conditioned on $p(0) = p_o$ in defining the detrended log-price process, it is a slight abuse of terminology to call these moments "unconditional". However, in this case the distinction is primarily semantic since the conditioning variable is more of an initial condition than an information variable—if we define the beginning of time as $t = 0$ and the fully observable starting value of $p(0)$ as p_o, then (9.3.49)–(9.3.52) are unconditional moments relative to these initial conditions. We shall adopt this definition of an unconditional moment throughout the remainder of this chapter.

[21] An implication of trend-stationarity is that the variance of τ-period returns has a finite limit as τ increases without bound, in this case σ^2/γ, whereas this variance increases linearly with τ under a random walk. While trend-stationary processes are often simpler to estimate, they have been criticized as unrealistic models of financial asset prices since they do not accord well with the common intuition that longer-horizon asset returns exhibit more risk or that price forecasts exhibit more uncertainty as the forecast horizon grows. However, if the source of such intuition is empirical observation, it may well be consistent with trend-stationarity since it is now well-known that for any finite set of data, trend-stationarity and difference-stationarity are virtually indistinguishable (see, for example, Section 2.7 in Chapter 2, Campbell and Perron [1991], Hamilton [1994, Chapters 17–18], and the many other "unit root" papers they cite).

Note that the first-order autocorrelation (9.3.52) of the trending O-U increments is always less than or equal to zero, bounded below by $-\frac{1}{2}$, and approaches $-\frac{1}{2}$ as τ increases without bound. These prove to be serious restrictions for many empirical applications, and they motivate the alternative processes introduced in Lo and Wang (1995) which have considerably more flexible autocorrelation functions. But as an illustration of the impact of serial correlation on option prices, the trending O-U process is ideal: despite the differences between the trending O-U process and an arithmetic Brownian motion, both data-generating processes yield the same risk-neutralized price process (9.3.44), hence the Black-Scholes formula still applies to options on stocks with log-price dynamics given by (9.3.46).

However, although the Black-Scholes formula is the same for (9.3.46), the σ in (9.3.46) is not necessarily the same as the σ in the geometric Brownian motion specification (9.2.2). Specifically, the two data-generating processes (9.2.2) and (9.3.46) must fit the same price data—they are, after all, two competing specifications of a single price process, the "true" DGP. Therefore, in the presence of serial correlation, e.g., specification (9.3.46), the *numerical value* for the Black-Scholes input σ will be different than in the case of geometric Brownian motion (9.2.2).

To be concrete, denote by $\overline{r_t(\tau)}$, $s^2[r_t(\tau)]$, and $\rho_1(\tau)$ the unconditional mean, variance, and first-order autocorrelation of $\{r_t(\tau)\}$, respectively, which may be defined without reference to any particular data-generating process.[22] The numerical values of these quantities may also be fixed without reference to any particular data-generating process. All competing specifications for the true data-generating process must come close to matching these moments to be plausible descriptions of that data (of course, the best specification is one that matches *all* the moments, in which case the true data-generating process will have been discovered). For the arithmetic Brownian motion, this implies that the parameters (μ, σ^2) must satisfy the following relations:

$$\overline{r_t(\tau)} \;=\; \mu\tau \tag{9.3.53}$$

$$s^2[r_t(\tau)] \;=\; \sigma^2\tau \tag{9.3.54}$$

$$\rho_1(\tau) \;=\; 0. \tag{9.3.55}$$

From (9.3.54), we obtain the well-known result that the Black-Scholes input σ^2 may be estimated by the sample variance of continuously compounded returns $\{r_t(\tau)\}$.

Nevertheless, Lo and Wang (1995) provide a generalization of the trending O-U process that contains stochastic trends, in which case the variance of returns will increase with the holding period τ.

[22]Of course, it must be assumed that the moments exist. However, even if they do not, a similar but more involved argument may be based on location, scale, and association parameters.

In the case of the trending O-U process, the parameters (μ, γ, σ^2) must satisfy

$$\overline{r_t(\tau)} \;=\; \mu\tau \tag{9.3.56}$$

$$s^2[r_t(\tau)] \;=\; \frac{\sigma^2}{\gamma}\left[1 - e^{-\gamma\tau}\right], \qquad \tau \geq 0 \tag{9.3.57}$$

$$\rho_1(\tau) \;=\; -\frac{1}{2}\left[1 - e^{-\gamma\tau}\right], \tag{9.3.58}$$

Observe that these relations must hold for the *population* values of the parameters if the trending O-U process is to be a plausible description of the DGP. Moreover, while (9.3.56)–(9.3.58) involve population values of the parameters, they also have implications for estimation. In particular, under the trending O-U specification, the sample variance of continuously compounded returns is clearly *not* an appropriate estimator for σ^2.

Holding the unconditional variance of returns fixed, the particular value of σ^2 now depends on γ. Solving (9.3.57) and (9.3.58) for γ and σ^2 yields:

$$\gamma \;=\; -\frac{1}{\tau}\log\bigl(1 + 2\rho_1(\tau)\bigr) \tag{9.3.59}$$

$$\sigma^2 \;=\; s^2(r_\tau)\,\gamma\bigl(1 - e^{-\gamma\tau}\bigr)^{-1} \;=\; \frac{s^2(r_\tau)}{\tau}\bigl[\,\gamma\tau\bigl(1 - e^{-\gamma\tau}\bigr)^{-1}\,\bigr], \tag{9.3.60}$$

which shows the dependence of σ^2 on γ explicitly.

In the second equation of (9.3.60), σ^2 has been re-expressed as the product of two terms: the first is the standard Black-Scholes input under the assumption that arithmetic Brownian motion is the data-generating process, and the second term is an adjustment factor required by the trending O-U specification. Since this adjustment factor is an increasing function of γ, as returns become more highly (negatively) autocorrelated, options on the stock will become more valuable *ceteris paribus*. More specifically, (9.3.60) may be rewritten as the following explicit function of $\rho_1(\tau)$:

$$\sigma^2 \;=\; \frac{s^2[r_t(\tau)]}{\tau} \cdot \frac{\log(1 + 2\rho_1(\tau))}{2\rho_1(\tau)}, \qquad \rho_1(\tau) \in (-\tfrac{1}{2}, 0]. \tag{9.3.61}$$

Holding fixed the unconditional variance of returns $s^2[r_t(\tau)]$, as the absolute value of the autocorrelation increases from 0 to $\frac{1}{2}$, the value of σ^2 increases without bound.[23] This implies that a specification error in the dynamics of $s(t)$ can have dramatic consequences for pricing options.

---

[23]We focus on the absolute value of the autocorrelation to avoid confusion in making comparisons between results for negatively autocorrelated and positively autocorrelated asset returns. See Lo and Wang (1995) for further details.

As the return interval τ decreases, it can be shown that the adjustment factor to $s^2[r_t(\tau)]/\tau$ in (9.3.61) approaches unity (use L'Hôpital's rule). In the continuous-time limit, the standard deviation of continuously compounded returns is a consistent estimator for σ and the effects of predictability on σ vanish. The intuition comes from the fact that σ is a measure of *local volatility*—the volatility of infinitesimal price changes—and there is no predictability over any infinitesimal time interval by construction (see Section 9.1.1). Therefore, the influence of predictability on estimators for σ is an empirical issue which depends on the degree of predictability relative to how finely the data is sampled, and must be addressed on a case-by-case basis. However, we provide a numerical example in the next section in which the magnitude of these effects is quantified for the Black-Scholes case.

Adjusting the Black-Scholes Formula for Predictability
Expression (9.3.61) provides the necessary input to the Black-Scholes formula for pricing options on an asset with the trending O-U dynamics. If the unconditional variance of daily returns is $s^2[r_t(1)]$, and if the first-order autocorrelation of τ-period returns is $\rho_1(\tau)$, then the price of a call option is given by:

$$C_{ou}(P(t), t; , K, T, r, \sigma) = P(t)\,\Phi(d_1) - Ke^{-r(T-t)}\,\Phi(d_2), \qquad (9.3.62)$$

where

$$\sigma^2 \equiv \frac{s^2[r_t(1)]}{\tau} \cdot \frac{\log(1 + 2\rho_1(\tau))}{([1 + 2\rho_1(\tau)]^{1/\tau} - 1)}, \qquad \rho_1(\tau) \in (-\tfrac{1}{2}, 0], \quad (9.3.63)$$

and d_1 and d_2 are defined in (9.2.17) and (9.2.18), respectively.

Expression (9.3.62) is simply the Black-Scholes formula with an adjusted volatility input. The adjustment factor multiplying $s^2[r_t(1)]/\tau$ in (9.3.63) is easily tabulated (see Lo and Wang [1995]); hence in practice it is a simple matter to adjust the Black-Scholes formula for negative autocorrelation of the form (9.3.58): Multiply the usual variance estimator $s^2[r_t(1)]/\tau$ by the appropriate factor from Table 3 of Lo and Wang (1995), and use this as σ^2 in the Black-Scholes formula.

Note that for all values of $\rho_1(\tau)$ in $(-\tfrac{1}{2}, 0]$, the factor multiplying $s^2[r_t(1)]/\tau$ in (9.3.63) is greater than or equal to one and increases in the absolute value of the first-order autocorrelation coefficient. This implies that option prices under the trending O-U specification are always greater than or equal to prices under the standard Black-Scholes specification, and that option prices are an increasing function of the absolute value of the first-order autocorrelation coefficient. These are purely features of the trending O-U process and do not generalize to other specifications of the drift (see Lo and Wang [1995] for examples of other patterns).

Table 9.5.   *Option prices on assets with negatively autocorrelated returns.*

Strike Price	Black-Scholes Price	Trending O-U Price, with Daily $\rho_\tau(1) =$					
		$-.05$	$-.10$	$-.20$	$-.30$	$-.40$	$-.45$
Time-to-Maturity $T-t = 7$ Days							
30	10.028	10.028	10.028	10.028	10.028	10.028	10.028
35	5.036	5.037	5.038	5.042	5.051	5.074	5.108
40	0.863	0.885	0.910	0.973	1.062	1.216	1.368
45	0.011	0.013	0.016	0.024	0.041	0.082	0.137
50	0.000	0.000	0.000	0.000	0.000	0.001	0.005
Time-to-Maturity $T-t = 182$ Days							
30	11.285	11.336	11.394	11.548	11.786	12.238	12.725
35	7.558	7.646	7.746	7.998	8.365	9.014	9.668
40	4.740	4.851	4.976	5.286	5.728	6.491	7.244
45	2.810	2.922	3.048	3.361	3.812	4.595	5.375
50	1.592	1.687	1.797	2.073	2.482	3.214	3.963
Time-to-Maturity $T-t = 364$ Days							
30	12.753	12.845	12.950	13.218	13.620	14.349	15.102
35	9.493	9.622	9.769	10.133	10.661	11.582	12.501
40	6.908	7.061	7.234	7.660	8.269	9.315	10.343
45	4.941	5.102	5.283	5.732	6.374	7.478	8.566
50	3.489	3.645	3.821	4.261	4.896	6.003	7.106

Comparison of Black-Scholes call option prices on a hypothetical $40 stock under an arithmetic Brownian motion versus a trending Ornstein-Uhlenbeck process for log-prices, assuming a standard deviation of 2% for daily continuously compounded returns, and a daily continuously compounded riskfree rate of $\log(1.05)/364$. As autocorrelation becomes larger in absolute value, option prices increase.

An Empirical Illustration

To gauge the empirical relevance of this adjustment for autocorrelation, Table 9.5 reports a comparison of Black-Scholes prices under arithmetic Brownian motion and under the trending Ornstein-Uhlenbeck process for various holding periods, strike prices, and daily autocorrelations from -5 to -45% for a hypothetical $40 stock. The unconditional standard deviation of daily returns is held fixed at 2% per day. The Black-Scholes price is calculated according to (9.2.16), setting σ equal to the unconditional standard deviation. The trending O-U prices are calculated by solving (9.3.57) and (9.3.58) for σ given τ and the return autocorrelations $\rho_1(\tau)$ of -0.05, -0.10, -0.20, -0.30, -0.40, and -0.45, and using these values of σ in the Black-Scholes formula (9.2.16), where $\tau \equiv 1$.

The first panel of Table 9.5 shows that even extreme autocorrelation in daily returns does not affect short-maturity in-the-money call option prices very much. For example, a daily autocorrelation of -45% has no impact on the \$30 7-day call; the price under the trending O-U process is identical to the standard Black-Scholes price of \$10.028. But even for such a short maturity, differences become more pronounced as the strike price increases; the at-the-money call is worth \$0.863 in the absence of autocorrelation, but increases to \$1.368 with an autocorrelation of -45%.

However, as the time to maturity increases, the remaining panels of Table 9.5 show that the impact of autocorrelation also increases. With a -10% daily autocorrelation, an at-the-money 1-year call is \$7.234 and rises to \$10.343 with a daily autocorrelation of -45%, compared to the standard Black-Scholes price of \$6.908. This is not surprising since the sensitivity of the Black-Scholes formula to σ—the option's vega—is an increasing function of the time-to-maturity (see Section 9.2.1). From (9.2.28), we see that for shorter-maturity options, changes in σ have very little impact on the call price, but longer-maturity options will be more sensitive.

In general, the effects of asset return predictability on the price of derivatives depends intimately on the precise nature of the predictability. For example, the importance of autocorrelation for option prices hinges critically on the degree of autocorrelation for a given return horizon τ and, of course, on the data-generating process which determines how rapidly this autocorrelation decays with τ. For this reason, Lo and Wang (1995) introduce several new stochastic processes that are capable of matching more complex patterns of autocorrelation and predictability than the trending O-U process.

9.3.5 Implied Volatility Estimators

Suppose the current market price of a one-year European call option on a nondividend-paying stock is \$7.382. Suppose further that its strike price is \$35, the current stock price is \$40, and the annual simple riskfree interest rate is 5%. If the Black-Scholes model holds, then the volatility σ implied by the values given above can only take on one value—0.200—because the Black-Scholes formula (9.2.16) yields a one-to-one relation between the option's price and σ, holding all other parameters fixed. Therefore, the option described above is said to have an *implied volatility* of 0.200 or 20%. So common is this notion of implied volatility that options traders often quote prices not in dollars but in units of volatility, e.g., "The one-year European call with \$35.000 strike is trading at 20%."

Because implied volatilities are linked directly to current market prices (via the Black-Scholes formula), some investment professionals have argued that they are better estimators of volatility than estimators based on historical data such as $\hat{\sigma}^2$. Implied volatilities are often said to be "forward looking" since they are based on current prices which presumably have expectations of the future impounded in them.

However, such an argument overlooks the fact that an implied volatility is intimately related to a specific *parametric* option-pricing model—typically the Black-Scholes model—which, in turn, is intimately related to a particular set of dynamics for the underlying stock price (geometric Brownian motion in the Black-Scholes case). Herein lies the problem with implied volatilities: If the Black-Scholes formula holds, then the parameter σ can be recovered *without error* by inverting the Black-Scholes formula for any one option's price (each of which yields the same numerical value for σ); if the Black-Scholes formula does not hold, then the implied volatility is difficult to interpret since it is obtained by inverting the Black-Scholes formula. Therefore, using the implied volatility of one option to obtain a more accurate forecast of volatility to be used in pricing other options is either unnecessary or logically inconsistent.

To see this more clearly, consider the argument that implied volatilities are better forecasts of future volatility because changing market conditions cause volatilities vary through time stochastically, and historical volatilities cannot adjust to changing market conditions as rapidly. The folly of this argument lies in the fact that stochastic volatility contradicts the assumptions required by the Black-Scholes model—if volatilities do change stochastically through time, the Black-Scholes formula is no longer the correct pricing formula and an implied volatility derived from the Black-Scholes formula provides no new information.

Of course, in this case the historical volatility estimator is equally useless, since it need not enter into the correct stochastic volatility option-pricing formula (in fact it does not, as shown by Hull and White [1987], Wiggins [1987] and others—see Section 9.3.6). The correct approach is to use a historical estimator of the unknown parameters entering into the pricing formula—in the Black-Scholes case, the parameter σ is related to the historical volatility estimator of continuously compounded returns, but under other assumptions for the stock price dynamics, historical volatility need not play such a central role.

This raises an interesting issue regarding the validity of the Black-Scholes formula. If the Black-Scholes formula is indeed correct, then the implied volatilities of any set of options on the same stock must be *numerically identical.* Of course, in practice they never are; thus the assumptions of the Black-Scholes model cannot literally be true. This should not come as a complete surprise; after all the assumptions of the Black-Scholes model imply that options are redundant securities, which eliminates the need for organized options markets altogether.

The difficulty lies in determining which of the many Black-Scholes assumptions are violated. If, for example, the Black-Scholes model fails empirically because stock prices do not follow a lognormal diffusion, we may be able to specify an alternate price process that fits the data better, in which case the "implied" parameter(s) of options on the same stock may indeed be numerically identical. Alternatively, if the Black-Scholes model fails empirically because in practice it is impossible to trade continuously due to transactions costs and other institutional constraints, then markets are never dynamically complete, options are never redundant securities, and we should never expect "implied" parameters of options on the same stock to be numerically identical for any option-pricing formula. In this case, the degree to which implied volatilities disagree may be an indication of how "redundant" options really are.

The fact that options traders quote prices in terms of Black-Scholes implied volatilities has no direct bearing on their usefulness from a pricing point of view, but is a remarkable testament to the popularity of the Black-Scholes formula as a convenient heuristic. Quoting prices in terms of "ticks" rather than dollars has no far-reaching economic implications simply because there is a well-known one-to-one mapping between ticks and dollars. Moreover, just because options traders quote prices in terms of Black-Scholes implied volatilities, this does not imply that they are using the Black-Scholes model to *set* their prices. Implied volatilities do convey information, but this information is identical to the information contained in the market prices on which the implied volatilities are based.

9.3.6 Stochastic-Volatility Models

Several empirical studies have shown that the geometric Brownian motion (9.2.2) is not an appropriate model for certain security prices. For example, Beckers (1983), Black (1976), Blattberg and Gonedes (1974), Christie (1982), Fama (1965), Lo and MacKinlay (1988, 1990c), and Mandelbrot (1963, 1971) have documented important departures from (9.2.2) for US stock returns: skewness, excess kurtosis, serial correlation, and time-varying volatilities. Although each of these empirical regularities has implications for option pricing, it is the last one that has received the most attention in the recent derivatives literature,[24] partly because volatility plays such a central role in the Black-Scholes/Merton formulation and in industry practice.

If, in the geometric Brownian motion model (9.2.2) the σ is a known deterministic function of time $\sigma(t)$, then the Black-Scholes formula still applies but with σ replaced by the integral $\int_t^T \sigma(s)\, ds$ over the option's life. However, if σ is stochastic, the situation becomes more complex. For

---

[24]See, for example, Amin and Ng (1993), Ball and Roma (1994), Beckers (1980), Cox (1975), Goldenberg (1991), Heston (1993), Hofmann, Platen, and Schweizer (1992), Hull and White (1987), Johnson and Shanno (1987), Scott (1987), and Wiggins (1987).

example, suppose that the fundamental asset's dynamics are given by:

$$dP = \mu P dt + \sigma P dB_p \tag{9.3.64}$$

$$d\sigma = \alpha(\sigma)dt + \beta(\sigma)dB_\sigma, \tag{9.3.65}$$

where $\alpha(\cdot)$ and $\beta(\cdot)$ are arbitrary functions of volatility σ, and B_p and B_σ are standard Brownian motions with instantaneous correlation $dB_p\, dB_s = \rho\, dt$. In this case, it may not be possible to determine the price of an option by arbitrage arguments alone, for the simple reason that there may not exist a dynamic self-financing portfolio strategy involving stocks and riskless bonds that can perfectly replicate the option's payoff.

Heuristically, stochastic volatility introduces a second source of uncertainty into the replicating portfolio and if this uncertainty (B_σ) is not perfectly correlated with the uncertainty inherent in the stock price process (B_p), the replicating portfolio will not be able to "span" the possible outcomes that an option may realize at maturity (see Harrison and Kreps [1979] and Duffie and Huang [1985] for a more rigorous discussion). Of course, if σ were the price of a traded asset, then under relatively weak regularity conditions there would exist a dynamic self-financing portfolio strategy consisting of stocks, bonds, and the volatility asset that could perfectly replicate the option.

In the absence of this additional hedging security, the only available method for pricing options in the presence of stochastic volatility of the form (9.3.65) is to appeal to a dynamic equilibrium model. Perhaps the simplest approach is to assert that the risk associated with stochastic volatility is not priced in equilibrium. This is the approach taken by Hull and White (1987) for the case where volatility follows a geometric Brownian motion

$$dP = \mu P dt + \sigma P dB_p \tag{9.3.66}$$

$$d\sigma^2 = \alpha\sigma^2 dt + \xi\sigma^2 dB_\sigma. \tag{9.3.67}$$

By assuming that volatility is uncorrelated with aggregate consumption, they show that equilibrium option prices are given by the expectation of the Black-Scholes formula, where the expectation is taken with respect to the average volatility over the option's life.

Using the dynamic equilibrium models of Garman (1976b) and Cox, Ingersoll, and Ross (1985b), Wiggins (1987) derives the equilibrium price of volatility risk in an economy where agents possess logarithmic utility functions, yielding an equilibrium condition—in the form of a PDE with certain boundary conditions—for the instantaneous expected return of the option price. Other derivative-pricing models with stochastic volatility take similar approaches, the differences coming from the type of equilibrium model employed or the choice of preferences that agents exhibit.

Parameter Estimation

One of the most challenging aspects of stochastic-volatility models, is the fact that realizations of the volatility process are unobservable yet option-pricing formulas are invariably functions of the parameters of the process driving σ. To date, there has been relatively little attention devoted to this important issue for continuous-time processes like (9.3.64)–(9.3.65) primarily because of the difficulties inherent in estimating continuous-time models with discretely sampled data. However, a great deal of attention has been devoted to a related discrete-time model: the autoregressive conditional heteroskedasticity (ARCH) process of Engle (1982) and its many variants (see Chapter 12 and Bollerslev, Chou, and Kroner [1992]).

Although originally motivated by issues other than option pricing, ARCH models does capture the spirit of some of the corresponding continuous-time models. Recent studies by Nelson and Foster (1994), Nelson and Ramaswamy (1990), and Nelson (1991, 1992, 1996) provide some important links between the two. In particular, Nelson (1996) and Nelson and Foster (1994) derive the continuous-record asymptotics for several discrete-time ARCH processes, some of which converge to the continuous-time processes of Hull and White (1987) and Wiggins (1987). The empirical properties of these estimators have yet to be explored but will no doubt be the subject of future research.

Discrete-Time Models

Another approach is to begin with a discrete-time dynamic equilibrium model for option prices in which the fundamental asset's price dynamics are governed by an ARCH model. Although it is typically impossible to price securities by arbitrage in discrete time, continuous-time versions must appeal to equilibrium arguments as well in the case of stochastic volatility; hence there is little loss of generality in leaving the continuous-time framework altogether in this case. This is the approach taken by Amin and Ng (1993), who derive option-pricing formulas for a variety of price dynamics— stochastic volatility, stochastic consumption growth variance, stochastic interest rates, and systematic jumps—by applying the discrete-time dynamic equilibrium models of Brennan (1979) and Rubinstein (1976).

Discrete-time models are also generally easier to implement empirically since virtually all historical data are sampled discretely, financial transactions are typically recorded at discrete intervals, parameter estimation and hypothesis testing involve discrete data records, and forecasts are produced at discrete horizons. For these reasons, there may be an advantage in modeling stochastic volatility via ARCH and pricing derivatives within a discrete-time equilibrium model.

However, continuous-time models do offer other insights that are harder to come by within a discrete-time framework. For example, the dynamics of nonlinear functions of the data-generating process are almost impossible to obtain in discrete time, but in continuous time Itô's differentiation rule gives an explicit expression for such dynamics. Theoretical insights into the equilibrium structure of derivatives prices—for example, which state variables affect derivatives prices and which do not—are also more readily obtained in a continuous-time framework such as Cox, Ingersoll, and Ross (1985b). Therefore, each set of models offers some valuable insights that are not contained in the other.

9.4 Pricing Path-Dependent Derivatives Via Monte Carlo Simulation

Consider a contract at date 0 that gives the holder the right but not the obligation to sell one share of stock at date T for a price equal to the maximum of that stock's price over the period from 0 to T. Such a contract, often called a *lookback* option, is clearly a put option since it gives the holder the option to sell at a particular price at maturity. However, in this case the strike price is stochastic and determined only at the maturity date. Because the strike price depends on the *path* that the stock price takes from 0 to T, and not just on the terminal stock price $P(T)$, such a contract is called a *path-dependent* option.

Path-dependent options have become increasingly popular as the hedging needs of investors become ever more complex. For example, many multinational corporations now expend great efforts to hedge against exchange-rate fluctuations since large portions of their accounts receivable and accounts payable are denominated in foreign currencies. One of the most popular path-dependent options are foreign currency *average rate* or *Asian* options which gives the holder the right to buy foreign currency at a rate equal to the average of the exchange rates over the life of the contract.[25]

Path-dependent options may be priced by the dynamic-hedging approach of Section 9.2.1, but the resulting PDE is often intractable. The risk-neutral pricing method offers a considerably simpler alternative in which the power of high-speed digital computers may be exploited. For example, consider the pricing of the option to sell at the maximum. If $P(t)$ denotes the date t stock price and $H(0)$ is the initial value of this put, we have

$$H(0) \;=\; e^{-rT}\, \mathrm{E}^* \left[\max_{0 \le t \le T} P(t) - P(T) \right] \qquad (9.4.1)$$

---

[25] The term "Asian" comes from the fact that such options were first actively written on stocks trading on Asian exchanges. Because these exchanges are usually smaller than their European and American counterparts, with relatively thin trading and low daily volume, prices on such exchanges are somewhat easier to manipulate. To minimize an option's exposure to the risk of stock-price manipulation, a new option was created with the average of the stock prices over the option's life playing the role of the terminal stock price.

$$= e^{-rT} \, \mathrm{E}^* \left[\underset{0 \leq t \leq T}{\mathrm{Max}} \, P(t) \right] - e^{-rT} \, \mathrm{E}^* \, [P(T)] \qquad (9.4.2)$$

$$= e^{-rT} \, \mathrm{E}^* \left[\underset{0 \leq t \leq T}{\mathrm{Max}} \, P(t) \right] - P(0), \qquad (9.4.3)$$

where E^* is the expectations operator with respect to the risk-neutral probability distribution or equivalent martingale measure.

Observe that in going from (9.4.2) to (9.4.3) we have used the fact that the expected present value of $P(T)$ discounted at the riskless rate r is $P(0)$. This holds because we have used the risk-neutral expectations operator E^*, and under the risk-neutral probabilities implicit in E^* all assets must earn an expected return of r; hence $e^{-rT} \, \mathrm{E}^*[P(T)] = P(0)$.

To evaluate (9.4.3) via Monte Carlo simulation, we simulate many sample paths of $\{P(t)\}$, find the maximum value for each sample path, or *replication*, and average the present discounted value of the maxima over all the replications to yield an expected value over all replications, i.e., an estimate of $H(0)$. Two issues arise immediately: How do we simulate a continuous sample path, and how many replications do we need for a reasonably precise estimate of $H(0)$?

9.4.1 Discrete Versus Continuous Time

By their very nature, digital computers are incapable of simulating truly continuous phenomena; but as a practical matter they are often capable of providing excellent approximations. In particular, if we divide our time interval $[0, T]$ into n discrete intervals each of length h, and simulate prices at each discrete date kh, $k = 0, \ldots, n$, the result will be an approximation to a continuous sample path which can be made successively more precise by allowing n to grow and h to shrink so as to keep T fixed.

For example, consider the case of geometric Brownian motion (9.2.2) for which the risk-neutral dynamics are given by

$$dP^*(t) = rP^*(t) \, dt + \sigma P^*(t) \, dB(t), \qquad (9.4.4)$$

and consider simulating the following approximate sample path P_n^*:

$$P_n^* = P^*(0) \exp \left[\sum_{k=1}^{n} r_k^*(h) \right], \qquad r_k^*(h) \sim \mathcal{N}(rh, \sigma^2 h). \qquad (9.4.5)$$

Despite the fact that the simulated path P_n varies only at multiples of h, the approximation may be made arbitrarily precise by increasing n and therefore decreasing h—as n increases without bound, P_n^* converges *weakly* to (9.4.4) (see Section 9.1.1 for further discussion). Unfortunately, there are no general rules for how large n must be to yield an adequate approximation—choosing n must be done on a case-by-case basis.

9.4.2 How Many Simulations to Perform

We *can*, however, provide some clear guidelines for choosing the number of replications m to simulate. Recall that our Monte Carlo estimate of $H(0)$ involves a simple average across replications:

$$\hat{H}(0) \ = \ e^{-rT} \frac{1}{m} \sum_{j=1}^{m} Y_{jn} - P(0), \qquad Y_{jn} \equiv \underset{0 \leq k \leq n}{\text{Max}} P_{jk}^{*}, \qquad (9.4.6)$$

where $\{P_{jk}^{*}\}_{k=0}^{n}$ is the jth replication or sample path of the stock price process under the risk-neutral distribution which, in the case of (9.4.4), implies that $\mu = r - \frac{\sigma^2}{2}$. But since by construction the Y_{jn}'s are IID random variables with finite positive variance, the Central Limit Theorem implies that for large m:

$$\sqrt{m} \left(\hat{H}(0) - H(0) \right) \overset{a}{\sim} \mathcal{N}\big(0, \sigma_y^2(n)\big), \qquad \sigma_y^2(n) \equiv \text{Var}\big[e^{-rT} Y_{jn}\big]. \quad (9.4.7)$$

Therefore, for large m an approximate 95% confidence interval for $H(0)$ may be readily constructed from (9.4.7):

$$\text{Pr}\left(\hat{H}(0) - \frac{1.96\sigma_y(n)}{\sqrt{m}} \ \leq \ H(0) \ \leq \ \hat{H}(0) + \frac{1.96\sigma_y(n)}{\sqrt{m}} \right) \overset{a}{=} \ 0.95.$$
$$(9.4.8)$$

The choice of m thus depends directly on the desired accuracy of $\hat{H}(0)$. If, for example, we require a $\hat{H}(0)$ that is within \$0.001 of $H(0)$ with 95% confidence, m must be chosen so that:

$$\frac{1.96\sigma_y(n)}{\sqrt{m}} \ \leq \ 0.001 \qquad \Rightarrow \qquad m \ \geq \ \left(\frac{1.96}{0.001} \right)^2 \sigma_y^2(n). \qquad (9.4.9)$$

Typically $\text{Var}[Y_{jn}]$ is not known, but it can be readily estimated from the simulations in the obvious way:

$$\widehat{\text{Var}}[Y_{jn}] \ = \ \frac{1}{m} \sum_{j=1}^{m} (Y_{jn} - \overline{Y}_n)^2, \qquad \overline{Y}_n \equiv \frac{1}{m} \sum_{j=1}^{m} Y_{jn}. \qquad (9.4.10)$$

Since the replications are IID by construction, estimators such as (9.4.10) will generally be very well-behaved, converging in probability to their expectations rapidly and, when properly normalized, converging in distribution just as rapidly to their limiting distributions.

9.4.3 Comparisons with a Closed-Form Solution

In the special case of the option to sell at the maximum with a geometric Brownian motion price process, a closed-form solution for the option price is given by Goldman, Sosin, and Gatto (1979):

$$H(0) = P(0)e^{-rT}\Phi\left(-\frac{\alpha T}{\sigma\sqrt{T}}\right)\left[1 - \frac{\sigma^2}{2r}\right] - P(0)$$

$$+ P(0)\left(1 + \frac{\sigma^2}{2r}\right)\left[1 - \Phi\left(-\frac{(\alpha + \sigma^2)T}{\sigma\sqrt{T}}\right)\right] \quad (9.4.11)$$

where $\alpha \equiv r - \sigma^2/2$.

Therefore, in this case we may compare the accuracy of the Monte Carlo estimator $\hat{H}(0)$ with the theoretical value $H(0)$. Table 9.6 provides such a comparison under the following assumptions (for simple returns):

$$\text{Annual Riskfree Interest Rate} \quad = \quad 5\%$$

$$\text{Annual Expected Stock Return} \quad = \quad 15\%$$

$$\text{Annual Standard Deviation of Stock Return} \quad = \quad 20\%$$

$$\text{Initial Stock Price } P(0) \quad = \quad \$40$$

$$\text{Time to Maturity } T \quad = \quad 1 \text{ Year.}$$

From the entries in Table 9.6, we see that large differences between the continuous-time price $H(0) = \$4.7937$ and the *crude* Monte Carlo estimator $\hat{H}(0)$ can arise, even when m and n are relatively large (the *antithetic* estimator is defined and discussed in the next section). For example, $H(0)$ and $\hat{H}(0)$ differ by 30 cents when $n = 250$, a nontrivial discrepancy given the typical sizes of options portfolios.

The difference between $\hat{H}(0)$ and $H(0)$ arises from two sources: sampling variation in $\hat{H}(0)$ and the discreteness of the simulated sample paths of prices. The former source of discrepancy is controlled by the number of replications m, while the latter source is controlled by the number of observations n in each simulated sample path. Increasing m will allow us to estimate $\mathrm{E}^*[\hat{H}(0)]$ with arbitrary accuracy, but if n is fixed then $\mathrm{E}^*[\hat{H}(0)]$ need not converge to the continuous-time price $H(0)$. Does this discrepancy imply that Monte Carlo estimators are inferior to closed-form solutions when such solutions are available? Not necessarily.

This difference highlights the importance of discretization in the pricing of path-dependent securities. Since we are selecting the *maximum* over k exponentials of the (discrete) partial sum $\sum_{t=1}^{k} r_t^*$, where k ranges from 0 to n, as n increases the maximum is likely to increase as well.[26] Heuristically,

---

[26]Although it is probable that the maximum of the partial sum will increase with n, it is not guaranteed. As we increase n in Table 9.6, we generate a new independent random sequence $\{r_t^*\}_{t=1}^{n}$, and there is always some chance that this new sequence with more terms will nevertheless yield smaller partial sums.

Table 9.6.   *Monte Carlo estimation of lookback option price.*

n	Crude		Antithetic	
	$\hat{H}(0)$	SE$[\hat{H}(0)]$	$\tilde{H}(0)$	SE$[\tilde{H}(0)]$
100	4.3818	0.0165	4.3644	0.0066
250	4.4911	0.0164	4.5136	0.0066
365	4.5479	0.0165	4.5603	0.0066
500	4.5746	0.0165	4.6007	0.0066
750	4.6529	0.0166	4.6414	0.0066
1,000	4.6448	0.0166	4.6493	0.0066
2,000	4.6706	0.0166	4.7001	0.0067
5,000	4.7175	0.0165	4.7269	0.0066

Monte Carlo estimator of the price of a one-year look-back put option with continuous-time Goldman-Sosin-Gatto price $H(0)$=\$4.7937. Each row corresponds to an independent set of simulations of 100,000 replications of sample paths of length n. For the antithetic-variates simulations, each sequence of IID random variates is used twice—the original sequence and its negative—yielding a total of 200,000 sample paths, or 100,000 negatively correlated pairs of paths. SE$[\hat{H}(0)]$ and SE$[\tilde{H}(0)]$ are the standard errors of $\hat{H}(0)$ and $\hat{H}(0)$, respectively.

the maximum of the daily closing prices of P over the year ($n = 250$ trading days) must be lower than the maximum of the daily highs over that same year ($n \rightarrow \infty$). Therefore, the continuous-time price $H(0)$, which is closer to the maximum of the daily highs, will almost always exceed the simulation price $\hat{H}(0)$ which is discretized.

Which price is more relevant depends of course on the terms of the particular contract. For example, average rate options on foreign exchange usually specify particular dates on which the exchange rate is measured, and it is almost always either a market closing rate (such as the corresponding spot rate of the IMM futures closing) or a central bank fixing rate. In both cases, the more relevant price would be the simulation price, since the path dependence is with respect to the discrete set of measured rates, and not an idealized continuous process.

9.4.4 Computational Efficiency

The two main concerns of any Monte Carlo simulation are accuracy and computational cost, and in most cases there will be tradeoffs between the two. As we saw in Section 9.4.2, the standard error of the Monte Carlo estimator $\hat{H}(0)$ is inversely proportional to the square root of the number of replications m, hence a 50% reduction in the standard error requires four times the number of replications, and so on. This type of Monte Carlo procedure is often described as *crude* Monte Carlo (see Hammersley and Handscomb [1964] for example), for obvious reasons. Therefore, a number of *variance-reduction* techniques have been developed to improve the efficiency of simulation estimators. Although a thorough discussion of these techniques is beyond the scope of this text, we shall briefly review a few of them here.[27]

A simple technique for improving the performance of Monte Carlo estimators is to replace estimates by their population counterparts whenever possible, for this reduces sampling variation in the estimator. For example, when simulating risk-neutralized asset returns, the sample mean of each replication will almost never be equal to its population mean (the riskless rate), but we can correct this sampling variation easily by adding the difference between the riskless rate and the sample mean to each observation of the replication. If this is done for each replication, the result will be a set of replications with no sampling error for the mean. The efficiency gain depends on the extent to which sampling errors for the mean contributes to the overall sampling variation of the simulation, but in many cases the improvement can be dramatic.

A related technique is to exploit other forms of population information. For example, suppose we wish to estimate $E^*[f(X)]$ and we find a random variable $g(Y)$ such that $E^*[g(Y)]$ is close to $E^*[f(X)]$ and $E^*[g(Y)]$ is known (this is the population information to be exploited). $E^*[f(X)]$ might be the price of newly created path-dependent derivative which must be estimated, and $E^*[g(Y)]$ the market price of an existing derivative with similar characteristics, hence a similar expectation. By expressing $E^*[f(X)]$ as the sum of $E^*[g(Y)]$ and $E^*[f(X) - g(Y)]$, the expectation to be estimated is decomposed into two terms where the first term is known and the second term can be simulated with much smaller sampling variation. This technique is known as the *control variate* method—$g(Y)$ is the control variate for $f(X)$—and its success depends on how close $E^*[g(Y)]$ is to $E^*[f(X)]$.

Another form of population information that can be exploited is symmetry. If, for example, the population distribution is symmetric about its mean and this mean is known (as in the case of risk-neutralized asset returns), then $m/2$ replications can yield m sample paths since each replication can

---

[27]Several texts provide excellent coverage of this material. Hammersley and Handscomb (1964) is a classic, concise but complete. Kalos and Whitlock (1986) provide a more detailed and updated exposition of similar material. Fishman (1996) is considerably more comprehensive and covers several advanced topics not found in other Monte Carlo texts such as Markov chain sampling, Gibbs sampling, random tours, and simulated annealing. Fishman (1996) also contains many applications, explicit algorithms for many of the techniques covered, and FORTRAN software (from an ftp site) for random number generation. Finally, Fang and Wang (1994) present a compact introduction to a new approach to Monte Carlo simulation based on purely deterministic sampling. Although it is still too early to tell how this approach compares to the more traditional methods, Fang and Wang (1994) provide some intriguing examples that look quite promising.

be "reflected" through its mean to produce a mirror-image which has the same statistical properties. This approach yields an added benefit: negative correlation among pairs of replications. If the summands of the Monte Carlo estimator are monotone functions of the replications they will also be negatively correlated, implying a smaller variance for the estimator.

This is a simple example of a more general technique known as the *antithetic variates* method in which correlation is induced across replications to reduce the variance of the sum. A more formal motivation for this approach comes from the following theorem: for any estimator which can be expressed as the sum of random variables, it is always possible to create a strict functional dependence between the summands which leaves the estimator unbiased but yields a variance that comes arbitrarily close to the minimum variance possible with these random variables (see Hammersley and Mauldon [1956]). Of course, the challenge is to construct such a functional dependence, but even if the optimal transformation is not apparent, substantial efficiency gains can be achieved by simpler kinds of dependence.

Variance reduction can also be accomplished by more sophisticated sampling methods. In *stratified sampling*, the support of the basic random variable X being simulated is partitioned into a finite number of intervals and crude Monte Carlo simulations are performed in each interval. If there is less variation in $f(X)$ *within* intervals than *across* the intervals, the sampling variation of the estimator of $\mathrm{E}^*[f(X)]$ will be reduced.

Importance sampling is a more sophisticated version, sampling more frequently in regions of the support where there is more variation in $f(X)$—where sampling is more "important"—instead of sampling at regular intervals. An even more sophisticated version of this method has recently been proposed by Fang and Wang (1994) in which replications are generated deterministically, not randomly, accordingly to an algorithm that is designed to minimize the sampling variation of the estimator directly. It is still too early to say how this approach—called the *number-theoretic* method—compares to the more traditional Monte Carlo estimators, but it has already found its way into the financial community (see, for example, Paskov and Traub [1995]) and the preliminary findings seem encouraging.

An Illustration of Variance Reduction

To illustrate the potential power of variance-reduction techniques, we construct an antithetic-variates estimator of the price of the one-year lookback put option of Section 9.4.3. For each simulated price path $\left\{P_{jk}^*\right\}_{k=0}^n$, another can be obtained without further simulation by reversing the sign of each of the randomly generated IID standard normal variates on which the price path is based, yielding a second path $\left\{\tilde{P}_{jk}^*\right\}_{k=0}^n$ which is negatively correlated with the first. If m sample paths of $\left\{P_{jk}^*\right\}_{k=0}^n$ are generated, the resulting antithetic-variates estimator $\tilde{H}(0)$ is simply the average across all $2m$ paths

$$\tilde{H}(0) = e^{-rT} \frac{1}{2m} \left(\sum_{j=1}^{m} Y_{jn} + \sum_{j=1}^{m} \tilde{Y}_{jn} \right) - P(0) \tag{9.4.12}$$

where

$$Y_{jn} \equiv \operatorname*{Max}_{0 \le k \le n} P_{jk}^{*}, \qquad \tilde{Y}_{jn} \equiv \operatorname*{Max}_{0 \le k \le n} \tilde{P}_{jk}^{*}.$$

The relation between antithetic-variates and crude Monte Carlo can be more easily seen by rewriting (9.4.12) as

$$\tilde{H}(0) = \left(\frac{1}{2} e^{-rT} \frac{1}{m} \sum_{j=1}^{m} Y_{jn} + \frac{1}{2} e^{-rT} \frac{1}{m} \sum_{j=1}^{m} \tilde{Y}_{jn} \right) - P(0) \tag{9.4.13}$$

$$= e^{-rT} \frac{1}{m} \sum_{j=1}^{m} \frac{Y_{jn} + \tilde{Y}_{jn}}{2} - P(0). \tag{9.4.14}$$

Equation (9.4.13) shows that $\tilde{H}(0)$ is based on a simple average of two averages, one based on the sample paths $\{P_{jk}^{*}\}_{k=0}^{n}$ and the other based on $\{\tilde{P}_{jk}^{*}\}_{k=0}^{n}$. The fact that these two averages are negatively correlated leads to a reduction in variance.

Equation (9.4.14) combines the two sums of (9.4.13) into one, with the averages of the antithetic pairs as the summands. This sum is particularly easy to analyze because the summands are IID—the correlation is confined *within* each summand, not across the summands—hence the variance of the sum is simply the sum of the variances. An expression for the variance of $\tilde{H}(0)$ then follows readily

$$\operatorname{Var}[\tilde{H}(0)] = e^{-2rT} \frac{1}{m} \operatorname{Var} \left[\frac{Y_{jn} + \tilde{Y}_{jn}}{2} \right] \tag{9.4.15}$$

$$= e^{-2rT} \frac{1}{m} \left(\frac{1}{2} \operatorname{Var}[Y_{jn}] + \frac{1}{2} \operatorname{Cov}[Y_{jn}, \tilde{Y}_{jn}] \right)$$

$$= \frac{\sigma_y^2(n)}{2m} (1 + \rho) \tag{9.4.16}$$

where $\sigma_y^2(n) \equiv \operatorname{Var}[e^{-rT} Y_{jn}] = \operatorname{Var}[e^{-rT} \tilde{Y}_{jn}]$ and $\rho \equiv \operatorname{Corr}[e^{-rT} Y_{jn}, e^{-rT} \tilde{Y}_{jn}]$. Equation (9.4.15) shows that the variance of $\tilde{H}(0)$ can be estimated by the product of e^{-rT} / m and the sample variance of the IID sequence $\{(Y_{jn} + \tilde{Y}_{jn})/2\}$. There is no need to account for the correlation between antithetic pairs because this is implicitly accounted for in the sample variance of $\{(Y_{jn} + \tilde{Y}_{jn})/2\}$.

Equation (9.4.16) provides additional insight into the variance reduction that antithetic variates affords. The reduction in variance comes from two sources: a doubling of the number of replications from m to $2m$, and the factor $1+\rho$ which should be less than one if the correlation between the antithetic variates is negative. Note that even if the correlation is positive, the variance of $\tilde{H}(0)$ will still be lower than the crude Monte Carlo estimator $\hat{H}(0)$ unless there is perfect correlation, i.e., $\rho=1$. Also, while we have doubled the number of replications, we have done so in a computationally trivial way: changing signs. Since the computations involved in pseudo-random number generation are typically more demanding than mere sign changes, this is another advantage of antithetic-variates simulations.

A comparison of the crude Monte Carlo estimator $\hat{H}(0)$ to the antithetic-variates estimator $\tilde{H}(0)$ is provided in Table 9.6. For most of the simulations, the ratio of the standard error of $\tilde{H}(0)$ to the standard error of $\hat{H}(0)$ is $0.0066/0.0165=0.400$, a reduction of about 60%. In comparison, a doubling of the number of replications from m to $2m$ for the crude Monte Carlo estimator would yield a ratio of $1/\sqrt{2}=0.707$, only a 29% reduction. More formally, observe from (9.4.7) and (9.4.16) that the ratio of the standard error of $\tilde{H}(0)$ to the standard error of $\hat{H}(0)$ is an estimator of $\sqrt{(1+\rho)/2}$, hence the ratio $0.0066/0.0165=0.400$ implies a correlation of -68% between the antithetic pairs of the simulations in Table 9.6, a substantial value which is responsible for the dramatic reduction in variance of $\tilde{H}(0)$.

9.4.5 Extensions and Limitations

The Monte Carlo approach to pricing path-dependent options is quite general and may be applied to virtually any European derivative security. For example, to price average-rate foreign currency options we would simulate price paths as above (perhaps using a different stochastic process more appropriate for exchange rates), compute the *average* for each replication, repeat this many times, and compute the average *across* the replications. Thus the power of the Cox-Ross risk-neutral pricing method is considerable. However, there are several important limitations to this approach that should be emphasized.

First, the Monte Carlo approach may only be applied to European options, options that cannot be exercised early. The early exercise feature of American options introduces the added complication of determining an optimal exercise policy, which must be done recursively using a dynamic-programming-like analysis. In such cases, numerical solution of the corresponding PDE is currently the only available method for obtaining prices.

Second, to apply the Cox-Ross technique to a given derivative security, we must first prove that the security *can* be priced by arbitrage considerations alone. Recall that in the Black-Scholes framework, the no-arbitrage condition was sufficient to completely determine the option price only because we were able to construct a dynamic portfolio of stocks, bonds, and options that was riskless. In effect, this implies that the option is "spanned" by stocks and bonds or, more precisely, the option's payoff at date T can be perfectly replicated by a particular dynamic trading strategy involving only stocks and bonds. The no-arbitrage condition translates into the requirement that the option price must equal the cost of the dynamic trading strategy that replicates the option's payoff.

But there are situations where the derivative security cannot be replicated by any dynamic strategy involving existing securities. For example, if we assume that the diffusion parameter σ in (9.2.2) is stochastic, then it may be shown that without further restrictions on σ there exists no nondegenerate dynamic trading strategy involving stocks, bonds, and options that is riskless. Heuristically, because there are now two sources of uncertainty, the option is no longer "spanned" by a dynamic portfolio of stocks and bonds (see Section 9.4.6 and Huang [1992] for further discussion).

Therefore, before we can apply the risk-neutral pricing method to a particular derivative security, we must first check that it is spanned by other traded assets. Since Goldman, Sosin, and Gatto (1979) demonstrate that the option to sell at the maximum is indeed spanned, we can apply the Cox-Ross method to that case with the assurance that the resulting price is in fact the no-arbitrage price and that deviations from this price necessarily imply riskless profit opportunities. But it may be more difficult to verify spanning for more complex path-dependent derivatives. In those cases, we may have to embed the security in a model of economic equilibrium, with specific assumptions about agents' preferences and their investment opportunity sets as, for example, in the stochastic-volatility model of Section 9.3.6.

9.5 Conclusion

The pricing of derivative securities is one of the unqualified successes of modern economics. It has changed the way economists view dynamic models of securities prices, and it has had an enormous impact on the investment community. The creation of ever more complex financial instruments has been an important stimulus for academic research and for the establishment of a bona fide "financial engineering" discipline. Recent innovations in derivative securities include: average rate options, more general "lookback" options, barrier options (also known as "down and out" or "birth and death" options), compound options, dual-currency or dual-equity options, synthetic convertible bonds, spread-lock interest rate swaps, rainbow options, and many other exotic securities. In each of these cases, closed-form pricing formulas are available only for a very small set of processes for the underlying asset's price, and a great deal of further research is needed to check whether such processes actually fit the data. Moreover, in many of these cases, analytical expressions for hedging positions in these securities do not exist and must also be determined empirically.

There are many unsettled issues in the statistical inference of continuous-time processes with discretely sampled data. Currently, the most pressing issue is the difficulty in obtaining consistent estimates of the parameters of Itô processes with nonlinear drift and/or diffusion coefficients. For many Itô processes of interest, we do not have closed-form expressions for their transition densities and hence maximum likelihood estimation is not feasible. The GMM approach of Hansen and Scheinkman (1995) may be the most promising alternative, and empirical applications and Monte Carlo studies are sure to follow.

Another area of active current research involves developing better models of fundamental asset price dynamics. For example, casual empirical observation suggests the presence of jump components in asset prices that are responsible for relatively large and sudden movements, but occur relatively infrequently and are therefore considerably more challenging to estimate precisely.[28] Indeed, there is even some doubt as to whether such jump processes can ever be identified from discretely sampled price data since the very act of discrete-sampling destroys the one clear distinction between diffusion processes and jump processes—the continuity of sample paths.

The difficulties in estimating parametric models of asset price dynamics have led to several attempts to capture the dynamics *nonparametrically*. For example, by placing restrictions on the drift coefficient of a diffusion process, Aït-Sahalia (1993) proposes a nonparametric estimator of its diffusion coefficient and applies this estimator to the pricing of interest rate options. Longstaff (1995) proposes a test of option-pricing models by focusing on the risk-neutral distribution implicit in option prices. And Hutchinson, Lo, and Poggio (1994) attempt to price derivative securities via neural network models. Although it is still too early to tell if these nonparametric and highly data-intensive methods will offer improvements over their parametric counterparts, the preliminary evidence is quite promising. In Chapter 12, we review some of these techniques and present an application to the pricing and hedging of derivative securities.

Closely related to the issue of stock price dynamics are several open questions regarding the pricing of options in incomplete markets, markets in which the sources of uncertainty affecting the fundamental asset are not spanned by traded securities. For example, if the volatility of the fundamental asset's price is stochastic, it is only under the most restrictive set of assumptions that the price of an option on such an asset may be determined by arbitrage arguments. Since there is almost universal agreement

---

[28]See, for example, Ball and Torous (1983, 1985). Merton (1976b) develops an option-pricing formula for combined diffusion/jump processes. See also Merton (1976a) for more general discussion of the impact of misspecifying stock price dynamics on the pricing of options.

that volatilities do shift over time in random fashion, it is clear that issues regarding market incompleteness are central to the pricing of derivative securities.

In this chapter we have only touched upon a small set of issues that surround derivatives research, those that have received the least attention in the extant literature, with the hope that a wider group of academics and investment professionals will be encouraged to join in the fray and quicken the progress in this exciting area.

Problems—Chapter 9

9.1 Show that the continuous-time process $p_n(t)$ of Section 9.1.1 converges in distribution to a normally distributed continuous-time process $p(t)$ by calculating the the moment-generating function of $p_n(t)$ and taking limits.

9.2 Derive (9.3.30) and (9.3.31) explicitly by evaluating and inverting the Fisher information matrix in (9.3.7) for the maximum likelihood estimators $\hat{\mu}$ and $\hat{\sigma}^2$ of the parameters of a geometric Brownian motion based on regularly sampled data.

9.3 Derive the maximum likelihood estimators $\hat{\mu}$, $\hat{\sigma}^2$, and $\hat{\gamma}$ of the parameters of the trending Ornstein-Uhlenbeck process (9.3.46), and calculate their asymptotic distribution explicitly using (9.3.7). How do these three estimators differ in their asymptotic properties under standard asymptotics and under continuous-record asymptotics?

9.4 You are currently managing a large pension fund and have invested most of it in IBM stock. Exactly one year from now, you will have to liquidate your entire IBM holdings, and you are concerned that it may be an inauspicious time to sell your position. CLM Financial Products Corporation has come to you with the following proposal: For a fee to be negotiated, they will agree to buy your entire IBM holdings exactly one year from now, but at a price per share equal to the *maximum* of the daily closing prices over the one-year period. What fee should you expect in your negotiations with CLM? Specifically:

9.4.1 Estimate the current (time 0) fair market price $H(0)$ of the option to sell at the maximum using Monte Carlo simulation. For simplicity, assume that IBM's stock price $P(t)$ follows a geometric Brownian motion (9.2.2) so that

$$\log \frac{P(t_2)}{P(t_1)} \sim \mathcal{N}\left(\mu(t_2 - t_1), \sigma^2(t_2 - t_1)\right), \qquad (9.5.1)$$

and use daily returns of IBM stock over the most recent five-year period to estimate the parameters μ and σ^2 to calibrate your simulations. Assume that there are 253 trading days in a year and that market prices have no volatility when markets are closed, i.e., weekends, holidays.

9.4.2 Provide a 95% confidence interval for $\hat{H}(0)$ and an estimate of the number of simulations needed to yield a price estimate that is within $.05 of the true price.

9.4.3 How does this price compare with the price given by the Goldman-Sosin-Gatto formula? Can you explain the discrepancy? Which price would you use to decide whether to accept or reject CLM's proposal?

10

Fixed-Income Securities

IN THIS CHAPTER and the next we turn our attention to the bond markets. We study bonds that have no call provisions or default risk, so that their payments are fully specified in advance. Such bonds deserve the name *fixed-income securities* that is often used more loosely to describe bonds whose future payments are in fact uncertain. In the US markets, almost all true fixed-income securities are issued by the US Treasury. Conventional Treasury securities make fixed payments in nominal terms, but in early 1996 the Treasury announced plans to issue *indexed bonds* whose nominal payments are indexed to inflation so that their payments are fixed in real terms.[1]

Many of the ideas discussed in earlier chapters can be applied to fixed-income securities as well as to any other asset. But there are several reasons to devote special attention to fixed-income securities. First, the fixed-income markets have developed separately from the equity markets. They have their own institutional structure and their own terminology. Likewise the academic study of fixed-income securities has its own traditions. Second, the markets for Treasury securities are extremely large regardless of whether size is measured by quantities outstanding or quantities traded. Third, fixed-income securities have a special place in finance theory because they have no cash-flow uncertainty, so their prices vary only as discount rates vary. By studying fixed-income securities we can explore the effects of changing discount rates without having to face the complications introduced by changing expectations of future cash flows. The prices of conventional Treasury securities carry information about nominal discount rates, while the prices of indexed securities carry information about real discount rates. Finally, many other assets can be seen as combinations of fixed-income securities and derivative securities; a callable bond, for example, is a fixed-income security less a put option.

---

[1] Such bonds have already been issued by the UK, Canadian, and several other governments. See Campbell and Shiller (1996) for a review.

The literature on fixed-income securities is vast.[2] We break it into two main parts. First, in this chapter we introduce basic concepts and discuss empirical work on linear time-series models of bond yields. This work is only loosely motivated by theory and has the practical aim of exploring the forecasting power of the term structure of interest rates. In Chapter 11 we turn to more ambitious, fully specified term-structure models that can be used to price interest-rate derivative securities.

10.1 Basic Concepts

In principle a fixed-income security can promise a stream of future payments of any form, but there are two classic cases.

Zero-coupon bonds, also called *discount bonds*, make a single payment at a date in the future known as the *maturity date*. The size of this payment is the *face value* of the bond. The length of time to the maturity date is the *maturity* of the bond. US Treasury bills (Treasury obligations with maturity at issue of up to 12 months) take this form.

Coupon bonds make *coupon payments* of a given fraction of face value at equally spaced dates up to and including the maturity date, when the face value is also paid. US Treasury notes and bonds (Treasury obligations with maturity at issue above 12 months) take this form. Coupon payments on Treasury notes and bonds are made every six months, but the coupon rates for these instruments are normally quoted at an annual rate; thus a 7% Treasury bond actually pays 3.5% of face value every six months up to and including maturity.[3]

Coupon bonds can be thought of as packages of discount bonds, one corresponding to each coupon payment and one corresponding to the final coupon payment together with the repayment of principal. This is not merely an academic concept, as the principal and interest components of US Treasury bonds have been traded separately under the Treasury's STRIPS (Separate Trading of Registered Interest and Principal Securities) program since 1985, and the prices of such Treasury *strips* at all maturities have been reported daily in the *Wall Street Journal* since 1989.

---

[2]Fortunately it has increased in quality since Ed Kane's judgement: "It is generally agreed that, ceteris paribus, the fertility of a field is roughly proportional to the quantity of manure that has been dumped upon it in the recent past. By this standard, the term structure of interest rates has become ... an extraordinarily fertile field indeed" (Kane [1970]). See Melino (1988) or Shiller (1990) for excellent recent surveys, and Sundaresan (1996) for a book-length treatment.

[3]See a textbook such as Fabozzi and Fabozzi (1995) or Fabozzi (1996) for further details on the markets for US Treasury securities.

10.1.1 Discount Bonds

We first define and illustrate basic bond market concepts for discount bonds. The *yield to maturity* on a bond is that discount rate which equates the present value of the bond's payments to its price. Thus if P_{nt} is the time t price of a discount bond that makes a single payment of \$1 at time $t + n$, and Y_{nt} is the bond's yield to maturity, we have

$$P_{nt} = \frac{1}{(1 + Y_{nt})^n}, \tag{10.1.1}$$

so the yield can be found from the price as

$$(1 + Y_{nt}) = P_{nt}^{-\left(\frac{1}{n}\right)}. \tag{10.1.2}$$

It is common in the empirical finance literature to work with log or continuously compounded variables. This has the usual advantage that it transforms the nonlinear equation (10.1.2) into a linear one. Using lowercase letters for logs the relationship between log yield and log price is

$$y_{nt} = -\left(\frac{1}{n}\right) p_{nt}. \tag{10.1.3}$$

The *term structure of interest rates* is the set of yields to maturity, at a given time, on bonds of different maturities. The *yield spread* $S_{nt} \equiv Y_{nt} - Y_{1t}$, or in log terms $s_{nt} \equiv y_{nt} - y_{1t}$, is the difference between the yield on an n-period bond and the yield on a one-period bond, a measure of the shape of the term structure. The *yield curve* is a plot of the term structure, that is, a plot of Y_{nt} or y_{nt} against n on some particular date t. The solid line in Figure 10.1.1 shows the log zero-coupon yield curve for US Treasury securities at the end of January 1987.[4] This particular yield curve rises at first, then falls at longer maturities so that it has a hump shape. This is not unusual, although the yield curve is most commonly upward-sloping over the whole range of maturities. Sometimes the yield curve is *inverted,* sloping down over the whole range of maturities.

Holding-Period Returns

The *holding-period return* on a bond is the return over some holding period less than the bond's maturity. In order to economize on notation, we specialize at once to the case where the holding period is a single period.[5] We

---

[4]This curve is not based on quoted strip prices, which are readily available only for recent years, but is estimated from the prices of coupon-bearing Treasury bonds. Figure 10.1.1 is due to McCulloch and Kwon (1993) and uses McCulloch's (1971, 1975) estimation method as discussed in section 10.1.3 below.

[5]Shiller (1990) gives a much more comprehensive treatment, which requires more complicated notation.

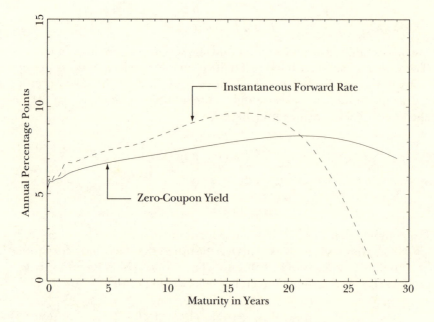

Figure 10.1.   *Zero-Coupon Yield and Forward-Rate Curves in January 1987*

define $R_{n,t+1}$ as the one-period holding-period return on an n-period bond purchased at time t and sold at time $t+1$. Since the bond will be an $(n-1)$-period bond when it is sold, the sale price is $P_{n-1,t+1}$ and the holding-period return is

$$(1 + R_{n,t+1}) \ = \ \frac{P_{n-1,t+1}}{P_{nt}} \ = \ \frac{(1+Y_{nt})^n}{(1+Y_{n-1,t+1})^{n-1}}. \tag{10.1.4}$$

The holding-period return in (10.1.4) is high if the bond has a high yield when it is purchased at time t, and if it has a low yield when it is sold at time $t+1$ (since a low yield corresponds to a high price).

Moving to logs for simplicity, the log holding-period return, $r_{n,t+1} \equiv \log(1 + R_{n,t+1})$, is

$$
\begin{aligned}
r_{n,t+1} \ = \ p_{n-1,t+1} - p_{nt} \ &= \ n\, y_{nt} - (n-1)y_{n-1,t+1} \\
&= \ y_{nt} - (n-1)(y_{n-1,t+1} - y_{nt}). \tag{10.1.5}
\end{aligned}
$$

The last equality in (10.1.5) shows how the holding-period return is determined by the beginning-of-period yield (positively) and the change in the yield over the holding period (negatively).

Equation (10.1.5) can be rearranged so that it relates the log bond price today to the log price tomorrow and the return over the next period: $p_{n,t} = -r_{n,t+1} + p_{n-1,t+1}$. One can solve this difference equation forward, substituting out future log bond prices until the maturity date is reached (and noting that the log price at maturity equals zero) to obtain $p_{nt} = -\sum_{i=0}^{n-1} r_{n-i,t+1+i}$, or in terms of the yield

$$y_{nt} = \left(\frac{1}{n}\right) \sum_{i=0}^{n-1} r_{n-i,t+1+i}. \tag{10.1.6}$$

This equation shows that the log yield to maturity on a zero-coupon bond equals the average log return per period if the bond is held to maturity.

Forward Rates
Bonds of different maturities can be combined to guarantee an interest rate on a fixed-income investment to be made in the future; the interest rate on this investment is called a *forward rate*.[6]

To guarantee at time *t* an interest rate on a one-period investment to be made at time $t + n$, an investor can proceed as follows. The desired future investment will pay \$1 at time $t + n + 1$ so she first buys one $(n + 1)$-period bond; this costs $P_{n+1,t}$ at time *t* and pays \$1 at time $t + n + 1$. The investor wants to transfer the cost of this investment from time *t* to time $t + n$; to do this she sells $P_{n+1,t}/P_{nt}$ *n*-period bonds. This produces a positive cash flow of $P_{nt}(P_{n+1,t}/P_{nt}) = P_{n+1,t}$ at time *t*, exactly enough to offset the negative time *t* cash flow from the first transaction. The sale of *n*-period bonds implies a negative cash flow of $P_{n+1,t}/P_{nt}$ at time $t + n$. This can be thought of as the cost of the one-period investment to be made at time $t + n$. The cash flows resulting from these transactions are illustrated in Figure 10.2.

The forward rate is defined to be the return on the time $t+n$ investment of $P_{n+1,t}/P_{nt}$:

$$(1 + F_{nt}) = \frac{1}{(P_{n+1,t}/P_{nt})} = \frac{(1 + Y_{n+1,t})^{n+1}}{(1 + Y_{nt})^n}. \tag{10.1.7}$$

In the notation F_{nt} the first subscript refers to the number of periods ahead that the one-period investment is to be made, and the second subscript refers to the date at which the forward rate is set. At the cost of additional complexity in notation we could also define forward rates for multiperiod investments, but we do not pursue this further here.

---

[6]An example of forward trading is the *when-issued* market in US Treasury securities. After an auction of new securities is announced but before the securities are issued, the securities are traded in the when-issued market, with settlement to occur when the securities are issued.

	time t	$t+n$	$t+n+1$
Transactions	⊢————————————+————————————⊣		
Buy 1 $(n+1)$-period bond	$-P_{n+1,t}$		1
Sell $P_{n+1,t}/P_{nt}$ n-period bonds	$\left(\dfrac{P_{n+1,t}}{P_{nt}}\right) P_{nt}$	$-\dfrac{P_{n+1,t}}{P_{nt}}$	
Net	0	$-\dfrac{P_{n+1,t}}{P_{nt}}$	1

Figure 10.2.   *Cash Flows in a Forward Transaction*

Moving to logs for simplicity, the n-period-ahead log forward rate is

$$
\begin{aligned}
f_{nt} &= p_{nt} - p_{n+1,t} \\
&= (n+1)\, y_{n+1,t} - n\, y_{nt} \\
&= y_{n+1,t} + n(y_{n+1,t} - y_{nt}) \\
&= y_{nt} + (n+1)(y_{n+1,t} - y_{nt}). \qquad (10.1.8)
\end{aligned}
$$

Equation (10.1.8) shows that the forward rate is positive whenever discount bond prices fall with maturity. Also, the forward rate is above both the n-period and the $(n+1)$-period discount bond yields when the $(n+1)$-period yield is above the n-period yield, that is, when the yield curve is upward-sloping.[7] This relation between a yield to maturity and the instantaneous forward rate at that maturity is analogous to the relation between marginal and average cost. The yield to maturity is the average cost of borrowing for n periods, while the forward rate is the marginal cost of extending the time period of the loan.

Figure 10.1 illustrates the relation between the forward-rate curve (shown as a dashed line) and the yield curve (a solid line). The forward-rate curve lies above the yield curve when the yield curve is upward-sloping, and below it when the yield curve is downward-sloping. The two curves cross when the yield curve is flat. These are the standard properties of marginal and average cost curves. When the cost of a marginal unit exceeds the cost of an average unit then the average cost increases with the addition of the

---

[7]As the time unit shrinks relative to the bond maturity n, the formula (10.1.8) approaches $f_{nt} = y_{nt} + n\, \partial y_{nt}/\partial n$, the n-period yield plus n times the slope of the yield curve at maturity n.

marginal unit, so the average cost rises when the marginal cost is above the average cost. Conversely, the average cost falls when the marginal cost is below the average cost.

10.1.2 Coupon Bonds

As we have already emphasized, a coupon bond can be viewed as a package of discount bonds, one with face value equal to the coupon for each date at which a coupon is paid, and one with the same face value and maturity as the coupon bond itself. Figure 10.3 gives a time line to illustrate the time pattern of payments on a coupon bond.

The price of a coupon bond depends not only on its maturity n and the date t, but also on its coupon rate. To keep notation as simple as possible, we define a period as the time interval between coupon payments and C as the coupon rate *per period*. In the case of US Treasury bonds a period is six months, and C is one half the conventionally quoted annual coupon rate. We write the price of a coupon bond as P_{cnt} to show its dependence on the coupon rate.

The per-period yield to maturity on a coupon bond, Y_{cnt}, is defined as that discount rate which equates the present value of the bond's payments to its price, so we have

$$P_{cnt} = \frac{C}{(1 + Y_{cnt})} + \frac{C}{(1 + Y_{cnt})^2} + \cdots + \frac{1 + C}{(1 + Y_{cnt})^n}. \qquad (10.1.9)$$

In the case of US Treasury bonds, where a period is six months, Y_{cnt} is the six-month yield and the annual yield is conventionally quoted as twice Y_{cnt}.

Equation (10.1.9) cannot be inverted to get an analytical solution for Y_{cnt}. Instead it must be solved numerically, but the procedure is straightforward since all future payments are positive so there is a unique positive real solution for Y_{cnt}.[8] Unlike the yield to maturity on a discount bond, the yield to maturity on a coupon bond does not necessarily equal the per-period return if the bond is held to maturity. That return is not even defined until one specifies the reinvestment strategy for coupons received prior to maturity. The yield to maturity equals the per-period return on the coupon bond held to maturity only if coupons are reinvested at a rate equal to the yield to maturity.

The implicit yield formula (10.1.9) simplifies in two important special cases. First, when $P_{cnt} = 1$, the bond is said to be selling at *par*. In this case the yield just equals the coupon rate: $Y_{cnt} = C$. Second, when maturity n

---

[8]With negative future payments, there can be multiple positive real solutions to (10.1.9). In the analysis of investment projects, the discount rate that equates the present value of a project to its cost is known as the *internal rate of return*. When projects have some negative cash flows in the future, there can be multiple solutions for the internal rate of return.

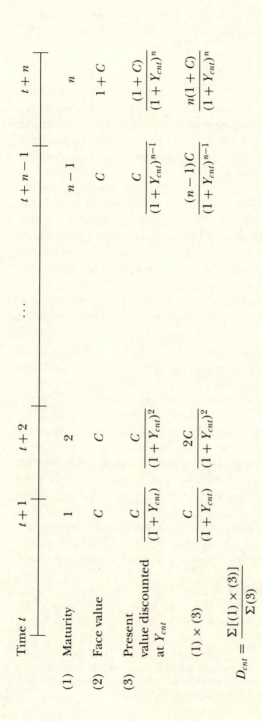

Time t	$t+1$	$t+2$	$\ldots$	$t+n-1$	$t+n$
(1) Maturity	1	2		$n-1$	n
(2) Face value	C	C		C	$1+C$
(3) Present value discounted at Y_{cnt}	$\dfrac{C}{(1+Y_{cnt})}$	$\dfrac{C}{(1+Y_{cnt})^2}$		$\dfrac{C}{(1+Y_{cnt})^{n-1}}$	$\dfrac{(1+C)}{(1+Y_{cnt})^n}$
(1) $\times$ (3)	$\dfrac{C}{(1+Y_{cnt})}$	$\dfrac{2C}{(1+Y_{cnt})^2}$		$\dfrac{(n-1)C}{(1+Y_{cnt})^{n-1}}$	$\dfrac{n(1+C)}{(1+Y_{cnt})^n}$

$$D_{cnt} = \frac{\Sigma[(1) \times (3)]}{\Sigma(3)}$$

Figure 10.3. *Calculation of Duration for a Coupon Bond*

is infinite, the bond is called a *consol* or *perpetuity*. In this case the yield just equals the ratio of the bond price to the coupon rate: $Y_{c\infty t} = C/P_{c\infty t}$.

Duration and Immunization

For discount bonds, maturity measures the length of time that a bondholder has invested money. But for coupon bonds, maturity is an imperfect measure of this length of time because much of a coupon bond's value comes from payments that are made before maturity. *Macaulay's duration*, due to Macaulay (1938), is intended to be a better measure; like maturity, its units are time periods. To understand Macaulay's duration, think of a coupon bond as a package of discount bonds. Macaulay's duration is a weighted average of the maturities of the underlying discount bonds, where the weight on each maturity is the present value of the corresponding discount bond calculated using the coupon bond's yield as the discount rate:[9]

$$
\begin{aligned}
D_{cnt} & = \frac{\frac{C}{(1+Y_{cnt})} + 2\frac{C}{(1+Y_{cnt})^2} + \cdots + n\frac{(1+C)}{(1+Y_{cnt})^n}}{P_{cnt}} \\[2ex]
& = \frac{C\sum_{i=1}^{n}\frac{i}{(1+Y_{cnt})^i} + \frac{n}{(1+Y_{cnt})^n}}{P_{cnt}}.
\end{aligned} \tag{10.1.10}
$$

The maturity of the first component discount bond is one period and this receives a weight of $C/(1 + Y_{cnt})$, the present value of this bond when Y_{cnt} is the discount rate; the maturity of the second discount bond is two and this receives a weight of $C/(1 + Y_{cnt})^2$; and so on until the last discount bond of maturity n gets a weight of $(1 + C)/(1 + Y_{cnt})^n$. To convert this into an average, we divide by the sum of the weights $C/(1 + Y_{cnt}) + C/(1 + Y_{cnt})^2 + \cdots + (1 + C)/(1 + Y_{cnt})^n$, which from (10.1.9) is just the bond price P_{cnt}. These calculations are illustrated graphically in Figure 10.3.

When $C = 0$, the bond is a discount bond and Macaulay's duration equals maturity. When $C > 0$, Macaulay's duration is less than maturity and it declines with the coupon rate. For a given coupon rate, duration declines with the bond yield because a higher yield reduces the weight on more distant payments in the average (10.1.10). The duration formula simplifies when a coupon bond is selling at par or has an infinite maturity. A par bond has price $P_{cnt} = 1$ and yield $Y_{cnt} = C$, so duration becomes $D_{cnt} = (1 - (1 + Y_{cnt})^{-n})/(1 - (1 + Y_{cnt})^{-1})$. A consol bond with infinite maturity has yield $Y_{c\infty t} = C/P_{c\infty t}$ so duration becomes $D_{c\infty t} = (1 + Y_{c\infty t})/Y_{c\infty t}$.

Numerical examples that illustrate these properties are given in Table 10.1. The table shows Macaulay's duration (and modified duration, defined in (10.1.12) below, in parentheses) for bonds with yields and coupon

---

[9]Macaulay also suggests that one could use yields on discount bonds rather than the yield on the coupon bond to calculate the present value of each coupon payment. However this approach requires that one measure a complete zero-coupon term structure.

Table 10.1. *Macaulay's and modified duration for selected bonds.*

		1	2	5	10	30	∞
Coupon rate	0%						
Yield	0%	1.000	2.000	5.000	10.000	30.000	—
		(1.000)	(2.000)	(5.000)	(10.000)	(30.000)	
	5%	1.000	2.000	5.000	10.000	30.000	—
		(0.976)	(1.951)	(4.878)	(9.756)	(29.268)	
	10%	1.000	2.000	5.000	10.000	30.000	—
		(0.952)	(1.905)	(4.762)	(9.524)	(28.571)	
Coupon rate	5%						
Yield	0%	0.988	1.932	4.550	8.417	21.150	—
		(0.988)	(1.932)	(4.550)	(8.417)	(21.150)	
	5%	0.988	1.928	4.485	7.989	15.841	20.500
		(0.964)	(1.881)	(4.376)	(7.795)	(15.454)	(20.000)
	10%	0.988	1.924	4.414	7.489	10.957	10.500
		(0.940)	(1.832)	(4.204)	(7.132)	(10.436)	(10.000)
Coupon rate	10%						
Yield	0%	0.977	1.875	4.250	7.625	18.938	—
		(0.977)	(1.875)	(4.250)	(7.625)	(18.938)	
	5%	0.977	1.868	4.156	7.107	14.025	20.500
		(0.953)	(1.823)	(4.054)	(6.933)	(13.683)	(20.000)
	10%	0.976	1.862	4.054	6.543	9.938	10.500
		(0.930)	(1.773)	(3.861)	(6.231)	(9.465)	(10.000)

Maturity (years)

The table reports Macaulay's duration and, in parentheses, modified duration for bonds with selected yields and maturities. Duration, yield, and maturity are stated in annual units but the underlying calculations assume that bond payments are made at six-month intervals.

rates of 0%, 5%, and 10%, and maturities ranging from one year to infinity. Duration is given in years but is calculated using six-month periods as would be appropriate for US Treasury bonds.

If we take the derivative of (10.1.9) with respect to Y_{cnt}, or equivalently with respect to $(1 + Y_{cnt})$, we find that Macaulay's duration has another very important property. It is the negative of the elasticity of a coupon bond's price with respect to its gross yield $(1 + Y_{cnt})$:[10]

$$D_{cnt} = -\frac{dP_{cnt}}{d(1 + Y_{cnt})}\frac{(1 + Y_{cnt})}{P_{cnt}}. \qquad (10.1.11)$$

In industry applications, Macaulay's duration is often divided by the gross yield $(1 + Y_{cnt})$ to get what is called *modified duration*:

$$\frac{D_{cnt}}{(1 + Y_{cnt})} = -\frac{dP_{cnt}}{dY_{cnt}}\frac{1}{P_{cnt}}. \qquad (10.1.12)$$

Modified duration measures the proportional sensitivity of a bond's price to a small absolute change in its yield. Thus if modified duration is 10, an increase in the yield of 1 basis point (say from 3.00% to 3.01%) will cause a 10 basis point or 0.10% drop in the bond price.[11]

Macaulay's duration and modified duration are sometimes used to answer the following question: What single coupon bond best approximates the return on a zero-coupon bond with a given maturity? This question is of practical interest because many financial intermediaries have long-term zero-coupon liabilities, such as pension obligations, and they may wish to match or *immunize* these liabilities with coupon-bearing Treasury bonds.[12] Although today stripped zero-coupon Treasury bonds are available, they may be unattractive because of tax clientele and liquidity effects, so the immunization problem remains relevant. If there is a *parallel* shift in the yield curve so that bond yields of all maturities move by the same amount, then a change in the zero-coupon yield is accompanied by an equal change in the coupon bond yield. In this case equation (10.1.11) shows that a coupon bond whose Macaulay duration equals the maturity of the zero-coupon liability (equivalently, a coupon bond whose modified duration equals the modified duration of the zero-coupon liability) has, to a first-order approximation, the same return as the zero-coupon liability. This bond—or any portfolio of bonds with the same duration—solves the immunization problem for small, parallel shifts in the term structure.

Although this approach is attractively simple, there are several reasons why it must be used with caution. First, it assumes that yields of all maturities move by the same amount, in a parallel shift of the term structure. We

---

[10]The elasticity of a variable B with respect to a variable A is defined to be the derivative of B with respect to A, times A/B: $(dB/dA)(A/B)$. Equivalently, it is the derivative of $\log(B)$ with respect to $\log(A)$.

[11]Note that if duration is measured in six-month time units, then yields should be measured on a six-month basis. One can convert to an annual basis by halving duration and doubling yields. The numbers in Table 10.1 have been annualized in this way.

[12]Immunization was originally defined by Reddington (1952) as "the investment of the assets in such a way that the existing business is immune to a general change in the rate of interest". Fabozzi and Fabozzi (1995), Chapter 42, gives a comprehensive discussion.

show in Section 10.2.1 that historically, movements in short-term interest rates have tended to be larger than movements in longer-term bond yields. Some modified approaches have been developed to handle the more realistic case where short yields move more than long yields, so that there are *nonparallel* shifts in the term structure (see Bierwag, Kaufman, and Toevs [1983], Granito [1984], Ingersoll, Skelton, and Weil [1978]).

Second, (10.1.11) and (10.1.12) give first-order derivatives so they apply only to infinitesimally small changes in yields. Figure 10.4 illustrates the fact that the relationship between the log price and the yield on a bond is convex rather than linear. The slope of this relationship, modified duration, increases as yields fall (a fact shown also in Table 10.1). This may be taken into account by using a second-order derivative. The *convexity* of a bond is defined as

$$\text{Convexity} \equiv \frac{\partial^2 P_{cnt}}{\partial Y_{cnt}^2} \frac{1}{P_{cnt}} = \frac{C \sum_{i=1}^{n} \frac{i(i+1)}{(1+Y_{cnt})^{i+2}} + \frac{n(n+1)}{(1+Y_{cnt})^{n+2}}}{P_{cnt}}, \quad (10.1.13)$$

and convexity can be used in a second-order Taylor series approximation of the price impact of a change in yield:

$$\frac{dP_{cn}(Y_{cn})}{P_{cn}} \approx \frac{dP_{cn}}{dY_{cn}} \frac{1}{P_{cn}} dY_{cn} + \frac{1}{2} \frac{d^2 P_{cn}}{dY_{cn}^2} \frac{1}{P_{cn}} (dY_{cn})^2$$

$$= (- \text{ modified duration}) \, dY_{cn}$$

$$+ \frac{1}{2} \text{ convexity } (dY_{cn})^2. \quad (10.1.14)$$

Finally, both Macaulay's duration and modified duration assume that cash flows are fixed and do not change when interest rates change. This assumption is appropriate for Treasury securities but not for callable securities such as corporate bonds or mortgage-backed securities, or for securities with default risk if the probability of default varies with the level of interest rates. By modelling the way in which cash flows vary with interest rates, it is possible to calculate the sensitivity of prices to interest rates for these more complicated securities; this sensitivity is known as *effective duration*.[13]

A Loglinear Model for Coupon Bonds
The idea of duration has also been used in the academic literature to find approximate linear relationships between log coupon bond yields, holding-period returns, and forward rates that are analogous to the exact relationships for zero-coupon bonds. To understand this approach, start from the

---

[13]See Fabozzi and Fabozzi (1995), Chapters 28–30, and Fabozzi (1996) for a discussion of various methods used by fixed-income analysts to calculate effective duration.

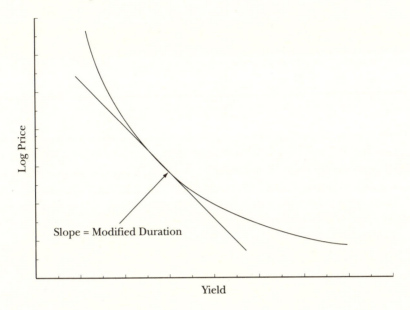

Figure 10.4. *The Price-Yield Relationship*

loglinear approximate return formula (7.1.19) derived in Chapter 7, and apply it to the one-period return $r_{c,n,t+1}$ on an n-period coupon bond:

$$r_{c,n,t+1} \approx k + \rho p_{c,n-1,t+1} + (1-\rho)c - p_{cnt}. \tag{10.1.15}$$

Here the log nominal coupon c plays the role of the dividend on stock, but of course it is fixed rather than random. The parameters ρ and k are given by $\rho \equiv 1/(1 + \exp(\overline{c-p}))$ and $k \equiv -\log(\rho) - (1-\rho)\log(1/\rho - 1)$. When the bond is selling at par, then its price is \$1 so its log price is zero and $\rho = 1/(1+C) = (1+Y_{cnt})^{-1}$. It is standard to use this value for ρ, which gives a good approximation for returns on bonds selling close to par.

One can treat (10.1.15), like the analogous zero-coupon expression (10.1.5), as a difference equation in the log bond price. Solving forward to the maturity date one obtains

$$p_{cnt} = \sum_{i=0}^{n-1} \rho^i [k + (1-\rho)c - r_{c,n-i,t+1+i}]. \tag{10.1.16}$$

This equation relates the price of a coupon bond to its stream of coupon payments and the future returns on the bond. A similar approximation of the log yield to maturity y_{cnt} shows that it satisfies an equation of the same form:

$$p_{cnt} \approx \sum_{i=0}^{n-1} \rho^i [k + (1 - \rho)c - y_{cnt}]$$

$$= \frac{(1 - \rho^n)}{(1 - \rho)} [k + (1 - \rho)c - y_{cnt}]. \qquad (10.1.17)$$

Equations (10.1.16) and (10.1.17) together imply that the n-period coupon bond yield satisfies $y_{cnt} \approx \left((1 - \rho)/(1 - \rho^n) \right) \sum_{i=0}^{n-1} \rho^i r_{c,n-i,t+1+i}$. Thus although there is no exact relationship there is an approximate equality between the log yield to maturity on a coupon bond and a weighted average of the returns on the bond when it is held to maturity.

Equation (10.1.11) tells us that Macaulay's duration for a coupon bond is the derivative of its log price with respect to its log yield. Equation (10.1.17) gives this derivative as

$$D_{cn} \approx \frac{(1 - \rho^n)}{(1 - \rho)} = \frac{1 - (1 + Y_{cnt})^{-n}}{1 - (1 + Y_{cnt})^{-1}}, \qquad (10.1.18)$$

where the second equality uses $\rho = (1 + Y_{cnt})^{-1}$. As noted above, this relation between duration and yield holds exactly for a bond selling at par.

Substituting (10.1.17) and (10.1.18) into (10.1.15), we obtain a loglinear relation between holding-period returns and yields for coupon bonds:

$$r_{c,n,t+1} \approx D_{cn} y_{cnt} - (D_{cn} - 1) y_{c,n-1,t+1}. \qquad (10.1.19)$$

This equation was first derived by Shiller, Campbell, and Schoenholtz (1983).[14] It is analogous to (10.1.5) for zero-coupon bonds; maturity in that equation is replaced by duration here, and of course the two equations are consistent with one another for a zero-coupon bond whose duration equals its maturity.

A similar analysis for forward rates shows that the n-period-ahead 1-period forward rate implicit in the coupon-bearing term structure is

$$f_{nt} \approx \frac{D_{c,n+1} y_{c,n+1,t} - D_{cn} y_{cnt}}{D_{c,n+1} - D_{cn}}. \qquad (10.1.20)$$

This formula, which is also due to Shiller, Campbell, and Schoenholtz (1983), reduces to the discount bond formula (10.1.8) when duration equals maturity.

---

[14]Shiller, Campbell, and Schoenholtz use Y_{cnt} instead of y_{cnt}, but these are equivalent to the same first-order approximation used to derive (10.1.19). They also derive formulas relating multiperiod holding returns to yields.

10.1.3 Estimating the Zero-Coupon Term Structure

The classic immunization problem is that of finding a coupon bond or portfolio of coupon bonds whose return has the same sensitivity to small interest-rate movements as the return on a given zero-coupon bond. Alternatively, one can try to find a portfolio of coupon bonds whose cash flows exactly match those of a given zero-coupon bond. In general, this portfolio will involve shortselling some bonds. This procedure has academic interest as well; one can extract an implied zero-coupon term structure from the coupon term structure.

If the complete zero-coupon term structure—that is, the prices of discount bonds $P_1 \ldots P_n$ maturing at each coupon date—is known, then it is easy to find the price of a coupon bond as

$$P_{cn} = P_1 C + P_2 C + \cdots + P_n(1 + C). \tag{10.1.21}$$

Time subscripts are omitted here and throughout this section to economize on notation.

Similarly, if a complete coupon term structure—the prices of coupon bonds $P_{c1} \ldots P_{cn}$ maturing at each coupon date—is available, then (10.1.21) can be used to back out the implied zero-coupon term structure. Starting with a one-period coupon bond, $P_{c1} = P_1(1 + C)$ so $P_1 = P_{c1}/(1 + C)$. We can then proceed iteratively. Given discount bond prices $P_1, \ldots, P_{n-1}$, we can find P_n as

$$P_n = \frac{P_{cn} - P_{n-1}C - \cdots - P_1 C}{1 + C}. \tag{10.1.22}$$

Sometimes the coupon term structure may be more-than-complete in the sense that at least one coupon bond matures on each coupon date and several coupon bonds mature on some coupon dates. In this case (10.1.21) restricts the prices of some coupon bonds to be exact functions of the prices of other coupon bonds. Such restrictions are unlikely to hold in practice because of tax effects and other market frictions. To handle this Carleton and Cooper (1976) suggest adding a bond-specific error term to (10.1.21) and estimating it as a cross-sectional regression with all the bonds outstanding at a particular date. If these bonds are indexed $i = 1 \ldots I$, then the regression is

$$P_{c_i n_i} = P_1 C_i + P_2 C_i + \cdots + P_{n_i}(1 + C_i) + u_i, \qquad i = 1 \ldots I, \tag{10.1.23}$$

where C_i is the coupon on the ith bond and n_i is the maturity of the ith bond. The regressors are coupon payments at different dates, and the coefficients are the discount bond prices $P_j, j = 1 \ldots N$, where $N = \max_i n_i$ is the longest coupon bond maturity. The system can be estimated by OLS provided that the coupon term structure is complete and that $I \geq N$.

Spline Estimation

In practice the term structure of coupon bonds is usually incomplete, and this means that the coefficients in (10.1.23) are not identified without imposing further restrictions. It seems natural to impose that the prices of discount bonds should vary smoothly with maturity. McCulloch (1971, 1975) suggests that a convenient way to do this is to write P_n, regarded as a function of maturity $P(n)$, as a linear combination of certain prespecified functions:

$$P_n = P(n) = 1 + \sum_{j=1}^{J} a_j f_j(n). \qquad (10.1.24)$$

McCulloch calls $P(n)$ the *discount function*. The $f_j(n)$ in (10.1.24) are known functions of maturity n, and the a_j are coefficients to be estimated. Since $P(0) = 1$, we must have $f_j(0) = 0$ for all j.

Substituting (10.1.24) into (10.1.23) and rearranging, we obtain a regression equation

$$\Pi_i = \sum_{j=1}^{J} a_j X_{ij} + u_i, \qquad i = 1 \ldots I, \qquad (10.1.25)$$

where $\Pi_i \equiv P_{c_i n_i} - 1 - C_i n_i$, the difference between the coupon bond price and the undiscounted value of its future payments, and $X_{ij} \equiv f_j(n_i) + C_i \sum_{l=1}^{n_i} f_j(l)$. Like equation (10.1.23), this equation can be estimated by OLS, but there are now only J coefficients rather than N.[15]

A key question is how to specify the functions $f_j(n)$ in (10.1.24). One simple possibility is to make $P(n)$, the discount function, a polynomial. To do this one sets $f_j(n) = n^j$. Although a sufficiently high-order polynomial can approximate any function, in practice one may want to use more parameters to fit the discount function at some maturities rather than others. For example one may want a more flexible approximation in maturity ranges where many bonds are traded.

To meet this need McCulloch suggests that $P(n)$ should be a *spline* function.[16] An rth-order spline, defined over some finite interval, is a piecewise rth-order polynomial with $r-1$ continuous derivatives; its rth derivative is a step function. The points where the rth derivative changes discontinuously (including the points at the beginning and end of the interval over which the spline is defined) are known as *knot points*. If there are K knot

---

[15]The bond pricing errors are unlikely to be homoskedastic. McCulloch argues that the standard deviation of u_i is proportional to the bid-ask spread for bond i, and thus weights each observation by the reciprocal of its spread. This is not required for consistency, but may improve the efficiency of the estimates.

[16]Suits, Mason, and Chan (1978) give an accessible introduction to spline methodology.

points, there are $K - 1$ subintervals in each of which the spline is a polynomial. The spline has $K - 2 + r$ free parameters, r for the first subinterval and 1 (that determines the unrestricted rth derivative) for each of the $K - 2$ following subintervals. McCulloch suggests that the knot points should be chosen so that each subinterval contains an equal number of bond maturity dates.

If forward rates are to be continuous, the discount function must have at least one continuous derivative. Hence a quadratic spline, estimated by McCulloch (1971), is the lowest-order spline that can fit the discount function. If we require that the forward-rate curve should also be continuously differentiable, then we need to use a cubic spline, estimated by McCulloch (1975) and others. McCulloch's papers give the rather complicated formulas for the functions $f_j(n)$ that make $P(n)$ a quadratic or cubic spline.[17]

Tax Effects

OLS estimation of (10.1.25) chooses the parameters a_j so that the bond pricing errors u_i are uncorrelated with the variables X_{ij} that define the discount function. If a sufficiently flexible spline is used, then the pricing errors will be uncorrelated with maturity or any nonlinear function of maturity. Pricing errors may, however, be correlated with the coupon rate which is the other defining characteristic of a bond. Indeed McCulloch (1971) found that his model tended to underprice bonds that were selling below par because of their low coupon rates.

McCulloch (1975) attributes this to a tax effect. US Treasury bond coupons are taxed as ordinary income while price appreciation on a coupon-bearing bond purchased at a discount is taxed as capital gains. If the capital gains tax rate τ_g is less than the ordinary income tax rate τ (as has often been the case historically), then this can explain a price premium on bonds selling below par. For an investor who holds a bond to maturity the pricing formula (10.1.21) should be modified to

$$P_{cn} = [1 - \tau_g(1 - P_{cn})]P(n) + (1 - \tau)C \sum_{i=1}^{n} P(i). \tag{10.1.26}$$

The spline approach can be modified to handle tax effects like that in (10.1.26), at the cost of some additional complexity in estimation. Once tax effects are included, coupon bond prices must be used to construct the variables X_{ij} on the right-hand side of (10.1.25). This means that the bond pricing errors are correlated with the regressors so the equation must be

---

[17]Adams and van Deventer (1994) argue for the use of a fourth-order spline, with the cubic term omitted, in order to maximize the "smoothness" of the forward-rate curve, where smoothness is defined to be minus the average squared second derivative of the forward-rate curve with respect to maturity.

estimated by instrumental variables rather than simple OLS. Litzenberger and Rolfo (1984) apply a tax-adjusted spline model of this sort to bond market data from several different countries.

The tax-adjusted spline model assumes that the same tax rates are relevant for all bonds. The model cannot handle "clientele" effects, in which differently taxed investors specialize in different bonds. Schaefer (1981, 1982) suggests that clientele effects can be handled by first finding a set of tax-efficient bonds for an investor in a particular tax bracket, then estimating an implied zero-coupon yield curve from those bonds alone.

Nonlinear Models

Despite the flexibility of the spline approach, spline functions have some unappealing properties. First, since splines are polynomials they imply a discount function which diverges as maturity increases rather than going to zero as required by theory. Implied forward rates also diverge rather than converging to any fixed limit. Second, there is no simple way to ensure that the discount function always declines with maturity (i.e., that all forward rates are positive). The forward curve illustrated in Figure 10.1 goes negative at a maturity of 27 years, and this behavior is not uncommon (see Shea [1984]). These problems are related to the fact that a flat zero-coupon yield curve implies an exponentially declining discount function, which is not easily approximated by a polynomial function. Since any plausible yield curve flattens out at the long end, splines are likely to have difficulties with longer-maturity bonds.

These difficulties have led some authors to suggest nonlinear alternatives to the linear specification (10.1.24). One alternative, suggested by Vasicek and Fong (1982), is to use an *exponential spline*, a spline applied to a negative exponential transformation of maturity. The exponential spline has the desirable property that forward rates and zero-coupon yields converge to a fixed limit as maturity increases. More generally, a flat yield curve is easy to fit with an exponential spline.

Although the exponential spline is appealing in theory, it is not clear that it performs better than the standard spline in practice (see Shea [1985]). The exponential spline does not make it easier to restrict forward rates to be positive. As for its long-maturity behavior, it is important to remember that forward rates cannot be directly estimated beyond the maturity of the longest coupon bond; they can only be identified by restricting the relation between long-horizon forward rates and shorter-horizon forward rates. The exponential spline, like the standard spline, fits the observed maturity range flexibly, leaving the limiting forward rate and speed of convergence to this rate to be determined more by the restrictions of the spline than by any characteristics of the long-horizon data. Since the exponential spline involves nonlinear estimation of a parameter used to transform maturity, it is more difficult to use than the standard spline and this cost may outweigh the exponential spline's desirable long-horizon properties. In any case, forward rate and yield curves should be treated with caution if they are extrapolated beyond the maturity of the longest traded bond.

Some other authors have solved the problem of negative forward rates by restricting the shape of the zero-coupon yield curve. Nelson and Siegel (1987), for example, model the instantaneous forward rate at maturity n as the solution to a second-order differential equation with equal roots: $f(n) = \beta_0 + \beta_1 \exp(-\alpha n) + \alpha n \beta_2 \exp(-\alpha n)$. This implies that the discount function is double-exponential:

$$P(n) = \exp[-\beta_0 n + (\beta_1 + \beta_2)(1 - \exp(-\alpha n))/\alpha - n\beta_2 \exp(-\alpha n)].$$

This specification generates forward-rate and yield curves with a desirable range of shapes, including upward-sloping, inverted, and hump-shaped. Svensson (1994) has developed this specification further. Other recent work has generated bond-price formulas from fully specified general-equilibrium models of the term structure, which we discuss in Chapter 11.

10.2 Interpreting the Term Structure of Interest Rates

There is a large empirical literature which tests statements about expected-return relationships among bonds without deriving these statements from a fully specified equilibrium model. For simplicity we discuss this literature assuming that zero-coupon bond prices are observed or can be estimated from coupon bond prices.

10.2.1 The Expectations Hypothesis

The most popular simple model of the term structure is known as the *expectations hypothesis*. We distinguish the *pure expectations hypothesis (PEH)* (PEH), which says that expected excess returns on long-term over short-term bonds are zero, from the *expectations hypothesis* (EH), which says that expected excess returns are constant over time. This terminology is due to Lutz (1940).

Different Forms of the Pure Expectations Hypothesis
We also distinguish different forms of the PEH, according to the time horizon over which expected excess returns are zero. A first form of the PEH equates the one-period expected returns on one-period and n-period bonds. The one-period return on a one-period bond is known in advance to be $(1 + Y_{1t})$, so this form of the PEH implies

$$(1 + Y_{1t}) = E_t[1 + R_{n,t+1}] = (1 + Y_{nt})^n E_t\left[(1 + Y_{n-1,t+1})^{-(n-1)}\right], \quad (10.2.1)$$

where the second equality follows from the definition of holding-period return and the fact that $(1 + Y_{nt})$ is known at time t.

A second form of the PEH equates the n-period expected returns on one-period and n-period bonds:

$$(1 + Y_{nt})^n = E_t\left[(1 + Y_{1t})(1 + Y_{1,t+1})\ldots(1 + Y_{1,t+n-1})\right]. \qquad (10.2.2)$$

Here $(1 + Y_{nt})^n$ is the n-period return on an n-period bond, which equals the expected return from rolling over one-period bonds for n periods. It is straightforward to show that if (10.2.2) holds for all n, it implies

$$1 + F_{n-1,t} \equiv \frac{(1 + Y_{nt})^n}{(1 + Y_{n-1,t})^{n-1}} = E_t[1 + Y_{1,t+n-1}]. \qquad (10.2.3)$$

Under this form of the PEH, the $(n - 1)$-period-ahead one-period forward rate equals the expected $(n - 1)$-period-ahead spot rate.

It is also straightforward to show that if (10.2.2) holds for all n, it implies

$$(1 + Y_{nt})^n = (1 + Y_{1t}) E_t\left[(1 + Y_{n-1,t+1})^{n-1}\right]. \qquad (10.2.4)$$

But (10.2.4) is inconsistent with (10.2.1) whenever interest rates are random. The problem is that by Jensen's Inequality, the expectation of the reciprocal of a random variable is not the reciprocal of the expectation of that random variable. Thus the pure expectations hypothesis cannot hold in both its one-period form and its n-period form.[18]

One can understand this problem more clearly by assuming that interest rates are lognormal and homoskedastic and taking logs of the one-period PEH equation (10.2.1) and the n-period PEH equation (10.2.4). Noting that from equation (10.1.5) the excess one-period log return on an n-period bond is

$$r_{n,t+1} - y_{1t} = (y_{nt} - y_{1t}) - (n - 1)(y_{n-1,t+1} - y_{nt}), \qquad (10.2.5)$$

equation (10.2.1) implies that

$$E[r_{n,t+1} - y_{1t}] = -(1/2) \operatorname{Var}[r_{n,t+1} - y_{1t}], \qquad (10.2.6)$$

while (10.2.4) implies that

$$E[r_{n,t+1} - y_{1t}] = (1/2) \operatorname{Var}[r_{n,t+1} - y_{1t}]. \qquad (10.2.7)$$

The difference between the right-hand sides of (10.2.6) and (10.2.7) is

[18]Cox, Ingersoll, and Ross (1981a) make this point very clearly. They also argue that in continuous time, only expected equality of instantaneous returns (a model corresponding to (10.2.1)) is consistent with the absence of arbitrage. But McCulloch (1993) has shown that this result depends on restrictive assumptions and does not hold in general.

Table 10.2. *Means and standard deviations of term-structure variables.*

Variable	Long bond maturity (n)						
	2	3	6	12	24	48	120
Excess return	0.385	0.564	0.848	0.917	0.709	0.614	−0.048
$r_{n,t+1} - y_{1t}$	(0.644)	(1.222)	(2.954)	(6.218)	(11.33)	(19.40)	(37.08)
Change in yield	0.010	0.010	0.010	0.010	0.011	0.011	0.012
$y_{n,t+1} - y_{nt}$	(0.592)	(0.576)	(0.570)	(0.547)	(0.488)	(0.410)	(0.310)
Change in yield	−0.188	−0.119	−0.056	−0.014	0.011	0.011	0.012
$y_{n-1,t+1} - y_{nt}$	(0.608)	(0.586)	(0.573)	(0.555)	(0.488)	(0.410)	(0.310)
Yield spread	0.197	0.326	0.570	0.765	0.958	1.153	1.367
$y_{nt} - y_{1t}$	(0.212)	(0.303)	(0.438)	(0.594)	(0.797)	(1.012)	(1.237)

Long bond maturities are measured in months. For each variable the table reports the sample mean and sample standard deviation (in parentheses) using monthly data over the period 1952:1-1991:2. The units are annualized percentage points. The underlying data are zero-coupon bond yields from McCulloch and Kwon (1993).

$\mathrm{Var}[r_{n,t+1} - y_{1t}]$, which measures the quantitative importance of the Jensen's Inequality effect in a lognormal homoskedastic model.

Table 10.2 reports unconditional sample means and standard deviations for several term-structure variables over the period 1952:1 to 1991:2.[19] All data are monthly, but are measured in annualized percentage points; that is, the raw variables are multiplied by 1200. The first row shows the mean and standard deviation of excess returns on n-month zero-coupon bonds over one-month bills. The mean excess return is positive and rising with maturity at first, but it starts to fall at a maturity of one year and is even slightly negative for ten-year zero-coupon bonds.

This pattern can be understood by breaking excess returns into the two components on the right-hand side of equation (10.2.5): the yield spread ($y_{nt} - y_{1t}$) between n-period and one-period bonds, and $-(n-1)$ times the change in yield ($y_{n-1,t+1} - y_{nt}$) on the n-period bond. Interest rates of all fixed maturities rise during the sample period, as shown in the second row of Table 10.2 and illustrated for one-month and ten-year rates in Figure 10.5. At the short end of the term structure this effect is offset by the decline in maturity from n to $n-1$ as the bond is held for one month; thus the change

---

[19]Table 10.2 is an expanded version of a table shown in Campbell (1995). The numbers given here are slightly different from the numbers in that paper because the sample period used in that paper was 1951:1 to 1990:2, although it was erroneously reported to be 1952:1 to 1991:2.

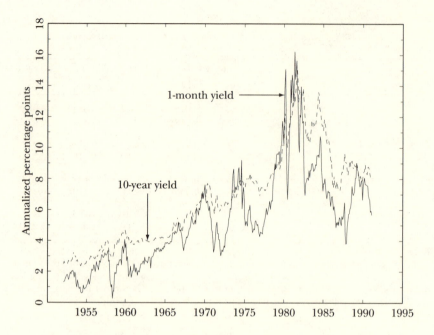

Figure 10.5.   *Short- and Long-Term Interest Rates 1952 to 1991*

in yield $(y_{n-1,t+1} - y_{nt})$, shown in the third row of Table 10.2, is negative for short bonds, contributing positively to their return.[20] At the long end of the term structure, however, the decline in maturity from n to $n-1$ is negligible, and so the change in yield $(y_{n-1,t+1} - y_{nt})$ is positive, causing capital losses on long zero-coupon bonds which outweigh the higher yields offered by these bonds, shown in the fourth row of Table 10.2.

The standard deviation of excess returns rises rapidly with maturity. If excess bond returns are white noise, then the standard error of the sample mean is the standard deviation divided by the square root of the sample size (469 months). The standard error for $n = 2$ is only 0.03%, whereas the standard error for $n = 120$ is 1.71%. Thus the pattern of mean returns is imprecisely estimated at long maturities.

The standard deviation of excess returns also determines the size of the wedge between the one-period and n-period forms of the pure expectations hypothesis. The difference between mean annualized excess returns under (10.2.6) and (10.2.7) is only 0.0003% for $n = 2$. It is still only 0.11% for

---

[20]Investors who seek to profit from this tendency of bond yields to fall as maturity shrinks are said to be "riding the yield curve."

$n = 24$. But it rises to 1.15% for $n = 120$. This calculation shows that the differences between different forms of the PEH are small except for very long-maturity zero-coupon bonds. Since these bonds have the most imprecisely estimated mean returns, the data reject all forms of the PEH at the short end of the term structure, but reject no forms of the PEH at the long end of the term structure. In this sense the distinction between different forms of the PEH is not critical for evaluating this hypothesis.

Most empirical research uses neither the one-period form of the PEH (10.2.6), nor the n-period form (10.2.7), but a log form of the PEH that equates the expected log returns on bonds of all maturities:

$$E[r_{n,t+1} - y_{1t}] = 0. \tag{10.2.8}$$

This model is halfway between equations (10.2.6) and (10.2.7) and can be justified as an approximation to either of them when variance terms are small. Alternatively, it can be derived directly as in McCulloch (1993).

Implications of the Log Pure Expectations Hypothesis
Once the PEH is formulated in logs, it is comparatively easy to state its implications for longer-term bonds. The log PEH implies, first, that the one-period log yield (which is the same as the one-period return on a one-period bond) should equal the expected log holding return on a longer n-period bond held for one period:

$$y_{1t} = E_t[r_{n,t+1}]. \tag{10.2.9}$$

Second, a long-term n-period log yield should equal the expected sum of n successive log yields on one-period bonds which are rolled over for n periods:

$$y_{nt} = (1/n) \sum_{i=0}^{n-1} E_t[y_{1,t+i}]. \tag{10.2.10}$$

Finally, the $(n-1)$-period-ahead one-period log forward rate should equal the expected one-period spot rate $(n-1)$ periods ahead:

$$f_{n-1,t} = E_t[y_{1,t+n-1}]. \tag{10.2.11}$$

This implies that the log forward rate for a one-period investment to be made at a particular date in the future should follow a martingale:

$$f_{nt} = E_t[y_{1,t+n}] = E_t[E_{t+1}[y_{1,t+n}]] = E_t[f_{n-1,t+1}]. \tag{10.2.12}$$

If any of equations (10.2.9), (10.2.10), and (10.2.11) hold for all n and t, then the other equations also hold for all n and t. Also, if any of these equations hold for $n = 2$ at some date t, then the other equations also hold for $n = 2$ and the same date t. Note however that (10.2.9)–(10.2.11) are not generally equivalent for particular n and t.

Alternatives to the Pure Expectations Hypothesis

The expectations hypothesis (EH) is more general than the PEH in that it allows the expected returns on bonds of different maturities to differ by constants, which can depend on maturity but not on time. The differences between expected returns on bonds of different maturities are sometimes called *term premia*. The PEH says that term premia are zero, while the EH says that they are constant through time.[21] Like the PEH, the EH can be formulated for one-period simple returns, for n-period simple returns, or for log returns. If bond returns are lognormal and homoskedastic, as in Singleton (1990), then these formulations are consistent with one another because the Jensen's Inequality effects are constant over time. Recent empirical research typically concentrates on the log form of the EH.

Early discussions of the term structure tended to ignore the possibility that term premia might vary over time, concentrating instead on their sign. Hicks (1946) and Lutz (1940) argued that lenders prefer short maturities while borrowers prefer long maturities, so that long bonds should have higher average returns than short bonds. Modigliani and Sutch (1966) argued that different lenders and borrowers might have different *preferred habitats*, so that term premia might be negative as well as positive. All these authors disputed the PEH but did not explicitly question the EH. More recent work has used intertemporal asset pricing theory to derive both the average sign and the time-variation of term premia; we discuss this work in Chapter 11.

10.2.2 Yield Spreads and Interest Rate Forecasts

We now consider empirical evidence on the expectations hypothesis (EH). Since the EH allows constant differences in the expected returns on short- and long-term bonds, it does not restrict constant terms so for convenience we drop constants from all equations in this section.

So far we have stated the implications of the expectations hypothesis for the levels of nominal interest rates. In post-World War II US data, nominal interest rates seem to follow a highly persistent process with a root very close to unity, so much empirical work uses yield spreads instead of yield levels.[22]

---

[21] This usage is the most common one in the literature. Fama (1984), Fama (1990), and Fama and Bliss (1987), however, use "term premia" to refer to realized, rather than expected, excess returns on long-term bonds.

[22] See Chapters 2 and 7 for a discussion of unit roots. The persistence of the short-rate

Recall that the yield spread between the n-period yield and the one-period yield is $s_{nt} \equiv y_{nt} - y_{1t}$. Equation (10.1.6) implies that

$$
\begin{aligned}
s_{nt} &= \left(\frac{1}{n}\right) E_t \left[\sum_{i=1}^{n} \left[(y_{1,t+i} - y_{1t}) + (r_{n+1-i,t+i} - y_{1,t+i}) \right] \right] \\
&= \left(\frac{1}{n}\right) E_t \left[\sum_{i=1}^{n} \left[(n-i) \Delta y_{1,t+i} + (r_{n+1-i,t+i} - y_{1,t+i}) \right] \right]. \quad (10.2.13)
\end{aligned}
$$

The second equality in equation (10.2.13) replaces multiperiod interest rate changes by sums of single-period interest rate changes. The equation says that the yield spread equals a weighted average of expected future interest rate changes, plus an unweighted average of expected future excess returns on long bonds. If changes in interest rates are stationary (that is, if interest rates themselves have one unit root but not two), and if excess returns are stationary (as would be implied by any model in which risk aversion and bonds' risk characteristics are stationary), then the yield spread is also stationary. This means that yields of different maturities are *cointegrated*.[23]

The expectations hypothesis says that the second term on the right-hand side of (10.2.13) is constant. This has important implications for the relation between the yield spread and future interest rates. It means that the yield spread is (up to a constant) the optimal forecaster of the change in the long-bond yield over the life of the short bond, and the optimal forecaster of changes in short rates over the life of the long bond. Recalling that we have dropped all constant terms, the relations are

$$
\left(\frac{1}{n-1}\right) s_{nt} = E_t[y_{n-1,t+1} - y_{nt}], \quad (10.2.14)
$$

and

$$
s_{nt} = E_t \left[\sum_{i=1}^{n-1} (1 - i/n) \Delta y_{1,t+i} \right]. \quad (10.2.15)
$$

Equation (10.2.14) can be obtained by substituting the definition of $r_{n,t+1}$, (10.1.5), into (10.2.9) and rearranging. It shows that when the yield spread is high, the long rate is expected to rise. This is because a high yield spread gives the long bond a yield advantage which must be offset by an anticipated capital loss. Such a capital loss can only come about through an increase in the long-bond yield. Equation (10.2.15) follows directly from (10.2.13) with constant expected excess returns. It shows that when the yield spread is

---

process is discussed further in Chapter 11.

[23] See Campbell and Shiller (1987) for a discussion of cointegration in the term structure of interest rates.

Table 10.3. *Regression coefficients $\hat{\beta}_n$ and $\hat{\gamma}_n$.*

Dependent variable	Long bond maturity (n)						
	2	3	6	12	24	48	120
Long-yield							
changes	0.003	−0.145	−0.835	−1.435	−1.448	−2.262	−4.226
(10.2.16)	(0.191)	(0.282)	(0.442)	(0.599)	(1.004)	(1.458)	(2.076)
Short-rate							
changes	0.502	0.467	0.320	0.272	0.363	0.442	1.402
(10.2.18)	(0.096)	(0.148)	(0.146)	(0.208)	(0.223)	(0.384)	(0.147)

Long bond maturities are measured in months. The first row reports the estimated regression coefficient $\hat{\beta}_n$ from (10.2.16), with an asymptotic standard error (in parentheses) calculated to allow for heteroskedasticity in the manner described in the Appendix. The second row reports the the the estimated regression coefficient $\hat{\gamma}_n$ from (10.2.18), with an asymptotic standard error calculated in the same manner, allowing also for residual autocorrelation. The expectations hypothesis of the term structure implies that both $\hat{\beta}_n$ and $\hat{\gamma}_n$ should equal one. The underlying data are monthly zero-coupon bond yields over the period 1952:1 to 1991:2, from McCulloch and Kwon (1993).

high, short rates are expected to rise so that the average short rate over the life of the long bond equals the initial long-bond yield. Near-term increases in short rates are given greater weight than further-off increases, because they affect the level of short rates during a greater part of the life of the long bond.

Yield Spreads and Future Long Rates

Equation (10.2.14), which says that high yield spreads should forecast increases in long rates, fares poorly in the data. Macaulay (1938) first noted the fact that high yield spreads actually tend to precede decreases in long rates. He wrote: "The yields of bonds of the highest grade should *fall* during a period in which short-term rates are higher than the yields of the bonds and *rise* during a period in which short-term rates are lower. Now experience is more nearly the opposite" (Macaulay [1938, p. 33]).

Table 10.3 reports estimates of the coefficient β_n and its standard error in the regression

$$y_{n-1,t+1} - y_{n,t} = \alpha_n + \beta_n \left(\frac{s_{nt}}{n-1} \right) + \epsilon_{n,t}. \qquad (10.2.16)$$

The maturity n varies from 3 months to 120 months (10 years).[24] According

---

[24]For maturities above one year the table uses the approximation $y_{n-1,t+1} \approx y_{n,t+1}$. Note

to the expectations hypothesis, we should find $\beta_n = 1$. In fact all the estimates in Table 10.3 are negative; all are significantly less than one, and some are significantly less than zero. When the long-short yield spread is high the long yield tends to fall, amplifying the yield differential between long and short bonds, rather than rising to offset the yield differential as required by the expectations hypothesis.

The regression equation (10.2.16) contains the same information as a regression of the excess one-period return on an n-period bond onto the yield spread s_{nt}. Equation (10.2.5) relating excess returns to yields implies that the excess-return regression would have a coefficient of $(1 - \beta_n)$. Thus the negative estimates of β_n in Table 10.3 correspond to a strong positive relationship between yield spreads and excess returns on long bonds. This is similar to the positive relationship between dividend yields and stock returns discussed in Chapter 7.[25]

One difficulty with the regression (10.2.16) is that it is particularly sensitive to measurement error in the long-term interest rate (see Stambaugh [1988]). Since the long rate appears both in the regressor with a positive sign and in the dependent variable with a negative sign, measurement error would tend to produce the negative signs found in Table 10.3. Campbell and Shiller (1991) point out that this can be handled by using instrumental variables regression where the instruments are correlated with the yield spread but not with the bond yield measurement error. They try a variety of instruments and find that the negative regression coefficients are quite robust.

Yield Spreads and Future Short Rates

There is much more truth in proposition (10.2.15), that high yield spreads should forecast long-term increases in short rates. This can be tested either directly or indirectly. The direct approach is to form the *ex post* value of the short-rate changes that appear on the right-hand side of (10.2.15) and to regress this on the yield spread. We define

$$s_{nt}^{*} \equiv \sum_{i=1}^{n-1}(1 - i/n)\Delta y_{1,t+i}, \qquad (10.2.17)$$

that this is not the same as approximating $p_{n-1,t+1}$ by $p_{n,t+1}$. The numbers given differ slightly from those in Campbell (1995) because that paper uses the sample period 1951:1 to 1990:2, erroneously reported as 1952:1 to 1991:2.

[25] Campbell and Ammer (1993), Fama and French (1989), and Keim and Stambaugh (1986) show that yield spreads help to forecast excess returns on bonds as well as on other long-term assets. Campbell and Shiller (1991) and Shiller, Campbell, and Schoenholtz (1983) show that yield spreads tend to forecast declines in long-bond yields.

and run the regression

$$s_{nt}^* = \mu_n + \gamma_n s_{nt} + \epsilon_{nt}. \tag{10.2.18}$$

The expectations hypothesis implies that $\gamma_n = 1$ for all n.[26]

Table 10.3 reports estimated $\hat{\gamma}_n$ coefficients with standard errors, correcting for heteroskedasticity and overlap in the equation errors in the manner discussed in the Appendix. The estimated coefficients have a U shape: For small n they are smaller than one but significantly positive; up to a year or so they decline with n, becoming insignificantly different from zero; beyond one year the coefficients increase and at ten years the coefficient is even significantly greater than one. Thus Table 10.3 shows that yield spreads have forecasting power for short-rate movements over a horizon of two or three months, and again over horizons of several years. Around one year, however, yield-spread variation seems almost unrelated to subsequent movements in short rates.

The regression equation (10.2.18) contains the same information as a regression of $(1/n)$ times the excess n-period return on an n-period bond onto the yield spread s_{nt}. The relation between excess returns and yields implies that the excess-return regression would have a coefficient of $(1-\gamma_n)$. Table 10.3 implies that yield spreads forecast excess returns out to horizons of several years, but the forecasting power diminishes towards ten years.

There are several econometric difficulties with the direct approach just described. First, one loses n periods of data at the end of the sample period. This can be quite serious: For example, the ten-year regression in Table 10.3 ends in 1981, whereas the three-month regression ends in 1991. This makes a substantial difference to the results, as discussed by Campbell and Shiller (1991). Second, the error term ϵ_{nt} is a moving average of order $(n-1)$, so standard errors must be corrected in the manner described in the Appendix. This can lead to finite-sample problems when $(n-1)$ is not small relative to the sample size. Third, the regressor is serially correlated and correlated with lags of the dependent variable, and this too can cause finite-sample problems (see Mankiw and Shapiro [1986], Richardson and Stock [1990], and Stambaugh [1986]).

Although these econometric problems are important, they do not seem to account for the U-shaped pattern of coefficients. Campbell and Shiller (1991) find similar results using a vector autoregressive (VAR) methodology like that described in Section 7.2.3 of Chapter 7. They find that the long-term yield spread is highly correlated with an unrestricted VAR forecast of future short-rate movements, while the intermediate-term yield spread is much more weakly correlated with the VAR forecast.

---

[26]Fama (1984) and Shiller, Campbell, and Schoenholtz (1983) use this approach at the short end of the term structure, while Fama and Bliss (1987) extend it to the long end. Campbell and Shiller (1991) provide a comprehensive review.

To interpret Table 10.3, it is helpful to return to equation (10.2.13) and rewrite it as

$$s_{nt} = sy_{nt} + sr_{nt}, \tag{10.2.19}$$

where

$$sy_{nt} \equiv E_t[s_{nt}^*] = \left(\frac{1}{n}\right) E_t \left[\sum_{i=1}^{n} (n-i) \Delta y_{1,t+i} \right],$$

and

$$sr_{nt} \equiv \left(\frac{1}{n}\right) E_t \left[\sum_{i=1}^{n} (r_{n+1-i,t+i} - y_{1,t+i}) \right].$$

In general the yield spread is the sum of two components, one that forecasts interest rate changes (sy_{nt}) and one that forecasts excess returns on long bonds (sr_{nt}). This means that the regression coefficient γ_n in equation (10.2.18) is

$$\gamma_n = \frac{\text{Cov}[s_{nt}^*, s_{nt}]}{\text{Var}[s_{nt}]}$$

$$= \frac{\text{Var}[sy_{nt}] + \text{Cov}[sy_{nt}, sr_{nt}]}{\text{Var}[sy_{nt}] + \text{Var}[sr_{nt}] + 2\,\text{Cov}[sy_{nt}, sr_{nt}]}. \tag{10.2.20}$$

For any given variance of excess-return forecasts sr_{nt}, as the variance of interest rate forecasts sy_{nt} goes to zero the coefficient γ_n goes to zero, but as the variance of sy_{nt} increases the coefficient γ_n goes to one. The U-shaped pattern of regression coefficients in Table 10.3 may be explained by reduced forecastability of interest rate movements at horizons around one year. There may be some short-run forecastability arising from Federal Reserve operating procedures, and some long-run forecastability arising from business-cycle effects on interest rates, but at a one-year horizon the Federal Reserve may smooth interest rates so that the variability of sy_{nt} is small. Balduzzi, Bertola, and Foresi (1993), Rudebusch (1995), and Roberds, Runkle, and Whiteman (1996) argue for this interpretation of the evidence. Consistent with this explanation, Mankiw and Miron (1986) show that the predictions of the expectations hypothesis fit the data better in periods when interest rate movements have been highly forecastable, such as the period immediately before the founding of the Federal Reserve System.

10.3 Conclusion

The results in Table 10.3 imply that naive investors, who judge bonds by their yields to maturity and buy long bonds when their yields are relatively high, have tended to earn superior returns in the postwar period in the United

States. This finding is reminiscent of the finding discussed in Chapter 7, that stock returns tend to be higher when dividend yields are high at the start of the holding period. As in the stock market case, it is not clear whether this result reflects a failure of rationality on the part of investors or the presence of time-varying risk premia. Froot (1989) has used survey data to argue that bond market investors have irrational expectations, but there is also much theoretical work, discussed in the next chapter, that explores the impact of time-varying risk on the term structure of interest rates.

This chapter has concentrated on the forecasting power of yield spreads for future movements in nominal interest rates. Yield spreads are also useful in forecasting other variables. For example, one can decompose nominal rates into inflation rates and real interest rates; the evidence is that most of the long-run forecasting power of the term structure is for inflation rather than real interest rates (see Fama [1975, 1990] and Mishkin [1990a, 1990b]). We mentioned in Chapter 8 that the slope of the term structure has some ability to forecast excess returns on stocks as well as bonds. Other recent studies by Chen (1991b) and Estrella and Hardouvelis (1991) have shown that the term structure forecasts real economic activity, since inverted yield curves tend to precede recessions and steeply upward-sloping yield curves tend to precede expansions.

Problems—Chapter 10

10.1   You are told that an 8-year nominal zero-coupon bond has a log yield to maturity of 9.1%, and a 9-year nominal zero-coupon bond has a log yield of 8.0%.

10.1.1   Can the pure expectations theory of the term structure describe these data?

10.1.2   A year goes by, and the bonds in part (a) still have the same yields to maturity. Can the pure expectations theory of the term structure describe these new data?

10.1.3   How would your answers change if you were told that the bonds have an 8% coupon rate per year, rather than zero coupons?

10.2   Suppose that the monetary authority controls short-term interest rates by setting

$$y_{1t} = y_{1,t-1} + \lambda(y_{2t} - y_{1t}) + \epsilon_t,$$

with $\lambda > 0$. Intuitively, the monetary authority tries to smooth interest rates but raises them when the yield curve is steep. Suppose also that the two-period bond yield satisfies

$$y_{2t} = (y_{1t} + E_t[y_{1,t+1}])/2 + x_t,$$

where x_t is a term premium that represents the deviation of the two-period yield from the log pure expectations hypothesis, equation (10.2.10). The variable x_t follows an AR(1) process

$$x_t = \phi x_{t-1} + \eta_t.$$

The error terms ϵ_t and η_t are serially uncorrelated and uncorrelated with each other.

10.2.1 Show that this model can be solved for an interest-rate process of the form

$$y_{1t} = y_{1,t-1} + \gamma x_t + \epsilon_t.$$

Express the coefficient γ as a function of the other parameters in the model.

10.2.2 The expectations hypothesis of the term structure is often tested in the manner of equation (10.2.17) by regressing the scaled change in the short rate onto the yield spread,

$$(y_{1,t+1} - y_{1t})/2 = \alpha + \beta(y_{2t} - y_{1t}) + u_{t+1},$$

and testing the hypothesis that the coefficient $\beta = 1$. If the model described above holds, what is the population value of the regression coefficient β?

10.2.3 Now consider a version of the problem involving n-period bonds. The monetary authority sets short-term interest rates as

$$y_{1t} = y_{1,t-1} + \lambda(y_{nt} - y_{1t}) + \epsilon_t,$$

and the n-period bond yield is determined by

$$y_{nt} - y_{1t} = (n-1)E_t[y_{n,t+1} - y_{nt}] + x_t,$$

where x_t now measures the deviation of the n-period yield from the log pure expectations hypothesis (10.2.14). (This formulation ignores the distinction between y_{nt} and $y_{n-1,t}$.) As before, x_t follows an AR(1) process. What is the coefficient γ in this case? What is the regression coefficient β in a regression of the form (10.2.16),

$$(y_{n,t+1} - y_{nt}) = \alpha + \beta(y_{nt} - y_{1t})/(n-1) + u_{t+1} ?$$

10.2.4 Do you find the model you have studied in this problem to be a plausible explanation of empirical findings on the term structure? Why or why not?

Note: This problem is based on McCallum (1994).

11

Term-Structure Models

THIS CHAPTER EXPLORES the large modern literature on fully specified general-equilibrium models of the term structure of interest rates. Much of this literature is set in continuous time, which simplifies some of the theoretical analysis but complicates empirical implementation. Since we focus on the econometric testing of the models and their empirical implications, we adopt a discrete-time approach; however we take care to relate all our results to their continuous-time equivalents. We follow the literature by first developing models for real bonds, but we discuss in some detail how these models can be used to price nominal bonds.

All the models in this chapter start from the general asset pricing condition introduced as (8.1.3) in Chapter 8: $1 = E_t[(1 + R_{i,t+1})M_{t+1}]$, where $R_{i,t+1}$ is the real return on some asset i and M_{t+1} is the *stochastic discount factor*. As we explained in Section 8.1 of Chapter 8, this condition implies that the expected return on any asset is negatively related to its covariance with the stochastic discount factor. In models with utility-maximizing investors, the stochastic discount factor measures the marginal utility of investors. Assets whose returns covary positively with the stochastic discount factor tend to pay off when marginal utility is high—they deliver wealth at times when wealth is most valuable to investors. Investors are willing to pay high prices and accept low returns on such assets.

Fixed-income securities are particularly easy to price using this framework. When cash flows are random, the stochastic properties of the cash flows help to determine the covariance of an asset's return with the stochastic discount factor. But a fixed-income security has deterministic cash flows, so it covaries with the stochastic discount factor only because there is time-variation in discount rates. This variation in discount rates is driven by the time-series behavior of the stochastic discount factor, so term-structure models are equivalent to time-series models for the stochastic discount factor.

From (10.1.4) in Chapter 10, we know that returns on n-period real zero-coupon bonds are related to real bond prices in a particularly simple way: $(1 + R_{n,t+1}) = P_{n-1,t+1}/P_{nt}$. Substituting this into (8.1.3), we find that the real price of an n-period real bond, P_{nt}, satisfies

$$P_{nt} = E_t[P_{n-1,t+1} M_{t+1}]. \qquad (11.0.1)$$

This equation lends itself to a recursive approach. We model P_{nt} as a function of those state variables that are relevant for forecasting the M_{t+1} process. Given that process and the function relating $P_{n-1,t}$ to state variables, we can calculate the function relating P_{nt} to state variables. We start the calculation by noting that $P_{0t} = 1$.

Equation (11.0.1) can also be solved forward to express the n-period bond price as the expected product of n stochastic discount factors:

$$P_{nt} = E_t[M_{t+1} \ldots M_{t+n}]. \qquad (11.0.2)$$

Although we emphasize the recursive approach, in some models it is more convenient to work directly with (11.0.2).

Section 11.1 explores a class of simple models in which all relevant variables are conditionally lognormal and log bond yields are linear in state variables. These *affine-yield models* include all the most commonly used term-structure models. Section 11.2 shows how these models can be fit to nominal interest rate data, and reviews their strengths and weaknesses. One of the main uses of term-structure models is in pricing interest-rate derivative securities; we discuss this application in Section 11.3. We show how standard term-structure models can be modified so that they fit the current term structure exactly. We then use the models to price forwards, futures, and options on fixed-income securities.

11.1 Affine-Yield Models

To keep matters simple, we assume throughout this section that the distribution of the stochastic discount factor M_{t+1} is conditionally lognormal. We specify models in which bond prices are jointly lognormal with M_{t+1}. We can then take logs of (11.0.1) to obtain

$$p_{nt} = E_t[m_{t+1} + p_{n-1,t+1}] + (1/2)\,\mathrm{Var}_t[m_{t+1} + p_{n-1,t+1}], \qquad (11.1.1)$$

where as usual lowercase letters denote the logs of the corresponding uppercase letters so for example $m_{t+1} \equiv \log(M_{t+1})$. This is the basic equation we shall use.

We begin with two models in which a single state variable forecasts the stochastic discount factor. Section 11.1.1 discusses the first model, in which m_{t+1} is homoskedastic, while Section 11.1.2 discusses the second model, in which the conditional variance of m_{t+1} changes over time. These are discrete-time versions of the well-known models of Vasicek (1977) and Cox, Ingersoll, and Ross (1985a), respectively. Section 11.1.3 then considers a more general model with two state variables, a discrete-time version of the model of Longstaff and Schwartz (1992). All of these models have the property that log bond prices, and hence log bond yields, are linear or *affine* in the state variables. This ensures the desired joint lognormality of bond prices with the stochastic discount factor. Section 11.1.4 describes the general properties of these *affine-yield models*, and discusses some alternative modelling approaches.[1]

11.1.1 A Homoskedastic Single-Factor Model

It is convenient to work with the negative of the log stochastic discount factor, $-m_{t+1}$. Without loss of generality, this can be expressed as the sum of its one-period-ahead conditional expectation x_t and an innovation ϵ_{t+1}:

$$- m_{t+1} = x_t + \epsilon_{t+1}. \tag{11.1.2}$$

We assume that ϵ_{t+1} is normally distributed with constant variance.

Next we assume that x_{t+1} follows the simplest interesting time-series process, a univariate AR(1) process with mean μ and persistence ϕ. The shock to x_{t+1} is written ξ_{t+1}:

$$x_{t+1} = (1 - \phi)\mu + \phi x_t + \xi_{t+1}. \tag{11.1.3}$$

The innovations to m_{t+1} and x_{t+1} may be correlated. To capture this, we write ϵ_{t+1} as

$$\epsilon_{t+1} = \beta\xi_{t+1} + \eta_{t+1}, \tag{11.1.4}$$

where ξ_{t+1} and η_{t+1} are normally distributed with constant variances and are uncorrelated with each other.

The presence of the uncorrelated shock η_{t+1} only affects the average level of the term structure and not its average slope or its time-series behavior. To simplify notation, we accordingly drop it and assume that $\epsilon_{t+1} = \beta\xi_{t+1}$. Equation (11.1.2) can then be rewritten as

$$- m_{t+1} = x_t + \beta\xi_{t+1}. \tag{11.1.5}$$

The innovation ξ_{t+1} is now the only shock in the system; accordingly we can write its variance simply as σ^2 without causing confusion.

Equations (11.1.5) and (11.1.3) imply that $-m_{t+1}$ can be written as an ARMA(1,1) process since it is the sum of an AR(1) process and white noise.

---

[1] Our discrete-time presentation follows Singleton (1990), Sun (1992), and especially Backus (1993). Sun (1992) explores the relation between discrete-time and continuous-time models in more detail.

In fact, $-m_{t+1}$ has the same structure as asset returns did in the example of Chapter 7, Section 7.1.4. As in that example, it is important to realize that $-m_{t+1}$ is not a univariate process even though its conditional expectation x_t is univariate. Thus the univariate autocorrelations of $-m_{t+1}$ do not tell us all we need to know for asset pricing; different sets of parameter values, with different implications for asset pricing, could be consistent with the same set of univariate autocorrelations for $-m_{t+1}$. For example, these autocorrelations could all be zero because $\sigma^2 = 0$, which would make interest rates constant, but they could also be zero for $\sigma^2 \neq 0$ if β takes on a particular value, and in this case interest rates would vary over time.

We can determine the price of a one-period bond by noting that when $n = 1$, $p_{n-1,t+1} = p_{0,t+1} = 0$, so the terms involving $p_{n-1,t+1}$ in equation (11.1.1) drop out. Substituting (11.1.5) and (11.1.3) into (11.1.1), we have

$$p_{1t} = E_t[m_{t+1}] + (1/2)\,\text{Var}_t[m_{t+1}] = -x_t + \beta^2\sigma^2/2. \qquad (11.1.6)$$

The one-period bond yield $y_{1t} = -p_{1t}$, so

$$y_{1t} = x_t - \beta^2\sigma^2/2. \qquad (11.1.7)$$

The short rate equals the state variable less a constant term, so it inherits the AR(1) dynamics of the state variable. Indeed, we can think of the short rate as measuring the state of the economy in this model. Note that there is nothing in equation (11.1.7) that rules out a negative short rate.

We now guess that the form of the price function for an n-period bond is

$$- p_{nt} = A_n + B_n\,x_t. \qquad (11.1.8)$$

Since the n-period bond yield $y_{nt} = -p_{nt}/n$, we are guessing that the yield on a bond of any maturity is linear or *affine* in the state variable x_t (Brown and Schaefer [1991]). We already know that bond prices for $n = 0$ and $n = 1$ satisfy equation (11.1.8), with $A_0 = B_0 = 0$, $A_1 = -\beta^2\sigma^2/2$, and $B_1 = 1$. We proceed to verify our guess by showing that it is consistent with the pricing relation (11.1.1). At the same time we can derive recursive formulas for the coefficients A_n and B_n.

Our guess for the price function (11.1.8) implies that the two terms on the right-hand side of (11.1.1) are

$$E_t[m_{t+1} + p_{n-1,t+1}] = -x_t - A_{n-1} - B_{n-1}(1 - \phi)\mu - B_{n-1}\phi\,x_t,$$

$$\text{Var}_t[m_{t+1} + p_{n-1,t+1}] = (\beta + B_{n-1})^2\sigma^2. \qquad (11.1.9)$$

Substituting (11.1.8) and (11.1.9) into (11.1.1), we get

$$A_n + B_n\,x_t - x_t - A_{n-1} - B_{n-1}(1 - \phi)\mu - B_{n-1}\phi\,x_t$$
$$+ (\beta + B_{n-1})^2\sigma^2/2 = 0. \qquad (11.1.10)$$

This must hold for any x_t, so the coefficients on x_t must sum to zero and the remaining coefficients must also sum to zero. This implies

$$B_n = 1 + \phi B_{n-1} = (1 - \phi^n)/(1 - \phi),$$

$$A_n - A_{n-1} = (1 - \phi)\mu B_{n-1} - (\beta + B_{n-1})^2\sigma^2/2. \tag{11.1.11}$$

We have now verified the guess (11.1.8), since with the coefficients in (11.1.11) the price function (11.1.8) satisfies the asset pricing equation (11.1.1) and its assumption that bond returns are conditionally lognormal.

Implications of the Homoskedastic Model
The homoskedastic bond pricing model has several interesting implications. First, the coefficient B_n measures the fall in the log price of an n-period bond when there is an increase in the state variable x_t or equivalently in the one-period interest rate y_{1t}. It therefore measures the sensitivity of the n-period bond return to the one-period interest rate. Equation (11.1.11) shows that the coefficient B_n follows a simple univariate linear difference equation in n, with solution $(1 - \phi^n)/(1 - \phi)$. As n increases, B_n approaches a limit $B = 1/(1 - \phi)$. Thus bond prices fall when short rates rise, and the sensitivity of bond returns to short rates increases with maturity.

Note that B_n is different from duration, defined in Section 10.1.2 of Chapter 10. Duration measures the sensitivity of the n-period bond return to the n-period bond yield, and for zero-coupon bonds duration equals maturity. B_n measures the sensitivity of the n-period bond return to the one-period interest rate; it is always less than maturity because the n-period bond yield moves less than one-for-one with the one-period interest rate.

A second implication of the model is that the expected log excess return on an n-period bond over a one-period bond, $E_t[r_{n,t+1}] - y_{1t} = E_t[p_{n-1,t+1}] - p_{nt} + p_{1t}$, is given by

$$
\begin{aligned}
E_t[r_{n,t+1}] - y_{1t} &= -\text{Cov}_t[r_{n,t+1}, m_{t+1}] - \text{Var}_t[r_{n,t+1}]/2 \\
&= B_{n-1}\text{Cov}_t[x_{t+1}, m_{t+1}] - B_{n-1}^2\text{Var}_t[x_{t+1}]/2 \\
&= -B_{n-1}\beta\sigma^2 - B_{n-1}^2\sigma^2/2. \tag{11.1.12}
\end{aligned}
$$

The first equality in (11.1.12) is a general result, discussed in Chapter 8, that holds for the excess log return on any asset over the riskfree interest rate. It can be obtained by taking logs of the fundamental relation $1 = E_t[(1 + R_{i,t+1})M_{t+1}]$ for the n-period bond and the short interest rate, and then taking the difference between the two equations. It says that the expected excess log return is the sum of a risk premium term and a Jensen's Inequality term in the own variance which appears because we are working in logs.

The second equality in (11.1.12) uses the fact that the unexpected component of the log return on an n-period bond is just $-B_{n-1}$ times the innovation in the state variable. The third equality in (11.1.12) uses the fact that the conditional variance of x_{t+1} and its conditional covariance with m_{t+1} are constants to show that the expected log excess return on any bond is constant over time, so that the log expectations hypothesis—but not the log pure expectations hypothesis—holds.

$-B_{n-1}$ is the coefficient from a regression of n-period log bond returns on state variable innovations, so we can interpret $-B_{n-1}$ as the bond's loading on the single source of risk and $\beta\sigma^2$ as the reward for bearing a unit of risk. Alternatively, following Vasicek (1977) and others, we might calculate the price of risk as the ratio of the expected excess log return on a bond, plus one half its own variance to adjust for Jensen's Inequality, to the standard deviation of the excess log return on the bond. Defined this way, the price of risk is just $-\beta\sigma$ in this model.

The homoskedastic bond pricing model also has implications for the pattern of forward rates, and hence for the shape of the yield curve. To derive these implications, we note that in any term-structure model the n-period-ahead forward rate f_{nt} satisfies

$$
\begin{aligned}
f_{nt} &= p_{nt} - p_{n+1,t} \\
&= -p_{1t} + (\mathrm{E}_t[p_{n,t+1}] - p_{n+1,t} + p_{1t}) - (\mathrm{E}_t[p_{n,t+1}] - p_{nt}) \\
&= y_{1t} + (\mathrm{E}_t[r_{n+1,t+1}] - y_{1t}) - (\mathrm{E}_t[p_{n,t+1}] - p_{nt}). \quad (11.1.13)
\end{aligned}
$$

In this model $\mathrm{E}_t[p_{n,t+1}] - p_{nt} = -B_n \mathrm{E}_t[\Delta x_{t+1}]$, and $\mathrm{E}_t[r_{n+1,t+1}] - y_{1t}$ is given by (11.1.12). Substituting into (11.1.13) and using $B_n = (1 - \phi^n)/(1 - \phi)$, we get

$$
\begin{aligned}
f_{nt} &= \mu - \left[\beta + \left(\frac{1 - \phi^n}{1 - \phi}\right)\right]^2 \frac{\sigma^2}{2} + \phi^n(x_t - \mu) \\
&= \left[\mu - \left(\beta + \frac{1}{1 - \phi}\right)^2 \frac{\sigma^2}{2}\right] + \left[(x_t - \mu) + \left(\frac{1 + \beta(1 - \phi)}{(1 - \phi)^2}\right)\sigma^2\right]\phi^n \\
&\quad - \left[\left(\frac{1}{1 - \phi}\right)^2 \frac{\sigma^2}{2}\right]\phi^{2n}. \quad (11.1.14)
\end{aligned}
$$

The first equality in (11.1.14) shows that the change in the n-period forward rate is ϕ^n times the change in x_t. Thus movements in the forward rate die out geometrically at rate ϕ. This can be understood by noting that the log expectations hypothesis holds in this model, so forward-rate movements reflect movements in the expected future short rate which are given by ϕ^n times movements in the current short rate.

As maturity n increases, the forward rate approaches

$$\mu - \left(\beta + 1/(1 - \phi)\right)^2 \sigma^2/2,$$

a constant that does not depend on the current value of the state variable x_t. Equation (11.1.7) implies that the average short rate is $\mu - \beta^2 \sigma^2/2$. Thus the difference between the limiting forward rate and the average short rate is

$$-\left(1/(1 - \phi)\right)^2 \sigma^2/2 - \left(\beta/(1 - \phi)\right)\sigma^2.$$

This is the same as the limiting expected log excess return on a long-term bond. Because of the Jensen's Inequality effect, the log forward-rate curve tends to slope downwards towards its limit unless β is sufficiently negative, $\beta < -1/2(1 - \phi)$.

As x_t varies, the forward-rate curve may take on different shapes. The second equality in (11.1.14) shows that the forward-rate curve can be written as the sum of a component that does not vary with n, a component that dies out with n at rate ϕ, and a component that dies out with n at rate ϕ^2. The third component has a constant coefficient with a negative sign; thus there is always a steeply rising component of the forward-rate curve. The second component has a coefficient that varies with x_t, so this component may be slowly rising, slowly falling, or flat. Hence the forward-rate curve may be rising throughout, falling throughout (*inverted*), or may be rising at first and then falling (*hump-shaped*) if the third component initially dominates and then is dominated by the second component further out along the curve. These are the most common shapes for nominal forward-rate curves. Thus, if one is willing to apply the model to nominal interest rates, disregarding the fact that it allows interest rates to go negative, one can fit most observed nominal term structures. However the model cannot generate a forward-rate curve which is falling at first and then rising (*inverted hump-shaped*), as occasionally seen in the data.

It is worth noting that when $\phi = 1$, the one-period interest rate follows a random walk. In this case the coefficients A_n and B_n never converge as n increases. We have $B_n = n$ and $A_n - A_{n-1} = -(\beta + n - 1)^2 \sigma^2/2$. The forward rate becomes $f_{nt} = x_t - (\beta + n)^2 \sigma^2/2$, which may increase with maturity at first if β is negative but eventually decreases with maturity forever. Thus the homoskedastic bond pricing model does not allow the limiting forward rate to be both finite and time-varying; either $\phi < 1$, in which case the limiting forward rate is constant over time, or $\phi = 1$, in which case there is no finite limiting forward rate. This restriction may seem rather counterintuitive; in fact it follows from the very general result—derived by Dybvig, Ingersoll, and Ross (1996)—that the limiting forward rate, if it exists, can never fall. In the homoskedastic model with $\phi < 1$ the limiting forward rate never falls because it is constant; in the homoskedastic model with $\phi = 1$ the limiting forward rate does not exist.

The discrete-time model developed in this section is closely related to the continuous-time model of Vasicek (1977). Vasicek specifies a continuous-time AR(1) or Ornstein-Uhlenbeck process for the short interest rate r, given by the following stochastic differential equation:

$$dr = \kappa(\theta - r)dt + \sigma\,dB, \qquad (11.1.15)$$

where κ, θ, and σ are constants.[2] Also, Vasicek assumes that the *price of interest rate risk*—the ratio of the expected excess return on a bond to the standard deviation of the excess return on the bond—is a constant that does not depend on the level of the short interest rate. The model of this section derives an AR(1) process for the short rate and a constant price of risk from primitive assumptions on the stochastic discount factor.

Equilibrium Interpretation of the Model

Our analysis has shown that the sign of the coefficient β determines the sign of all bond risk premia. To understand this, consider the effects of a positive shock ξ_{t+1} which increases the state variable x_{t+1} and lowers all bond prices. When β is positive the shock also drives down m_{t+1}, so bond returns are positively correlated with the stochastic discount factor. This correlation has hedge value, so risk premia on bonds are negative. When β is negative, on the other hand, bond returns are negatively correlated with the stochastic discount factor, and risk premia are positive.

We can get more intuition by considering the case where the stochastic discount factor reflects the power utility function of a representative agent, as in Chapter 8. In this case $M_{t+1} = \delta(C_{t+1}/C_t)^{-\gamma}$, where δ is the discount factor and γ is the risk-aversion coefficient of the representative agent. Taking logs, we have

$$m_{t+1} = \log(\delta) - \gamma\,\Delta c_{t+1}. \qquad (11.1.16)$$

It follows that $x_t \equiv E_t[-m_{t+1}] = -\log(\delta) + \gamma E_t[\Delta c_{t+1}]$, and $\epsilon_{t+1} \equiv -m_{t+1} - E_t[-m_{t+1}] = \gamma(\Delta c_{t+1} - E_t[\Delta c_{t+1}])$. x_t is a linear function of expected consumption growth, and ϵ_{t+1} is proportional to the innovation in consumption growth. The term-structure model of this section then implies that expected consumption growth is an AR(1) process, so that realized consumption growth is an ARMA(1,1) process. The coefficient β governs the covariance between consumption innovations and revisions in expected future consumption growth. If β is positive, then a positive consumption shock today drives up expected future consumption growth and increases interest rates; the resulting fall in bond prices makes bonds covary negatively with consumption and gives them negative risk premia. If

---

[2]As in Chapter 9, dB in (11.1.15) denotes the increment to a Brownian motion; it should not be confused with the bond price coefficients B_n of this section.

β is negative, a positive shock to consumption lowers interest rates so bonds have positive risk premia.

Campbell (1986) explores the relation between bond risk premia and the time-series properties of consumption in a related model. Campbell's model is similar to the one here in that consumption and asset returns are conditionally lognormal and homoskedastic. It is more restrictive than the model here because it makes consumption growth (rather than expected consumption growth) a univariate stochastic process, but it is more general in that it does not require expected consumption growth to follow an AR(1) process. Campbell shows that the sign of the risk premium for an n-period bond depends on whether a consumption innovation raises or lowers consumption growth expected over $(n-1)$ periods. Backus and Zin (1994) explore this model in greater detail. Backus, Gregory, and Zin (1989) also relate bond risk premia to the time-series properties of consumption growth and interest rates.

Cox, Ingersoll, and Ross (1985a) show how to derive a continuous-time term-structure model like the one in this section from an underlying production model. Sun (1992) and Backus (1993) restate their results in discrete time. Assume that there is a representative agent with discount factor δ and time-separable log utility. Suppose that the agent faces a budget constraint of the form

$$K_{t+1} = (K_t - C_t)X_t V_{t+1}, \qquad (11.1.17)$$

where K_t is capital at the start of the period, $(K_t - C_t)$ is invested capital, and $X_t V_{t+1}$ is the return on capital. This budget constraint has constant returns to scale because the return on capital does not depend on the level of capital. X_t is the anticipated component of the return and V_{t+1} is an unanticipated technology shock. With log utility it is well-known that the agent chooses $C_t/K_t = (1-\delta)$. Substituting this into (11.1.17) and taking logs we find that

$$\Delta c_{t+1} = \log(\delta) + x_t + v_{t+1}, \qquad (11.1.18)$$

where $v_{t+1} \equiv \log(V_{t+1})$, and $-m_{t+1} = -\log(\delta) + \Delta c_{t+1} = x_t + \epsilon_{t+1}$. This derivation allows x_t to follow any process, including the AR(1) assumed by the term-structure model.

11.1.2 A Square-Root Single-Factor Model

The homoskedastic model of the previous section is appealing because of its simplicity, but it has several unattractive features. First, it assumes that interest rate changes have constant variance. Second, the model allows interest rates to go negative. This makes it applicable to real interest rates, but less appropriate for nominal interest rates. Third, it implies that risk premia are constant over time, contrary to the evidence presented in Section 10.2.1 of Chapter 10. One can alter the model to handle these problems, while retaining much of the simplicity of the basic structure, by allowing the state variable x_t to follow a conditionally lognormal but heteroskedastic *square-root* process. This change is entirely consistent with the equilibrium foundations for the model given in the previous section.

The square-root model, which is a discrete-time version of the famous Cox, Ingersoll, and Ross (1985a) continuous-time model, replaces (11.1.5) and (11.1.3) with

$$- m_{t+1} = x_t + x_t^{1/2} \epsilon_{t+1} = x_t + x_t^{1/2} \beta \xi_{t+1}, \qquad (11.1.19)$$

$$x_{t+1} = (1 - \phi)\mu + \phi x_t + x_t^{1/2} \xi_{t+1}. \qquad (11.1.20)$$

The new element here is that the shock ξ_{t+1} is multiplied by $x_t^{1/2}$. To understand the importance of this, recall that in the homoskedastic model x_{t+i} and m_{t+i} are normal conditional on x_t for all $i \geq 1$. This means that one can analyze the homoskedastic model either by taking logs of (11.0.1) to get the recursive equation (11.1.1), or by taking logs of (11.0.2) to get an n-period loglinear equation:

$$p_{nt} = \mathrm{E}_t[m_{t+1} + \cdots + m_{t+n}] + (1/2)\operatorname{Var}_t[m_{t+1} + \cdots + m_{t+n}]. \quad (11.1.21)$$

Calculations based on (11.1.21) are more cumbersome than the analysis presented in the previous section, but they give the same result. In the square-root model, by contrast, x_{t+1} and m_{t+1} are normal conditional on x_t but x_{t+i} and m_{t+i} are nonnormal conditional on x_t for all $i > 1$. This means that one can only analyze the square-root model using the recursive equation (11.1.1); the n-period loglinear relation (11.1.21) does not hold in the square-root model.

Proceeding with the recursive analysis as before, we can determine the price of a one-period bond by substituting (11.1.19) into (11.1.1) to get

$$p_{1t} = \mathrm{E}_t[m_{t+1}] + (1/2)\operatorname{Var}_t[m_{t+1}] = -x_t(1 - \beta^2 \sigma^2/2). \qquad (11.1.22)$$

The one-period bond yield $y_{1t} = -p_{1t}$ is now proportional to the state variable x_t. Once again the short rate measures the state of the economy in the model.

Since the short rate is proportional to the state variable, it inherits the property that its conditional variance is proportional to its level. Many authors have noted that interest rate volatility tends to be higher when interest rates are high; in Section 11.2.2 we discuss the empirical evidence on this point. This property also makes it hard for the interest rate to go negative, since the upward drift in the state variable tends to dominate the random shocks as x_t declines towards zero. Cox, Ingersoll, and Ross (1985a) show that negative interest rates are ruled out in the continuous-time version of this model, where the instantaneous interest rate follows the process $dr = \kappa(\theta - r)dt + \sigma r^{1/2}dB$.[3] Time-variation in volatility also produces time-variation in term premia, so that the log expectations hypothesis no longer holds in this model.

We now guess that the price function for an n-period bond has the same linear form as before, $-p_{nt} = A_n + B_n x_t$, equation (11.1.8). In this model $A_0 = B_0 = 0$, $A_1 = 0$, and $B_1 = 1 - \beta^2\sigma^2/2$. It is straightforward to verify the guess and to show that A_n and B_n obey

$$B_n = 1 + \phi B_{n-1} - (\beta + B_{n-1})^2\sigma^2/2,$$

$$A_n - A_{n-1} = (1 - \phi)\mu B_{n-1}. \tag{11.1.23}$$

Comparing (11.1.23) with (11.1.11), we see that the term in σ^2 has been moved from the equation describing A_n to the equation describing B_n. This is because the variance is now proportional to the state variable, so it affects the slope coefficient rather than the intercept coefficient for the bond price. The limiting value of B_n, which we write as B, is now the solution to a quadratic equation, but for realistic parameter values this solution is close to the limit $1/(1 - \phi)$ from the previous model. Thus B_n is positive and increasing in n.

The expected excess log bond return in the square-root model is given by

$$
\begin{aligned}
E_t[r_{n,t+1}] - y_{1t} &= -\text{Cov}_t[r_{n,t+1}, m_{t+1}] - \text{Var}_t[r_{n,t+1}]/2 \\
&= B_{n-1}\text{Cov}_t[x_{t+1}, m_{t+1}] - B_{n-1}^2\text{Var}_t[x_{t+1}]/2 \\
&= (-B_{n-1}\beta\sigma^2 - B_{n-1}^2\sigma^2/2)x_t. \tag{11.1.24}
\end{aligned}
$$

The first two equalities here are the same as in the previous model. The third equality is the formula from the previous model, (11.1.12), multiplied by the state variable x_t. Thus the expected log excess return is proportional to the state variable x_t or, equivalently, to the short interest rate y_{1t}. This is the expected result since the conditional variance of interest rates is proportional to x_t. Once again the sign of β determines the sign of the risk premium term in (11.1.24). Since the standard deviation of excess bond returns is proportional to the square root of x_t, the price of interest rate risk—the ratio of the expected excess log return on a bond, plus one half its own variance to adjust for Jensen's Inequality, to the standard deviation of

---

[3]Depending on the parameter values, it may be possible for the interest rate to be zero in the continuous-time model. Longstaff (1992) discusses alternative ways to model this possibility.

the excess log return on the bond—is also proportional to the square root of x_t.

The forward rate in the square-root model is given by

$$
\begin{aligned}
f_{nt} &= y_{1t} + B_n(\mathrm{E}_t[\Delta x_{t+1}] - \mathrm{Cov}_t[x_{t+1}, m_{t+1}]) - B_n^2 \mathrm{Var}_t[x_{t+1}]/2 \\
&= (1 - \beta^2 \sigma^2/2) x_t - B_n[(1 - \phi)(x_t - \mu) + x_t \beta \sigma^2] \\
&\quad - B_n^2 x_t \sigma^2/2.
\end{aligned}
\tag{11.1.25}
$$

The first equality in (11.1.25) is the same as in the homoskedastic model, while the second equality multiplies variance terms by x_t where appropriate. It can be shown that the square-root model permits the same range of shapes for the yield curve—upward-sloping, inverted, and humped—as the homoskedastic model.

Pearson and Sun (1994) have shown that the square-root model can be generalized to allow the variance of the state variable to be linear in the level of the state variable, rather than proportional to it. One simply replaces the $x_t^{1/2}$ terms, multiplying the shocks in (11.1.19) and (11.1.20) with terms of the form $(\alpha_0 + \alpha_1 x_t)^{1/2}$. The resulting model is tractable because it remains in the affine-yield class, and it nests both the homoskedastic model (the case $\alpha_0 = 1, \alpha_1 = 0$) and the basic square-root model (the case $\alpha_0 = 0$, $\alpha_1 = 1$).

11.1.3 A Two-Factor Model

So far we have only considered single-factor models. Such models imply that all bond returns are perfectly correlated. While bond returns do tend to be highly correlated, their correlations are certainly not one and so it is natural to ask how this implication can be avoided.

We now present a simple model in which there are two factors rather than one, so that bond returns are no longer perfectly correlated.[4] The model is a discrete-time version of the model of Longstaff and Schwartz (1992). It replaces (11.1.19) with

$$
- m_{t+1} = x_{1t} + x_{2t} + x_{1t}^{1/2} \epsilon_{t+1},
\tag{11.1.26}
$$

and replaces (11.1.20) with a pair of equations for the state variables:

$$
x_{1,t+1} = (1 - \phi_1)\mu_1 + \phi_1 x_{1t} + x_{1t}^{1/2} \xi_{1,t+1},
\tag{11.1.27}
$$

$$
x_{2,t+1} = (1 - \phi_2)\mu_2 + \phi_2 x_{2t} + x_{2t}^{1/2} \xi_{2,t+1}.
\tag{11.1.28}
$$

---

[4]Although bond returns are not perfectly correlated in this model, the covariance matrix of bond returns has rank two and hence is singular whenever we observe more than two bonds. We discuss this point further in Section 11.1.4.

Finally, the relation between the shocks is

$$\epsilon_{t+1} = \beta \xi_{1,t+1}, \tag{11.1.29}$$

and the shocks $\xi_{1,t+1}$ and $\xi_{2,t+1}$ are uncorrelated with each other. We will write σ_1^2 for the variance of $\xi_{1,t+1}$ and σ_2^2 for the variance of $\xi_{2,t+1}$.

In this model, minus the log stochastic discount factor is forecast by two state variables, x_{1t} and x_{2t}. The variance of the innovation to the log stochastic discount factor is proportional to the level of x_{1t}, as in the square-root model; and each of the two state variables follows a square-root autoregressive process. Finally, the log stochastic discount factor is conditionally correlated with x_1 but not with x_2. This last assumption is required to keep the model in the tractable affine-yield class. Note that the two-factor model nests the single-factor square-root model, which can be obtained by setting $x_{2t} = 0$, but does not nest the single-factor homoskedastic model.

Proceeding in the usual way, we find that the price of a one-period bond is

$$p_{1t} = \mathrm{E}_t[m_{t+1}] + (1/2)\,\mathrm{Var}_t[m_{t+1}] = -x_{1t} - x_{2t} + x_{1t}\beta^2\sigma_1^2/2. \tag{11.1.30}$$

The one-period bond yield $y_{1t} = -p_{1t}$ is no longer proportional to the state variable x_{1t}, because it depends also on x_{2t}. The short interest rate is no longer sufficient to measure the state of the economy in this model. Longstaff and Schwartz (1992) point out, however, that the conditional variance of the short rate is a different linear function of the two state variables:

$$\mathrm{Var}_t[y_{1,t+1}] = (1 - \beta^2\sigma_1^2/2)^2\sigma_1^2\,x_{1t} + \sigma_2^2\,x_{2t}. \tag{11.1.31}$$

Thus the short rate and its conditional volatility summarize the state of the economy, and one can always state the model in terms of these two variables.

We guess that the price function for an n-period bond is linear in the two state variables: $-p_{nt} = A_n + B_{1n}x_{1t} + B_{2n}x_{2t}$. We already know that $A_0 = B_{10} = B_{20} = 0$, $A_1 = 0$, $B_{11} = 1 - \sigma_\epsilon^2/2$, and $B_{21} = 1$. It is straightforward to show that A_n, B_{1n}, and B_{2n} obey

$$B_{1n} = 1 + \phi_1 B_{1,n-1} - (\beta + B_{1,n-1})^2\sigma_1^2/2,$$

$$B_{2n} = 1 + \phi_2 B_{2,n-1} - B_{2,n-1}^2\sigma_2^2/2,$$

$$A_n - A_{n-1} = (1 - \phi_1)\mu_1 B_{1,n-1} + (1 - \phi_2)\mu_2 B_{2,n-1}. \tag{11.1.32}$$

The difference equation for B_{1n} is the same as in the single-factor square-root model, (11.1.23), but the difference equation for B_{2n} includes only a term in the own variance of x_2 because x_2 is uncorrelated with m and does not affect the variance of m. The difference equation for A_n is just the sum of two terms, each of which has the familiar form from the single-factor square-root model.

The expected excess log bond return in the two-factor model is given by

$$
\begin{aligned}
E_t[r_{n,t+1}] - y_{1t} &= -\mathrm{Cov}_t[r_{n,t+1}, m_{t+1}] - \mathrm{Var}_t[r_{n,t+1}]/2 \\
&= B_{1,n-1}\,\mathrm{Cov}_t[x_{1,t+1}, m_{t+1}] - B_{1,n-1}^2\,\mathrm{Var}_t[x_{1,t+1}]/2 \\
&\quad - B_{2,n-1}^2\,\mathrm{Var}_t[x_{2,t+1}]/2 \\
&= [-B_{1,n-1}\beta\sigma_1^2 - B_{1,n-1}^2\sigma_1^2/2]x_{1t} \\
&\quad - [B_{2,n-1}^2\sigma_2^2/2]x_{2t}.
\end{aligned}
\tag{11.1.33}
$$

This is the same as in the square-root model, with the addition of an extra term, arising from Jensen's Inequality, in the variance of $x_{2,t+1}$.

The forward rate in the two-factor model is given by

$$
\begin{aligned}
f_{nt} &= y_{1t} + B_{1n}(E_t[\Delta x_{1,t+1}] - \mathrm{Cov}_t[x_{1,t+1}, m_{t+1}]) + B_{2n}E_t[\Delta x_{2,t+1}] \\
&\quad - B_{1n}^2\,\mathrm{Var}_t[x_{1,t+1}]/2 - B_{2n}^2\,\mathrm{Var}_t[x_{2,t+1}]/2 \\
&= (1 - \beta^2\sigma_1^2/2)x_{1t} + x_{2t} - B_{1n}(1 - \phi_1)(x_{1t} - \mu_1) \\
&\quad - B_{2n}(1 - \phi_2)(x_{2t} - \mu_2) - B_{1n}x_{1t}\beta\sigma_1^2 \\
&\quad - B_{1n}^2 x_{1t}\sigma_1^2/2 - B_{2n}^2 x_{2t}\sigma_2^2/2.
\end{aligned}
\tag{11.1.34}
$$

This is the obvious generalization of the square-root model. Importantly, it can generate more complicated shapes for the yield curve, including inverted hump shapes, as the independent movements of both x_{1t} and x_{2t} affect the term structure.

The analysis of this model illustrates an important principle. As Cox, Ingersoll, and Ross (1985a) and Dybvig (1989) have emphasized, under certain circumstances one can construct multifactor term-structure models simply by "adding up" single-factor models. Whenever the stochastic discount factor m_{t+1} can be written as the sum of two independent processes, then the resulting term structure is the sum of the term structures that would exist under each of these processes. In the Longstaff and Schwartz (1992) model the stochastic discount factor is the sum of $-x_{1t} - x_{1t}^{1/2}\beta\xi_{1,t+1}$ and $-x_{2t}$, and these components are independent of each other. Inspection of (11.1.34) shows that the resulting term structure is just the sum of a general square-root term structure driven by the x_{1t} process and a special square-root term structure with parameter restriction $\beta = 0$ driven by the x_{2t} process.

11.1.4 Beyond Affine-Yield Models

We have considered a sequence of models, each of which turns out to have the property that log bond yields are linear or *affine* in the underlying state variables. Brown and Schaefer (1991) and Duffie and Kan (1993) have clarified the primitive assumptions necessary to get an affine-yield model. In the discrete-time framework used here, these conditions are most easily stated by defining a vector $\mathbf{x}_t$ which contains the log stochastic discount factor m_t and the time t values of the state variables relevant for forecasting future m_{t+i}, $i = 1 \ldots n$. If the conditional forecast of $\mathbf{x}$ one period ahead, $E_t[\mathbf{x}_{t+1}]$, is affine in the state variables, and if the conditional distribution of $\mathbf{x}$ one period ahead is normal with a variance-covariance matrix $\mathrm{Var}_t[\mathbf{x}_{t+1}]$ which is affine in the state variables, then the resulting term-structure model is an affine-yield model.

To see this, consider the steps we used to derive the implications of each successive term-structure model. We first calculated the log short-term interest rate; this is affine in the underlying state variables if m_{t+1} is conditionally normal and $E_t[m_{t+1}]$ and $\mathrm{Var}_t[m_{t+1}]$ are affine in the state variables. We next guessed that log bond yields were affine and proceeded to verify the guess. If yields are affine, and if $\mathbf{x}$ is conditionally normal with affine variance-covariance matrix, then the risk premium on any bond is affine. Finally we derived log forward rates; these are affine if the short rate, risk premium, and the expected change in the state variable are all affine. Affine forward rates imply affine yields, verifying that the model is in the affine-yield class.

Brown and Schaefer (1991) and Duffie and Kan (1993) state conditions on the short rate which deliver an affine-yield model in a continuous-time setting. They show that the risk-adjusted drift in the short rate—the expected change in the short rate less the covariance of the short rate with the stochastic discount factor—and the variance of the short rate must both be affine to get an affine-yield model. The models of Vasicek (1977), Cox, Ingersoll, and Ross (1985a), and Pearson and Sun (1994) satisfy these requirements, but some other continuous-time models such as that of Brennan and Schwartz (1979) do not.

Affine-yield models have a number of desirable properties which help to explain their appeal. First, log bond yields inherit the conditional normality assumed for the underlying state variables. Second, because log bond yields are linear functions of the state variables we can renormalize the model so that the yields themselves are the state variables. This is obvious in a one-factor model where the short rate is the state variable, but it is equally possible in a model with any number of factors. Longstaff and Schwartz (1992) present their two-factor model as one in which the volatility of the short rate and the level of the short rate are the factors; the model could be written equally well in terms of any two bond yields of fixed maturities. Third, affine-yield models with K state variables imply that the term structure of interest rates can be summarized by the levels of K bond yields at each point in time and the constant coefficients relating other bond yields to the K basis yields. In this sense affine-yield models are linear; their nonlinearity is confined to the process governing the intertemporal evolution of the K basis yields and the relation between the cross-sectional coefficients and the underlying parameters of the model.

Affine-yield models also have some disadvantages. The linear relations among bond yields mean that the covariance matrix of bond returns has rank K—equivalently, we can perfectly fit the return on any bond using a regression on K other contemporaneous bond returns. This implication will always be rejected by a data set containing more than K bonds, unless we add extra error terms to the model. Affine-yield models also limit the way in which interest rate volatility can change with the level of interest rates; for example a model in which volatility is proportional to the square of the interest rate is not affine. Finally, as Constantinides (1992) emphasizes, single-factor affine-yield models imply that risk premia on long-term bonds always have the same sign.

If we move outside the affine-yield class of models, we can no longer work with equation (11.1.1) but must return to the underlying nonlinear difference equation (11.0.1) or its n-period representation (11.0.2). In general these equations must be solved numerically. One common method is to set up a binomial tree for the short-term interest rate. Black, Derman, and Toy (1990) and Black and Karasinski (1991), for example, assume that the simple one-period yield Y_{1t} is conditionally lognormal (as opposed to the assumption of affine-yield models that $(1 + Y_{1t})$ is conditionally lognormal). They use a binomial tree to solve their models for the implied term structure of interest rates. Constantinides (1992), however, presents a model that can be solved in closed form. His model makes the log stochastic discount factor a sum of noncentral chi-squared random variables rather than a normal random variable, and Constantinides is then able to calculate the expectations in (11.0.2) analytically.

11.2 Fitting Term-Structure Models to the Data

11.2.1 Real Bonds, Nominal Bonds, and Inflation

The term-structure models described so far apply to bonds whose payoffs are riskless in real terms. Almost all actual bonds instead have payoffs that are riskless in nominal terms.[5] We now discuss how the models can be adapted to deal with this fact.

To study nominal bonds we need to introduce some new notation. We write the nominal price index at time t as Q_t, and the gross rate of inflation from t to $t+1$ as $\Pi_{t+1} \equiv Q_{t+1}/Q_t$. We have already defined P_{nt} to be the real price of an n-period real bond which pays one goods unit at time $t+n$; we now define $P_{nt}^{\$}$ to be the nominal price of an n-period nominal bond which pays \$1 at time $t+n$. From these definitions it follows that the nominal price of an n-period real bond is $P_{nt} Q_t$, and the real price of an n-period nominal bond is $P_{nt}^{\$}/Q_t$. We do not adopt any special notation for these last two concepts.

If we now apply the general asset pricing condition,

$$1 = \mathrm{E}_t[(1 + R_{i,t+1})M_{t+1}],$$

to the real return on an n-period nominal bond, we find that

$$\frac{P_{nt}^{\$}}{Q_t} = \mathrm{E}_t\left[\frac{P_{n-1,t+1}^{\$}}{Q_{t+1}} M_{t+1}\right]. \qquad (11.2.1)$$

Multiplying through by Q_t, we have

$$\begin{aligned}
P_{nt}^{\$} &= \mathrm{E}_t\left[P_{n-1,t+1}^{\$} M_{t+1} \frac{Q_t}{Q_{t+1}}\right] \\
&= \mathrm{E}_t\left[P_{n-1,t+1}^{\$} \frac{M_{t+1}}{\Pi_{t+1}}\right] \\
&= \mathrm{E}_t[P_{n-1,t+1}^{\$} M_{t+1}^{\$}], \qquad (11.2.2)
\end{aligned}$$

where $M_{t+1}^{\$} \equiv M_{t+1}/\Pi_{t+1}$ can be thought of as a *nominal* stochastic discount factor that prices nominal returns.

The empirical literature on nominal bonds uses this result in one of two ways. The first approach is to take the primitive assumptions that we made about M_{t+1} in Section 11.1 and to apply them instead to $M_{t+1}^{\$}$. The real term-structure models of the last section are then reinterpreted as nominal term-structure models. Brown and Dybvig (1986), for example, do this when

---

[5] Some governments, notably those of Canada, Israel, and the UK, have issued bonds whose nominal payoffs are linked to a nominal price index. In 1996 the US Treasury is considering issuing similar securities. These index-linked bonds approximate real bonds but are rarely exactly equivalent to real bonds. Brown and Schaefer (1994) give a lucid discussion of the imperfections in the UK indexing system, and apply the Cox, Ingersoll, and Ross (1985a) model to UK index-linked bonds. See also Barr and Campbell (1995) and Campbell and Shiller (1996).

they apply the Cox, Ingersoll, and Ross (1985a) square-root model directly to data on US nominal bond prices. The square-root model restricts interest rates to be positive, and in this respect it is more appropriate for nominal interest rates than for real interest rates.

The second approach is to assume that the two components of the nominal stochastic discount factor, M_{t+1} and $1/\Pi_{t+1}$, are independent of each other. To see how this assumption facilitates empirical work, take logs of the nominal stochastic discount factor to get

$$m_{t+1}^{\$} = m_{t+1} - \pi_{t+1}. \tag{11.2.3}$$

When the components m_{t+1} and π_{t+1} are independent, we can price nominal bonds by using the insights of Cox, Ingersoll, and Ross (1985a) and Dybvig (1989). Recall from Section 11.1.3 their result that the log bond price in a model with two independent components of the stochastic discount factor is the sum of the log bond prices implied by each component. We can, for example, apply the Longstaff and Schwartz (1992) model to nominal bonds by assuming that m_{t+1} is described by a square-root single-factor model, $-m_{t+1} = x_{1t} + x_{1t}^{1/2}\beta\xi_{1,t+1}$, and that π_{t+1} is known at t and equal to a state variable x_{2t}. We then get $-m_{t+1}^{\$} = -m_{t+1} + \pi_{t+1} = x_{1t} + x_{1t}^{1/2}\beta\xi_{1,t+1} + x_{2t}$, and the Longstaff-Schwartz model describes nominal bonds.

More generally, the assumption that M_{t+1} and $1/\Pi_{t+1}$ are independent implies that prices of nominal bonds are just prices of real bonds multiplied by the expectation of the future real value of money, and that expected real returns on nominal bonds are the same as expected real returns on real bonds. To see this, consider equation (11.2.2) with maturity $n = 1$, and note that the independence of M_{t+1} and $1/\Pi_{t+1}$ allows us to replace the expectation of their product by the product of their expectations:

$$P_{1t}^{\$} = \mathrm{E}_t[M_{t+1}^{\$}] = \mathrm{E}_t[M_{t+1}]\,\mathrm{E}_t\left[\frac{1}{\Pi_{t+1}}\right] = P_{1t}\,Q_t\,\mathrm{E}_t\left[\frac{1}{Q_{t+1}}\right], \tag{11.2.4}$$

since $P_{1t} = \mathrm{E}_t[M_{t+1}]$ and $1/\Pi_{t+1} = Q_t/Q_{t+1}$. Thus the nominal price of a bond which pays \$1 tomorrow is the nominal price of a bond which pays one unit of goods tomorrow, times the expectation of the real value of \$1 tomorrow.

We now guess that a similar relationship holds for all maturities n, and we prove this by induction. If the $(n-1)$-period relationship holds, $P_{n-1,t}^{\$} = P_{n-1,t}\,Q_t\,\mathrm{E}_t[1/Q_{t+n-1}]$, then

$$
\begin{aligned}
P_{nt}^{\$} &= \mathrm{E}_t\left[P_{n-1,t+1}^{\$}\,M_{t+1}\frac{Q_t}{Q_{t+1}}\right] \\
&= \mathrm{E}_t\left[P_{n-1,t+1}\,Q_{t+1}\,\mathrm{E}_{t+1}\left[\frac{1}{Q_{t+n}}\right]M_{t+1}\frac{Q_t}{Q_{t+1}}\right]
\end{aligned}
$$

$$= Q_t \, \mathrm{E}_t \left[P_{n-1,t+1} \, M_{t+1} \, \mathrm{E}_{t+1} \left[\frac{1}{Q_{t+n}} \right] \right]$$

$$= P_{nt} \, Q_t \, \mathrm{E}_t \left[\frac{1}{Q_{t+n}} \right], \qquad (11.2.5)$$

where the last equality uses both the independence of real variables from the price level (which enables us to replace the expectation of a product by the product of expectations), and the fact that $P_{nt} = \mathrm{E}_t[P_{n-1,t+1} \, M_{t+1}]$. Equation (11.2.5) is the desired result that the nominal price of a bond which pays \$1 at time $t + n$ is the nominal price of a bond which pays one unit of goods at time $t + n$, times the expected real value of \$1 at time $t + n$. Dividing (11.2.5) by Q_t, we can see that the same relationship holds between the real prices of nominal bonds and the real prices of real bonds. Further, (11.2.5) implies that the expected real return on a nominal bond equals the expected real return on a real bond:

$$\mathrm{E}_t \left[\frac{P_{n-1,t+1}^{\$}}{P_{nt}^{\$}} \frac{Q_t}{Q_{t+1}} \right] = \mathrm{E}_t \left[\frac{\mathrm{E}_{t+1}[1/Q_{t+n}] P_{n-1,t+1} \, Q_{t+1}}{\mathrm{E}_t[1/Q_{t+1}] P_{nt} \, Q_t} \frac{Q_t}{Q_{t+1}} \right]$$

$$= \mathrm{E}_t \left[\frac{P_{n-1,t+1}}{P_{nt}} \right]. \qquad (11.2.6)$$

Gibbons and Ramaswamy (1993) use these results to test the implications of real term-structure models for econometric forecasts of real returns on nominal bonds.

Although it is extremely convenient to assume that inflation is independent of the real stochastic discount factor, this assumption may be unrealistic. Barr and Campbell (1995), Campbell and Ammer (1993), and Pennacchi (1991), using respectively UK data on indexed and nominal bonds, rational-expectations methodology applied to US data, and survey data, all find that innovations to expected inflation are negatively correlated in the short run with innovations to expected future real interest rates. More directly, Campbell and Shiller (1996) find that inflation innovations are correlated with stock returns and real consumption growth, proxies for the stochastic discount factor suggested by the traditional CAPM of Chapter 5 and the consumption CAPM of Chapter 8.

11.2.2 Empirical Evidence on Affine-Yield Models

All the models we have discussed so far need additional error terms if they are to fit the data. To see why, consider a model in which the real stochastic discount factor is driven by a single state variable. In such a model, returns on all real bonds are perfectly correlated because the model has only a single shock. Similarly, returns on all nominal bonds are perfectly correlated in any model where a single state variable drives the nominal stochastic discount factor. In reality there are no deterministic linear relationships among returns on different bonds, so these implications are bound to be rejected by the data. Adding extra state variables increases the rank of the variance-covariance matrix of bond returns from one to K, where K is the number of state variables, but whenever there are more than K bonds the matrix remains singular—equivalently, there are deterministic linear relationships among bond returns. So these models, too, are trivially rejected by the data.

To handle this problem empirical researchers allow additional error terms to affect bond prices. These errors may be thought of as measurement errors in bond prices, errors in calculating implied zero-coupon prices from an observed coupon-bearing term structure, or model specification errors arising from tax effects or transactions costs. Alternatively, if one uses a model for the real stochastic discount factor and tests it on nominal bonds in the manner of Gibbons and Ramaswamy (1993), the errors may arise from unexpected inflation.

Whatever the source of the additional errors, auxiliary assumptions about their behavior are needed to keep the model testable. One common assumption is that bond-price errors are serially uncorrelated, although they may be correlated across bonds. This assumption makes it easy to examine the time-series implications of term-structure models. Other authors assume that bond-price errors are uncorrelated across bonds, although they may be correlated over time.

Affine-Yield Models as Latent-Variable Models

Stambaugh (1988) and Heston (1992) show that under fairly weak assumptions about the additional bond price errors, an affine-yield model implies a *latent-variable* structure for bond returns. Variables that forecast bond returns can do so only as proxies for the underlying state variables of the model; if there are fewer state variables than forecasting variables, this puts testable restrictions on forecasting equations for bond returns.

A general affine-yield model with K state variables takes the form

$$- p_{nt} = A_n + B_{1n} x_{1t} + \cdots + B_{Kn} x_{Kt}, \tag{11.2.7}$$

where x_{kt}, $k = 1 \ldots K$, are the state variables, and A_n and B_{kn}, $k = 1 \ldots K$, are constants. The model also implies that expected excess returns on long bonds over the short interest rate can be written as

$$E_t[r_{n,t+1} - y_{1t}] = A_n^* + B_{1n}^* x_{1t} + \cdots + B_{Kn}^* x_{Kt}, \tag{11.2.8}$$

where A_n^* and B_{kn}^*, $k = 1 \ldots K$, are constants. The model puts cross-sectional restrictions on these constants which are related to the time-series process driving the state variables, but we ignore this aspect of the model here.

Now suppose that we do not observe the true excess returns on long bonds, but instead observe a noisy measure

$$e_{n,t+1} = r_{n,t+1} - y_{1t} + \eta_{n,t+1}, \tag{11.2.9}$$

where $\eta_{n,t+1}$ is an error term. We assume that $\eta_{n,t+1}$ is orthogonal to a vector $\mathbf{h}_t$ containing J instruments h_{jt}, $j = 1 \ldots J$:

$$E[\eta_{n,t+1} \mid \mathbf{h}_t] = 0. \tag{11.2.10}$$

The vector $\mathbf{h}_t$ might contain lagged variables, for example, if the return error $\eta_{n,t+1}$ is serially uncorrelated. We further assume that for each state variable x_{kt}, $k = 1 \ldots K$, the expectation of the state variable conditional on the instruments is linear in the instruments:

$$E[x_{kt} \mid \mathbf{h}_t] = \sum_{j=1}^{J} \theta_{kj} h_{jt} \tag{11.2.11}$$

for some constant coefficients θ_{kj}.

These assumptions imply that the expectation of $e_{n,t+1}$ conditional on the instruments, which from (11.2.10) is the same as the expectation of the true excess return $r_{n,t+1} - y_{1t}$ conditional on the instruments, is linear in the instruments:

$$E[e_{n,t+1} \mid \mathbf{h}_t] = E[r_{n,t+1} - y_{1t} \mid \mathbf{h}_t] =$$

$$A_n^* + \sum_{k=1}^{K} B_{kn}^* E[x_{kt} \mid \mathbf{h}_t] = A_n^* + \sum_{k=1}^{K} B_{kn}^* \sum_{j=1}^{J} \theta_{kj} h_{jt}. \tag{11.2.12}$$

If we define $\mathbf{e}_{t+1}$ to be the vector $[e_{1,t+1} \ldots e_{N,t+1}]$ for assets $n = 1 \ldots N$, then (11.2.12) can be rewritten in vector form as

$$\mathbf{e}_{t+1} = \mathbf{A}^* + \mathbf{C}\mathbf{h}_t + \boldsymbol{\eta}_{t+1}, \tag{11.2.13}$$

where $\mathbf{A}^*$ is a vector whose nth element is A_n^* and $\mathbf{C}$ is a matrix of coefficients whose (n, j) element is

$$C_{nl} = \sum_{k=1}^{K} B_{kn}^* \theta_{kj}. \tag{11.2.14}$$

Equations (11.2.13) and (11.2.14) define a latent-variable model for expected excess bond returns with K latent variables. Equation (11.2.14) says that the $(N \times J)$ matrix of coefficients of N assets on J instruments has rank at most K, where K is the number of state variables in the underlying term-structure model. The instruments forecast excess bond returns only through their ability to proxy for the state variables (measured by the θ_{kj}

coefficients) and the role of the state variables in determining excess bond returns (measured by the B_{kn}^* coefficients). The system is particularly easy to understand in the single-factor case. Here $K = 1$, we can drop the k subscripts, and (11.2.14) becomes

$$C_{nj} = B_n^* \theta_j. \tag{11.2.15}$$

Equation (11.2.15) says that each row of the matrix $\mathbf{C}$ is proportional to each other row, and the coefficients of proportionality are ratios of B_n^* coefficients. Note that the rank of the matrix $\mathbf{C}$ could be less than K; for example, it is zero in a homoskedastic model with K state variables because in such a model the coefficients B_{kn}^* are zero for all k and n.

Latent-variable models of the form (11.2.14) or (11.2.15) have been applied to financial data by Campbell (1987), Gibbons and Ferson (1985), and Hansen and Hodrick (1983). They can be estimated by Generalized Method of Moments applied to the system of regression equations (11.2.13). Heston (1992) points out that one can equivalently estimate a system of instrumental variables regressions of excess returns on K basis excess returns, where the elements of $\mathbf{h}_t$ are the instruments.

A key issue is how to choose instruments $\mathbf{h}_t$ that satisfy (11.2.10) (orthogonality of instruments and bond pricing errors) and (11.2.11) (state variables linear in the instruments). In an affine-yield model without bond pricing errors, bond yields and forward rates are linear in the state variables; hence the state variables are linear in yields and forward rates. This property survives the addition of normally distributed bond pricing errors. Thus it is natural to choose yields or forward rates as instruments satisfying (11.2.11).

To satisfy (11.2.10), one must be more specific about the nature of the bond pricing errors. The error in a bond price measured at time t affects both the time t bond yield and the excess return on the bond from t to $t + 1$. Hence yields and forward rates measured at time t are not likely to be orthogonal to errors in excess bond returns from t to $t + 1$. If the bond price errors are uncorrelated across time, however, then yields and forward rates measured at time $t - 1$ will be orthogonal to excess bond return errors from t to $t + 1$; and if the bond price errors are uncorrelated across bonds, then one can choose a set of yields or forward rates measured at different maturities than those used for excess returns. Stambaugh (1988) applies both these strategies to monthly data on US Treasury bills of maturities two to six months over the period 1959:3 to 1985:11. He finds strong evidence against a model with one state variable and weaker evidence against a model with two state variables. Heston (1992) studies a more recent period, 1970:2 to 1988:5, and a data set including longer maturities (6, 12, 36, and 60 months) and finds little evidence against a model with one state variable.

Evidence on the Short-Rate Process

If one is willing to assume that there is negligible measurement error in the short-term nominal interest rate, then time-series analysis of short-rate behavior may be a useful first step in building a nominal term-structure model. Chan, Karolyi, Longstaff, and Sanders (1992) estimate a discrete-time model for the short rate of the form

$$y_{1,t+1} - y_{1t} = \alpha + \beta y_{1t} + \epsilon_{t+1}, \tag{11.2.16}$$

where

$$E_t[\epsilon_{t+1}] = 0, \qquad E_t[\epsilon_{t+1}^2] = \sigma^2 y_{1t}^{2\gamma}. \tag{11.2.17}$$

This specification nests the single-factor models we discussed in Section 11.1; the homoskedastic model has $\gamma = 0$, while the square-root model has $\gamma = 0.5$. It also approximates a continuous-time diffusion process for the instantaneous short rate $r(t)$ of the form $dr = (\beta_0 + \beta_1 r)dt + \sigma r^\gamma dB$. Such a diffusion process nests the major single-factor continuous-time models for the short rate. The Vasicek (1977) model, for example, has $\gamma = 0$; the Cox, Ingersoll, and Ross (1985a) model has $\gamma = 0.5$, and the Brennan and Schwartz (1979) model has $\gamma = 1$.[6]

Chan et al. (1992) estimate (11.2.16) and (11.2.17) by Generalized Method of Moments. They define an error vector with two elements, the first being $y_{1,t+1} - (1+\beta)y_{1t} - \alpha$ and the second being $\left(y_{1,t+1} - (1+\beta)y_{1t} - \alpha\right)^2 - \sigma^2 y_{1t}^{2\gamma}$. These errors are orthogonal to any instruments known at time t; a constant and the level of the short rate y_{1t} are used as the instruments. In monthly data on a one-month Treasury bill rate over the period 1964:6 to 1989:12, Chan et al. find that α and β are small and often statistically insignificant. The short-term interest rate is highly persistent so it is hard to reject the hypothesis that it follows a random walk. They also find that γ is large and precisely estimated. They can reject all models which make $\gamma < 1$, and their unrestricted estimate of γ is about 1.5 and almost two standard errors above 1.

To understand these results, consider the case where $\alpha = \beta = 0$, so the short rate is a random walk without drift. Then the error term ϵ_{t+1} in (11.2.16) is just the change in the short rate $y_{1,t+1} - y_{1t}$, and (11.2.17) says that the expectation of the squared change in the short rate, $E_t[(y_{1,t+1} - y_{1t})^2] = \sigma^2 y_{1t}^{2\gamma}$. Equivalently,

$$E_t\left[\left(\frac{y_{1,t+1} - y_{1t}}{y_{1t}^\gamma}\right)^2\right] = \sigma^2, \tag{11.2.18}$$

so when the change in the short rate is scaled by the appropriate power of the short rate, it becomes homoskedastic. Figures 11.1a through d illustrate

---

[6]Note however that (11.2.16) and (11.2.17) do not nest the Pearson-Sun model.

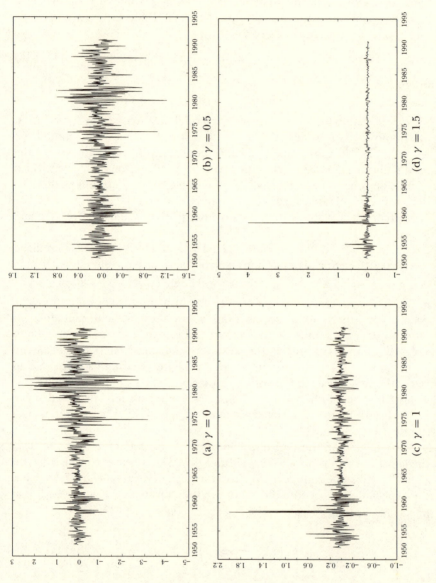

Figure 11.1. *Change in Short Rate Divided by Short Rate to the Power γ*

the results of Chan et al. by plotting changes in short rates scaled by various powers of short rates. The figures show $(y_{1,t+1} - y_{1t})/(y_{1t}^\gamma)$ for $\gamma = 0, 0.5,$ 1, and 1.5, using the data of McCulloch and Kwon (1993) over the period 1952:1 to 1991:2. Over the period since 1964 studied by Chan et al., it is striking how the variance of the series appears to stabilize as one increases γ from 0 to 1.5.

These results raise two problems for single-factor affine-yield models of the nominal term structure. First, when there is no mean-reversion in the short rate, forward rates and bond yields may rise with maturity initially, but they eventually decline with maturity and continue to do so forever. Second, single-factor affine-yield models require that $\gamma = 0$ or 0.5 in (11.2.17). The estimated value of 1.5 takes one outside the tractable class of affine-yield models and forces one to solve the term-structure model numerically.

There is as yet no consensus about how to resolve these problems. Aït-Sahalia (1996b) argues that existing parametric models are too restrictive; he proposes a nonparametric method for estimating the drift and volatility of the short interest rate. He argues that the short rate is very close to a random walk when it is in the middle of its historical range (roughly, between 4% and 17%), but that it mean-reverts strongly when it gets outside this range. Chan et al. miss this because their linear model does not allow mean-reversion to depend on the level of the interest rate. Aït-Sahalia also argues that interest-rate volatility is related to the level of the interest rate in a more complicated way than is allowed by any standard model. His most general parametric model, and the only one he does not reject statistically, has the short interest rate following the diffusion $dr = (\beta_0 + \beta_1 r + \beta_2 r^2 + \beta_3/r)dt + (\sigma_0 + \sigma_1 r + \sigma_2 r^\gamma)dB$. He estimates γ to be about 2, but the other parameters of the volatility function also play an important role in determining volatility.

Following Hamilton (1989), an alternative view is that the short rate randomly switches among different regimes, each of which has its own mean and volatility parameters. Such a model may have mean-reversion within each regime, but the short rate may appear to be highly persistent when one averages data from different regimes. If regimes with high mean parameters are also regimes with high volatility parameters, then such a model may also explain the apparent sensitivity of interest rate volatility to the level of the interest rate without invoking a high value of γ. Figures 11.1a–d show that no single value of γ makes scaled interest rate changes homoskedastic over the whole period since 1952; the choice of $\gamma = 1.5$ works very well for 1964 to 1991 but worsens heteroskedasticity in the 1950s and early 1960s.[7] Thus at least some regime changes are needed to fit the data, and it may be that a model with $\gamma = 0$ or $\gamma = 0.5$ is adequate once regime changes

---

[7]Although this is not shown in the figures, the $\gamma = 1.5$ model also breaks down in the 1990s.

are allowed. Gray (1996) explores this possibility but estimates only slightly lower values of γ than Chan et al., while Naik and Lee (1994) solve for bond and bond-option prices in a regime-shift model with $\gamma = 0$.

Brenner, Harjes, and Kroner (1996) move in a somewhat different direction. They allow for GARCH effects on interest rate volatility, as described in Section 12.2 of Chapter 12, as well as the level effect on volatility described by (11.2.17). They replace (11.2.17) by $E_t[\epsilon_{t+1}^2] = \sigma_t^2 y_{1t}^{2\gamma}$ and $\sigma_t^2 = \omega + \theta\epsilon_t^2 + \phi\sigma_{t-1}^2$, a standard GARCH(1,1) model. They find that a model with $\gamma = 0.5$ fits the short rate series quite well once GARCH effects are included in the model; however they do not explore the implications of this for bond or bond-option pricing.

Cross-Sectional Restrictions on the Term Structure

So far we have emphasized the time-series implications of affine-yield models and have ignored their cross-sectional implications. Brown and Dybvig (1986) and Brown and Schaefer (1994) take the opposite approach, ignoring the models' time-series implications and estimating all the parameters from the term structure of interest rates observed at a point in time. If this procedure is repeated over many time periods, it generates a sequence of parameter estimates which should in theory be identical for all time periods but which in practice varies over time. The procedure is analogous to the common practice of calculating implied volatility by inverting the Black-Scholes formula using traded option prices; there too the model requires that volatility be constant over time, but implied volatility tends to move over time.

Of course, bond pricing errors might cause estimated parameters to shift over time even if true underlying parameters are constant. But in simple term-structure models there also appear to be some systematic differences between the parameter values needed to fit cross-sectional term-structure data and the parameter values implied by the time-series behavior of interest rates. These systematic differences are indicative of misspecification in the models. To understand the problem, we will choose parameters in the single-factor homoskedastic and square-root models to fit various simple moments of the data and will show that the resulting model does not match some other characteristics of the data.

In the homoskedastic single-factor model, the important parameters of the model can be identified by considering the following four moments of the data:

$$\text{Corr}[y_{1t}, y_{1,t-1}] = \phi$$

$$\text{Var}[y_{1t}] = \frac{\sigma^2}{1 - \phi^2}$$

$$\lim_{n \to \infty} E[r_{n,t+1} - y_{1t}] = \lim_{n \to \infty} E[f_{nt} - y_{1t}]$$

$$= -\left(\frac{1}{1-\phi}\right)^2 \sigma^2/2 - \left(\frac{\beta}{1-\phi}\right)\sigma^2$$

$$E[y_{1t}] = \mu - \beta^2 \sigma^2/2. \tag{11.2.19}$$

The first-order autocorrelation of the short rate identifies the autoregressive parameter ϕ. Given ϕ, the variance of the short rate then identifies the innovation variance σ^2. Given ϕ and σ^2, the average excess return on a very long-term bond, or equivalently the average difference between a very long-term forward rate and the short rate, identify the parameter β. Finally, given ϕ, σ^2, and β, the mean short rate identifies μ.

In the zero-coupon yield data of McCulloch and Kwon (1993) over the period 1952 to 1991, the monthly first-order autocorrelation of the short rate is 0.98, implying $\phi = 0.98$. The standard deviation of the short rate is 3.064% at an annual rate or 0.00255 in natural units, implying $\sigma = 0.00051$ in natural units or 0.610% at an annual rate.

In the data there is some discrepancy between the average excess return on long bonds, which from Table 10.2 is negative at -0.048% at an annual rate for $n = 120$, and the average slope of the forward-rate curve, which is positive at 1.507% at an annual rate when measured by the difference between a 60–120 month forward rate and the 1-month short rate. The difference occurs because interest rates rose over the period 1952 to 1991; stationary term-structure models force the true mean change in interest rates to be zero, but an increase in interest rates in a particular sample can make the sample mean excess return on long bonds negative even when the sample mean slope of the forward-rate curve is positive. The value of β required to fit the average slope of the forward-rate curve is -122. The implied value for $\mu - \sigma^2/2$, expressed at an annual rate, is 7.632%.

The difficulty with the homoskedastic single-factor model is that with these parameters the average forward-rate term-structure curves very gradually from its initial value to its asymptote, as shown by the dashed line in Figure 11.2. The sample average forward-rate curve over the 1952 to 1991 period, shown by the solid line in Figure 11.2, rises much more steeply at first and then flattens out at about five years maturity.

This problem arises because the theoretical average forward-rate curve approaches its asymptote approximately at geometric rate ϕ. One could match the sample average forward-rate curve more closely by choosing a smaller value of ϕ. Unfortunately this would be inconsistent not only with the observed persistence of the short rate, but also with the observed pattern of volatility in forward rates. Equation (11.1.14) shows that the standard

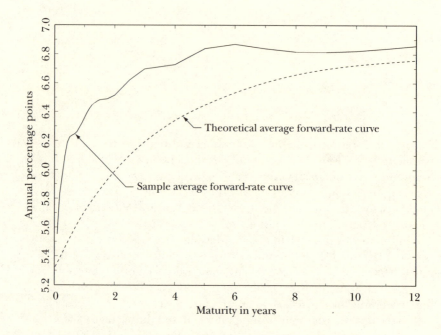

Figure 11.2. *Sample and Theoretical Average Forward-Rate Curves*

deviation of the forward rate declines at rate ϕ. In the 1952 to 1991 period the standard deviation of the n-period forward rate barely declines at all with maturity n, and this feature of the data can only be fit by an extremely persistent short-rate process. Backus and Zin (1994) discuss this problem in detail and suggest that a higher-order model which allows both transitory and persistent movements in the short rate can fit the term structure more successfully.

Parameter identification is somewhat more difficult in the square-root model. Here the moments given in equation (11.2.19) become

$$\text{Corr}[y_{1t}, y_{1,t-1}] = \phi$$

$$\text{Var}[y_{1t}] = (1 - \beta^2 \sigma^2/2)^2 \frac{\sigma^2 \mu}{1 - \phi^2}$$

$$\lim_{n \to \infty} \text{E}[r_{n,t+1} - y_{1t}] = \lim_{n \to \infty} \text{E}[f_{nt} - y_{1t}] = [-\beta B \sigma^2 - B^2 \sigma^2/2]\mu$$

$$\text{E}[y_{1t}] = \mu(1 - \beta^2 \sigma^2/2),$$

$$(11.2.20)$$

where B is the limiting value of B_n from equation (11.1.23). As before, we can identify $\phi = 0.98$ from the estimated first-order autocorrelation of the short rate, but now the other parameters of the model are simultaneously determined. One can of course estimate them by Generalized Method of Moments. The square-root model, like the homoskedastic model, produces an average forward-rate curve that approaches its asymptote very slowly when the short rate is highly persistent; thus the model has many of the same empirical limitations as the homoskedastic model.

In summary, the single-factor affine-yield models we have described in this chapter are too restrictive to fit the behavior of nominal interest rates. The latent-variable structure of the data, the nature of the short rate process, and the shape of the average term structure are all hard to fit with these models. In response to this researchers are exploring more general models, including affine-yield models in which the single state variable follows a higher-order ARMA process (Backus and Zin [1994]), affine-yield models with several state variables (Longstaff and Schwartz [1992]), regime-switching models (Gray [1996], Naik and Lee [1994]), and GARCH models of interest rate volatility (Brenner, Harjes, and Kroner [1996]). No one model has yet emerged as the consensus choice for modeling the nominal term structure. We note however that Brown and Schaefer (1994) and Gibbons and Ramaswamy (1993) have achieved some success in fitting simple models to prices of UK index-linked bonds and econometric forecasts of real returns on US nominal bonds. Thus single-factor affine-yield models may be more appropriate for modeling real interest rates than for modeling nominal interest rates.

11.3 Pricing Fixed-Income Derivative Securities

One of the main reasons for the explosion of interest in term-structure models is the practical need to price and hedge fixed-income derivative securities. In this section we show how term-structure models can be used in this context. Section 11.3.1 begins by discussing ways to augment standard term-structure models so that they fit the current yield curve exactly. Derivatives traders usually want to take this yield curve as given, and so they want to use a pricing model that is fully consistent with all current bond prices. We explain the popular approaches of Ho and Lee (1986), Black, Derman, and Toy (1990), and Heath, Jarrow, and Morton (1992). Section 11.3.2 shows how term-structure models can be used to price forward and futures contracts on fixed-income securities, while Section 11.3.3 explores option pricing in the context of a term-structure model.

11.3.1 Fitting the Current Term Structure Exactly

In general a model gives an exact fit to as many data points as it has parameters. The homoskedastic single-factor model presented in Section 11.1, for example, has four parameters, ϕ, β, σ^2, and μ. Inevitably this model does not fit the whole term structure exactly. To allow for this the empirical work of the previous section added error terms, reflecting model specification error and measurement error in bond prices.

In pricing fixed-income derivative securities it may be desirable to have a model that does fit the current term structure exactly. To achieve this, we can use the result of Cox, Ingersoll, and Ross (1985a) and Dybvig (1989) that one can add independent term-structure models together. A simple approach, due originally to Ho and Lee (1986), is to break observed forward rates f_{nt} into two components:

$$f_{nt} = f_{nt}^a + f_{nt}^b, \tag{11.3.1}$$

where f_{nt}^a is the forward rate implied by a standard tractable model and f_{nt}^b is the residual. The residual component is then attributed to a deterministic term-structure model. Since a deterministic process is independent of any stochastic process, the decomposition (11.3.1) is always legitimate. There is a corresponding decomposition of the stochastic discount factor,

$$m_{t+1} = m_{t+1}^a + m_{t+1}^b. \tag{11.3.2}$$

In a deterministic model, the absence of arbitrage requires that

$$f_{nt}^b = y_{1,t+n}^b = m_{t+n}^b. \tag{11.3.3}$$

Thus we are postulating that future stochastic discount factors contain a deterministic component that is reflected in future short-term interest rates and current forward rates.

Although this procedure works well in any one period, there is nothing to ensure that it will be consistent from period to period. A typical application of the approach sets $y_{1t}^b = 0$, so that the current short rate is used as an input into the stochastic term-structure model without any adjustment for a deterministic component. Deterministic components of future short rates $y_{1,t+n}^b$ are then set to nonzero values to fit the time t term structure. When time $t + n$ arrives, however, this procedure is repeated; now $y_{1,t+n}^b$ is set to zero and deterministic components of more distant future short rates are made nonzero to fit the time $t + n$ term structure. As Dybvig (1989) emphasizes, this time inconsistency is troublesome although the procedure may work well for some purposes.

It is also important to understand that fitting one set of asset prices exactly does not guarantee that a model will fit other asset prices accurately.

Backus, Foresi, and Zin (1996) illustrate this problem as follows. They assume that the homoskedastic single-factor model of subsection 11.1.1 holds, with a mean-reverting short rate so $\phi < 1$. They show that one can exactly fit the current term structure with a homoskedastic random walk model, a lognormal version of Ho and Lee (1986). The model uses equation (11.1.5), but replaces equation (11.1.3) with

$$x_{t+i} = x_{t+i-1} + g_{t+i} + \xi_{t+i}, \tag{11.3.4}$$

where g_{t+i} is a deterministic drift term that is specified at time t for all future dates $t + i$ in order to fit the time t term structure of interest rates, and as before ξ_{t+i} is a normally distributed shock with constant variance σ^2. Backus, Foresi, and Zin (1996) show that this model does not capture the conditional means or variances of future interest rates, and so it misprices options on bonds. Problem 11.1 works this out in detail.

A somewhat more sophisticated procedure for fitting the term structure of interest rates specifies future deterministic volatilities of short rate movements, as well as future deterministic drifts. Black, Derman, and Toy (1990) do this in a lognormal model for the short rate. In the present model one can replace the constant variance of ξ_{t+i}, σ^2, with a deterministically time-varying one-period-ahead conditional variance σ_{t+i}^2. Backus, Foresi, and Zin (1996) show that if the true model is the mean-reverting homoskedastic model, the misspecified random walk model with deterministic volatilities and drifts can fit any two of the current term structure, the conditional means of future short rates, and the conditional variances of future short rates. However it still cannot fit all three of these simultaneously, and so it cannot correctly price a complete set of bond options. The lesson of this example is that fixed-income derivative security prices depend on the dynamic behavior of interest rates, so it is important to model interest rate dynamics as accurately as possible even if one is interested only in pricing derivative securities today.

A related approach that has become very popular is due to Heath, Jarrow, and Morton (1992). These authors start from the current forward-rate curve discussed in Chapter 10, and they suggest that one should specify a term structure of forward volatilities to determine the movements of future risk-adjusted forward rates. To understand this approach as simply as possible, suppose that interest-rate risk is unpriced, so there are no risk premia in bond markets and the objective process for forward rates coincides with the risk-adjusted process. In this case bonds of all maturities must have the same expected instantaneous return in a continuous-time setting, and the same expected one-period return in a discrete-time setting. That is, the one-period version of the pure expectations hypothesis of the term structure (PEH) holds, so from (10.2.6) of Chapter 10 we have

$$E_t[r_{n,t+1} - y_{1t}] = -(1/2)\operatorname{Var}_t[r_{n,t+1} - y_{1t}]. \tag{11.3.5}$$

The expected log excess return on a bond of any maturity over the one-period interest rate is minus one-half the variance of the log excess return.

Now recall the relation between an n-period-ahead 1-period log forward rate f_{nt} and log bond prices, given as (10.1.8) in Chapter 10: $f_{nt} = p_{nt} - p_{n+1,t}$. This implies that the change from time t to time $t+1$ in a forward rate for an investment to be made at time $t+n$ is

$$
\begin{aligned}
f_{n-1,t+1} - f_{nt} &= (p_{n-1,t+1} - p_{n,t+1}) - (p_{nt} - p_{n+1,t}) \\
&= r_{n,t+1} - r_{n+1,t+1} \\
&= (r_{n,t+1} - y_{1t}) - (r_{n+1,t+1} - y_{1t}).
\end{aligned}
\tag{11.3.6}
$$

Taking expectations of (11.3.6) and using (11.3.5), we find that

$$
E_t[f_{n-1,t+1} - f_{nt}] = \left(\frac{1}{2}\right)\left(\text{Var}_t[r_{n+1,t+1} - y_{1t}] - \text{Var}_t[r_{n,t+1} - y_{1t}]\right).
$$
$$
\tag{11.3.7}
$$

The conditional variances of future excess bond returns determine the expected changes in forward rates, and these expected changes together with the current forward-rate curve determine the forward-rate curves and yield curves that are expected to prevail at every date in the future. Similar properties hold for the risk-adjusted forward-rate process even when interest-rate risk is priced.

Heath, Jarrow, and Morton (1992) exploit this insight in a continuous-time setting and show how it can be used to price fixed-income derivative securities. It is still important to model interest-rate dynamics accurately in this framework, but now the parameters of the model are expressed as volatilities; many participants in the markets for fixed-income securities find it easier to work with these parameters than with the parameters that govern short-rate dynamics and interest-rate risk prices in traditional models. A drawback of this approach, however, is that the implied process for the short-term interest rate is generally extremely complicated.

11.3.2 Forwards and Futures

A particularly simple kind of derivative security is a forward contract. An n-period forward contract, negotiated at time t on an underlying security with price S_{t+n} at time $t+n$, specifies a price at which the security will be purchased at time $t+n$. Thus the forward price, which we write G_{nt}, is determined at time t but no money changes hands until time $t+n$.[8]

Cox, Ingersoll, and Ross (1981b) show that the forward price G_{nt} is the time t price of a claim to a payoff of S_{t+n}/P_{nt} at time $t+n$. Equivalently, $G_{nt} P_{nt}$

---

[8]The n-period forward rate defined in Section 10.1.1 of Chapter 10 is the yield on a forward contract to buy a zero-coupon bond with maturity date $t+n+1$ at time $t+n$.

is the price of a claim to a payoff of S_{t+n}. Intuitively, the P_{nt} terms appear because no money need be paid until time $t + n$; thus the purchaser of a forward contract has the use of money between t and $t + n$. Cox, Ingersoll, and Ross establish this proposition using a simple arbitrage argument. They consider the following investment strategy: At time t, take a long position in $1/P_{nt}$ forward contracts and put G_{nt} into n-period bonds. By doing this one can purchase G_{nt}/P_{nt} bonds. The payoff from this strategy at time $t + n$ is

$$\frac{1}{P_{nt}}[S_{t+n} - G_{nt}] + \frac{G_{nt}}{P_{nt}} = \frac{S_{t+n}}{P_{nt}}, \tag{11.3.8}$$

where the first term is the profit or loss on the forward contracts and the second term is the payoff on the bonds. Since this investment strategy costs G_{nt} at time t and pays S_{t+n}/P_{nt} at time $t + n$, the proposition is established. It can also be stated using stochastic-discount-factor notation as

$$G_{nt} = E_t[M_{n,t+n}S_{t+n}/P_{nt}], \tag{11.3.9}$$

where the n-period stochastic discount factor $M_{n,t+n}$ is the product of n successive one-period stochastic discount factors: $M_{n,t+n} \equiv M_{t+1} \ldots M_{t+n}$.

A futures contract differs from a forward contract in one important respect: It is *marked to market* each period during the life of the contract, so that the purchaser of a futures contract receives the futures price increase or pays the futures price decrease each period. Because of these margin payments, futures pricing—unlike forward pricing—generally involves more than just the two periods t and $t + n$.[9] If we write the price of an n-period futures contract as H_{nt}, then we have

$$H_{nt} = E_t[M_{t+1}H_{n-1,t+1}/P_{1t}]. \tag{11.3.10}$$

This can be established using a similar argument to that of Cox, Ingersoll, and Ross. Consider the following investment strategy: At time t, take a long position in $1/P_{1t}$ futures contracts and put H_{nt} into one-period bonds. By doing this one can purchase H_{nt}/P_{1t} bonds. At time $t + 1$, liquidate the futures contracts. The payoff from this strategy at time $t + 1$ is

$$\frac{1}{P_{1t}}[H_{n-1,t+1} - H_{nt}] + \frac{H_{nt}}{P_{1t}} = \frac{H_{n-1,t+1}}{P_{1t}}, \tag{11.3.11}$$

---

[9]The Treasury-bond and Treasury-note futures contracts traded on the Chicago Board of Trade also have a number of special option features that affect their prices. A trader with a short position can choose to deliver on any day within the settlement month and can choose to deliver a number of alternative bonds. The short trader also has a "wild card option" to announce delivery at a particular day's settlement price any time in the six hours after that price is determined. The discussion here abstracts from these option features; see Hull (1993, Chapter 4) for an introduction to them.

where the first term is the mark-to-market payment on the futures contracts purchased at time t and the second term is the payoff on the bonds. Because the futures contracts are marked to market, the entire position can be liquidated at time $t+1$ without generating any further cash flows at time $t+n$. Since this investment strategy costs H_{nt} at time t and pays $H_{n-1,t+1}/P_{1t}$ at time $t+1$, we have shown that (11.3.10) holds. Furthermore, we can solve (11.3.10) forward to time $t+n$, using the fact that $H_{0,t+n} = S_{t+n}$, to obtain

$$H_{nt} = E_t \left[M_{n,t+n} S_{t+n} \middle/ \prod_{i=0}^{n-1} P_{1,t+i} \right]. \tag{11.3.12}$$

Comparing equations (11.3.9) and (11.3.12), we can see that there are some circumstances where forward contracts and futures contracts written on the same underlying asset with the same maturity have equal prices. First, if bond prices are not random then absence of arbitrage requires that $P_{nt} = \prod_{i=0}^{n-1} P_{1,t+i}$, so $G_{nt} = H_{nt}$. This means that forward and futures prices are equal in any model with a constant interest rate. Second, if there is only one period to maturity then $P_{nt} = P_{1t}$ and again $G_{nt} = H_{nt}$. Since futures contracts are marked to market daily the period here must be one day, so this result is of limited interest. Third, if the price of the underlying asset is not random, then forward and futures prices both equal the underlying asset price. To see this, note that if $S_{t+n} = V$, a constant, then (11.3.9) becomes

$$G_{nt} = E_t[M_{n,t+n}V/P_{nt}] = (V/P_{nt}) E_t[M_{n,t+n}] = V, \tag{11.3.13}$$

since $P_{nt} = E_t[M_{n,t+n}]$. Under the same conditions $H_{1t} = V$, and we can show that $H_{nt} = V$ if $H_{n-1,t+1} = V$ because (11.3.10) becomes

$$H_{nt} = E_t[M_{t+1}V/P_{1t}] = (V/P_{1t}) E_t[M_{t+1}] = V. \tag{11.3.14}$$

Thus $H_{nt} = V$ for all n, so forward and futures prices are equal.

More generally, however, forward and futures prices may differ. In the case where the underlying asset is an $n+\tau$-period zero-coupon bond at time t, which will be a τ-period bond at time $t+n$, we can write the forward price as $G_{\tau nt}$ and the futures price as $H_{\tau nt}$. The forward price is easy to calculate in this case:

$$G_{\tau nt} = (1/P_{nt}) E_t[M_{n,t+n} P_{\tau,t+n}] = P_{\tau+n,t}/P_{nt}. \tag{11.3.15}$$

When $\tau = 1$ the yield on this forward contract is the forward rate defined in Section 10.1.1 of Chapter 10: $F_{nt} = 1/G_{1nt}$.

The futures price must be calculated recursively from equation (11.3.10). In a particular term-structure model one can do the calculation explicitly and solve for the relation between forward and futures prices.

Problem 11.2 is to do this for the homoskedastic single-factor model developed in Section 11.1.1. The problem is to show that the ratio of forward to futures prices is constant in that model, and that it exceeds one so that forward prices are always greater than futures prices.

11.3.3 Option Pricing in a Term-Structure Model

Suppose one wants to price a European call option written on an underlying security with price S_t.[10] If the option has n periods to expiration and exercise price X, then its terminal payoff is $\text{Max}(S_{t+n} - X, 0)$. It can be priced like any other n-period asset using the n-period stochastic discount factor $M_{n,t+n} \equiv M_{t+1} \ldots M_{t+n}$. Writing the option price as $C_{nt}(X)$, we have

$$
\begin{aligned}
C_{nt}(X) &= \text{E}_t[M_{n,t+n} \, \text{Max}(S_{t+n} - X, 0)] \\
&= \text{E}_t[M_{n,t+n} S_{t+n} \mid S_{t+n} \geq X] \\
&\quad - X \text{E}_t[M_{n,t+n} \mid S_{t+n} \geq X].
\end{aligned}
\tag{11.3.16}
$$

In general equation (11.3.16) must be evaluated using numerical methods, but it simplifies dramatically in one special case. Suppose that $M_{n,t+n}$ and S_{t+n} are jointly lognormal conditional on time t information, with conditional expectations of their logs μ_m and μ_s, and conditional variances and covariance of their logs σ_{mm}, σ_{ss}, and σ_{ms}. All these moments may depend on t and n, but we suppress this for notational simplicity. Then we have

$$
\begin{aligned}
\text{E}_t[M_{n,t+n} S_{t+n} \mid S_{t+n} \geq X] \\
= \exp\left(\mu_m + \mu_s + \frac{\sigma_{mm} + \sigma_{ss} + 2\sigma_{ms}}{2}\right) \\
\times \Phi\left(\frac{\mu_s + \sigma_{ms} - x}{\sigma_s} + \sigma_s\right),
\end{aligned}
\tag{11.3.17}
$$

and

$$
\text{E}_t[M_{n,t+n} \mid S_{t+n} \geq X] = \exp\left(\mu_m + \frac{\sigma_{mm}}{2}\right) \Phi\left(\frac{\mu_s + \sigma_{ms} - x}{\sigma_s}\right),
\tag{11.3.18}
$$

where $\Phi(\cdot)$ is the cumulative distribution function of a standard normal random variable, and $x \equiv \log(X)$.[11]

Equations (11.3.17) and (11.3.18) hold for any lognormal random variables M and S and do not depend on any other properties of these variables.

---

[10] The notation here differs from the notation used in Chapter 9. There P_t is used for the underlying security price, but here we reserve P for zero-coupon bond prices and use S_t for a generic security price.

[11] These results were derived by Rubinstein (1976); see also Huang and Litzenberger (1988).

But we know from asset pricing theory that the underlying security price S_t must satisfy

$$S_t = E_t[M_{n,t+n} S_{t+n}] = \exp\left(\mu_m + \mu_s + \frac{\sigma_{mm} + \sigma_{ss} + 2\sigma_{ms}}{2}\right). \quad (11.3.19)$$

We also know that the price of an n-period zero-coupon bond, P_{nt}, must satisfy

$$P_{nt} = E_t[M_{n,t+n}] = \exp\left(\mu_m + \frac{\sigma_{mm}}{2}\right). \quad (11.3.20)$$

Using (11.3.19) and (11.3.20) to simplify (11.3.17) and (11.3.18), and substituting into (11.3.16), we get an expression for the price of a call option when the underlying security is jointly lognormal with the multiperiod stochastic discount factor:

$$\begin{aligned}
C_{nt}(X) &= S_t \Phi\left(\frac{\mu_s + \sigma_{ms} - x + \sigma_{ss}}{\sqrt{\sigma_{ss}}}\right) - XP_{nt} \Phi\left(\frac{\mu_s + \sigma_{ms} - x}{\sqrt{\sigma_{ss}}}\right) \\
&= S_t \Phi\left(\frac{s_t - x - p_{nt} + \sigma_{ss}/2}{\sqrt{\sigma_{ss}}}\right) \\
&\quad -XP_{nt} \Phi\left(\frac{s_t - x - p_{nt} - \sigma_{ss}/2}{\sqrt{\sigma_{ss}}}\right).
\end{aligned} \quad (11.3.21)$$

To get the standard option pricing formula of Black and Scholes (1973), we need two further assumptions. First, assume that the conditional variance of the underlying security price n periods ahead, σ_{ss}, is proportional to n: $\sigma_{ss} = n\sigma^2$ for some constant σ^2. Second, assume that the term structure is flat so that $P_{nt} = e^{-rn}$ for some constant interest rate r. With these additional assumptions, (11.3.21) yields the Black-Scholes formula,[12]

$$\begin{aligned}
C_{nt}(X) &= S_t \Phi\left(\frac{s_t - x + (r + \sigma^2/2)n}{\sqrt{n}\,\sigma}\right) \\
&\quad - Xe^{-rn} \Phi\left(\frac{s_t - x + (r - \sigma^2/2)n}{\sqrt{n}\,\sigma}\right).
\end{aligned} \quad (11.3.22)$$

For fixed-income derivatives, however, the extra assumptions needed to get the Black-Scholes formula (11.3.22) are not reasonable. Suppose that the asset on which the call option is written is a zero-coupon bond which currently has $n+\tau$ periods to maturity. If the option has exercise price X and n periods to expiration, the option's payoff at expiration will be $\text{Max}(P_{\tau,t+n} -$

---

[12]Of course, for any given n we can always define $\sigma^2 = \sigma_{ss}/n$ and $r = -p_{nt}/n$ so that the Black-Scholes formula applies for that n. The assumptions given are needed for the Black-Scholes formula to apply to all n with the same r and σ^2.

$X, 0$). The relevant bond price at expiration is the τ-period bond price since the maturity of the bond shrinks over time. In a term- structure model the conditional volatility of the τ-period bond price n periods ahead is not generally n times the conditional volatility of the $(n + \tau - 1)$-period bond price one period ahead. Also, of course, the term structure is generally not flat in a term-structure model.

To get closed-form solutions for interest-rate derivatives prices we need a term-structure model in which bond prices and stochastic discount factors are conditionally lognormal at all horizons; that is, we need the homoskedastic single-factor model of Section 11.1.1 or some multifactor generalization of it. In the single-factor model we can use the option pricing formula (11.3.21) with the following inputs: $S_t = P_{n+\tau,t} = \exp(-A_{n+\tau} - B_{n+\tau} x_t)$, $P_{nt} = \exp(-A_n - B_n x_t)$, and

$$
\begin{aligned}
\sigma_{ss} &= \text{Var}_t[p_{\tau,t+n}] = \text{Var}_t[-A_\tau - B_\tau x_{t+n}] \\
&= B_\tau^2 \text{Var}_t[x_{t+n}] = \frac{(1 - \phi^\tau)^2 \sigma^2 (1 - \phi^{2n})}{(1 - \phi)^2 (1 - \phi^2)}.
\end{aligned}
\tag{11.3.23}
$$

This expression for σ_{ss} does not grow linearly with n. Hence if one uses the Black-Scholes formula (11.3.22) and calculates implied volatility, the implied volatility will depend on the maturity of the option; there will be a *term structure of implied volatility* that will depend on the parameters of the underlying term- structure model. Jamshidian (1989) presents a continuous-time version of this result, and Turnbull and Milne (1991) derive it in discrete time along with numerous results for other types of derivative securities. Option pricing is considerably more difficult in a square-root model, but Cox, Ingersoll, and Ross (1985a) present some useful results.

Investment professionals often want to price options in a way that is exactly consistent with the current term structure of interest rates. To do this, we can break the n-period stochastic discount factor into two components:

$$
M_{n,t+n} = M_{n,t+n}^a M_{n,t+n}^b,
\tag{11.3.24}
$$

where, as in Section 11.3.1, the *a*-component is stochastic while the *b*-component is deterministic. There is a corresponding decomposition of bond prices for any maturity j: $P_{jt} = P_{jt}^a P_{jt}^b$. Then it is easy to show that

$$
\begin{aligned}
C_{nt}(X) &= E_t[M_{n,t+n}^a M_{n,t+n}^b \text{ Max}(P_{\tau,t+n}^a P_{\tau,t+n}^b - X, 0)] \\
&= M_{n,t+n}^b P_{\tau,t+n}^b E_t[M_{n,t+n}^a \text{ Max}(P_{\tau,t+n}^a - X/P_{\tau,t+n}^b, 0)] \\
&= P_{nt}^b P_{\tau,t+n}^b C_{nt}^a(X/P_{\tau,t+n}^b) \\
&= P_{n+\tau,t}^b C_{nt}^a(X/P_{\tau,t+n}^b),
\end{aligned}
\tag{11.3.25}
$$

where C^a is the call option price that would prevail if the stochastic discount factor were M^a. In other words options can be priced using the stochastic term-structure model, using the deterministic model only to adjust the exercise price and the final solution for the option price. This approach was first used by Ho and Lee (1986); however as Dybvig (1989) points out, Ho and Lee choose as their *a*-model the single-factor homoskedastic model with $\phi = 1$, which has numerous unappealing properties. Black, Derman, and Toy (1990), Heath, Jarrow, and Morton (1992), and Hull and White (1990a) use similar approaches with different choices for the *a*-model.

11.4 Conclusion

In this chapter we have thoroughly explored a tractable class of interest-rate models, the so-called affine-yield models. In these models log bond yields are linear in state variables, which simplifies the analysis of the term structure of interest rates and of fixed-income derivative securities. We have also seen that affine-yield models have some limitations, particularly in describing the dynamics of the short-term nominal interest rate. There is accordingly great interest in developing more flexible models that allow for such phenomena as multiple regimes, nonlinear mean-reversion, and serially correlated interest-rate volatility, and that fully exploit the information in the yield curve.

As the term-structure literature moves forward, it will be important to integrate it with the rest of the asset pricing literature. We have seen that term-structure models can be viewed as time-series models for the stochastic discount factor. The research on stock returns discussed in Chapter 8 also seeks to characterize the behavior of the stochastic discount factor. By combining the information in the prices of stocks and fixed-income securities it should be possible to gain a better understanding of the economic forces that determine the prices of financial assets.

Problems—Chapter 11

11.1 Assume that the homoskedastic lognormal bond pricing model given by equations (11.1.3) and (11.1.5) holds with $\phi < 1$.

11.1.1 Suppose you fit the current term structure of interest rates using a random walk model augmented by deterministic drift terms, equation (11.3.4). Derive an expression relating the drift terms to the state variable x_t and the parameters of the true bond pricing model.

11.1.2 Compare the expected future log short rates implied by the true bond pricing model and the random walk model with deterministic drifts.

11.1.3 Compare the time t conditional variances of log bond prices at time $t + 1$ implied by the true bond pricing model and the random walk model with deterministic drifts.

11.1.4 Compare the prices of bond options implied by the true bond pricing model and the random walk model with deterministic drifts.

Note: This question is based on Backus and Zin (1994).

11.2 Define $G_{\tau n t}$ to be the price at time t of an n-period forward contract on a zero-coupon bond which matures at time $t + n + \tau$. Define $H_{\tau n t}$ to be the price at time t of an n-period futures contract on the same zero-coupon bond. Assume that the homoskedastic single-factor term-structure model of Section 11.1.1 holds.

11.2.1 Show that both the log forward price $g_{\tau n t}$ and the log futures price $h_{\tau n t}$ are affine in the state variable x_t. Solve for the coefficients determining these prices as functions of the term-structure coefficients A_n and B_n.

11.2.2 Show that the ratio of forward to futures prices is constant and greater than one. Give some economic intuition for this result.

11.2.3 For the parameter values in Section 11.2.2, plot the ratio of forward prices to futures prices as a function of maturity n.

Note: This question is based on Backus, Foresi, and Zin (1996).

12

Nonlinearities in Financial Data

THE ECONOMETRIC METHODS we discuss in this text are almost all designed to detect *linear* structure in financial data. In Chapter 2, for example, we develop time-series tests for predictability of asset returns that use weighted combinations of return autocorrelations—linear predictability is the focus. The event study of Chapter 4, and the CAPM and APT of Chapters 5 and 6, are based on linear models of expected returns. And even when we broaden our focus in later chapters to include other economic variables such as consumption, dividends, and interest rates, the models remain linear. This emphasis on linearity should not be too surprising since many of the economic models that drive financial econometrics are linear models.

However, many aspects of economic behavior may not be linear. Experimental evidence and casual introspection suggest that investors' attitudes towards risk and expected return are nonlinear. The terms of many financial contracts such as options and other derivative securities are nonlinear. And the strategic interactions among market participants, the process by which information is incorporated into security prices, and the dynamics of economy-wide fluctuations are all inherently nonlinear. Therefore, a natural frontier for financial econometrics is the modeling of nonlinear phenomena.

This is quite a challenge, since the collection of nonlinear models is much "larger" than the collection of linear models—after all, everything which is not linear is nonlinear. Moreover, nonlinear models are generally more difficult to analyze than linear ones, rarely producing closed-form expressions which can be easily manipulated and empirically implemented. In some cases, the only mode of analysis is computational, and this is unfamiliar territory to those of us who are accustomed to thinking analytically, intuitively, and linearly.

But economists of a new generation are creating new models and tools that can capture nonlinearities in economic phenomena, and some of these models and tools are the focus of this chapter. Exciting advances in dynam-

467

ical systems theory, nonlinear time-series analysis, stochastic-volatility models, nonparametric statistics, and artificial neural networks have fueled the recent interest in nonlinearities in financial data, and we shall explore each of these topics in the following sections.

Section 12.1 revisits some of the issues raised in Chapter 2 regarding predictability, but from a linear-versus-nonlinear perspective. We present a taxonomy of models that distinguishes between models that are nonlinear in mean and hence depart from the martingale hypothesis, and models that are nonlinear in variance and hence depart from independence but not from the martingale hypothesis.

Section 12.2 explores in greater detail models that are nonlinear in variance, including univariate and multivariate Generalized Autoregressive Conditionally Heteroskedastic (GARCH) and stochastic-volatility models.

In Sections 12.3 and 12.4 we move beyond parametric time-series models to explore nonparametric methods for fitting nonlinear relationships between variables, including smoothing techniques and artificial neural networks. Although these techniques are able to uncover a variety of nonlinearities, they are heavily data-dependent and computationally intensive. To illustrate the power of these techniques, we present an application to the pricing and hedging of derivative securities and to estimating state-price densities.

We also discuss some of the limitations of these techniques in Section 12.5. The most important limitations are the twin problems of overfitting and data-snooping, which plague linear models too but not nearly to the same degree. Unfortunately, we have very little to say about how to deal with these issues except in very special cases, hence this is an area with many open research questions to be answered.

12.1 Nonlinear Structure in Univariate Time Series

A typical time-series model relates an observed time series x_t to an underlying sequence of shocks ϵ_t. In *linear* time-series analysis the shocks are assumed to be uncorrelated but are not necessarily assumed to be IID. By the Wold Representation Theorem any time series can be written as an infinite-order linear moving average of such shocks, and this linear moving-average representation summarizes the unconditional variance and autocovariances of the series.

In *nonlinear* time-series analysis the underlying shocks are typically assumed to be IID, but we seek a possibly nonlinear function relating the series x_t to the history of the shocks. A general representation is

$$x_t = f(\epsilon_t, \epsilon_{t-1}, \epsilon_{t-2}, \ldots),\qquad (12.1.1)$$

where the shocks are assumed to have mean zero and unit variance, and $f(\cdot)$ is some unknown function. The generality of this representation makes it very hard to work with—most models used in practice fall into a somewhat more restricted class that can be written as

$$x_t = g(\epsilon_{t-1}, \epsilon_{t-2}, \ldots) + \epsilon_t h(\epsilon_{t-1}, \epsilon_{t-2}, \ldots). \qquad (12.1.2)$$

The function $g(\cdot)$ represents the mean of x_t conditional on past information, since $E_{t-1}[x_t] = g(\epsilon_{t-1}, \epsilon_{t-2}, \ldots)$. The innovation in x_t is proportional to the shock ϵ_t, where the coefficient of proportionality is the function $h(\cdot)$. The square of this function is the variance of x_t conditional on past information, since $E_{t-1}[(x_t - E_{t-1}[x_t])^2] = h(\epsilon_{t-1}, \epsilon_{t-2}, \ldots)^2$. Models with nonlinear $g(\cdot)$ are said to be *nonlinear in mean*, whereas models with nonlinear $h(\cdot)^2$ are said to be *nonlinear in variance*.

To understand the restrictions imposed by (12.1.2) on (12.1.1), consider expanding (12.1.1) in a Taylor series around $\epsilon_t = 0$ for given $\epsilon_{t-1}, \epsilon_{t-2}, \ldots$:

$$\begin{aligned} x_t &= f(0, \epsilon_{t-1}, \ldots) + \epsilon_t f_1(0, \epsilon_{t-1}, \ldots) \\ &\quad + (1/2)\epsilon_t^2 f_{11}(0, \epsilon_{t-1}, \ldots) + \cdots, \end{aligned} \qquad (12.1.3)$$

where f_1 is the derivative of f with respect to ϵ_t, its first argument; f_{11} is the second derivative of f with respect to ϵ_t; and so forth. To obtain (12.1.2), we drop the higher-order terms in the Taylor expansion and set $g(\epsilon_{t-1}, \ldots) = f(0, \epsilon_{t-1}, \ldots)$ and $h(\epsilon_{t-1}, \ldots) = f_1(0, \epsilon_{t-1}, \ldots)$. By dropping higher-order terms we link the time-variation in the higher conditional moments of x_t inflexibly with the time-variation in the second conditional moment of x_t, since for all powers $p \geq 2$, $E_{t-1}[(x_t - E_{t-1}[x_t])^p] = h(\cdot)^p E[\epsilon_t^p]$. Those who are interested primarily in the first two conditional moments of x_t regard this restriction as a price worth paying for the greater tractability of (12.1.2).

Equation (12.1.2) leads to a natural division in the nonlinear time-series literature between models of the conditional mean $g(\cdot)$ and models of the conditional variance $h(\cdot)^2$. Most time-series models concentrate on one form of nonlinearity or the other. A simple nonlinear moving-average model, for example, takes the form

$$x_t = \epsilon_t + \alpha \epsilon_{t-1}^2. \qquad (12.1.4)$$

Here $g(\cdot) = \alpha \epsilon_{t-1}^2$ and $h(\cdot) = 1$. This model is nonlinear in mean but not in variance. The first-order Autoregressive Conditionally Heteroskedastic (ARCH) model of Engle (1982), on the other hand, takes the form

$$x_t = \epsilon_t \sqrt{\alpha \epsilon_{t-1}^2}. \qquad (12.1.5)$$

Here $g(\cdot) = 0$ and $h(\cdot) = \sqrt{\alpha \epsilon_{t-1}^2}$. This model is nonlinear in variance but not in mean.

One way to understand the distinction between nonlinearity in mean and nonlinearity in variance is to consider the moments of the x_t process. As we have emphasized, nonlinear models can be constructed so that second moments (autocovariances) $E[x_t x_{t-i}]$ are all zero for $i>0$. In the two examples above it is easy to confirm that this is the case provided that ϵ_t is symmetrically distributed, i.e., its third moment is zero. For the nonlinear moving average (12.1.4), for example, we have $E[x_t x_{t-1}] = E[(\epsilon_t + \alpha\epsilon_{t-1}^2)(\epsilon_{t-1} + \alpha\epsilon_{t-2}^2)] = \alpha E[\epsilon_{t-1}^3] = 0$ when $E[\epsilon_{t-1}^3] = 0$.

Now consider the behavior of higher moments of the form

$$E[x_t x_{t-i} x_{t-j} x_{t-k} \cdots].$$

Models that are nonlinear in the mean allow these higher moments to be nonzero when $i, j, k, \ldots > 0$. Models that are nonlinear in variance but obey the martingale property have $E[x_t \mid x_{t-1}, \ldots] = 0$, so their higher moments are zero when $i, j, k, \ldots > 0$. These models can only have nonzero higher moments if at least one time lag index $i, j, k, \ldots$ is zero. In the nonlinear-moving-average example, (12.1.4), the third moment with $i=j=1$,

$$
\begin{aligned}
E[x_t x_{t-1}^2] &= E[(\epsilon_t + \alpha\epsilon_{t-1}^2)(\epsilon_{t-1} + \alpha\epsilon_{t-2}^2)^2] \\
&= \alpha E[\epsilon_{t-1}^4] + 2\alpha^2 E[\epsilon_{t-2}^2] E[\epsilon_{t-1}^3] \neq 0.
\end{aligned}
$$

In the first-order ARCH example, (12.1.5), the same third moment $E[x_t x_{t-1}^2]$ $= E[(\epsilon_t\sqrt{\alpha\epsilon_{t-1}^2})\epsilon_{t-1}^2\alpha\epsilon_{-2}^2] = 0$. But for this model the fourth moment with $i=0$, $j=k=1$, $E[x_t^2 x_{t-1}^2] = E[\epsilon_t^2 \alpha^2 \epsilon_{t-1}^4 \epsilon_{t-2}^2] \neq 0$.

We discuss ARCH and other models of changing variance in Section 12.2; for the remainder of this section we concentrate on nonlinear models of the conditional mean. In Section 12.1.1 we explore several alternative ways to parametrize nonlinear models, and in Section 12.1.2 we use these parametric models to motivate and explain some commonly used tests for nonlinearity in univariate time series, including the test of Brock, Dechert, and Scheinkman (1987).

12.1.1 Some Parametric Models

It is impossible to provide an exhaustive account of all nonlinear specifications, even when we restrict our attention to the subset of parametric models. Priestley (1988), Teräsvirta, Tjøstheim, and Granger (1994), and Tong (1990) provide excellent coverage of many of the most popular nonlinear time-series models, including more-specialized models with some very intriguing names, e.g., *self-exciting threshold autoregression* (SETAR), *amplitude-dependent exponential autoregression* (EXPAR), and *state-dependent models* (SDM). To provide a sense of the breadth of this area, we discuss four examples in this section: polynomial models, piecewise-linear models, Markov-switching models, and deterministic chaotic models.

Polynomial Models

One way to represent the function $g(\cdot)$ is expand it in a Taylor series around $\epsilon_{t-1}=\epsilon_{t-2}=\cdots=0$, which yields a discrete-time *Volterra series* (see Volterra [1959]):

$$g(\epsilon_{t-1}, \epsilon_{t-2}, \ldots) = \sum_{i=1}^{\infty} a_i \epsilon_{t-i} + \sum_{i=1}^{\infty} \sum_{j=i}^{\infty} b_{ij} \epsilon_{t-i} \epsilon_{t-j}$$

$$+ \sum_{i=1}^{\infty} \sum_{j=i}^{\infty} \sum_{k=j}^{\infty} c_{ijk} \epsilon_{t-i} \epsilon_{t-j} \epsilon_{t-k} + \cdots. \quad (12.1.6)$$

The single summation in (12.1.6) is a standard linear moving average, the double summation captures the effects of lagged cross-products of two innovations, the triple summation captures the effects of lagged cross-products of three innovations, and so on. The summations indexed by j start at i, the summations indexed by k start at j, and so on to avoid counting a given cross-product of innovations more than once. The idea is to represent the true nonlinear function of past innovations as a weighted sum of polynomial functions of the innovations. Equation (12.1.4) is a simple example of a model of this form. Robinson (1979) and Priestley (1988) make extensive use of this specification.

Polynomial models may also be written in autoregressive form. The function $g(\epsilon_{t-1}, \epsilon_{t-2}, \ldots)$ relating the conditional mean to past shocks may be rewritten as a function $g^*(x_{t-1}, x_{t-2}, \ldots)$ relating the conditional mean to lags of x_t. The autoregressive version of (12.1.6) is then

$$g^*(x_{t-1}, x_{t-2}, \ldots) = \sum_{i=1}^{\infty} a_i^* x_{t-i} + \sum_{i=1}^{\infty} \sum_{j=i}^{\infty} b_{ij}^* x_{t-i} x_{t-j}$$

$$+ \sum_{i=1}^{\infty} \sum_{j=i}^{\infty} \sum_{k=j}^{\infty} c_{ijk}^* x_{t-i} x_{t-j} x_{t-k} + \cdots. \quad (12.1.7)$$

It is also possible to obtain mixed autoregressive/moving-average representations, the nonlinear equivalent of ARMA models. The bilinear model, for example, uses lagged values of x_t, lagged values of ϵ_t, and cross-products of the two:

$$g^{**}(\epsilon_{t-1}, x_{t-1}, \ldots) = \sum_{i=1}^{\infty} \alpha_i \epsilon_{t-i} + \sum_{i=1}^{\infty} \beta_i x_{t-i} + \sum_{i=1}^{\infty} \sum_{j=1}^{\infty} \gamma_{ij} x_{t-i} \epsilon_{t-j}. \quad (12.1.8)$$

This model can capture nonlinearities parsimoniously (with a finite, short lag length) when pure nonlinear moving-average or nonlinear autoregressive models fail to do so. Granger and Andersen (1978) and Subba Rao and Gabr (1984) explore bilinear models in detail.

Piecewise-Linear Models

Another popular way to fit nonlinear structure is to use piecewise-linear functions, as in the first-order *threshold autoregression* (TAR):

$$x_t = \begin{cases} \alpha_1 + \beta_1 x_{t-1} + \epsilon_t & \text{if } x_{t-1} < k \\ \alpha_2 + \beta_2 x_{t-1} + \epsilon_t & \text{if } x_{t-1} \geq k. \end{cases} \tag{12.1.9}$$

Here the intercept and slope coefficient in a regression of x_t on its lag x_{t-1} depend on the value of x_{t-1} in relation to the *threshold k*. This model can be generalized to higher orders and multiple thresholds, as explained in detail in Tong (1983, 1990).

Piecewise-linear models also include *change-point* models or, as they are known in the economics literature, models with *structural breaks.* In these models, the parameters are assumed to shift—typically once—during a fixed sample period, and the goal is to estimate the two sets of parameters as well as the change point or structural break. Perron (1989) applies this technique to macroeconomic time series, and Brodsky (1993) and Carlstein, Muller, and Siegmund (1994) present more recent methods for dealing with change points, including nonparametric estimators and Bayesian inference.

Change-point methods are very well-established in the statistics and operations research literature, but their application to economic models is not without controversy. Unlike the typical engineering application where a structural break is known to exist in a given dataset, we can never say with certainty that a structural break exists in an economic time series. And if we think a structural break has occurred because of some major economic event, e.g., a stock market crash, this data-driven specification search can bias our inferences dramatically towards finding breaks where none exist (see, for example, Leamer [1978] and Lo and MacKinlay [1990]).

Markov-Switching Models

The Markov-switching model of Hamilton (1989, 1990, 1993) and Sclove (1983a, 1983b) is closely related to the TAR. The key difference is that changes in regime are determined not by the level of the process, but by an unobserved state variable which is typically modeled as a Markov chain. For example,

$$x_t = \begin{cases} \alpha_1 + \beta_1 x_{t-1} + \epsilon_{1t} & \text{if } s_t = 1 \\ \alpha_2 + \beta_2 x_{t-1} + \epsilon_{2t} & \text{if } s_t = 0 \end{cases} \tag{12.1.10}$$

where s_t is an unobservable two-state Markov chain with some transition probability matrix $\mathbf{P}$. Note the slightly different timing convention in (12.1.10): s_t determines the regime at time t, not s_{t-1}. In both regimes, x_t is an AR(1), but the parameters (including the variance of the error term) differ across regimes, and the change in regime is stochastic and possibly serially correlated.

This model has obvious appeal from an economic perspective. Changes in regime are caused by factors other than the series we are currently modeling (s_t determines the regime, not x_t), rarely do we know which regime we are in (s_t is unobservable), but after the fact we can often identify which regime we were in with some degree of confidence (s_t can be estimated, via Hamilton's [1989] filtering process). Moreover, the Markov-switching model does not suffer from some of the statistical biases that models of structural breaks do; the regime shifts are "identified" by the interaction between the data and the Markov chain, not by *a priori* inspection of the data. Hamilton's (1989) application to business cycles is an excellent illustration of the power and scope of this technique.

Deterministic Nonlinear Dynamical Systems

There have been many exciting recent advances in modeling deterministic *nonlinear dynamical systems*, and these have motivated a number of techniques for estimating nonlinear relationships. Relatively simple systems of ordinary differential and difference equations have been shown to exhibit extremely complex dynamics. The popular term for such complexity is the *Butterfly Effect*, the notion that "a flap of a butterfly's wings in Brazil sets off a tornado in Texas".[1] This refers, only half-jokingly, to the following simple system of deterministic ordinary differential equations proposed by Lorenz (1963) for modeling weather patterns:

$$\dot{x} = 10(y - x) \qquad (12.1.11)$$

$$\dot{y} = xz + 28x - y \qquad (12.1.12)$$

$$\dot{z} = xy + \frac{8}{3}z. \qquad (12.1.13)$$

Lorenz (1963) observed that even the slightest change in the starting values of this system—in the fourth decimal place, for example—produces dramatically different sample paths, even after only a short time. This *sensitivity to initial conditions* is a hallmark of the emerging field of *chaos theory*.

---

[1]This is adapted from the title of Edward Lorenz's address to the American Association for the Advancement of Science in Washington, D.C., December 1979. See Gleick (1987) for a lively and entertaining layman's account of the emerging science of nonlinear dynamical systems, or chaos theory.

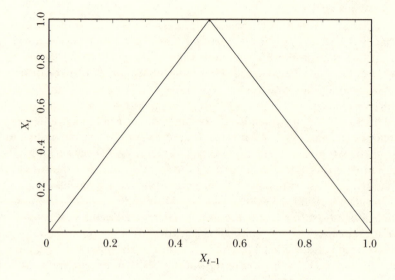

Figure 12.1.   *The Tent Map*

An even simpler example of a chaotic system is the well-known tent map:

$$x_t = \begin{cases} 2x_{t-1} & \text{if } x_{t-1} < \frac{1}{2} \\ 2(1-x_{t-1}) & \text{if } x_{t-1} \geq \frac{1}{2} \end{cases}, \qquad x_0 \in (0, 1). \quad (12.1.14)$$

The tent map can be viewed as a first-order threshold autoregression with no shock ϵ_t and with parameters $\alpha_1=0$, $\beta_1=2$, $\alpha_2=2$, and $\beta_2=-2$. If x_{t-1} lies between 0 and 1, x_t also lies in this interval; thus the tent map maps the unit interval back into itself as illustrated in Figure 12.1. Data generated by (12.1.14) appear random in that they are uniformly distributed on the unit interval and are serially uncorrelated. Moreover, the data also exhibit sensitive dependence to initial conditions, which will be verified in Problem 12.1. Hsieh (1991) presents several other leading examples, while Brock (1986), Holden (1986), and Thompson and Stewart (1986) provide more formal discussions of the mathematics of chaotic systems.

Although the many important breakthroughs in nonlinear dynamical systems do have immediate implications for physics, biology, and other "hard" sciences, the impact on economics and finance has been less dramatic. While a number of economic applications have been considered,[2] none are especially compelling, particularly from an empirical perspective.

---

[2]See, for example, Boldrin and Woodford (1990), Brock and Sayers (1988), Craig, Kohlase, and Papell (1991), Day (1983), Grandmont and Malgrange (1986), Hsieh (1993), Kennan

There are two serious problems in modeling economic phenomena as deterministic nonlinear dynamical systems. First, unlike the theory that is available in many natural sciences, economic theory is generally not specific about functional forms. Thus economists rarely have theoretical reasons for expecting to find one form of nonlinearity rather than another. Second, economists are rarely able to conduct controlled experiments, and this makes it almost impossible to deduce the parameters of a deterministic dynamical system governing economic phenomena, even if such a system exists and is low-dimensional. When controlled experiments are feasible, e.g., in particle physics, it is possible to recover the dynamics with great precision by taking many "snapshots" of the system at closely spaced time intervals. This technique, known as a *stroboscopic map* or a *Poincaré section*, has given empirical content to even the most abstract notions of nonlinear dynamical systems, but unfortunately cannot be applied to non-experimental data.

The possibility that a relatively simple set of nonlinear deterministic equations can generate the kind of complexities we see in financial markets is tantalizing, but it is of little interest if we cannot recover these equations with any degree of precision. Moreover, the impact of statistical sampling errors on a system with sensitive dependence to initial conditions makes dynamical systems theory even less practical. Of course, given the rapid pace at which this field is advancing, these reservations may be much less serious in a few years.

12.1.2 Univariate Tests for Nonlinear Structure

Despite the caveats of the previous section, the mathematics of chaos theory has motivated several new statistical tests for independence and nonlinear structure which are valuable in their own right, and we now discuss these tests.

Tests Based on Higher Moments
Our earlier discussion of higher moments of nonlinear models can serve as the basis for a statistical test of nonlinearity. Hsieh (1989), for example, defines a scaled third moment:

$$\varphi(i, j) \equiv \frac{\mathrm{E}[x_t\, x_{t-i}\, x_{t-j}]}{\mathrm{E}[x_t^2]^{3/2}} \qquad (12.1.15)$$

and observes that $\varphi(i, j)=0$ for all $i, j>0$ for IID data, or data generated by a martingale model that is nonlinear only in variance. He suggests estimating

and O'Brien (1993), Pesaran and Potter (1992), Scheinkman and LeBaron (1989), and Scheinkman and Woodford (1994).

$\varphi(i, j)$ in the obvious way:

$$\hat{\varphi}(i, j) \equiv \frac{\frac{1}{T} \sum_t x_t \, x_{t-i} \, x_{t-j}}{\left[\frac{1}{T} \sum_t x_t^2\right]^{3/2}}. \tag{12.1.16}$$

Under the null hypothesis that $\varphi(i, j)=0$, and with sufficient regularity conditions imposed on x_t so that higher moments exist, $\sqrt{T}\hat{\varphi}(i, j)$ is asymptotically normal and its variance can be consistently estimated by

$$\hat{V} \equiv \frac{\frac{1}{T} \sum_t x_t^2 \, x_{t-i}^2 \, x_{t-j}^2}{\left[\frac{1}{T} \sum_t x_t^2\right]^3}. \tag{12.1.17}$$

Hsieh's test uses one particular third moment of the data, but it is also possible to look at several moments simultaneously. The autoregressive polynomial model (12.1.7), for example, suggests that a simple test of nonlinearity in the mean is to regress x_t onto its own lags and cross-products of its own lags, and to test for the joint significance of the nonlinear terms. Tsay (1986) proposes a test of this sort using second-order terms and M lags for a total of $M(M+1)/2$ nonlinear regressors. One can calculate heteroskedasticity-consistent standard errors so that the test becomes robust to the presence of nonlinearity in variance.

The Correlation Integral and the Correlation Dimension

To distinguish a deterministic, chaotic process from a truly random process, it is essential to view the data in a sufficiently high-dimensional form. In the case of the tent map, for example, the data appear random if one plots x_t on the unit interval since x_t has a uniform distribution. If one plots x_t and x_{t-1} on the unit square, however, the data will all fall on the tent-shaped line shown in Figure 12.1.

This straightforward approach can yield surprising insights, as we saw in analyzing stock price discreteness in Chapter 3. However it becomes difficult to implement when higher dimensions or more complicated nonlinearities are involved. Grassberger and Procaccia (1983) have suggested a formal approach to capture this basic idea. Their approach begins by organizing the data (prefiltered, if desired, to remove linear structure) into *n-histories* x_t^n, defined by

$$x_t^n = \{x_{t-n+1}, \ldots, x_t\}. \tag{12.1.18}$$

The parameter n is known as the *embedding dimension*.

The next step is to calculate the fraction of pairs of n-histories that are "close" to one another. To measure closeness, we pick a number k and call a pair of n-histories x_s^n and x_t^n close to one another if the greatest absolute difference between the corresponding members of the pair is smaller than

k: $\max_{i=0,\dots,n-1} |x_{s-i}-x_{t-i}| < k$. We define a closeness indicator K_{st} that is one if the two n-histories are close to one another and zero otherwise:

$$K_{st} = \begin{cases} 1 & \text{if } \max_{i=0,\dots,n-1} |x_{s-i} - x_{t-i}| < k \\ 0 & \text{otherwise.} \end{cases} \qquad (12.1.19)$$

We define $C_{n,T}(k)$ to be the fraction of pairs that are close in this sense, in a sample of n-histories of size T:

$$C_{n,T}(k) \equiv \frac{\sum_{s=1}^{T}\sum_{t=s}^{T} K_{st}}{T(T-1)/2}. \qquad (12.1.20)$$

The *correlation integral* $C_n(k)$ is the limit of this fraction as the sample size increases:

$$C_n(k) \equiv \lim_{T\to\infty} C_{n,T}(k). \qquad (12.1.21)$$

Equivalently, it is the probability that a randomly selected pair of n-histories is close.

Obviously the correlation integral will depend on both the embedding dimension n and the parameter k. To see how k can matter, set the embedding dimension $n=1$ so that n-histories consist of single data points, and consider the case where the data are IID and uniformly distributed on the unit interval $(0, 1)$. In this case the fraction of data points that are within a distance k of a benchmark data point is $2k$ when the benchmark data point is in the middle of the unit interval (between k and $1-k$), but it is smaller when the benchmark data point lies near the edge of the unit interval. In the extreme case where the benchmark data point is zero or one, only a fraction k of the other data points are within k of the benchmark. The general formula for the fraction of data points that are close to a benchmark point b is $\min(k+b, 2k, k+1-b)$. As k shrinks, however, the complications caused by this "edge problem" become negligible and the correlation integral approaches $2k$.

Grassberger and Procaccia (1983) investigate the behavior of the correlation integral as the distance measure k shrinks. They calculate the ratio of $\log C_n(k)$ to $\log k$ for small k:

$$v_n = \lim_{k\to 0} \frac{\log C_n(k)}{\log k} \qquad (12.1.22)$$

which measures the proportional decrease in the fraction of points that are close to one another as we decrease the parameter that defines closeness. In the IID uniform case with $n=1$, the ratio $\log C_1(k)/\log k$ approaches $\log 2k/\log k=(\log 2+\log k)/\log k=1$ as k shrinks. Thus $v_1=1$ for IID uniform data; for small k, the fraction of points that are close to one another shrinks at the same rate as k.

Now consider the behavior of the correlation integral with higher embedding dimensions n. When $n=2$, we are plotting 2-histories of the data on a 2-dimensional diagram such as Figure 12.1 and asking what fraction of the 2-histories lie within a square whose center is a benchmark 2-history and whose sides are of length $2k$. With uniformly distributed IID data, a fraction $4k^2$ of the data points lie within such a square when the benchmark 2-history is sufficiently far away from the edges of the unit square. Again we handle the edge problem by letting k shrink, and we find that the ratio $\log C_2(k)/\log k$ approaches $\log 4k^2/\log k = (\log 4 + 2\log k)/\log k = 2$ as k shrinks. Thus $v_2=2$ for IID uniform data; for small k, the fraction of pairs of points that are close to one another shrinks twice as fast as k. In general $v_n=n$ for IID uniform data; for small k, the fraction of n-histories that are close to one another shrinks n times as fast as k.

The correlation integral behaves very differently when the data are generated by a nonlinear deterministic process. To see this, consider data generated by the tent map. In one dimension, such data fall uniformly on the unit line so we again get $v_1=1$. But in two dimensions, all the data points fall on the tent-shaped line shown in Figure 12.4. For small k, the fraction of pairs of points that are close to one another shrinks at the same rate as k so $v_2=1$. In higher dimensions a similar argument applies, and $v_n=1$ for all n when data are generated by the tent map.

The *correlation dimension* is defined to be the limit of v_n as n increases, when this limit exists:

$$v = \lim_{n \to \infty} v_n. \qquad (12.1.23)$$

Nonlinear deterministic processes are characterized by finite v.

The contrast between nonlinear deterministic data and IID uniform data generalizes to IID data with other distributions, since $v_n=n$ for IID data regardless of the distribution. The effect of the distribution averages out because we take each n-history in turn as a benchmark n-history when calculating the correlation integral. Thus Grassberger and Procaccia (1983) suggest that one can distinguish nonlinear deterministic data from IID random data by calculating v_n for different n and seeing whether it grows with n or converges to some fixed limit. This approach requires large amounts of data since one must use very small k to calculate v_n and no distribution theory is available for v_n.

The Brock-Dechert-Scheinkman Test

Brock, Dechert, and Scheinkman (1987) have developed an alternative approach that is better suited to the limited amounts of data typically available in economics and finance. They show that even when k is finite, if the data are IID then for any n

$$C_n(k) = C_1(k)^n. \qquad (12.1.24)$$

To understand this result, note that the ratio $C_{n+1}(k)/C_n(k)$ can be interpreted as a conditional probability:

$$\frac{C_{n+1}(k)}{C_n(k)} = \Pr\left(\max_{i=0,\ldots,n} |x_{s-i} - x_{t-i}| < k \;\middle|\; \max_{i=1,\ldots,n} |x_{s-i} - x_{t-i}| < k \right)$$

$$= \Pr\left(|x_s - x_t| < k \;\middle|\; \max_{i=1,\ldots,n} |x_{s-i} - x_{t-i}| < k \right). \quad (12.1.25)$$

That is, $C_{n+1}(k)/C_n(k)$ is the probability that two data points are close, given that the previous n data points are close. If the data are IID, this must equal the unconditional probability that two data points are close, $C_1(k)$. Setting $C_{n+1}(k)/C_n(k)=C_1(k)$ for all positive n, we obtain (12.1.24).

Brock, Dechert, and Scheinkman (1987) propose the *BDS* test statistic,

$$J_{n,T}(k) = \sqrt{T}\, \frac{C_{n,T}(k) - C_{1,T}(k)^n}{\hat{\sigma}_{n,T}(k)}, \quad (12.1.26)$$

where $C_{n,T}(k)$ and $C_{1,T}(k)$ are the sample correlation integrals defined in (12.1.20), and $\hat{\sigma}_{n,T}(k)$ is an estimator of the asymptotic standard deviation of $C_{n,T}(k)-C_{1,T}(k)^n$. The BDS statistic is asymptotically standard normal under the IID null hypothesis; it is applied and explained by Hsieh (1989) and Scheinkman and LeBaron (1989), who provide explicit expressions for $\hat{\sigma}_{n,T}(k)$. Hsieh (1989) and Hsieh (1991) report Monte Carlo results on the size and power of the BDS statistic in finite samples.

While there are some pathological nonlinear models for which $C_n(k)=C_1(k)^n$ as in IID data, the BDS statistic appears to have good power against the most commonly used nonlinear models. It is important to understand that it has power against models that are nonlinear in variance but not in mean, as well as models that are nonlinear in mean. Thus a BDS rejection does not necessarily imply that a time-series has a time-varying conditional mean; it could simply be evidence for a time-varying conditional variance. Hsieh (1991), for example, strongly rejects the hypothesis that common stock returns are IID using the BDS test. He then estimates models of the time-varying conditional variance of returns and gets much weaker evidence against the hypothesis that the residuals from such models are IID.

12.2 Models of Changing Volatility

In this section we consider alternative ways to model the changing volatility of a time-series η_{t+1}. Section 12.2.1 presents univariate Autoregressive Conditionally Heteroskedastic (ARCH) and stochastic-volatility models, and Section 12.2.2 shows how these may be generalized to a multivariate setting. Section 12.2.3 covers models in which time-variation in the conditional mean is linked to time-variation in the conditional variance; these models are non-linear in both mean and variance.

In order to concentrate on volatility, we assume that η_{t+1} is an innovation, that is, it has mean zero conditional on time t information. In a finance application, η_{t+1} might be the innovation in an asset return. We define σ_t^2 to be the time t conditional variance of η_{t+1} or equivalently the conditional expectation of η_{t+1}^2. We assume that conditional on time t information, the innovation is normally distributed:

$$\eta_{t+1} \sim \mathcal{N}(0, \sigma_t^2). \tag{12.2.1}$$

The unconditional variance of the innovation, σ^2, is just the unconditional expectation of σ_t^2:[3]

$$\sigma^2 \equiv E[\eta_{t+1}^2] = E\big[E_t[\eta_{t+1}^2]\big] = E[\sigma_t^2].$$

Thus variability of σ_t^2 around its mean does not change the unconditional variance σ^2.

The variability of σ_t^2 does, however, affect higher moments of the unconditional distribution of η_{t+1}. In particular, with time-varying σ_t^2 the unconditional distribution of η_{t+1} has fatter tails than a normal distribution. To show this, we first write:

$$\eta_{t+1} = \sigma_t \epsilon_{t+1}, \tag{12.2.2}$$

where ϵ_{t+1} is an IID random variable with zero mean and unit variance (as in the previous section) that is normally distributed (an assumption we did not make in the previous section).

As we discussed in Chapter 1, a useful measure of tail thickness for the distribution of a random variable y is the normalized fourth moment, or kurtosis, defined by $K(y) \equiv E[y^4]/E[y^2]^2$. It is well known that the kurtosis of a normal random variable is 3; hence $K(\epsilon_{t+1}) = 3$. But for innovations η_{t+1}, we have

$$\begin{aligned}
K(\eta_{t+1}) &= \frac{E[\sigma_t^4]\,E[\epsilon_{t+1}^4]}{(E[\sigma_t^2])^2} \\
&= \frac{3E[\sigma_t^4]}{(E[\sigma_t^2])^2} \\
&\geq \frac{3(E[\sigma_t^2])^2}{(E[\sigma_t^2])^2} = 3, \tag{12.2.3}
\end{aligned}$$

[3]This result holds only because we are working with an innovation series that has a constant (zero) conditional mean. For a series with a time-varying conditional mean, the unconditional variance is not the same as the unconditional expectation of the conditional variance.

where the first equality follows from the independence of σ_t and ϵ_{t+1}, and the inequality is implied by Jensen's Inequality. Intuitively, the unconditional distribution is a mixture of normal distributions, some with small variances that concentrate mass around the mean and some with large variances that put mass in the tails of the distribution. Thus the mixed distribution has fatter tails than the normal.

We now consider alternative ways of modeling and estimating the σ_t^2 process. The literature on this subject is enormous, and so our review is inevitably selective. Bollerslev, Chou, and Kroner (1992), Bollerslev, Engle, and Nelson (1994), Hamilton (1994) provide much more comprehensive surveys.

12.2.1 Univariate Models

Early research on time-varying volatility extracted volatility estimates from asset return data before specifying a parametric time-series model for volatility. Officer (1973), for example, used a rolling standard deviation—the standard deviation of returns measured over a subsample which moves forward through time—to estimate volatility at each point in time. Other researchers have used the difference between the high and low prices on a given day to estimate volatility for that day (Garman and Klass [1980], Parkinson [1980]). Such methods implicitly assume that volatility is constant over some interval of time.

These methods are often quite accurate if the objective is simply to measure volatility at a point in time; as Merton (1980) observed, if an asset price follows a diffusion with constant volatility, e.g., a geometric Brownian motion, volatility can be estimated arbitrarily accurately with an arbitrarily short sample period if one measures prices sufficiently frequently.[4] Nelson (1992) has shown that a similar argument can be made even when volatility changes through time, provided that the conditional distribution of returns is not too fat-tailed and that volatility changes are sufficiently gradual.

It is, however, both logically inconsistent and statistically inefficient to use volatility measures that are based on the assumption of constant volatility over some period when the resulting series moves through time. To handle this, more recent work specifies a parametric model for volatility first, and then uses the model to extract volatility estimates from the data on returns.

ARCH Models

A basic observation about asset return data is that large returns (of either sign) tend to be followed by more large returns (of either sign). In other

---

[4]See Section 9.3.2 of Chapter 9. Note however that high-frequency price data are often severely affected by microstructure problems of the sort discussed in Chapter 3. This has limited the usefulness of the high-low method of Garman and Klass (1980) and Parkinson (1980).

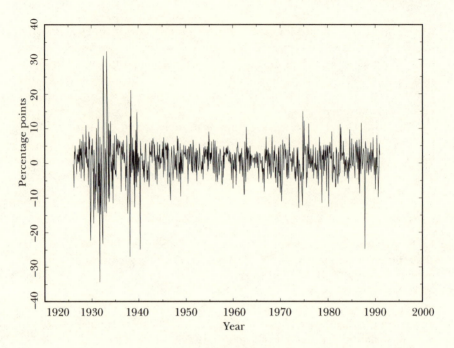

Figure 12.2. *Monthly Excess Log US Stock Returns, 1926 to 1994*

words, the volatility of asset returns appears to be serially correlated. This can be seen visually in Figure 12.2, which plots monthly excess returns on the CRSP value-weighted stock index over the period from 1926 to 1994. The individual monthly returns vary wildly, but they do so within a range which itself changes slowly over time. The range for returns is very wide in the 1930s, for example, and much narrower in the 1950s and 1960s.

An alternative way to understand this is to calculate serial correlation coefficients for squared excess returns or absolute excess returns. At 0.23 and 0.21, respectively, the first-order serial correlation coefficients for these series are about twice as large as the first-order serial correlation coefficient for returns themselves, 0.11, and are highly statistically significant since the standard error under the null of no serial correlation is $1/\sqrt{T} = 0.036$. The difference is even more dramatic in the average of the first 12 auto-correlation coefficients: 0.20 for squared excess returns, 0.21 for absolute excess returns, and 0.02 for excess returns themselves. This reflects the fact that the autocorrelations of squared and absolute returns die out only very slowly.

To capture the serial correlation of volatility, Engle (1982) proposed the class of Autoregressive Conditionally Heteroskedastic, or ARCH, models. These write conditional variance as a distributed lag of past squared innovations:

$$\sigma_t^2 = \omega + \alpha(L)\eta_t^2, \tag{12.2.4}$$

where $\alpha(L)$ is a polynomial in the lag operator. To keep the conditional variance positive, ω and the coefficients in $\alpha(L)$ must be nonnegative.

As a way to model persistent movements in volatility without estimating a very large number of coefficients in a high-order polynomial $\alpha(L)$, Bollerslev (1986) suggested the Generalized Autoregressive Conditionally Heteroskedastic, or GARCH, model:

$$\sigma_t^2 = \omega + \beta(L)\sigma_{t-1}^2 + \alpha(L)\eta_t^2, \tag{12.2.5}$$

where $\beta(L)$ is also a polynomial in the lag operator. By analogy with ARMA models, this is called a GARCH(p, q) model when the order of the polynomial $\beta(L)$ is p and the order of the polynomial $\alpha(L)$ is q. The most commonly used model in the GARCH class is the simple GARCH(1,1) which can be written as

$$
\begin{aligned}
\sigma_t^2 &= \omega + \beta\sigma_{t-1}^2 + \alpha\eta_t^2 \\
&= \omega + (\alpha + \beta)\sigma_{t-1}^2 + \alpha(\eta_t^2 - \sigma_{t-1}^2) \\
&= \omega + (\alpha + \beta)\sigma_{t-1}^2 + \alpha\sigma_{t-1}^2(\epsilon_t^2 - 1). \tag{12.2.6}
\end{aligned}
$$

In the second equality in (12.2.6), the term $(\eta_t^2 - \sigma_{t-1}^2)$ has mean zero, conditional on time $t-1$ information, and can be thought of as the shock to volatility. The coefficient α measures the extent to which a volatility shock today feeds through into next period's volatility, while $(\alpha + \beta)$ measures the rate at which this effect dies out over time. The third equality in (12.2.6) rewrites the volatility shock as $\sigma_{t-1}^2(\epsilon_t^2 - 1)$, the square of a standard normal less its mean—that is, a demeaned $\chi^2(1)$ random variable—multiplied by past volatility σ_{t-1}^2.

The GARCH(1,1) model can also be written in terms of its implications for squared innovations η_{t+1}^2. We have

$$\eta_{t+1}^2 = \omega + (\alpha + \beta)\eta_t^2 + (\eta_{t+1}^2 - \sigma_t^2) - \beta(\eta_t^2 - \sigma_{t-1}^2). \tag{12.2.7}$$

This representation makes it clear that the GARCH(1,1) model is an ARMA(1,1) model for squared innovations; but a standard ARMA(1,1) model has homoskedastic shocks, while here the shocks $(\eta_{t+1}^2 - \sigma_t^2)$ are themselves heteroskedastic.

Persistence and Stationarity

In the GARCH(1,1) model it is easy to construct multiperiod forecasts of volatility. When $\alpha + \beta < 1$, the unconditional variance of η_{t+1}, or equivalently the unconditional expectation of σ_t^2, is $\omega/(1-\alpha-\beta)$. Recursively substituting in (12.2.6), and using the law of iterated expectations, the conditional expectation of volatility j periods ahead is

$$E_t[\sigma_{t+j}^2] = (\alpha + \beta)^j \left(\sigma_t^2 - \frac{\omega}{1 - \alpha - \beta}\right) + \frac{\omega}{1 - \alpha - \beta}. \qquad (12.2.8)$$

The multiperiod volatility forecast reverts to its unconditional mean at rate $(\alpha + \beta)$. This relation between single-period and multiperiod forecasts is the same as in a linear ARMA(1,1) model with autoregressive coefficient $(\alpha + \beta)$. Multiperiod forecasts can be constructed in a similar fashion for higher-order GARCH models.

When $\alpha + \beta = 1$, the conditional expectation of volatility j periods ahead is instead

$$E_t[\sigma_{t+j}^2] = \sigma_t^2 + j\omega. \qquad (12.2.9)$$

The GARCH(1,1) model with $\alpha + \beta = 1$ has a unit autoregressive root so that today's volatility affects forecasts of volatility into the indefinite future. It is therefore known as an integrated GARCH, or IGARCH(1,1), model.

The IGARCH(1,1) process for σ_t^2 looks very much like a linear random walk with drift ω. However Nelson (1990) shows that this analogy must be treated with caution. A linear random walk is nonstationary in two senses. First, it has no stationary distribution, hence the process is not *strictly stationary*. Second, it has no unconditional first or second moments, hence it is not *covariance stationary*. In the IGARCH(1,1) model, on the other hand, σ_t^2 is strictly stationary even though its stationary distribution generally lacks unconditional moments. Thus the IGARCH(1,1) model is strictly stationary but not generally covariance stationary.

It is particularly easy to show that the IGARCH(1,1) model has a stationary distribution in the case where $\omega = 0$. Here (12.2.9) simplifies to $E_t[\sigma_{t+j}^2] = \sigma_t^2$, so volatility is a martingale. At the same time, volatility remains bounded because it cannot go negative. But the martingale convergence theorem states that a bounded martingale must converge; in this case, the only value to which it can converge is zero. The stationary distribution for σ_t^2 is then a degenerate distribution with point mass at zero, and this implies that the stationary distribution for η_{t+1} is also degenerate at zero. In this case the stationary distributions for σ_t^2 and η_{t+1} have moments, but they are all trivially zero.

When $\omega > 0$, Nelson (1990) shows that there exists a nondegenerate stationary distribution for σ_t^2. But this distribution does not have a finite mean or higher moments. The innovation η_{t+1} then has a stationary distribution with a zero mean, but with tails that are so thick that no second- or higher-order moments exist.[5]

---

[5]Nelson shows that these properties hold more generally for GARCH(1,1) models with $\alpha + \beta > 1$ but with $E[\log(\beta + \alpha\epsilon_t^2)] < 0$.

Alternative Functional Forms

In the standard GARCH model, forecasts of future variance are linear in current and past variances and squared returns drive revisions in the forecasts. An alternative model, sometimes known as the absolute value GARCH model, makes forecasts of future standard deviation linear in current and past standard deviations and has absolute values of returns driving revisions in the forecasts. An absolute value GARCH(1,1) model, for example, would be

$$\sigma_t = \omega + \beta\sigma_{t-1} + \alpha\sigma_{t-1}|\epsilon_t|. \tag{12.2.10}$$

Schwert (1989) and Taylor (1986) estimate absolute value ARCH models, while Nelson and Foster (1994) discuss the absolute value GARCH(1,1).

The models we have considered so far are symmetric in that negative and positive shocks ϵ_{t+1} have the same effect on volatility. However Black (1976) and many others have pointed out that there appears to be an asymmetry in stock market data: Negative innovations to stock returns tend to increase volatility more than positive innovations of the same magnitude. Possible explanations for this asymmetry are discussed in Section 12.2.3. To handle this, one can generalize the absolute value GARCH model to

$$\sigma_t = \omega + \beta\sigma_{t-1} + \alpha\sigma_{t-1}f(\epsilon_t), \tag{12.2.11}$$

where

$$f(\epsilon_t) = |\epsilon_t - b| - c(\epsilon_t - b). \tag{12.2.12}$$

Here the shift parameter b and the tilt parameter c measure two different types of asymmetry. b is unrestricted but we need $|c| \leq 1$ to ensure that $f(\epsilon_t) \geq 0$. When $c=0$ but $b \neq 0$, the effect of a shock on volatility depends on its distance from b, so that volatility increases more when there is no shock than when there is a shock of size b. When $b=0$ but $c \neq 0$, a zero shock has the smallest impact on volatility but there is a distinction between positive and negative shocks; a shock of given size may have a larger effect when it is negative than when it is positive, or vice versa. Following Hentschel (1995), a nice way to understand (12.2.12) is to plot $f(\epsilon_t)$ against ϵ_t, as in Figure 12.3.[6] Panel (a) of the figure shows the absolute-value function ($b=0$, $c=0$); this is plotted again as a dashed line in each of the other panels. Panel (b) shows the shifted absolute-value function ($b=0.5$, $c=0$), panel (c) shows the tilted absolute-value function ($b=0$, $c=0.25$), and panel (d) shows a shifted and tilted absolute-value function ($b=0.5$, $c=-0.25$).

Hentschel (1995) further generalizes (12.2.11) to allow a power of $f(\epsilon_t)$, rather than $f(\epsilon_t)$ itself, to affect volatility, and to allow a power of σ_t, rather

---

[6]This is similar to the "news impact curve" of Pagan and Schwert (1990) and Engle and Ng (1993), which plots σ_t^2 against η_t, holding any other relevant state variables at their unconditional means.

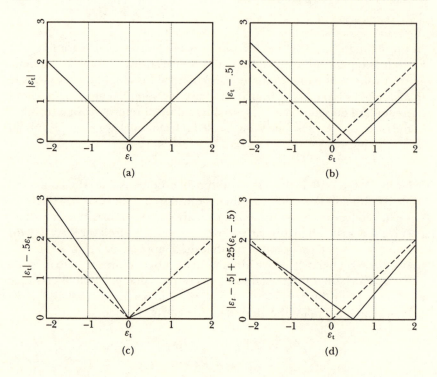

Figure 12.3. *Shifted and Tilted Absolute-Value Function*

than σ_t itself, to be the variable that follows a linear difference equation. The resulting equation is

$$\frac{\sigma_t^\lambda - 1}{\lambda} = \omega + \beta \left(\frac{\sigma_{t-1}^\lambda - 1}{\lambda} \right) + \alpha \sigma_{t-1}^\lambda [f(\epsilon_t)]^\nu. \qquad (12.2.13)$$

Equation (12.2.13) defines a family of models that includes most of the popular GARCH-type models in the literature.[7] The standard GARCH model sets $\lambda = \nu = 2$, and $b = c = 0$. Glosten, Jagannathan, and Runkle (1993) have generalized the standard GARCH model to allow nonzero c. Engle and Ng (1993) have instead allowed nonzero b. The absolute value GARCH model sets $\lambda = \nu = 1$ with free b and c. Another particularly important member of the family (12.2.12) is the exponential GARCH or EGARCH model of Nelson (1990), which is obtained by setting $\lambda = 0$, $\nu = 1$, and $b = 0$ to get

$$\log(\sigma_t) = \omega + \beta \log(\sigma_{t-1}) + \alpha \left[|\epsilon_t| - c\epsilon_t \right]. \qquad (12.2.14)$$

[7] See also Ding, Granger, and Engle (1993) for a related family of models.

This model is appealing because it does not require any parameter restrictions to ensure that the conditional variance of the return is always positive. Also it becomes both strictly nonstationary and covariance nonstationary when $\alpha + \beta = 1$, so it does not share the unusual statistical properties of the IGARCH(1,1) model. On the other hand, multiperiod forecasts of future variances are harder to calculate in the EGARCH model; no closed-form expressions like (12.2.8) are available.

Estimation

We have introduced an almost bewildering variety of volatility models. To discover which features of these models are important in fitting financial data, one must be able to estimate the models' parameters. Fortunately this is fairly straightforward for GARCH models and other models in the class defined by (12.2.13). Conditional on the parameters of the model and an initial variance estimate, the data are normally distributed and we can construct a likelihood function recursively. We write the vector of model parameters as θ, define $\sigma_t(\theta)$ to be the conditional standard deviation at time t implied by the parameters and the history of returns, and define $\epsilon_{t+1}(\theta) \equiv \eta_{t+1}/\sigma_t(\theta)$. When θ contains the true parameters of the model, $\epsilon_{t+1}(\theta)$ is IID with density function $g(\epsilon_{t+1}(\theta))$ which we have assumed to be standard normal:

$$g(\epsilon_{t+1}(\theta)) = \frac{1}{\sqrt{2\pi}} e^{-\epsilon_{t+1}(\theta)^2/2}. \tag{12.2.15}$$

The conditional log likelihood of η_{t+1} is therefore

$$
\begin{aligned}
\ell_t(\eta_{t+1}; \theta) &= \log\big(g(\eta_{t+1}/\sigma_t(\theta))\big) - \log(\sigma_t^2(\theta))/2 \\
&= -\log(\sqrt{2\pi}) - \eta_{t+1}^2/2\sigma_t^2(\theta) \\
&\quad - \log(\sigma_t^2(\theta))/2, \tag{12.2.16}
\end{aligned}
$$

where the last term is a Jacobian term that appears because we observe η_{t+1} and not $\eta_{t+1}/\sigma_t(\theta)$. The log likelihood of the whole data set $\eta_1, \ldots, \eta_T$ is

$$\mathcal{L}(\eta_1, \ldots, \eta_T) = \sum_{t=1}^{T} \ell_t(\eta_{t+1}; \theta). \tag{12.2.17}$$

The maximum likelihood estimator is the choice of parameters θ that maximizes (12.2.17).[8]

---

[8] In practice one needs an initial σ_0^2 to begin calculating the conditional likelihoods in (12.2.16). The influence of the initial condition diminishes over time and becomes negligible asymptotically; thus the choice of initial condition does not affect the consistency of the estimator.

Although it is easy to show that the maximum likelihood estimator is consistent, it is harder to prove that it is asymptotically normal. The difficulty is that this requires regularity conditions which are hard to verify for GARCH processes. Lee and Hansen (1994) give some results for the GARCH(1,1) model but few other results are available. Empirical researchers typically ignore this problem and assume that the usual regularity conditions hold. Some simulation evidence (Bollerslev and Wooldridge [1992] and Lumsdaine [1995]) supports this practice.

Hentschel (1995) provides maximum likelihood estimates for a great variety of models in the family (12.2.13) using daily and monthly stock return data over the period from 1926 to 1990. To estimate the parameters λ and ν with any precision, Hentschel finds that he needs the very large number of observations provided by daily data. These data suggest that λ is close to one (as in the absolute value GARCH model), but that ν is greater than one, in fact close to 1.5. In both daily and monthly data, Hentschel finds that asymmetry is better modeled with the shift parameter b than with the tilt parameter c. Thus US stock returns are well-described by a GARCH model for the conditional standard deviation, driven by the shifted absolute value of shocks raised to the power three halves. The volatility process is highly persistent in all the models estimated, although the degree of persistence is sensitive to specification in the post-World War II period.

Additional Explanatory Variables
Up to this point we have modeled volatility using only the past history of returns themselves. It is straightforward to add other explanatory variables: For example, one can write an augmented GARCH(1,1) model as

$$\sigma_t^2 = \omega + \gamma X_t + \beta \sigma_{t-1}^2 + \alpha \eta_t^2, \qquad (12.2.18)$$

where X_t is any variable known at time t. Provided that $X_t \geq 0$ and $\gamma \geq 0$, this model still constrains volatility to be positive. Alternatively, one can add explanatory variables to the EGARCH model without any sign restrictions. Glosten, Jagannathan, and Runkle (1993) add a short-term nominal interest rate to various GARCH models and show that it has a significant positive effect on stock market volatility.

Conditional Nonnormality
The GARCH models we have considered imply that the distribution of returns, conditional on the past history of returns, is normal. Equivalently, the standardized residuals of these models, $\epsilon_{t+1}(\theta) = \eta_{t+1}/\sigma_t(\theta)$, should be normal. Unfortunately, in practice there is excess kurtosis in the standardized residuals of GARCH models, albeit less than in the raw returns (see, for example, Bollerslev [1987] and Nelson [1991]).

One way to handle this problem is to continue to work with the conditional normal likelihood function defined by (12.2.16) and (12.2.17), but to interpret the estimator as a quasi-maximum likelihood estimator (White [1982]). Standard errors for parameter estimates can then be calculated using a robust covariance matrix estimator as discussed by Bollerslev and Wooldridge (1992).

Alternatively, one can explicitly model the fat-tailed distribution of the shocks driving a GARCH process. Bollerslev (1987), for example, suggests a Student-*t* distribution with *k* degrees of freedom:

$$g(\epsilon_{t+1}(\boldsymbol{\theta})) = \Gamma\left(\frac{k+1}{2}\right)\Gamma\left(\frac{k}{2}\right)^{-1}(k-2)^{-1/2}\left(1+\frac{\epsilon_{t+1}(\boldsymbol{\theta})}{k-2}\right)^{-(k+1)/2},$$

$$(12.2.19)$$

where $\Gamma(\cdot)$ is the gamma function. The *t* distribution converges to the normal distribution as *k* increases, but has excess kurtosis; indeed its fourth moment is infinite when $k \leq 4$. In a similar spirit Nelson (1991) uses a Generalized Error Distribution, while Engle and Gonzalez-Rivera (1991) estimate the error density nonparametrically.

GARCH models can also be estimated by Generalized Method of Moments (GMM). This is appealing when the conditional volatility σ_t^2 can be written as a fairly simple function of observed past variables (past squared returns and additional variables such as interest rates). Then the model implies that squared returns, less the appropriate function of the observed variables, are orthogonal to the observed variables. GMM estimation has the usual attraction that one need not specify a density for shocks to returns.

Stochastic-Volatility Models

Another response to the nonnormality of returns conditional upon past returns is to assume that there is a random variable conditional upon which returns are normal, but that this variable—which we may call *stochastic volatility*—is not directly observed. This kind of assumption is often made in continuous-time theoretical models, where asset prices follow diffusions with volatility parameters that also follow diffusions. Melino and Turnbull (1990) and Wiggins (1987) argue that discrete-time stochastic-volatility models are natural approximations to such processes. If we parametrize the discrete-time process for stochastic volatility, we then have a filtering problem: to process the observed data to estimate the parameters driving stochastic volatility and to estimate the level of volatility at each point in time.

A simple example of a stochastic-volatility model is the following:

$$\eta_t = \epsilon_t e^{\alpha_t/2}, \qquad \alpha_t = \phi\alpha_{t-1} + \xi_t, \qquad (12.2.20)$$

where $\epsilon_t \sim \mathcal{N}(0, \sigma_\epsilon^2)$, $\xi_t \sim \mathcal{N}(0, \sigma_\xi^2)$, and we assume that ϵ_t and ξ_t are serially uncorrelated and independent of each other. Here α_t measures the difference between the conditional log standard deviation of returns and its mean; it follows a zero-mean AR(1) process.

We can rewrite this system by squaring the return equation and taking logs to get

$$\log(\eta_t^2) = \alpha_t + \log(\epsilon_t^2), \qquad \alpha_t = \phi\alpha_{t-1} + \xi_t. \tag{12.2.21}$$

This is in linear state-space form except that the first equation of (12.2.21) has an error with a $\log \chi^2$ distribution instead of a normal distribution. To appreciate the importance of the nonnormality, one need only consider the fact that when ϵ_t is very close to zero (an "inlier"), $\log(\epsilon_t^2)$ is a very large negative outlier.

The system can be estimated in a variety of ways. Melino and Turnbull (1990) and Wiggins (1987) use GMM estimators. While this is straightforward, it is not efficient. Harvey, Ruiz, and Shephard (1994) suggest a quasi-maximum-likelihood estimator which ignores the nonnormality of $\log(\epsilon_t^2)$ and proceeds as if both equations in (12.2.21) had normal error terms. More recently, Jacquier, Polson, and Rossi (1994) have suggested a Bayesian approach and Shephard and Kim (1994) have proposed a simulation-based exact maximum-likelihood estimator.

12.2.2 Multivariate Models

So far we have considered only the volatility of a single asset return. More generally, we may have a vector of asset returns whose conditional covariance matrix evolves through time. Suppose we have N assets with return innovations $\eta_{i,t+1}$, $i=1\ldots N$. We stack these innovations into a vector $\boldsymbol{\eta}_{t+1}=[\ \eta_{1,t+1} \ \cdots \ \eta_{N,t+1}]'$ and define $\sigma_{ii,t}=\text{Var}_t(\eta_{i,t+1})$ and $\sigma_{ij,t}=\text{Cov}_t(\eta_{i,t+1},\eta_{j,t})$; hence $\boldsymbol{\Sigma}_t=[\sigma_{ij,t}]$ is the conditional covariance matrix of all the returns. It is often convenient to stack the nonredundant elements of $\boldsymbol{\Sigma}_t$—those on and below the main diagonal—into a vector. The operator which performs this stacking is known as the *vech* operator: $\text{vech}(\boldsymbol{\Sigma}_t)$ is a vector with $N(N+1)/2$ elements.

Multivariate GARCH Models
Many of the ideas we have considered in a univariate context translate naturally to the multivariate setting. The simplest generalization of the univariate GARCH(1,1) model (12.2.6) relates $\text{vech}(\boldsymbol{\Sigma}_t)$ to $\text{vech}(\boldsymbol{\eta}_t\boldsymbol{\eta}_t')$ and to $\text{vech}(\boldsymbol{\Sigma}_{t-1})$:

$$\text{vech}(\boldsymbol{\Sigma}_t) = \boldsymbol{\omega} + \boldsymbol{\Psi}\,\text{vech}(\boldsymbol{\Sigma}_{t-1}) + \boldsymbol{\Lambda}\,\text{vech}(\boldsymbol{\eta}_t\boldsymbol{\eta}_t'). \tag{12.2.22}$$

Here $\boldsymbol{\omega}$ is a vector with $N(N+1)/2$ elements, and $\boldsymbol{\Psi}$ and $\boldsymbol{\Lambda}$ are $N(N+1)/2 \times N(N+1)/2$ matrices; hence the total number of parameters in this model is $N^2(N+1)^2/2 + N(N+1)/2$ which grows with the fourth power of N. It is clear that this model becomes unmanageable very quickly; much of the literature on multivariate GARCH models therefore seeks to place plausible restrictions on (12.2.22) to reduce the number of parameters. Another important goal of the literature is to find restrictions which guarantee that the covariance matrix Σ_t is positive definite. Such restrictions are comparatively straightforward in a univariate setting—for example, all the parameters in a univariate GARCH(1,1) model must be positive—but are much less obvious in a multivariate model.

Kroner and Ng (1993) provide a nice survey of the leading multivariate GARCH models. A first specification, the VECH model of Bollerslev, Engle, and Wooldridge (1988) (named after the vech operator), writes the covariance matrix as a set of univariate GARCH models. Each element of Σ_t follows a univariate GARCH model driven by the corresponding element of the cross-product matrix $\boldsymbol{\eta}_t\boldsymbol{\eta}_t'$. The (i, j) element of Σ_t is given by

$$\sigma_{ij,t} = \omega_{ij} + \beta_{ij}\,\sigma_{ij,t-1} + \alpha_{ij}\,\eta_{it}\,\eta_{jt}. \tag{12.2.23}$$

This model is obtained from (12.2.22) by making the matrices $\boldsymbol{\Lambda}$ and $\boldsymbol{\Psi}$ diagonal. The implied conditional covariance matrix is always positive definite if the matrices of parameters $[\omega_{ij}]$, $[\beta_{ij}]$, and $[\alpha_{ij}]$ are all positive definite. The model has three parameters for each element of Σ_t and thus $3N(N+1)/2$ parameters in all.

A second specification, the BEKK model of Engle and Kroner (1995) (named after an earlier working paper by Bollerslev, Engle, Kraft, and Kroner), guarantees positive definiteness by working with quadratic forms rather than the individual elements of Σ_t. The model is

$$\Sigma_t = \mathbf{C}'\mathbf{C} + \mathbf{B}'\Sigma_{t-1}\mathbf{B} + \mathbf{A}'\boldsymbol{\eta}_t\boldsymbol{\eta}_t'\mathbf{A}, \tag{12.2.24}$$

where $\mathbf{C}$ is a lower triangular matrix with $N(N+1)/2$ parameters, and $\mathbf{B}$ and $\mathbf{A}$ are square matrices with N^2 parameters each, for a total parameter count of $(5N^2+N)/2$. Weak restrictions on $\mathbf{B}$ and $\mathbf{A}$ guarantee that Σ_t is always positive definite.

A special case of the BEKK model is the single-factor GARCH(1,1) model of Engle, Ng, and Rothschild (1990). In this model we define N-vectors $\boldsymbol{\lambda}$ and $\mathbf{w}$ and scalars α and β, and then have

$$\Sigma_t = \mathbf{C}'\mathbf{C} + \boldsymbol{\lambda}\boldsymbol{\lambda}'[\beta\mathbf{w}'\Sigma_{t-1}\mathbf{w} + \alpha(\mathbf{w}'\boldsymbol{\eta}_t)^2]. \tag{12.2.25}$$

Here $\mathbf{C}$ is restricted as in the previous equation. We can impose one normalizing restriction on this model; it is convenient to set $\iota'\mathbf{w}=1$, where ι is a vector of ones. The vector $\mathbf{w}$ can then be thought of as a vector of portfolio weights. We define $\eta_{pt} = \mathbf{w}'\boldsymbol{\eta}_t$ and $\sigma_{pp,t} = \mathbf{w}'\boldsymbol{\Sigma}_t\mathbf{w}$. The model can now be restated as

$$
\begin{aligned}
\sigma_{ij,t} &= \omega_{ij} + \lambda_i \lambda_j \sigma_{pp,t} \\
\sigma_{pp,t} &= \omega_{pp} + \beta \sigma_{pp,t-1} + \alpha \eta_{p,t}^2.
\end{aligned}
\tag{12.2.26}
$$

The covariances of any two asset returns move through time only with the variance of the portfolio return, which follows a univariate GARCH(1,1) model. The single-factor GARCH(1,1) model is a special case of the BEKK model where the matrices $\mathbf{A}$ and $\mathbf{B}$ have rank one: $\mathbf{A} = \sqrt{\alpha}\mathbf{w}\lambda'$ and $\mathbf{B} = \sqrt{\beta}\mathbf{w}\lambda'$. It has $(N^2+5N+2)/2$ free parameters. The model can be extended straightforwardly to allow for multiple factors or a higher-order GARCH structure.

Finally, Bollerslev (1990) has proposed a constant-correlation model in which each asset return variance follows a univariate GARCH(1,1) model and the covariance between any two assets is given by a constant-correlation coefficient multiplying the conditional standard deviations of the returns:

$$
\begin{aligned}
\sigma_{ii,t} &= \omega_{ii} + \beta_{ii} \sigma_{ii,t-1} + \alpha_{ii} \eta_{it}^2, \\
\sigma_{ij,t} &= \rho_{ij}\sqrt{\sigma_{ii,t}\sigma_{jj,t}}.
\end{aligned}
\tag{12.2.27}
$$

This model has $N(N+5)/2$ parameters. It gives a positive definite covariance matrix provided that the correlations ρ_{ij} make up a well-defined correlation matrix and the parameters ω_{ii}, α_{ii}, and β_{ii} are all positive.

To understand the differences between these models, it is instructive to consider what happens to the conditional covariance between two asset returns after large shocks of opposite signs hit the two assets. In the VECH model with a positive α_{ij} coefficient, the negative cross-product $\eta_{it}\eta_{jt}$ lowers the conditional covariance. In the constant correlation model, on the other hand, the sign of the cross-product $\eta_{it}\eta_{jt}$ is irrelevant; any event that increases the variances of two positively correlated assets raises the covariance between them. In the factor ARCH model $\sigma_{ij,t}$ only moves with $\sigma_{pp,t}$, so the effect of a negative cross-product $\eta_{it}\eta_{jt}$ depends on the weights in portfolio p.

As in the univariate case, return volatilities may be persistent in multivariate GARCH models. Multivariate models allow for the possibility that some asset volatilities may share common persistent components; for example, there might be one persistent component in a set of volatilities, so that all changes in one volatility relative to another are transitory. Bollerslev and Engle (1993) explore this idea, which is analogous to the concept of cointegration in the literature on linear unit-root processes.

Multivariate Stochastic-Volatility Models

The univariate stochastic-volatility model given in (12.2.20) is also easily extended to a multivariate setting. We have

$$\boldsymbol{\eta}_t = \boldsymbol{\epsilon}_t e^{\boldsymbol{\alpha}_t/2}, \qquad \boldsymbol{\alpha}_t = \boldsymbol{\Phi}\boldsymbol{\alpha}_{t-1} + \boldsymbol{\xi}_t, \qquad (12.2.28)$$

where $\boldsymbol{\eta}_t$, $\boldsymbol{\epsilon}_t$, $\boldsymbol{\alpha}_t$, and $\boldsymbol{\xi}_t$ are now $(N \times 1)$ vectors and $\boldsymbol{\Phi}$ is an $(N \times N)$ matrix. This model has N^2 parameters in the matrix $\boldsymbol{\Phi}$, $N(N+1)/2$ parameters in the covariance matrix of $\boldsymbol{\epsilon}_t$, and $N(N+1)/2$ parameters in the covariance matrix of $\boldsymbol{\eta}_t$, so the total number of parameters is $N(2N+1)$. There is no need to restrict $\boldsymbol{\alpha}_t$ to be positive and it is straightforward to estimate the $\boldsymbol{\epsilon}_t$ and $\boldsymbol{\eta}_t$ covariance parameters in square-root form to ensure that the implied covariance matrix is positive definite. Harvey, Ruiz, and Shephard (1994) suggest restricted versions of this model in which $\boldsymbol{\Phi}$ is diagonal (reducing the number of parameters to $N(N+2)$) or is even the identity matrix (further reducing the number of parameters to $N(N+1)$).

Even without such extra restrictions, it is important to understand that the specification (12.2.28) imposes constant conditional correlations of asset returns. In this respect it is as restrictive as Bollerslev's (1990) constant-correlation GARCH model, and it has more parameters than that model whenever $N > 3$.

A Conditional Market Model

Even the most restrictive of the models we have discussed so far are hard to apply to a large cross-sectional data set because the number of their parameters grows with the square of the number of assets N. The problem is that these models take the whole conditional covariance matrix of returns as the object to be studied. An alternative approach, paralleling the much earlier development of static mean-variance analysis, is to work with a conditional market model. Continuing to ignore nonzero mean returns, we write

$$\eta_{i,t+1} = \beta_{it}\eta_{m,t+1} + \zeta_{i,t+1}, \qquad (12.2.29)$$

where $\beta_{it} \equiv \sigma_{im,t}/\sigma_{mm,t}$ is the conditional beta of asset i with the market, and $\zeta_{i,t+1}$ is an idiosyncratic shock which is assumed to be uncorrelated across assets. Within this framework we might model $\sigma_{mm,t}$, the conditional variance of the market return as a univariate GARCH(1,1) process; we might model $\beta_{im,t}$ or equivalently $\sigma_{im,t}$ as depending on $\sigma_{mm,t}$, $\beta_{im,t-1}$, and the returns η_{it} and η_{mt}; and we might model the conditional variance of the idiosyncratic shock to return as another univariate GARCH(1,1) process. The covariance matrix implied by a model of this sort is guaranteed to be positive definite, and the number of parameters in the model grows at rate N rather than N^2, which makes the model applicable to much larger numbers of assets. Braun,

Nelson, and Sunier (1995) take this approach, using EGARCH functional forms for the individual components of the model.

12.2.3 Links between First and Second Moments

We have reviewed some extremely sophisticated models of time-varying second moments in time series whose first moments are assumed to be constant and zero. But the essence of finance theory is that it relates the first and second moments of asset returns. Accordingly we now discuss models in which conditional mean returns may change with the conditional variances and covariances.

The GARCH-M Model

Engle, Lilien, and Robins (1987) suggest adding a time-varying intercept to the basic univariate model (12.2.2). Writing r_{t+1} for a continuously compounded asset return which is the time series of interest (since we no longer work with a mean-zero innovation), we have

$$r_{t+1} \; = \; \mu_t + \sigma_t \epsilon_{t+1}, \qquad \mu_t \; = \; \gamma_0 + \gamma_1 \sigma_t^2, \tag{12.2.30}$$

where ϵ_{t+1} is an IID random variable as before, and σ_t^2 can follow any GARCH process. This *GARCH-in-mean* or GARCH-M model makes the conditional mean of the return linear in the conditional variance. It can be straightforwardly estimated by maximum likelihood, although it is not known whether the model satisfies the regularity conditions for asymptotic normality of the maximum likelihood estimator.

The GARCH-M model can also be specified so that the conditional mean is linear in the conditional standard deviation rather than the conditional variance. It has been generalized to a multivariate setting by Bollerslev, Engle, and Wooldridge (1988) and others, but the number of parameters increases rapidly with the number of returns and the model is typically applied to only a few assets.

The Instrumental Variables Approach

As an alternative to the GARCH-M model, Campbell (1987) and Harvey (1989, 1991) have suggested that one can estimate the parameters linking first and second moments by GMM. These authors start with a model for the "market" return that makes the expected market return linear in its own variance, conditional on some vector $\mathbf{H}_t$ containing L instruments or forecasting variables:

$$\mathrm{E}[r_{m,t+1} | \mathbf{H}_t] \; = \; \gamma_0 + \gamma_1 \mathrm{Var}[r_{m,t+1} | \mathbf{H}_t]. \tag{12.2.31}$$

Campbell and Harvey assume that conditional expected returns are linear in the instruments and define errors

$$u_{m,t+1} \equiv r_{m,t+1} - \mathbf{H}_t\mathbf{b}_m,$$

$$e_{m,t+1} \equiv r_{m,t+1} - \gamma_0 - \gamma_1(r_{m,t+1} - \mathbf{H}_t\mathbf{b}_m)^2. \tag{12.2.32}$$

Here $\mathbf{b}_m$ is a vector of regression coefficients of the market return on the instruments. The error $u_{m,t+1}$ is the difference between the market return and a linear combination of the instruments, while the error $e_{m,t+1}$ is the difference between the market return and a linear function of $u_{m,t+1}^2$. The model (12.2.31) implies that the errors $u_{m,t+1}$ and $e_{m,t+1}$ are both orthogonal to the instruments $\mathbf{H}_t$. With L instruments, there are $2L$ orthogonality conditions available to estimate $L+2$ parameters (γ_0, γ_1, and the L coefficients in $\mathbf{b}_m$). Thus GMM delivers both parameter estimates and a test for the overidentifying restrictions of the model.

This approach can easily be generalized to include other assets whose expected returns are given by

$$\mathrm{E}[r_{i,t+1} \mid \mathbf{H}_t] = \gamma_0 + \gamma_1 \mathrm{Cov}[r_{i,t+1}, r_{m,t+1} \mid \mathbf{H}_t]. \tag{12.2.33}$$

If there are N such assets, we define a vector $\mathbf{r}_{t+1} \equiv [r_{1,t+1}, \ldots, r_{N,t+1}]'$. The conditional expectation of $\mathbf{r}_{t+1}$ is given by $\mathrm{E}[\mathbf{r}_{t+1} \mid \mathbf{H}_t] = \mathbf{H}_t\mathbf{B}$, where $\mathbf{B}$ is a matrix with NL coefficients. We define errors

$$\mathbf{u}_{t+1} \equiv \mathbf{r}_{t+1} - \mathbf{H}_t\mathbf{B},$$

$$\mathbf{e}_{t+1} \equiv \mathbf{r}_{t+1} - \gamma_0 - \gamma_1(\mathbf{r}_{t+1} - \mathbf{H}_t\mathbf{B})(r_{m,t+1} - \mathbf{H}_t\mathbf{b}_m), \tag{12.2.34}$$

and we get $2NL$ extra orthogonality conditions to identify $NL + 1$ extra parameters. The total number of orthogonality conditions in (12.2.33) and (12.2.34) is $2(N + 1)L$ and the total number of parameters is $N(L + 1) + L + 2$. Thus the model is identified whenever two or more instruments are available.

Harvey (1989) further generalizes the model to allow for a time-varying price of risk. He replaces (12.2.33) by

$$\mathrm{E}[r_{i,t+1} \mid \mathbf{H}_t] = \gamma_0 + \gamma_{1t} \mathrm{Cov}[r_{i,t+1}, r_{m,t+1} \mid \mathbf{H}_t], \tag{12.2.35}$$

where γ_{1t} varies through time but is common to all assets. Since (12.2.35) holds for the market portfolio itself,

$$\gamma_{1t} = \frac{\mathrm{E}[r_{m,t+1} \mid \mathbf{H}_t] - \gamma_0}{\mathrm{Var}[r_{m,t+1} \mid \mathbf{H}_t]}, \tag{12.2.36}$$

and Harvey uses this to estimate the model. He substitutes (12.2.36) into (12.2.35), multiplies through by $\mathrm{Var}[r_{m,t+1} \mid \mathbf{H}_t]$, and uses $\mathrm{E}[r_{m,t+1}\mid\mathbf{H}_t] =$

$\mathbf{H}_t\mathbf{b}_m$ and $\mathrm{E}[r_{t+1} \mid \mathbf{H}_t] = \mathbf{H}_t\mathbf{B}$ to construct a new error vector

$$
\begin{aligned}
\mathbf{v}_{t+1} &= (r_{m,t+1} - \mathbf{H}_t\mathbf{B}_m)^2(\mathbf{H}_t\mathbf{B} - \gamma_0\iota) \\
&\quad -(\mathbf{r}_{t+1} - \mathbf{H}_t\mathbf{B})(r_{m,t+1} - \mathbf{H}_t\mathbf{b}_m)(\mathbf{H}_t\mathbf{b}_m - \gamma_0). \quad (12.2.37)
\end{aligned}
$$

Harvey replaces $\mathbf{e}_{t+1}$ in (12.2.34) with $\mathbf{v}_{t+1}$ in (12.2.37), and drops the error $e_{m,t+1}$ in (12.2.32). This gives a system with L fewer orthogonality conditions and one less parameter to estimate (since γ_1 drops out of the model). The number of overidentifying restrictions declines by $L - 1$. Harvey (1989) finds some evidence that the price of risk varies when a US stock index is used as the market portfolio; however he also rejects the overidentifying restrictions of the model. Harvey (1991) uses a world stock index as the market portfolio and obtains similar results.

The Conditional CAPM and the Unconditional CAPM
Equations (12.2.35) and (12.2.36) can be rewritten as

$$
\mathrm{E}[r_{i,t+1} \mid \mathbf{H}_t] = \gamma_0 + \beta_{it}\lambda_t, \qquad (12.2.38)
$$

where $\beta_{it} \equiv \mathrm{Cov}[r_{i,t+1}, r_{m,t+1} \mid \mathbf{H}_t]/\mathrm{Var}[r_{m,t+1} \mid \mathbf{H}_t]$, the conditional beta of asset i with the market return, and $\lambda_t \equiv \mathrm{E}[r_{m,t+1} \mid \mathbf{H}_t] - \gamma_0$, the expected excess return on the market over a riskless return.

Jagannathan and Wang (1996) emphasize that this conditional version of the CAPM need not imply the unconditional CAPM that was discussed in Chapter 5. If we take unconditional expectations of (12.2.38), we get

$$
\mathrm{E}[r_{i,t+1}] = \gamma_0 + (\mathrm{E}[\beta_{it}])(\mathrm{E}[\lambda_t]) + \mathrm{Cov}(\beta_{it}, \lambda_t). \qquad (12.2.39)
$$

Here $\mathrm{E}[\lambda_t]$ is the unconditional expected excess return on the market. $\mathrm{E}[\beta_{it}]$ is the unconditional expectation of the conditional beta, which need not be the same as the unconditional beta, although the difference is likely to be small. Most important, the covariance between the conditional beta and the expected excess market return λ_t appears in (12.2.39). Assets whose betas are high when the market risk premium is high will have higher un-conditional mean returns than would be predicted by the unconditional CAPM. Jagannathan and Wang (1996) argue that the high average returns on small stocks might be explained by this effect if small-stock betas tend to rise at times when the expected excess return on the stock market is high. They present some indirect evidence for this story although they do not directly model the time-variation of small-stock betas.

Volatility Innovations and Return Innovations
Empirical researchers have found little evidence that periods of high volatil-ity in stock returns are periods of high expected stock returns. Some pa-pers report weak evidence for this relationship (see Bollerslev, Engle, and

Wooldridge [1988], French, Schwert, and Stambaugh [1987], and Harvey [1989]), but other papers which use the short-term nominal interest rate as an instrument find a negative relationship between the mean and volatility of returns (see Campbell [1987] and Glosten, Jagannathan, and Runkle [1993]).

As French, Schwert, and Stambaugh (1987) emphasize, there is much stronger evidence that positive *innovations* to volatility are correlated with negative *innovations* to returns. We have already discussed how asymmetric GARCH models can fit this correlation. At a deeper level, it can be explained in one of two ways. One possibility is that negative shocks to returns drive up volatility. The *leverage hypothesis,* due originally to Black (1976), says that when the total value of a levered firm falls, the value of its equity becomes a smaller share of the total. Since equity bears the full risk of the firm, the percentage volatility of equity should rise. Even if a firm is not financially levered with debt, this may occur if the firm has fixed commitments to workers or suppliers. Although there is surely some truth to this story, it is hard to account for the magnitude of the return-volatility correlation using realistic leverage estimates (see Christie [1982] and Schwert [1989]).

An alternative explanation is that causality runs the other way: Positive shocks to volatility drive down returns. Campbell and Hentschel (1992) call this the *volatility-feedback hypothesis.* If expected stock returns increase when volatility increases, and if expected dividends are unchanged, then stock prices should fall when volatility increases. Campbell and Hentschel build this into a formal model by using the loglinear approximation for returns (7.2.26):

$$r_{t+1} = E_t[r_{t+1}] + \eta_{d,t+1} - \eta_{r,t+1}, \qquad (12.2.40)$$

where

$$\eta_{d,t+1} \equiv E_{t+1}\left[\sum_{j=0}^{\infty} \rho^j \Delta d_{t+1+j}\right] - E_t\left[\sum_{j=0}^{\infty} \rho^j \Delta d_{t+1+j}\right]$$

is the change in expectations of future dividends in (7.2.25), and

$$\eta_{r,t+1} \equiv E_{t+1}\left[\sum_{j=1}^{\infty} \rho^j r_{t+1+j}\right] - E_t\left[\sum_{j=1}^{\infty} \rho^j r_{t+1+j}\right]$$

is the change in expectations of future returns.

Campbell and Hentschel model the dividend news variable $\eta_{d,t+1}$ as a GARCH(1,1) process with a zero mean: $\eta_{d,t+1} \sim \mathcal{N}(0, \sigma_t^2)$, where $\sigma_t^2 = \omega + \beta\sigma_{t-1}^2 + \alpha\eta_{dt}^2$.[9] They model the expected return as linear in the variance

---

[9]In fact they use a more general asymmetric model, the quadratic GARCH or QGARCH model of Sentana (1991). This is to allow the model to fit asymmetry in returns even in the absence of volatility feedback. However the basic idea is more simply illustrated using a standard GARCH model.

of dividend news: $E_t[r_{t+1}] = \gamma_0 + \gamma_1 \sigma_t^2$. These assumptions imply that the revision in expectations of all future returns is a multiple of today's volatility shock $(\eta_{d,t+1}^2 - \sigma_t^2)$:

$$
\begin{aligned}
\eta_{r,t+1} &= E_{t+1}\left[\sum_{j=1}^{\infty} \rho^j r_{t+1+j}\right] - E_t\left[\sum_{j=1}^{\infty} \rho^j r_{t+1+j}\right] \\
&= \theta(\eta_{d,t+1}^2 - \sigma_t^2), \quad\quad\quad\quad\quad\quad (12.2.41)
\end{aligned}
$$

where $\theta = \gamma_1 \rho \alpha / (1 - \rho(\alpha + \beta))$. The coefficient θ is large when γ_1 is large (for then expected returns move strongly with volatility), when α is large (for then shocks feed strongly into future volatility), and when $\alpha + \beta$ is large (for then volatility shocks have persistent effects on expected returns). Substituting into (12.2.40), the implied process for returns is

$$
r_{t+1} = \gamma_0 + \gamma_1 \sigma_t^2 + \eta_{d,t+1} - \theta(\eta_{d,t+1}^2 - \sigma_t^2). \quad\quad (12.2.42)
$$

This is not a GARCH process, but a quadratic function of a GARCH process. It implies that returns are negatively skewed because a large negative realization of $\eta_{d,t+1}$ will be amplified by the quadratic term whereas a large positive realization will be damped by the quadratic term. The intuition is that any large shock of either sign raises expected future volatility and required returns, driving down the stock return today. Conversely, "no news is good news"; if $\eta_{d,t+1}=0$ this lowers expected future volatility and raises the stock return today. Campbell and Hentschel find much stronger evidence for a positive price of risk γ_1 when they estimate the model (12.2.42) than when they simply estimate a standard GARCH-M model. Their results suggest that both the volatility feedback effect and the leverage effect contribute to the asymmetric behavior of stock market volatility.

12.3 Nonparametric Estimation

In some financial applications we may be led to a functional relation between two variables Y and X without the benefit of a structural model to restrict the parametric form of the relation. In these situations, we can use *nonparametric* estimation techniques to capture a wide variety of nonlinearities without recourse to any one particular specification of the nonlinear relation. In contrast to the relatively highly structured or *parametric* approach to estimating nonlinearities described in Sections 12.1 and 12.2, nonparametric estimation requires few assumptions about the nature of the nonlinearities. However, this is not without cost—nonparametric estimation is highly data-intensive and is generally not effective for smaller sample sizes. Moreover, nonparametric estimation is especially prone to *overfitting*, a problem that cannot be easily overcome by statistical methods (see Section 12.5 below).

Perhaps the most commonly used nonparametric estimators are *smooth-ing* estimators, in which observational errors are reduced by averaging the data in sophisticated ways. Kernel regression, orthogonal series expansion, projection pursuit, nearest-neighbor estimators, average derivative estima-tors, splines, and artificial neural networks are all examples of smoothing. To understand the motivation for such averaging, suppose that we wish to estimate the relation between two variables Y_t and X_t which satisfy

$$Y_t = m(X_t) + \epsilon_t, \qquad t = 1, \ldots, T, \qquad (12.3.1)$$

where $m(\cdot)$ is an arbitrary fixed but unknown nonlinear function and $\{\epsilon_t\}$ is a zero-mean IID process.

Consider estimating $m(\cdot)$ at a particular date t_0 for which $X_{t_0} = x_0$, and suppose that for this one observation X_{t_0}, we can obtain *repeated* indepen-dent observations of the variable Y_{t_0}, say $Y_{t_0}^1 = y_1, \ldots, Y_{t_0}^n = y_n$. Then a natural estimator of the function $m(\cdot)$ at the point x_0 is

$$\hat{m}(x_0) = \frac{1}{n}\sum_{i=1}^{n} y_i = \frac{1}{n}\sum_{i=1}^{n} [\, m(x_0) + \epsilon_t^i \,] \qquad (12.3.2)$$

$$= m(x_0) + \frac{1}{n}\sum_{i=1}^{n} \epsilon_t^i, \qquad (12.3.3)$$

and by the Law of Large Numbers, the second term in (12.3.3) becomes negligible for large n.

Of course, if $\{Y_t\}$ is a time series, we do not have the luxury of repeated observations for a given X_t. However, if we assume that the function $m(\cdot)$ is sufficiently smooth, then for time-series observations X_t near the value x_0, the corresponding values of Y_t should be close to $m(x_0)$. In other words, if $m(\cdot)$ is sufficiently smooth, then in a small neighborhood around x_0, $m(x_0)$ will be nearly constant and may be estimated by taking an average of the Y_t's that correspond to those X_t's near x_0. The closer the X_t's are to the value x_0, the closer an average of corresponding Y_t's will be to $m(x_0)$. This argues for a *weighted* average of the Y_t's, where the weights decline as the X_t's get farther away from x_0. This weighted average procedure of estimating $m(x)$ is the essence of smoothing. More formally, for any arbitrary x, a smoothing estimator of $m(x)$ may be expressed as

$$\hat{m}(x) \equiv \frac{1}{T}\sum_{t=1}^{T} \omega_{t,T}(x) Y_t, \qquad (12.3.4)$$

where the weights $\{\omega_{t,T}(x)\}$ are large for those Y_t's paired with X_t's near x, and small for those Y_t's with X_t's far from x.

To implement such a procedure, we must define what we mean by "near" and "far". If we choose too large a neighborhood around x to compute the average, the weighted average will be too smooth and will not exhibit the genuine nonlinearities of $m(\cdot)$. If we choose too small a neighborhood around x, the weighted average will be too variable, reflecting noise as well as the variations in $m(\cdot)$. Therefore, the weights $\{\omega_{t,T}(x)\}$ must be chosen carefully to balance these two considerations. We shall address this and other related issues explicitly in Sections 12.3.1 to 12.3.3 and Section 12.5.

12.3.1 Kernel Regression

An important smoothing technique for estimating $m(\cdot)$ is *kernel regression*. In the kernel regression model, the weight function $\omega_{t,T}(x)$ is constructed from a probability density function $K(x)$, also called a *kernel*:

$$K(x) \geq 0, \qquad \int K(u)\,du = 1. \tag{12.3.5}$$

Despite the fact that $K(x)$ is a probability density function, it plays no probabilistic role in the subsequent analysis—it is merely a convenient method for computing a weighted average, and does *not* imply, for example, that X is distributed according to $K(x)$ (which would be a parametric assumption).

By rescaling the kernel with respect to a variable $h>0$, we can change its spread by varying h if we define:

$$K_h(u) \equiv \frac{1}{h}K(u/h), \qquad \int K_h(u)\,du = 1. \tag{12.3.6}$$

Now we can define the weight function to be used in the weighted average (12.3.4) as

$$\omega_{t,T}(x) \equiv K_h(x - X_t)/g_h(x) \tag{12.3.7}$$

$$g_h(x) \equiv \frac{1}{T}\sum_{t=1}^{T} K_h(x - X_t). \tag{12.3.8}$$

If h is very small, the averaging will be done with respect to a rather small neighborhood around each of the X_t's. If h is very large, the averaging will be over larger neighborhoods of the X_t's. Therefore, controlling the degree of averaging amounts to adjusting the smoothing parameter h, also known as the *bandwidth*.[10] Substituting (12.3.8) into (12.3.4) yields the *Nadaraya-Watson* kernel estimator $\hat{m}_h(x)$ of $m(x)$:

$$\hat{m}_h(x) = \frac{1}{T}\sum_{t=1}^{T} \omega_{t,T}(x)Y_t = \frac{\sum_{t=1}^{T} K_h(x - X_t)Y_t}{\sum_{t=1}^{T} K_h(x - X_t)}. \tag{12.3.9}$$

---

[10]Choosing the appropriate bandwidth is discussed more fully in Section 12.3.2.

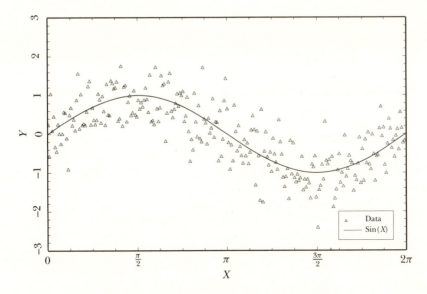

Figure 12.4. *Simulation of $Y_t = \mathrm{Sin}(X_t) + 0.5\epsilon_t$*

Under certain regularity conditions on the shape of the kernel K and the magnitudes and behavior of the weights as the sample size grows, it may be shown that $\hat{m}_h(x)$ converges to $m(x)$ asymptotically in several ways (see Härdle [1990] for further details). This convergence property holds for a wide class of kernels, but for the remainder of this chapter and in our empirical examples we shall use the most popular choice of kernel, the Gaussian kernel:

$$\mathrm{K}_h(x) = \frac{1}{h\sqrt{2\pi}} e^{-\frac{x^2}{2h^2}}. \tag{12.3.10}$$

An Illustration of Kernel Regression

To illustrate the power of kernel regression in capturing nonlinear relations, we apply this smoothing technique to an artificial dataset constructed by Monte Carlo simulation. Denote by $\{X_t\}$ a sequence of 500 observations which take on values between 0 and 2π at evenly spaced increments, and let $\{Y_t\}$ be related to $\{X_t\}$ through the following nonlinear relation:

$$Y_t = \mathrm{Sin}(X_t) + 0.5\epsilon_t \tag{12.3.11}$$

where $\{\epsilon_t\}$ is a sequence of IID pseudorandom standard normal variates. Using the simulated data $\{X_t, Y_t\}$ (see Figure 12.4), we shall attempt to estimate the conditional expectation $\mathrm{E}[Y_t \mid X_t] = \mathrm{Sin}(X_t)$, using kernel regression. To do this, we apply the Nadaraya-Watson estimator (12.3.9) with a Gaussian kernel to the data, and vary the bandwidth parameter h between $0.1\hat{\sigma}_x$ and $0.5\hat{\sigma}_x$ where $\hat{\sigma}_x$ is the sample standard deviation of $\{X_t\}$. By varying h in units of standard deviation, we are implicitly normalizing the explanatory variable X_t by its own standard deviation, as (12.3.10) suggests.

For each value of h, we plot the kernel estimator as a function of X_t, and these plots are given in Figures 12.5a to 12.5c. Observe that for a bandwidth of $0.1\hat{\sigma}_x$, the kernel estimator is too choppy—the bandwidth is too small to provide sufficient local averaging to recover $\text{Sin}(X_t)$. While the kernel estimator does pick up the cyclical nature of the data, it is also picking up random variations due to noise, which may be eliminated by increasing the bandwidth and consequently widening the range of local averaging.

Figure 12.5b shows the kernel estimator for a larger bandwidth of $0.3\hat{\sigma}_x$, which is much smoother and a closer fit to the true conditional expectation.

As the bandwidth is increased, the local averaging is performed over successively wider ranges, and the variability of the kernel estimator (as a function of x) is reduced. Figure 12.5c plots the kernel estimator with a bandwidth of $0.5\sigma_x$, which is too smooth since some of the genuine variation of the sine function has been eliminated along with the noise. In the limit, the kernel estimator approaches the sample average of $\{Y_t\}$, and all the variability of Y_t as a function of X_t is lost.

12.3.2 Optimal Bandwidth Selection

It is apparent from the example in Section 12.3.1 that choosing the proper bandwidth is critical in any application of kernel regression. There are several methods for selecting an optimal bandwidth; the most common of these is the method of *cross-validation*, popular because of its robustness and asymptotic optimality (see Härdle [1990, Chapter 5] for further details). In this approach, the bandwidth is chosen to minimize a weighted-average squared error of the kernel estimator. In particular, for a sample of T observations $\{X_t, Y_t\}_{t=1}^{t=T}$, let

$$\hat{m}_{h,j}(X_j) = \frac{1}{T} \sum_{t \neq j} \omega_{t,T}(X_j) Y_t \tag{12.3.12}$$

which is simply the kernel estimator based on the dataset with observation j deleted, *evaluated* at the jth observation X_j. Then the cross-validation function $\text{CV}(h)$ is defined as

$$\text{CV}(h) = \frac{1}{T} \sum_{t=1}^{T} [Y_t - \hat{m}_{h,t}(X_t)]^2 \delta(X_t), \tag{12.3.13}$$

where $\delta(X_t)$ is a nonnegative weight function that is required to reduce boundary effects (see Härdle [1990, p. 162] for further discussion). The

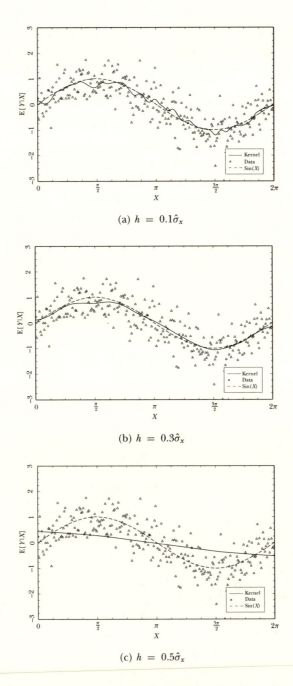

(a) $h = 0.1\hat{\sigma}_x$

(b) $h = 0.3\hat{\sigma}_x$

(c) $h = 0.5\hat{\sigma}_x$

Figure 12.5. *Kernel Estimator*

function CV(h) is called the cross-validation function because it validates the success of the kernel estimator in fitting $\{Y_t\}$ across the T subsamples $\{X_t, Y_t\}_{t \neq j}$, each with one observation omitted. The optimal bandwidth is the one that minimizes this function.

12.3.3 Average Derivative Estimators

For many financial applications, we wish to relate Y_t to *several* variables $X_{1t}, \ldots, X_{kt}$ nonparametrically. For example, we may wish to model the expected returns of stocks and bonds as a nonlinear function of several factors: the market return, interest rate spreads, dividend yield, etc. (see Lo and MacKinlay [1996]). Such a task is considerably more ambitious than the univariate example of Section 12.3.1. To see why, consider the case of five independent variables and, without loss of generality, let these five variables all take on values in the interval $[0, 1]$. Even if we divide the domain of each variable into only ten equally spaced pieces, this would yield a total of $10^5 = 100{,}000$ neighborhoods each of width 0.10; hence we would need at least 100,000 observations to ensure an average of just one data point per neighborhood! This *curse of dimensionality* can only be solved by placing restrictions on the kinds of nonlinearities that are allowable.

For example, suppose a *linear* combination of the X_{it}'s is related to Y_t nonparametrically. This has the advantage of capturing important nonlinearities while providing sufficient structure to permit estimation with reasonable sample sizes. Specifically, consider the following multivariate nonlinear model:

$$Y_t = m(\mathbf{X}_t'\boldsymbol{\beta}) + \epsilon_t, \qquad \mathrm{E}[\epsilon_t|\mathbf{X}_t] = 0 \qquad (12.3.14)$$

where $\mathbf{X}_t = [X_{1t} \ldots X_{kt}]'$ is now a $(k \times 1)$ vector and $m(\cdot)$ is some arbitrary but fixed nonlinear function. The function $m(\cdot)$ may be estimated by the following two-step procedure: (1) estimate $\boldsymbol{\beta}$ with an average derivative estimator $\hat{\boldsymbol{\beta}}$; and (2) estimate $m(\cdot)$ with a kernel regression of Y_t on $\mathbf{X}_t'\hat{\boldsymbol{\beta}}$.

Stoker (1986) observes that the coefficients $\boldsymbol{\beta}$ of (12.3.14) may be estimated up to a scale factor by ordinary least squares if either of the following two conditions is true: (1) the $\mathbf{X}_t$'s are multivariate normal vectors; or, more generally, (2) $\mathrm{E}[X_{it} \mid \mathbf{X}_t'\boldsymbol{\beta}]$ is linear in $\mathbf{X}_t'\boldsymbol{\beta}$ for $i = 1, \ldots, k$.[11] If neither of these conditions holds, Stoker (1986) proposes an ingenious estimator, the *average derivative* estimator, which can estimate $\boldsymbol{\beta}$ consistently (see also Stoker [1992]).

---

[11] This second condition is satisfied by multivariate normal $\mathbf{X}_t$'s but is also satisfied for non-normal elliptically symmetric distributions. See Chamberlain (1983b), Chung and Goldberger (1984), Deaton and Irish (1984), and Ruud (1983).

Average derivative estimators are based on the fact that the expectation of the derivative of $m(\cdot)$ with respect to the $\mathbf{X}_t$'s is proportional to β:

$$\mathrm{E}\left[\frac{\partial m}{\partial \mathbf{X}_t}\right] = \mathrm{E}[m'(\mathbf{X}_t'\beta)]\beta \propto \beta. \qquad (12.3.15)$$

Therefore, an estimator of the average derivative is equivalent to an estimator of β up to a scale factor, and this scale factor is irrelevant for our purposes since it may be subsumed by $m(\cdot)$ and consistently estimated by kernel regression.

There are several average derivative estimators available: the *direct*, *indirect*, and *slope* estimators. Stoker (1991, Theorem 1) shows that they are all asymptotically equivalent; however, Stoker (1992, Chapter 3) favors the *indirect slope estimator* (ISE) for two reasons. First, if the relation between Y_t and $\mathbf{X}_t$ is truly linear, the indirect slope estimator is still unbiased whereas the others are not. Second, the indirect slope estimator requires less precision from its nonparametric component estimators because of the ISE's ratio form (see below).

Heuristically, the indirect slope estimator $\hat{\beta}_{\mathrm{ISE}}$ exploits the fact that the unknown parameter vector β is proportional to the covariance between the dependent variable Y and the negative of the derivative of the logarithm of the marginal density of independent variables $\mathbf{X}_t$, denoted by $l(\cdot)$. Therefore, by estimating $\mathrm{Cov}[Y, l(\cdot)]$, we obtain a consistent estimator of β up to scale. This covariance may be estimated by computing the sample covariance between Y and the sample counterpart to $l(\cdot)$.

More formally, $\hat{\beta}_{\mathrm{ISE}}$ may be viewed as an instrumental variables (IV) estimator (see Section A.1 of the Appendix) of the regression of Y_t on $\mathbf{X}_t$ with the instrument matrix $\mathbf{H}$:

$$\hat{\beta}_{\mathrm{ISE}} = (\mathbf{H'X})^{-1}\mathbf{H'Y}, \qquad (12.3.16)$$

where $\mathbf{Y} \equiv [Y_1 \ldots Y_T]'$,

$$\mathbf{H} \equiv \begin{bmatrix} 1 & \mathbf{I}_b(\mathbf{X}_1)\hat{l}(\mathbf{X}_1)' \\ \vdots & \vdots \\ 1 & \mathbf{I}_b(\mathbf{X}_t)\hat{l}(\mathbf{X}_t)' \\ \vdots & \vdots \\ 1 & \mathbf{I}_b(\mathbf{X}_T)\hat{l}(\mathbf{X}_T)' \end{bmatrix}, \qquad \mathbf{X} \equiv \begin{bmatrix} 1 & \mathbf{X}_1' \\ \vdots & \vdots \\ 1 & \mathbf{X}_t' \\ \vdots & \vdots \\ 1 & \mathbf{X}_T' \end{bmatrix}, \qquad (12.3.17)$$

$\hat{l}(\cdot)$ is an estimator of the negative of the derivative of the log of the marginal density of $\mathbf{X}_t$, and $\mathbf{I}_b(\mathbf{x})$ is an indicator function that trims a portion of the sample with estimated marginal densities lower than a fixed constant b:

$$\mathbf{I}_b(\mathbf{x}) \equiv \mathbf{1}[\hat{f}(\mathbf{x}) > b]. \qquad (12.3.18)$$

In most empirical applications, the constant b is set so that between 1% and 5% of the sample is trimmed.

To obtain $\hat{l}(\cdot)$, observe that if $f(\mathbf{x})$ denotes the marginal density of $\mathbf{X}_t$, then the Gaussian kernel estimator of $f(\mathbf{x})$ is given by[12]

$$\hat{f}(\mathbf{x}) \;=\; \frac{1}{T}\frac{1}{h^k}\sum_{t=1}^{T}\mathrm{K}\left(\frac{\mathbf{x}-\mathbf{X}_t}{h}\right), \tag{12.3.19}$$

where

$$\mathrm{K}\left(\frac{\mathbf{x}-\mathbf{X}_t}{h}\right) \;\equiv\; \prod_{i=1}^{k}\mathrm{K}_i\left(\frac{x_i-X_{it}}{h}\right) \tag{12.3.20}$$

$$\;=\; (2\pi)^{-k/2}\exp\left[-\frac{1}{2h^2}(\mathbf{x}-\mathbf{X}_t)'(\mathbf{x}-\mathbf{X}_t)\right]. \tag{12.3.21}$$

Therefore, we have

$$\hat{f}'(\mathbf{x}) \;=\; \frac{1}{T}\frac{1}{h^{k+1}}\sum_{t=1}^{T}\mathrm{K}'\left(\frac{\mathbf{x}-\mathbf{X}_t}{h}\right) \tag{12.3.22}$$

$$\;=\; -\frac{1}{T}\frac{1}{h^{k+1}}\sum_{t=1}^{T}\mathrm{K}\left(\frac{\mathbf{x}-\mathbf{X}_t}{h}\right)\cdot(\mathbf{x}-\mathbf{X}_t)/h, \tag{12.3.23}$$

and we can define $\hat{l}(\mathbf{x})$ to be

$$\hat{l}(\mathbf{x}) \;\equiv\; -\frac{\hat{f}'(\mathbf{x})}{\hat{f}(\mathbf{x})}, \tag{12.3.24}$$

Despite the multivariate nature of $f(\cdot)$, observe that there is still only a single bandwidth to adjust in the kernel estimator (12.3.19). As in the univariate case, the bandwidth controls the degree of local averaging, but now over multidimensional neighborhoods. As a practical matter, the numerical properties of this local averaging procedure may be improved by normalizing all the X_{it}'s by their own standard deviations before computing $\hat{f}(\cdot)$, and then multiplying each of the β_i's by the standard deviation of the corresponding X_{it} to undo the normalization.

---

[12]Note that the bandwidth h implicit in $\hat{f}(\mathbf{x})$ is, in general, different from the bandwidth of the nonparametric estimator of $m(\cdot)$ in (12.3.14). Cross-validation techniques may be used to select both; however, this may be computationally too demanding and simple rules-of-thumb may suffice.

12.3.4 Application: Estimating State-Price Densities

One of the most important theoretical advances in the economics of invest-ment under uncertainty is the time-state preference model of Arrow (1964) and Debreu (1959) in which they introduce primitive securities, each pay-ing $1 in one specific state of nature and nothing otherwise. Now known as *Arrow-Debreu* securities, they are the fundamental building blocks from which we have derived much of our current understanding of economic equilibrium in an uncertain environment.

In practice, since true Arrow-Debreu securities are not yet traded on any organized exchange, Arrow-Debreu prices are not observable.[13] However, using nonparametric techniques—specifically, multivariate kernel regres-sion—Aït-Sahalia and Lo (1996) develop estimators for such prices, known as a *state-price density* (SPD) in the continuous-state case. The SPD contains a wealth of information concerning the pricing (and hedging) of risky assets in an economy. In principle, it can be used to price other assets, even assets that are currently not traded (see Aït-Sahalia and Lo [1995] for examples).[14]

More importantly, SPDs contain much formation about preferences and asset price dynamics. For example, if parametric restrictions are imposed on the data-generating process of asset prices, the SPD estimator may be used to infer the preferences of the representative agent in an equilibrium model of asset prices (see, for example, Bick [1990] and He and Leland [1993]). Alternatively, if specific preferences are imposed, the SPD estima-tor may be used to infer the data-generating process of asset prices (see, for example, Derman and Kani [1994], Dupire [1994], Jackwerth and Ru-binstein [1995], Longstaff [1992, 1994], Rady [1994], Rubinstein [1985], and Shimko [1991, 1993]). Indeed, Rubinstein (1985) has observed that any two of the following implies the third: (1) the representative agent's preferences; (2) asset price dynamics; and (3) the SPD.

Definition of the State-Price Density
To define the SPD formally, consider a standard dynamic exchange economy (see Chapter 8) in which the equilibrium price p_t of a security at date t with a single liquidating payoff $Y(C_T)$ at date T that is a function of aggregate consumption C_T is given by:

$$P_t = E_t[Y(C_T)M_{t,T}], \qquad M_{t,T} \equiv \frac{\delta^{T-t}U'(C_T)}{U'(C_t)} \qquad (12.3.25)$$

---

[13]This may soon change with the advent of *supershares*, first proposed by Garman (1978) and Hakansson (1976, 1977) and currently under development by Leland O'Brien Rubinstein Associates, Inc. See Mason, Merton, Perold, and Tufano (1995) for further details.

[14]Of course, markets must be dynamically complete for such prices to be meaningful—see, for example, Constantinides (1982). This assumption is almost always adopted, either explicitly or implicitly, in parametric derivative pricing models, and we adopt it as well.

where $M_{t,T}$ is the marginal rate of substitution between dates t and T, and δ is the rate of time preference. This well-known equilibrium asset-pricing relation equates current price of the security to its expected discounted future payoff, discounted using the stochastic discount factor.

Lucas (1978) observes that (12.3.25) need not imply a martingale process for $\{P_t\}$, supporting Leroy's (1973) contention that the martingale property is neither a necessary nor sufficient condition for rationally determined asset prices. However, assuming that the conditional distribution of future consumption has a density representation $f_t(\cdot)$, the conditional expectation in (12.3.25) can be re-expressed in the following way:

$$
\mathrm{E}_t[Y(C_T)M_{t,T}] = \int Y(C_T)\frac{\delta^{T-t}U_T'(C_T)}{U_t'(C_t)}f_t(C_T)\,dC_T \tag{12.3.26}
$$

$$
= e^{-r_{t,T}(T-t)}\int Y(C_T)f_t^*(C_T)\,dC_T \tag{12.3.27}
$$

$$
= e^{-r_{t,T}(T-t)}\mathrm{E}_t^*[Y(C_T)], \tag{12.3.28}
$$

where

$$
f_t^*(C_T) \equiv \frac{M_{t,T}\,f_t(C_T)}{\int M_{t,T}\,f_t(C_T)\,dC_T}, \tag{12.3.29}
$$

and $r_{t,T}$ is the continuously compounded net rate of return between t and T of an asset promising one unit of consumption at T; i.e., it is the return on the riskless asset.

This version of the Euler equation shows that an asset's current price can be expressed as its discounted expected payoff, discounted at the riskless rate of interest (see Chapter 8 for a more detailed discussion). However, the expectation is taken with respect to the SPD f^*, a marginal-rate-of-substitution-weighted probability density function, not the original probability density function f of future consumption. In a continuous-time setting, f^* is also known as the *risk-neutral pricing density* (Cox and Ross [1976]) or the *equivalent martingale measure* (Harrison and Kreps [1979]).[15]

Once f_t^* is obtained, it can be used to price any asset at date t with a single liquidating payoff at date T that is an arbitrary function of consumption C_T.[16] SPDs also provide the link between preference-based equilibrium models of the type discussed in Chapter 8 and arbitrage-based derivative pricing models of the type discussed in Chapter 9. Indeed, implicit in the

---

[15]See Huang and Litzenberger (1988, Chapter 5) for a more detailed discussion of SPDs.

[16]Securities with multiple payoffs and infinite horizons can also be priced by the SPD, but in these cases the SPD must be appropriately redefined to capture the time-variation in the marginal rates of substitution—see Breeden and Litzenberger (1978) and Radner (1982) for further discussion.

prices of *all* financial securities—derivatives or not—are the prices of Arrow-Debreu securities, and these prices may be used to value all other securities, no matter how complex.

Pricing Derivatives with SPDs
Under some regularity conditions, we may express f^* as an explicit function of t and T so that a single SPD $f^*(C_T; t, T)$ may be used to price an asset at any date t with a single liquidating payoff $Y(C_T)$ at any future date $T \geq t$ (see footnote 16):

$$P_t = e^{-r_{t,T}(T-t)} \int Y(C_T) f^*(C_T; t, T) dC_T, \qquad (12.3.30)$$

and we shall adopt this convention for notational simplicity. For example, a European call option on date-T aggregate consumption C_T with strike price X has a payoff function $Y(C_T) = \max[C_T - X, 0]$ and hence its date-t price G_t is simply

$$G_t = e^{-r_{t,T}(T-t)} \int \max[C_T - X, 0] f^*(C_T; t, T) dC_T. \qquad (12.3.31)$$

Even the most complex path-independent derivative security can be priced and hedged according to (12.3.30). For example, consider a security with the highly nonlinear payoff function:

$$Y(C) = \frac{a - b}{1 + \exp[-\beta(C - \alpha)]} + b,$$
$$a > 0, \quad b < 0 \qquad (12.3.32)$$

$$\alpha \equiv c + \frac{1}{\beta} \log(-a/b). \qquad (12.3.33)$$

This payoff function is a smoothed version of the payoff to an option portfolio commonly known as *bullish vertical spread*, in which a call option with a low strike is purchased and a call option with a high strike price is written (see Figure 12.5 and Cox and Rubinstein [1985, Chapter 1] for further details).

Extracting SPDs from Derivatives Prices
There is an even closer relation between option prices and SPDs than (12.3.30) suggests, which Ross (1976), Banz and Miller (1978), and Breeden and Litzenberger (1978) first discovered. In particular, they show that the second derivative of the call-pricing function G_t with respect to the strike

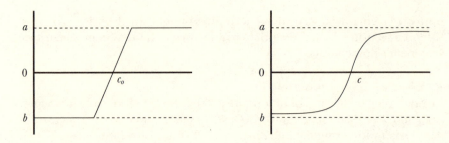

Figure 12.6. *Bullish Vertical Spread Payoff Function and Smoothed Version*

price X must equal the SPD:

$$\frac{\partial^2 G_t}{\partial X^2} = e^{-r_{t,T}(T-t)}f^*. \tag{12.3.34}$$

Therefore, impounded in every option pricing formula is the SPD f^*.

To estimate the SPD using (12.3.34), we require a call option pricing formula. Although many parametric pricing formulas exist (see Hull [1993, Chapter 17] for some popular examples), Aït-Sahalia and Lo (1996) construct a *nonparametric* pricing formula that places fewer restrictions—primarily smoothness and weak dependence—on the data-generating process of the underlying asset's price. While parametric formulas such as those of Black and Scholes (1973) and Merton (1973) offer great advantages when the parametric assumptions (e.g., geometric Brownian motion) are satisfied, nonparametric methods are robust to violations of these assumptions. Since there is some empirical evidence that casts doubt on such assumptions, at least for stock indexes,[17] the nonparametric approach may have some important advantages.[18]

Given observed call option prices $\{G_i, X_i, \tau_i\}$ (where $\tau_i \equiv T_i - t_i$), the prices of the underlying asset $\{P_i\}$, and the riskless rate of interest $\{r_{\tau_i}\}$, we may construct the smooth nonparametric call-pricing function as

$$\hat{G}(P, X, \tau, r_\tau) = \hat{E}[G \mid P, X, \tau, r_\tau] \tag{12.3.35}$$

using a multivariate kernel K, formed as a product of $d=4$ univariate kernels:

$$K_h(P, X, \tau, r_\tau) \equiv k_{h_p}(P)k_{h_x}(X)k_{h_\tau}(\tau)k_{h_r}(r_\tau), \tag{12.3.36}$$

---

[17]See Lo and MacKinlay (1988), for example.

[18]See Hutchinson, Lo, and Poggio (1994) and Aït-Sahalia (1996a) for other nonparametric option pricing alternatives.

and hence

$$\hat{G}(P, X, \tau, r_\tau) = \frac{\sum_{i=1}^n k_{h_p}(P - P_i)k_{h_x}(X - X_i)k_{h_\tau}(\tau - \tau_i)k_{h_r}(r_\tau - r_{\tau_i})C_i}{\sum_{i=1}^n k_{h_p}(P - P_i)k_{h_x}(X - X_i)k_{h_\tau}(\tau - \tau_i)k_{h_r}(r_\tau - r_{\tau_i})}.$$
(12.3.37)

The option's delta and SPD estimator then follow by differentiating $\hat{P}$:

$$\hat{\Delta}(P, X, \tau, r_\tau) = \frac{\partial \hat{G}(P, X, \tau, r_\tau)}{\partial P}$$
(12.3.38)

$$\hat{f}^*(P_T \mid P, \tau, r_\tau) = e^{r_\tau \tau}\left[\frac{\partial^2 \hat{G}(P, X, \tau, r_\tau)}{\partial X^2}\right]_{X=P_T}.$$
(12.3.39)

Under standard regularity assumptions on the data-generating process as well as smoothness assumptions on the true call-pricing function, Aït-Sahalia and Lo (1996) show that the estimators of the option price, the option's delta, and the SPD are all consistent and asymptotically normal, and they provide explicit expressions for the asymptotic variances.

Armed with the SPD, any derivative security with characteristic ζ and payoff function $Y(\zeta, P_T)$ at $T=t+\tau$ can now be priced at date t by the pricing function:

$$G(P, \zeta, \tau, r_\tau) = e^{-r_\tau \tau}\int_0^\infty Y(\zeta, P_T)\,\hat{f}^*(P_T \mid P, \tau, r_\tau)\,dP_T.$$
(12.3.40)

If the payoff function $Y(\cdot)$ is twice-differentiable in P_T, then

$$G(P, \zeta, \tau, r_\tau) = e^{-r_\tau \tau}\int_0^\infty Y(\zeta, P_T)\,\hat{f}^*(P_T \mid P, \tau, r_\tau)\,dP_T$$
(12.3.41)

$$= \int_0^\infty Y(\zeta, P_T)\frac{\partial^2 \hat{G}}{\partial P_T^2}\,dP_T$$
(12.3.42)

$$= \int_0^\infty \frac{\partial^2 Y(\zeta, P_T)}{\partial P_T^2}\,\hat{G}\,dP_T.$$
(12.3.43)

Integrating against $\hat{G}$ instead of its second derivative speeds up the convergence rate of the estimator—$\hat{G}$ converges at speed $n^{1/2}h^{4/2}$ and its integral against a smooth function of P_T converges at speed $n^{1/2}h^{3/2}$, whereas the second derivative of $\hat{G}$ converges at $n^{1/2}h^{8/2}$ and its integral against a smooth function of P_T at $n^{1/2}h^{6/2}$. A factor of $h^{3/2}$ is gained in the speed of convergence by integrating the second derivative of the payoff function—when it exists—against $\hat{G}$ instead of integrating the payoff function itself against the second derivative of $\hat{G}$.

Aït-Sahalia and Lo (1996) apply this estimator to the pricing and delta-hedging of S&P 500 call and put options using daily data obtained from the Chicago Board Options Exchange for the sample period from January 4, 1993 to December 31, 1993, yielding a total sample size of 14,431 observations. The estimates of the SPDs exhibit negative skewness and excess kurtosis, a common feature of historical stock returns (see Chapter 1 for example). Also, unlike many parametric option pricing models, the SPD-generated option pricing formula is capable of capturing persistent volatility "smiles" and other empirical features of market prices.

12.4 Artificial Neural Networks

An alternative to nonparametric regression that has received much recent attention in the engineering and business communities is the *artificial neural network*. Artificial neural networks may be viewed as a nonparametric technique, hence these models would fit quite naturally in Section 12.3. However, because initially they drew their motivation from biological phenomena—in particular, from the physiology of nerve cells—they have become part of a separate, distinct, and burgeoning literature (see Hertz, Krogh, and Palmer [1991], Hutchinson, Lo, and Poggio [1994], Poggio and Girosi [1990], and White [1992] for overviews of this literature).

To underscore the common nonparametric origins of artificial neural networks, we describe three kinds of networks in this section, collectively known as *learning networks* (see Barron and Barron [1988]). In Section 12.4.1 we introduce the multilayer perceptron, perhaps the most popular type of artificial neural network in the recent literature—this is what the term "neural network" is usually taken to mean. In Sections 12.4.2 and 12.4.3 we present two other techniques that also have network interpretations: radial basis functions, and projection pursuit regression.

12.4.1 Multilayer Perceptrons

Perhaps the simplest example of an artificial neural network is the *binary threshold model* of McCulloch and Pitts (1943), in which an *output* variable Y taking on only the values zero and one is nonlinearly related to a collection of J *input* variables X_j, $j = 1, \ldots, J$ in the following way:

$$Y = g\left(\sum_{j=1}^{J} \beta_j X_j - \mu \right) \qquad (12.4.1)$$

$$g(u) = \begin{cases} 1 & \text{if } u \geq 0 \\ 0 & \text{if } u < 0. \end{cases} \qquad (12.4.2)$$

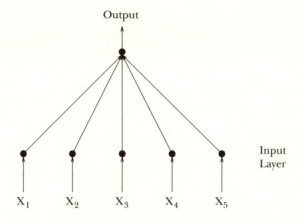

Figure 12.7. *Binary Threshold Model*

According to (12.4.1), each input X_j is weighted by a coefficient β_j, called the *connection strength,* and then summed across all inputs. If this weighted sum exceeds the *threshold* μ, then the artificial neuron is switched on or *activated* via the *activation function* $g(\cdot)$; otherwise it remains dormant. This simple network is often represented graphically as in Figure 12.7, in which the *input layer* is said to be *connected* to the *output layer.*

Generalizations of the binary threshold model form the basis of most current applications of artificial neural network models. In particular, to allow for continuous-valued outputs, the Heaviside activation function (12.4.2) is replaced by the logistic function (see Figure 12.8):

$$g(u) = \frac{1}{1 + e^{-u}}. \tag{12.4.3}$$

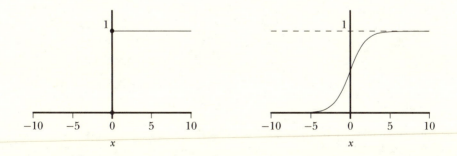

Figure 12.8. *Comparison of Heaviside and Logistic Activation Functions*

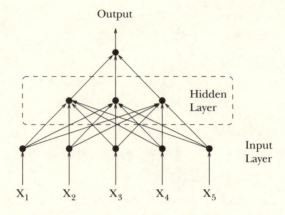

Figure 12.9. *Multilayer Perceptron with a Single Hidden Layer*

Also, without loss of generality, we set μ to zero since it is always possible to model a nonzero activation level by defining the first input $X_1=1$ in which case the negative of that input's connection strength $-\beta_1$ becomes the activation level.

But perhaps the most important extension of the binary threshold model is the introduction of a *hidden layer* between the input layer and the output layer. Specifically, let

$$Y = h\left(\sum_{k=1}^{K} \alpha_k g(\beta_k' \mathbf{X})\right) \tag{12.4.4}$$

$$\beta_k = \begin{bmatrix} \beta_{k1} & \beta_{k2} & \cdots & \beta_{kJ} \end{bmatrix}', \quad \mathbf{X} = \begin{bmatrix} X_1 & X_2 & \cdots & X_J \end{bmatrix}',$$

where $h(\cdot)$ is another arbitrary nonlinear activation function. In this case, the inputs are connected to multiple *hidden units*, and at each hidden unit they are weighted (differently) and transformed by the (same) activation function $g(\cdot)$. The output of each hidden unit is then weighted yet again—this time by the α_k's—and summed and transformed by a second activation function $h(\cdot)$. Such a network configuration is an example of a *multilayer perceptron* (MLP)—a single (hidden) layer in this case—and is perhaps the most common type of artificial neural network among recent applications. In contrast to Figure 12.7, the multilayer perceptron has a more complex *network topology* (see Figure 12.9). This can be generalized in the obvious way by adding more hidden layers, hence the term *multilayer* perceptron.

For a given set of inputs and outputs $\{\mathbf{X}_t, Y_t\}$, MLP approximation amounts to estimating the parameters of the MLP network—the vectors β_k and scalars α_k, $k=1, \ldots, K$—typically by minimizing the sum of squared deviations between the output and the network, i.e., $\sum_t [Y_t - \sum_k \alpha_k g(\beta_k' \mathbf{X})]^2$.

In the terminology of this literature, the process of parameter estimation is called *training* the network. This is less pretentious than it may appear to be—an early method of parameter estimation was *backpropagation*, and this does mimic a kind of learning behavior (albeit a very simplistic one).[19] However, White (1992) cites a number of practical disadvantages with backpropagation (numerical instabilities, occasional non-convergence, etc.), hence the preferred method for estimating the parameters of (12.4.4) is nonlinear least-squares.

Even the single hidden-layer MLP (12.4.4) possesses the *universal approximation property*: It can approximate any nonlinear function to an arbitrary degree of accuracy with a suitable number of hidden units (see White [1992]). However, the universal approximation property is shared by many nonparametric estimation techniques, including the nonparametric regression estimator of Section 12.3, and the techniques in Sections 12.4.2 and 12.4.3. Of course, this tells us nothing about the performance of such techniques in practice, and for a given set of data it is possible for one technique to dominate another in accuracy and in other ways.

Perhaps the most important advantage of MLPs is their ability to approximate complex nonlinear relations through the composition of a network of relatively simple functions. This specification lends itself naturally to *parallel processing*, and although there are currently no financial applications that exploit this feature of MLPs, this may soon change as parallel-processing software and hardware become more widely available.

To illustrate the MLP model, we apply it to the artificial dataset generated by (12.3.11). For a network with one hidden layer and five hidden units, denoted by MLP(1,5), with $\Theta(\cdot)$ set to the identity function, we obtain the following model:

$$
\begin{aligned}
\hat{Y}_t \;=\;\; & 5.282 - 14.576g(-1.472 + 1.869X_t) \\
& - 5.411g(-2.628 + 0.641X_t) \\
& - 3.071g(13.288 - 2.347X_t) + 6.320g(-2.009 + 4.009X_t) \\
& + 7.892g(-3.316 + 2.484X_t)
\end{aligned}
\tag{12.4.5}
$$

where $g(u) = 1/(1 + e^{-u})$. This model is plotted in Figure 12.10 and compares well with the kernel estimator described in Section 12.3.1. Despite the fact that (12.4.5) looks nothing like the sine function, nevertheless the MLP performs quite well numerically and is relatively easy to estimate.

---

[19]Backpropagation is essentially the method of *stochastic approximation* first proposed by Robbins and Monro (1951a). See White (1992) for further details.

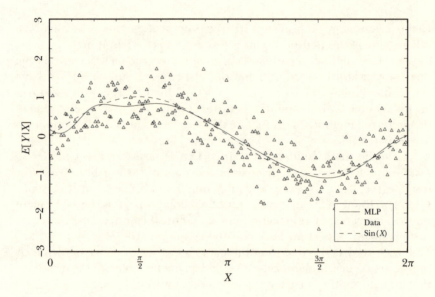

Figure 12.10.   *MLP(1,5) Model of $Y_t = \mathrm{Sin}(X_t) + 0.5\epsilon_t$*

12.4.2 Radial Basis Functions

The class of *radial basis functions* (RBFs) were first used to solve *interpolation* problems—fitting a curve exactly through a set of points (see Powell [1987] for a review). More recently, RBFs have been extended by several researchers to perform the more general task of approximation (see Broomhead and Lowe [1988], Moody and Darken [1989],and Poggio and Girosi [1990]). In particular, Poggio and Girosi (1990) show how RBFs can be derived from the classical *regularization* problem in which some unknown function $Y=m(\mathbf{X})$ is to be approximated given a sparse dataset $(\mathbf{X}_t, Y_t)$ and some smoothness constraints. In terms of our multiple-regression analogy, the d-dimensional vector $\mathbf{X}_t$ are the explanatory variables, Y_t the dependent variable, and $m(\cdot)$ the possibly nonlinear function that is the conditional expectation of Y_t given $\mathbf{X}_t$, and hence

$$Y_t = m(\mathbf{X}_t) + \epsilon_t, \qquad \mathrm{E}[\epsilon_t|\mathbf{X}_t] = 0. \tag{12.4.6}$$

The regularization (or nonparametric estimation) problem may then be viewed as the minimization of the following objective functional:

$$V(m) \equiv \sum_{t=1}^{T} \left(\|\hat{Y}_t - m(\mathbf{X}_t)\|^2 + \lambda \|\mathcal{D}m(\mathbf{X}_t)\|^2 \right), \tag{12.4.7}$$

where $\| \cdot \|$ is some vector norm and $\mathcal{D}$ is a differential operator. The first term of the sum in (12.4.7) is simply the distance between $m(\mathbf{X}_t)$ and the observation Y_t, the second term is a penalty function that is a decreasing function of the smoothness of $m(\cdot)$, and λ controls the tradeoff between smoothness and fit.

In its most general form, and under certain conditions (see, for example, Poggio and Girosi [1990]), the solution to the minimization of (12.4.7) is given by the following expression:

$$\hat{m}(\mathbf{X}_t) = \sum_{k=1}^{K} \beta_k \hat{m}_k(\|\mathbf{X}_t - \mathbf{U}_k\|) + \mathcal{P}(\mathbf{X}_t), \qquad (12.4.8)$$

where $\{\mathbf{U}_k\}$ are d-dimensional vector *centers* (similar to the *knots* of spline functions), $\{\beta_k\}$ are scalar coefficients, $\{\hat{m}_k\}$ are scalar functions, $\mathcal{P}(\cdot)$ is a polynomial, and K is typically much less than the number of observations T in the sample. Such approximants have been termed *hyperbasis functions* by Poggio and Girosi (1990) and are closely related to splines, smoothers such as kernel estimators, and other nonparametric estimators.[20]

For our current purposes, we shall take the vector norm to be a weighted Euclidean norm defined by a $(d \times d)$ weighting-matrix $\mathbf{W}$, and we shall take the polynomial term to be just the linear and constant terms, yielding the following specification for $\hat{m}(\cdot)$:

$$\hat{m}(\mathbf{X}_t) = \alpha_0 + \boldsymbol{\alpha}_1' \mathbf{X}_t + \sum_{k=1}^{k} \beta_k \hat{m}_k \left((\mathbf{X}_t - \mathbf{U}_k)' \mathbf{W}' \mathbf{W} (\mathbf{X}_t - \mathbf{U}_k) \right), \qquad (12.4.9)$$

where α_0 and $\boldsymbol{\alpha}_1$ are the coefficients of the polynomial $\mathcal{P}(\cdot)$. Miccheli (1986) shows that a large class of basis functions $\hat{m}_k(\cdot)$ are appropriate, but the most common choices for basis functions are Gaussians e^{-x/σ^2} and multiquadrics $\sqrt{x+\sigma^2}$.

Networks of this type can generate any real-valued output, but in applications where we have some *a priori* knowledge of the range of the desired outputs, it is computationally more efficient to apply some nonlinear transfer function to the outputs to reflect that knowledge. This will be the case in our application to derivative pricing models, in which some of the RBF networks will be augmented with an *output sigmoid*, which maps the range $(-\infty, \infty)$ into the fixed range $(0, 1)$. In particular, the augmented network will be of the form $g(\hat{m}(\mathbf{x}))$ where $g(u) = 1/(1 + e^{-u})$.

As with MLPs, RBF approximation for a given set of inputs and outputs $(\mathbf{X}_t, Y_t)$, involves estimating the parameters of the RBF network—the

---

[20]To economize on terminology, here we use RBFs to encompass both the interpolation techniques used by Powell (1987) and their subsequent generalizations.

$d(d+1)/2$ unique entries of the matrix $W'W$, the dk elements of the centers $\{\mathbf{U}_k\}$, and the $d+k+1$ coefficients α_0, $\boldsymbol{\alpha}_1$, and $\{\beta_k\}$—typically by nonlinear least-squares, i.e., by minimizing $\sum_t [Y_t - m(\mathbf{X}_t)]^2$ numerically.

12.4.3 Projection Pursuit Regression

Projection pursuit is a method that emerged from the statistics community for analyzing high-dimensional datasets by looking at their low-dimensional projections. Friedman and Stuetzle (1981) developed a version for the nonlinear regression problem called projection pursuit regression (PPR). Similar to MLPs, PPR models are composed of projections of the data, i.e., products of the data with estimated coefficients, but unlike MLPs they also estimate the nonlinear combining functions from the data. Following the notation of Section 12.4.1, the formulation for PPR with a univariate output can be written as

$$m(\mathbf{X}_t) \quad = \quad \alpha_0 + \sum_{k=1}^{K} \alpha_k m_k(\beta_k' \mathbf{X}_t) \tag{12.4.10}$$

where the functions $m_k(\cdot)$ are estimated from the data (typically with a smoother), the $\{\alpha_k\}$ and $\{\beta_k\}$ are coefficients, K is the number of *projections*, and α_0 is commonly taken to be the sample mean of the outputs $m(\mathbf{X}_t)$. The similarities between PPR, RBF, and MLP networks should be apparent from (12.4.10).

12.4.4 Limitations of Learning Networks

Despite the many advantages that learning networks possess for approximating nonlinear functions, they have several important limitations. In particular, there are currently no widely accepted procedures for determining the network architecture in a given application, e.g., the number of hidden layers, the number of hidden units, the specification of the activation function(s), etc. Although some rules of thumb have emerged from casual empirical observation, they are heuristic at best.

Difficulties also arise in training the network. Typically, network parameters are obtained by minimizing the sum of squared errors, but because of the nonlinearities inherent in these specifications, the objective function may not be globally convex and can have many local minima.

Finally, traditional techniques of statistical inference such as significance testing cannot always be applied to network models because of the nesting of layers. For example, if one of the α_k's in (12.4.4) is zero, then the connection strengths β_k of that hidden unit are unidentified. Therefore, even simple significance tests and confidence intervals require complex combinations of maintained hypotheses to be interpreted properly.

12.4.5 Application: Learning the Black-Scholes Formula

Given the power and flexibility of neural networks to approximate complex nonlinear relations, a natural application is to derivative securities whose pricing formulas are highly nonlinear even when they are available in closed form. In particular, Hutchinson, Lo, and Poggio (1994) pose the following challenge: If option prices were truly determined by the Black-Scholes formula exactly, can neural networks "learn" the Black-Scholes formula? In more standard statistical jargon: Can the Black-Scholes formula be estimated nonparametrically via learning networks with a sufficient degree of accuracy to be of practical use?

Hutchinson, Lo, and Poggio (1994) face this challenge by performing Monte Carlo simulation experiments in which various neural networks are trained on artificially generated Black-Scholes option prices and then compared to the Black-Scholes formula both analytically and in out-of-sample hedging experiments to see how close they come. Even with training sets of only six months of daily data, learning network pricing formulas can approximate the Black-Scholes formula with reasonable accuracy.

Specifically, they begin by simulating a two-year sample of daily stock prices, and creating a cross-section of options each day according to the rules used by the Chicago Board Options Exchange with prices given by the Black-Scholes formula. They refer to this two-year sample of stock and (multiple) option prices as a single *training path*, since the network is trained on this sample.[21] Given a simulated training path $\{P(t)\}$ of daily stock prices, they construct a corresponding path of option prices according to the rules of the Chicago Board Options Exchange (CBOE) for introducing options on stocks.

A typical training path is shown in Figure 12.11. Because the options generated for a particular sample path are a function of the (random) stock price path, the size of this data matrix (in terms of number of options and total number of data points) varies across sample paths. For their training set, the number of options per sample path range from 71 to 91, with an average of 81. The total number of data points range from 5,227 to 6,847, with an average of 6,001.

The nonlinear models obtained from neural networks yield estimates

---

[21]They assume that the underlying asset for the simulation experiments is a typical NYSE stock, with an initial price $P(0)$ of $50.00, an annual continuously compounded expected rate of return μ of 10%, and an annual volatility σ of 20%. Under the Black-Scholes assumption of a geometric Brownian motion,

$$dP = \mu P dt + \sigma P dB,$$

and taking the number of days per year to be 253, they draw 506 pseudorandom variates $\{\epsilon_t\}$ from the distribution $\mathcal{N}(\mu/253, \sigma^2/253)$ to obtain two years of daily continuously compounded returns, which are converted to prices with the usual relation $P(t) = P(0)\exp[\sum_{i=1}^{t} \epsilon_i]$ for $t > 0$.

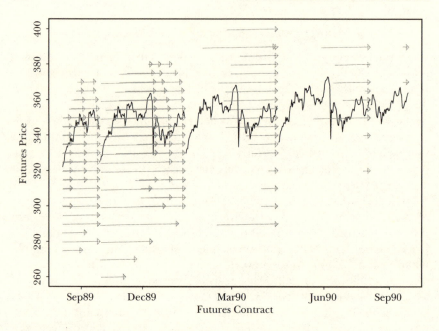

Figure 12.11. *Typical Simulated Training Path (see the text for parameters)*
*Dashed line represents stock price, while the arrows represent the options on the stock. The
y-coordinate of the tip of the arrow indicates the strike price (arrows are slanted to make different
introduction and expiration dates visible).*

of option prices and deltas that are difficult to distinguish visually from the
true Black-Scholes values. An example of the estimates and errors for an
RBF network is shown in Figure 12.12. The estimated equation for this
particular RBF network is

$$
\begin{aligned}
\widehat{G/X} \;=\; & -0.06\sqrt{\begin{bmatrix} P/X - 1.35 \\ \tau - 0.45 \end{bmatrix}' \begin{bmatrix} 59.79 & -0.03 \\ -0.03 & 10.24 \end{bmatrix} \begin{bmatrix} P/X - 1.35 \\ \tau - 0.45 \end{bmatrix}} + 2.55 \\[2ex]
& -0.03\sqrt{\begin{bmatrix} P/X - 1.18 \\ \tau - 0.24 \end{bmatrix}' \begin{bmatrix} 59.79 & -0.03 \\ -0.03 & 10.24 \end{bmatrix} \begin{bmatrix} P/X - 1.18 \\ \tau - 0.24 \end{bmatrix}} + 1.97 \\[2ex]
& +0.03\sqrt{\begin{bmatrix} P/X - 0.98 \\ \tau + 0.20 \end{bmatrix}' \begin{bmatrix} 59.79 & -0.03 \\ -0.03 & 10.24 \end{bmatrix} \begin{bmatrix} P/X - 0.98 \\ \tau + 0.20 \end{bmatrix}} + 0.00
\end{aligned}
$$

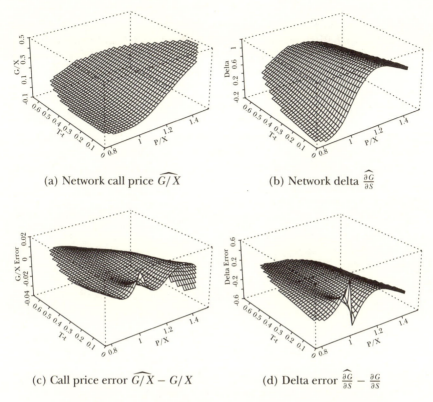

(a) Network call price $\widehat{G/X}$ (b) Network delta $\widehat{\frac{\partial G}{\partial S}}$

(c) Call price error $\widehat{G/X} - G/X$ (d) Delta error $\widehat{\frac{\partial G}{\partial S}} - \frac{\partial G}{\partial S}$

Figure 12.12.   *Typical Behavior of Four-Nonlinear-Term RBF Model*

$$+ 0.10\sqrt{\begin{bmatrix} P/X - 1.05 \\ \tau + 0.10 \end{bmatrix}' \begin{bmatrix} 59.79 & -0.03 \\ -0.03 & 10.24 \end{bmatrix} \begin{bmatrix} P/X - 1.05 \\ \tau + 0.10 \end{bmatrix}} + 1.62$$

$$+ 0.14P/X - 0.24\tau - 0.01, \tag{12.4.11}$$

where $\tau \equiv T-t$. Observe from (12.4.11) that the centers in the RBF model are not constrained to lie within the range of the inputs, and in fact do not in the third and fourth centers in this example. The largest errors in these networks tend to occur at the kink-point for options at the money at expiration, and also along the boundary of the sample points.

While the accuracy of the learning network *prices* is obviously of great interest, this alone is not sufficient to ensure the practical relevance of the nonparametric approach. In particular, the ability to *hedge* an option position is as important, since the very existence of an arbitrage-based pricing formula is predicated on the ability to replicate the option through a dynamic hedging strategy (see the discussion in Chapter 9). This additional constraint provides additional motivation for regularization techniques and, specifically, the RBF networks used by Hutchinson, Lo, and Poggio (1994).

In particular, delta-hedging strategies require an accurate approximation of the derivative of the underlying pricing formula, and the need for accurate approximations of derivatives leads directly to the smoothness constraint imposed by regularization techniques such as RBF networks.[22] Hutchinson, Lo, and Poggio (1994) show that both RBF and MLP networks provide excellent delta-hedging capabilities for the simulated Black-Scholes data as well as in an empirical application to S&P 500 futures options, in a few cases outperforming the Black-Scholes formula (recall that the formula is derived under the assumption that delta-hedging is performed continuously, whereas these simulations assume daily delta-hedging).

Although parametric derivative pricing formulas are preferred when they are available, the results of Hutchinson, Lo, and Poggio (1994) show that nonparametric learning-network alternatives can be useful substitutes when parametric methods fail. While their findings are promising, we cannot yet conclude that such an approach will be successful in general—their simulations have focused only on the Black-Scholes model, and their empirical application consists of only a single instrument and time period, S&P 500 futures options for 1987 to 1991.

However, this general approach points to a number of promising directions for future research. Perhaps the most pressing item on this agenda is the specification of additional inputs, inputs that are not readily captured by parametric models, e.g., the return on the market, general market volatility, and other measures of business conditions.

Other research directions are motivated by the need for proper statistical inference in the specification of learning networks. First, we require some method of matching the network architecture—number of nonlinear units, number of centers, type of basis functions, etc.—to the specific dataset at hand in some optimal and, preferably, automatic fashion.

Second, the relation between sample size and approximation error should be explored, either analytically or through additional Monte Carlo simulation experiments. Perhaps some data-dependent metric can be con-

---

[22] In fact, it is well known that the problem of numerical differentiation is ill-posed. The classical approach [Reinsch (1967)] is to regularize it by finding a sufficiently smooth function that solves the variational problem in (12.4.7). As we discussed earlier, RBF networks as well as splines and several forms of MLP networks follow directly from the regularization approach and are therefore expected to approximate not only the pricing formula but also its derivatives (provided the basis function corresponding to a smoothness prior is of a sufficient degree, see Poggio and Girosi (1990): in particular, the Gaussian is certainly sufficiently smooth for our problem). A special case of this general argument is the result of Gallant and White (1992) and Hornik, Stinchcombe, and White (1990) who show that single-hidden-layer MLP networks can approximate the derivative of an arbitrary nonlinear mapping arbitrarily well as the number of hidden units increases.

structed, that can provide real-time estimates of approximation errors in much the same way that standard errors may be obtained for typical statistical estimators.

And finally, the need for better performance measures is clear. While typical measures of goodness-of-fit such as R^2 do offer some guidance for model selection, they are only incomplete measures of performance. Moreover, the notion of degrees of freedom is no longer well-defined for nonlinear models, and this has implications for all statistical measures of fit.

12.5 Overfitting and Data-Snooping

While each of the nonlinear methods discussed in this chapter has its own costs and benefits, the problems of *overfitting* and *data-snooping* affect all of them to the same degree. Overfitting occurs when a model fits "too well," in the sense that the model has captured both random noise as well as genuine nonlinearities. Heuristically, the primary source of overfitting is having too few "degrees of freedom" or too many parameters relative to the number of datapoints, and a typical symptom is an excellent in-sample fit but poor out-of-sample performance.[23] Data-snooping is a related problem that can lead to excellent but spurious out-of-sample performance. Data-snooping biases arise when we ignore the fact that many specification searches have been conducted to obtain the final specification of a model we are fitting to the data.[24] Even if a model is in fact incorrect, by searching long enough over various datasets and/or parameter values, we are likely to find some combination that *will* fit the data. However, this fit is spurious and is merely a symptom of our extensive search procedure.

Unfortunately, there are no simple remedies to these two problems since the procedures that give rise to them are the same procedures that produce genuine empirical discoveries. The source of both problems is the inability to perform controlled experiments and, consequently, the heavy reliance on statistical inference for our understanding of the data. As with all forms of statistical inference, there is always a margin of error, and this margin is often sensitive to small changes in the way we process the data and revise our models.

---

[23]The degrees of freedom of a nonlinear model are often difficult to determine because the notion of a "parameter" may be blurred. For example, the kernel regression may seem to have only one free parameter—the bandwidth h—but this is clearly misleading since each datapoint serves as a center for local averaging. See Hampel (1986) and Wahba (1990) for further discussion.

[24]See Leamer (1978) and Lo and MacKinlay (1990b) for formal analyses of such biases, and Black (1993) for a recent example in the finance literature.

Nevertheless, there are several ways to mitigate the effects of overfitting and data-snooping. For example, the impact of systematic specification searches may often be calculated explicitly, as in Lo and MacKinlay (1990b). In such instances, using a corrected statistical distribution for inference will safeguard against finding significant results where none exist. Careful out-of-sample performance evaluation can uncover overfitting problems, and if relatively few out-of-sample tests are conducted, or if they are conducted over different (and weakly correlated) datasets, this will minimize the effects of data-snooping.

But perhaps the most effective means of reducing the impact of over-fitting and data-snooping is to impose some discipline on the specification search by *a priori* theoretical considerations. These considerations may be in the form of well-articulated mathematical models of economic behavior, or behavioral models motivated by psychological phenomena, or simply heuristic rules of thumb based on judgment, intuition, and past experience. While all of these sources are also affected by data-snooping and overfitting to some extent—no form of inference can escape these problems—they are less susceptible and offer a less data-dependent means of model validation.

All this suggests the need for an *a priori* framework or specification for the model before confronting the data. By proposing such a specification, along with the kinds of phenomena one is seeking to capture and the relevant variables to be used in the search, the chance of coming upon a spuriously successful model is reduced.

12.6 Conclusion

Nonlinearities are clearly playing a more prominent role in financial applications, thanks to increases in computing power and the availability of large datasets. Unlike the material presented in earlier chapters, some of the ideas in this chapter are less well-established and more tentative. Within a short time many of the techniques we have covered will be refined, and some may become obsolete. Nevertheless, it is important to develop a sense of the direction of research and the open questions to be addressed, especially at the early stages of these explorations.

Despite the flexibility of the nonlinear models we have considered, they do have some serious limitations. They are typically more difficult to estimate precisely, more sensitive to outliers, numerically less stable, and more prone to overfitting and data-snooping biases than comparable linear models. Contrary to popular belief, nonlinear models require *more* economic structure and *a priori* considerations, not less. And their interpretation often requires more effort and care. However, nonlinearities are often a fact of economic life, and for many financial applications the sources and nature of nonlinearity can be readily identified or, at the very least, characterized in some fashion. In such situations, the techniques described in this chapter are powerful additions to the armory of the financial econometrician.

Problems—Chapter 12

12.1   Most pseudorandom number generators implemented on digital computers are *multiplicative linear congruential generators* (MLCG), in which $X_n = (aX_{n-1} + c)$ mod m, where a is some "well-chosen" multiplier, c is an optional constant, and m is equal to or slightly smaller than the largest integer that can be represented in one computer word. (For example, let $a = 1664525$, $c = 0$, and $m = 2^{32}$.) In contrast to MLCG numbers, consider the following two nonlinear recursions: the *tent map* (see Section 12.1.1) and the logistic map, respectively:

$$X_n = \begin{cases} 2X_{n-1} & \text{if } X_{n-1} < \frac{1}{2} \\ 2(1 - X_{n-1}) & \text{if } X_{n-1} \geq \frac{1}{2} \end{cases}, \quad X_o \in (0, 1) \quad (12.6.1)$$

$$X_n = 4X_{n-1}(1 - X_{n-1}), \qquad X_o \in (0, 1). \quad (12.6.2)$$

These recursions are examples of *chaotic* systems, which exhibit extreme sensitive dependence to initial conditions and unusually complex dynamic behavior.

12.1.1   What are good properties for pseudorandom number generators to have, and how should you make comparisons between distinct generators in practice (not in theory)?

12.1.2   Perform various Monte Carlo simulations comparing MLCG to the tent and logistic maps to determine which is the better pseudorandom number generator. Which is better and why? In deciding which criteria to use, think about the kinds of applications for which you will be using the pseudorandom number generators. Hint: Use 1.99999999 instead of 2 in your implementation of (12.6.1), and 3.99999999 instead of 4 in your implementation of (12.6.2)—for extra credit: Explain why.

12.2   Estimate a multilayer perceptron model for monthly returns on the S&P 500 index from 1926:1 to 1994:12 using five lagged returns as inputs and one hidden layer with ten units. Calculate the in-sample root-mean-squared-error (RMSE) of the one-step-ahead forecast of your model and compare it to the corresponding out-of-sample results for the test period 1986:1 to 1994:12. Can you explain the differences in performance (if any)?

12.3   Use kernel regression to estimate the relation between the monthly returns of IBM and the S&P 500 from 1965:1 to 1994:12. How would a conventional beta be calculated from the results of the kernel estimator? Construct at least two measures that capture the incremental value of kernel estimation over ordinary least squares.

Appendix

THIS APPENDIX PROVIDES a brief introduction to the most commonly used estimation techniques in financial econometrics. Many other good reference texts cover this material in more detail, hence we focus only on those aspects that are most relevant for our immediate purposes. Readers looking for a more systematic and comprehensive treatment should consult Hall (1992), Hamilton (1994), Ogaki (1992), and White (1984).

We begin by following Hall's (1992) exposition of linear instrumental variables (IV) estimation in Section A.1 as an intuitive introduction to Hansen's (1982) Generalized Method of Moments (GMM) estimator. We develop the GMM method itself in Section A.2, and discuss methods for handling serially correlated and heteroskedastic errors in Section A.3. In Section A.4 we relate GMM to maximum likelihood (ML) estimation.

A.1 Linear Instrumental Variables

Consider a linear relationship between a scalar y_t and a vector $\mathbf{x}_t$: $y_t = \mathbf{x}'_t \boldsymbol{\theta}_0 + \epsilon_t(\boldsymbol{\theta}_0)$, $t = 1 \ldots T$. Stacking the T observations, this can be written as

$$\mathbf{y} = \mathbf{X}\boldsymbol{\theta}_0 + \boldsymbol{\epsilon}(\boldsymbol{\theta}_0), \tag{A.1.1}$$

where $\mathbf{y}$ is a $(T \times 1)$ vector containing T observations of y_t, $\mathbf{X}$ is a $(T \times N_X)$ matrix containing T observations of the N_X independent variables in $\mathbf{x}_t$, $\boldsymbol{\theta}_0$ is an $(N_X \times 1)$ parameter vector, and $\boldsymbol{\epsilon}(\boldsymbol{\theta}_0)$ is a $(T \times 1)$ vector containing T observations of the error term ϵ_t. The error term is written as a function of the true parameter vector so that the notation ϵ can be used for both the true equation error and the residual of an estimated equation. For simplicity, assume that the error term is serially uncorrelated and homoskedastic, with variance σ^2; thus the variance of $\boldsymbol{\epsilon}(\boldsymbol{\theta}_0)$ is $\mathrm{Var}[\boldsymbol{\epsilon}(\boldsymbol{\theta}_0)] = \sigma^2 \mathbf{I}_T$, where $\mathbf{I}_T$ is a $(T \times T)$ identity matrix.

There are also available N_H instruments in an $(N_H \times 1)$ column vector $\mathbf{h}_t$. The T observations of this vector form a $(T \times N_H)$ matrix $\mathbf{H}$. The instruments have the property that $\mathrm{E}(\mathbf{h}'_t \epsilon_t(\theta_0))$ is an $(N_H \times 1)$ vector of zeroes; that is, the instruments are contemporaneously uncorrelated with the error ϵ_t.[1] The statement that a particular instrument is uncorrelated with the equation error is known as an *orthogonality condition*, and IV regression uses the N_H available orthogonality conditions to estimate the model.

Given an arbitrary coefficient vector θ, we can form the corresponding residual $\epsilon_t(\theta) \equiv y_t - \mathbf{x}'_t \theta$. Stacking this residual into a vector, we get $\epsilon(\theta) \equiv \mathbf{y} - \mathbf{X}\theta$. We can also define an $(N_H \times 1)$ column vector containing the cross-product of the instrument vector with the residual,

$$\mathbf{f}_t(\theta) \equiv \mathbf{h}_t \epsilon_t(\theta). \qquad (A.1.2)$$

The expectation of this cross-product is an $(N_H \times 1)$ vector of zeroes at the true parameter vector:

$$\mathrm{E}[\mathbf{f}_t(\theta_0)] = 0. \qquad (A.1.3)$$

The basic idea of IV estimation is to choose coefficients to satisfy this condition as closely as possible. Of course, we do not observe the true expectation of $\mathbf{f}$ and so we must work instead with the sample average of $\mathbf{f}$. We write this as $\mathbf{g}_T(\theta)$, using the subscript T to indicate dependence on the sample:

$$\mathbf{g}_T(\theta) \equiv T^{-1} \sum_{t=1}^{T} \mathbf{f}_t(\theta) = T^{-1} \sum_{t=1}^{T} \mathbf{h}_t \epsilon_t(\theta) = T^{-1} \mathbf{H}' \epsilon(\theta). \qquad (A.1.4)$$

Minimum Distance Criterion

In general there may be more elements of $\mathbf{g}_T(\theta)$ than there are coefficients, and so in general it is not possible to set all the elements of $\mathbf{g}_T(\theta)$ to zero. Instead, we minimize a quadratic form, a weighted sum of squares and cross-products of the elements of $\mathbf{g}_T(\theta)$. We define the quadratic form $\mathbf{Q}_T(\theta)$ as

$$\mathbf{Q}_T(\theta) \equiv \mathbf{g}_T(\theta)' \mathbf{W}_T \mathbf{g}_T(\theta) = [T^{-1}\epsilon(\theta)'\mathbf{H}]\mathbf{W}_T[T^{-1}\mathbf{H}'\epsilon(\theta)], \qquad (A.1.5)$$

where $\mathbf{W}_T$ is an $(N_H \times N_H)$ symmetric, positive definite weighting matrix.

IV regression chooses $\hat{\theta}_T$ as the value of θ that minimizes $\mathbf{Q}_T(\theta)$. Substituting the definition of $\epsilon(\theta)$ into (A.1.5), the first-order condition for the

---

[1] In many applications, ϵ_t is a forecast error that is uncorrelated with any variables known in advance. In this case the instrument vector $\mathbf{h}_t$ will include only lagged variables that are known at time $t - 1$ or earlier. Nonetheless we write it as $\mathbf{h}_t$ for notational simplicity and generality.

minimization problem is

$$\mathbf{X}'\mathbf{H}\mathbf{W}_T\,\mathbf{H}'\mathbf{y} \;=\; \mathbf{X}'\mathbf{H}\mathbf{W}_T\,\mathbf{H}'\mathbf{X}\hat{\boldsymbol{\theta}}_T. \tag{A.1.6}$$

When the number of instruments, N_H, equals the number of parameters to be estimated, N_X, and the matrix $\mathbf{H}'\mathbf{X}$ is nonsingular, then $\mathbf{X}'\mathbf{H}\mathbf{W}_T$ cancels out of the left- and right-hand sides of (A.1.6) and the minimization gives

$$\hat{\boldsymbol{\theta}}_T \;=\; (\mathbf{H}'\mathbf{X})^{-1}\mathbf{H}'\mathbf{y}. \tag{A.1.7}$$

This estimate is independent of the weighting matrix $\mathbf{W}_T$, since with $N_H = N_X$ all the orthogonality conditions can be satisfied exactly and there is no need to trade off one against another. It is easy to see that (A.1.7) gives the usual formula for an OLS regression coefficient when the instruments $\mathbf{H}$ are the same as the explanatory variables $\mathbf{X}$.

More generally, N_H may exceed N_X so that there are more orthogonality conditions to be satisfied than parameters to be estimated. In this case the model is overidentified and the solution for $\hat{\boldsymbol{\theta}}_T$ is

$$\hat{\boldsymbol{\theta}}_T \;=\; (\mathbf{X}'\mathbf{H}\mathbf{W}_T\,\mathbf{H}'\mathbf{X})^{-1}\mathbf{X}'\mathbf{H}\mathbf{W}_T\,\mathbf{H}'\mathbf{y}. \tag{A.1.8}$$

Asymptotic Distribution Theory
The next step is to calculate the asymptotic distribution of the parameter estimate $\hat{\boldsymbol{\theta}}_T$. Substituting in for $\mathbf{y}$ from (A.1.1) and rearranging, we find that

$$\sqrt{T}(\hat{\boldsymbol{\theta}}_T - \boldsymbol{\theta}_0) \;=\; (T^{-1}\mathbf{X}'\mathbf{H}\mathbf{W}_T\,T^{-1}\mathbf{H}'\mathbf{X})^{-1}\,T^{-1}\mathbf{X}'\mathbf{H}\mathbf{W}_T\,T^{-1/2}\mathbf{H}'\epsilon(\boldsymbol{\theta}_0). \tag{A.1.9}$$

Now suppose that as T increases, $T^{-1}\mathbf{H}'\mathbf{H}$ converges to $\mathbf{M}_{HH}$, a nonsingular moment matrix, and $T^{-1}\mathbf{X}'\mathbf{H}$ converges to $\mathbf{M}_{XH}$, a moment matrix of rank N_X. Suppose also that as T increases the weighting matrix $\mathbf{W}_T$ converges to some symmetric, positive definite limit $\mathbf{W}$. Because we have assumed that the error $\epsilon(\boldsymbol{\theta}_0)$ is serially uncorrelated and homoskedastic, when the orthogonality conditions hold $T^{-1/2}\mathbf{H}'\epsilon(\boldsymbol{\theta}_0)$ converges in distribution to a normal vector with mean zero and variance-covariance matrix $\sigma^2\mathbf{M}_{HH}$. We use the notation $\mathbf{S}$ for this asymptotic variance-covariance matrix:

$$\mathbf{S} \;\equiv\; \lim_{T\to\infty} \mathrm{Var}[\,T^{-1/2}\mathbf{H}'\epsilon(\boldsymbol{\theta}_0)\,] \;=\; \sigma^2\mathbf{M}_{HH}. \tag{A.1.10}$$

Using (A.1.4), $\mathbf{S}$ can be interpreted more generally as the asymptotic variance of $T^{1/2}$ times the sample average of $\mathbf{f}$, that is, $T^{1/2}$ times $\mathbf{g}_T$:

$$\mathbf{S} \;=\; \lim_{T\to\infty} \mathrm{Var}\!\left[\,T^{1/2}\sum_{t=1}^{T}\mathbf{f}_t(\boldsymbol{\theta}_0)\right] \;=\; \lim_{T\to\infty} \mathrm{Var}[\,T^{1/2}\mathbf{g}_T(\boldsymbol{\theta}_0)\,]. \tag{A.1.11}$$

With these convergence assumptions, (A.1.9) implies that

$$\sqrt{T}(\hat{\boldsymbol{\theta}}_T - \boldsymbol{\theta}_0) \overset{d}{\to} N(0, \mathbf{V}), \tag{A.1.12}$$

where

$$\begin{aligned}
\mathbf{V} &= (\mathbf{M}_{XH}\mathbf{W}\mathbf{M}_{HX})^{-1}\mathbf{M}_{XH}\mathbf{W}\mathbf{S}\mathbf{W}\mathbf{M}_{HX}(\mathbf{M}_{XH}\mathbf{W}\mathbf{M}_{HX})'^{-1} \\
&= \sigma^2 (\mathbf{M}_{XH}\mathbf{W}\mathbf{M}_{HX})^{-1}\mathbf{M}_{XH}\mathbf{W}\mathbf{M}_{HH}\mathbf{W}\mathbf{M}_{HX}(\mathbf{M}_{XH}\mathbf{W}\mathbf{M}_{HX})'^{-1},
\end{aligned} \tag{A.1.13}$$

and $\mathbf{M}_{HX} = \mathbf{M}'_{XH}$.

Optimal Weighting Matrix

We have now shown that the estimator $\hat{\boldsymbol{\theta}}_T$ is consistent and asymptotically normal. The final step of the analysis is to pick a weighting matrix $\mathbf{W}$ that minimizes the asymptotic variance matrix $\mathbf{V}$ and hence delivers an asymptotically efficient estimator. It turns out that $\mathbf{V}$ is minimized by picking $\mathbf{W}$ equal to any positive scalar times $\mathbf{S}^{-1}$. Recall that $\mathbf{S}$ is the asymptotic variance-covariance matrix of the sample average orthogonality conditions $\mathbf{g}_T(\boldsymbol{\theta})$. Intuitively, one wants to downweight noisy orthogonality conditions and place more weight on orthogonality conditions that are precisely measured. Since here $\mathbf{S}^{-1} = \sigma^{-2}\mathbf{M}_{HH}^{-1}$, it is convenient to set $\mathbf{W}$ equal to

$$\mathbf{W}^* = \mathbf{M}_{HH}^{-1}; \tag{A.1.14}$$

the formula for $\mathbf{V}$ then simplifies to

$$\mathbf{V}^* = \sigma^2 (\mathbf{M}_{XH}\mathbf{M}_{HH}^{-1}\mathbf{M}_{HX})^{-1}. \tag{A.1.15}$$

In practice one can choose a weighting matrix

$$\mathbf{W}_T^* = (T^{-1}\mathbf{H}'\mathbf{H})^{-1}. \tag{A.1.16}$$

As T increases, $\mathbf{W}_T^*$ will converge to $\mathbf{W}^*$.

With this weighting matrix the formula for $\hat{\boldsymbol{\theta}}_T$ becomes

$$\hat{\boldsymbol{\theta}}_T^* = [\mathbf{X}'\mathbf{H}(\mathbf{H}'\mathbf{H})^{-1}\mathbf{H}'\mathbf{X}]^{-1}\mathbf{X}'\mathbf{H}(\mathbf{H}'\mathbf{H})^{-1}\mathbf{H}'\mathbf{y} = (\hat{\mathbf{X}}'\hat{\mathbf{X}})^{-1}\hat{\mathbf{X}}'\mathbf{y}, \tag{A.1.17}$$

where $\hat{\mathbf{X}} \equiv \mathbf{H}(\mathbf{H}'\mathbf{H})^{-1}\mathbf{H}'\mathbf{X}$ is the predicted value of $\mathbf{X}$ in a regression of $\mathbf{X}$ on $\mathbf{H}$. This is the well-known two-stage least squares (2SLS) estimator. It can be thought of as a two-stage procedure in which one first regresses $\mathbf{X}$ on $\mathbf{H}$, then regresses $\mathbf{y}$ on the fitted value from the first stage to estimate the parameter vector $\boldsymbol{\theta}_0$.

Alternatively, one can think of 2SLS as regressing both $\mathbf{X}$ and $\mathbf{y}$ on $\mathbf{H}$ in the first stage, and then regressing the fitted value of $\mathbf{y}$ on the fitted value of $\mathbf{X}$;

exactly the same coefficient estimate (A.1.17) is implied. Note that under this alternative interpretation, the second-stage regression asymptotically has an R^2 statistic of unity because the error term in (A.1.1) is orthogonal to the instruments and therefore has a fitted value of zero when projected on the instruments. This implies that asymptotically, if (A.1.1) and the orthogonality conditions hold, then the coefficient estimates should not depend on which variable is chosen to be the dependent variable in (A.1.1) and which are chosen to be regressors. Asymptotically, the same coefficient estimates will be obtained (up to a normalization) whichever way the regression is written.

The variance-covariance matrix of 2SLS coefficient estimates, $\mathbf{V}^*$, can be estimated by substituting consistent estimates of the various moment matrices into (A.1.15) to obtain

$$\hat{\mathbf{V}}_T^* = \hat{\sigma}^2 (T^{-1}\mathbf{X}'\mathbf{H}(\mathbf{H}'\mathbf{H})^{-1}\mathbf{H}'\mathbf{X})^{-1}, \qquad (A.1.18)$$

where $\hat{\sigma}^2$ is a consistent estimate of the variance of the equation error. This formula is valid for just-identified IV and OLS coefficient estimates as well.

In place of the weighting matrix $\mathbf{W}^*$ defined above, it is always possible to use $k\mathbf{W}^*$ where k is any positive scalar. Similarly, in place of the weighting matrix $\mathbf{W}_T^*$ one can use $k_T\mathbf{W}_T^*$, where k_T is any positive scalar that converges to k. This rescaling does not affect the formula for the instrumental variables estimator (A.1.17). One possible choice for the scalar k is σ^{-2}, the reciprocal of the variance of the equation error ϵ_t; this makes the weighting matrix equal to $\mathbf{S}^{-1}$. The corresponding choice for the scalar k_T is some consistent estimate $\hat{\sigma}^{-2}$ of σ^{-2}. Hansen (1982) has shown that with this scaling, T times the minimized value of the objective function is asymptotically distributed χ^2 with $(N_H - N_X)$ degrees of freedom under the null hypothesis that (A.1.1) holds and the instruments are orthogonal to the equation error.

Hansen's test of the null hypothesis is related to the intuition that under the null, the residual from the IV regression equation should be uncorrelated with the instruments and a regression of the residual on the instruments should have a "small" R^2 statistic. To understand this, note that when $\mathbf{W}_T = (\hat{\sigma}^2 T^{-1}\mathbf{H}'\mathbf{H})^{-1}$, the minimized objective function is

$$[T^{-1}\epsilon(\hat{\boldsymbol{\theta}}_T^*)'\mathbf{H}](\hat{\sigma}^2 T^{-1}\mathbf{H}'\mathbf{H})^{-1}[T^{-1}\mathbf{H}'\epsilon(\hat{\boldsymbol{\theta}}_T^*)]. \qquad (A.1.19)$$

Now consider regressing the residual $\epsilon(\hat{\boldsymbol{\theta}}_T^*)$ on the instruments $\mathbf{H}$. The fitted value is $\mathbf{H}(\mathbf{H}'\mathbf{H})^{-1}\mathbf{H}'\epsilon(\hat{\boldsymbol{\theta}}_T^*)$, and the R^2 statistic of the regression converges to the same limit as (A.1.19). Thus Hansen's result implies that T times the R^2 in a regression of the residual on the instruments is asymptotically χ^2 with $(N_H - N_X)$ degrees of freedom. This is a standard test of overidentifying restrictions in two-stage least squares (Engle [1984]).

A.2 Generalized Method of Moments

The Generalized Method of Moments (Hansen [1982]) can be understood as an extension of the linear IV regression we have discussed. Suppose now that we have a model which defines a vector $\epsilon_t = \epsilon(\mathbf{x}_t, \boldsymbol{\theta})$, where $\mathbf{x}_t$ now includes all the data relevant for the model (that is, we have dropped the distinction between y_t and $\mathbf{x}_t$), and $\boldsymbol{\theta}$ is a vector of N_β coefficients. This formulation generalizes the linear IV regression in three ways. First, $\epsilon(\mathbf{x}_t, \boldsymbol{\theta})$ can be a column vector with N_ϵ elements rather than a scalar. Second, $\epsilon(\mathbf{x}_t, \boldsymbol{\theta})$ can be a nonlinear rather than a linear function of the data and the parameters. Third, $\epsilon(\mathbf{x}_t, \boldsymbol{\theta})$ can be heteroskedastic and serially correlated rather than homoskedastic white noise. Our model tells us only that there is some true set of parameters $\boldsymbol{\theta}_0$ for which $\epsilon(\mathbf{x}_t, \boldsymbol{\theta}_0)$ is orthogonal to a set of instruments; as before these are written in an $(N_H \times 1)$ column vector $\mathbf{h}_t$.

By analogy with (A.1.2) we define

$$\mathbf{f}_t(\boldsymbol{\theta}) \equiv \mathbf{h}_t \otimes \epsilon(\mathbf{x}_t, \boldsymbol{\theta}). \tag{A.2.1}$$

The notation $\otimes$ denotes the *Kronecker product* of the two vectors. That is, $\mathbf{f}$ is a vector containing the cross-product of each instrument in $\mathbf{h}$ with each element of ϵ. $\mathbf{f}$ is therefore a column vector with $N_f = N_\epsilon N_H$ elements, and the model implies by analogy with (A.1.3) that

$$\mathrm{E}\left[\mathbf{f}_t(\boldsymbol{\theta}_0)\right] = 0. \tag{A.2.2}$$

Just as in (A.1.4), we define a vector $\mathbf{g}_T(\boldsymbol{\theta})$ containing the sample averages corresponding to the elements of $\mathbf{f}$ in (A.1.19):

$$\mathbf{g}_T(\boldsymbol{\theta}) = T^{-1} \sum_{t=1}^{T} \mathbf{f}_t(\boldsymbol{\theta}). \tag{A.2.3}$$

By analogy with (A.1.5), GMM minimizes the quadratic form

$$\mathbf{Q}_T(\boldsymbol{\theta}) \equiv \mathbf{g}_T(\boldsymbol{\theta})' \mathbf{W}_T \mathbf{g}_T(\boldsymbol{\theta}). \tag{A.2.4}$$

Since the problem is now nonlinear, this minimization must be performed numerically. The first-order condition is

$$\mathbf{D}_T(\hat{\boldsymbol{\theta}}_T)' \mathbf{W}_T \mathbf{g}_T(\hat{\boldsymbol{\theta}}_T) = 0, \tag{A.2.5}$$

where $\mathbf{D}_T(\boldsymbol{\theta})$ is a matrix of partial derivatives defined by

$$\mathbf{D}_T(\boldsymbol{\theta}) = \partial \mathbf{g}_T(\boldsymbol{\theta})/\partial \boldsymbol{\theta}'. \tag{A.2.6}$$

The (i, j) element of $\mathbf{D}_T(\boldsymbol{\theta})$ is $\partial \mathbf{g}_{Ti}(\boldsymbol{\theta})/\partial \beta_j$.

Asymptotic Distribution Theory

The asymptotic distribution of the coefficient estimate $\hat{\boldsymbol{\theta}}_T$ is

$$\sqrt{T}(\hat{\boldsymbol{\theta}}_T - \boldsymbol{\theta}_0) \overset{d}{\rightarrow} N(0, \mathbf{V}), \tag{A.2.7}$$

where

$$\mathbf{V} = (\mathbf{D}_0'\mathbf{W}\mathbf{D}_0)^{-1}\mathbf{D}_0'\mathbf{W}\mathbf{S}\mathbf{W}\mathbf{D}_0(\mathbf{D}_0'\mathbf{W}\mathbf{D}_0)^{-1}. \tag{A.2.8}$$

These expressions are directly analogous to (A.1.12) and (A.1.13) for the linear instrumental variables case. $\mathbf{D}_0$ is a generalization of $\mathbf{M}_{HX}$ in those equations and is defined by $\mathbf{D}_0 \equiv \mathrm{E}[\partial \mathbf{f}(\mathbf{x}_t, \boldsymbol{\theta}_0)/\partial \boldsymbol{\theta}_0]$. $\mathbf{D}_T(\boldsymbol{\theta})$ converges asymptotically to $\mathbf{D}_0$. $\mathbf{S}$ is defined as in (A.1.11) by

$$\mathbf{S} \equiv \lim_{T \to \infty} \mathrm{Var}\left[T^{1/2} \sum_{t=1}^{T} \mathbf{f}_t(\boldsymbol{\theta}_0) \right] = \lim_{T \to \infty} \mathrm{Var}[T^{-1/2}\mathbf{g}_T(\boldsymbol{\theta}_0)]. \tag{A.2.9}$$

Optimal Weighting Matrix

Just as in the linear IV case, the optimal weighting matrix that minimizes $\mathbf{V}$ is any positive scalar times $\mathbf{S}^{-1}$. With an optimal weighting matrix the asymptotic variance of $T^{1/2}$ times the coefficient estimate $\hat{\boldsymbol{\theta}}_T^*$ is

$$\mathbf{V}^* = (\mathbf{D}_0'\mathbf{S}^{-1}\mathbf{D}_0)^{-1}. \tag{A.2.10}$$

Also, when the weighting matrix $\mathbf{S}^{-1}$ is used, T times the minimized objective function is distributed χ^2 with $(N_f - N_\beta)$ degrees of freedom, where N_f is the number of orthogonality conditions and N_β is the number of parameters to be estimated.

In practice, of course, $\mathbf{S}$ and the other quantities in (A.2.8) must be estimated. To do this, one starts with an arbitrary weighting matrix $\mathbf{W}_T$; this could be the identity matrix or could be chosen using some prior information about the relative variances of the different orthogonality conditions. Using $\mathbf{W}_T$, one minimizes (A.2.4) to get an initial consistent estimate $\hat{\boldsymbol{\theta}}_T$. To estimate $\mathbf{V}$ in (A.2.8), one replaces its elements by consistent estimates. $\mathbf{D}_0$ can be replaced by $\mathbf{D}_T(\hat{\boldsymbol{\theta}}_T)$, $\mathbf{W}$ can be replaced by $\mathbf{W}_T$, and $\mathbf{S}$ can be replaced by a consistent estimate $\mathbf{S}_T(\hat{\boldsymbol{\theta}}_T)$. Given these estimates, one can construct a new weighting matrix $\mathbf{W}_T^* = \mathbf{S}_T(\hat{\boldsymbol{\theta}}_T)^{-1}$ and minimize (A.2.4) again to get a second-stage estimate $\hat{\boldsymbol{\theta}}_T^*$. The asymptotic variance of $T^{1/2}$ times the second-stage estimate can be estimated as

$$\hat{\mathbf{V}}_T^* = (\mathbf{D}_T(\hat{\boldsymbol{\theta}}_T^*)'\mathbf{S}_T(\hat{\boldsymbol{\theta}}_T^*)^{-1}\mathbf{D}_T(\hat{\boldsymbol{\theta}}_T^*))^{-1}, \tag{A.2.11}$$

and the second-stage minimized objective function is distributed χ^2 with $(N_f - N_\beta)$ degrees of freedom. Although a two-stage procedure is asymptotically efficient, it is also possible to iterate the procedure further until the parameter estimates and minimized objective function converge. This eliminates any dependence of the estimator on the initial weighting matrix, and it appears to improve the finite-sample performance of GMM when the number of parameters is large (Ferson and Foerster [1994]).

A.3 Serially Correlated and Heteroskedastic Errors

One of the most important steps in implementing GMM estimation is estimating the matrix $\mathbf{S}$. From (A.2.9),

$$
\mathbf{S} = \lim_{T \to \infty} \mathrm{E}\left[T^{-1} \left(\sum_{t=1}^{T} \mathbf{f}_t(\boldsymbol{\theta}_0) \right) \left(\sum_{t=1}^{T} \mathbf{f}_t(\boldsymbol{\theta}_0)' \right) \right]
$$

$$
= \boldsymbol{\Gamma}_0(\boldsymbol{\theta}_0) + \sum_{j=1}^{\infty} \left(\boldsymbol{\Gamma}_j(\boldsymbol{\theta}_0) + \boldsymbol{\Gamma}_j'(\boldsymbol{\theta}_0) \right), \tag{A.3.1}
$$

where

$$
\boldsymbol{\Gamma}_j(\boldsymbol{\theta}_0) \equiv \mathrm{E}\left[\mathbf{f}_t(\boldsymbol{\theta}_0)\, \mathbf{f}_{t+1-j}(\boldsymbol{\theta}_0)' \right] \tag{A.3.2}
$$

is the jth autocovariance matrix of $\mathbf{f}_t(\boldsymbol{\theta}_0)$. The matrix $\mathbf{S}$ is the variance-covariance matrix of the time-average of $\mathbf{f}_t(\boldsymbol{\theta}_0)$; equivalently, it is the spectral density matrix of $\mathbf{f}_t(\boldsymbol{\theta}_0)$ at frequency zero. It can be written as an infinite sum of autocovariance matrices of $\mathbf{f}_t(\boldsymbol{\theta}_0)$.

If the autocovariances of $\mathbf{f}_t(\boldsymbol{\theta}_0)$ are zero beyond some lag, then one can simplify the formula (A.3.1) for $\mathbf{S}$ by dropping the zero autocovariances. The autocovariances of $\mathbf{f}_t(\boldsymbol{\theta}_0)$ are zero if the corresponding autocovariances of $\epsilon(\mathbf{x}_t, \boldsymbol{\theta}_0)$ are zero. In the linear IV case with serially uncorrelated errors discussed earlier, for example, $\epsilon(\mathbf{x}_t, \boldsymbol{\theta}_0)$ is white noise and so $\mathbf{f}_t(\boldsymbol{\theta}_0)$ is white noise; in this case one can drop all the autocovariances $\boldsymbol{\Gamma}_j$ for $j > 0$ and $\mathbf{S}$ is just $\boldsymbol{\Gamma}_0$, the variance of $\mathbf{f}_t(\boldsymbol{\theta}_0)$. The same result holds in the consumption CAPM with one-period returns studied in Chapter 8. However in regressions with K-period returns, like those studied in Chapter 7, $K-1$ autocovariances of $\mathbf{f}_t(\boldsymbol{\theta}_0)$ are nonzero and the expression for $\mathbf{S}$ is correspondingly more complicated.

The Newey-West Estimator

To estimate $\mathbf{S}$ it would seem natural to replace the true autocovariances of $\mathbf{f}_t(\boldsymbol{\theta}_0)$, $\boldsymbol{\Gamma}_j(\boldsymbol{\theta}_0)$, with sample autocovariances

$$
\boldsymbol{\Gamma}_{j,T}(\hat{\boldsymbol{\theta}}_T) \equiv T^{-1} \sum_{t=j+1}^{T} \mathbf{f}_t(\hat{\boldsymbol{\theta}}_T)\, \mathbf{f}_{t-j}(\hat{\boldsymbol{\theta}}_T)', \tag{A.3.3}
$$

and substitute into (A.3.1). However there are two difficulties that must be faced. First, in a finite sample one can estimate only a finite number of autocovariances; and to get a consistent estimator of $\mathbf{S}$ one cannot allow the number of estimated autocovariances to increase too rapidly with the sample size. Second, there is no guarantee that an estimator of $\mathbf{S}$ formed by substituting (A.3.3) into (A.3.1) will be positive definite. To handle these two problems Newey and West (1987) suggested the following estimator:

$$\mathbf{S}_T(q, \hat{\boldsymbol{\theta}}_T) = \boldsymbol{\Gamma}_{0,T}(\hat{\boldsymbol{\theta}}_T) + \sum_{j=1}^{q} \left(\frac{q-j}{q} \right) \left(\boldsymbol{\Gamma}_{j,T}(\hat{\boldsymbol{\theta}}_T) + \boldsymbol{\Gamma}'_{j,T}(\hat{\boldsymbol{\theta}}_T) \right), \quad \text{(A.3.4)}$$

where q increases with the sample size but not too rapidly. $q-1$ is the maximum lag length that receives a nonzero weight in the Newey and West (1987) estimator. The estimator guarantees positive definiteness by downweighting higher-order autocovariances, and it is consistent because the downweighting disappears asymptotically.

In models where autocovariances are known to be zero beyond lag $K-1$, it is tempting to use the Newey and West (1987) estimator with $q = K$. This is legitimate when $K=1$, so that only the variance $\boldsymbol{\Gamma}_{0,T}(\hat{\boldsymbol{\theta}}_T)$ appears in the estimator; but when $K>1$ this approach can severely downweight some nonzero autocovariances; depending on the sample size, it may be better to use $q>K$ in this situation.

Although the Newey and West (1987) weighting scheme is the most commonly used, there are several alternative estimators in the literature including those of Andrews (1991), Andrews and Monahan (1992), and Gallant (1987). Hamilton (1994) provides a useful overview.

The Linear Instrumental Variables Case
The general formulas given here apply in both nonlinear and linear models, but they can be understood more simply in linear IV regression models. Return to the linear model of Section A.1, but allow the error term $\epsilon_t(\boldsymbol{\theta}_0)$ to be serially correlated and heteroskedastic. Equation (A.1.10) becomes

$$\mathbf{S} \equiv \lim_{T \to \infty} \text{Var}[T^{-1/2}\mathbf{H}'\boldsymbol{\epsilon}(\boldsymbol{\theta}_0)] = \lim_{T \to \infty} T^{-1}\mathbf{H}'\boldsymbol{\Omega}(\boldsymbol{\theta}_0)\mathbf{H}, \quad \text{(A.3.5)}$$

where $\boldsymbol{\Omega}(\boldsymbol{\theta}_0)$ is the variance-covariance matrix of $\boldsymbol{\epsilon}(\boldsymbol{\theta}_0)$. This can be estimated by

$$\mathbf{S}_T(\hat{\boldsymbol{\theta}}_T) = T^{-1}\mathbf{H}'\boldsymbol{\Omega}_T(\hat{\boldsymbol{\theta}}_T)\mathbf{H}, \quad \text{(A.3.6)}$$

where $\boldsymbol{\Omega}_T(\hat{\boldsymbol{\theta}}_T)$ is an estimator of $\boldsymbol{\Omega}(\boldsymbol{\theta}_0)$. Equation (A.2.11) now becomes

$$\hat{\mathbf{V}}_T^* = (T^{-1}\mathbf{X}'\mathbf{H}(\mathbf{H}'\boldsymbol{\Omega}_T(\hat{\boldsymbol{\theta}}_T)\mathbf{H})^{-1}\mathbf{H}'\mathbf{X})^{-1}. \quad \text{(A.3.7)}$$

In the homoskedastic white noise case considered earlier, $\boldsymbol{\Omega} = \sigma^2\mathbf{I}_T$ so we used an estimate $\boldsymbol{\Omega}_T(\hat{\boldsymbol{\theta}}_T) \equiv \hat{\sigma}^2\mathbf{I}_T$ where $\hat{\sigma}^2 = T^{-1}\sum_{t=1}^{T} \epsilon_t^2(\hat{\boldsymbol{\theta}}_T)$. Substituting this into (A.3.7) gives (A.1.18).

When the error term is serially uncorrelated but heteroskedastic, then Ω is a diagonal matrix with different variances on each element of the main diagonal. One can construct a sample equivalent of each element as follows. For each element on the main diagonal of the matrix, $\Omega_{T,tt}(\hat{\boldsymbol{\theta}}_T) = \epsilon_t(\hat{\boldsymbol{\theta}}_T)^2$, while each off-diagonal element $\Omega_{T,st}(\hat{\boldsymbol{\theta}}_T) = 0$ for $s \neq t$. Substituting the resulting matrix $\Omega_T(\hat{\boldsymbol{\theta}}_T)$ into (A.3.6) one gets a consistent estimator of $\mathbf{S}_T(\hat{\boldsymbol{\theta}})$, and substituting it into (A.3.7) one gets a consistent estimator $\hat{\mathbf{V}}_T^*$. This is true even though the matrix $\Omega(\hat{\boldsymbol{\theta}}_T)$ is not itself a consistent estimator of Ω because the number of elements of Ω that must be estimated equals the sample size.

When the error term is serially correlated and homoskedastic, then one can construct each element of the matrix $\Omega_T(\hat{\boldsymbol{\theta}}_T)$ as follows:

$$\Omega_{T,st}(\hat{\boldsymbol{\theta}}_T) = \begin{cases} T^{-1} \sum_{i=l+1}^{T} \left(\frac{q-l}{q}\right) \epsilon_i(\hat{\boldsymbol{\theta}}_T)\, \epsilon_{i-l}(\hat{\boldsymbol{\theta}}_T) & \text{if } l \equiv |t-s| < q, \\ 0 & \text{otherwise} \end{cases}$$

$$(A.3.8)$$

where the Newey and West (1987) weighting scheme with maximum lag length q is used. Alternatively, one can replace the triangular weights $(q - l)/q$ with unit weights to get the estimator of Hansen and Hodrick (1980), but this is not guaranteed to be positive definite.

When the error term is serially correlated and heteroskedastic, then one can construct $\Omega_T(\hat{\boldsymbol{\theta}}_T)$ as:

$$\Omega_{T,st}(\hat{\boldsymbol{\theta}}_T) = \begin{cases} \left(\frac{q-l}{q}\right) \epsilon_s(\hat{\boldsymbol{\theta}}_T)\, \epsilon_t(\hat{\boldsymbol{\theta}}_T) & \text{if } l \equiv |t-s| < q, \\ 0 & \text{otherwise} \end{cases}$$

$$(A.3.9)$$

where the Newey and West (1987) weighting scheme is used. Again one can replace the triangular weights with unit weights to get the estimator of Hansen and Hodrick (1980). In each case substituting $\Omega(\hat{\boldsymbol{\theta}}_T)$ into (A.3.6) gives a consistent estimate of $\mathbf{S}$, and substituting it into equation (A.3.7) gives a consistent estimator $\hat{\mathbf{V}}_T^*$, even though the matrix $\Omega(\hat{\boldsymbol{\theta}}_T)$ is not itself a consistent estimator of Ω because the number of nonzero elements increases too rapidly with the sample size. White (1984) gives a comprehensive treatment of the linear model with serially correlated and heteroskedastic errors.

A.4 GMM and Maximum Likelihood

Following Hamilton (1994), we now show how some well-known properties of Maximum Likelihood estimators (MLE) can be understood in relation to GMM. We first lay out some notation. We use L_t to denote the density of

$\mathbf{x}_{t+1}$ conditional on the history of $\mathbf{x}_t$ and a parameter vector $\boldsymbol{\theta}$:

$$L_t(\mathbf{x}_{t+1}, \boldsymbol{\theta}) = L(\mathbf{x}_{t+1} \mid \mathbf{x}_t, \mathbf{x}_{t-1}, \dots, \boldsymbol{\theta}). \tag{A.4.1}$$

We use the notation ℓ_t for the log of L_t, the conditional log likelihood:

$$\ell_t(\mathbf{x}_{t+1}, \boldsymbol{\theta}) = \log L_t(\mathbf{x}_{t+1}, \boldsymbol{\theta}). \tag{A.4.2}$$

The log likelihood $\mathcal{L}$ of the whole data set $\mathbf{x}_1, \dots, \mathbf{x}_T$ is just the sum of the conditional log likelihoods:

$$\mathcal{L} = \sum_{t=1}^{T} \ell_t. \tag{A.4.3}$$

Since L_t is a conditional density, it must integrate to 1:

$$\int L_t(\mathbf{x}_{t+1}, \boldsymbol{\theta}) \, d\mathbf{x}_{t+1} = 1. \tag{A.4.4}$$

Given certain regularity conditions, it follows that the partial derivative of L_t with respect to $\boldsymbol{\theta}$ must integrate to zero. A series of simple manipulations then shows that

$$
\begin{aligned}
0 &= \int \frac{\partial L_t(\mathbf{x}_{t+1}, \boldsymbol{\theta})}{\partial \boldsymbol{\theta}} \, dx_{t+1} = \int \frac{\partial L_t(\mathbf{x}_{t+1}, \boldsymbol{\theta})}{\partial \boldsymbol{\theta}} \frac{1}{L_t} L_t \, dx_{t+1} \\
&= \int \frac{\partial \ell_t(\mathbf{x}_{t+1}, \boldsymbol{\theta})}{\partial \boldsymbol{\theta}} L_t \, dx_{t+1} \\
&= \mathrm{E}_t \frac{\partial \ell_t(\mathbf{x}_{t+1}, \boldsymbol{\theta})}{\partial \boldsymbol{\theta}} = \mathrm{E} \frac{\partial \ell_t(\mathbf{x}_{t+1}, \boldsymbol{\theta})}{\partial \boldsymbol{\theta}}.
\end{aligned} \tag{A.4.5}
$$

The partial derivative of the conditional log likelihood with respect to the parameter vector, $\partial \ell_t(\mathbf{x}_{t+1}, \boldsymbol{\theta})/\partial \boldsymbol{\theta}$, is a vector with N_β elements. It is known as the *score vector*. From (A.4.5), it has conditional expectation zero when the data are generated by (A.4.1). It also has unconditional expectation zero and thus plays a role analogous to the vector of orthogonality conditions $\mathbf{f}_t$ in GMM analysis. The sample average $(1/T) \sum_{t=1}^{T} \partial \ell_t(\mathbf{x}_{t+1}, \boldsymbol{\theta})/\partial \boldsymbol{\theta}$ plays a role analogous to $\mathbf{g}_T(\boldsymbol{\theta})$ in GMM analysis.

The maximum likelihood estimate of the parameters is just the solution $\hat{\boldsymbol{\theta}}$ to $\mathrm{Max}\, \mathcal{L}(\boldsymbol{\theta}) = \sum_{t=1}^{T} \ell_t$. The first-order condition for the maximization can be written as

$$\mathbf{g}_T(\hat{\boldsymbol{\theta}}) = T^{-1} \sum_{t=1}^{T} \partial \ell_t(\mathbf{x}_{t+1}, \hat{\boldsymbol{\theta}})/\partial \boldsymbol{\theta} = 0, \tag{A.4.6}$$

which also characterizes the GMM parameter estimate for a just-identified model. Thus the MLE is the same as GMM based on the orthogonality conditions in (A.4.5).

Asymptotic Distribution Theory

The asymptotic distribution of ML parameter estimates is given by the following result:

$$\sqrt{T}(\hat{\theta} - \theta_0) \overset{a}{\sim} \mathcal{N}\left(0, \mathcal{I}^{-1}(\theta_0)\right), \tag{A.4.7}$$

where $\mathcal{I}$ given by:

$$\mathcal{I}(\theta) \equiv \lim_{n \to \infty} -\mathrm{E}\left[\frac{1}{n}\frac{\partial^2 \mathcal{L}(\theta)}{\partial\theta\,\partial\theta'}\right], \tag{A.4.8}$$

and is known as the *information matrix*. $\mathcal{I}$ can be estimated by the sample counterpart:

$$\hat{\mathcal{I}}_a = -\frac{1}{T}\sum_{t=1}^{T}\frac{\partial^2 \ell_t(\hat{\theta})}{\partial\theta\partial\theta'}. \tag{A.4.9}$$

The information matrix gives us a measure of the sensitivity of the value of the likelihood is to the values of the parameters in the neighborhood of the maximum. If small changes in the parameters produce large changes in likelihood near the maximum, then the parameters can be precisely estimated. Since the likelihood function is flat at the maximum, the local sensitivity of the likelihood to the parameters is measured by the local curvature (the second derivative) of likelihood with respect to the parameters, evaluated at the maximum.

Information-Matrix Equality

An alternative estimator of the information matrix, $\hat{\mathcal{I}}_b$, uses the average outer product or sample variance of the score vectors:

$$\hat{\mathcal{I}}_b \equiv T^{-1}\sum_{t=1}^{T}\frac{\partial \ell_t(\hat{\theta})}{\partial\theta}\frac{\partial \ell_t(\hat{\theta})'}{\partial\theta}. \tag{A.4.10}$$

To see why $\hat{\mathcal{I}}_b$ converges to the same limit as $\hat{\mathcal{I}}_a$, differentiate the third equality of equation (A.4.5) with respect to θ' to get

$$
\begin{aligned}
0 &= \int \frac{\partial^2 \ell_t(\mathbf{x}_{t+1}, \theta)}{\partial\theta\partial\theta'} L_t\, dx_{t+1} + \int \frac{\partial \ell_t(\mathbf{x}_{t+1}, \theta)}{\partial\theta}\frac{\partial L_t(\mathbf{x}_{t+1}, \theta)'}{\partial\theta}\, dx_{t+1} \\
&= \int \frac{\partial^2 \ell_t(\mathbf{x}_{t+1}, \theta)}{\partial\theta\partial\theta'} L_t\, dx_{t+1} + \int \frac{\partial \ell_t(\mathbf{x}_{t+1}, \theta)}{\partial\theta}\frac{\partial \ell_t(\mathbf{x}_{t+1}, \theta)'}{\partial\theta} L_t\, dx_{t+1} \\
&= \mathrm{E}_t \frac{\partial^2 \ell_t(\mathbf{x}_{t+1}, \theta)}{\partial\theta\partial\theta'} + \mathrm{E}_t \frac{\partial \ell_t(\mathbf{x}_{t+1}, \theta)}{\partial\theta}\frac{\partial \ell_t(\mathbf{x}_{t+1}, \theta)'}{\partial\theta} \\
&= \mathrm{E} \frac{\partial^2 \ell_t(\mathbf{x}_{t+1}, \theta)}{\partial\theta\partial\theta'} + \mathrm{E} \frac{\partial \ell_t(\mathbf{x}_{t+1}, \theta)}{\partial\theta}\frac{\partial \ell_t(\mathbf{x}_{t+1}, \theta)'}{\partial\theta}.
\end{aligned} \tag{A.4.11}
$$

This is known as the *information-matrix equality*, and implies that the expectations to which the sample averages $\hat{\mathcal{I}}_a$ and $\hat{\mathcal{I}}_b$ converge are equal. The information matrix equality holds under the assumption that the data are generated by (A.4.1).

GMM analysis gives an alternative formula for the distribution of ML parameter estimates. Recall from (A.2.11) that the GMM estimator is asymptotically normal with asymptotic variance estimator

$$\hat{\mathbf{V}}_T^* = (\mathbf{D}_T(\hat{\boldsymbol{\theta}}_T^*)'\mathbf{S}_T(\hat{\boldsymbol{\theta}}_T^*)^{-1}\mathbf{D}_T(\hat{\boldsymbol{\theta}}_{T}*))^{-1}.$$

In this case

$$\mathbf{D}_T(\hat{\boldsymbol{\theta}}_T^*) = \frac{\partial g_T(\hat{\boldsymbol{\theta}}_T^*)}{\partial\boldsymbol{\theta}} = T^{-1}\sum_{t=1}^{T}\frac{\partial^2\ell_t(\hat{\boldsymbol{\theta}})}{\partial\boldsymbol{\theta}\partial\boldsymbol{\theta}'} = \hat{\mathcal{I}}_a, \qquad (A.4.12)$$

while

$$\mathbf{S}_T(\hat{\boldsymbol{\theta}}_T^*) = T^{-1}\sum_{t=1}^{T}\frac{\partial\ell_t(\hat{\boldsymbol{\theta}})}{\partial\boldsymbol{\theta}}\frac{\partial\ell_t(\hat{\boldsymbol{\theta}})'}{\partial\boldsymbol{\theta}} = \hat{\mathcal{I}}_b \qquad (A.4.13)$$

since the score vector is serially uncorrelated so **S** can be estimated from its sample variance. Therefore, the distribution of the GMM estimator can be expressed as:

$$\sqrt{T}(\hat{\boldsymbol{\theta}} - \boldsymbol{\theta}_0) \overset{a}{\sim} \mathcal{N}\left(0, [\mathcal{I}_a(\boldsymbol{\theta}_0)\mathcal{I}_b^{-1}(\boldsymbol{\theta}_0)\mathcal{I}_a(\boldsymbol{\theta}_0)]^{-1}\right), \qquad (A.4.14)$$

where $\mathcal{I}_a$ and $\mathcal{I}_b$ are the limits of $\hat{\mathcal{I}}_a$ and $\hat{\mathcal{I}}_b$ as T increases without bound, evaluated at the true parameter vector $\boldsymbol{\theta}_0$.

When the model is correctly specified, $\hat{\mathcal{I}}_a$ and $\hat{\mathcal{I}}_b$ both converge to the information matrix $\mathcal{I}$, hence (A.4.14) simplifies in the limit to $(\mathcal{I}\mathcal{I}^{-1}\mathcal{I})^{-1} = \mathcal{I}^{-1}$ which reduces to the conventional expression for the asymptotic variance in (A.4.7). Therefore, either $\hat{\mathcal{I}}_a$ or $\hat{\mathcal{I}}_b$ (or both) can be used to estimate $\mathcal{I}$ in this case.

However, when the model is misspecified, $\hat{\mathcal{I}}_a$ and $\hat{\mathcal{I}}_b$ converge to different limits in general; this has been used as the basis for a specification test by White (1982). But ML estimates of the misspecified model are still consistent provided that the orthogonality conditions hold, and one can use the general variance formula (A.4.14) provided that the score vector is serially uncorrelated. White (1982) suggests this approach, which is known as *quasi-maximum likelihood* estimation.

Hypothesis Testing
The asymptotic variances in (A.4.7) and (A.4.14) can be used in a straightforward manner to construct Wald tests of restrictions on the parameters.

The idea of such tests is to see whether the unrestricted parameter estimates are significantly different from their restricted values, where the variance of the unrestricted estimates is calculated without imposing the restrictions.

Alternatively, one may want to test restrictions using estimates only of the restricted model. Once restrictions are imposed, the minimized GMM objective function is no longer identically zero. Instead, the Hansen (1982) result is that T times the minimized objective function has a χ^2 distribution with degrees of freedom equal to the number of restrictions. In this case T times the minimized objective function is just

$$T\mathbf{g}_T(\hat{\boldsymbol{\theta}})'\,\hat{\mathcal{I}}_b^{-1}\,\mathbf{g}_T(\hat{\boldsymbol{\theta}}), \qquad\qquad (A.4.15)$$

which is the Lagrange multiplier test statistic for a restricted model estimated by maximum likelihood.

The Delta Method

More complicated inferences for arbitrary nonlinear functions of the estimator $\hat{\boldsymbol{\theta}}$ may be performed via Taylor's Theorem or the *delta method*. If $\sqrt{T}(\hat{\boldsymbol{\theta}} - \boldsymbol{\theta}_0) \overset{a}{\sim} \mathcal{N}(0, V_{\theta})$, then a nonlinear function $f(\hat{\boldsymbol{\theta}})$ has the following asymptotic distribution:

$$\sqrt{T}\left(f(\hat{\boldsymbol{\theta}}) - f(\boldsymbol{\theta})\right) \overset{a}{\sim} \mathcal{N}(0, V_f), \qquad V_f \equiv \frac{\partial f}{\partial \boldsymbol{\theta}'} V_{\theta} \frac{\partial f}{\partial \boldsymbol{\theta}} \qquad (A.4.16)$$

which follows from a first-order Taylor series approximation for $f(\boldsymbol{\theta})$ around θ_0. Higher-order terms converge to zero faster than $1/\sqrt{T}$ hence only the first term of the expansion matters for the asymptotic distribution of $f(\hat{\boldsymbol{\theta}})$.

References

Abel, A., 1990, "Asset Prices under Habit Formation and Catching Up with the Joneses," in *American Economic Review* 80, *Papers and Proceedings*, 38–42.

———, 1996, "Risk Premia and Term Premia in General Equilibrium," unpublished paper, University of Pennsylvania.

Abel, A., N. G. Mankiw, L. Summers, and R. Zeckhauser, 1989, "Assessing Dynamic Efficiency: Theory and Evidence," *Review of Economic Studies*, 56, 1–20.

Acharya, S., 1988, "A Generalized Econometric Model and Tests of a Signalling Hypothesis with Two Discrete Signals," *Journal of Finance*, 43, 413–429.

———, 1993, "Value of Latent Information: Alternative Event Study Methods," *Journal of Finance*, 48, 363–385.

Adams, K., and D. van Deventer, 1994, "Fitting Yield Curves and Forward Rate Curves with Maximum Smoothness," *Journal of Fixed Income*, 4, 52–62.

Admati, A., and P. Pfleiderer, 1988, "A Theory of Intraday Patterns: Volume and Price Variability," *Review of Financial Studies*, 1, 3–40.

———, 1989, "Divide and Conquer: A Theory of Intraday and Day-of-the-Week Mean Effects," *Review of Financial Studies*, 2, 189–224.

Affleck-Graves, J., and B. McDonald, 1989, "Nonnormalities and Tests of Asset Pricing Theories," *Journal of Finance*, 44, 889–908.

Affleck-Graves, J., S. Hegde, and R. Miller, 1994, "Trading Mechanisms and the Components of the Bid-Ask Spread," *Journal of Finance*, 49, 1471–1488.

Ainslie, G., 1992, *Picoeconomics*, Cambridge University Press, Cambridge.

Aitchison, J., and S. Silvey, 1957, "The Generalization of Probit Analysis to the Case of Multiple Responses," *Biometrika*, 44, 131–140.

Aït-Sahalia, Y., 1993, "Nonparametric Functional Estimation with Applications to Financial Models," unpublished Ph.D. dissertation, Department of Economics, Massachusetts Institute of Technology.

———, 1996a, "Nonparametric Pricing of Interest Rate Derivative Securities," *Econometrica*, 64, 527–560.

———, 1996b, "Testing Continuous-Time Models of the Spot Interest Rate," *Review of Financial Studies*, 9, 385–426.

Aït-Sahalia, Y., and A. Lo, 1996, "Nonparametric Estimation of State-Price Densities Implicit in Financial Asset Prices", Working Paper LFE–1015–96, MIT Laboratory for Financial Engineering.

Aiyagari, S., and M. Gertler, 1991, "Asset Returns with Transaction Costs and Uninsured Individual Risk: A Stage III Exercise," *Journal of Monetary Economics*, 27, 309–331.

Aldous, D., 1989, *Probability Approximations via the Poisson Clumping Heuristic*, Springer-Verlag, New York.

Aldous, D., and P. Diaconis, 1986, "Shuffling Cards and Stopping Times," *American Mathematical Monthly*, 8, 333–348.

Alexander, S., 1961, "Price Movements in Speculative Markets: Trends or Random Walks," *Industrial Management Review*, 2, 7–26.

————, 1964, "Price Movements in Speculative Markets: Trends or Random Walks, No. 2," in P. Cootner (ed.), *The Random Character of Stock Market Prices*, Massachusetts Institute of Technology Press, Cambridge, MA.

Amihud, Y., and H. Mendelson, 1980, "Dealership Markets: Market Making with Uncertainty," *Journal of Financial Economics*, 8, 31–54.

————, 1986, "Asset Pricing and the Bid-Ask Spread," *Journal of Financial Economics*, 17, 223–250.

————, 1987, "Trading Mechanisms and Stock Returns: An Empirical Investigation," *Journal of Finance*, 42, 533–553.

Amin, K., and V. Ng, 1993, "Option Valuation with Systematic Stochastic Volatility," *Journal of Finance*, 48, 881–910.

Anderson, T., 1984, *An Introduction to Multivariate Statistical Analysis* (2nd ed.), John Wiley and Sons, New York.

Andrews, D., 1991, "Heteroskedasticity and Autocorrelation Consistent Covariance Matrix Estimation," *Econometrica*, 59, 817–858.

Andrews, D., and J. Monahan, 1992, "An Improved Heteroskedasticity and Autocorrelation Consistent Covariance Matrix Estimator," *Econometrica*, 60, 953–966.

Arnold, L., 1974, *Stochastic Differential Equations: Theory and Applications*, John Wiley and Sons, New York.

Arrow, K., 1964, "The Role of Securities in the Optimal Allocation of Risk Bearing," *Review of Economic Studies*, 31, 91–96.

Aschauer, D., 1985, "Fiscal Policy and Aggregate Demand," *American Economic Review*, 75, 117–127.

Ashford, J., 1959, "An Approach to the Analysis of Data for Semi-Quantal Responses in Biological Response," *Biometrics*, 26, 535–581.

Ashley, J., 1962, "Stock Prices and Changes in Earnings and Dividends: Some Empirical Results," *Journal of Political Economy*, 82–85.

Asquith, P., and D. Mullins, 1986, "Equity Issues and Offering Dilution," *Journal of Financial Economics*, 15, 61–89.

Atchison, M., K. Butler, and R. Simonds, 1987, "Nonsynchronous Security Trading and Market Index Autocorrelation," *Journal of Finance*, 42, 111–118.

Bachelier, L., 1900, "Theory of Speculation," in Cootner, P. (ed.), *The Random Character of Stock Market Prices*, Massachusetts Institute of Technology Press, Cambridge, MA, 1964; Reprint.

Backus, D., 1993, "Cox-Ingersoll-Ross in Discrete Time," unpublished paper, New York University.

Backus, D., and S. Zin, 1994, "Reverse Engineering the Yield Curve," Working Paper 4676, NBER, Cambridge, MA.

Backus, D., S. Foresi, and S. Zin, 1996, "Arbitrage Opportunities in Arbitrage-Free Models of Bond Pricing," Working Paper 5638, NBER, Cambridge, MA.

Backus, D., A. Gregory, and S. Zin, 1989, "Risk Premiums in the Term Structure: Evidence from Artificial Economies," *Journal of Monetary Economics*, 24, 371–399.

Badrinath, S., Kale, J., and T. Noe, 1995, "Of Shepherds, Sheep, and the Cross-Autocorrelations in Equity Returns," *Review of Financial Studies*, 8, 401–430.

Bagehot, W., (a.k.a. Jack Treynor), 1971, "The Only Game in Town," *Financial Analysts Journal*, 22, 12–14.

Bakshi, G., and Z. Chen, 1996, "The Spirit of Capitalism and Stock Market Prices," *American Economic Review*, 86, 133–157.

Balduzzi, P., G. Bertola, and S. Foresi, 1993, "A Model of Target Changes and the Term Structure of Interest Rates," Working Paper 4347, NBER, Cambridge, MA.

Ball, C., 1988, "Estimation Bias Induced by Discrete Security Prices," *Journal of Finance*, 43, 841–865.

Ball, C., and A. Roma, 1994, "Stochastic Volatility Option Pricing," *Journal of Financial and Quantitative Analysis*, 29, 589–607.

Ball, C., and W. Torous, 1983, "A Simplified Jump Process for Common Stock Returns," *Journal of Financial and Quantitative Analysis*, 18, 53–65.

———, 1985, "On Jumps in Common Stock Prices and Their Impact on Call Option Pricing," *Journal of Finance*, 40, 155–174.

———, 1988, "Investigating Security-Price Performance in the Presence of Event-Date Uncertainty," *Journal of Financial Economics*, 22, 123–154.

Ball, R., and P. Brown, 1968, "An Empirical Evaluation of Accounting Income Numbers," *Journal of Accounting Research*, 159–178.

Ball, C., W. Torous, and A. Tschoegl, 1985, "The Degree of Price Resolution: The Case of the Gold Market," *Journal of Futures Markets*, 5, 29–43.

Banz, R., 1981, "The Relation between Return and Market Value of Common Stocks," *Journal of Financial Economics*, 9, 3–18.

Banz, R., and M. Miller, 1978, "Prices for State-Contingent Claims: Some Estimates and Applications," *Journal of Business*, 51, 653–672.

Barberis, N., A. Shleifer, and R. Vishny, 1996, "A Model of Investor Sentiment with both Underreaction and Overreaction," unpublished paper, University of Chicago and Harvard University.

Barclay, M., and R. Litzenberger, 1988, "Announcement Effects of New Equity Issues and the Use of Intraday Price Data," *Journal of Financial Economics*, 21, 71–100.

Barker, C., 1956, "Effective Stock Splits," *Harvard Business Review*, 34(1), January–February, 101–106.

———, 1957, "Stock Splits in a Bull Market," *Harvard Business Review*, 35(3), May–June, 72–79.

———, 1958, "Evaluation of Stock Dividends," *Harvard Business Review*, 36(4), July–August, 99–114.

Barr, D., and J. Campbell, 1995, "Inflation, Real Interest Rates, and the Bond Market: A Study of UK Nominal and Index-Linked Government Bond Prices," Discussion Paper 1732, Harvard Institute of Economic Research, Harvard University.

Barron, A., 1993, "Universal Approximation Bounds for Superpositions of a Sigmoidal Function," *IEEE Trans. Info. Theory*, 39, 930–945.

————, 1994, "Approximation and Estimation Bounds for Artificial Neural Networks," *Machine Learning*, 14, 115–133.

Barron, A., and R. Barron, 1988, "Statistical Learning Networks: A Unifying View," in *20th Symposium on the Interface: Computing Science and Statistics*, pp. 192–203, Reston, Virginia.

Barsky, R., and J. De Long, 1993, "Why Does the Stock Market Fluctuate?," *Quarterly Journal of Economics*, 108, 291–311.

Basu, S., 1977, "The Investment Performance of Common Stocks in Relation to Their Price to Earnings Ratios: A Test of the Efficient Market Hypothesis," *Journal of Finance*, 32, 663–682.

Beckers, S., 1980, "The Constant Elasticity of Variance Model and Its Implications for Option Pricing," *Journal of Finance*, 35, 661–673.

————, 1983, "Variances of Security Price Returns Based on High, Low, and Closing Prices," *Journal of Business*, 56, 97–112.

Benartzi, S., and R. Thaler, 1995, "Myopic Loss Aversion and the Equity Premium Puzzle," *Quarterly Journal of Economics*, 110, 73–92.

Benston, G., and R. Hagerman, 1974, "Determinants of Bid-Asked Spreads in the Over-the-Counter Market," *Journal of Financial Economics*, 1, 353–364.

Benveneto, R., 1984, "The Occurrence of Sequence Patterns in Ergodic Markov Chains," *Stochastic Processes and Their Applications*, 17, 369–373.

Bernard, V., 1987, "Cross-Sectional Dependence and Problems in Inference in Market-Based Accounting Research," *Journal of Accounting Research*, 25, 1–48.

Berndt, E., B. Hall, R. Hall, and J. Hausman, 1974, "Estimation and Inference in Nonlinear Structural Models," *Annals of Economic and Social Measurement*, 3, 653–665.

Bernstein, P., 1992, *Capital Ideas: The Improbable Origins of Modern Wall Street*, Free Press, New York.

Bertsimas, D., and A. Lo, 1996, "Optimal Control of Execution Costs," Working Paper LFE–1025–96, Massachusetts Institute of Technology Laboratory for Financial Engineering, Cambridge, MA.

Bertsimas, D., L. Kogan, and A. Lo, 1996, "When Is Time Continuous?," Working Paper LFE–1045–96, Massachusetts Institute of Technology Laboratory for Financial Engineering.

Bhattacharya, M., 1983, "Transactions Data Tests of Efficiency of the Chicago Board Options Exchange," *Journal of Financial Economics*, 12, 181–185.

Bick, A., 1990, "On Viable Diffusion Price Processes of the Market Portfolio," *Journal of Finance*, 45, 673–689.

Bierwag, G., G. Kaufman, and A. Toevs (eds.), 1983, *Innovations in Bond Portfolio Management: Duration Analysis and Immunization,* JAI Press, Westport, CT.

Biggans, J., and C. Cannings, 1987, "Markov Renewal Processes, Counters and Repeated Sequences in Markov Chains," *Advances in Applied Probability,* 19, 521–545.

Billingsley, P., 1968, *Convergence of Probability Measures,* John Wiley and Sons, New York.

Black, F., 1971, "Toward a Fully Automated Stock Exchange," *Financial Analysts Journal,* July–August, 29–44.

———, F., 1972, "Capital Market Equilibrium with Restricted Borrowing," *Journal of Business,* 45, July, 444–454.

———, 1976, "Studies of Stock Price Volatility Changes," in *Proceedings of the 1976 Meetings of the Business and Economic Statistics Section, American Statistical Association,* pp. 177–181.

———, 1993, "Return and Beta," *Journal of Portfolio Management,* 20, 8–18.

Black, F., and P. Karasinski, 1991, "Bond and Option Pricing when Short Rates Are Lognormal," *Financial Analysts Journal,* July–August, 52–59.

Black, F., and M. Scholes, 1972, "The Valuation of Option Contracts and a Test of Market Efficiency," *Journal of Finance,* 27, 399–418.

———, 1973, "The Pricing of Options and Corporate Liabilities," *Journal of Political Economy,* 81, 637–654.

Black, F., E. Derman, and W. Toy, 1990, "A One-Factor Model of Interest Rates and Its Application to Treasury Bond Options," *Financial Analysts Journal,* January–February, 33–39.

Black, F., M. Jensen, and M. Scholes, 1972, "The Capital Asset Pricing Model: Some Empirical Tests," in Jensen, M. (ed.), *Studies in the Theory of Capital Markets,* Praeger, New York.

Blanchard, O., and M. Watson, 1982, "Bubbles, Rational Expectations and Financial Markets," in P. Wachtel (ed.), *Crises in the Economic and Financial Structure: Bubbles, Bursts, and Shocks,* Lexington, Lexington, MA.

Blattberg, R., and N. Gonedes, 1974, "A Comparison of Stable and Student Distributions as Statistical Models for Stock Prices," *Journal of Business,* 47, 244–280.

Blume, M., and I. Friend, 1973, "A New Look at the Capital Asset Pricing Model," *Journal of Finance,* 28, 19–33.

———, 1978, *The Changing Role of the Individual Investor,* John Wiley and Sons, New York.

Blume, M., and R. Stambaugh, 1983, "Biases in Computed Returns: An Application to the Size Effect," *Journal of Financial Economics,* 12, 387–404.

Blume, L., D. Easley, and M. O'Hara, 1994, "Market Statistics and Technical Analysis: The Role of Volume," *Journal of Finance,* 49, 153–181.

Blume, M., C. MacKinlay, and B. Terker, 1989, "Order Imbalances and Stock Price Movements on October 19 and 20, 1987," *Journal of Finance,* 44, 827–848.

Boehmer, E., J. Musumeci, and A. Poulsen, 1991, "Event-Study Methodology under Conditions of Event Induced Variance," *Journal of Financial Economics*, 30, 253–272.

Boldrin, M., and M. Woodford, 1990, "Equilibrium Models Displaying Endogenous Fluctuations and Chaos: A Survey," *Journal of Monetary Economics*, 25, 189–222.

Bollerslev, T., 1986, "Generalized Autoregressive Conditional Heteroskedasticity," *Journal of Econometrics*, 31, 307–327.

———, 1987, "A Conditional Heteroskedastic Time Series Model for Speculative Prices and Rates of Return," *Review of Economics and Statistics*, 69, 542–547.

———, 1990, "Modelling the Coherence in Short-Run Nominal Exchange Rates: A Multivariate Generalized ARCH Approach," *Review of Economics and Statistics*, 72, 498–505.

Bollerslev, T., and R. Engle, 1993, "Common Persistence in Conditional Variances," *Econometrica*, 61, 166–187.

Bollerslev, T., and J. Wooldridge, 1992, "Quasi-Maximum Likelihood Estimation and Inference in Dynamic Models with Time Varying Covariances," *Econometric Reviews*, 11, 143–172.

Bollerslev, T., R. Chou, and K. Kroner, 1992, "ARCH Modelling in Finance: A Review of the Theory and Empirical Evidence," *Journal of Econometrics*, 52, 5–59.

Bollerslev, T., R. Engle, and D. Nelson, 1994, "ARCH Models," in R. Engle and D. McFadden (eds.), *Handbook of Econometrics*, Vol. IV, Elsevier, Amsterdam.

Bollerslev, T., R. Engle, and J. Wooldridge, 1988, "A Capital Asset Pricing Model with Time Varying Covariances," *Journal of Political Economy*, 96, 116–131.

Bonomo, Marco, and René Garcia, 1993, "Disappointment Aversion as a Solution to the Equity Premium and the Risk-Free Rate Puzzles," CRDE Discussion Paper 2793. University of Montreal.

Boudoukh, J., and M. Richardson, 1994, "The Statistics of Long-Horizon Regressions Revisited," *Mathematical Finance*, 4, 103–119.

Boudoukh, J., Richardson, M., Stanton, R. and R. Whitelaw, 1995, "Pricing Mortgage-Backed Securities in a Multifactor Interest Rate Environment: A Multivariate Density Estimation Approach," working paper, Stern School of Business, New York University.

Boudoukh, J., M. Richardson, and R. Whitelaw, 1994, "A Tale of Three Schools: Insights on Autocorrelations of Short-Horizon Stock Returns," *Review of Financial Studies*, 7, 539–573.

Box, G., and D. Cox, 1964, "An Analysis of Transformations," *Journal of the Royal Statistical Society*, Series B(26), 211–243.

Box, G., and D. Pierce, 1970, "Distribution of Residual Autocorrelations in Autoregressive-Integrated Moving Average Time Series Models," *Journal of the American Statistical Association*, 65, 1509–1526.

Boyle, P., 1977, "Options: A Monte Carlo Approach," *Journal of Financial Economics*, 4, 323–338.

———, 1988, "A Lattice Framework for Option Pricing with Two State Variables," *Journal of Financial and Quantitative Analysis*, 1–12.

Brainard, W., W. Nelson, and M. Shapiro, 1991, "The Consumption Beta Explains Expected Returns at Long Horizons," unpublished paper, Yale University and University of Michigan.

Branch, B., and W. Freed, 1977, "Bid-Asked Spreads on the AMEX and the Big Board," *Journal of Finance*, 32, 159–163.

Braun, P., D. Nelson, and A. Sunier, 1995, "Good News, Bad News, Volatility, and Betas," *Journal of Finance*, 50, 1575–1603.

Breeden, D., 1979, "An Intertemporal Asset Pricing Model with Stochastic Consumption and Investment Opportunities," *Journal of Financial Economics*, 7, 265–296.

Breeden, D., and R. Litzenberger, 1978, "Prices of State-Contingent Claims Implicit in Option Prices," *Journal of Business*, 51, 621–651.

Breeden, D., M. Gibbons, and R. Litzenberger, 1989, "Empirical Tests of the Consumption-Oriented CAPM," *Journal of Finance*, 44, 231–262.

Breen, W., and R. Korajczyk, 1993, "On Selection Biases in Book-to-Market Based Tests of Asset Pricing Models," Working Paper 167, Northwestern University, Evanston, IL.

Brennan, M., 1979, "The Pricing of Contingent Claims in Discrete-Time Models," *Journal of Finance*, 34, 53–68.

Brennan, M., and T. Copeland, 1988, "Stock Splits, Stock Prices, and Transaction Costs," *Journal of Financial Economics*, 22, 83–101.

Brennan, M., and E. Schwartz, 1977a, "Convertible Bonds: Valuation and Optimal Strategies for Call and Conversion," *Journal of Finance*, 32, 1699–1715.

———, 1977b, "The Valuation of American Put Options," *Journal of Finance*, 32, 449–462.

———, 1978, "Finite Difference Methods and Jump Processes Arising in the Pricing of Contingent Claims: A Synthesis," *Journal of Financial and Quantitative Analysis*, 13, 461–474.

———, 1979, "A Continuous-Time Approach to the Pricing of Bonds," *Journal of Banking and Finance*, 3, 133–155.

Brennan, M., N. Jegadeesh, and B. Swaminathan, 1993, "Investment Analysis and the Adjustment of Stock Prices to Common Information," *Review of Financial Studies*, 6, 799–824.

Brenner, R., R. Harjes, and K. Kroner, 1996, "Another Look at Alternative Models of the Short-Term Interest Rate," *Journal of Financial and Quantitative Analysis*, 31, 85–107.

Brock, W., 1986, "Distinguishing Random and Deterministic Systems: Abridged Version," *Journal of Economic Theory*, 40, 168–195.

Brock, W., and C. Sayers, 1988, "Is The Business Cycle Characterized By Deterministic Chaos?," *Journal of Monetary Economics*, 22, 71–90.

Brock, W., W. Dechert, and J. Scheinkman, 1987, "A Test for Independence Based on the Correlation Dimension," unpublished paper, University of Wisconsin at Madison, University of Houston, and University of Chicago.

Brock, W., J. Lakonishok, and B. LeBaron, 1992, "Simple Technical Trading Rules and the Stochastic Properties of Stock Returns," *Journal of Finance*, 47, 1731–1764.

Brodsky, B., 1993, *Nonparametric Methods in Change-Point Problems*, Kluwer Academic Publishers, Boston.

Bronfman, C., 1991, "From Trades to Orders on the NYSE: Pitfalls in Inference Using Transactions Data," working paper, Department of Finance and Real Estate, College of Business and Public Administration, University of Arizona, Tucson, AZ.

Broomhead, D., and D. Lowe, 1988, "Multivariable Functional Interpolation and Adaptive Networks," *Complex Systems*, 2, 321–355.

Brown, S., and P. Dybvig, 1986, "The Empirical Implications of the Cox, Ingersoll, Ross Theory of the Term Structure of Interest Rates," *Journal of Finance*, 41, 617–632.

Brown, D., and R. Jennings, 1989, "On Technical Analysis," *Review of Financial Studies*, 2, 527–552.

Brown, R., and S. Schaefer, 1991, "Interest Rate Volatility and the Term Structure," unpublished paper, London Business School.

———, 1994, "The Term Structure of Real Interest Rates and the Cox, Ingersoll, and Ross Model," *Journal of Financial Economics*, 35, 3–42.

Brown, S., and J. Warner, 1980, "Measuring Security Price Performance," *Journal of Financial Economics*, 8, 205–258.

———, 1985, "Using Daily Stock Returns: The Case of Event Studies," *Journal of Financial Economics*, 14, 3–31.

Brown, S., and M. Weinstein, 1985, "Derived Factors in Event Studies," *Journal of Financial Economics*, 14, 491–495.

Brown, S., W. Goetzmann, and S. Ross, 1995, "Survival," *Journal of Finance*, 50, 853–873.

Burnside, C., 1994, "Hansen-Jagannathan Bounds as Classical Tests of Asset Pricing Models," *Journal of Business and Economic Statistics*, 12, 57–79.

Campbell, C., and C. Wasley, 1993, "Measuring Security Price Performance Using Daily NASDAQ Returns," *Journal of Financial Economics*, 33, 73–92.

Campbell, J., 1986, "Bond and Stock Returns in a Simple Exchange Model," *Quarterly Journal of Economics*, 101, 785–803.

———, 1987, "Stock Returns and the Term Structure," *Journal of Financial Economics*, 18, 373–399.

———, 1991, "A Variance Decomposition for Stock Returns," *Economic Journal*, 101, 157–179.

———, 1993a, "Intertemporal Asset Pricing without Consumption Data," *American Economic Review*, 83, 487–512.

———, 1993b, "Why Long Horizons? A Study of Power against Persistent Alternatives," unpublished paper, Princeton University.

———, 1995, "Some Lessons from the Yield Curve," *Journal of Economic Perspectives*, 9(3), 129–152.

———, 1996a, "Understanding Risk and Return," *Journal of Political Economy*, 104, 298–345.

———, 1996b, "Consumption and the Stock Market: Interpreting International Evidence," NBER Working Paper 5610, National Bureau of Economic Research, Cambridge, MA.

Campbell, J., and J. Ammer, 1993, "What Moves the Stock and Bond Markets? A Variance Decomposition for Long-Term Asset Returns," *Journal of Finance*, 48, 3–37.

Campbell, J., and J. Cochrane, 1995, "By Force of Habit: A Consumption-Based Explanation of Aggregate Stock Market Behavior," unpublished paper, Harvard University and University of Chicago.

Campbell, J., and L. Hentschel, 1992, "No News Is Good News: An Asymmetric Model of Changing Volatility in Stock Returns," *Journal of Financial Economics*, 31, 281–318.

Campbell, J., and H. Koo, 1996, "A Comparison of Numerical and Analytical Approximate Solutions to an Intertemporal Consumption Choice Problem," *Journal of Economic Dynamics and Control*, forthcoming.

Campbell, J., and A. Kyle, 1993, "Smart Money, Noise Trading, and Stock Price Behavior," *Review of Economic Studies*, 60, 1–34.

Campbell, J., and N. G. Mankiw, 1987, "Are Output Fluctuations Transitory?," *Quarterly Journal of Economics*, 102, 857–880.

———, 1990, "Permanent Income, Current Income, and Consumption," *Journal of Business and Economic Statistics*, 8, 265–278.

Campbell, J., and P. Perron, 1991, "Pitfalls and Opportunities: What Macroeconomists Should Know about Unit Roots," *NBER Macroeconomics Annual*, 6, 141–201.

Campbell, J., and R. Shiller, 1987, "Cointegration and Tests of Present Value Models," *Journal of Political Economy*, 95, 1062–1087.

———, 1988a, "The Dividend-Price Ratio and Expectations of Future Dividends and Discount Factors," *Review of Financial Studies*, 1, 195–227.

———, 1988b, "Stock Prices, Earnings, and Expected Dividends," *Journal of Finance*, 43, 661–676.

———, 1991, "Yield Spreads and Interest Rate Movements: A Bird's Eye View," *Review of Economic Studies*, 58, 495–514.

———, 1996, "A Scorecard for Indexed Government Debt," *NBER Macroeconomics Annual*, forthcoming.

Campbell, J., S. Grossman, and J. Wang, 1993, "Trading Volume and Serial Correlation in Stock Returns," *Quarterly Journal of Economics*, 108, 905–939.

Carlstein, E., H. Muller, and D. Siegmund, eds., 1994, *Change-Point Problems*, Institute of Mathematical Statistics, Hayward, CA.

Carleton, W., and I. Cooper, 1976, "Estimation and Uses of the Term Structure of Interest Rates," *Journal of Finance*, 31, 1067–1083.

Carverhill, A., 1988, "Numerical Methods in Pricing," Preprint 88/1, Financial Options Research Centre, University of Warwick, UK.

Carverhill, A., and N. Webber, 1988, "American Options: Validation of Numerical Methods," Preprint 88/2, Financial Options Research Centre, University of Warwick, UK.

Cecchetti, S., P. Lam, and N. Mark, 1990, "Mean Reversion in Equilibrium Asset Prices," *American Economic Review*, 80, 398–418.

———, 1994, "Testing Volatility Restrictions on Intertemporal Marginal Rates of Substitution Implied by Euler Equations and Asset Returns," *Journal of Finance*, 49, 123–152.

Chamberlain, G., 1983a, "Funds, Factors, and Diversification in Arbitrage Pricing Models," *Econometrica*, 51, 1305–1323.

———, 1983b, "A Characterization of the Distributions that Imply Mean-Variance Utility Functions," *Journal of Economic Theory*, 29, 1985–201.

Chamberlain, G., and M. Rothschild, 1983, "Arbitrage, Factor Structure, and Mean-Variance Analysis on Large Asset Markets," *Econometrica*, 51, 1281–1304.

Chan, K., 1988, "On the Contrarian Investment Strategy," *Journal of Business*, 61, 147–163.

Chan, K., N. Chen, and D. Hsieh, 1985, "An Exploratory Investigation of the Firm Size Effect," *Journal of Financial Economics*, 14, 451–472.

Chan, K., W. Christie, and P. Schultz, 1995, "Market Structure and the Intraday Evolution of Bid-Ask Spreads for NASDAQ Securities," *Journal of Business*, 68, 35–60.

Chan, K., G. Karolyi, F. Longstaff, and A. Sanders, 1992, "An Empirical Comparison of Alternative Models of the Short-Term Interest Rate," *Journal of Finance*, 47, 1209–1227.

Chan, L., and J. Lakonishok, 1993a, "Are the Reports of Beta's Death Premature?," *Journal of Portfolio Management*, 19, 51–62.

———, 1993b, "Institutional Trades and Intra-Day Stock Price Behavior," *Journal of Financial Economics*, 33, 173–199.

———, 1995, "The Behavior of Stock Prices around Institutional Trades," *Journal of Finance*, 50, 1147–1174.

Chen, H., 1991a, "Estimation of a Projection-Pursuit Type Regression Model," *Annals of Statistics*, 19, 142–157.

Chen, N., 1983, "Some Empirical Tests of Arbitrage Pricing," *Journal of Finance*, 38, 1393–1414.

Chen, N., 1991b, "Financial Investment Opportunities and the Macroeconomy," *Journal of Finance*, 46, 529–554.

Chen, N., and J. Ingersoll, 1983, "Exact Pricing in Linear Factor Models with Finitely Many Assets," *Journal of Finance*, 38, 985–988.

Chen, N., R. Roll, and S. Ross, 1986, "Economic Forces and the Stock Market," *Journal of Business*, 59, 383–403.

Chiras, D., and S. Manaster, 1978, "The Information Content of Option Prices and a Test of Market Efficiency," *Journal of Financial Economics*, 6, 213–234.

Cho, D., and E. Frees, 1988, "Estimating the Volatility of Discrete Stock Prices," *Journal of Finance*, 43, 451–466.

Choi, J., D. Salandro, and K. Shastri, 1988, "On the Estimation of Bid-Ask Spreads: Theory and Evidence," *Journal of Financial and Quantitative Analysis*, 23, 219–230.

Christie, A., 1982, "The Stochastic Behavior of Common Stock Variances: Value, Leverage, and Interest Rate Effects," *Journal of Financial Economics*, 10, 407–432.

Christie, W., and P. Schultz, 1994, "Why Do NASDAQ Market Makers Avoid Odd-Eighth Quotes?," *Journal of Finance*, 49, 1813–1840.

Christie, W., J. Harris, and P. Schultz, 1994, "Why Did NASDAQ Market Makers Stop Avoiding Odd-Eighth Quotes?," *Journal of Finance*, 49, 1841–1860.

Chung, C., and A. Goldberger, 1984, "Proportional Projects in Limited Dependent Variables Models," *Econometrica*, 52, 531–534.

Chung, K., and R. Williams, 1990, *Introduction to Stochastic Integration* (2d ed.), Birkhäuser, Boston, MA.

Clark, P., 1973, "A Subordinated Stochastic Process Model with Finite Variance for Speculative Prices," *Econometrica*, 41, 135–156.

Clewlow, L., 1990, "Finite Difference Techniques for One and Two Dimensional Option Valuation Problems," Preprint 90/10, Financial Options Research Centre, University of Warwick, UK.

Cochrane, J., 1988, "How Big Is the Random Walk in GNP?," *Journal of Political Economy*, 96, 893–920.

———, 1991, "Volatility Tests and Efficient Markets: A Review Essay," *Journal of Monetary Economics*, 27, 463–487.

Cochrane, J., and L. Hansen, 1992, "Asset Pricing Explorations for Macroeconomics," in *NBER Macroeconomics Annual 1992*, Massachusetts Institute of Technology Press, Cambridge, MA, 115–165.

Cohen, K., G. Hawawini, S. Maier, R. Schwartz, and D. Whitcomb, 1983a, "Estimating and Adjusting for the Intervalling-Effect Bias in Beta," *Management Science*, 29, 135–148.

———, 1983b, "Friction in the Trading Process and the Estimation of Systematic Risk," *Journal of Financial Economics*, 12, 263–278.

Cohen, K., S. Maier, R. Schwartz, and D. Whitcomb, 1978, "The Returns Generation Process, Returns Variance, and the Effect of Thinness in Securities Markets," *Journal of Finance*, 33, 149–167.

———, 1979, "On the Existence of Serial Correlation in an Efficient Securities Market," *TIMS Studies in the Management Sciences*, 11, 151–168.

———, 1981, "Transaction Costs, Order Placement Strategy and Existence of the Bid-Ask Spread," *Journal of Political Economy*, 89, 287–305.

———, 1986, *The Microstructure of Securities Markets*, Prentice-Hall, Englewood Cliffs, NJ.

Collins, D., and W. Dent, 1984, "A Comparison of Alternative Testing Methodologies Used In Capital Market Research," *Journal of Accounting Research*, 22, 48–84.

Connor, G., 1984, "A Unified Beta Pricing Theory," *Journal of Economic Theory*, 34, 13–31.

Connor, G., and R. Korajczyk, 1986, "Performance Measurement with the Arbitrage Pricing Theory: A New Framework for Analysis," *Journal of Financial Economics*, 15, 373–394.

———, 1988, "Risk and Return in an Equilibrium APT: Application of a New Test Methodology," *Journal of Financial Economics*, 21, 255–290.

———, 1993, "A Test for the Number of Factors in an Approximate Factor Structure," *Journal of Finance*, 48, 1263–1291.

Conrad, J., and G. Kaul, 1993, "Long-Term Market Overreaction or Biases in Computed Returns?," *Journal of Finance*, 48, 39–63.

Conrad, J., G. Kaul, and M. Nimalendran, 1991, "Components of Short-Horizon Individual Security Return," *Journal of Financial Economics*, 29, 365–384.

Constantinides, G., 1982, "Intertemporal Asset Pricing with Heterogeneous Consumers and without Demand Aggregation," *Journal of Business*, 55, 253–268.

———, 1986, "Capital Market Equilibrium with Transaction Costs," *Journal of Political Economy*, 94, 842–862.

———, 1990, "Habit Formation: A Resolution of the Equity Premium Puzzle," *Journal of Political Economy*, 98, 519–543.

———, 1992, "A Theory of the Nominal Term Structure of Interest Rates," *Review of Financial Studies*, 5, 531–552.

Constantinides, G., and D. Duffie, 1996, "Asset Pricing with Heterogeneous Consumers," *Journal of Political Economy*, 104, 219–240.

Cootner, P. (ed.), 1964, *The Random Character of Stock Market Prices*, Massachusetts Institute of Technology Press, Cambridge, MA.

Copeland, T., and D. Galai, 1983, "Information Effects on the Bid-Ask Spread," *Journal of Finance*, 38, 1457–1469.

Corrado, C., 1989, "A Nonparametric Test for Abnormal Security Price Performance in Event Studies," *Journal of Financial Economics*, 23, 385–395.

Courtadon, G., 1982, "A More Accurate Finite Difference Approximation for the Valuation of Options," *Journal of Financial and Quantitative Analysis*, 17, 697–703.

Cowles, A., 1933, "Can Stock Market Forecasters Forecast?," *Econometrica*, 1, 309–324.

———, 1960, "A Revision of Previous Conclusions Regarding Stock Price Behavior," *Econometrica*, 28, 909–915.

Cowles, A., and H. Jones, 1937, "Some A Posteriori Probabilities in Stock Market Action," *Econometrica*, 5, 280–294.

Cox, D., and H. Miller, 1965, *The Theory of Stochastic Processes*, Chapman and Hall, London.

Cox, J., 1975, "Notes on Option Pricing I: Constant Elasticity of Variance Diffusions," unpublished lecture notes, Graduate School of Business, Stanford University.

Cox, J., and S. Ross, 1976, "The Valuation of Options for Alternative Stochastic Processes," *Journal of Financial Economics*, 3, 145–166.

Cox, J., and M. Rubinstein, 1985, *Options Markets*, Prentice-Hall, Englewood Cliffs, New Jersey.

Cox, J., J. Ingersoll, and S. Ross, 1981a, "A Reexamination of Traditional Hypotheses about the Term Structure of Interest Rates," *Journal of Finance*, 36, 769–799.

———, 1981b, "The Relation between Forward Prices and Futures Prices," *Journal of Financial Economics*, 9, 321–346.

———, 1985a, "A Theory of the Term Structure of Interest Rates," *Econometrica*, 53, 385–408.

———, 1985b, "An Intertemporal General Equilibrium Model of Asset Prices," *Econometrica*, 53, 363–384.

Cox, J., S. Ross, and M. Rubinstein, 1979, "Option Pricing: A Simplified Approach," *Journal of Financial Economics*, 7, 229–264.

Crack, T. and O. Ledoit, 1996, "Robust Structure Without Predictability: The 'Compass Rose' Pattern of the Stock Market," *Journal of Finance*, 51, 751–762.

Craig, S., J. Kohlase, and D. Papell, 1991, "Chaos Theory and Microeconomics: An Application to Model Specification and Hedonic Estimation," *Review of Economics and Statistics*, 73, 208–215.

Cumby, R., and D. Modest, 1987, "Testing for Market Timing Ability: A Framework for Forecast Evaluation," *Journal of Financial Economics*, 19, 169–190.

Cutler, D., J. Poterba, and L. Summers, 1991, "Speculative Dynamics," *Review of Economic Studies*, 58, 529–546.

Cybenko, G., 1989, "Approximation by Superpositions of a Sigmoidal Function," *Mathematics of Control, Signals, and Systems*, 2, 303–314.

Dann, L., and C. James, 1982, "An Analysis of the Impact of Deposit Rate Ceilings on the Market Values of Thrift Institutions," *Journal of Finance*, 37, 1259–1275.

David, F., and D. Barton, 1962, *Combinatorial Chance*, Hafner, New York.

Davies, R., and D. Harte, 1987, "Tests for Hurst Effect," *Biometrika*, 74, 95–101.

Davis, D., and C. Holt, 1993, *Experimental Economics*, Princeton University Press, Princeton, NJ.

Davis, M., and A. Norman, 1990, "Portfolio Selection with Transaction Costs," *Mathematics of Operations Research*, 15, 676–713.

Day, R., 1983, "The Emergence of Chaos from Classical Economic Growth," *Quarterly Journal of Economics*, 98, 201–214.

Deaton, A., and M. Irish, 1984, "Statistical Models for Zero Expenditures in Household Budgets," *Journal of Public Economics*, 23, 59–80.

DeBondt, W., and R. Thaler, 1985, "Does the Stock Market Overreact?," *Journal of Finance*, 40, 793–805.

———, 1987, "Further Evidence on Investor Overreaction and Stock Market Seasonality," *Journal of Finance*, 42, 557–582.

Debreu, G., 1959, *Theory of Value*, John Wiley and Sons, New York.

DeLong, B., A. Shleifer, L. Summers, and R. Waldmann, 1990a, "Positive Feedback Investment Strategies and Destabilizing Speculation," *Journal of Finance*, 45, 379–396.

———, 1990b, "Noise Trader Risk in Financial Markets," *Journal of Political Economy*, 98, 703–738.

Demsetz, H., 1968, "The Cost of Transacting," *Quarterly Journal of Economics*, 82, 33–53.

Derman, E., and I. Kani, 1994, "Riding on the Smile," *RISK*, 7, February, 32–39.

Dhrymes, P., I. Friend, B. Gultekin, and M. Gultekin, 1984, "A Critical Reexamination of the Empirical Evidence on the Arbitrage Pricing Theory," *Journal of Finance*, 39, 323–346.

Diaconis, P., 1988, *Group Representations in Probability and Statistics*, Institute of Mathematical Statistics, Hayward, CA.

Diaconis, P., and M. Shahshahani, 1984, "On Nonlinear Functions of Linear Combinations," *SIAM Journal on Scientific and Statistical Computing*, 5(1), 175–191.

Diamond, P., 1965, "National Debt in a Neoclassical Growth Model," *American Economic Review*, 55, 1126–1150.

Diba, B., and H. Grossman, 1988, "The Theory of Rational Bubbles in Stock Prices," *Economic Journal*, 98, 746–757.

Dickey, D., and W. Fuller, 1979, "Distribution of the Estimators for Autoregressive Time Series with a Unit Root," *Journal of the American Statistical Association*, 74, 427–431.

Dimson, E., 1979, "Risk Measurement When Shares Are Subject to Infrequent Trading," *Journal of Financial Economics*, 7, 197–226.

Ding, Z., C. Granger, and R. Engle, 1993, "A Long Memory Property of Stock Returns and a New Model," *Journal of Empirical Finance*, 1, 83–106.

Dolley, J., 1933, "Characteristics and Procedure of Common Stock Split-Ups," *Harvard Business Review*, 316–326.

Donaldson, R., and M. Kamstra, 1996, "A New Dividend Forecasting Procedure that Rejects Bubbles in Asset Prices: The Case of 1929's Stock Crash," *Review of Financial Studies*, 9, 333–383.

Donoho, D., and I. Johnstone, 1989, "Projection-Based Approximation and A Duality with Kernel Methods," *Annals of Statistics*, 17, 58–106.

Duffie, D., 1992, *Dynamic Asset Pricing Theory*, Princeton University Press, Princeton, NJ.

Duffie, D., and C. Huang, 1985, "Implementing Arrow-Debreu Equilibria by Continuous Trading of Few Long-Lived Securities," *Econometrica*, 53, 1337–1356.

Duffie, D., and R. Kan, 1993, "A Yield-Factor Model of Interest Rates," unpublished paper, Stanford University.

Dufour, J., 1981, "Rank Tests for Serial Dependence," *Journal of Time Series Analysis*, 2, 117–128.

Dufour, J., and R. Roy, 1985, "Some Robust Exact Results on Sample Autocorrelations and Tests of Randomness," *Journal of Econometrics*, 29, 257–273.

Dunn, K., and K. Singleton, 1986, "Modelling the Term Structure of Interest Rates under Habit Formation and Durability of Goods," *Journal of Financial Economics*, 17, 27–55.

Dupire, B., 1994, "Pricing with a Smile," *RISK*, 7, January, 18–20.

Durlauf, S., and R. Hall, 1989, "Measuring Noise in Stock Prices," unpublished paper, Stanford University.

Durlauf, S., and P. Phillips, 1988, "Trends versus Random Walks in Time Series Analysis," *Econometrica*, 56, 1333–1357.

Dybvig, P., 1985, "An Explicit Bound on Individual Assets' Deviations from APT Pricing in a Finite Economy," *Journal of Financial Economics*, 12, 483–496.

———, 1989, "Bond and Bond Option Pricing Based on the Current Term Structure," unpublished paper, Washington University.

Dybvig, P., and J. Ingersoll, 1982, "Mean-Variance Theory in Complete Markets," *Journal of Business*, 55, 233–252.

Dybvig, P., and S. Ross, 1985, "Yes, The APT Is Testable," *Journal of Finance*, 40, 1173–1188.

Dybvig, P., J. Ingersoll, Jr., and S. Ross, 1996, "Long Forward and Zero-Coupon Rates Can Never Fall," *Journal of Business*, 69, 1–25.

Easley, D., and M. O'Hara, 1987, "Price, Trade Size, and Information in Securities Markets," *Journal of Financial Economics*, 19, 69–90.

———, 1992, "Time and the Process of Security Price Adjustment," *Journal of Finance*, 47, 577–605.

Eberlein, E., and M. Taqqu, 1986, *Dependence in Probability and Statistics: A Survey of Recent Result*, Progress in Probability and Statistics, Vol. 11, Birkhäuser, Boston.

Eckbo, B., 1983, "Horizontal Mergers, Collusion, and Stockholder Wealth," *Journal of Financial Economics*, 11, 241–276.

Eckbo, E., V. Maksimovic, and J. Williams, 1990, "Consistent Estimation of Cross-Sectional Models in Event-Studies," *Review of Financial Studies*, 3(3), 343–365.

Edwards, R., and J. Magee, 1966, *Technical Analysis of Stock Trends* (revised 5th ed.), John Magee, Boston.

Eichenbaum, M., L. Hansen, and K. Singleton, 1988, "A Time Series Analysis of Representative Agent Models of Consumption and Leisure Choice under Uncertainty," *Quarterly Journal of Economics*, 103, 51–78.

Eikeboom, A., 1993, "The Dynamics of the Bid-Ask Spread," working paper, Sloan School of Management, Massachusetts Institute of Technology, Cambridge, MA.

Einstein, A., 1905, "Ueber die von der molekular-kinetischen Theorie der Wärme geforderte Bewegung von in ruhenden Flüssigkeiten suspendierten Teilchen," *Annalen der Physik*, 17, 549–560.

Engle, R., 1982, "Autoregressive Conditional Heteroskedasticity with Estimates of the Variance of UK Inflation," *Econometrica*, 50, 987–1008.

———, 1984, "Wald, Likelihood Ratio, and Lagrange Multiplier Tests in Econometrics," in Z. Griliches and M. Intriligator (eds.), *Handbook of Econometrics, Volume II*, North-Holland, Amsterdam, chap. 13.

Engle, R., and G. Gonzalez-Rivera, 1991, "Semiparametric ARCH Models," *Journal of Business and Economic Statistics*, 9, 345–359.

Engle, R., and C. Granger, 1987, "Cointegration and Error-Correction: Representation, Estimation, and Testing," *Econometrica*, 55, 251–276.

Engle, R., and K. Kroner, 1995, "Multivariate Simultaneous Generalized ARCH," *Econometric Theory*, 11, 122–150.

Engle, R., and V. Ng, 1993, "Measuring and Testing the Impact of News on Volatility," *Journal of Finance*, 48, 1749–1778.

Engle, R., D. Lilien, and R. Robins, 1987, "Estimating Time-Varying Risk Premia in the Term Structure: The ARCH-M Model," *Econometrica*, 55, 391–407.

Engle, R., V. Ng, and M. Rothschild, 1990, "Asset Pricing with a Factor ARCH Covariance Structure: Empirical Estimates for Treasury Bills," *Journal of Econometrics*, 45, 213–238.

Epstein, L., and S. Zin, 1989, "Substitution, Risk Aversion, and the Temporal Behavior of Consumption and Asset Returns: A Theoretical Framework," *Econometrica*, 57, 937–968.

———, 1990, "First-Order Risk Aversion and the Equity Premium Puzzle," *Journal of Monetary Economics*, 26, 387–407.

———, 1991, "Substitution, Risk Aversion, and the Temporal Behavior of Consumption and Asset Returns: An Empirical Investigation," *Journal of Political Economy*, 99, 263–286.

Estrella, A., and G. Hardouvelis, 1991, "The Term Structure as a Predictor of Real Economic Activity," *Journal of Finance*, 46, 555–576.

Eytan, T., and G. Harpaz, 1986, "The Pricing of Futures and Options Contracts on the Value Line Index," *Journal of Finance*, 41, 843–856.

Fabozzi, F., 1996, *Bond Markets, Analysis and Strategies* (3rd ed.), Prentice-Hall, Upper Saddle River, NJ.

Fabozzi, F., and T. Fabozzi (eds.), 1995, *The Handbook of Fixed-Income Securities* (4th ed.), Irwin, Burr Ridge, IL.

Fama, E., 1965, "The Behavior of Stock Market Prices," *Journal of Business*, 38, 34–105.

———, 1970, "Efficient Capital Markets: A Review of Theory and Empirical Work," *Journal of Finance*, 25, 383–417.

———, 1975, "Short-Term Interest Rates as Predictors of Inflation," *American Economic Review*, 65, 269–282.

———, 1976, *Foundations of Finance*, Basic Books, New York.

———, 1984, "The Information in the Term Structure," *Journal of Financial Economics*, 13, 509–521.

———, 1990, "Term-Structure Forecasts of Interest Rates, Inflation, and Real Returns," *Journal of Monetary Economics*, 25, 59–76.

———, 1991, "Efficient Capital Markets: II," *Journal of Finance*, 46, 1575–1618.

———, 1993, "Multifactor Portfolio Efficiency and Multifactor Asset Pricing Models," working paper, CRSP, University of Chicago, Chicago, IL.

Fama, E., and R. Bliss, 1987, "The Information in Long-Maturity Forward Rates," *American Economic Review*, 77, 680–692.

Fama, E., and M. Blume, 1966, "Filter Rules and Stock Market Trading Profits," *Journal of Business*, 39, 226–241.

Fama, E., and K. French, 1988a, "Dividend Yields and Expected Stock Returns," *Journal of Financial Economics*, 22, 3–27.

———, 1988b, "Permanent and Temporary Components of Stock Prices," *Journal of Political Economy*, 96, 246–273.

———, 1989, "Business Conditions and Expected Returns on Stocks and Bonds," *Journal of Financial Economics*, 25, 23–49.

———, 1992, "The Cross-Section of Expected Stock Returns," *Journal of Finance*, 47, 427–465.

———, 1993, "Common Risk Factors in the Returns on Stocks and Bonds," *Journal of Financial Economics*, 33, 3–56.

———, 1996a, "Multifactor Explanations of Asset Pricing Anomalies," *Journal of Finance*, 51, 55–84.

———, 1996b, "The CAPM Is Wanted, Dead or Alive," *Journal of Finance*, forthcoming.

Fama, E., and J. MacBeth, 1973, "Risk, Return, and Equilibrium: Empirical Tests," *Journal of Political Economy*, 71, 607–636.

Fama, E., and R. Roll, 1971, "Parameter Estimates for Symmetric Stable Distributions," *Journal of the American Statistical Association*, 66, 331–338.

Fama, E., L. Fisher, M. Jensen, and R. Roll, 1969, "The Adjustment of Stock Prices to New Information," *International Economic Review*, 10, 1–21.

Fang, K., and Y. Wang, 1994, *Number-Theoretic Methods in Statistics*, Chapman and Hall, London.

Faust, J., 1992, "When Are Variance Ratio Tests For Serial Dependence Optimal?," *Econometrica*, 60, 1215–1226.

Feller, W., 1968, *An Introduction to Probability Theory and Its Applications*, John Wiley and Sons, New York.

Ferson, W., and G. Constantinides, 1991, "Habit Persistence and Durability in Aggregate Consumption: Empirical Tests," *Journal of Financial Economics*, 29, 199–240.

Ferson, W., and S. Foerster, 1994, "Finite Sample Properties of the Generalized Method of Moments in Tests of Conditional Asset Pricing Models," *Journal of Financial Economics*, 36, 29–55.

Fielitz, B., 1976, "Further Results on Asymmetric Stable Distributions of Stock Prices Changes," *Journal of Financial and Quantitative Analysis*, 11, 39–55.

Fielitz, B., and J. Rozell, 1983, "Stable Distributions and Mixtures of Distributions Hypotheses for Common Stock Returns," *Journal of the American Statistical Association*, 78, 28–36.

Fisher, L., 1966, "Some New Stock Market Indexes," *Journal of Business*, 39, 191–225.

Fishman, G., 1996, *Monte Carlo: Concepts, Algorithms, and Applications*, Springer-Verlag, New York.

Flavin, M., 1983, "Excess Volatility in the Financial Markets: A Reassessment of the Empirical Evidence," *Journal of Political Economy*, 91, 929–956.

Frankel, J., G. Galli, and A. Giovannini, eds., 1996, *The Microstructure of Foreign Exchange Markets* (NBER Conference Report), University of Chicago Press, Chicago, IL.

French, K., and R. Roll, 1986, "Stock Return Variances: The Arrival of Information and the Reaction of Traders," *Journal of Financial Economics*, 17, 5–26.

French, K., G. Schwert, and R. Stambaugh, 1987, "Expected Stock Returns and Volatility," *Journal of Financial Economics*, 19, 3–30.

Friedman, J., and W. Stuetzle, 1981, "Projection Pursuit Regression," *Journal of the American Statistical Association*, 76(376), December.

Friend, I., and M. Blume, 1975, "The Demand for Risky Assets," *American Economic Review*, 65, 900–922.

Froot, K., 1989, "New Hope for the Expectations Hypothesis of the Term Structure of Interest Rates," *Journal of Finance*, 44, 283–305.

Froot, K., and M. Obstfeld, 1991, "Intrinsic Bubbles: The Case of Stock Prices," *American Economic Review*, 81, 1189–1217.

Fuller, W., 1976, *Introduction to Statistical Time Series*, Wiley, New York.

Furbush, D., and J. Smith, 1996, "Quoting Behavior on NASDAQ: The Determinants of Clustering and Relative Spreads," Economists Inc., Washington, D.C.

Galai, D., 1977, "Tests of Market Efficiency of the Chicago Board Options Exchange," *Journal of Business*, 50, 167–197.

———, 1978, "Empirical Tests of Boundary Conditions for CBOE Options," *Journal of Financial Economics*, 6, 187–211.

Gallant, A., 1987, *Nonlinear Statistical Models*, John Wiley and Sons, New York.

Gallant, A., and H. White, 1992, "On Learning the Derivatives of an Unknown Mapping with Multilayer Feedforward Networks," *Neural Networks*, 5, 128–138.

Gallant, R., P. Rossi, and G. Tauchen, 1991, "Stock Prices and Volume," *Review of Financial Studies*, 5, 199–242.

Garber, P., 1989, "Tulipmania," *Journal of Political Economy*, 97, 535–560.

Garman, M., 1976a, "Market Microstructure," *Journal of Financial Economics*, 3, 257–275.

———, 1976b, "A General Theory of Asset Valuation under Diffusion State Processes," Working Paper 50, University of California, Berkeley.

————, 1978, "The Pricing of Supershares," *Journal of Financial Economics*, 6, 3–10.

Garman, M., and M. Klass, 1980, "On the Estimation of Security Price Volatilities from Historical Data," *Journal of Business*, 53, 67–78.

George, T., G. Kaul, and M. Nimalendran, 1991, "Estimation of the Bid-Ask Spread and Its Components: A New Approach," *Review of Financial Studies*, 4, 23–656.

Gerber, H., and S. Li, 1981, "The Occurrence of Sequence Patterns in Repeated Experiments and Hitting Times in a Markov Chain," *Stochastic Processes and Their Applications*, 11, 101–108.

Geske, R., and K. Shastri, 1985, "Valuation by Approximation: A Comparison of Option Valuation Techniques," *Journal of Financial and Quantitative Analysis*, 20, 45–72.

Gibbons, M., 1982, "Multivariate Tests of Financial Models: A New Approach," *Journal of Financial Economics*, 10, 3–27.

Gibbons, M., and W. Ferson, 1985, "Testing Asset Pricing Models with Changing Expectations and an Unobservable Market Portfolio," *Journal of Financial Economics*, 14, 217–236.

Gibbons, M., and K. Ramaswamy, 1993, "A Test of the Cox, Ingersoll, and Ross Model of the Term Structure," *Review of Financial Studies*, 6, 619–658.

Gibbons, M., S. Ross, and J. Shanken, 1989, "A Test of the Efficiency of a Given Portfolio," *Econometrica*, 57, 1121–1152.

Gilles, C., and S. LeRoy, 1991, "Econometric Aspects of the Variance Bounds Tests: A Survey," *Review of Financial Studies*, 4, 753–791.

Giovannini, A., and P. Weil, 1989, "Risk Aversion and Intertemporal Substitution in the Capital Asset Pricing Model," Working Paper 2824, NBER, Cambridge, MA.

Gleick, J., 1987, *Chaos: Making a New Science*, Viking Penguin Inc., New York.

Glosten, L., 1987, "Components of the Bid-Ask Spread and the Statistical Properties of Transaction Prices," *Journal of Finance*, 42, 1293–1307.

Glosten, L., and L. Harris, 1988, "Estimating the Components of the Bid/Ask Spread," *Journal of Financial Economics*, 21, 123–142.

Glosten, L., and P. Milgrom, 1985, "Bid, Ask and Transaction Prices in a Specialist Market with Heterogeneously Informed Traders," *Journal of Financial Economics*, 14, 71–100.

Glosten, L., R. Jagannathan, and D. Runkle, 1993, "On the Relation Between the Expected Value and the Volatility of the Nominal Excess Return on Stocks," *Journal of Finance*, 48, 1779–1801.

Godek, P., 1996, "Why NASDAQ Market Makers Avoid Odd-Eighth Quotes," *Journal of Financial Economics*, 41, 465–474.

Goldenberg, D., 1991, "A Unified Method for Pricing Options on Diffusion Processes," *Journal of Financial Economics*, 29, 3–34.

Goldman, B., H. Sosin, and M. Gatto, 1979, "Path Dependent Options: 'Buy at the Low, Sell at the High,'" *Journal of Finance*, 34, 1111–1127.

Goldman, B., H. Sosin, and L. Shepp, 1979, "On Contingent Claims that Insure Ex-Post Optimal Stock Market Timing," *Journal of Finance*, 34, 401–414.

Goldstein, M., 1993, *Bid-Ask Spreads on U.S. Equity Markets*, Unpublished Ph.D. dissertation, Wharton School, University of Pennsylvania.

Goodhart, C., and R. Curcio, 1990, "Asset Price Discovery and Price Clustering in the Foreign Exchange Market," unpublished working paper, London School of Economics.

Gordon, M., 1962, *The Investment, Financing, and Valuation of the Corporation*, Irwin, Homewood, IL.

Gottlieb, G., and A. Kalay, 1985, "Implications of the Discreteness of Observed Stock Prices," *Journal of Finance*, 40, 135–154.

Gourieroux, C., A. Monfort, and A. Trognon, 1985, "A General Approach to Serial Correlation," *Econometric Theory*, 1, 315–340.

Gourlay, A., and S. McKee, 1977, "The Construction of Hopscotch Methods for Parabolic and Elliptic Equations in Two Space Dimensions with a Mixed Derivative," *Journal of Computational and Applied Mathematics*, 201–206.

Graham, R., D. Knuth, and O. Patashnik, 1989, *Concrete Mathematics: A Foundation for Computer Science*, Addison-Wesley, Reading, MA.

Grandmont, J., and P. Malgrange, 1986, "Introduction to Nonlinear Economic Dynamics," *Journal of Economic Theory*, 40, 3–12.

Granger, C., 1966, "The Typical Spectral Shape of an Economic Variable," *Econometrica*, 34, 150–161.

———, 1969, "Investigating Causal Relations by Econometric Models and Cross-Spectral Methods," *Econometrica*, 37, 424–438.

———, 1980, "Long Memory Relationships and the Aggregation of Dynamic Models," *Journal of Econometrics*, 14, 227–238.

Granger, C., and A. Andersen, 1978, *An Introduction to Bilinear Time Series Models*, Vandenhoeck and Ruprecht, Göttingen.

Granger, C., and R. Joyeux, 1980, "An Introduction to Long Memory Time Series Models and Fractional Differencing," *Journal of Time Series Analysis*, 1, 15–29.

Granger, C., and O. Morgenstern, 1963, "Spectral Analysis of New York Stock Market Prices," *Kyklos*, 16, 1–27.

Granger, C., and O. Morgenstern, 1970, *Predictability of Stock Market Prices*, Heath-Lexington, Lexington, MA.

Granito, M., 1984, *Bond Portfolio Immunization*, Lexington, Lexington, MA.

Grassberger, P., and I. Procaccia, 1983, "Measuring the Strangeness of Strange Attractors," *Physica*, 9D, 189–208.

Gray, S., 1996, "Modeling the Conditional Distribution of Interest Rates as a Regime-Switching Process," *Journal of Financial Economics*, 42, 27–62.

Grinblatt, M., and S. Titman, 1985, "Factor Pricing in a Finite Economy," *Journal of Financial Economics*, 12, 497–507.

Grossman, S., 1989, *The Informational Role of Prices*, Massachusetts Institute of Technology Press, Cambridge, MA.

Grossman, S., and R. Shiller, 1981, "The Determinants of the Variability of Stock Market Prices," *American Economic Review*, 71, 222–227.

———, 1982, "Consumption Correlatedness and Risk Measurement in Economies with Non-Traded Assets and Heterogeneous Information," *Journal of Financial Economics*, 10, 195–210.

Grossman, S., and J. Stiglitz, 1980, "On the Impossibility of Informationally Efficient Markets," *American Economic Review*, 70, 393–408.

Grossman, S., and Z. Zhou, 1996, "Equilibrium Analysis of Portfolio Insurance," *Journal of Finance*, 51, 1379–1403.

Grossman, S., A. Melino, and R. Shiller, 1987, "Estimating the Continuous Time Consumption Based Asset Pricing Model," *Journal of Business and Economic Statistics*, 5, 315–328.

Grossman, S., M. Miller, D. Fischel, K. Cone, and D. Ross, 1995, "Clustering and Competition in Asset Markets," Lexecon Inc. Report.

Grundy, B., and M. McNichols, 1989, "Trade and Revelation of Information through Prices and Direct Disclosure," *Review of Financial Studies*, 2, 495–526.

Gultekin, N., R. Rogalski, and S. Tiniç, 1982, "Option Pricing Model Estimates: Some Empirical Results," *Financial Management*, 11, 58–69.

Gurland, J., T. Lee, and P. Dahm, 1960, "Polychotomous Quantal Response in Biological Assay," *Biometrics*, 16, 382–398.

Hagerman, R., 1978, "More Evidence on the Distribution of Security Returns," *Journal of Finance*, 33, 1213–1220.

Hakansson, N., 1976, "Purchasing Power Funds: A New Kind of Financial Intermediary," *Financial Analysts Journal*, 32, 49–59.

———, 1977, "The Superfund: Efficient Paths towards Efficient Capital Markets in Large and Small Countries," in H. Levy and M. Sarnat (eds.), *Financial Decision Making Under Uncertainty*, Academic Press, New York.

Hald, A., 1990, *A History of Probability and Statistics and Their Applications before 1750*, John Wiley and Sons, New York.

Hall, A., 1992, "Some Aspects of Generalized Method of Moments Estimation," in G. Maddala, C. Rao, and H. Vinod (eds.), *Handbook of Statistics, Volume 11: Econometrics*, North-Holland, Amsterdam.

Hall, R., 1988, "Intertemporal Substitution in Consumption," *Journal of Political Economy*, 96, 221–273.

Halpern, P., and S. Turnbull, 1985, "Empirical Tests of Boundary Conditions for Toronto Stock Exchange Options," *Journal of Finance*, 40, 481–500.

Hamilton, J., 1989, "A New Approach to the Economic Analysis of Nonstationary Time Series and the Business Cycle," *Econometrica*, 57, 357–384.

———, 1990, "Analysis of Time Series Subject to Changes in Regime," *Journal of Econometrics*, 45, 39–70.

———, 1993, "Estimation, Inference, and Forecasting of Time Series Subject to Changes in Regime," in G. Maddala, C. Rao, and H. Vinod, eds., *Handbook of Statistics*, Volume 11, North-Holland, New York.

Hamilton, J., 1994, *Time Series Analysis*, Princeton University Press, Princeton, NJ.

Hammersley, J., and D. Handscomb, 1964, *Monte Carlo Methods*, Chapman and Hall, London.

Hammersley, J., and J. Mauldon, 1956, "General Principles of Antithetic Variates," *Proceedings of the Cambridge Philosophical Society*, 52, 476–481.

Hampel, F., 1986, *Robust Statistics: The Approach Based on Influence Functions*, John Wiley and Sons, New York.

Hansen, L., 1982, "Large Sample Properties of Generalized Method of Moments Estimators," *Econometrica*, 50, 1029–1054.

———, 1985, "A Method for Calculating Bounds on the Asymptotic Covariance Matrices of Generalized Method of Moments Estimators," *Journal of Econometrics*, 30, 203–238.

Hansen, L., and R. Hodrick, 1980, "Forward Exchange Rates as Optimal Predictors of Future Spot Rates: An Econometric Analysis," *Journal of Political Economy*, 88, 829–853.

———, 1983, "Risk Averse Speculation in the Forward Foreign Exchange Market: An Econometric Analysis of Linear Models," in J. Frenkel (ed.), *Exchange Rates and International Macroeconomics*, University of Chicago Press, Chicago, IL.

Hansen, L., and R. Jagannathan, 1991, "Implications of Security Market Data for Models of Dynamic Economies," *Journal of Political Economy*, 99, 225–262.

Hansen, L., and S. Richard, 1987, "The Role of Conditioning Information in Deducing Testable Restrictions Implied by Dynamic Asset Pricing Models," *Econometrica*, 55, 587–613.

Hansen, L., and J. Scheinkman, 1995, "Back to the Future: Generating Moment Implications for Continuous-Time Markov Processes," *Econometrica*, 63, 767–804.

Hansen, L., and K. Singleton, 1982, "Generalized Instrumental Variables Estimation of Nonlinear Rational Expectations Models," *Econometrica*, 50, 1269–1288.

———, 1983, "Stochastic Consumption, Risk Aversion and the Temporal Behavior of Asset Returns," *Journal of Political Economy*, 91, 249–268.

Hansen, L., J. Heaton, and E. Luttmer, 1995, "Econometric Evaluation of Asset Pricing Models," *Review of Financial Studies*, 8, 237–274.

Hansen, L., J. Heaton, and M. Ogaki, 1988, "Efficiency Bounds Implied by Multiperiod Conditional Moment Restrictions," *Journal of the American Statistical Association*, 83, 863–871.

Härdle, W., 1990, *Applied Nonparametric Regression*, Cambridge University Press, Cambridge, UK.

Harris, L., 1990, "Estimation of Stock Variances and Serial Covariances from Discrete Observations," *Journal of Financial and Quantitative Analysis*, 25, 291–306.

———, 1991, "Stock Price Clustering and Discreteness," *Review of Financial Studies*, 4, 389–415.

Harris, L., G. Sofianos, and J. Shapiro, 1994, "Program Trading and Intraday Volatility," *Review of Financial Studies*, 7, 653–685.

Harrison, M., 1985, *Brownian Motion and Stochastic Flow Systems*, John Wiley and Sons, New York.

Harrison, M., and D. Kreps, 1979, "Martingales and Arbitrage in Multiperiod Securities Markets," *Journal of Economic Theory*, 20, 381–408.

Harrison, M., and S. Pliska, 1981, "Martingales and Stochastic Integrals in the Theory of Continuous Trading," *Stochastic Processes and Their Applications*, 11, 215–260.

Harvey, A., E. Ruiz, and N. Shephard, 1994, "Multivariate Stochastic Variance Models," *Review of Economic Studies*, 61, 247–264.

Harvey, C., 1988, "The Real Term Structure and Consumption Growth," *Journal of Financial Economics*, 22, 305–334.

———, 1989, "Time-Varying Conditional Covariances in Tests of Asset Pricing Models," *Journal of Financial Economics*, 24, 289–317.

———, 1991, "The World Price of Covariance Risk," *Journal of Finance*, 46, 111–157.

Harvey, C., and G. Zhou, 1990, "Bayesian Inference in Asset Pricing Tests," *Journal of Financial Economics*, 26, 221–254.

Hasbrouck, J., 1988, "Trades, Quotes, Inventories, and Information," *Journal of Financial Economics*, 22, 229–252.

———, 1991a, "Measuring the Information Content of Stock Trades," *Journal of Finance*, 46, 179–208.

———, 1991b, "The Summary Informativeness of Stock Trades: An Econometric Analysis," *Review of Financial Studies*, 4, 571–595.

Hasbrouck, J., and T. Ho, 1987, "Order Arrival, Quote Behavior, and the Return-Generating Process," *Journal of Finance*, 42, 1035–1048.

Hausman, J., 1978, "Specification Tests in Econometrics," *Econometrica*, 46, 1251–1271.

Hausman, J., A. Lo, and C. MacKinlay, 1992, "An Ordered Probit Analysis of Transaction Stock Prices," *Journal of Financial Economics*, 31, 319–379.

He, H., and H. Leland, 1993, "On Equilibrium Asset Price Processes," *Review of Financial Studies*, 6, 593–617.

He, H., and D. Modest, 1995, "Market Frictions and Consumption-Based Asset Pricing," *Journal of Political Economy*, 103, 94–117.

Heath, D., R. Jarrow, and A. Morton, 1992, "Bond Pricing and the Term Structure of Interest Rates: A New Methodology for Contingent Claims Valuation," *Econometrica*, 60, 77–105.

Heaton, J., 1995, "An Empirical Investigation of Asset Pricing with Temporally Dependent Preference Specifications," *Econometrica*, 681–717.

Heaton, J., and D. Lucas, 1996, "Evaluating the Effects of Incomplete Markets on Risk Sharing and Asset Pricing," *Journal of Political Economy*, 104, 668–712.

Helson, H., and D. Sarason, 1967, "Past and Future," *Mathematica Scandinavia*, 21, 5–16.

Henriksson, R., and R. Merton, 1981, "On Market Timing and Investment Performance, II: Statistical Procedures for Evaluating Forecasting Skills," *Journal of Business*, 54, 513–533.

Hentschel, L., 1995, "All in the Family: Nesting Symmetric and Asymmetric GARCH Models," *Journal of Financial Economics*, 39, 71–104.

Herrndorf, N., 1984, "A Functional Central Limit Theorem for Weakly Dependent Sequences of Random Variables," *Annals of Probability*, 12, 141–153.

Hertz, J., A. Krogh, and R. Palmer, 1991, *Introduction to the Theory of Neural Computation*, Addison-Wesley Publishing Company, Reading, MA.

Heston, S., 1992, "Testing Continuous-Time Models of the Term Structure of Interest Rates," unpublished paper, Yale University.

———, 1993, "A Closed-Form Solution for Options with Stochatic Volatility with Applications to Bond and Currency Options," *Review of Financial Studies*, 6, 327–343.

Hicks, J., 1946, *Value and Capital* (2d ed.), Oxford University Press, Oxford.

Hinich, M., and D. Patterson, 1985, "Evidence of Nonlinearity in Daily Stock Returns," *Journal of Business and Economic Statistics*, 3, 69–77.

Ho, T., and S. Lee, 1986, "Term Structure Movements and Pricing Interest Rate Contingent Claims," *Journal of Finance*, 41, 1011–1029.

Ho, T., and H. Stoll, 1980, "On Dealership Markets under Competition," *Journal of Finance*, 35, 259–267.

———, 1981, "Optimal Dealer Pricing under Transactions and Return Uncertainty," *Journal of Financial Economics*, 9, 47–73.

Hodrick, R., 1992, "Dividend Yields and Expected Stock Returns: Alternative Procedures for Inference and Measurement," *Review of Financial Studies*, 5, 357–386.

Hoel, P., S. Port, and C. Stone, 1972, *Introduction to Stochastic Processes*, Houghton Mifflin, Boston, MA.

Hofmann, N., E. Platen, and M. Schweizer, 1992, "Option Pricing under Incompleteness and Stochastic Volatility," *Mathematical Finance*, 2, 153–187.

Hogarth, R., and M. Reder, eds., 1987, *Rational Choice: The Contrast Between Economics and Psychology*, University of Chicago Press, Chicago, IL.

Holden, A., ed., 1986, *Chaos*, Princeton University Press, Princeton, NJ.

Hornik, K., 1989, "Multilayer Feedforward Networks Are Universal Approximators," *Neural Networks*, 2(5), 359–366.

Hornik, K., M. Stinchcombe, and H. White, 1990, "Universal Approximation of an Unknown Mapping and Its Derivatives," *Neural Networks*, 3, 551–560.

Hosking, J., 1981, "Fractional Differencing," *Biometrika*, 68, 165–176.

Hsieh, D., 1989, "Testing for Nonlinear Dependence in Daily Foreign Exchange Rates," *Journal of Business*, 62, 339–368.

———, 1991, "Chaos and Nonlinear Dynamics: Application to Financial Markets," *Journal of Finance*, 46, 1839–1877.

———, 1993, "Implications of Nonlinear Dynamics for Financial Risk Management," *Journal of Financial and Quantitative Analysis*, 1993, 28, 41–64.

Hsu, D., R. Miller, and D. Wichern, 1974, "On the Stable Paretian Behavior of Stock Market Prices," *Journal of the American Statistical Association*, 69, 108–113.

Huang, C., 1992, *Lecture Notes on the Theory of Financial Markets in Continuous Time*.

Huang, C., and R. Litzenberger, 1988, *Foundations for Financial Economics*, North-Holland, New York.

Huang, R., and H. Stoll, 1995a, "The Components of the Bid-Ask Spread: A General Approach," Financial Markets Research Center Working Paper 94–33, Owen Graduate School of Management, Vanderbilt University.

———, 1995b, "Dealer Versus Auction Markets: A Paired Comparison of Execution Costs on NASDAQ and the NYSE," Financial Markets Research Center Working Paper 95–16, Owen Graduate School of Management, Vanderbilt University.

Huber, P., 1985, "Projection Pursuit," *Annals of Statistics*, 13(2), 435–525.

Huberman, G., 1982, "A Simple Approach to Arbitrage Pricing Theory," *Journal of Economic Theory*, 28, 183–191.

Huberman, G., S. Kandel, and R. Stambaugh, 1987, "Mimicking Portfolios and Exact Arbitrage Pricing," *Journal of Finance*, 42, 1–9.

Huberman, G., and S. Kandel, 1987, "Mean-Variance Spanning," *Journal of Finance*, 42(4), 873–888.

Hull, J., 1993, *Options, Futures, and Other Derivative Securities* (2d ed.), Prentice-Hall, Englewood Cliffs, New Jersey.

Hull, J., and A. White, 1987, "The Pricing of Options on Assets with Stochastic Volatilities," *Journal of Finance*, 42, 281–300.

———, 1990a, "Pricing Interest-Rate-Derivative Securities," *Review of Financial Studies*, 3, 573–592.

———, 1990b, "Valuing Derivative Securities Using the Explicit Finite Difference Method," *Journal of Financial and Quantitative Analysis*, 25, 87–100.

Hurst, H., 1951, "Long Term Storage Capacity of Reservoirs," *Transactions of the American Society of Civil Engineers*, 116, 770–799.

Hutchinson, J., A. Lo, and T. Poggio, 1994, "A Nonparametric Approach to the Pricing and Hedging of Derivative Securities Via Learning Networks," *Journal of Finance*, 49, 851–889.

Ingersoll, J., 1987, *Theory of Financial Decision Making*, Rowman & Littlefield, Totowa, NJ.

Ingersoll, J. Jr., J. Skelton, and R. Weil, 1978, "Duration Forty Years Later," *Journal of Financial and Quantitative Analysis*, 13, 627–650.

Itô, K., 1951, "On Stochastic Differential Equations," *Memoirs of the American Mathematical Society*, 4, 1–51.

Jackwerth, J., and M. Rubinstein, 1995, "Recovering Probability Distributions from Contemporary Security Prices," working paper, Haas School of Business, University of California at Berkeley.

Jacquier, E., N. Polson, and P. Rossi, 1994, "Bayesian Analysis of Stochastic Volatility Models," *Journal of Business and Economic Statistics*, 12, 371–389.

Jagannathan, R., and Z. Wang, 1996, "The Conditional CAPM and the Cross-Section of Expected Returns," *Journal of Finance*, 51, 3–53.

Jain, P., 1986, "Analyses of the Distribution of Security Market Model Prediction Errors for Daily Returns Data," *Journal of Accounting Research*, 24, 76–96.

Jamshidian, F., 1989, "An Exact Bond Option Formula," *Journal of Finance*, 44, 205–209.

Jarrell, G., and A. Poulsen, 1989, "The Returns to Acquiring Firms in Tender Offers: Evidence from Three Decades," *Financial Management*, 18, 12–19.

Jarrell, G., J. Brickley, and J. Netter, 1988, "The Market for Corporate Control: The Empirical Evidence Since 1980," *Journal of Economic Perspectives*, 2, 639–658.

Jarrow, R., and A. Rudd, 1982, "Approximate Option Valuation for Arbitrary Stochastic Processes," *Journal of Financial Economics*, 10, 347–369.

Jegadeesh, N., 1990, "Evidence of Predictable Behavior of Security Returns," *Journal of Finance*, 45, 881–898.

———, 1991, "Seasonality in Stock Price Mean Reversion: Evidence from the U.S. and the U.K.," *Journal of Finance*, 46, 1427–1444.

Jegadeesh, N., and S. Titman, 1993, "Returns to Buying Winners and Selling Losers: Implications for Stock Market Efficiency," *Journal of Finance*, 48, 65–91.

———, 1995, "Overreaction, Delayed Reaction, and Contrarian Profits," *Review of Financial Studies*, 8, 973–993.

Jensen, M., and R. Ruback, 1983, "The Market for Corporate Control: The Scientific Evidence," *Journal of Financial Economics*, 11, 5–50.

Jerison, D., I. Singer, and D. Stroock (eds.), 1996, *The 1994 Wiener Symposium Proceedings*, American Mathematical Society, Providence, RI.

Jobson, D., and R. Korkie, 1982, "Potential Performance and Tests of Portfolio Efficiency," *Journal of Financial Economics*, 10, 433–466.

———, 1985, "Some Tests of Linear Asset Pricing with Multivariate Normality," *Canadian Journal of Administrative Sciences*, 2, 114–138.

Johnson, H., 1983, "An Analytic Approximation of the American Put Price," *Journal of Financial and Quantitative Analysis*, 18, 141–148.

Johnson, H., and D. Shanno, 1987, "Option Pricing when the Variance Is Changing," *Journal of Financial and Quantitative Analysis*, 22, 143–151.

Jones, L., 1987, "On a Conjecture of Huber Concerning the Convergence of Projection Pursuit Regression," *Annals of Statistics*, 15(2), 880–882.

Jöreskog, K., 1967, "Some Contributions to Maximum Likelihood Factor Analysis," *Psychometrika*, 34, 183–202.

Judge, G., W. Griffiths, C. Hill, H. Lïkepohl, and T. Lee, 1985, *The Theory and Practice of Econometrics*, John Wiley and Sons, New York.

Kagel, J., and A. Roth, eds., 1995, *Handbook of Experimental Economics*, Princeton University Press, Princeton, NJ.

Kahneman, D., and A. Tversky, 1979, "Prospect Theory: An Analysis of Decision Under Risk," *Econometrica*, 47, 263–291.

Kalos, M., and P. Whitlock, 1986, *Monte Carlo Methods, Volume I: Basics,* John Wiley and Sons, New York.

Kandel, E., and L. Marx, 1996, "NASDAQ Market Structure and Spread Patterns," unpublished working paper, Simon Graduate School of Business, University of Rochester.

Kandel, S., 1984, "The Likelihood Ratio Test of Mean-Variance Efficiency without a Riskless Asset," *Journal of Financial Economics,* 13, 575–592.

Kandel, S., R. McCulloch, and R. Stambaugh, 1995, "Bayesian Inference and Portfolio Efficiency," *Review of Financial Studies,* 8, 1–53.

Kandel, S., and R. Stambaugh, 1987, "On Correlations and Inferences about Mean-Variance Efficiency," *Journal of Financial Economics,* 18, 61–90.

———, 1989, "Modelling Expected Stock Returns for Long and Short Horizons," Working Paper 42-88, Rodney L. White Center, Wharton School, University of Pennsylvania.

———, 1990, "A Mean-Variance Framework for Tests of Asset Pricing Models," *Review of Financial Studies,* 2, 125–156.

———, 1991, "Asset Returns and Intertemporal Preferences," *Journal of Monetary Economics,* 27, 39–71.

———, 1995, "Portfolio Inefficiency and the Cross-Section of Expected Returns," *Journal of Finance,* 50, 157–184.

Kane, E., 1970, "The Term Structure of Interest Rates: An Attempt to Reconcile Teaching with Practice," *Journal of Finance,* 25, May, 361–374.

———, 1983, "Nested Tests of Alternative Term Structure Theories," *Review of Economics and Statistics,* 65, 115–123.

Kane, E., and H. Unal, 1988, "Change in Assessments of Deposit Institution Riskiness," *Journal of Financial Services Research,* 1, 207–229.

Karpoff, J., 1986, "A Theory of Trading Volume," *Journal of Finance,* 41, 1069–1088.

———, 1987, "The Relation between Price Changes and Trading Volume: A Survey," *Journal of Financial and Quantitative Analysis,* 22, 109–126.

Keim, D., 1989, "Trading Patterns, Bid-Ask Spreads, and Estimated Security Returns: The Case of Common Stocks at Calendar Turning Points," *Journal of Financial Economics,* 25, 75–97.

Keim, D., and A. Madhavan, 1995a, "Anatomy of the Trading Process: Empirical Evidence on the Behavior of Institutional Traders," *Journal of Financial Economics,* 37, 371–398.

———, 1995b, "Execution Costs and Investment Performance: An Empirical Analysis of Institutional Equity Trades," working paper, School of Business Administration, University of Southern California.

———, 1996, "The Upstairs Market for Large-Block Transactions: Analysis and Measurement of Price Effects," *Review of Financial Studies,* 9, 1–36.

Keim, D., and R. Stambaugh, 1986, "Predicting Returns in Stock and Bond Markets," *Journal of Financial Economics,* 17, 357–390.

Kendall, M., 1953, "The Analysis of Economic Time Series—Part I: Prices," *Journal of the Royal Statistical Society*, 96, 11–25.

———, 1954, "Note on Bias in the Estimation of Autocorrelation," *Biometrika*, 41, 403–404.

Kennan, D., and M. O'Brien, 1993, "Competition, Collusion, and Chaos," *Journal of Economic Dynamics and Control*, 17, 327–353.

Kennedy, D., 1976, "The Distribution of the Maximum Brownian Excursion," *Journal of Applied Probability*, 13, 371–376.

Kim, M., C. Nelson, and R. Startz, 1988, "Mean Reversion in Stock Prices? A Reappraisal of the Empirical Evidence," Technical Report 2795, NBER, Cambridge, MA; to appear in *Review of Economic Studies*.

Kindleberger, C., 1989, *Manias, Panics, and Crashes: A History of Financial Crises*, revised ed., Basic Books, New York.

Kleidon, A., 1986, "Variance Bounds Tests and Stock Price Valuation Models," *Journal of Political Economy*, 94, 953–1001.

Kleidon, A., and R. Willig, 1995, "Why Do Christie and Schultz Infer Collusion from Their Data?," unpublished working paper.

Kocherlakota, N., 1996, "The Equity Premium: It's Still a Puzzle," *Journal of Economic Literature*, 34, 42–71.

Korajczyk, R., and C. Viallet, 1989, "An Empirical Investigation of International Asset Pricing," *Review of Financial Studies*, 2, 553–586.

Kothari, S., J. Shanken, and R. Sloan, 1995, "Another Look at the Cross-Section of Expected Returns," *Journal of Finance*, 50, 185–224.

Kreps, D., and E. Porteus, 1978, "Temporal Resolution of Uncertainty and Dynamic Choice Theory," *Econometrica*, 46, 185–200.

Kreps, D., 1988, *Notes on the Theory of Choice*, Westview Press, Boulder, CO.

Kroner, K., and V. Ng, 1993, "Modelling the Time Varying Comovement of Asset Returns," unpublished paper, University of Arizona and International Monetary Fund.

Kyle, A., 1985, "Continuous Auctions and Insider Trading," *Econometrica*, 53, 1315–1335.

Laibson, D., 1996, "Hyperbolic Discount Functions, Undersaving, and Savings Policy," Working Paper 5635, NBER, Cambridge, MA.

Lakonishok, J., A. Shleifer, and R. Vishny, 1994, "Contrarian Investment, Extrapolation, and Risk," *Journal of Finance*, 49, 1541–1578.

Lanen, W., and R. Thompson, 1988, "Stock Price Reactions as Surrogates for the Net Cashflow Effects of Corporate Financial Decisions," *Journal of Accounting and Economics*, 10, 311–334.

Lang, S., 1973, *Calculus of Several Variables*, Addison-Wesley, Reading, MA.

Leamer, E., 1978, *Specification Searches*, John Wiley and Sons, New York.

LeBaron, B., 1996, "Technical Trading Rule Profitability and Foreign Exchange Intervention," Working Paper 5505, NBER, Cambridge, MA.

Lee, C., and M. Ready, 1991, "Inferring Trade Direction from Intraday Data," *Journal of Finance*, 46, 733–746.

Lee, S., and B. Hansen, 1994, "Asymptotic Theory for the GARCH(1,1) Quasi-Maximum Likelihood Estimator," *Econometric Theory*, 10, 29–52.

Lehmann, B., 1987, "Orthogonal Frontiers and Alternative Mean Variance Efficiency Tests," *Journal of Finance*, 42, 601–619.

———, 1990, "Fads, Martingales, and Market Efficiency," *Quarterly Journal of Economics*, 105, 1–28.

———, 1991, "Earnings, Dividend Policy, and Present Value Relations: Building Blocks of Dividend Policy Invariant Cash Flows," Working Paper 3676, NBER, Cambridge, MA.

———, "Empirical Testing of Asset Pricing Models," in P. Newman, M. Milgate, and J. Eatwell (eds.), *The New Palgrave Dictionary of Money and Finance*, Stockton Press, New York, pp. 749–759.

Lehmann, B., and D. Modest, 1988, "The Empirical Foundations of the Arbitrage Pricing Theory," *Journal of Financial Economics*, 21, 213–254.

Leroy, S., 1973, "Risk Aversion and the Martingale Property of Stock Returns," *International Economic Review*, 14, 436–446.

LeRoy, S., 1989, "Efficient Capital Markets and Martingales," *Journal of Economic Literature*, 27, 1583–1621.

LeRoy, S., and R. Porter, 1981, "The Present Value Relation: Tests Based on Variance Bounds," *Econometrica*, 49, 555–577.

LeRoy, S., and D. Steigerwald, 1992, "Volatility," Working Paper 6-92, Department of Economics, University of California Santa Barbara.

Levy, H., 1985, "Upper and Lower Bounds of Put and Call Option Values: Stochastic Dominance Approach," *Journal of Finance*, 40, 1197–1218.

Lévy, P., 1924, "Théorie des Erreurs. La Loi de Gauss et Les Lois Exceptionelles," *Bull. Soc. Math.*, 52, 49–85.

———, 1925, *Calcul des Probabilités*, Gauthier-Villers, Paris.

Li, S., 1980, "A Martingale Approach to the Study of Occurrence of Sequence Patterns in Repeated Experiments," *Annals of Probability*, 8, 1171–1176.

Lintner, J., 1965a, "Security Prices, Risk and Maximal Gains from Diversification," *Journal of Finance*, 20, 587–615.

———, 1965b, "The Valuation of Risky Assets and the Selection of Risky Investments in Stock Portfolios and Capital Budgets," *Review of Economics and Statistics*, 47, 13–37.

Litzenberger, R., and K. Ramaswamy, 1979, "The Effect of Personal Taxes and Dividends on Capital Asset Prices: Theory and Evidence," *Journal of Financial Economics*, 7, 163–196.

Litzenberger, R., and J. Rolfo, 1984, "An International Study of Tax Effects on Government Bonds," *Journal of Finance*, 39, 1–22.

Liu, C., and J. He, 1991, "A Variance-Ratio Test of Random Walks in Foreign Exchange Rates," *Journal of Finance*, 46, 777–786.

Ljung, G., and G. Box, 1978, "On a Measure of Lack of Fit in Time Series Models," *Biometrika*, 66, 67–72.

Ljung, L., and T. Söderström, 1986, *Theory and Practice of Recursive Identification*, Massachusetts Institute of Technology Press, Cambridge, MA.

Lo, A., 1986, "Statistical Tests of Contingent Claims Asset-Pricing Models: A New Methodology," *Journal of Financial Economics*, 17, 143–173.

———, 1987, "Semiparametric Upper Bounds for Option Prices and Expected Pay-offs," *Journal of Financial Economics*, 19, 373–388.

———, 1988, "Maximum Likelihood Estimation of Generalized Itô Processes with Discretely Sampled Data," *Econometric Theory*, 4, 231–247.

———, 1991, "Long Term Memory in Stock Market Prices," *Econometrica*, 59, 1279–1313.

———, ed., 1995, *The Industrial Organization and Regulation of the Securities Industry* (NBER Conference Report), University of Chicago Press, Chicago, IL.

———, ed., 1996, *Market Efficiency: Stock Market Behaviour in Theory and Practice*, Edward Elgar Publishing, Ltd., London.

Lo, A., and A. C. MacKinlay, 1988, "Stock Market Prices Do Not Follow Random Walks: Evidence from a Simple Specification Test," *Review of Financial Studies*, 1, 41–66.

———, 1989, "The Size and Power of the Variance Ratio Test in Finite Samples: A Monte Carlo Investigation," *Journal of Econometrics*, 40, 203–238.

———, 1990a, "An Econometric Analysis of Nonsynchronous-Trading," *Journal of Econometrics*, 45, 181–212.

———, 1990b, "Data-Snooping Biases in Tests of Financial Asset Pricing Models," *Review of Financial Studies*, 3, 431–468.

———, 1990c, "When Are Contrarian Profits Due to Stock Market Overreaction?," *Review of Financial Studies*, 3, 175–208.

———, 1996, "Maximizing Predictability in the Stock and Bond Markets," Working Paper LFE–1019–96, MIT Laboratory for Financial Engineering.

Lo, A., and J. Wang, 1995, "Implementing Option Pricing Models when Asset Returns Are Predictable," *Journal of Finance*, 50, 87–129.

Loewenstein, G., and D. Prelec, 1992, "Anomalies in Intertemporal Choice: Evidence and an Interpretation," *Quarterly Journal of Economics*, 107, 573–598.

Longstaff, F., 1989, "A Nonlinear General Equilibrium Model of the Term Structure of Interest Rates," *Journal of Financial Economics*, 23, 195–224.

———, 1992, "Multiple Equilibria and Term Structure Models," *Journal of Financial Economics*, 32, 333–344.

———, 1995, "Option Pricing and the Martingale Restriction," *Review of Financial Studies*, 8, 1091–1124.

Longstaff, F., and E. Schwartz, 1992, "Interest Rate Volatility and the Term Structure: A Two-Factor General Equilibrium Model," *Journal of Finance*, 47, 1259–1282.

Lorenz, E., 1963, "Deterministic Aperiodic Flow," *Journal of Atmospheric Sciences*, 20, 130–141.

Lucas, R., Jr., 1978, "Asset Prices in an Exchange Economy," *Econometrica*, 46, 1429–1446.

Lumsdaine, R., 1995, "Finite-Sample Properties of the Maximum Likelihood Estimator in GARCH(1,1) and IGARCH(1,1) Models: A Monte Carlo Investigation," *Journal of Business and Economic Statistics*, 13, 1–10.

Luttmer, E., 1994, "Asset Pricing in Economies with Frictions," unpublished paper, Kellogg Graduate School of Management, Northwestern University.

Lutz, F., 1940, "The Structure of Interest Rates," *Quarterly Journal of Economics*, 55, 36–63.

Macaulay, F., 1938, *Some Theoretical Problems Suggested by the Movements of Interest Rates, Bond Yields, and Stock Prices in the United States Since 1856*, National Bureau of Economic Research, New York.

MacBeth, J., and L. Merville, 1979, "An Empirical Examination of the Black-Scholes Call Option Pricing Model," *Journal of Finance*, 34, 1173–1186.

———, 1980, "Tests of the Black-Scholes and Cox Call Option Valuation Models," *Journal of Finance*, 35, 285–300.

Mackay, C., 1852, *Memoirs of Extraordinary Popular Delusions and the Madness of Crowds*, 2nd ed., Office Nat. Illustrated Library, London.

MacKinlay, A. C., 1987, "On Multivariate Tests of the CAPM," *Journal of Financial Economics*, 18, 341–372.

———, 1995, "Multifactor Models Do Not Explain Deviations from the CAPM," *Journal of Financial Economics*, 38, 3–28.

MacKinlay, A. C., and M. Richardson, 1991, "Using Generalized Methods of Moments to Test Mean-Variance Efficiency," *Journal of Finance*, 46, 511–527.

Maddala, G., 1983, *Limited-Dependent and Qualitative Variables in Econometrics*, Cambridge University Press, Cambridge, UK.

Madhavan, A., and S. Smidt, 1991, "A Bayesian Model of Intraday Specialist Pricing," *Journal of Financial Economics*, 30, 99–134.

Magnus, J., and H. Neudecker, 1988, *Matrix Differential Calculus*, John Wiley and Sons, New York.

Malatesta, P., and R. Thompson, 1985, "Partially Anticipated Events: A Model of Stock Price Reactions with an Application to Corporate Acquisitions," *Journal of Financial Economics*, 14, 237–250.

Malkiel, B., 1992, "Efficient Market Hypothesis," in Newman, P., M. Milgate, and J. Eatwell (eds.), *New Palgrave Dictionary of Money and Finance*, Macmillan, London.

Mandelbrot, B., 1963, "The Variation of Certain Speculative Prices," *Journal of Business*, 36, 394–419.

———, 1967, "The Variation of Certain Speculative Prices," *Journal of Business*, 36, 394–419.

————, 1971, "When Can Price Be Arbitraged Efficiently? A Limit to the Validity of the Random Walk and Martingale Models," *Review of Economics and Statistics*, 53, 225–236.

————, 1972, "Statistical Methodology for Non-Periodic Cycles: From the Covariance to R/S Analysis," *Annals of Economic and Social Measurement*, 1, 259–290.

————, 1975, "Limit Theorems on the Self-Normalized Range for Weakly and Strongly Dependent Processes," *Z. Wahrscheinlichkeitstheorie verw.*, Gebiete 31, 271–285.

Mandelbrot, B., and M. Taqqu, 1979, "Robust R/S Analysis of Long Run Serial Correlation," *Bulletin of the International Statistical Institute*, 48 (Book 2), 59–104.

Mandelbrot, B., and H. Taylor, 1967, "On the Distribution of Stock Price Differences," *Operations Research*, 15, 1057–1062.

Mandelbrot, B., and J. Van Ness, 1968, "Fractional Brownian Motion, Fractional Noises and Applications," *S.I.A.M. Review*, 10, 422–437.

Mandelbrot, B., and J. Wallis, 1968, "Noah, Joseph and Operational Hydrology," *Water Resources Research*, 4, 909–918.

————, 1969a, "Computer Experiments with Fractional Gaussian Noises. Parts 1, 2, 3," *Water Resources Research*, 5, 228–267.

————, 1969b, "Some Long Run Properties of Geophysical Records," *Water Resources Research*, 5, 321–340.

Mankiw, N. G., 1986, "The Equity Premium and the Concentration of Aggregate Shocks," *Journal of Financial Economics*, 17, 211–219.

Mankiw, N. G., and J. Miron, 1986, "The Changing Behavior of the Term Structure of Interest Rates," *Quarterly Journal of Economics*, 101, 211–221.

Mankiw, N. G., and M. Shapiro, 1986, "Do We Reject Too Often? Small Sample Properties of Tests of Rational Expectations Models," *Economics Letters*, 20, 139–145.

Mankiw, N. G., and S. Zeldes, 1991, "The Consumption of Stockholders and Non-Stockholders," *Journal of Financial Economics*, 29, 97–112.

Mankiw, N. G., D. Romer, and M. Shapiro, 1985, "An Unbiased Reexamination of Stock Market Volatility," *Journal of Finance*, 40, 677–687.

Manne, H., 1965, "Mergers and the Market for Corporate Control," *Journal of Political Economy*, 73, 110–120.

Mark, N., 1995, "Exchange Rates and Fundamentals: Evidence on Long-Horizon Predictability," *American Economic Review*, 85, 201–218.

Markowitz, H., 1959, *Portfolio Selection: Efficient Diversification of Investments*, John Wiley, New York.

Marsh, T., and R. Merton, 1986, "Dividend Variability and Variance Bounds Tests for the Rationality of Stock Market Prices," *American Economic Review*, 76, 483–498.

Marsh, T., and E. Rosenfeld, 1986, "Non-Trading, Market Making, and Estimates of Stock Price Volatility," *Journal of Financial Economics*, 15, 359–372.

Mason, S., R. Merton, A. Perold, and P. Tufano, 1995, *Cases in Financial Engineering: Applied Studies of Financial Innovation*, Prentice-Hall, Englewood Cliffs, NJ.

Mayers, D., 1972, "Nonmarketable Assets and Capital Market Equilibrium under Uncertainty," in Jensen, M. (ed.), *Studies in the Theory of Capital Markets*, Praeger, New York, 223–248.

McCallum, B., 1994, "Monetary Policy and the Term Structure of Interest Rates," Working Paper 4938, NBER, Cambridge, MA.

McCullagh, P., 1980, "Regression Models for Ordinal Data," *Journal of the Royal Statistical Society*, Series B(42), 109–142.

McCulloch, J., 1971, "Measuring the Term Structure of Interest Rates," *Journal of Business*, 44, 19–31.

———, 1975, "The Tax-Adjusted Yield Curve," *Journal of Finance*, 30, 811–830.

———, 1993, "A Reexamination of Traditional Hypotheses About the Term Structure: A Comment," *Journal of Finance*, 48, 779–789.

McCulloch, J., and H. Kwon, 1993, "US Term Structure Data, 1947–1991," Working Paper 93-6, Ohio State University.

McCulloch, W., and W. Pitts, 1943, "A Logical Calculus of Ideas Immanent in Nervous Activity," *Bulletin of Mathematical Biophysics*, 5, 115–133.

McQueen, G., and V. Roley, 1993, "Stock Prices, News, and Business Conditions," *Review of Financial Studies*, 6, 683–707.

Mech, T., 1993, "Portfolio Return Autocorrelation," *Journal of Financial Economics*, 34, 307–344.

Mehra, R., and E. Prescott, 1985, "The Equity Premium: A Puzzle," *Journal of Monetary Economics*, 15, 145–161.

Mei, J., 1993, "A Semiautoregression Approach to the Arbitrage Pricing Theory," *Journal of Finance*, 48, 599–620.

Melino, A., 1988, "The Term Structure of Interest Rates: Evidence and Theory," *Journal of Economic Surveys*, 2, 335–366.

Melino, A., and S. Turnbull, 1990, "Pricing Foreign Currency Options with Stochastic Volatility," *Journal of Econometrics*, 45, 239–265.

Merton, R., 1969, "Lifetime Portfolio Selection under Uncertainty: The Continuous Time Case," *Review of Economics and Statistics*, 51, 247–257.

———, 1972, "An Analytic Derivation of the Efficient Portfolio Frontier," *Journal of Financial and Quantitative Analysis*, 7, 1851–1872.

———, 1973a, "An Intertemporal Capital Asset Pricing Model," *Econometrica*, 41, 867–887.

———, 1973b, "Rational Theory of Option Pricing," *Bell Journal of Economics and Management Science*, 4, 141–183.

———, 1976a, "The Impact on Option Pricing of Specification Error in the Underlying Stock Price Distribution," *Journal of Finance*, 31, 333–350.

———, 1976b, "Option Pricing when Underlying Stock Returns Are Discontinuous," *Journal of Financial Economics*, 3, 125–144.

———, 1980, "On Estimating the Expected Return on the Market: An Exploratory Investigation," *Journal of Financial Economics*, 8, 323–361.

———, 1981, "On Market Timing and Investment Performance, I: An Equilibrium Theory of Value for Market Forecasts," *Journal of Business*, 54, 363–406.

———, 1990, *Continuous-Time Finance*, Blackwell Publishers, Cambridge, MA.

Miccheli, C., 1986, "Interpolation of Scattered Data: Distance Matrices and Conditionally Positive Definite Functions," *Constructive Approximation*, 2, 11–22.

Mikkelson, W., and M. Partch, 1986, "Valuation Effects of Security Offerings and the Issuance Process," *Journal of Financial Economics*, 15, 31–60.

Mishkin, F., 1988, "The Information in the Term Structure: Some Further Results," *Journal of Applied Econometrics*, 3, 307–314.

———, 1990a, "The Information in the Longer-Maturity Term Structure about Future Inflation," *Quarterly Journal of Economics*, 105, 815–821.

———, 1990b, "What Does the Term Structure Tell Us about Future Inflation?," *Journal of Monetary Economics*, 25, 77–95.

Mitchell, M., and J. Netter, 1994, "The Role of Financial Economics in Securities Fraud Cases: Applications at the Securities and Exchange Commission," *The Business Lawyer*, 49, 545–590.

Modest, D., and M. Sundaresan, 1983, "The Relationship between Spot and Futures Prices in Stock Index Futures Markets: Some Preliminary Evidence," *Journal of Futures Markets*, 3, 15–42.

Modigliani, F., and R. Sutch, 1966, "Innovations in Interest Rate Policy," *American Economic Review*, 56, 178–197.

Mood, A., 1940, "The Distribution Theory of Runs," *Annals of Mathematical Statistics*, 11, 367–392.

Moody, J., and C. Darken, 1989, "Fast Learning in Networks of Locally Tuned Processing Units," *Neural Computations*, 1, 281–294.

Morrison, D., 1990, *Multivariate Statistical Methods*, McGraw Hill, New York.

Morse, D., 1984, "An Econometric Analysis of the Choice of Daily Versus Monthly Returns in Tests of Information Content," *Journal of Accounting Research*, 22, 605–623.

Mossin, J., 1966, "Equilibrium in a Capital Asset Market," *Econometrica*, 35, 768–783.

Muirhead, R., 1983, *Aspects of Multivariate Statistical Theory*, John Wiley and Sons, New York.

Murphy, J., 1986, *Technical Analysis of the Futures Markets*, New York Institute of Finance, New York.

Muth, J., 1960, "Optimal Properties of Exponentially Weighted Forecasts," *Journal of the American Statistical Association*, 55, 299–306.

Muthuswamy, J., 1988, "Asynchronous Closing Prices and Spurious Autocorrelations in Portfolio Returns," working paper, Graduate School of Business, University of Chicago.

Myers, J., and A. Bakay, 1948, "Influence of Stock Split-Ups on Market Price," *Harvard Business Review*, 251–265.

Myers, S., and N. Majluf, 1984, "Corporate Financing and Investment Decisions When Firms Have Information that Investors Do Not Have," *Journal of Financial Economics*, 13, 187–221.

Naik, V., and M. Lee, 1994, "The Yield Curve and Bond Option Prices with Discrete Shifts in Economic Regimes," unpublished paper, University of British Columbia and University of Saskatchewan.

Neftci, S., 1991, "Naive Trading Rules in Financial Markets and Wiener-Kolmogorov Prediction Theory: A Study of 'Technical Analysis'," *Journal of Business*, 64, 549–572.

Nelson, D., 1990, "Stationarity and Persistence in the GARCH(1,1) Model," *Econometric Theory*, 6, 318–334.

———, 1991, "Conditional Heteroskedasticity in Asset Returns: A New Approach," *Econometrica*, 59, 347–370.

———, 1992, "Filtering and Forecasting with Misspecified ARCH Models I: Getting the Right Variance with the Wrong Model," *Journal of Econometrics*, 52, 61–90.

———, 1996, "Asymptotically Optimal Smoothing with ARCH Models," *Econometrica*, 64, 561–573.

Nelson, C., and M. Kim, 1993, "Predictable Stock Returns: The Role of Small Sample Bias," *Journal of Finance*, 48, 641–661.

Nelson, C., and A. Siegel, 1987, "Parsimonious Modelling of Yield Curves," *Journal of Business*.

Nelson, C., and R. Startz, 1990, "The Distribution of the Instrumental Variables Estimator and Its *t*-Ratio when the Instrument Is a Poor One," *Journal of Business*, 63, S125–S140.

Nelson, D., and D. Foster, 1994, "Asymptotic Filtering Theory for Univariate ARCH Models," *Econometrica*, 62, 1–41.

Nelson, D., and K. Ramaswamy, 1990, "Simple Binomial Processes as Diffusion Approximations in Financial Models," *Review of Financial Studies*, 3, 393–430.

New York Stock Exchange Fact Book: 1992 Data, 1993, New York Stock Exchange, April.

Newey, W., 1985, "Semiparametric Estimation of Limited Dependent Variable Models with Endogenous Explanatory Variables," *Annales de L'Insee*, 59/60, 219–237.

Newey, W., and K. West, 1987, "A Simple, Positive Semi-Definite, Heteroscedasticity and Autocorrelation Consistent Covariance Matrix," *Econometrica*, 55, 703–708.

Niederhoffer, V., 1965, "Clustering of Stock Prices," *Operations Research*, 13, 258–265.

———, 1966, "A New Look at Clustering of Stock Prices," *Journal of Business*, 39, 309–313.

Niederhoffer, V., and M. Osborne, 1966, "Market Making and Reversal on the Stock Exchange," *Journal of the American Statistical Association*, 61, 897–916.

Niyogi, P., and F. Girosi, 1996, "On the Relationship between Generalization Error, Hypothesis Complexity, and Sample Complexity for Radial Basis Functions," *Neural Computation*, 8, 819–842.

Officer, R., 1972, "The Distribution of Stock Returns," *Journal of the American Statistical Association*, 67, 807–812.

———, 1973, "The Variability of the Market Factor of the New York Stock Exchange," *Journal of Business*, 46, 434–453.

Ogaki, M., 1992, "Generalized Method of Moments: Econometric Applications," in G. Maddala, C. Rao, and H. Vinod (eds.), *Handbook of Statistics, Volume 11: Econometrics*, North-Holland, Amsterdam.

O'Hara, M., 1995, *Market Microstructure Theory*, Blackwell Publishers, Cambridge, MA.

Oldfield, G., R. Rogalski, and R. Jarrow, 1977, "An Autoregressive Jump Process for Common Stock Returns," *Journal of Financial Economics*, 6, 389–418.

Osborne, M., 1959, "Brownian Motion in the Stock Market," *Operations Research*, 7, 145–173.

———, 1962, "Periodic Structure in the Brownian Motion of Stock Prices," *Operations Research*, 10, 345–379.

Pagan, A., and G. Schwert, 1990, "Alternative Models for Conditional Stock Volatility," *Journal of Econometrics*, 45, 267–290.

Parker, D., 1985, "Learning Logic," Working Paper 47, Center for Computational Research in Economics and Management Science, Massachusetts Institute of Technology.

Parkinson, M., 1980, "The Extreme Value Method for Estimating the Variance of the Rate of Return," *Journal of Business*, 53, 61–65.

Paskov, S., and J. Traub, 1995, "Faster Valuation of Financial Derivatives," *Journal of Portfolio Management*, 22, 113–120.

Pau, L., 1991, "Technical Analysis for Portfolio Trading by Syntactic Pattern Recognition," *Journal of Economic Dynamics and Control*, 15, 715–730.

Pearson, N., and T. Sun, 1994, "Exploiting the Conditional Density in Estimating the Term Structure: An Application to the Cox, Ingersoll, and Ross Model," *Journal of Finance*, 49, 1279–1304.

Pennacchi, G., 1991, "Identifying the Dynamics of Real Interest Rates and Inflation: Evidence Using Survey Data," *Review of Financial Studies*, 4, 53–86.

Perrakis, S., 1986, "Option Bounds in Discrete Time: Extensions and the Price of the American Put," *Journal of Business*, 59, 119–142.

Perrakis, S., and P. Ryan, 1984, "Option Pricing Bounds in Discrete Time," *Journal of Finance*, 39, 519–525.

Perron, P., 1989, "The Great Crash, the Oil Price Shock, and the Unit Root Hypothesis," *Econometrica*, 57, 1361–1402.

———, 1991, "Test Consistency With Varying Sampling Frequency," *Econometric Theory*, 7, 341–368.

Pesaran, M., and S. Potter, 1992, "Nonlinear Dynamics and Econometrics: An Introduction," *Journal of Applied Econometrics*, 7(Supp), S1–S8.

Petersen, M., and S. Umlauf, 1990, "An Empirical Examination of the Intraday Behavior of the NYSE Specialist," working paper, Massachusetts Institute of Technology, Cambridge, MA.

Phillips, S., and C. Smith, 1980, "Trading Costs for Listed Options: The Implications for Market Efficiency," *Journal of Financial Economics*, 8, 179–201.

Poggio, T., and F. Girosi, 1990, "Networks for Approximation and Learning," *Proceedings of the IEEE*, special issue: *Neural Networks I: Theory and Modeling*, 78, 1481–1497.

Poterba, J., and L. Summers, 1986, "The Persistence of Volatility and Stock Market Fluctuations," *American Economic Review*, 76, 1142–1151.

————, 1988, "Mean Reversion in Stock Returns: Evidence and Implications," *Journal of Financial Economics*, 22, 27–60.

Powell, M., 1987, "Radial Basis Functions for Multivariable Interpolation: A Review," in J. Mason and M. Cox (eds.), *Algorithms for Approximation*, Clarendon Press, Oxford, UK.

Prabhala, N., 1995, "Conditional Methods in Event-Studies and An Equilibrium Justification for Using Standard Event-Study Procedures," School of Management, Yale University, New Haven, CT.

Praetz, P., 1972, "The Distribution of Share Price Changes," *Journal of Business*, 45, 49–55.

Priestley, M., 1988, *Non-Linear and Non-Stationary Time Series Analysis*, Academic Press, San Diego.

Radner, R., 1982, "Equilibrium Under Uncertainty," in K. Arrow and M. Intriligator (eds.), *Handbook of Mathematical Economics*, Volume II, North-Holland, New York, 923–1006.

Rady, S., 1994, "State Prices Implicit in Valuation Formulae for Derivative Securities: A Martingale Approach," Discussion Paper 181, LSE Financial Markets Group, London, UK.

Randles, R., and D. Wolfe, 1979, *Introduction to the Theory of Nonparametric Statistics*, John Wiley and Sons, New York.

Reddington, F., 1952, "Review of the Principle of Life-Office Valuations," *Journal of the Institute of Actuaries*, 78, 286–340.

Reinsch, C., 1967, "Smoothing by Spline Functions," *Numer Math*, 10, 177–183.

Restoy, F., and P. Weil, 1993, "Approximate Equilibrium Asset Pricing," unpublished paper, Bank of Spain and ECARE.

Richard, S., 1978, "An Arbitrage Model of the Term Structure of Interest Rates," *Journal of Financial Economics*, 7, 38–58.

Richardson, M., 1993, "Temporary Components of Stock Prices: A Skeptic's View," *Journal of Business and Economic Statistics*, 11, 199–207.

Richardson, M., and T. Smith, 1991, "Tests of Financial Models with the Presence of Overlapping Observations," *Review of Financial Studies*, 4, 227–254.

————, 1994, "A Unified Approach to Testing for Serial Correlation in Stock Returns," *Journal of Business*, 67, 371–399.

Richardson, M., and J. Stock, 1989, "Drawing Inferences from Statistics Based on Multi-Year Asset Returns," *Journal of Financial Economics*, 25, 323–348.

Rietz, T., 1988, "The Equity Risk Premium: A Solution?," *Journal of Monetary Economics*, 21, 117–132.

Ritchken, P., 1985, "On Option Pricing Bounds," *Journal of Finance*, 40, 1219–1233.

Ritter, J., 1990, "Long-Run Performance of Initial Public Offerings," *Journal of Finance*.

Robbins, H., and S. Monro, 1951a, "A Stochastic Approximation Method," *Annals of Mathematical Statistics*, 25, 737–744.

———, 1951b, "A Stochastic Approximation Model," *Annals of Mathematical Statistics*, 22, 400–407.

Roberds, W., D. Runkle, and C. Whiteman, 1996, "A Daily View of Yield Spreads and Short-Term Interest Rate Movements," *Journal of Money, Credit and Banking*, 28, 34–53.

Roberts, H., 1959, "Stock-Market 'Patterns' and Financial Analysis: Methodological Suggestions," *Journal of Finance*, 14, 1–10.

———, 1967, "Statistical versus Clinical Prediction of the Stock Market," unpublished manuscript, Center for Research in Security Prices, University of Chicago, May.

Robinson, M., 1988, "Block Trades on the Major Canadian and U.S. Stock Exchanges: A Study of Pricing Behavior and Market Efficiency," unpublished Ph.D. dissertation, School of Business Administration, University of Western Ontario, Ontario, Canada.

Robinson, P., 1979, "The Estimation of a Non-Linear Moving Average Model," *Stochastic Processes and Their Applications*, 5, 81–90.

Roll, R., 1977, "A Critique of the Asset Pricing Theory's Tests: Part I," *Journal of Financial Economics*, 4, 129–176.

———, 1980, "Orthogonal Portfolios," *Journal of Financial and Quantitative Analysis*, 15, 1005–1023.

———, 1984, "A Simple Implicit Measure of the Effective Bid-Ask Spread in an Efficient Market," *Journal of Finance*, 39, 1127–1140.

Roll, R., and S. Ross, 1980, "An Empirical Investigation of the Arbitrage Pricing Theory," *Journal of Finance*, 35, 1073–1103.

———, 1984, "A Critical Reexamination of the Empirical Evidence on the Arbitrage Pricing Theory: A Reply," *Journal of Finance*, 39, 347–350.

———, 1994, "On the Cross-Sectional Relation between Expected Returns and Betas," *Journal of Finance*, 49, 101–122.

Romano, J., and L. Thombs, 1996, "Inference for Autocorrelations under Weak Assumptions," *Journal of the American Statistical Association*, 91, 590–600.

Rosenblatt, F., 1962, *Principles of Neurodynamics*, Spartan Books, New York.

Ross, S., 1976, "The Arbitrage Theory of Capital Asset Pricing," *Journal of Economic Theory*, 13, 341–360.

———, 1977, "Risk, Return, and Arbitrage," in I. Friend and J. Bicksler (eds.), *Risk and Return in Finance I*, Ballinger, Cambridge, MA.

Rubin, D., and D. Thayer, 1982, "EM Algorithms for ML Factor Analysis," *Psychometrika*, 57, 69–76.

Rubinstein, M., 1976, "The Valuation of Uncertain Income Streams and the Pricing of Options," *Bell Journal of Economics*, 7, 407–425.

———, 1985, "Nonparametric Tests of Alternative Option Pricing Models Using All Reported Trades and Quotes on the 30 Most Active CBOE Option Classes from August 23, 1976 through August 31, 1978," *Journal of Finance*, 40, 455–480.

———, 1994, "Implied Binomial Trees," *Journal of Finance*, 49, 771–818.

Rudebusch, G., 1995, "Federal Reserve Interest Rate Targeting, Rational Expectations, and the Term Structure," *Journal of Monetary Economics*, 35, 245–274.

Rumelhart, D., G. Hinton, and R. Williams, 1986, "Learning Internal Representation by Error Propagation," in D. Rumelhart and J. McClelland (eds.), *Parallel Distributed Processing: Explorations in the Microstructure of Cognition*, Volume 1: *Foundations*, Massachusetts Institute of Technology Press, Cambridge, MA, chap. 8.

Ruud, P., 1983, "Sufficient Conditions for the Consistency of Maximum Likelihood Estimation Despite Misspecification of Distribution in Multinomial Discrete Choice Models," *Econometrica*, 51, 225–228.

Samuelson, P., 1965, "Proof that Properly Anticipated Prices Fluctuate Randomly," *Industrial Management Review*, 6, 41–49.

———, 1967, "Efficient Portfolio Selection for Pareto-Lévy Investments," *Journal of Financial and Quantitative Analysis*, 2, 107–122.

———, 1969, "Lifetime Portfolio Selection by Dynamic Stochastic Programming," *Review of Economics and Statistics*, 51, 239–246.

———, 1972, "Mathematics of Speculative Price," in Day, R., and S. Robinson (eds.), *Mathematical Topics in Economic Theory and Computation*, Society for Industrial and Applied Mathematics, Philadelphia, PA.

———, 1973, "Proof that Properly Discounted Present Values of Assets Vibrate Randomly," *Bell Journal of Economics and Management Science*, 4, 369–374.

———, 1976, "Limited Liability, Short Selling, Bounded Utility, and Infinite-Variance Stable Distributions," *Journal of Financial and Quantitative Analysis*, 485–503.

Schaefer, S., 1981, "Measuring a Tax-Specific Term Structure of Interest Rates in the Market for British Government Securities," *Economic Journal*, 91, 415–431.

———, 1982, "Tax-Induced Clientele Effects in the Market for British Government Securities," *Journal of Financial Economics*.

Scheinkman, J., and B. LeBaron, 1989, "Nonlinear Dynamics and Stock Returns," *Journal of Business*, 62, 311–338.

Scheinkman, J., and M. Woodford, 1994, "Self-Organized Criticality and Economic Fluctuations," *American Economic Review*, 84, 417–421.

Schipper, K., and R. Thompson, 1983, "The Impact of Merger-Related Regulations on the Shareholders of Acquiring Firms," *Journal of Accounting Research*, 21, 184–221.

———, 1985, "The Impact of Merger-Related Regulations Using Exact Test Statistics," *Journal of Accounting Research*, 23, 408–415.

Scholes, M., and J. Williams, 1977, "Estimating Betas from Nonsynchronous Data," *Journal of Financial Economics*, 5, 309–328.

Schuss, Z., 1980, *Theory and Application of Stochastic Differential Equations*, John Wiley and Sons, New York.

Schwartz, E., 1977, "The Valuation of Warrants: Implementing a New Approach," *Journal of Financial Economics*, 4, 79–93.

Schwert, G., 1981, "Using Financial Data to Measure the Effects of Regulation," *Journal of Law and Economics*, 24, 121–157.

———, 1989, "Why Does Stock Market Volatility Change Over Time?," *Journal of Finance*, 44, 1115–1153.

Schwert, W., 1990, "Stock Market Volatility," *Financial Analysts Journal*, May–June, 23–34.

Sclove, S., 1983a, "Time-Series Segmentation: A Model and a Method," *Information Sciences*, 29, 7–25.

———, 1983b, "On Segmentation of Time Series," in S. Karlin, T. Amemiya, and L. Goodman, eds., *Studies in Econometrics, Time Series, and Multivariate Statistics*, Academic Press, New York.

Scott, L., 1985, "The Present Value Model of Stock Prices: Regression Tests and Monte Carlo Results," *Review of Economics and Statistics*, 67, 599–607.

———, 1987, "Option Pricing when the Variance Changes Randomly: Theory, Estimation, and an Application," *Journal of Financial and Quantitative Analysis*, 22, 419–438.

Securities and Exchange Commission, 1994, *Market 2000: An Examination of Current Equity Market Developments*, US Government Printing Office, Washington, DC.

Sentana, E., 1991, "Quadratic ARCH Models: A Potential Reinterpretation of ARCH Models as Second-Order Taylor Approximations," unpublished paper, London School of Economics.

Serfling, R., 1980, *Approximation Theorems of Mathematical Statistics*, John Wiley and Sons, New York.

Shanken, J., 1982, "The Arbitrage Pricing Theory: Is It Testable?," *Journal of Finance*, 37, 1129–1140.

———, 1985a, "Multi-Beta CAPM or Equilibrium APT? A Reply," *Journal of Finance*, 40, 1189–1196.

———, 1985b, "Multivariate Tests of the Zero-Beta CAPM," *Journal of Financial Economics*, 14, 327–348.

———, 1986, "Testing Portfolio Efficiency When the Zero-Beta Rate Is Unknown," *Journal of Finance*, 41, 269–276.

————, 1987a, "Multivariate Proxies and Asset Pricing Relations: Living with the Roll Critique," *Journal of Financial Economics*, 18, 91–110.

————, 1987b, "Nonsynchronous Data and the Covariance-Factor Structure of Returns," *Journal of Finance*, 42, 221–232.

————, 1987c, "A Bayesian Approach to Testing Portfolio Efficiency," *Journal of Financial Economics*, 19, 195–215.

————, 1992a, "The Current State of the Arbitrage Pricing Theory," *Journal of Finance*, 47, 1569–1574.

————, 1992b, "On the Estimation of Beta-Pricing Models," *Review of Financial Studies*, 5, 1–34.

Sharpe, W., 1964, "Capital Asset Prices: A Theory of Market Equilibrium under Conditions of Risk," *Journal of Finance*, 19, 425–442.

————, 1970, *Portfolio Theory and Capital Markets*, McGraw-Hill, New York, NY.

Sharpe, W., G. Alexander, and J. Bailey, 1995, *Investments*, Fifth Edition, Prentice-Hall, Englewood Cliffs, NJ.

Shea, G., 1984, "Pitfalls in Smoothing Interest Rate Term Structure Data: Equilibrium Models and Spline Approximations," *Journal of Financial and Quantitative Analysis*, 19, 253–269.

————, 1985, "Interest Rate Term Structure Estimation with Exponential Splines: A Note," *Journal of Finance*, 40, 319–325.

Shefrin, H., and M. Statman, 1985, "The Disposition to Ride Winners Too Long and Sell Lowers Too Soon: Theory and Evidence," *Journal of Finance*, 41, 774–790.

Shephard, N., and S. Kim, 1994, "Stochastic Volatility: Likelihood Inference and Comparison with ARCH Models," unpublished paper, Nuffield College, Oxford, and Princeton University.

Shiller, R., 1981, "Do Stock Prices Move Too Much to Be Justified by Subsequent Changes in Dividends?," *American Economic Review*, 71, 421–436.

————, 1984, "Stock Prices and Social Dynamics," *Brookings Papers on Economic Activity*, 2, 457–498.

————, 1989, *Market Volatility*, Massachusetts Institute of Technology Press, Cambridge, MA.

————, 1990, "The Term Structure of Interest Rates," in B. Friedman and F. Hahn (eds.), *Handbook of Monetary Economics*, North-Holland, Amsterdam.

Shiller, R., and P. Perron, 1985, "Testing the Random Walk Hypothesis: Power Versus Frequency of Observation," *Economics Letters*, 18, 381–386.

Shiller, R., J. Campbell, and K. Schoenholtz, 1983, "Forward Rates and Future Policy: Interpreting the Term Structure of Interest Rates," *Brookings Papers on Economic Activity*, 1, 173–217.

Shimko, D., 1991, "Beyond Implied Volatility: Probability Distributions and Hedge Ratios Implied by Option Prices," working paper, University of Southern California.

————, 1993, "Bounds of Probability," *RISK*, 6, 33–37.

Shorack, G., and J. Wellner, 1986, *Empirical Processes with Applications to Statistics*, John Wiley and Sons, New York.

Sias, R., and L. Starks, 1994, "Institutions, Individuals and Return Autocorrelations," Working Paper, University of Texas, Austin.

Siegel, J., 1994, *Stocks for the Long Run*, Norton, New York.

Silvey, S., 1975, *Statistical Inference*, Chapman and Hall, London.

Simkowitz, M., and W. Beedles, 1980, "Asymmetric Stable Distributed Security Returns," *Journal of the American Statistical Association*, 75, 306–312.

Sims, C., 1974, "Output and Labor Input in Manufacturing," *Brookings Papers on Economic Activity*, 3, 695–728.

———, 1977, "Exogeneity and Causal Ordering in Macroeconomic Models," in *New Methods in Business Cycle Research: Proceedings from a Conference*, Federal Reserve Bank of Minneapolis.

Singleton, K., 1990, "Specification and Estimation of Intertemporal Asset Pricing Models," in B. Friedman and F. Hahn (eds.), *Handbook of Monetary Economics*, North-Holland, Amsterdam.

Smith, A., 1968, *The Money Game*, Random House, New York.

Smith, C., 1976, "Option Pricing: A Review," *Journal of Financial Economics*, 3, 3–51.

Stambaugh, R., 1982, "On the Exclusion of Assets from Tests of the Two Parameter Model," *Journal of Financial Economics*, 10, 235–268.

———, 1986, "Bias in Regressions with Lagged Stochastic Regressors," CRSP Working Paper 156, University of Chicago.

———, 1988, "The Information in Forward Rates: Implications for Models of the Term Structure," *Journal of Financial Economics*, 21, 41–70.

Startz, R., 1989, "The Stochastic Behavior of Durable and Non-Durable Consumption," *Review of Economics and Statistics*, 71, 356–363.

Stein, E., and J. Stein, 1991, "Stock Price Distributions with Stochastic Volatility: An Analytic Approach," *Review of Financial Studies*, 4, 727–753.

Stoker, T., 1986, "Consistent Estimation of Scaled Coefficients," *Econometrica*, 54, 1461–1481.

———, 1991, "Equivalence of Direct, Indirect and Slope Estimators of Average Derivatives," in W. Barnett, J. Powell, and G. Tauchen (eds.), *Nonparametric and Semiparametric Methods in Econometrics and Statistics*, Cambridge University Press, Cambridge, UK.

———, 1992, *Lectures on Semiparametric Econometrics*, CORE Lecture Series, CORE Foundation, Louvain-la-Neuve, Belgium.

Stoll, H., 1978, "The Supply of Dealer Services in Securities Markets," *Journal of Finance*, 33, 1133–1151.

———, 1985, *The Stock Exchange Specialist System: An Economic Analysis*, Salomon Brothers Center, New York University, New York.

———, 1989, "Inferring the Components of the Bid-Ask Spread: Theory and Empirical Tests," *Journal of Finance*, 44, 115–134.

Stoll, H., and R. Whaley, 1990, "Stock Market Structure and Volatility," *Review of Financial Studies*, 3, 37–71.

Strang, G., 1976, *Linear Algebra and Its Applications*, Academic Press, New York.

Stuart, A., and K. Ord, 1987, *Kendall's Advanced Theory of Statistics*, Vols. I–III, Oxford University Press, New York.

Stutzer, M., 1995, "A Simple Nonparametric Approach to Derivative Security Valuation," working paper, Carlson School of Management, University of Minnesota.

Subba Rao, T., and M. Gabr, 1984, *An Introduction to Bispectral Analysis and Bilinear Time Series Models*, Springer-Verlag, Berlin.

Suits, D., A. Mason, and L. Chan, 1978, "Spline Functions Fitted by Standard Regression Methods," *Review of Economics and Statistics*, 60, 132–139.

Summers, L., 1986, "Does the Stock Market Rationally Reflect Fundamental Values?," *Journal of Finance*, 41, 591–600.

Sun, T., 1992, "Real and Nominal Interest Rates: A Discrete-Time Model and Its Continuous-Time Limit," *Review of Financial Studies*, 5, 581–611.

Sundaresan, S., 1989, "Intertemporally Dependent Preferences and the Volatility of Consumption and Wealth," *Review of Financial Studies*, 2, 73–88.

———, 1996, *Fixed-Income Securities*, forthcoming.

Svensson, L., 1994, "Estimating and Interpreting Forward Interest Rates: Sweden 1992–1994," Working Paper 4871, NBER, Cambridge, MA.

Taylor, S., 1986, *Modelling Financial Time Series*, John Wiley and Sons, London.

Taylor, M., and H. Allen, 1992, "The Use of Technical Analysis in the Foreign Exchange Market," *Journal of International Money and Finance*, 11, 304–314.

Teräsvirta, T., D. Tjøstheim, and C. Granger, 1994, "Aspects of Modelling Nonlinear Time Series," in R. Engle and D. McFadden (eds.), *Handbook of Econometrics*, Vol. IV, Elsevier, Amsterdam.

Thisted, R., 1991, "Assessing the Effect of Allergy Medications: Models for Paired Comparisons on Ordered Categories," *Statistics of Medicine*, forthcoming.

Thompson, J., and H. Stewart, 1986, *Nonlinear Dynamics and Chaos*, John Wiley and Sons, New York.

Tiniç, S., 1972, "The Economics of Liquidity Services," *Quarterly Journal of Economics*, 86, 79–93.

Tirole, J., 1982, "On the Possibility of Speculation under Rational Expectations," *Econometrica*, 50, 1163–1181.

———, 1985, "Asset Bubbles and Overlapping Generations," *Econometrica*, 53, 1499–1527.

Tong, H., 1983, *Threshold Models in Nonlinear Time Series Analysis*, Springer-Verlag, New York.

———, 1990, *Non-linear Time Series: A Dynamic System Approach*, Oxford University Press, Oxford.

Treynor, J., and R. Ferguson, 1985, "In Defense of Technical Analysis," *Journal of Finance*, 40, 757–773.

Trzcinka, C., 1986, "On the Number of Factors in the Arbitrage Pricing Model," *Journal of Finance*, 41, 347–368.

Tsay, R., 1986, "Nonlinearity Tests for Time Series," *Biometrika*, 73, 461–466.

Tucker, A., 1992, "A Reexamination of Finite- and Infinite-Variance Distributions as Models of Daily Stock Returns," *Journal of Business and Economic Statistics*, 10, 73–81.

Turnbull, S., and F. Milne, 1991, "A Simple Approach to Interest-Rate Option Pricing," *Review of Financial Studies*, 4, 87–120.

Tversky, A., and D. Kahneman, 1992, "Advances in Prospect Theory: Cumulative Representation of Uncertainty," *Journal of Risk and Uncertainty*, 5, 297–323.

Vapnik, V., 1982, *Estimation of Dependences Based on Empirical Data*, Springer-Verlag, Berlin.

Vasicek, O., 1977, "An Equilibrium Characterization of the Term Structure," *Journal of Financial Economics*, 5, 177–188.

Vasicek, O., and H. Fong, 1982, "Term Structure Modelling Using Exponential Splines," *Journal of Finance*, 37, 339–341.

Vayanos, D., 1995, "Transaction Costs and Asset Prices: A Dynamic Equilibrium Model," unpublished paper, Stanford University.

Volterra, V., 1959, *Theory of Functionals and of Integro-Differential Equations*, Dover, New York.

Wahba, G., 1990, *Spline Models for Observational Data*, Regional Conference Series in Applied Mathematics, Vol. 59, SIAM Press, Philadelphia.

Wallis, W., and H. Roberts, 1956, *Statistics: A New Approach*, Free Press, New York.

Wang, J., 1993, "A Model of Intertemporal Asset Prices Under Asymmetric Information," *Review of Economic Studies*, 60, 249–282.

———, 1994, "A Model of Competitive Stock Trading Volume," *Journal of Political Economy*, 102, 127–168.

Weil, P., 1989, "The Equity Premium Puzzle and the Risk-Free Rate Puzzle," *Journal of Monetary Economics*, 24, 401–421.

West, K., 1988a, "Bubbles, Fads, and Stock Price Volatility Tests: A Partial Evaluation," *Journal of Finance*, 43, 639–656.

———, 1988b, "Dividend Innovations and Stock Price Volatility," *Econometrica*, 56, 37–61.

Wheatley, S., 1988, "Some Tests of the Consumption-Based Asset Pricing Model," *Journal of Monetary Economics*, 22, 193–218.

White, H., 1980, "A Heteroskedasticity-Consistent Covariance Matrix Estimator and a Direct Test for Heteroskedasticity," *Econometrica*, 48, 817–838.

———, 1982, "Maximum Likelihood Estimation of Misspecified Models," *Econometrica*, 50, 1–25.

———, 1984, *Asymptotic Theory for Econometricians*, Academic Press, Orlando, FL.

———, 1992, *Artificial Neural Networks: Approximation and Learning Theory*, Blackwell Publishers, Cambridge, MA.

White, H., and I. Domowitz, 1984, "Nonlinear Regression with Dependent Observations," *Econometrica*, 52, 143–162.

Widrow, B., and S. Stearns, 1985, *Adaptive Signal Processing*, Prentice-Hall, Englewood Cliffs, NJ.

Wiener, N., 1923, "Differential-Space," *Journal of Mathematics and Physics*, 2, 131–174.

Wiggins, J., 1987, "Option Values Under Stochastic Volatility: Theory and Empirical Estimates," *Journal of Financial Economics*, 19, 351–372.

Wilcox, D., 1992, "The Construction of U.S. Consumption Data: Some Facts and Their Implications for Empirical Work," *American Economic Review*, 82, 922–941.

Wood, R., T. McInish, and K. Ord, 1985, "An Investigation of Transactions Data for NYSE Stocks," *Journal of Finance*, 40, 723–738.

Working, H., 1960, "Note on the Correlation of First Differences of Averages in a Random Chain," *Econometrica*, 28, 916–918.

Yaari, M., 1987, "The Dual Theory of Choice Under Risk," *Econometrica*, 55, 95–115.

Zarowin, P., 1989, "Short-Run Overreaction: Size and Seasonality Effect," *Journal of Portfolio Management*, 15, 26–29.

Zehna, P., 1966, "Invariance of Maximum Likelihood Estimation," *Annals of Mathematical Statistics*, 37, 744–744.

Author Index

Subject Index